Interrogations

Following the suicide of Robert Ley on 24 October 1945, guards were posted for twenty-four hours a day outside each prisoner's door. They had to observe the prisoner at least once each minute.

Richard Overy

Interrogations

The Nazi Elite in Allied Hands, 1945

VIKING

VIKING
Published by the Penguin Group
Penguin Putnam Inc., 375 Hudson Street,
New York, New York 10014, U.S.A.
Penguin Books Ltd, 80 Strand,
London WC2R ORL, England
Penguin Books Australia Ltd, Ringwood,
Victoria, Australia
Penguin Books Canada Ltd, 10 Alcorn Avenue,
Toronto, Ontario, Canada M4V 3B2
Penguin Books (N.Z.) Ltd, 182–190 Wairau Road,
Auckland 10, New Zealand

Penguin Books Ltd, Registered Offices:
Harmondsworth, Middlesex, England

First Published in 2001 by Viking Penguin,
a member of Penguin Putnam Inc.

1 3 5 7 9 10 8 6 4 2

LIBRARY OF CONGRESS CATALOGING IN PUBLICATION DATA
Overy, R. J.
Interrogations : the Nazi elite in Allied hands, 1945 / Richard Overy.
p.   cm.
Includes bibliographical references and index.
ISBN 0-670-03008-2
1.War criminals — Germany—Biography. 2. Nazis—Biography.
3. World War,1939–1945—Atrocites. 4. Nuremberg Trial of
Major German War Criminals,
Nuremberg, Germany, 1945–1946. I. Title
D736.O94 2001
364.1'38'092243—dc21   2001026722

This book is printed on acid–free paper. ∞

Printed in the United States of America
Set in Sabon

This book is dedicated to
ALICE TEICHOVA and MIKULÁŠ TEICH,
remarkable survivors of an evil age

Contents

List of Illustrations

All Imperial War Museum material is reproduced by permission of the Trustees of the Imperial War Museum, London.

Acknowledgements

I have many debts to acknowledge for help, advice and support in the writing of *Interrogations*. I am grateful to the Controller of Her Majesty's Stationery Office and the National Archives in Washington, DC for permission to reproduce the interrogation material. The Documents Department at the Imperial War Museum, London, and the Museum archives centre at Duxford, Cambridge, have been more than helpful, and I should like to thank Stephen Walton and Pam Wright in particular. At the National Archives in Washington I received much needed assistance from Wilbert Mahoney and John Taylor. I am grateful for the use of material in the Liddell Hart Archive in my own institution, King's College, London, which was brought to my attention by Professor Albert Kiralfy, himself a former interrogator and interpreter. David Cesarani and Ken Follett gave up valuable time to comment on an earlier draft, for which I am deeply grateful. Michael Smith looked at the legal passages to save me from howlers in legal theory. I would also like to thank Claudia Baldoli, Nicholas Davidson, Gerald Fleming, Isabel Heinemann, Ian Kershaw, Sergei Kudryashev, Joachim Lund and Cecilia Mackay. I would like to thank my editor at Penguin, Simon Winder, for his unflagging support of the project, and my agent Gill Coleridge for all her help and efforts over the years. Finally, and not least, my love and thanks to my family for putting up with my endless preoccupation with such grim subjects.

Richard Overy
April 2001

Preface

As Hitler faced the reality of defeat in April 1945 he reflected on the
future facing the German people: 'It fills me with horror to think of
our Reich hacked to pieces by the victors, our peoples exposed to the
savage excesses of the Bolsheviks and the American gangsters.' His
outlook was suicidal. He could not contemplate life in the 'transition
period'. He confessed himself unable to understand how Germany
could survive without the elite 'which led her to the very pinnacles of
heroism'. He comforted himself with the thought that the more
Germany suffered, the 'more glorious' would be its historical revival.
Nourished by these fantasies, tormented by these fears, Hitler killed
himself and left the German people to cope without him.[1]

The transition period was grim for most Germans. Defeat was
complete. The elite in which Hitler placed so much trust melted away,
some into hiding, some abroad, some dead by their own hand. Most
of them ended up in Allied hands as wanted war criminals, members
of what Churchill called the 'Hitler gang'. Cooped up in high-security
internment camps, they appeared 'a sorry, uneasy lot'.[2] The Allies
argued about how they should be treated. They agreed in August 1945
to hold a trial to expose the reality of the Hitler regime to world
opinion. The idea was to re-educate the Germans to make them useful
European citizens again.

First the Allies had to educate themselves. They knew something of
conditions in the Third Reich, but their collective view of Germany
and the Germans bordered at times on caricature. The thousands of
prisoners in Allied hands were the gateway to understanding how it
had been possible for Hitler so to captivate an entire people that
it proved willing to follow him blindly along the path to war and
destruction. The prisoners themselves became one of the chief sources

used by the Allied powers to incriminate them. Slowly a picture emerged from the thousands of interrogations of how the Third Reich had operated and with what frightful consequences. It was a story at times hard to credit. 'The Nazi political set-up,' wrote one British official, 'was as fantastic as any Münchhausen tale. It is incredible that such things could have happened.'[3]

The story of the trial of Hitler's fallen elite at Nuremberg has been told often and well. The interval between their capture in May and June 1945 and the start of the trial on 20 November 1945 is, by comparison, shrouded in shadows. The 'transition period' has come to be regarded as a mere intermission between catastrophic defeat and well-earned retribution. It was that, but much more. The story of the incarceration and interrogation of the German elite in 1945 has its own portion of drama and pathos. Here were men in acute stress, squirming under the glare of hostile opinion. They had been transported in a matter of weeks from the comfortable status of high office, with all its perquisites and props, to the rigours of Allied imprisonment with 'minimum clothing, accommodation and medical care' and a daily diet of 1,550 calories.[4] The realization that the Allies would actually imprison an entire government, military leadership and diplomatic corps produced a variety of traumatic responses – shock, profound disorientating disgrace, hysterical behaviour, even amnesia. For the fraction tortured by a genuine sense of guilt there was a smothering depression. 'Why don't you just shoot us?' asked one prisoner.

The months of interrogation produced a rich vein of evidence for the Allied prosecution teams. In an odd sense it gave the German leaders an opportunity to ask themselves what they had been doing under Hitler's spell and why they had acted in the way they did. This self-examination did not often provoke contrition or remorse, but it did expose their expectations and behaviour to searching review. None of those interrogated hour after hour could fail to betray something about themselves and the system they served however hard they tried to deny or dissimulate. Very seldom have historians had the opportunity to examine the oral evidence of an entire leadership corps taken down verbatim only weeks after their fall from power. The interrogations provide a window into the Third Reich of remarkable range and complexity. It is all the more surprising that they should have attracted so little scholarly attention. They are viewed here as a whole for the first time, freed from association with the more accessible and popularized cross-examinations of the trial itself.

They should none the less be treated with caution. The examples reproduced in the second part of the book must be viewed not as the truth, but for what they are: statements of a point of view, greatly influenced by the questions the interrogator chooses to ask and by the willingness of the interviewee to respond with candour or deceit. Interrogation is not the same as conversation. The prisoners were brought up from the cells under armed guard to sit in front of a uniformed officer, an interpreter and a court stenographer. A few understood English, but most did not. They were not allowed to ask questions; only seldom could they take initiatives. When one frightened police chief kept throwing anxious queries back, his exasperated interrogator finally turned on the interpreter: 'Did you tell him to answer the questions and that *I* would ask them?'[5]

The prisoners did all talk, sometimes at great length, and willingly. None sat in stony silence. The interviews bore few of the hallmarks of the modern criminal interrogation, where prisoners' rights are protected, including the right to silence, and attorneys sit in close attendance watching for breaches of procedure. When asked to sign sworn statements most did so without demur, though the occasional argument arose over mistranslation. The beaten enemy was neither defiant nor openly obstructive; the transcripts reveal a surprising degree of compliance alongside more devious strategies of misrepresentation and forgetfulness. Defeat produced a dull sense of resignation even among the most unreconstructed National Socialists. 'Over the past months,' wrote an Allied Control Council officer early in 1946, 'the average German has been variously described as stupefied, punch-drunk, bomb-happy, and other epithets, intended to explain the apparent lethargy and indifference.'[6] The prisoners were no more immune from these states of temporary debilitation than their countrymen.

The interrogation transcripts selected for this volume cover only a fraction of the interviews conducted in 1945. They have been chosen either because of the historical significance of their content, or because they help to illuminate the more acute manifestations of psychological crisis among the cohort of prisoners. Some minor changes have been made to the way the transcripts were originally prepared, including the correction of spelling mistakes. The details of these corrections can be found immediately before the transcript section. Every care has been taken to ensure that the sense has not been altered or distorted, and the transcripts of those few prisoners who replied in English have been kept in the original form. Most of the idiosyncrasies of spelling and grammar were the consequences of long, tiring typing sessions for secretaries who knew little or no German, and who faced gruelling deadlines to get the transcripts finished. A few of the interrogations have been reproduced in full, but most are lengthy excerpts from interviews that usually lasted two or three hours. Some of the 'interrogations' were presented in the form of written answers to a set of questions supplied by the interrogator. Some were written as short reports for the prosecution, without a formal question and answer format. These variations are noted in the text. Brief notes are attached to each transcript to clarify the context of the subject-matter or to provide additional factual information. In general the interrogations speak for themselves, without need of elaboration.

Abbreviations

BAB	Bundesarchiv, Berlin Lichterfelde
BAK	Bundesarchiv, Koblenz
BAOR	British Army of the Rhine
BIOS	British Intelligence Objectives Sub-Committee
BWCE	British War Crimes Executive
CAB	Cabinet papers
CIA	Criminal Investigation Agency
CIOS	Combined Intelligence Objectives Sub-Committee
EDS	Enemy Documents Section, Cabinet Office
FIAT	Field Intelligence Agency Technical
FO	British Foreign Office
IMT	International Military Tribunal
IWM	Imperial War Museum
LCO	Lord Chancellor's Office
LHA	Liddell Hart Archive, King's College, London
NA II	National Archives and Records Administration II, College Park, Maryland
OKH	Oberkommando des Heeres (Supreme Command of the Army)
OKW	Oberkommando der Wehrmacht (Supreme Command of the Armed Forces)
OSS	Office of Strategic Services
OUSCC	Office of the United States Chief of Counsel
PREM	Prime Minister's papers
PRO	Public Record Office, Kew, London
RAF	Royal Air Force
RG	Record Group
RSHA	Reichssicherheitshauptamt (Reich Main Security Office)

SA	Sturmabteilung
SD	Sicherheitsdienst
SHAEF	Supreme Headquarters, Allied Expeditionary Force
SIS	Secret Intelligence Service
SS	Schutzstaffel
TS	Treasury Solicitor
UNWCC	United Nations War Crimes Commission
USFET	United States Forces, European Theater
USSBS	United States Strategic Bombing Survey
WO	War Office

Part I

Interrogations: an Introduction

Outlaw Country

What is now proposed is that a duly constituted military tribunal should undertake the execution without any re-trial when the outlaw reaches its hand. That corresponds with the rule that the Sheriff did not try the outlaw or bring him before any court for trial; he merely hanged him.

Lord Simon, the Lord Chancellor, 10 November 1943

In Caesar's day the enemy were treated as enemies, i.e. slaughtered out of hand if they were not enslaved. In Napoleonic times there was banishment and imprisonment by what was called political action, – now we would impose death – surely this is retrogression rather than progress.

Murray Bernays, US war crimes team, 16 April 1945 [1]

The ruined city of Nuremberg following eleven major bomb attacks. More than 50 percent of the city was destroyed, leaving 250,000 homeless.

If Winston Churchill had got his way, there would have been no major German war criminals to prosecute in 1945 and no Nuremberg Military Tribunal to try them. It was Churchill's earnest wish, which he expressed repeatedly in the months running up to the end of the European war in May 1945, that captured German leaders, whether party bosses, soldiers, or ministers, should be identified positively on the say of any local army officer with the rank of major-general or above, and then shot within six hours.

Churchill felt a powerful animosity towards those he blamed for plunging the world into war. He did not believe that a formal judicial trial would be appropriate for what he termed the 'Hitler gang'. In November 1943 he penned a note which he hoped would form the basis for a decision by the British War Cabinet to declare German leaders 'world outlaws' alongside Italian and Japanese leaders and the Quislings spawned by their conquests. Churchill thought the number would amount to between 50 and 100 persons. They would benefit from nothing more than a brief kangaroo court at which their identity would be verified. Once identified they were, in Churchill's own words, to be 'shot to death . . . without reference to higher authority'. This blunt procedure, Churchill hoped, would avoid the 'tangles of legal procedure'.[2]

A few days later, the Lord Chancellor, Lord Simon, the British government's senior adviser on legal affairs, wrote a paper supporting Churchill's idea that the major Axis war criminals should be treated as common outlaws. Simon based his argument on ancient precedent. In medieval Britain a Grand Jury could declare a criminal an outlaw for failure to appear and account for heinous crimes. He could then legally be put to death by anyone who caught him. Under the fourteenth-century monarch Edward III, that general right was revoked and outlaws could only be executed by the local sheriff. Simon assumed that the United Nations fighting the Axis now constituted a latter-day Grand Jury, while the senior military officers who would see to it that the senior war criminals were killed at once were the modern equivalent of the sheriff. He accepted that killing outlaws was not 'a strictly legal principle', though he failed to point out that outlawry in criminal cases had in fact been abolished in English law in 1938. However, like Churchill he could see little advantage in staging a trial. Since it was out of the question to 'let these arch-criminals go free', the only option was to shoot first and ask questions later.[3]

It may now seem outrageous that the leaders of a liberal democracy rooted in respect for the law should discuss between them how best to kill prisoners without a trial, but the idea stemmed from a genuine uncertainty about how to call Hitler and his accomplices to account. When the treatment of war criminals had been discussed by Churchill's Cabinet in June 1942, the Foreign Secretary, Anthony Eden, recommended that every effort should be made to avoid the embarrassing failure to hang the Kaiser at the end of the First World War by abandoning from the outset any idea of judicial proceedings against Axis leaders. 'The guilt of such individuals is so black,' Eden suggested, 'that they fall outside and go beyond the scope of any judicial process.' His advice was to deal with them the way the Allied powers dealt with Napoleon in 1815, by a quick political decision. Lesser war criminals might be tried within the limits of established law on war crimes, but a Hitler trial would require new laws to be made up to match the crimes, and this was not only legally dubious, but would give the defence endless opportunities to argue so.[4]

This remained the British government's position right through to 1945. A judicial tribunal was regarded as a legal quagmire in which Hitler and his associates might make a great deal of mischief in the absence of a clear body of international law; they should be treated by a 'political act', agreed between the Allied powers, which in British eyes became a scarcely veiled euphemism for summary execution. There was no shortage of voices raised in bloodthirsty hue and cry. Churchill made no attempt to disguise either his contempt and loathing for the enemy, or his enthusiasm for capital punishment, swiftly imposed. In August 1944, for example, he wrote to his military secretary, General Hastings Ismay, suggesting that the Allies should publicly declare who the outlaws were and announce that 'Hitler, Goering, Himmler and other monsters' would be killed if they fell into Allied hands.[5] When Churchill prepared a telegram on war criminals for Stalin in September 1944 he included the term 'world outlaws' and inserted, against the advice of colleagues, the idea he had first raised in 1943, that they might be executed within six hours, perhaps on the assumption that Stalin habitually dealt with his enemies in that manner.[6] The telegram was not sent; but Churchill's sentiments were widely shared among Britain's elite. In the summer of 1944 the Labour Party leader, Clement Attlee, a man of humane and moderate outlook, asked the War Cabinet to consider executing a selection of senior German businessmen 'as an example to the others' not to pursue their 'nefarious ends' through war.[7] In a debate on war crimes in the House of Lords in March 1945 no less a figure than the Archbishop of York, second-in-command of the Anglican Church, commended the Churchill view that once formally identified, the major criminals should simply be 'done to death'. When Lord Simon hosted an international conference on war crimes in his office a few weeks later, shortly before the end of the war in Europe, the prevailing British view was still that summary execution would be the simplest solution.[8]

In the end it was Britain's two major allies, the Soviet Union and the United States, who rejected a quick execution in favour of a full trial. Of the two, the Soviet Union played the greater part in persuading both her partners that judicial procedure was the way forward. The Soviet view was first put to Churchill when he visited Moscow in October 1944. During the course of the discussions Churchill sounded Stalin out on summary justice. 'U[ncle]. J[oe]. took an unexpectedly ultra-respectable line,' Churchill wrote to Roosevelt, who was also inclined to accept the quick execution formula. 'There must be no executions without trial; otherwise the world would say we were afraid to try them . . . if there were no trials there must be no death sentences.'[9] Such a view was no doubt consistent with Soviet practice during the terror of the 1930s, when the victims, whether highly-placed Bolsheviks or humble workers and peasants, were forced to go through due process of law before execution or a spell in the camps. It was the view that the Soviet Foreign Minister, Vyacheslav Molotov, had first laid down in October 1942 when he urged the Allies to declare that the clique of German leaders and 'their cruel accomplices' should be named, arrested and tried according to the criminal code.[10] Such legal formalism bore little resemblance to the western idea of a trial. The Soviet side saw German defeat as the opportunity for a 'show trial' on a grand scale. The language used by Soviet officials echoed the violent vocabulary of denunciation and opprobrium used against 'deviationists' and 'counter-revolutionary filth' during the terror of the 1930s.

An article in *Pravda* in March 1945 called for the 'speedy and just trial' of the 'criminal Hitlerite gang', and of the 'Hitlerite hordes' and 'fascist bandits' who sustained their evil cause.[11]

There was more than a hint of irony in Soviet strictures to western leaders on the merits of trials over summary justice. Yet the Soviet insistence on a trial played a direct part in pushing the United States government down the same path. American opinion was divided on the treatment of the major war criminals. Henry Morgenthau, Roosevelt's Secretary of the Treasury, harboured, like Churchill, a brutal hostility towards the German enemy. In September 1944 he presented Roosevelt with a memorandum – now usually described as the Morgenthau Plan – for the treatment of post-war Germany in which he echoed the British idea that the major criminals should simply be apprehended, identified and 'put to death by firing squads'.[12] Roosevelt, whose fading energies were absorbed in the contest for a fourth term as President, was not unsympathetic to Morgenthau's tough stance on Germany. It was the Secretary of War, the ageing Republican Henry Stimson, who rallied those circles in Washington who believed that the American legal tradition would be ill-served by what amounted to the equivalent of lynch-law. He wrote to Roosevelt on 9 September condemning every aspect of the Morgenthau proposals. Stimson favoured procedures consistent with the American Bill of Rights: 'notification to the accused of the charge, the right to be heard and, within reasonable limits, to call witnesses in his defense'. That meant a trial, in effect 'an international tribunal'.[13]

Stimson had the advantage of Morgenthau. The investigation of war crimes and the organization to apprehend war criminals was the responsibility of his War Department. From the autumn of 1944, under the guidance of Assistant Secretary of War, John M. McCloy, legal officials wrestled with the problem of how to establish a judicial tribunal that could effectively try and punish the major war criminals. They drew inspiration from the Soviet insistence on what Molotov called 'the special international tribunal'. In November 1944 the War Department received a long précis of a book on 'The Criminal Responsibility of the Hitlerites' by the head of the Soviet Extraordinary State Commission for the Investigation of German War Crimes, Professor A. N. Trainin. He reiterated the Soviet demand for a tribunal at which the major war criminals would be tried for conspiring to wage aggressive war (crimes against peace) and for waging that war with premeditated brutality (crimes against the laws of war).[14] Trainin was seen by the War Department as a useful ally in their efforts to define how a tribunal might be established, and to isolate and outmanoeuvre those in Washington and London who favoured execution. The 'trial' lobby in America relied for its success on a strange alliance with a Soviet system almost entirely at odds with American conceptions of justice.

The shape of a future trial was first outlined in the War Department by General Myron C. Cramer, the Judge Advocate-General, in a memorandum in October 1944. Cramer regarded it as axiomatic that some kind of international military tribunal should be established and that the senior war criminals should have the same right to defend themselves against clearly stated charges as any other prisoner.[15] On 9 November McCloy hosted a meeting at the Pentagon on war crimes where the idea of a 'full dress war guilt-conspiracy trial, by international tribunal' was approved. The principle of a judicial trial was pitted against the British idea of a 'political act' of revenge. In January the War Department, supported by the Secretary of State and the US Attorney-General, presented Roosevelt with a firm proposal for an international tribunal to try the leading German war criminals on the basis of 'legal concepts firmly rooted in our law'.[16] Even Morgenthau offered grudging acceptance of the proposals. That same month the Treasury Secretary announced to McCloy that he also favoured a quick, simple and direct trial as long as Hitler could not use the courtroom as a platform to 'reargue the theories expounded in *Mein Kampf*'.[17]

A collision between the three Allies became unavoidable. At the Yalta Conference in the Crimea in February 1945, Churchill returned to the theme of summary execution but found neither Stalin nor Roosevelt willing to discuss the issue in detail. No decision was reached, and as the war neared an end the fate of German leaders who fell into Allied hands was no nearer resolution. Early in April 1945 Roosevelt sent to London his personal adviser on war crimes, Judge Samuel Rosenman, to try to bridge the gap between the American and British positions. On 8 April Rosenman called on Lord Simon in his office at the House of Lords. The treatment of the major war criminals was the main point of argument. Simon began the conference with a categorical rejection of the idea of a judicial tribunal – 'neither good nor practicable' – and suggested a compromise. An Instrument of Arraignment would be drawn up by the victors charging Hitler and his colleagues with plotting 'the domination of Europe and the World', the maltreatment of the Jews, and gross breaches of the laws of war. The charges would be heard before a tribunal of Allied personalities, who would decide if they were true. The tribunal would report to Allied leaders, who would make a political decision on how to dispose of them. The British Attorney-General, Sir David Maxwell-Fyfe, then presented the standard British argument for summary execution. Faced with a battery of views hostile to a judicial trial, Rosenman simply reminded the conference that the American position was broadly in favour of a judicial trial 'in accordance with accepted judicial norms'.[18]

American officials were puzzled chiefly by an evident paradox in the British attitude: 'Are the English,' wrote McCloy during a visit to London in mid-April, 'who are the ones in whom the concept of trial before punishment is fundamental, to be the only ones to argue against the procedure of trial?' McCloy found his answer on a walk around Hyde Park Corner near London's Marble Arch, where soap-box orators traditionally congregate to harangue passers-by on the great issues of the day. On the evening of 15 April he found among the gaggle of debates a lively exchange on war criminals. When the speaker urged his listeners to hang them all, he was interrupted by shouts from the audience: 'That's not British justice' – 'Try them for the crimes they committed'. To McCloy's ear the consensus among the crowd appeared to favour a trial. At a meeting the following day, he told Simon bluntly that in his view 'summary execution without trial is contrary to the fundamental conception of justice'.[19]

The British politicians who persisted in rejecting Britain's own judicial traditions became increasingly isolated. On 21 April Judge Rosenman was subjected to a final plea from Simon to avoid judicial proceedings. The Lord Chancellor began by insisting that a trial was redundant for those already condemned at the bar of world opinion: 'H[is]. M[ajesty's]. G[overnment]. assume that it is beyond question that Hitler and a number of arch-criminals associated with him (including Mussolini) must . . . suffer the penalty of death.' The introduction of even a cursory preliminary trial was so fraught with 'difficulties and dangers' that Simon, abandoning the compromise he had earlier suggested of an Instrument of Arraignment, urged for the last time the view that 'execution without trial is the preferable course'. The alternative, Simon insisted, was to hold a trial in which the British public's sense of fair play would simply allow Hitler all the usual freedoms of judicial procedure, which would certainly produce a lengthy trial, and might lead to a successful defence against loosely worded or ill-conceived charges of conspiracy. The public might then say, Simon continued, 'The man should be shot out of hand' to prevent the whole process from ending up as farce. Either way, the end result was a firing-squad, but the quickest and least politically dangerous solution was for the Allied powers to agree a political solution, and to do so as quickly as possible.[20]

The result was not what Simon wanted, but it could scarcely have surprised him. The American authorities began to prepare for a major trial regardless of the attitude of their ally. The day following Simon's entreaty, 22 April, McCloy wrote to Rosenman asking him to help select a Chief of Counsel for the United States to prepare the case against the main war criminals. On 26 April Henry Stimson instructed McCloy to set up a small planning group to prepare 'the trial of the major Axis leaders'.[21] After a little delay the choice of counsel fell on the Supreme Court Justice Robert Jackson, who had a string of anti-trust cases behind him, and was a former Roosevelt Attorney-General. On 2 May he was formally appointed by presidential order 9547 to the post of Chief of Counsel for preparing and prosecuting charges against 'the leaders of the European Axis powers and their principal agents and accessories'.[22] Jackson was a popular choice. He cut a serious and dignified figure in his smart three-piece suits, decked out with fob-watch and breast-pocket kerchief. He was determined that the trial would take place and would be a triumph for American notions of justice. It was said that he harboured ambitions for the presidency itself, but his commitment to the idea of a trial stemmed not from political ambition but from a genuine revulsion against the system whose representatives he laboured to convict.[23]

The moving spirit behind the decision to prepare a trial in defiance of the British was the American Vice-President, Harry S Truman, who succeeded Roosevelt when he died on 12 April. Truman, a former judge and a Senator for Missouri, met Rosenman on his return from London. Truman was implacably opposed to the British idea of

The American Chief Prosecuting Counsel, Robert Houghwout Jackson, seen here standing on the top of Claridges in Brook Street, London, during a visit to prepare the terms of the tribunal.

summary execution. He told Rosenman to reject any form of 'political disposition' of the major criminals and to insist on 'some kind of trial'.[24] In a statement issued from the White House on 2 May, the day of Jackson's appointment, Truman announced to the world America's commitment to the judicial path: 'It is our objective to establish as soon as possible an international military tribunal; and to provide a trial procedure which will be expeditious in nature and which will permit no evasion or delay – but one which is in keeping with our tradition of fairness toward those accused of crime.'[25] Truman instructed Rosenman to attend the founding meeting of the United Nations Organization in San Francisco and there to reach agreement with the British and Soviet representatives on the terms for a judicial process.

At San Francisco the idea of the outlaw was finally set aside. The American delegates took with them a draft proposal for an inter-Allied agreement on the prosecution of European war criminals. On 3 May the three Foreign Ministers met to hear the proposals, which were presented by Rosenman. For the previous two weeks American pressure on the British had been mounting. When Churchill's War Cabinet met on 26 April they had a message from Truman insisting that there must be some form of judicial process, but they remained adamantly opposed. By early May both Hitler and Mussolini were dead, the one at his own hand in the bunker in Berlin, the other killed by Italian anti-fascist partisans. Eden's initial instructions were to impress on the American and Soviet delegates that the dictators' deaths rendered a trial 'inappropriate and unnecessary', and to suggest that the remaining senior figures should be tried by the nations that had claims on them. Hermann Goering, for example, was wanted by the Czechs; Eden was asked to advise his Soviet and American colleagues, Molotov and the United States Secretary of State, Edward Stettinius, that Goering should stand trial in Prague.[26]

On 3 May, the day Rosenman was scheduled to open discussions in San Francisco, the War Cabinet met again to consider Eden's instructions. This time Simon, who continued to oppose a trial, found his colleagues less willing to endorse his proposals. Quite why the Cabinet finally turned is not clear, but there had been voices raised against summary justice on earlier occasions. This time there was an element of political calculation. The risks of opposing both the United States and the Soviet Union at the founding conference of the United Nations, and in the full glare of publicity, must have played a part. So too did Cabinet unease about the illiberal character of victor's justice, now that victory was in sight. Churchill penned a brief minute for Eden that the British government was at last willing to accept American and Soviet views 'in principle', so long as a satisfactory procedure for the trial could be elaborated. The difference of eight hours between London and San Francisco made it possible for Eden to receive the news that same day, in time to confirm to his fellow delegates that the British government had at last changed its mind.[27] Rosenman telegraphed Truman with the news later in the day. The British capitulated all down the line. On 6 May one of the American team, Colonel Ammi Cutter, wired to McCloy at the Pentagon the news that 'Progress is being made'. A tentative agreement had been reached between American, British, Soviet and, at the invitation of the Big Three, French delegations to establish an international military tribunal based on judicial principles, with one judge and one chief of counsel from each of the four states. Nothing was formally signed, but the scene was now set for the capture, incarceration and prosecution of those senior Axis leaders still to fall into Allied hands.[28]

The American victory at San Francisco came very late in the day. Four days later the Third Reich formally surrendered, with the Allies only in the very early stages of deciding what might be done with the senior leaders that remained. There was no common list which laid down who was, and was not, a major war criminal. No charges had been agreed, since there had been little inter-Allied discussion of the nature of the crimes for which their captives might have to answer. The precise nature of the international tribunal could not be established with ease since it required the reconciliation of very different approaches to law – the common law tradition of Anglo-American judicial practice, which Simon and his colleagues had been so eager to suspend, and the civil law traditions of France and the Soviet Union. Under civil law the accused cannot testify under oath on his own behalf, but may make a final unsworn statement at the end of the trial. Under common law the defendants can testify, but make no closing statement. The two systems also control the flow of witnesses in different ways: civil law trials are dictated largely by the judge on the basis of a prepared dossier of evidence, common law trials by the prosecution who introduce evidence as the trial goes along. In the end a clever compromise was reached in which the practices of both systems were operated in synthesis, but the trial could not disguise its mongrel character.[29]

Above all, no real thought had been given to the difficulties of extracting sufficient high-quality evidence, either documentary or oral, to make a conviction look plausible. Too much of the discussion before victory had been based on the assumption of guilt, and the decision to stage a trial proved difficult to take with full seriousness in the knowledge that everyone expected the defendants to be condemned to death in the course of time. This attitude was not confined, as is so often supposed, to the Soviet side. When Justice Jackson read the War Department proposals for a tribunal drawn up in April 1945 he told its authors that the language used gave the impression 'that it is setting up a court organized to convict'.[30] The British Treasury Solicitor, Sir Thomas Barnes, was of the opinion that whatever kind of trial was devised for the major war criminals 'there can be no doubt that these men will be executed'.[31] This reflected the view across the British establishment. The difference was that the Soviet authorities made no public pretence that the trials were anything else but a prelude to a well-earned death; British views were kept behind closed doors. During the summer the Soviet Tass news agency published profiles of the major prisoners in the English-language *Soviet Monitor*. Each one ended with a call for the severest penalty: 'so must the Hitlerite hangman Alfred Rosenberg . . . be punished by death'; 'Guilty, the gallows for the arch-murderer Frank', and so on.[32]

One consequence of the triumph of a trial over summary justice was that the United States came to play the major part in the subsequent organization of the Tribunal. The American team found that the British and Soviet authorities, for different reasons, were reluctant to work with the same enthusiasm or the necessary speed. The British side remained sceptical about the prospects for an effective trial, and were critical of the American intention to base the charges on the concept of a general conspiracy. British participation was constrained by the small numbers assigned to assist with trial preparation. The British team was dwarfed by the American personnel. In May 1945 the War Department shipped 30 legal officers and 25 stenographers by air to Europe to deal with war crimes; another 30 legal experts, 25

The four chief prosecutors (from left to right): Sir David Maxwell-Fyfe, Iona Nikitchenko, Robert Jackson and Robert Falco. The British and American teams played the largest part in preparing the trial and prosecution.

stenographers and 6 forensic evidence experts followed more slowly by ship. By September over 200 people were working for Jackson. When the British War Crimes Executive tried to recruit 67 additional personnel (including 55 translators) to cope with the demands of pre-trial preparation, the request was turned down. Even at the high point of the trial in 1946 the British team had only 34 members.[33] The French contingent was the smallest of all. In the complex efforts to re-establish a central French administration after German occupation and partition, there was little money or time to spare on the task of bringing those occupiers to book.[34]

Relations with the Soviet war crimes team was anything but satisfactory. The Soviet personnel were under orders to keep themselves apart from the western officials. Even informal contacts were frowned upon. Soviet negotiators had to refer all discussion back to Moscow, which proved cumbersome and time-consuming. Jackson had scant respect

Smiling Soviet soldiers are handed a weekly ration of American cigarettes and scarce consumer items. The penalties for fraternization with westerners could be severe, and co-operation was kept to a minimum.

for his ally. In May he told the British prosecutors that they should begin preparations regardless of whether the Soviet Union collaborated or not. In July he complained to the War Department that the Soviet view of a tribunal bore little resemblance to 'what Americans and British would regard as a fair trial'. The chief Soviet prosecutor, Major-General Iona T. Nikitchenko, Vice-President of the Soviet Supreme Court and a key figure in the Soviet show trials of the 1930s, assumed from the start of his negotiations with the American and British representatives that German leaders had already been convicted on the basis of the agreement reached at Yalta, and that the tribunal's main purpose was 'to determine the measure of guilt of each particular person and mete out the necessary punishment'.[35] Jackson found the endless procedural hold-ups deeply frustrating. When he was presented with a Swiss watch by his staff on his birthday he asked them where they had got it. 'Well, we got it from the Russians,' replied a wit. 'That's fine,' retorted Jackson. 'Up to now, I haven't been able to get even the time of day out of them.'[36]

The real difficulty lay in the nature of the trial itself. Though the American side had done a good deal of preliminary thinking about the Tribunal and the charges, there was no agreement among the four Allies on any of the central issues. At the end of May 1945 Jackson was sent a copy of an article from the current issue of *Newsweek* magazine highly critical of the information received from his infant organization: 'Nobody knew what a war criminal was – officially. Nobody knew what men were on the list of war criminals – officially. Nobody knew when they would be tried – officially.'[37] None of these issues was even close to resolution. A draft memorandum on the trial was produced on 13 May by Jackson's office, but it was marked as a 'tentative secret US project', to be shown to no one save those Americans working directly on it. The first outline of American thinking was communicated to the British on 22 May. Not until a week later did the British government finally appoint a chief of counsel, the Attorney-General, Sir David Maxwell-Fyfe. On 9 June a firm invitation was sent to the representatives of the four powers involved to meet in London later that month to begin the task of arranging and defining the Tribunal.[38] On 26 June the delegations finally met in London to thrash out a common plan.

The results were disillusioning for the American team who shared the largest responsibility for defining both the shape of the trial and the charges to be tried. At one point Jackson became so frustrated with the failure to reach agreement that he openly discussed the possibility of a trial organized by the Americans alone. Arguments over the actual location for the trials in July almost persuaded Jackson to resign his post. Until then, no decision had actually been reached about where the Tribunal should sit. The Americans and British briefly considered the merits of Leipzig, Munich and Luxemburg, but in Moscow there was strong feeling that Berlin, the capital city of the 'fascist conspirators', was the natural site. This presented problems, for Berlin was in the Soviet area of occupation; the city itself was divided into four separate zones, one for each of the major Allies, which left room for even more argument. The American Military Governor, General Lucius Clay, suggested the city of Nuremberg, which had once hosted the notorious annual Nazi Party rallies. Jackson flew to inspect it with British and French representatives and returned enthusiastic about the choice. The Soviet delegation in London dithered, and finally agreed to Nuremberg as the location for the trials only on the condition that Berlin would become the official home of the Tribunal authorities. Jackson was forced to accept the compromise.[39] Nothing would have been gained at that point by a hardening of tension between the Soviet Union and the west. Though the confrontation described by the term 'Cold War' was already taking shape, the Allies could not afford any public hint of discord for fear the defendants might exploit such differences for their own ends.

The endless negotiations over details created an unexpectedly tight schedule. The short time available to work out the practical management of the Tribunal, and to gather and assess the evidence, presented an almost impossible task. On 9 July Murray Bernays, one of the senior New York lawyers in Jackson's office, wrote to McCloy's department in Washington the following dispirited report:

We are deplorably behind schedule on the procurement of the evidence . . . the actual proof could be listed on a very few 3 × 5 filing cards written on one side . . . I do not want you to think that I feel beaten. We may not turn out the best job in the world, but I still believe we can do a workman-like job at least . . . The trouble is that to do *the job we started out to do, in the time allowed* it looks very much as though we will need a minor miracle, but day by day we are giving the good Lord (and ourselves) less time to work it.[40]

All four Allies wanted a quick trial, which increased the pressure on those struggling to prepare it. The British and American prosecutors assumed at first that a trial could be started in early September; the date was then shifted to early November at the latest. It was still expected to be over by Christmas.[41] The eventual ten-month trial was the very opposite of what the prosecution teams either wanted or expected.

The four-power Tribunal was finally confirmed at the Potsdam Conference of the Big Three Allied powers held from mid-July in the Cecilienhof palace outside Berlin. At the request of the British government war crimes were included on the agenda. Truman and the new British Prime Minister, Clement Attlee, who replaced Churchill part way through the conference, pressed Stalin to agree to a joint

The Big Three at the Potsdam Conference in July 1945. Churchill, Truman and Stalin agreed to establish a military tribunal to try the major war criminals. Churchill preferred the solution of quick execution. Stalin insisted on a trial.

communiqué. Stalin was as keen as they were to start a trial, but he wanted the defendants named in the statement. Since the final list was still far from agreement, Truman was against including any names. The Soviet side accepted the draft statement only after they had extracted the promise that a list would be published within thirty days. On 2 August the three Allies reaffirmed their common commitment to the trial of the major war criminals at the earliest possible opportunity. This public endorsement speeded up the final stages of discussion in London, and ended any thoughts Jackson might still have harboured for an all-American trial. On the same day the Nuremberg site was at last agreed. On 8 August the four delegations signed a formal agreement for an international military tribunal, with a Charter laying down the procedures and character of the trial and outlining the main charges.[42]

The subsequent Tribunal was founded, as Truman and Jackson had always intended, on American notions of justice. It was established to allow a formal judicial procedure, with the right for defendants to defend themselves against clearly stated charges. The assumption underlying a formal process was the possibility of innocence. Yet it was precisely the impossibility of such an outcome in the minds of Churchill and his colleagues that had first prompted the call for summary execution. For the same reason, Soviet officials took for granted the guilt of the accused, and saw the Tribunal, like the show trials of the 1930s, as an arena for displaying that guilt to public review before inevitable and deserved punishment. Even in the United States grave doubts remained about the wisdom of constructing a special judicial instrument which might result in long-drawn-out and indecisive legal arguments. In late November 1945 the editor of *Fortune* magazine sent Jackson the text of an article he intended to publish in the December issue. The item was a long and detailed demolition of the legal basis of the Tribunal and the failure to pursue 'political action' as the British had demanded. The idea that some Nazi war criminals might be acquitted 'would be the greatest crime of the age'. What was wanted was not a verdict but only a sentence. This was a view indistinguishable from the Soviet position Jackson had so forcefully opposed in the summer. It was said to match the sentiments of the American Attorney-General who had recently expressed the hope that the Nuremberg Tribunal would deal out 'what we in Texas call "law

west of the Pecos" – fast justice, particularly fast', in short a form
of lynch-law. 'Immediate capital punishment', concluded the article,
would have better satisfied a world 'that aches to be rid of the organizers of Nazi criminality'.[43] The idea of the outlaw was not so easily
set to rest.

The Criminals

So grotesque and preposterous are the principal characters in this galaxy of clowns and crooks in Ashcan, Dustbin and the other centres of detention that none but a 'thrice double ass' could have taken them for rulers.

Political Division report, Control Commission for Germany, Summer 1945[1]

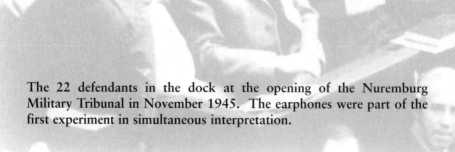

The 22 defendants in the dock at the opening of the Nuremburg Military Tribunal in November 1945. The earphones were part of the first experiment in simultaneous interpretation.

It was one thing to agree to hold a trial in 1945, quite another to decide who should be arraigned before it. From the moment when war crimes began to be discussed in detail, in the summer of 1942, a distinction was made between those guilty of local war crimes in a particular theatre of war and those major war criminals 'whose notorious offences,' as Churchill put it, 'have no special geographical location'.[2] The lesser criminals were to be sent back to be tried in the midst of the populations they had violated; the major criminals were to be dealt with by the Allies, all of whom had some claim against them. These major criminals were, according to the British Foreign Secretary, Anthony Eden, to be chosen because, from position or reputation, they personified 'the worst and most extreme features of Nazism and Fascism'.[3]

In September 1943 the United Nations (the term adopted to describe the Allied powers some years before the modern United Nations was formally founded in May 1945) established a War Crimes Commission. One of its principal tasks was to draw up lists of war criminals, that could be exploited once the war was over in order to expedite their capture and prosecution. The organizers took for granted the guilt of the main actors. As a result Hitler was not included on the United Nations list until incredulous Soviet officials pointed out the lapse. His name was added in March 1945, shortly before his suicide. Hitler's designated successor, Hermann Goering, was another absentee; his name was appended only in November 1944.[4] This confusion was understandable, since the major war criminals had been singled out for special treatment. The difficulty was still to decide who was, and was not, a major war criminal outside the circle of those whose criminality was deemed to be self-evident.

When Churchill launched the discussion of summary execution in November 1943 he suggested that the list of major criminals would exceed fifty but not be more than 100. These inflated figures were arbitrary ones, plucked from the air. Churchill assumed the trials would include Italian and Japanese leaders, as well as German. Most of the initial lists included Mussolini as a matter of course, and the first full list of major war criminals drawn up by the British Foreign

Office in June 1944 included thirty-three Germans and eight Italians. Many on the German list were already household names. The list was divided into two parts: those who should be included without question (Hitler, Goering, Himmler, Ribbentrop, Bormann and so on) and a second list of seven names whose significance as major criminals was in doubt, including the virtually unknown Erwin Kraus, head of the Nazi Party Car Corps. The Italians listed were, by contrast, anything but household names beyond Benito Mussolini, Italy's Prime Minister and architect of Italian participation in the war, and Marshal Rodolfo Graziani, who had led Italian forces in North Africa earlier in the war.[5]

A year later Italians had disappeared from the lists altogether. Although Jackson was appointed to prosecute 'Axis criminality', his first report to President Truman, submitted on 6 June 1945, made reference only to the 'international brigands' who led the German state and the Nazi Party.[6] The official American and British lists produced in June 1945 contained no Italian names. Marshal Graziani, caught in May 1945, was singled out as someone who still needed investigation, but he was eventually tried in 1948 by an Italian court. The decision to exclude Italian leaders had a political purpose behind it. Italy surrendered in 1943 and its southern and central areas had been occupied by Allied forces since 1944. Italian officials and soldiers collaborated with the Allies; northern Italy, where German forces continued to confront the Allies until the end of the war, came to be regarded as one of the occupied areas. Savage German reprisals against Italians put the population on a par with the other victims of German atrocity. The trial of Italian leaders after Mussolini's death in 1945 would have done little to help Anglo-American efforts to integrate Italy once again into the democratic bloc.[7]

The term 'Axis criminality' came to mean 'German criminality'. Defining the list of criminals became one of the major preoccupations in the last year of the war. A mere number was scarcely adequate as a criterion. Eden was aware that selection had to be seen to be 'systematic and not arbitrary', but the original list of 33 Germans contained only 14 of the eventual 22 defendants taken to Nuremberg for trial. The great majority were officials of the National Socialist Party, and they included one woman, the leader of the Reich Women's League, Gertrud von Scholz-Klink. Knowledge of their careers and offices was scanty. As if to justify their inclusion a number of names had special remarks appended: Bernhard Rust (Education Minister), 'spent some time in a mental home'; Robert Ley (head of the German Labour Front), 'a Party leader of old standing and of the worst type'; and so on.[8] One soldier was included, Field Marshal Wilhelm Keitel, chief-of-staff of the Supreme Command of the Armed Forces (wrongly described as Minister of Defence). The decision to include him was based on the need to have at least some representative of the military side of Germany's war effort. Eden rejected the inclusion of further officers on the grounds that it would be impossible to know where to draw the line; for the same reason no industrialist was included on the list.

The introduction of a specific set of names provoked immediate criticism. Clement Attlee urged the War Cabinet to consider indicting a great many German generals on the ground that 'officers who behave like gangsters should be shot'. He wanted a number of German capitalists included; all big businessmen, Attlee suggested, 'should be deprived of their property' along with the German 'Junker' landowners 'who form the hard core of German militarism'.[9] The War Cabinet was not persuaded to spread the net so far. The main criticism focused on the very large number of names, many of them unknown to the public. The Cabinet endorsed the idea of a list with only a dozen really prominent names and sent the Lord Chancellor away to revise it. When he reported back in September 1944 he had whittled the list down to five – Hitler, Himmler, Goering, Goebbels and Ribbentrop – with the proviso that the Allies might lengthen the list as they saw fit.[10] When negotiations with the other Allies began in earnest in May 1945, British thinking was still fixed on a small number of high-ranking war criminals.

Shortly before the conference assembled in London late in June 1945 to negotiate the Tribunal agreement, the Foreign Office wrote to the British Attorney-General naming those still regarded as the major criminals. Hitler and Goebbels had killed themselves in Hitler's Berlin bunker in April; dead, too, was the head of the SS, Heinrich Himmler, who committed suicide on 23 May in British custody. That left Goering and Ribbentrop from the original list. Robert Ley and Rudolf Hess, Hitler's deputy who had flown dramatically to Scotland in May 1941, to remain in British captivity throughout the war, were both added to the central cohort for trial. The Foreign Office also had slim lists of second- and third-rank criminals. The second list comprised representatives of what were described as 'the most obnoxious activities of the Nazi regime'. Keitel was made to represent German militarism; Julius Streicher, the Party's leading anti-semitic propagandist, and former Party leader in Franconia (Bavaria), was made to represent German anti-semitism; the Austrian Ernst Kaltenbrunner, head of the Reich Main Security Office (RSHA) from 1943, responsible for the Gestapo and the security services, was taken to stand for the system of state terror imposed on Germany and occupied Europe. The final list included prominent government leaders: Wilhelm Frick, Minister of the Interior from 1933 to 1943; Hans Frank, Party legal expert and General-Governor of that part of occupied Poland not absorbed into the Reich; and Alfred Rosenberg, the Nazi Party's leading ideologue and Minister for the Occupied Eastern Territories. Rather than try to distinguish between the three lists, the Foreign Office recommended to the British delegation that all nine should stand trial together.[11]

The American approach to who was a major war criminal differed from the British view in one important respect. From early on in the preparations for a trial it was assumed not only that specific named individuals would be indicted but whole organizations deemed by their very character to be criminal in intent. The inspiration behind the idea of collective guilt was Colonel Murray Bernays, a New York lawyer working in the personnel branch of the army General Staff. Bernays was one of the most important legal minds engaged on the American side from the autumn of 1944 in defining the nature of a trial and the charges involved. He argued that a major trial could indict organizations through a representative individual member; once convicted of conspiracy to commit crimes, both that individual and all other members of the organization would be deemed to be guilty. This highly questionable procedure – there was no precedent in either domestic American or in international law – would make it possible to attack the Gestapo or the SS as a body, rather than the one or two individuals who gave the orders at the top.[12] Stimson was enthusiastic about the proposal. When he and the Secretary of State explained to Roosevelt the basis of American war crimes policy in January they suggested that any future trial should arraign not only German leaders 'but the organizations employed by them'.[13] This became the formal American position when discussions began with the British in April. Little serious thought had been given to the organizations likely to be indicted beyond the SS, SA and Gestapo, but the concept of collective responsibility was regarded as a more effective way to attack the entire fabric of the Nazi state rather than the dozen men who ran it.

The definition of major war criminal was largely an academic exercise before the end of the war. Until, or unless, a substantial number of enemy leaders fell into Allied hands there was no question of a trial. As the news began to emerge that the central figures had been killed or had committed suicide, the nature of the trial began to change shape. So much of the discussion had been predicated on the capture of Hitler, Himmler and Goebbels that their deaths left an evident gap at the centre of any putative tribunal. Instructions were already in place well before the end of the war for American and British army personnel on how to apprehend and identify the lesser fry. Anyone suspected of criminal activities was to be interned in one of a number of civilian camps where they would be subjected to preliminary interrogation to ascertain whether they should be sent on for interrogation at a more senior level. A standard detention form was devised on which the arresting officers were to place a photograph of the detainee, his fingerprints and a detailed breakdown of his main physical characteristics, to be entered on a complicated grid that left nothing to chance. Under the entry 'legs' there was a bewildering choice of 'bow, bandy, left deformed, left limp, left missing, right deformed, right limp, right missing'. Hair ranged from black to turning grey (though there was no entry for white), and it could be waved, close-cropped, dyed or bobbed. Under 'back' there was the single entry 'humped' and under 'build' one box marked 'corpulent'. The final row of the grid left spaces for a description of any tattoos, with the helpful footnote that 'certain members of the SS have their blood group tattooed under left arm'.[14] Profiles of prison suspects produced later by the interrogation centres showed that the grids were obediently filled in. The following examples must have matched many inherited prejudices about the German enemy:

Figure: Tall muscular
Face: Round (head also round). Has a duelling scar on his left cheek.
Dark complexion
Hair: Dark brown
Eyes: Dark

Deformity: Partial amputation of one leg

or again:

Figure: Powerfully built
Face: Long, with protruding cheekbones. Brutal expression
Hair: Greying[15]

The task of sifting out the more important criminals on the basis of tens of thousands of such arrest reports from among the millions of German soldiers and officials who fell into Allied hands was a daunting one.

In the first post-war weeks it was very unclear who had been captured. Rumour was rife, and co-operation between the British, Americans and French less than amiable. On 21 May Bernays wrote to Jackson to find out if the Tribunal 'could go forward' on the basis of the haul of senior prisoners already accounted for. His list included Ley, Kaltenbrunner, Goering, Frick, Frank, and the former German Economics Minister, Hjalmar Schacht, who were all in American hands. The British had Hess and Arthur Seyss-Inquart (Reich Commissar in the Netherlands); the French captured Baron Constantin von Neurath, German Foreign Minister from 1933 to 1938, and later Reich Protector of German-occupied Bohemia. This was a meagre start, but within days of Bernays's letter the net began to fill up. On 23 May the British finally decided to end the short-lived regime of Admiral Karl Doenitz, former commander of the German submarine arm, who had been appointed Chancellor of Germany the day after Hitler's suicide. Doenitz set up his government at Flensburg in northern Germany, negotiated German surrender on 7 May, and then sat there, a king without a kingdom attended by courtiers with titles but no power. He was incarcerated together with General Alfred Jodl, Hitler's Chief of Operations, and Albert Speer, Hitler's pet architect and Minister of Armaments from 1942 to 1945, who was briefly Minister of Economics in the Doenitz Cabinet.

Others on the list of wanted leaders were caught through good fortune rather than solid detective work. Streicher was unexpectedly unearthed by American forces in the Tyrol on 22 May. He had disguised himself by growing a beard as part of an attempt to masquerade as an artist. During a routine interview an American officer joked that

The remnants of the Doenitz Government, set up following Hitler's death on 30 April, are arrested by British soldiers on 23 May 1945 at Flensburg in north Germany. Doenitz (centre) is seen standing with Alfred Jodl and Albert Speer.

he looked just like the wanted war criminal whose identity he was trying to conceal. Streicher was misled by the American's poor command of German, and gave himself up at once. Joachim von Ribbentrop came into British hands on 14 June by the strangest of routes. His picture was displayed on 'Wanted' posters all over Germany, but he succeeded in living in Hamburg for more than a month unrecognized. In growing desperation he contacted a wine merchant he knew in the city and asked him for temporary sanctuary until the time was ripe for him to reappear in public. 'This concerns the future of Germany,' he added darkly. The merchant's son reported the visit to the police. The next day soldiers arrived early in the morning outside the apartment he was staying in, hammering on the door with rifle butts. Ribbentrop was discovered inside asleep, dressed in pink and white striped pyjamas. He was made to dress; his request for a shave was brusquely swept aside. He took a wash-bag with him and set off into captivity. The bag was later found to contain 100,000 marks and a letter addressed to 'Vincent' Churchill. At his first interrogation Ribbentrop candidly explained that he needed the money to help him lie low until public opinion was less committed to the death penalty and he could be treated as befitted a man who had once been the Foreign Minister of a great state.[16]

The former head of the RSHA terror apparatus, Ernst Kaltenbrunner, hoped, like Ribbentrop, to hide out until the hue and cry died down. He and a number of companions made their way to a hunting lodge high in the Austrian Alps. His hiding-place was betrayed to the American army by a huntsman. He had assumed the identity and papers of a Dr Josef Unterwogen, but when his captors brought him face-to-face with his mistress, she rushed to embrace him in her anxiety and relief. Hans Frank tried to conceal himself in a large group of German prisoners-of-war, but on the first night behind barbed wire he slashed his wrists and his neck. He was narrowly saved from death, but his identity was quickly established and he joined the prisoners at 'Ashcan' when he was sufficiently recovered.[17] Lapses in communication held up the information that Walther Funk (Schacht's successor), Rosenberg, Franz von Papen (Hitler's Vice-Chancellor from 1933 to 1934) and Hitler's military deputy, Field Marshal Wilhelm Keitel, were also prisoners in American hands. The Soviet Union captured few senior war criminals. Only two of them, Hans Fritzsche, one of Goebbels's deputies, and Grand Admiral Erich Raeder, former commander-in-chief of the German navy, finally stood trial at Nuremberg.[18]

Now the task began in earnest to decide which of those in captivity should be made to feel the full weight of Allied retribution. There can be little doubt that availability played a part. At a meeting in June the British Attorney-General suggested a criterion for selection which was purely arbitrary: 'the test should be "Do we want the man for making a success of our trial? If Yes, we must have him." '[19] Under the principle approved by both the American and British teams that named individuals could be made to stand for entire organizations or corporate interests, it was merely a question of choosing the best candidate to take the part of the armed forces, or the Gestapo, or the forces of popular Party anti-semitism. The choice of Julius Streicher to stand

Robert Ley, head of the German Labour Front under Hitler, shortly after his capture in disguise in May 1945. Ley later committed suicide at Nuremberg.

Julius Streicher, the leading anti-semitic propagandist in the Third Reich, tried to escape detection by posing as an artist. He was caught by chance when he was challenged by a Jewish-American soldier who thought he saw a passing resemblance to one of the most-wanted war criminals.

for the Party racists ignored the fact that he had little to do with the formal implementation of genocide and had been forced from public life well before the Holocaust was unleashed. Streicher was included on grounds argued by the British Foreign Office that his presence 'would help to deal with the issue of anti-Jewish activities of the Nazis at an early stage and in a conclusive manner'.[20] Kaltenbrunner was taken to represent the Gestapo on the same grounds, though the actual head of the Gestapo, a brutal career policeman named Heinrich Mueller, was missing from every list of potential war criminals, as was the name of Adolf Eichmann, one of the handful of key personnel responsible for organizing the genocide.

By arraigning a small number of individual representatives it proved possible gradually to reduce the numbers likely to stand trial. The Soviet side wanted at least 100. In July the American list of named individuals extended to seventy-two, including Hitler, Himmler, Goebbels and Himmler's deputy, Reinhard Heydrich, who were already dead. Most of those named were Party leaders, senior businessmen and military commanders; the list did contain the names of the twenty-two men who were indicted later in the year to stand trial at Nuremberg.[21] The British list, as we have seen, was considerably shorter. In June the number of those considered with certainty to be ' "top-class" criminals' was still only six: Goering, Ribbentrop, Ley, Rosenberg, Kaltenbrunner and Frick. Another list circulating in the British War Office at the same time had nine names on it, adding Keitel, Doenitz and Streicher, but substituting the elderly Nazi Party treasurer, Franz Xavier Schwarz, for Kaltenbrunner.[22] In August a compromise between the American and British positions was arrived at when a list of twenty-four names was drawn up as the 'First List of Defendants'.[23]

The list masked a good deal of background argument which went on right up to the final days before the trial. The major stumbling-block proved to be the treatment of senior soldiers and businessmen. The initial decision to arraign Keitel as the token for German militarism was modified by the inclusion of Jodl, Raeder and Doenitz. Of these three it was Doenitz who caused the most anxiety. He was included on the list in May with the caveat that he would remain there only if the evidence supported a prosecution. By mid-August a War Office spokesman warned that the case against him was 'too weak to be presented'. Jackson was told a week later that there was simply 'insufficient evidence' to convict him. This prospect raised the real danger that Doenitz might be acquitted. The War Office regarded this outcome as 'disastrous to the whole purpose of the trial'. Doenitz complained in his memoirs that his name was simply pencilled in on the list during the Potsdam Conference as an afterthought, but he had been included on most official lists since May as head of the German government following Hitler's suicide. His name was raised at Potsdam by Molotov alongside a number of other prisoners (Goering, Hess, Ribbentrop, etc.) whom the Soviet side hoped to include by name in the Tribunal agreement drawn up on 8 August.[24] The case against Raeder was regarded as more secure, though not certain. He was in Soviet hands, and was returned only at British insistence, allegedly in exchange for former White Russian generals in British hands.[25] In the end Jackson was determined that German militarism should stand trial. With the support of Soviet prosecutors the four military commanders remained on the list.

The inclusion of economic leaders was the greater problem. From the initial planning of the trial there had existed strong popular pressure to include German business as a partner in the crimes of the regime. The Soviet view, expressed by Professor Trainin, was consistent with Marxist theory. The chief perpetrators were Hitler and the German government ('the most dangerous and ferocious group of international criminals'), but their 'social base' lay in a 'vast group of industrial and financial "Fuehrers"' who shared collective responsibility for the crimes of the regime as the 'aiders and abetters'. Trainin considered industrial and financial leaders to be penally liable in the same sense as political offenders.[26] Western socialists shared this interpretation. But so too did a great many American politicians and lawyers who had spent the 1930s locked in combat with America's web of giant corporations whose power they sought to restrain. The odd alliance of Marxist anti-capitalism and American populism made it almost certain that German businessmen would, sooner or later, find themselves in the war crimes net.

The economic case was, none the less, more difficult to prove at law. Jackson's team searched for a legal framework which would accommodate business complicity. Many of them had cut their legal teeth on American anti-trust cases in the 1930s, and now found themselves in surprisingly familiar territory. The Austrian émigré economist

Peter Drucker supplied a twenty-page paper on 'The Pattern of Nazi Economic Crimes' in June. A Senate report on 'Cartels and National Security' from November 1944 was added to the file entitled 'Industrial War Criminals' on the grounds that it provided an intellectual under-pinning to the case against cartelized German industry.[27] By July Jackson's team had added to the list of potential criminal activities a number of German economic policies, including compulsory carteliz-ation, the development of the synthetics industry and foreign exchange controls. These relatively innocuous practices, however, were common throughout the developed world. What was supposed to give them criminal intent in the German case was the link made between econ-omic policy and war preparation, and it was this link that brought senior economists and businessmen onto the list of defendants.

Jackson hoped that a number of prominent German businessmen would sit in the dock at Nuremberg. The chief among them was the banker Hjalmar Schacht, a Hitler sympathizer in 1933, though not a Nazi. Schacht as President of the central bank, then Economics Minis-ter, masterminded the economic revival of Germany until he fell foul of Goering's ambitions to dominate the economy. In 1937 he resigned as minister; in January 1939 he was sacked from the Reichsbank. Schacht was a nationalist of the old kind, anti-semitic but not geno-cidal, keen to rebuild Germany as a great power but not to squander that revival through war. He crossed swords with Hitler on both issues and was fortunate to avoid a fate worse than dismissal. He was suspected of complicity in the plot to assassinate Hitler in July 1944 and imprisoned. He was fortunate again to survive the orgy of killing in the camps in the last vengeful days of the regime. Alone of all the defendants, Schacht entered Allied captivity from a concentration camp. He was found in May 1945 at Dobbiaco, a camp just south of the Austro-Italian border, where he had been transferred from Dachau. After a short stop in Capri, he was moved to 'Ashcan' in June.[28]

Schacht appeared on none of the early lists of potential major war criminals. Only in July, as a result of American and Soviet pressure, was his name added. The British were unhappy from the start about including the economic case. In August the Attorney-General's office warned that the case against Schacht could not be sustained, and that acquittal would be the only responsible verdict.[29] The decision to include the elderly and ailing arms manufacturer Gustav Krupp as a

Members of the Economic Division of the Allied Control Commission in Berlin plough through hundreds of documents trying to demonstrate the responsibility of German business in preparing for and profiting from the war.

major war criminal was also contested on the grounds that the evidence of complicity in war crimes or political activity was non-existent, but Jackson held his ground. Krupp was made to stand for German heavy industry as Keitel was made to stand for the armed forces. When it became clear that Krupp was too infirm to be tried ('He is, I understand, virtually dead,' wrote a puzzled official of the British War Crimes Executive), Jackson wanted to substitute his son, Alfried, on the grounds that someone had to take the industrialists' part before the Tribunal.[30] Neither this decision, nor the American wish to include a further number of senior businessmen, was endorsed by the other three prosecution teams. Jackson protested shortly before the opening of the trial in November that he had promised the President that he would find an industrialist to prosecute and that 'the President had told the

United States public', but his colleagues were not prepared to add a new name so long after formal publication of the Indictment in October. The final list of defendants at Nuremberg counted only Schacht and his successor, Walther Funk, as the emblems of a corrupted German capitalism.[31]

The decision to adopt the Bernays proposals that entire organizations could also be indicted alongside individual criminals meant that the final list of defendants, agreed during August and September, were arraigned not only on grounds of personal responsibility for crimes committed but on grounds of their membership of organizations which the prosecution would demonstrate were criminal in intent. The first full list of these organizations was drawn up in July. The Nazi Party was represented by the Party leadership corps, the German Labour Front and the Hitler Youth; the other authorities singled out began with the Reich Cabinet, and included the RSHA, the SS, SA, Gestapo, the SD (the Party security agency), the Four Year Plan (set up in 1936 to oversee the development of the war economy), the German High Command, the General Staff and the High Commands of the three separate armed services.[32] The intention in prosecuting organizations was to expose the generally criminal character of the regime, but it was also expected that subsequent trials of lesser criminals could be accelerated if membership of a criminal organization could be demonstrated. There were powerful legal objections to this procedure, since it classified as criminal activities those not commonly regarded as such, and did so through retrospective action. The difficulties inherent in proving organizational responsibility forced the American prosecuting team to slim down the number of indicted organizations from sixteen to seven. The Reich Cabinet, the Party leadership corps, the SS, SA, Gestapo, the SD, and the General Staff and High Command of the Armed Forces, all took the stand alongside the individual defendants.

The list of individual major war criminals to stand trial was announced on 29 August; the organizations only appeared later in the Indictment, which was drafted in September and early October 1945 and finally agreed on 6 October. The list represented a series of compromises. It included names against whom the prosecution case was clearly weak: Karl Doenitz, Erich Raeder, Hjalmar Schacht, Gustav Krupp, and Hitler's first Foreign Minister, von Neurath. Others were included, in the absence of the chief decision-makers, because they stood for an important element of the regime – Keitel for the absent Hitler, Kaltenbrunner for the dead Himmler and the apparatus of terror, Fritzsche for Goebbels and the propaganda machine. The rest owed their place to their function, their office, or their reputation: Frick, Speer, Frank, von Ribbentrop, Hess, Funk, Rosenberg, Bormann, von Papen and the Hitler Youth leader Baldur von Schirach had been high-ranking ministers or Party leaders; Streicher, Seyss-Inquart and Fritz Sauckel were Party men of lesser rank whose place in the racism or imperialism of the regime gave added grounds for prosecution. Yet there remained curious omissions: the Gestapo chief Mueller, the tough Justice Minister, Otto Thierack, the Labour Minister, Franz Seldte, the Agriculture Minister and architect of the 'Blood and Soil' philosophy, Walther Darré, all of whom, with the exception of Mueller, whose identity escaped the investigation teams almost entirely, had been included in earlier versions of the Indictment.[33]

The long arguments over the final roster of defendants highlighted one of the most questionable aspects of the trial preparation: the inability to tell individual prisoners whether they would or would not stand trial. The final decision was not a lottery, but it must have appeared so to many of those awaiting the outcome of their incarceration. The reasons for the delay are easy to explain. When the war ended knowledge about the structure of the Third Reich and the activities of its elites was limited. The prosecution teams were desperate for reliable information. The one key source was the Office of Strategic Services (OSS), run by General Bill Donovan in Washington. The OSS supplied hundreds of brief biographical profiles to assist in the selection of defendants, but the supply failed to keep pace with the demand for knowledge. The other major source was the testimony of the prisoners themselves, many of whom were asked in the early weeks of their captivity to supply lengthy analyses of the power structures and patterns of decision-making of the regime they had recently served, uncertain whether or not they might incriminate themselves through their revelations. A second problem faced by the prosecution was uncertainty about the charges and the evidence needed to sustain them. Until the charges were properly defined it proved impossible to decide precisely which cohort of captives, beyond the 'first six', should stand trial for them.

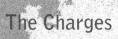

The Charges

Germans from the town of Ludwiglust are made to walk past the graves of concentration camp victims from the camp at Wobbelin in May 1945. German 're-education' included exposure to the atrocities of the Hitler regime.

Our case against the major defendants is concerned with the Nazi masterplan . . . The groundwork of our case must be factually authentic and constitute a well-documented history of what we are convinced was a grand, concerted pattern to incite and commit the aggressions and barbarities which have shocked the world.

Justice Robert Jackson, report to the President, 7 June 1945 [1]

The US draft indictment on the subject of the 'common plan' of the Nazis for preparing etc. a war of aggression suffers from the grave difficulty that it assumes that this plan was in existence, in the form in which it later developed, from the moment of the Nazi arrival in power, or even before . . . it is very seriously doubted whether anything like sufficient evidence can be produced to convince the Court on this crucial and fundamental point.

British Treasury Solicitor, [August] 1945 [2]

Few people in 1945 doubted that Adolf Hitler and his many accomplices had been nourished on ambitions of world conquest. This was the centrepiece of the case prosecuted at Nuremberg. In the course of waging aggressive war countless other atrocities were committed (and the German people were judged to have been enslaved and terrorized by their own government in order to wage it) but the driving force behind the barbarous regime was war. So obvious was German guilt deemed to be, in striking contrast to the bitter arguments about 'War Guilt' at the end of the First World War, that the necessity of proving the charge of warmongering was widely regarded as an irrelevance. The proof of the pudding was in the eating: Germany had occupied or invaded a dozen European states.* These were incontestable historical facts.

The case of the major war criminals nevertheless turned out to be anything but *prima facie*. The waging of aggressive war was not regarded by international lawyers as a war crime as such, though it might well result in numerous violations of the rules of war. When the United Nations War Crimes Commission sought to define the crimes for which it could legitimately seek redress, the best that could be done was to start with the list of war crimes drawn up in 1919 to cope with the misdemeanours of an earlier generation. The thirty-two crimes listed certainly included offences that had been perpetrated throughout the Second World War, and not only by Germans: 'murder and massacres', 'systematic terrorism', 'torture of civilians', 'deportation of civilians', 'forced labour of civilians', 'usurpation of sovereignty', as well as less heinous acts such as 'misuse of flags of truce' and 'poisoning of wells'.[3] The difficulty lay with ascribing responsibility for individual acts to the major war criminals. It was agreed that particular crimes were to be prosecuted in the country where they had been committed. A different basis had to be found for linking particular acts of terror and atrocity with a more general responsibility for the system that produced them.

* Austria, Czechoslovakia, Poland, Denmark, Norway, the Netherlands, Belgium, Luxemburg, France, Yugoslavia, Greece, the Soviet Union.

The missing link was found in the idea of a conspiracy. This too was inspired by Murray Bernays, who saw 'conspiracy to subjugate Europe' as a legal shortcut allowing a wider range of crimes to be introduced as part of a single general act.[4] Stimson approved of the idea that there existed a demonstrable 'unity of criminal purpose in all the acts of Nazism', since this would permit any future prosecution not only to demonstrate a conspiracy to commit war crimes against other injured populations, but to introduce the idea that domestic terror and racism were part and parcel of the same general conspiracy.[5] In November 1944 the War Department came down strongly in favour of conspiracy as the central instrument in demonstrating the criminality of the German leadership. Bernays was asked to present the legal arguments. He demonstrated that acts which were not war crimes in any technical sense, or not even crimes at all, could none the less be deemed to be part of a conspiracy if the end result was aggressive war and atrocity. 'The means of accomplishing the conspiracy,' he explained, 'will be as varied as the "sadistic ingenuity of the conspirators could devise".'[6] Under these circumstances it was possible for criminality to be imputed to everyone deemed to be part of the conspiracy, even if no 'provable act' could be allocated to each individual participant. Bernays saw no legal barrier to dating the conspiracy to 30 January 1933, the day Hitler was appointed Chancellor of Germany.

The conspiracy theory became firmly lodged in all American discussions of the future trial. It had about it a seductive simplicity. Stimson recommended it to Roosevelt on the grounds that such a charge removed the need for more than one major tribunal, while conspiracy embraced all the likely charges to be brought to bear, either from the waging of aggressive war, or from the pre-war terrorization of the German people, or those charges arising from the persecution of the Jews.[7] It also possessed the singular merit that the defence 'I was only obeying orders' could not be admitted. A conspiracy suggested some degree of voluntary participation or complicity even for those defendants remote from the actual machinery of war-making or genocide. By the time Jackson assumed responsibility for preparing the trial in May the underlying assumption of the American case was that at some time before 1 September 1939 the major war criminals 'entered into a common plan or enterprise aimed at the establishment of complete domination of Europe and eventually the world'.[8]

Conspiracy theories invite invention and provoke scepticism. The idea that Nazi policy at home and abroad could be reduced to a single common pattern of action compelled the American prosecutors to bend historical reality. The idea that 'the Nazis' (a term used interchangeably with German leaders, many of whom were not National Socialists) conspired together to conquer the world was scarcely credible, even in 1945, yet it was the centrepiece of the prosecution case. The object, however, was not simply to demonstrate that the Nazis planned and organized the conquest of Europe as a prelude to world domination, but to make it possible to link the wars of conquest with crimes committed even before 1939 against the German people, and the barbarities pursued in the occupied areas against Jews, forced labourers and civilian resisters. The 'master plan', as Jackson reported to President Truman in early June 1945, involved 'acts which have been regarded as criminal since the time of Cain'.[9] The enslavement of the German people through propaganda and terror was regarded as a premeditated attempt to hijack the German state as the instrument for waging wars of aggression. The promotion of the idea of 'Nordic superiority' was intended to create a new generation of young Germans wedded to the 'glorification of war'.[10] The deliberate indoctrination of the Gestapo, SS and other instruments of Nazi terror was designed to create a caste of brutalized enforcers who would carry to the occupied area the vicious habits of totalitarian Germany.

One of the driving forces of this interpretation was the desire to include the exclusion and murder of the Jews as a crime punishable by an international tribunal under international law. The American prosecutors wanted to avoid the approach taken by the UN War Crimes Commission where German anti-semitism was regarded either as a purely domestic matter, not capable of treatment under inter-national law, or as one element in the general wave of Nazi brutality and lawlessness, to be punished separately in national courts set up to prosecute local atrocities. Jewish lobby groups in the United States pressed the War Department to make the persecution of the Jews a specific charge.[11] A new crime of 'genocide' was defined by the Jewish academic Rafael Lemkin, but it was not a recognized category in international law. In a paper drafted in July 1945 for the Judge Advocate-General's office in Washington defining the new offence ('destruction of nations; genos = race, cide = killing') Lemkin focused on the idea of a general conspiracy to 'cripple in their development or to destroy completely, entire nations'. However, his suggestion for the indictment of Hitler on a charge of conspiracy to commit genocide did not even include anti-semitism, since the Jews in Europe did not in any recognized sense constitute a 'nation'. Instead Lemkin included specific charges that were trivial in comparison with the larger crimes of racial mass murder – 'Ordered the inclusion of groups of Belgian citizens as members of the Reichstag [German parliament]' or 'Encouraged prostitution and extramarital relations between Dutch and Norwegian women and members of the German armed forces'.[12] His appended list of potential defendants against the charge of genocide did not even include Himmler, its primary architect.

The problem of defining racial murder was side-stepped by devising a new category of international criminality: 'crimes against humanity'. These were crimes not covered by prior agreements arising from the laws of war; they were to include 'atrocities and persecutions on racial, religious or political grounds' committed by the Nazi regime since 30 January 1933.[13] By the middle of July 1945 Jackson had a clear view in his own mind about the charges to be levelled against the major war criminals. They were all derived from the common criminal plan, which formed the first charge of conspiracy. The remaining charges were grouped under three headings: the waging of aggressive war in violation of treaty agreements; the perpetrating of war crimes in violation of the rules, customs and laws of war; and the planning and perpetration of other persecutions both inside and outside Germany.[14] Following the line of argument developed by the Soviet team the first category was described as 'crimes against peace'.[15] These charges were repeated in the Agreement on the Tribunal signed on 8 August between the four Allied powers, and formed the basis of the final Indictment completed on 6 October.

The charges bore the unmistakable stamp of the American prosecution team. They were not universally approved, even by American lawyers. When the Acting Dean of the Harvard Law School, Edmund E. Morgan, was invited in January 1945 to pronounce judgement on the merits of using conspiracy theory to prosecute war crimes, he unambiguously rejected the idea on the grounds that it violated the spirit of 'Anglo-American legal thought' by making up the offence after it had been committed. Morgan urged the War Department to reconsider charges he regarded as 'unwise and unjustifiable', or risk losing the 'reasoned approval of civilized communities'.[16] Jackson was well aware that conventional international law not only failed to embrace the idea of conspiracy, but did not even regard aggressive war as a distinct crime. War was a relationship regarded in law as morally neutral, in which both parties enjoyed the same rights. The laws of war might well be broken during the course of the contest, but war itself was not illegal. Jackson challenged this view on the grounds that modern international law failed to make the medieval distinction between unjust and just wars, between 'the war of defense and the war of aggression'. This was not necessarily a distinction that his medieval legal experts would have recognized, but it served Jackson's purpose. He was able to argue that as a result of the international agreements made since the First World War, and he had in mind principally the Briand–Kellogg Pact signed in Paris in 1928 which outlawed war as an instrument for the settling of international disputes, there was now a basis in international law on which to found a precedent that 'aggressive war-making is illegal and criminal'.[17]

British doubts rested more on the basis that conspiracy would be very difficult to demonstrate on the evidence available. The British response to Jackson's draft indictment in August called for a case based on 'strictly provable facts'. The 'common plan', which Jackson regarded as the essence of the case, was little liked in London, where the historical reality of the Third Reich was viewed very differently. 'The Nazis, and Hitler in particular,' ran one British report, 'were supreme opportunists and, whilst they had almost certainly aggressive designs from the beginning, it is very probable that their aggressive plans only gradually took the shape in which they were carried through.'[18] A long analysis by the British Foreign Office of the contents of *Mein Kampf*, described as the 'master document' (and used invariably in this capacity by the Soviet prosecutors), was forced to conclude that the book 'does not reveal the Nazi aims of conquest and domination fully and explicitly'.[19] When the American prosecutors tried to recruit the émigré German historian and former National Socialist, Hermann Rauschning, to the team of prosecution witnesses in July 1945 he refused on the grounds that the general conspiracy charge was nonsense: 'in his opinion not over half a dozen men in Germany planned conquest of the world . . . he personally doubted if

Hitler had any such plan'.[20] The post-war debates in German history about whether Nazi foreign policy was based on a deliberate set of intentions or on opportunistic reaction, most famously exposed in the arguments generated by A. J. P. Taylor's *Origins of the Second World War*, published in 1961, had their roots in the interpretative arguments surrounding the Nuremberg trials.

The historical objections to a charge of conspiracy were evident to anyone familiar with the history of pre-war Germany. There were also serious legal objections. French and Soviet law did not embrace the concept of conspiracy as such; nor was this approach consistent with German practice. Robert Kempner, an émigré German lawyer working for Jackson, recalled in his memoirs that in Anglo-Saxon law complicity often proved sufficient for conviction: 'The gangster was at the hairdresser's on the day [of the crime], later he obtained a bit of the loot, but I don't need to prove that, because he was part of the gang anyway.'[21] Under German law direct participation in a stated crime had to be demonstrated in court. Both the Soviet and French prosecution teams wanted to avoid specifying conspiracy to wage aggressive war as the central charge, and to substitute instead the specific acts of violation and atrocity associated with the waging of war by the European Axis states. Though Soviet legal experts had provided the American war crimes team with the theoretical basis for 'crimes against peace', the Soviet prosecutor, Iona Nikitchenko, did not want aggressive war in general to be penalized in case the Soviet occupation of eastern Poland and the Soviet–Finnish 'Winter War' should be raised by the German defendants in order to embarrass the prosecution. So anxious was Moscow to avoid these revelations that a security team led by Colonel Likhachev was sent to Nuremberg to try to prevent any details of the Soviet Union's shady past from surfacing during the trial. All detailed references to German aggression against Poland originally included in the draft of the opening speech for the Soviet prosecution were deleted by the authorities in Moscow in order to avoid awkward questions in court.[22]

The Soviet insistence that the crime of aggressive war should be applied only to the European Axis countries (even though Italy was not represented among the defendants at Nuremberg) was finally conceded by Jackson at the very last meeting of the London conference, and the Tribunal eventually prosecuted Germans for specific acts of military aggression. The issue of conspiracy also had to be resolved. At the instigation of the British Treasury Solicitor, Sir Thomas Barnes, the Soviet and French reservations about conspiracy were met by removing from the charge of general conspiracy the references to war crimes and crimes against humanity, and confining conspiracy only to the waging of aggressive war. Both the French and Soviet representatives in London were keen for the persecution of their civilian populations to be included in the trial, and this could now be done without the difficulty, anticipated by most critics of the American scheme, of trying to demonstrate beyond doubt that the conspiracy extended to all the totalitarian practices of the Nazi regime.[23]

The final agreement still placed the burden of proof firmly at the Allies' door. It was incontestable that aggressive war had been waged and that atrocities beyond measure had been perpetrated. The uncertain factor was evidence. When the trial preparation began in April 1945 the prosecution teams had no idea whether or not material would be forthcoming to sustain a judicial process. The American conviction that a common conspiracy existed was an assertion, not yet a case that could be proved. Only on 26 April did the War Department authorize the collection of evidence to be used against the major war criminals. The Judge Advocate-General, Myron Cramer, informed McCloy on 5 May that the directive issued to him in November 1944 to begin assembling evidence for war crimes committed against American nationals had been so severely constrained by a lack of personnel and the sheer complexity of the task that it threatened to produce an *opéra bouffe* instead of a solemn judicial trial. The material gathered so far included published information on the Third Reich and on prominent Nazi personalities easily available from American sources, but did not constitute anything in the nature of adequate forensic evidence.[24] When original German documents became available in Europe towards the end of the war, there was an unseemly scramble for the spoils between all those institutions and offices with claims on evidence. 'Everyone is at cross purposes,' complained one American officer to the War Department, 'more or less grabbing in all directions.'[25]

The ambition to match evidence to charges that had not yet been properly defined defied all conventional legal practice. Only in mid-May did Jackson's new team explain the kind of proof they were looking for. This included the 'nature and purpose of the criminal plan or enterprise', which had no historical basis beyond the mere statement of its existence; and 'the facts and circumstances that made the wars launched by the defendants wars of aggression', a procedure that produced a mere tautology. Proof was also required of acts and conduct 'which may not have been criminal *per se*', but which were utilized in furthering the 'criminal plan'. To speed up the preparation of the trial the supply of proof was to be confined to any evidence that appeared to have probative value, and the final case was to rest on 'the best evidence *readily* available' rather than on evidence yet to be unearthed. 'Time is of the essence,' the report concluded, 'and a good case ready for trial at an early date will be far preferable to a perfect case unduly delayed.'[26]

The evidence itself was divided into a number of distinct categories: documentary evidence (including official state papers, correspondence, speeches, laws and decrees, treaties and diplomatic agreements); photographs (still, and motion picture); and last of all, oral testimony taken from film, tape-recordings and witnesses. Interrogation material, which eventually supplied one of the most important sources, was yet to feature in its own right. The collection and assessment of evidence was the responsibility of specific departments. On Jackson's team Colonel Robert Storey, a Texas lawyer who served in the Army Air Forces during the war, was given the job of sorting the documentary evidence captured by American forces in Europe. In Washington the OSS promised to deliver the fruits of their intelligence-gathering on Germany, but when it finally emerged it was found to amount to little more than a summary of material already supplied.[27] Quite by chance Bernays discovered the existence of the Jewish Central Information Office, which housed a wide assembly of books and materials on the Third Reich, brought to London in 1939 by Alfred Wiener, whose name was given to the collection after the war when it became known formally as the Wiener Library. The American team paid £20 for the privilege of unlimited access, on the condition that they should arrive at the library with a letter of recommendation.[28]

The British War Crimes Executive delayed sending a research group to Europe until late July 1945, and then dispatched only three officers and six clerks to Paris to deal with the mountain-range of archives unearthed by the British 21st Army Group, whose responsibility it was to seize anything of a documentary character, from ministerial files to telephone directories.[29] Under the circumstances the supply of high-grade evidence for the trial was a remarkable achievement. Officers sifted through material after it had been translated at high speed by a small team of German-speakers. Anything of importance was sent at once to Jackson, marked 'aggression' or 'war crimes', and filed. The key evidence of conspiracy grew very slowly. In late June a translation arrived of what has become known ever since as the 'Hossbach memorandum' – the minutes of a meeting called by Hitler on 5 November 1937 (and recorded later by the army adjutant Friedrich Hossbach), during which he outlined his foreign policy ambitions towards Austria and Czechoslovakia. On 2 August, only a few days before the Tribunal charter was finalized and published, Jackson received a translation of 'Case Green', the directive for the invasion of Czechoslovakia drawn up in late May 1938, though the British Foreign Office had been in possession of the document since early June following its discovery lying in the dust and rubble of Hitler's bombed Bavarian retreat at Berchtesgaden[30]. The 'Aggression' file also contained a potential bombshell: a translation of the 'Secret Additional Protocol to the German–Soviet Pact' concluded in August 1939, which divided Poland into Soviet and German spheres of interest. Tempting though its revelation must have been for Jackson as he wrestled with his Soviet counterparts in conference, Soviet collusion in German aggression remained locked away in the file.[31]

By August, three months of detective work had produced a great deal of the evidence felt to be necessary in order to be able to mount an effective prosecution at all. Further evidence emerged after the charges had been defined and the indictment drawn up and delivered to the defendants, and continued to surface even while the trial was in progress. Where the evidence was weakest, it has remained weak. The attempt to construct a master-plan and a general conspiracy has been sustained by few historians; there is little dispute that Hitler intended to wage war at some time, but the timing and nature of those wars owed much to shifting international circumstances, many of which had simply to be disregarded by the tribunal. No sane historian now disputes that the mass murder of the Jews is historical fact, yet the central documentary evidence on the decision for genocide could not be found, and the timing and motives for that decision remain live historical issues more than half a century later. The numerous gaps in the story could be filled only by finding witnesses or participants willing to testify on oath under interrogation or cross-examination. This necessity brought the process of interrogation into the limelight. On key aspects of the trial preparation, interrogation was indispensable. On 4 August Bernays wrote to the chief of the American Interrogation Division, Colonel John Amen, asking him to investigate the claim made by Ribbentrop that there was a concerted policy directed at 'Jews, Churches, Freemasons etc.'. This was an area of proof, Bernays conceded, which was not satisfactory, and he asked Amen to press all his interrogation subjects for further evidence of such a policy, how it was carried out, and by whom.[32] Vital interrogation evidence on the Jewish genocide was still being produced long after the Tribunal had begun its deliberations and long after the charges, laid out in the Indictment, had finally been made available to the defendants after months of uncertainty and speculation. Interrogation was to supply the missing links that remained after months of forensic investigation. From August to the opening of the trial in November the focus of the prosecution teams shifted from finding documents to asking questions.

Asking the Questions

Murray Bernays (centre), who developed the idea of 'conspiracy' in order to indict whole organizations for crimes against peace and against humanity, studies documents togther with the chief of the Interrogation Division, Colonel John Amen (right).

Confidence is the touchstone of all interrogations. No matter whether the P.[risoner of] W.[ar] has raped, pillaged and killed defenceless women and children, so long as that PW has a story to tell, it is the duty of the interrogator to put these unpleasant feelings out of his head and set himself to the task with a completely open mind.

Major Kenneth Hechler, War Department Historical Branch interrogator, 1945[1]

Under Anglo-Saxon law a criminal when arrested enjoys a number of rights, including the right to remain silent, the right to a defence counsel and the right, should he choose to talk under interrogation, to the usual warnings about incrimination. Above all, he must be formally charged after a specified period of time or allowed to go free. None of these procedures was allowed to the group of senior German prisoners from among whom the defendants at Nuremberg were eventually selected. In the summer of 1945 it would have been remarkable had such rights been considered at all. One of Justice Jackson's first tasks as Chief of Counsel was to instruct the American War Department to deny suspected German war criminals the normal privileges accorded to prisoners-of-war, however senior in rank they might be, and to keep them 'in close confinement and stern control', ready for interrogation.[2]

The process of systematic interrogation of prisoners and witnesses in preparation for the trial did not begin until August 1945, when they were moved in small batches to Nuremberg prison. Between the dates of their capture and the transfer to Nuremberg they were held at two main internment camps, one run by the Americans, the other by the British. The largest number were under American guard in Mondorf-les-Bains, a small spa town in Luxemburg. The camp was known by the derogatory code-name 'Ashcan'. A smaller number, mainly prisoners with a background in the business and technical life of Germany, were held at Kransberg Castle outside Frankfurt am Main under the British code-name 'Dustbin'. The regime in the two internment camps was strikingly different. At Kransberg, which had been converted into a German air force headquarters for Goering by Albert Speer in 1939, the prisoners were housed in a two-storey servant block. The rooms were clean and the food, basic military rations, generous by the standards of defeated Germany. The prisoners were allowed to walk and talk freely, to write occasional letters and to listen to the radio. A weekly cabaret was arranged. Schacht, who with Speer was one of only two prisoners at Kransberg to feature among the defendants at Nuremberg, entertained his fellows with poetry readings. Every now and again a team of interrogators from one of the technical intelligence agencies arrived, but for most of the prisoners the long summer in the mountains was a disconcerting interlude.[3]

The conditions at Mondorf were, by comparison, rigid and spartan. The forty prisoners held for war crimes trials were kept in the Grand Hotel, a shabby spa centre converted into a temporary prison camp. The building and an acre of grounds were surrounded by two fifteen-foot barbed wire fences, one with an electric current, and wooden watchtowers with machine-gun emplacements. Guards had orders to shoot if prisoners strayed too near the perimeter. An armoured car, a light tank and an anti-aircraft battery were installed on the approaches to the hotel against what must have been the remotest threat of rescue or escape. The prisoners slept in rooms stripped bare of everything save two army bunks, straw mattresses (which were removed as a punishment for any misdemeanour), a small table and a straight-backed chair. Pillows were allowed only to prisoners who fell ill. The food was limited to 1,550 calories per day, the amount allowed for ordinary German civilians. The regime was the brainchild of an American colonel, Burton C. Andrus, who was appointed to head the security division at 'Ashcan', and was later transferred to Nuremberg to run the prison there. Andrus was ideal for the job. He wore a brightly polished helmet over his grey crew-cut hair, a smart uniform, and small steel-framed spectacles. Under his arm he carried a riding crop. His expression was severe and unyielding. He took a distinct pleasure in doing his job by rules minutely calculated and inflexibly enforced. One of the interrogators who passed through Mondorf remembered him as a man known for his 'pettiness and naïveté', who displayed 'a little mind' when indulging his absolute power over the men in his charge. He told one visitor that he considered all the prisoners to be 'nuts'.[4] He was the instrument of the 'stern control' Jackson promised his President.

After weeks of incarceration it was easy to regard the tired and ill-dressed prisoners as creatures who deserved their fate. Their popular reputation for blind fanaticism and sordid brutality predisposed many of those who came into contact with them to assume the worst. The British diplomat Ivone Kirkpatrick visited 'Ashcan' in June 1945 and found the inhabitants repellent – 'nasty and in every respect third-rate'. He thought the efforts to prevent the prisoners from committing suicide were misplaced. 'It will save us a great deal of trouble,' he wrote to

Colonel Burton C. Andrus was the commander of the security detachment at 'Ashcan' camp, and later at Nuremberg. He was responsible for the welfare and discipline of the prisoners, and imposed on his charges a tough, no-nonsense regime. They were, he told one visitor, 'nuts'.

Eden, 'if all the inmates of "Ashcan" were to commit mass suicide.'[5] Many of the guards displayed an ill-concealed contempt for their charges. Andrus made no attempt to mask his own feelings. 'He knew how to keep those "S.O.B.s" in line,' he told one American investigating team, 'and he would see to it that they would give us the answers we wanted.'[6] The captives were seldom physically abused or threatened once in prison, out of the hands of their army captors, but they were subjected to intense psychological pressure. At one point early in his captivity Fritz Sauckel was told repeatedly by his interrogators that if he failed to tell them what they wanted to know he would be turned over to the Russians.[7]

The prisoners were allowed to speak to each other. Their conversations were bugged from a small house adjoining the camp. Occasionally four or five of them were moved to the house for a few days at a time in the hope that they might talk more freely together away from the main camp. These discussions were also recorded and transcribed. The prisoners were subject to interrogation by a permanent team of eight interrogators, whose identity was shielded from the prisoners by false names and ranks. The interrogations were not carried out systematically. For most of the period from May to August the prisoners were the object of fact-finding from intelligence agencies whose primary interest was not in trial preparation but in the discovery of technical information. Under the auspices of the Field Intelligence Agency Technical (FIAT), and the Combined Intelligence Objectives Sub-Committee (CIOS), numerous short interrogations were conducted on aspects of the German war economy, German scientific research, and on the structure of the Nazi state. Some prisoners were interviewed by members of the United States Strategic Bombing Survey, whose members were under heavy pressure of time to produce reports on the impact of Allied bombing on German production and morale.[8] In July a further layer of interrogations was imposed by the War Department's Shuster Commission, a committee of senior American academics appointed to reconstruct an operational history of the war from the German side. The Commission was established on 19 May by Stimson's deputy, Robert Patterson, who wanted interrogations done quickly in case prisoners were dispersed or killed, and to prevent them developing among themselves 'a sort of "*party line*" explanation of events'.[9] Only when a number of 'reputable scientific bodies' asked

Colonel Amen, head of the Interrogation Division, dictates transcripts to a secretary. The division worked round the clock to provide a regular record of every interrogation, but were always short of staff and competent linguists.

Jackson for permission to undertake systematic psychological examination of the prisoners, on the grounds that 'science will be helped' by the experiment, was a request turned down.[10]

Few of these many interrogations were used for the case to be prosecuted at Nuremberg. They were circulated to provide some background detail, but the questions asked in them were seldom directly related to the charges as they came to be defined by the prosecuting delegations in London. The responsibility for interrogating the major war criminals and the key witnesses for the trial lay with the prosecution. Bernays wrote to Jackson on 9 May, one week after his appointment, to suggest that a special section should be set up to conduct interrogations in Europe along the lines dictated by Jackson's view of the probable charges.[11] Jackson chose a New York lawyer working for the US Army Inspector-General, Colonel John Harlan Amen, to run what soon became the Interrogation Division. He was a well-respected trial lawyer with a successful record for prosecuting corruption cases, who was

convinced of the importance of oral evidence in preparing and conducting adversarial trials.[12] He accompanied Jackson to Europe in
mid-May and set up office at 7 rue de Presbourg in Paris.

There his Division began the task of establishing contacts with the
interrogation centres and internment camps run by the American and
British armies. During June his staff started to sift through and analyse
the first of 800 interrogation reports supplied by the agencies and army
intelligence centres.[13] This labour consumed a great deal of the energy
of the Division. By August only 500 had been processed on standard
'Information Analysis' forms, on which brief synopses of each interrogation were recorded. The task of interrogating the likely defendants
at the forthcoming Tribunal was postponed until the prisoners were
under exclusive American custody and ready for trial; the date for the
transfer to Nuremberg rested on the final agreement between the
powers on the nature of the Tribunal and the charges. This left Amen
and his team only a few weeks to extract oral testimony. Early in
August an advance party from his Division arrived in Nuremberg,
followed shortly after by a section of the British War Crimes Executive.
The British were prepared to rely on Amen and his Division rather
than establish a separate organization of their own. On 8 August, the
day agreement on the tribunal was reached, the Paris-based branch of
the Executive confirmed to the War Office in London that they intended
'to leave the interrogation of the major criminals to the Americans',
with the proviso that British investigators could 'weigh-in' on any
particular issue when it suited them to do so.[14]

The transfer of prisoners from 'Ashcan' and 'Dustbin' began in early
August. On 5 August General Dwight D. Eisenhower, the Supreme
Commander of Allied Forces in Europe, ordered the transfer of twenty-
seven named prisoners from Mondorf to Nuremberg. The number
included eleven of the thirteen prisoners held at 'Ashcan' who were
formally selected later that month to stand trial.[15] The transfers
were undertaken piecemeal. The first group of internees at Mondorf
were roused one morning at dawn and bundled into two army ambu-
lances. They were forbidden to talk to each other. Dressed in shabby
clothes, without ties, belts or shoelaces, they sat in silence as they drove
the twenty kilometres to Luxemburg airport. Here they boarded two
transport planes under heavily armed escort and flew southeastwards,
unaware of their destination or of the fact that they had been chosen

as likely defendants in a trial for war crimes.[16] Not all the prisoners and witnesses could be moved to Nuremberg together because of delays in converting the prison building to its new role. By 19 August twenty-one had been transferred, though the building was intended to house up to 200, and eventually held exactly 100.[17] The arrangements for the transfers were in army hands and Jackson's office had great difficulty trying to locate exactly where the prisoners were. On 22 August Colonel Andrus, who had accompanied the prisoners in person, notified Jackson of the whereabouts of all those on the most-wanted list. Some of the likely defendants remained at 'Dustbin'; others who were eventually to stand trial, including Raeder and von Neurath, failed to appear on the list at all.[18]

The transfer from Kransberg Castle was much slower. Not until the list of defendants was published on 29 August were Schacht and Speer given any inkling that they would be joining the other prisoners at Nuremberg. Schacht was sent off first in mid-September, first to an intermediate camp at Oberürsel known simply as 'the cage', where conditions were, as Schacht later recalled in his memoirs, the worst he experienced, either German or Allied. There were just two meals a day, one in the morning, one at four o'clock, consisting of half-cooked peas. The beds were wooden planks with a blanket drawn over them. One ten-minute walk in the open was permitted each day. After three weeks he was taken in a car under escort with two other prisoners to Nuremberg where he was placed, like all the prisoners, in solitary confinement.[19] Speer was allowed to enjoy the easy atmosphere a little longer, but in late September he was taken away by jeep to Oberürsel, and then by lorry to Nuremberg where he arrived late at night, to be placed in a bleak, sparsely furnished cell on the ground floor of Nuremberg prison, opposite Hermann Goering.[20]

The remaining defendants arrived during October and November. Rudolf Hess was flown in from Britain on 8 October; von Neurath, whose precise whereabouts the Americans did not know when they wanted to interrogate him in early September, was brought from French captivity; finally Raeder and Fritzsche, prisoners of the Soviet Union, were first transferred from Moscow to Berlin in October, then to Nuremberg two days before the opening of the trial on 20 November, too late for serious interrogation.[21] The two Soviet captives experienced Moscow very differently. The hapless Fritzsche, assistant to the hated Goebbels, was taken to the Lubyanka prison, the heart of the Stalinist apparatus of terror. Here he was put on a starvation diet and subjected to periods of solitary confinement, though not physically abused. He was relentlessly interrogated by men skilled in the art of extracting a full confession. Raeder, on the other hand, who was in poor health when he was captured, was allowed to rest at home until he had recovered enough to travel. He was plied with generous rations to speed his revival. In early July he was flown from Berlin to Moscow with his wife where he was placed in a comfortable dacha near the capital, with a guard on the door. Here he was allowed to write, given a reasonable diet and the medicines needed for his heart condition. As a result the few pictures of Raeder at Nuremberg show a figure less drawn and hungry than his fellow defendants.[22]

The Interrogation Division was transferred from Paris to Nuremberg in the middle of August. Like all the major prosecution personnel, they were housed in the Grand Hotel, one of the few buildings in the centre of Nuremberg still habitable after the bombing. Though badly damaged, the hotel could still accommodate several hundred staff, two or more to a room. Wooden planks were laid across the damaged floor to connect the two wings of the building. Water was supplied in large canvas drums installed in the corridors to avoid the risk from the city's contaminated water-supply. The ballroom and bar became the social centre of Nuremberg. Even the Soviet delegation, housed elsewhere in the city, would visit the hotel where they maintained 'a smiling taciturnity' until they were gripped by the urge to dance to the noisy jazz bands and orchestras that gave the hotel an atmosphere of degenerate hysteria amidst the grim business of dispensing justice. The press corps was housed outside the city, in a villa belonging to the wealthy Faber pencil manufacturers, but the reporters, too, gravitated to the Grand Hotel in search of decent food and gossip. Beyond the hotel lay the ruins of Nuremberg. Out of a city of 400,000, destined by Hitler to become the showpiece of the Party, 250,000 eked out an existence in the stark and gutted buildings. Visitors remarked on the strange silence of the shattered streets; beneath the rubble there lived thousands of Germans, noiselessly guarding their few possessions, cooking soups and potatoes by night, scrounging cigarettes from soldiers, deadened by defeat and disease.[23]

One of the other buildings to survive the bombing was the *Landes-*

Grand Admiral Erich Raeder (right) sits eating beans and crackers with Hans Fritzsche, a Propaganda Ministry official. Both had been in Soviet hands in Moscow, Raeder in a comfortable *dacha*, Fritzsche in the notorious Lubyanka prison.

gericht, the provincial court. Behind its left wing was a large prison block, consisting of five three-tier wings built around a central rotunda. One of the wings was partitioned off. It was here that the defendants and witnesses were brought. Each stone cell measured nine feet by thirteen, with a heavy wooden door on one side and a small barred window on the opposite wall. The door had a small window set into it at chin height covered with a wire grille. A wooden panel was attached which opened out to form a small tray on which the prisoners' food, in army mess tins, was delivered to them. Outside each cell, next to the door, was a spotlight. The furnishing was sparse – an army cot, a table and a chair. A copy of the Bible was supplied to each defendant.[24] During August Colonel Andrus supervised the introduction of modifications to ensure that prisoners could not kill themselves, or each other. Nets were installed under the upper corridors, and the window glass was replaced with plastic 'celloglass'; all metal projections and dangerous fixtures, which might tempt a hanging, were removed and

The Grand Hotel, Nuremberg, was only lightly damaged by bombing and became the centre of the American presence in the city. Jackson and his staff were housed in the hotel; the Soviet delegation chose to stay in villas outside the city.

At the end of the day in Nuremberg, soldiers and civilians indulged in a hectic nightlife in the ballroom of the Grand Hotel. Here a more restrained *thé dansant* produces a packed dancefloor.

A view of the prison attached to the Nuremberg Palace of Justice. The wooden walkway was hastily constructed for the prisoners after an SS dagger thrown from the wall landed close to Goering on his way to the court building.

The prison at Nuremberg, built in the nineteenth century, consisted of four wings that fanned outwards from the court building. The prisoners were housed on two floors of one wing.

the walls repaired.[25] Outside the prison block was a small exercise yard, enclosed by a high wall, where prisoners were permitted, two at a time, to walk up and down for fifteen minutes in silence.

The regime imposed on prisoners at Nuremberg was stricter still than at Mondorf. Andrus ran the Internal Security Detachment with an iron rod. The most onerous requirement was silence. Prisoners were not permitted to communicate with each other, or with the guards or workers. They could only talk to the prison staff 'on matters pertaining to the office of those individuals'. No other discussion was permitted and guards were under strict orders to enforce silence. The interrogations took place with men who were denied the habits of conversation for weeks at a time. The other limitations were more bearable. Books could be supplied from a prison library. Writing materials were freely available, and letters were permitted to family, the prison commandant, legal authorities and interrogators, though they had to pass under the gaze of the prison officials. Prisoners were allowed one shower a week, but had to remain silent as they washed in the communal shower room. They were only allowed one set of clothes, and nothing that could be used to craft a home-made noose. The older prisoners were eventually allowed two pieces of string, four inches in length, to tie up their shoes, to save them from the awkward shuffle in the exercise yard. Written instructions were given to all prisoners on attempting to escape: 'If such attempt is made they will be struck down or shot. Any injury they suffer will be their own fault. The guard will call *halt, if time permits.*'[26]

The prisoners were guarded night and day. The object was to ensure that a guard went past the cell every minute to check through the small panel that the prisoner was still visible. At night prisoners were forced to keep their hands and head in view from under the blanket at all times. The toilets were positioned in such a way that the feet of the prisoner could still be seen. This system of review placed a strain on both prisoners and keepers. On one occasion a guard fainted from the effect of having to stare every minute through the wire grid in the door at Kaltenbrunner's wide-check jacket.[27] The impact on the prisoners was mixed. Some coped with the conditions stoically enough. Others were already in a state of near nervous collapse when they arrived. The worst case was Ribbentrop, whom Andrus considered to be close to a complete breakdown. His sight was failing, he had lost a good

The water system in Nuremberg was contaminated as a result of the bombing. In the Grand Hotel the US Army placed large canvas water bags along the corridors for guests to use.

A German POW carries the daily ration of food in mess tins for the major war criminals. Most of the staff at the prison were German POWs, but they were forbidden from talking to the prisoners. The diet was fixed at 1,550 calories a day.

deal of weight at Mondorf, and he had abandoned the will to keep up what shabby appearances were permitted. Only two cases led to hospitalization. Kaltenbrunner suffered a spontaneous haemorrhage of the brain membrane three days before the trial and missed the first weeks in court. One of the witnesses, held under less severe conditions in the internment wing, was reported in early October to be close to suicide. A month later, in a clearly psychotic state, he was sent to a psychiatric institution.[28] Prisoners were visited by a doctor each day to check on their physical condition; two psychiatrists, Douglas Kelley and Gustave Gilbert, checked their mental states. Gilbert also arranged for the prisoners to be tested for intelligence with a German version of the Wechsler-Bellevue Adult Intelligence Test, which made allowance for the deterioration of intelligence with advancing age. Schacht achieved the highest score (143 against an adult average of 90–110), but did so with a generous age adjustment; Streicher achieved the lowest, a score of 106. The more surprising thing is how readily the prisoners agreed to participate. After weeks of enforced silence Kelley found them 'eager to talk', 'almost without probing or prompting'.[29]

Some effort had already been made to anticipate the psychological responses of a people experiencing the desolation of defeat after the fantastic promises of victory. In May 1945 the British Directorate of Army Psychiatry produced a lengthy memorandum on the variety of ways in which the Germans might react when confronted by 'national, social and personal disaster'.[30] The 'mental "buffers"' likely to result were described with the familiar vocabulary of contemporary psychiatry: dissociation, projection, manic denial, anarchy and delinquency, withdrawal, depression and realistic adaptation. Dissociation was regarded as the commonest response, leading in extreme cases to 'stupor or "loss of memory"' and 'inconsistent, self-contradictory behaviour, such as denial of former allegiance to National Socialism'. British psychiatrists assumed this was a particular expression of the German psyche: 'the line between this German capacity for forgetting . . . and conscious lying is often difficult to draw'.[31]

Projection was also expected to be a widespread reaction in the belief that Germans already possessed a 'stab-in-the-back' mentality following their experience in the First World War, and would seek once more to blame anyone but themselves for the catastrophe. Denial, nihilistic violence and withdrawal into a world of fantasy were less

The chief of the security apparatus of terror in the Third Reich, Ernst Kaltenbrunner, is led back to his cell after a spell in hospital following minor haemorrhages to the brain membrane in November 1945. Kaltenbrunner refused to acknowledge his responsibility.

common but already manifest among the prisoners in British hands. Depression and adaptation were the hallmarks of the guilty personality who was none the less capable of acknowledging that guilt. In extreme cases the consequence was expected to be suicide ('we can hope for the elimination of a certain percentage of people who would make the post-war period difficult'), but in most cases it was hoped that depression would be benign, allowing the guilty individual to sustain the strong sense of social responsibility so necessary to the psychological reconstruction of Germany.[32] Almost all of these reactions were to be found among the cohort of leading Germans in Allied hands, but because the interrogators were not experienced psychiatrists they reacted to the traumatized individuals in front of them without differentiation. In the end Kelley and Gilbert succeeded in getting the prisoners to speak more freely and more candidly in their cells than they did in the interrogation room.

The interrogations began on 15 August 1945, when Amen, accompanied by three of the four chief American interrogators, interviewed Alfred Jodl on the invasion of Norway. Much thought had gone into the format the interrogations should follow. The interrogation team was supplied with forty-four dossiers of detailed information on senior German prisoners drawn up by the Judge Advocate-General's office in Washington to be used as background briefs in preparing the questions. The OSS also supplied extensive analyses of the structure of the dictatorship and the major institutions that it spawned.[33] To simplify the arguments small illustrated information cards were produced: 'Aggressive Action 1938–1939' had four simple maps showing the 'conquest of Austria', 'absorption of Sudetenland', 'conquest of Czechoslovakia', 'invasion of Poland'. Helpful slogans were printed beneath each map to indicate a real unity of purpose between the four acts of aggression: 'Czechoslovakia encircled', 'Czechoslovakian defenses weakened', 'borders shortened – new bases acquired', and finally 'bases for attack on USSR'. The map of the conquest of Czechoslovakia failed to indicate that an independent Slovakian state was set up when German forces occupied Bohemia. The final map simply left the half of Poland occupied by the Red Army in 1939 as blank, with black arrows pointing menacingly across it towards the distant pre-1939 Soviet border.[34]

Armed with the background information, the interrogators were given regular instructions on subjects where more evidence was needed and some indication of the line of questioning they should pursue. The evidence acquired through interrogation then had to be systematically scrutinized by the Analysis Section of the Interrogation Division run by Lieutenant-Colonel Henry Otto and two assistant subalterns. At Bernays's suggestion the oral evidence was to be presented on special forms under the heading 'Staff Evidence Analysis'. The material had to be filed by crime and by individual criminal. The digest of interrogation evidence included a summary of the statements by main points based upon 'direct knowledge or participation' or on the more speculative 'information and belief'. The form also included a complicated cross-referencing system to other proof, points of law or possible defence,

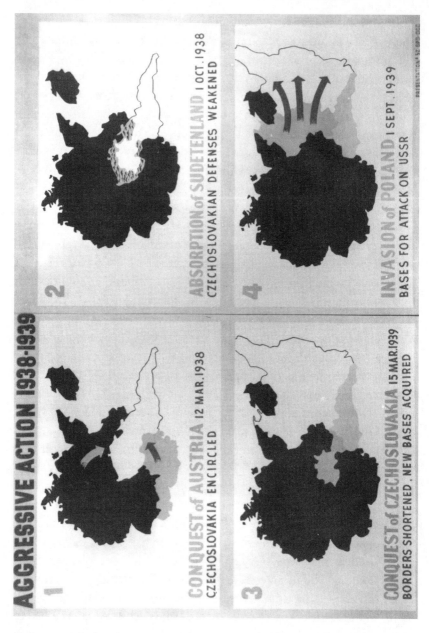

In this stylized OSS chart showing German aggression in central Europe, Germany has taken on the profile of a predatory wolf, though the equally predatory Soviet bear has been ignored in the map of the division of Poland.

and to other defendants and charges, all of which took a great deal of administrative time.[35] The interrogations were taken down in shorthand by a team of stenographers, and then typed up by the secretarial staff in full and filed in a safe. The stenographers wrote in English, taking down a second-hand version of every reply in German after it had been translated for them by one of the ten interpreters attached to the Division. Some defendants replied in English; few of those on Amen's team had a fluent command of German.

The interrogators themselves were grouped under the Staff Section of the Interrogation Division. Amen himself conducted few of the interrogations, unless there was good cause. He honoured Goering by conducting all of his. When von Ribbentrop failed to respond in very lengthy interrogations to any of the major questions he was asked, Amen took over the questioning in an attempt to bully out of him a better level of recollection.[36] Most interrogations were conducted by just four officers: Colonel Howard A. Brundage from the Judge Advocate-General's office; Colonel Thomas S. Hinkel, from the same department; Major John J. Monigan; and Thomas J. Dodd, the only civilian lawyer, who later became a member of the American trial counsel. Three more interrogators were later added to the section, but only two, Lieutenant-Colonel Smith Brookhart, Jr., and Lieutenant-Colonel Murray I. Gurfein (who did know German), conducted any substantial number of interviews.[37] The Soviet prosecution team also undertook short interrogations of some, though not all, of the major defendants. All but a handful of these interviews were the responsibility of Major-General Alexandrov, a member of the Soviet trial counsel, and Colonel Solomon Rosenblit, who also acted at times as an interpreter.

Each interrogation was conducted on standard lines. Most took place in a small room with large windows on the third floor of the court building. The room contained a table and a dozen chairs. There would usually be present the interrogator, an interpreter and a court reporter/stenographer. When they were assembled a small button was pushed, alerting a waiting military policeman outside to usher in the prisoner. The formal proceedings opened with the administration of an oath by the interrogator to the interpreter: 'Do you solemnly swear to translate from English into German the questions I am about to ask the witness, and his responses from German into English, to the best

A rare picture of the interrogators. Pictured with Colonel Amen (seated) are Howard Brundage (centre) and Judge Thomas Dodd. The interrogators were short of experience of German conditions, but were chosen for their reputations as trial lawyers.

of your ability, so help you God?' To which the interpreter replied solemnly as required: 'I swear, so help me God.' Only then did the interrogator turn to the prisoner and administer the standard legal oath requiring 'the truth, the whole truth and nothing but the truth'. Some replied simply 'yes', others with the full oath. Prisoners were not required to swear again before subsequent interrogations, though they were frequently, and necessarily, reminded by the interrogator that they remained under oath. The questioning then began. Each session lasted approximately two hours, but because of the cumbersome system of interpretation and record-keeping the substance of the interview was considerably less than the time allotted might have permitted. In many cases the interrogation of an individual prisoner was conducted over one or two days, with the same interrogator responsible for each of the three or four interviews. In other cases the interrogations were spread out over a number of weeks, which required the interrogator to remind the prisoner of the context of any earlier discussion and made continuity in the interrogation difficult.[38]

The interrogator carried with him a sheet suggesting the line of questioning or the questions themselves. Few of these are to be found among the pre-trial records. The pencil-written notes of the interrogation of Hermann Goering's brother, Albert, have survived. They show a list of ten questions ('relations with brother', 'acquaintance with Nazi bigshots', etc.), each one followed by a number of subordinate questions (after 'Why not a Nazi?' was added 'Every incentive. How opposed it? – Why – What did brother say? Wasn't it liability to him?'). The questions were based on a detailed brief from the US army intelligence branch (G2) at army headquarters in Europe on 'Corruption in the Nazi Party', sent in the belief that Albert Goering could reveal 'shady business transactions on the part of Party or SS leaders' and 'scandal or gossip' about high-placed Germans. A separate sheet shows the interrogator at work during the interview itself, scribbling down additional questions ('All he did for you, nothing in return from you?'), ticking off the subjects covered, highlighting key points in small doodled boxes, sketched perhaps during the regular breaks for interpretation.[39]

Soviet practice in interrogation differed from the American in numerous ways. The Soviet interrogator was accompanied by a bevy of Soviet officials and an interpreter who worked from Russian to

German and back again. At each Soviet interview there would be present a representative of the American Interrogation Division, an interpreter from Russian/German into English and a court reporter to record the interrogation in English. Only the American interpreter was required to swear an oath. The Soviet interrogator simply relayed to the witness that the Russian interpreter had 'been informed that he is responsible for an accurate translation', and knew, no doubt, the consequences of any dereliction.[40] Most Soviet interrogations lasted little more than an hour, despite the cumbersome process of translation into two other languages. They conformed to a standard pattern. The central issue for the Soviet delegation was to establish whether or not the prisoner was familiar enough with Hitler's *Mein Kampf* to confirm that invasion of the Soviet Union had been a Nazi plan since the 1920s. The answers they received were in general evasive. Goering told them that since they obviously had a copy, they could read it for themselves. Speer replied, 'I read it only superficially.'[41] Kaltenbrunner gave a guileful response: 'I never read it all of a piece. I read it chapter by chapter, and may have skipped some of them.' Alexandrov then asked him whether he could remember the contents of the book. Kaltenbrunner claimed to be able to remember the foreign policy passages 'particularly', but when he was then asked if he remembered the references to 'foreign policies in the East', he replied 'No' and the interrogation was terminated.[42]

Soviet interrogators laboured under the disadvantage that they could not use the techniques they were more familiar with in Moscow. It was noted with disapproval by the KGB that Alexandrov failed to respond with sufficient vigour to the occasional declaration of anti-Soviet sentiments by those he cross-examined.[43] The prisoners that were captured by the Soviet side proved more pliant than the internees at Nuremberg. The copy of an interrogation of Hans Fritzsche, a senior official in Goebbels's Ministry of Propaganda and Popular Enlightenment, which was sent to Jackson's office in September, betrayed all the hallmarks of Soviet judicial procedure, not only through the use of simple propagandistic language, but because of the willingness of the prisoner to confess everything attributed to him by his interlocutor without demur, as the following exchanges show:

Q. You were arrested as one of those guilty of the war begun by Hitler in Europe. Do you admit that you are guilty of this?
A. Yes, I admit it. . . . I took a direct part in the preparation of the second imperialistic war begun by Hitler.

Q. The Germans intended to make the Soviet Union a German colony?
A. Yes. (précis) I organized German propaganda in such a way as to inflame hatred of the German people not only for the peoples of the USSR but for the peoples of all democratic countries.[44]

When Speer was asked similar questions at Nuremberg in November, he retorted, 'I had nothing to do with the development of these plans', and was not pressed further.[45] The court eventually thought differently. Despite the damning confessions, Fritzsche was acquitted by the Tribunal a year later; Speer was given twenty years.

For the internees at Nuremberg interrogation was the principal activity before the trial began formally on 20 November. They were all accustomed to the experience. When the witness Wilhelm Keppler, one of Goering's deputies and Party economist, was chided by Thomas Hinkel for his attitude under interrogation, Keppler indignantly protested, 'I have been questioned thirty-six times up to this time and I have never been reproached for not being co-operative.'[46] Albert Speer was interrogated seventy-six times on technical questions before he arrived at Nuremberg, though he was only questioned five times by American interrogators after he finally arrived in October. None the less, the prisoners had to adjust to interrogations held on oath, and under the shadow of an impending war crimes trial whose precise dimensions were unknown until the Indictment was formally presented to each defendant on 19 October. They reacted to interrogation in different ways, and they responded to each interrogator differently.

The bridge between interviewer and interviewee was easier to cross when the language barrier was removed. At Mondorf prisoners were regularly interrogated by American German-speakers (one of the resident interrogation staff was a professor of German at Dartmouth College), which set many of them at their ease.[47] In Nuremberg almost none of the interrogators could speak German, and the clumsy process of reading out a prepared question in English, waiting for the translation, watching for the response and awaiting its translation into English (which could take several minutes) made it more difficult to establish a bond of confidence between the two parties. Some of the prisoners chose to speak in English in order to make the conversations more manageable. The prison guards soon discovered that most of the prisoners could speak at least a little English. Jodl's deputy as Chief of Operations, General Walther Warlimont, gave English lessons to fellow prisoners before his transfer to Nuremberg from 'Ashcan'. He was among a handful of defendants and witnesses who were willing to conduct their interrogations in the language of the enemy. Speer, though it was known he could speak English well, chose to reply in German. Goering also understood English, and betrayed as much in interrogations by his facial expression when he heard the questions, but he, too, insisted on the services of an interpreter.[48] Those who spoke in English did so from a more thorough familiarity. The two Foreign Ministers, von Neurath and von Ribbentrop, both spoke in English, though when the latter was flustered or uncertain he would ask to be allowed to lapse into German again. Franz von Papen spoke fluently in English in his first interrogations, but occasional misunderstandings which irritated his interrogator led to the presence of an interpreter. The stenographic record shows, however, that he was not needed, and von Papen persevered in English through what proved to be some of the longest of all the interrogations.[49] Only von Neurath, Hitler's first Foreign Minister, and a traditional career diplomat, spoke faultless English throughout his interviews.

The prisoners were generally in a sufficient state of physical and psychological health to be able to endure the hours of questioning, but some were evidently more robust than others. Only one witness, General Karl Bodenschatz, who had been an adjutant to Goering, had real difficulty both hearing and responding. He was injured in the bomb explosion at Hitler's headquarters on 20 July 1944, and suffered a 60 per cent hearing loss. 'I ask you to speak loudly to me,' he told his interrogator at the outset of his interview, 'otherwise, I will not understand.' He also suffered a head injury and severe burns: 'I would like you to give me time for an answer,' he continued, 'because my brain is injured and I should have time to consider everything I say.'[50] Ribbentrop, whose long rambling answers provoked the only evidence

Interpreters were in short supply at Nuremberg, but their job was vital. Here an interpreter puts a privileged registration document on the windscreen of his car, allowing him access to scarce fuel supplies.

of real irritation on the part of the interrogators, finally confessed that he had been taking bromide sleeping remedies for four years, which, according to the German doctors he had consulted, dulled the brain and restricted memory. Ribbentrop tried to mobilize the support of the prison psychiatrist, Douglas Kelley, for his case, but Amen too talked to Kelley who informed him that bromides, even in strong doses, might simulate the condition of 'a person who had had too much to drink', but would not have the 'slightest effect' on memory.[51] Other prisoners manifested increasing anxiety and depression as the time for the trial drew nearer, among them Robert Ley, who committed suicide on 24 October, Hans Frank, and Julius Streicher, whose sanity remained in doubt until the court pronounced him fit to stand. The worst case was Walther Funk.

Funk had an unfortunate name. The American guards pronounced 'funk' the English way, rather than the German, which appears phonetically as 'foonck'. Funk, in English, has several meanings, but the dictionary definition, 'cowering fear; a state of panic or terror', exactly matched his demeanour throughout the pre-trial months, as all those in the prison knew. He was an unprepossessing individual, short and flabby, with a balding head and a puffy oval face. 'Looking at this miserable figure,' wrote Major Airey Neave, who served the Indictment on Funk, 'it seemed amazing that he had become "Plenipotentiary for the War Economy".'[52] He had been chosen for this post by Goering, who wanted someone he could dominate with ease after the prickly Schacht had resigned in 1937. Funk became Minister of Economics at the same time and, in 1939, President of the Reichsbank, the German central bank. As the war progressed he became a marginal figure in the struggle for economic power between Goering, Speer and Himmler, out of his depth in the world of Nazi power politics.

Funk was in poor health, suffering from problems of the prostate gland and the urethra, and in regular pain, as he reminded his interrogators at intervals during interrogation. He was despised by the other prisoners, who were well aware of his reputation for homosexuality and drunkenness. He remained in a perpetual state of depression, crying openly during questioning, and uncontrollably at points where his guilt seemed unanswerable. When he was served with the Indictment he could not rise from his bunk until Colonel Andrus shouted, 'Stand up, Funk.' He continued to weep remorselessly, while Andrus yelled, 'Be a man, Funk.'[53] Of all the prisoners, save Rudolf Hess, whose amnesia prevented effective interrogation, Funk was the least capable of sustaining questioning. The constant pain in which he found himself was compounded with a profound and unendurable guilt, whose physical manifestation was matched by none of the other prisoners. His interrogators found his lachrymose behaviour, his capacity for denial and his faltering memory permanent barriers to useful interrogation.

On the other side of the table the interrogators had problems of their own. The American prosecution had a great deal to learn about Germany and the Germans; many of the early interviews displayed an understandable ignorance about fundamental aspects of the exotic regime they were investigating. But many of the problems were practical ones. There were serious shortages of the auxiliary staff necessary to type up interrogations, translate documents or act as interpreters. Advertisements in Britain and the United States for personnel capable

Walther Funk, head of the German Central Bank and Economics Minister, cut a sorry figure at Nuremberg. In poor health and shocked at being thought a war criminal, Funk denied almost everything about his close connection with the seizure of Jewish assets.

of translating and interpreting netted a surprisingly small number. The War Office found resistance among potential recruits because they would have to spend at least another year in uniform, away from their families. One volunteer who was keen to stay in the army, an injured guards officer, was found to speak no German.[54] When the State Department in Washington searched for translators in German, Russian and French they could not find one competent linguist from among the forty-five they interviewed and pressed the British to supply more. In the end native Germans were drafted in to swell the numbers.[55] The Soviet prosecutors faced the same difficulties. By the end of October 1945 they had only three translators working on Russian–German texts and six on Russian–English. They also lacked first-class interpreters. The duplication of documents brought additional headaches. Eisenhower's promise to make photostatic equipment available for the trial was not met, and during September a shuttle service had to be operated between Nuremberg and Frankfurt to reproduce trial materials in duplicate.[56] Copies of the interrogations proved particularly irksome. Staff were warned not to leave any material lying around either in their offices or in the Grand Hotel; during lunch breaks at least one member of staff was required to remain present in offices to prevent the loss of security-rated documents. So severe did the attrition of interrogation reports become that Amen was eventually left with only one complete set, his own master copies, held under lock and key. These were to be used only on the premises under the supervision of a responsible official.[57]

These were small irritations, but they slowed down the procurement and distribution of interrogation evidence, much of it vital to the conduct of the trial. However, the main problem confronting the interrogators was extracting from their subjects an accurate account of their role and responsibilities, and some sense of their degree of culpability. 'They can be easily interrogated,' ran a report to the Foreign Office in London on the 'Ashcan' camp at Mondorf. 'They are not all of them truthful.'[58] The key to successful interrogation was the ability to extract the truth, but it had to be extracted from men who with every comment might incriminate themselves further. No advantage flowed from confessing guilt, since no signed confessions were required of them. Silence might have protected them, but it seems to have occurred to none of them to refuse co-operation. At one point the Soviet prosecutor, Alexandrov, had to remind Speer that he was

Documents at Nuremberg were too valuable to be left lying around. Strict rules on use were introduced, and the master copies of transcripts and evidence locked away in a safe.

The reproduction of documents was a logistical nightmare at Nuremberg. Shortages of machinery and time meant that not even the four prosecution teams ended up with all they needed by the time the trial started. Work went on through the night to meet demand.

under no obligation to answer a question if he chose not to.[59] Instead many more of them were garrulous rather than taciturn. They talked because in all but a handful of cases they hoped to incriminate others or to present a reasoned defence of their position rather than openly admit their personal degree of responsibility. The psychological pressure to engage in denial and projection is a common feature of interrogation, as every schoolboy knows. Ordinary criminals do so habitually. The difficulty the internees faced at Nuremberg was to be confronted day after day with documentary evidence of the very activities of which they professed ignorance.

One of the interrogators at Mondorf, Major Kenneth Hechler, analysed the problem of conducting effective interrogation for the US Army Historical Division in a study published in 1949. He found that the men he interviewed did not react well to 'sympathy or over-friendliness', but they did respect 'a frank, precise approach'. This reaction he learned only from experience. For his first interrogation he was prepared for conflict: if his subject proved obstinate about answering, he and his assistant planned 'to shoot some fast, loud ones at him in sequence'. The reality was very different. When General Warlimont was brought in, Hechler stood awkwardly in silence. Warlimont proffered his hand; his interrogator shook it and offered him a cigarette. There followed a discussion which lasted all morning. Gradually the exchanges evolved from interrogation to conversation. Hechler became more confident in subsequent interrogations, but he kept the matter-of-fact, open approach and extracted a great deal from his subjects. When he suggested the same method of questioning to colleagues the reaction was unusually hostile ('Do you think this is a football game we have been through?' remarked one of them, 'Are we supposed to shake hands and just treat them like good sports?'), but it did pay dividends.[60]

At Nuremberg the interrogating style seldom resembled the sessions at Mondorf. The record of interrogations shows that some of the interrogation team were more effective than others in extracting hard information and focused answers. Judge Thomas Dodd came closest to Hechler. He interrogated Franz von Papen, a fellow Catholic, in lengthy, discursive and friendly exchanges. In his memoirs von Papen remembered Dodd as 'polite, correct, even kind'. When von Papen was later acquitted by the Tribunal, Dodd sent him a box of Havana

Fritz Sauckel was the organizational mind behind the vast recruitment of forced foreign labour in Germany during the war. Under interrogation he insisted that he was just a bureaucrat obeying orders. Foreign workers, he claimed, were treated just like Germans.

cigars. 'I still think of him warmly,' wrote von Papen.[61] Speer, on the other hand, found Dodd 'sharp and aggressive', while Major Monigan, who interrogated him on his arrival at Nuremberg, he found 'pleasant' and 'well-disposed'.[62] Monigan was responsible for interrogating Fritz Sauckel, the wartime Plenipotentiary for Labour Supply, and succeeded in long and not unfriendly discussions in extracting a great deal of information from a prisoner who resolutely refused to accept his guilt.[63] The other interrogators adopted a more adversarial relationship, though there are surprisingly few moments of tension or ill-temper throughout the interrogation transcripts. Amen was brusque and direct and enjoyed the advantage over the rest of the interrogation team that he was much more familiar with the historical background and the documentary proof and so could press a line of questioning with greater confidence. When prisoners could see that their interrogator was working on unfamiliar ground, they could argue points of fact or history, or indulge in deliberate obfuscation.

Over the months of interviews the tactics of interrogation were perfected and the knowledge at the disposal of the interrogators was magnified far beyond the partial and often ill-informed fund with which they began. Only Ribbentrop would not be broken down. After six fruitless interrogations in which he gave long-winded and evasive answers to every question, Jackson himself was invited to visit the interrogation room, where he questioned Ribbentrop for an hour and a half without any effective result.[64] Two days later, on 7 October, Amen, together with Ribbentrop's regular interrogator, Howard Brundage, and the President of the United Nations War Crimes Commission, Lord Wright, visited him again. Amen conducted the interview, clearly intent on breaking down his recalcitrant charge at last. There followed just over an hour of questioning. Amen's frustration rose in direct proportion to Ribbentrop's vapid posturing:

Q. The minute you say 'Probably', it makes all your testimony worthless, because anything is probable, and anything is possible. I mean, I want you to talk facts. You always say, 'Maybe', or 'Possibly', or 'Possible', and that makes it all worthless.
A. Yes, but what can I do if I don't remember exactly?
Q. You can stick to things that you know about. Something that you are willing to say definitely; do you understand?

A. All right. I can say this, for instance. You see, if this casual – if this talk there – I must have said during this –

Q. You see. That is another point. That is of no interest to anybody, 'I must have said.' It is just like somebody talking in a dream.

In the final minutes of the interrogation, Amen lost his temper. The following passage is one of very few in all the interrogation records where an interrogator failed to maintain his detachment:

Q. [Amen] You don't remember anything. That is obvious. But I am hoping that someday you will see how ridiculous it is to sit here and make these 'ifs', and 'buts', and 'maybes', and to say nothing, because it won't help you in the trial. You have got to find some kind of story and stick to it. Your position is that you don't know anything about anything, except what you heard through some third or fourth person.[65]

Ribbentrop was interrogated on three further occasions, where he continued to hover uncertainly at the edge of a self-induced amnesia.

Once the Indictment was served on the chief defendants on 19 October they had the right to refuse further interrogation. In respect of that right the number and frequency of interrogations declined thereafter. Instead, the interrogators concentrated their efforts on the more numerous witnesses housed at Nuremberg, many of whom were to stand trial in subsequent proceedings. The material gathered by interrogation was exploited during October and November as the cases against individual war criminals were finally put together. Some of the interrogations were written into the trial documents; the remainder were locked away in Amen's safe and, in many cases, have scarcely surfaced since.

The Absentees:
Hitler, Himmler, Bormann

Soviet soldiers act as impromptu tour guides in the ruins of Hitler's Reich Chancellery in the summer of 1945. Here they show cameramen the shallow grave where the bodies of Hitler and Eva Braun were supposed to have been found, and the petrol cans used to burn the bodies.

Behind a carefully prepared façade of conventional figures tied to their posts and going through their appropriate motions, Hitler governed the Reich, and although in the peerage of Pandemonium, within the façade, there was a shifting of precedence from Goering to Himmler, from Himmler to Bormann, the only real ruler of the place until the very end was Adolf Hitler.

Political Division report, Control Commission for Germany, Summer 1945[1]

One thing is certain: all [Hitler's] associates who had worked closely with him for a long time were entirely dependent and obedient to him. However forceful their behavior in their own sphere of influence, in his presence they were insignificant and timid. This timidity . . . has always been beyond my comprehension . . . Cowardice alone could not account for this . . . *They were under his spell, blindly obedient to him and with no will of their own, whatever the medical term for this phenomenon may be.*

Examination of Albert Speer, 1 October 1945[1]

Until his suicide on 30 April 1945, the Allies expected to put Adolf Hitler on trial as a war criminal. It was an intriguing proposition, for here was a man universally hated outside Germany, yet manifestly capable of exerting a morbid fascination even among his enemies. 'You will have to admit that Hitler was a genius,' Schacht told interrogators, 'but an evil genius.' A report sent back to the British Foreign Office in the late summer of 1945 confessed as much: 'He can and must be plainly labelled evil, but it will be no use trying to belittle his genius or to disparage his power – he can no more be laughed off than can Satan himself.'[3]

It was the very prospect of bringing such a man before a judicial tribunal that encouraged the idea of immediate execution. Hitler had been on trial once before, in Germany in 1924, charged with treason for his part in the abortive *Putsch* in November 1923 in Munich. On that occasion he had hijacked the trial to make capital for his brand of radical nationalism; instead of execution, which was within the judge's power to bestow, he was sentenced to only five years, and was let out in less than one.[4] There existed the very real danger that if Hitler stood trial again he might dominate the proceedings, or prove to be a final feeble rallying point for German nationalists in their hour of defeat. The problem of trying Hitler was one of the first issues addressed by the American War Department when serious planning for war crimes trials began in late 1944. The first legal hurdle was the principle established in international law that a head of state enjoyed the immunity of his status. This argument was not lightly set aside. The War Department view was that immunity was forfeit if it could be demonstrated that the head of state had ordered aggressive war as a deliberate act, but that required adequate proof to be shown in court, which Hitler would be free to challenge.[5] Justice Jackson developed a more philosophical case for trial. He rejected immunity as a relic of the doctrine of the Divine Right of Kings; he preferred the American doctrine of responsible government: 'We do not accept the paradox,' he reported to President Truman in June 1945, 'that legal responsibility should be the least where power is the greatest.' These were ancient arguments on sovereignty. Hitler was not to be Thomas Hobbes's

Leviathan; he stood, like John Locke's monarch, 'under God and the law'.[6]

Shorn of immunity, Hitler might still have had wide opportunity to make mischief. When Colonel William Chanler, one of the many New York lawyers working in the Pentagon, sketched out the scene of a Hitler trial in November 1944, the danger of allowing Hitler the space to argue issues of international law was evident. Chanler hoped that a future tribunal would invoke the Briand–Kellogg Pact outlawing war as the basis for the case against Hitler. To such a charge, thought Chanler, Hitler might offer three defences: that his aggressions were 'lawful acts of war'; that they were defensive wars, permitted under the Pact; and that the wars were necessary to correct the 'Crime of Versailles' and to achieve legitimate 'living-space'. The tribunal would then find the necessary proof to show that Hitler's wars were wars of aggression as defined by the Pact, and his defence invalid.[7] The risk in adopting such a procedure lay not only in the uncertainty that the Briand–Kellogg Pact had any real force in international law ('people in Europe haven't much respect for it,' rightly concluded one contributor to War Department discussions), but in the possibility that Hitler could stand and argue these issues with his enemies in the full glare of world publicity.

British politicians and officials based their criticism of the American conception of a tribunal on the fear that Hitler would gain more than he would lose from being exposed in court. 'Hitler's fate might have a great effect on the future history of the world,' warned Lord Simon in April 1945; 'German youth still regarded Hitler as a god.'[8] The British priority was to avoid any procedure through which Hitler could 'make himself appear as a martyr' by rejecting the legal basis of a tribunal and insisting that he was the victim of political injustice.[9] Among Jackson's files can be found a cartoon cut from a copy of *Free World* magazine in April 1945. Below the banner 'Court of International Justice' stood a row of sombre judges watching the floor of the court where journalists and cameramen crowded around a podium. There stood Hitler, gesturing and proclaiming above microphones marked CBS and NBC; beside him stood Goebbels, Goering, Himmler and Ribbentrop, their thumbs directed towards their Leader. Underneath was the caption 'I was only obeying orders, from above'.[10] These were real fears as long as the Allies were committed to a trial with some element of defence for Hitler to exploit. His death on the afternoon of 30 April 1945, announced on German radio the following morning, made a trial more likely, not less.

Hitler's ghost plainly haunted the pre-trial preparations. There was no certainty that he was actually dead. The Red Army discovered the charred bodies of Hitler and Eva Braun, the mistress he married in the bunker, on 4 May in the Reich Chancellery gardens, but they did not know their identity. The following day an officer from Smersh, the Soviet military counter-espionage service, arrived to take away the remains for autopsy. Dental records confirmed the identity, but the congenitally suspicious Stalin, unconvinced by the medical evidence, refused to tell his Allies of the find, or to halt the frantic efforts of his security services to track down a Hitler still possibly at large.[11] By contrast, the death of Goebbels and his family, whose remains were discovered close to Hitler's, was confirmed by the Soviet authorities on 6 May after the captive Fritzsche had identified the charred and shrivelled remains of his minister in an airless, improvised mortuary close to the Chancellery. The Soviet knowledge about Hitler leaked out unofficially. On 6 June at a Red Army press conference in Berlin, it was unexpectedly announced that Hitler's body had been discovered with 'fair certainty' on the basis of a surviving jawbone, and that he had died from taking poison.[12] The news was not corroborated from Moscow, which continued to take the line that Hitler was probably still at large, perhaps even secretly under the protection of the west. In mid-June the Soviet Tass news agency reported information from Cairo which suggested that Hitler, disguised as a woman, had landed secretly in Dublin and was in hiding somewhere in Ireland.[13]

The British and Americans thus had to make do with the flimsiest evidence of Hitler's fate. In June a former guard at the Chancellery bunker, Hermann Karnau, arrived at Field Marshal Montgomery's headquarters in northern Germany with the news that he had seen the bodies of Hitler and Eva Braun burning in the Chancellery gardens on 1 May (the date was in fact 30 April).[14] This account was the centrepiece of a long intelligence report produced by SHAEF on 'Hitler's Last Days' which was distributed at the end of July to allay public disquiet about Hitler's fate. The conclusions of the report were tentative, but, as it was revealed many years later, broadly correct:

A cartoon published in *Free World* in April 1945 expressed the real fears that the Allies had about the consequences of putting Hitler in a court which he might exploit to his own advantage. His death on 30 April 1945 made a war-crimes trial less problematic.

American soldiers on leave in Paris read a special edition of the army journal *Stars and Stripes* reporting the death of Adolf Hitler. Despite the official German announcement, rumours persisted throughout the year that Hitler had escaped and was on the run.

No one yet knows how Hitler met his end . . . He was, according to the OKW, transmitting messages up to the 28th April, and between then and the 1st May he probably met his death either by taking poison, shooting himself, or by ordering his dug-out to be blown up . . . One prisoner, a security service guard at the Reichs Chancellery, said that on the 1st May he saw Eva Braun in the Reichs Chancellery crying that she would rather die there as she did not want to escape. Later that evening when he opened the door of the emergency exit he saw the bodies of Hitler and Eva Braun burning on the floor. Hitler's head was split and his legs were already consumed. Hitler was said to have poisoned himself and Eva Braun in his office, and his personal servant, Lange, had carried out his orders to cremate their bodies. His body is said to be buried 2 yards [1.8 metres] away from the emergency exit in a bomb crater. This story can hardly be called firm evidence, and the Russians, who have publicly proclaimed their doubts as to whether Hitler is dead, state that their efforts to locate his corpse in the Reichs Chancellery met with no success. Despite Russian scepticism it seems probable that, from all we know of Hitler's last days, he chose to die in Berlin.[15]

The rumours, however, persisted. Early in September a radio report from Rome announced that Hitler had been seen in Hamburg, where he was living under an assumed identity.

The western Allies could not afford to ignore these claims from fear of Soviet recriminations. British intelligence officers scoured Hamburg for days. Sea patrols were sent out to try to intercept a mahogany yacht on which it was said that Hitler and Eva Braun had made their escape. A Dr Pleve came forward to claim that Hitler's appearance had been altered by a plastic operation. This particular revelation was greeted at the British Foreign Office with the following splenetic minute: 'I believe this to be sheer poppycock: the "plastic operation" which "changed Hitler's appearance" was probably carried out with a service revolver in the Führerbunker.'[16] Exasperated by the uncertainty surrounding Hitler's end, British military intelligence organized a thorough investigation of all the evidence available in the west which was undertaken by the intelligence officer and future historian, Major Hugh Trevor-Roper. His report, drafted at the end of October 1945 and given out in a condensed version to the press on 2 November, announced that Hitler had shot rather than poisoned himself, that Eva Braun had taken poison, and that both bodies had been taken into the Chancellery grounds and incinerated beyond recognition. The report was enough to convince the western Allies that they were not suddenly going to be confronted with a Hitler trial after all.[17]

Nevertheless, no stone could be left unturned. The civilian censors scoured German correspondence for clues. One letter, opened in January 1946, expressed the widespread public belief that Hitler was alive: 'Many say that he will come back as a social-democrat.'[18] The interrogators at Nuremberg were alert for any hint about Hitler's fate. When Ribbentrop mentioned in his interrogations that 'the Fuehrer is dead', Jackson was concerned enough to ask Ribbentrop in person to elaborate. His explanation was circumstantial – Hitler's remark to him ten days beforehand that he would never leave the Chancellery alive, the appointment of the Doenitz government – but he did confirm that Hitler had talked about committing suicide: 'it must have been the 20th or 21st of April, one or two or three days before I left Berlin, he evidently saw then that the war was definitely lost and he left, I think, the Military Operations Room saying that he wanted to shoot himself'. Goering was in no doubt that Hitler had decided on suicide: 'he said this only too clearly and too explicitly to different people . . . we all knew about this exactly'.[19] The testimony of Wilhelm Scheidt, official historian of the German army, recorded at the end of September 1945, showed that Hitler's decision had been taken only shortly before the end. Until 20 or 21 April (Scheidt could not be certain of the date) it had been Hitler's intention to move his headquarters from Berlin to Berchtesgaden and continue the fight. Keitel remembered that on the occasion of Hitler's bunker birthday party on 20 April, Hitler felt he was still 'destined to complete another task', but did not elaborate what it might be.[20]

The uncertainty surrounding Hitler's fate left the trial prosecutors with a difficult question. Could or should Hitler be indicted *in absentia* for the crimes he committed? This question was made more complicated by the decision to make conspiracy the central charge, for Hitler was the absent gang leader, whose other members had to be shown to have conspired with him. Under English law this was possible to do, for a single conspirator could, in theory, be tried for conspiring with 'divers other persons' even if those other persons were missing from the dock, or dead. The onus on the prosecution was to demonstrate that a conspiracy had taken place; once proven, all those named as conspirators were guilty.[21] The result was that Hitler remained on the list of major war criminals over the summer months to answer for his part of the conspiracy, as one of a number of 'persons now dead or not present'. When Jackson's office produced the first draft of the Indictment in September, the list of defendants included 'Adolf Hitler *alias* Adolf Schickelgruber' as well as Heinrich Himmler and Paul Joseph Goebbels, both of whom were known to be dead.[22] Jackson was anxious to avoid a situation in which Hitler might turn up during the course of the trial unindicted and force the embarrassed Allies to start proceedings all over again. However, when the British War Crimes Executive met late in September they discussed the question of whether to indict men almost certainly dead, and rejected the idea on the grounds that the Indictment itself specified that the defendants had conspired with Hitler. The meeting agreed to remove Hitler's name from all lists of major war criminals because to leave it there 'would merely stir up public curiosity about his survival'.[23] Hitler's place at the trial was taken by proxy.

The prosecution needed to know a great deal about the absent leader. They wanted to understand the nature of the power he exerted over his fellow-conspirators; they required hard detail on Hitler's decisions; they could not apportion blame until they were certain of the degree of responsibility each defendant enjoyed under Hitler's dictatorship. The search for answers raised a difficult problem: if Hitler did play the role the Allies ascribed to him of ruthless, centralizing dictator, it was going to be more difficult to convict his subordinates for their part in the conspiracy. On the other hand, the image of a dictator more figurehead than prime mover was convincing neither to the Allied prosecutors nor to the wider public. Everything they had on Hitler pointed to the conclusion that he did, indeed, hold his circle in thrall. 'If he told you you were a woman,' Goering was reported as saying, 'you would leave the room believing that you were.'[24] From the 'Ashcan' camp at Mondorf came the unsurprising conclusion that 'without exception, the Ministers and high officials of [Hitler's] government attribute the sole responsibility for all the decisions which led up to the war to Hitler himself . . .'[25]

Early on in the interrogation process the intelligence agencies looked for individuals who could fill in the missing parts of the jigsaw. Reports were commissioned on Hitler's personality and on the structure of Nazi rule. Rather than interrogate him again, Albert Speer was asked to write down his assessment of 'The Character of Adolf Hitler', which he did while at 'Dustbin' over the course of three weeks in July 1945. His report is the richest and freshest account of Hitler produced by any of the internees; it has about it a candour and vividness that Speer's later writing, though fluent and persuasive, seems to lack. The study was Speer's first attempt to write at length about the world he had recently inhabited as one of Hitler's inner circle. He was as anxious as his interrogators to explain the hold Hitler had exercised over all those around him, including Speer himself. He considered Hitler a man incapable of 'intimate personal relations', possessed of a personality that was 'inaccessible and unpredictable'. At the same time Hitler needed the psychological nourishment of complete loyalty from those around him. Men who on their own territory were powerful characters became 'insignificant and timid' in front of him. 'I noticed,' continued Speer, 'during my activities as architect that being in his presence for any length of time made me tired, exhausted and *void*. Capacity for independent work was paralysed.'[26]

The spell that Hitler cast on those in his immediate orbit Speer attributed to what has come to be called 'the myth of the Fuehrer'. Visitors came to Hitler already predisposed to be spellbound:

Without doubt [wrote Speer], there must have been some suggestive power of persuasion. On the other hand, one must not lose sight of the fact that there existed in the minds of the people a very powerful general conviction of Hitler's greatness and mission. *One must therefore bear in mind the feelings of reverence for his historical magnitude with which most visitors approached him, and the significance which they therefore attached to each word of his.*[27]

Speer found Hitler capable of extraordinary self-control, in contrast to the western image of a man who raged and chewed carpets. The effect of his calmness was to confirm in others the belief that they were 'in the presence of a man who stood above and was able to handle any situation'. At the same time he was incapable of giving clear orders, or acting decisively to remove ineffective subordinates. Orders were, in Speer's words, 'roughly outlined', often given 'as "an opinion" only', though Hitler expected them to be dealt with as if they were direct orders. Rather than sack a failing minister, he would '"freeze" them out by imperceptible degrees', and finally shunt them aside in some 'unobtrusive way'. His habit, Speer concluded, was to have 'two or three competitors for each important position, all of whom he directed immediately [personally]'. The result of these habits of authority was to create a dictatorship in which 'outwardly there was no apparent system'.[28]

This interpretation has become the stock-in-trade of recent historical accounts of the Third Reich where Hitler has been characterized as a 'weak dictator', governing a systemless state. Speer's summary of the dictatorship, composed only weeks after the end of the war, fits exactly with that analysis: 'To the imagination of the outsider Hitler was a keen, quick, brutally governing dictator. It is difficult to realize that in reality, he edged along hesitantly, almost fearfully. But that was the case.'[29] None the less, Hitler remained, on Speer's account, a man capable of exercising an unnatural power of personality on all those around him. His subordinates fed him with what he wanted to hear; in return Hitler promoted the most sycophantic and weak-willed characters, whom he could dominate absolutely. Moreover, however imprecise or general the 'orders' that Hitler gave, Speer also observed during the war *'the rigid line he took in his decisions and the obstinacy with which he followed it'*. As the war progressed Hitler changed from a man 'whose working methods were those of an artist', with bursts of 'abrupt, quick work' and intuitive solutions, to a leader who became, in Speer's words, 'work's slave':

Before the war he had known very well how to delegate work to others, which worked out to his advantage. Now, however, as his problems began to accumulate, he would increasingly concern himself with details with which he would never have bothered before. He forced himself to become a diligent, methodical worker, and that *neither suited his personality, nor benefited his decisions.*[30]

Prior to 1939 the turning-points, the 'world-shattering decisions', were taken at Hitler's mountain retreat at Obersalzburg in the Bavarian Alps, where he found the landscape and the atmosphere congenial for the artist-ruler. During the war they had to be taken in the stifling context of his military command centre.

The consequence was declining health and mental overstrain. Hitler had to squeeze decisions, Speer noted, out of a 'tortured brain'. He kept himself going with 'a naturally strong will'. He withdrew into a self-imposed isolation. The long evening dinners followed by a film were suspended. The busy lunchtimes were abandoned and Hitler took lunch on his own, or with his secretaries, or an occasional visitor. Speer found them 'monotonous and silent', though a relief from the 'soul-destroying entourage' of military men at Hitler's headquarters, with their endless discussions of hunting, careers, family gossip and the details of army life.[31] In the last years of the war Speer watched Hitler turn old: 'By his stubborn ways, his sustained outbursts of anger, he often reminded me of a senile man.' His complete inability to encompass the idea of defeat, right up until the month before his death, produced in him 'the petrification and hardening of his character and his mind' and magnified the elements of 'severity, injustice, and obstinacy'. Hitler was kept going, Speer concluded, by an exceptional, obsessive self-belief, 'his "faith" in the road prescribed to him by fate'. This sense of destiny defied rational explanation. The many witnesses to Hitler's final months failed to understand how their leader could sustain belief in ultimate victory. His confidence stemmed, Speer believed, from genuine 'inner conviction', and was not solely a device to keep his people fighting: *'If there was anything pathological in his ideas during the last few years, it was this unshakable faith in his lucky star.'*[32] Only in the very face of defeat did Hitler finally turn against the nation that had sustained him. At that point of acute self-awareness, Hitler *'consciously wanted to annihilate the German people, and to destroy the last foundations of its existence'.*[33]

None of the remaining internees generated any extended discussion of Hitler to match Speer's. They all had opinions about Hitler. In passing, they revealed important details and observations. General Warlimont remembered the day the Japanese attack on Pearl Harbor was reported because Hitler ordered champagne and uncharacteristically took two glasses himself, 'indicative of his emotional excitement at the attack'. He also recalled Hitler's demeanour on D-Day in June 1944, when he came into his daily military conference 'with his face beaming' to announce, in Austrian dialect, 'It's begun.'[34] Field Marshal Guderian remarked on Hitler's lack of reality: 'He . . . had a special picture of the world which actually was a picture of another world. As he believed, so must the world be, but in fact it was not.'[35] This was evident from the interrogation of Field Marshal Walther Brauchitsch, commander-in-chief of the army from 1938 to 1941, who asserted that Hitler never intended to fight a European war in 1939, but entirely misjudged the temper of the western states. Brauchitsch recalled from memory the following comment Hitler made at a military conference held on 23 May, which formed an important part of the evidence at the trial of conspiracy to launch aggressive war: 'I would be a fool if I would slide into a world war because of the Polish question. I shall not be so foolish as the people in 1914.'[36] (General Franz Halder, Brauchitsch's chief-of-staff, also recalled Hitler's remark, but he expressed it more vividly: 'I would have been an idiot if, on account of the measly Corridor question [the territorial dispute with Poland] I should slide into a war like the incapable nitwits did in 1914.')[37]

The trial defendants were seldom directly interrogated about Hitler. Most of them remained loyal to the Hitler they remembered, though Hess could not remember him at all. When Robert Ley was arrested in May he told his captors, 'you can torture me or beat me or impale me, but I will never doubt Hitler's acts'.[38] He was never shaken from this view. At Nuremberg he informed Amen that Hitler 'was one of the greatest men there ever was'.[39] Ribbentrop wanted to make it clear that in foreign affairs Hitler 'held everything firmly in his hands' and 'decided everything directly' (an interpretation that was nearer the truth than his frustrated interrogators would allow), but would not be persuaded that the same man was responsible for the atrocities of the regime. 'We were under his will, and we all worshipped this man,' Ribbentrop told Brundage. 'He was the symbol of Germany.' On another occasion, when Ribbentrop was discussing the 'queer people' around Hess, his interrogator interrupted to ask, 'Did you think Hitler was queer?' Ribbentrop asked to discuss his opinion off the record, and what may well have been a rare moment of candour remains tantalizingly lost.[40]

There was little other evidence that Hitler's lieutenants now thought more negatively about their leader in order to find favour with their prosecutors. They were more inclined to blame the dead Himmler, who was universally regarded as the malign *éminence grise* behind the perversion of the Third Reich. Even Speer, who clinically exposed the weaknesses of the dictatorship, wanted it on record that he did not want 'to be counted among those who malign him in order to exonerate themselves'.[41] Baldur von Schirach took much the same line when he told his interrogator that he had adopted Nazi race views 'because I considered it my duty to have the same conception as Hitler', but had now, as a result of reflections prompted by an earlier interrogation, arrived at a different view 'not only because of the trial – which is not interested in my present position – but in order to satisfy my conscience'.[42] When pressed to account for the German invasion of the Soviet Union, von Schirach took the opportunity to present his own conjecture on Hitler's state of mind. The career of Hitler's personality he divided into three periods: the years from 1920 to 1934 'was his humane period'; the next four years represented his 'superhuman period'; from 1938 to 1945 he had entered his 'inhuman' years. Von Schirach attributed the final deadly change of course to the only possible explanation, 'that he developed a mental illness'.[43] None of the other defendants referred to Hitler as mad, nor was it ever pursued as a line of questioning.

A more revealing side to Hitler was exposed in some of the subsidiary interrogations of Hitler's immediate staff. His adjutant and companion Julius Schaub, who had been with Hitler since January 1925, confirmed to Amen that Hitler's personal correspondence, which he had guarded in a safe in the Berghof, Hitler's retreat at Berchtesgaden, was burned on Hitler's orders shortly after 24 April 1945, when Schaub left Berlin for the south. Schaub confirmed what historians have since learned for themselves, that the volume of personal correspondence was surprisingly small. Amen pressed Schaub to admit that it had been a substantial documentary source ('Did it make a nice big fire?'), but the details made no difference to the fact that the record was now lost.[44] Hitler's secretaries, Christa Schroeder and Johanna Wolff, described how Hitler prepared the speeches and papers that formed an important part of the Nuremberg case. The following account of Hitler's drafting methods is taken from Amen's interrogation of Schroeder:

Q. Did he always dictate to you directly on the typewriter?

A. Yes, directly on the machine.

Q. What was the procedure which you followed?

A. He dictated in the rough, so to speak, and then he would correct it three or four times, as he was very fastidious with the language.

Q. Did he start off with any notes of his own?

A. Yes, he took down a series of key words which really were the framework of the speech.

Q. And then from those key words, he would dictate the first draft to you on the typewriter?

A. Yes. He dictated fluently, and at the same speed, and with the same kind of voice, and acting he would use when he actually would deliver a speech.

Q. Then when he received the first draft, what did he do with that?

A. Well, he left it alone for a few hours, or for a few days, as the case might be. It was his habit to dictate late at night, and to go to bed in the small hours. Then he might take it on the next morning and correct, or he might even let it be for a few days and then correct it . . .

Q. Was the procedure always the same?

A. Always.[45]

None of this proved the content of the documents, but by this stage there were over 200 separate items in Allied hands intended to prove the case that Hitler had conspired to wage aggressive war. If confirmation were needed, one of Hitler's adjutants from 1935 to 1939, Fritz Wiedemann, in response to the question posed in an interrogation in October 1945 'What was Hitler's Policy?', gave the disarming reply, 'To make war.' When his interrogator asked what facts he had to reach such an opinion, Wiedemann replied, 'His own words.'[46]

The fear expressed earlier in the year that Hitler might yet surface from the trial transformed into myth was not borne out by the interrogations. There was no prospect that the second absentee, Heinrich Himmler, could ever be rescued from a reputation that was low even among his own Nazi colleagues. Himmler died from taking a cyanide capsule in British custody a few days after he was arrested on 21 May by three Russian soldiers assigned to work for a British security patrol. His final movements were reconstructed from the interrogation of his principal adjutant, Werner Grothmann, at the 21st Army Group Interrogation Centre. On 2 May Himmler and a party of five other SS men arrived at the north German city of Flensburg, where Admiral Doenitz, recently appointed Hitler's successor, was establishing a new German government. Himmler changed into civilian clothes in Flensburg, removed his glasses and added a black patch over one eye. After discussing with Doenitz whether he should remain a member of the government, he left Flensburg on 6 May to stay on a farmstead south of the city. On 11 May they made their way to Friedrichskoog, where they looked for a small boat to cross the Elbe river to Neuhaus, and thence to the Harz mountains, where Himmler hoped he could remain undetected for some time.

His object was to flee southwards to the Alps and to stay there out of Allied hands as long as possible (there was no question, Grothmann told his interrogator, that Himmler wanted to set up an Alpine redoubt for a last stand against the Allies). On 15 or 16 May (Grothmann was uncertain), they found a fishing-boat and crossed the Elbe, making their way to the town of Meinstedt. When Himmler, Grothmann, and an SS man named Macher made their way into the town on 21 May they were arrested and sent to a camp at Bremervörde. Under interrogation Himmler gave his name as Hitzinger. The three men were moved to a camp at Lüneburg, where Himmler finally decided to reveal his identity. The British camp officials then separated their three captives and Himmler committed suicide in the course of being strip-searched.[47] Grothmann, described in his British interrogation report as 'a swaggering, unpenitent young Nazi', was subsequently interrogated in ignorance of Himmler's fate. He regarded Himmler 'as a benevolent personality'. He insisted, as Himmler might have done in his own defence, that his chief knew nothing of conditions in the concentration camps, because he had never visited one. The pictures he was shown of the camp at Bergen-Belsen he rejected as propaganda; at the most he conceded that camp commanders were left to their own devices, and that any of the evils exposed in the system were not Himmler's responsibility, but theirs.[48]

The absence of Himmler from the trial had few ramifications. The institutions he ran – the SS, the SD, the Gestapo – were arraigned as criminal organizations (though not the RSHA, which was the umbrella organization for them all). Ernst Kaltenbrunner was indicted as his proxy, despite his fruitless and mendacious efforts under interrogation to explain that his position as chief of the RSHA had nothing to do with the SS, the Gestapo or the camps. Himmler's suicide did not deter the Allies from taking Himmler's family into custody. His wife, Margaret, was interrogated by Amen in late September, but could tell him little. She claimed to have seen him only fifteen to twenty times throughout the war. When told about the camps she defended her husband by blaming Hitler (the only person to do so). Amen then asked her how she got along with her husband, but she refused to reply. Amen coaxed her with the assurance (dishonestly given) that the interrogation was 'entirely confidential', to be read by no one other than himself. Finally she blurted out: 'Well I think the Americans and the British know just as well as I do that my husband was not faithful to me.'[49] Himmler's elder brother, Gebhard, a schoolteacher, was also interrogated following his arrest as a member of the SS leadership corps on the night of 16 May. He had little of substance to add to the Tribunal case. He told his interrogators at the 21st Army Group about the plans his brother had nursed for the years following a German victory, which included the development of herbal medicines 'on the theory that this was a science of pure Germanic origin', and the creation of a new 'Staats-Schutz-Korps' (state protection corps) from the ranks of the SS. Under interrogation Gebhard Himmler was said to fluctuate between 'the intolerably arrogant Nazi' and a subservience so abject 'as to rival an Eastern beggar'. He was, in short, as his interrogation centre report concluded, 'a thoroughly despicable specimen of humanity',[50] but his contribution to the case against the apparatus of terror and racial persecution his brother constructed was negligible.

The third absentee, Martin Bormann, the head of Hitler's Party Chancellery and one of the most powerful figures in German domestic politics by 1945, played a larger part at Nuremberg. He was included in the list of defendants in the Indictment, and eventually condemned to death by the Tribunal in October 1946. He could not be presumed dead, like Goebbels, because no body was found. The evidence surrounding his alleged survival was circumstantial, but the possibility remained open, and has fuelled historical speculation ever since. The Bormann case had to be prepared on the assumption that one day he might be apprehended or, like Himmler, reveal his identity. The OSS investigated the Bormann case over the summer and produced a biographical report in August 1945 which concluded that, on the best available evidence, Bormann died in the battle of Berlin. But one month later Justice Jackson was informed by the OSS that there was new intelligence information on Bormann which could be acted upon 'unless we have been definitely advised by the Russians that Bormann is in custody', which was a possibility, given Soviet reluctance to be entirely open with their ally. Earlier in the summer a group of Soviet soldiers visiting SHAEF informed their startled hosts that it was quite possible for them to interrogate Bormann, only for the Soviet authorities to issue a strongly worded denial a few days later.[51]

The intelligence on Bormann was flimsy in the extreme. The Danish Kalundborg radio station reported that Bormann had made a speech from a secret radio station 'a few days ago' (dated 21 September); another contact suggested he was in hiding in Mecklenburg, where he had served in the early 1920s in the Rossbach Freikorps, a group of German veterans who fought their own brutal campaign against the Polish claims on German territory.[52] The presumption was made that

Bormann might still be alive and in Germany, and could therefore be indicted. A formal procedure was worked out to give Bormann notice that his presence was required in court. Once a week for four weeks between 22 October and the planned opening of the trial on 20 November the notice of indictment was to be read out on the radio and published in the newspaper of Bormann's home town. The notice included the one residue of the theory of outlawry drawn up by Lord Simon in 1943: if Bormann failed to appear and was found guilty and sentenced by the court, the sentence could be carried out 'without further hearing' whenever, and wherever, he was apprehended. The British major charged with issuing the notice could not decide where Bormann's home city was, and instead ordered the notice displayed throughout Germany. Two hundred thousand 'Wanted' posters were distributed.[53]

By November a definite decision had to be taken over how to proceed. The British prosecution team drew up a detailed report on Bormann's probable fate which was presented on 16 November, the day before a meeting called by Jackson to determine whether Bormann should stand trial *in absentia*. The story was pieced together from the interrogation of three men who were with Bormann on the day he attempted to break out from the bunker on 1 May, the day following Hitler's suicide, but the chief witness was Hitler's chauffeur, Erich Kempka. According to this version of events, the men set off in a tank in an attempt to cross the river Spree. The tank was stopped as it tried to cross the bridge; Soviet soldiers tossed a grenade inside. Two of the survivors recalled that Bormann was probably killed by the explosion, one that he was badly wounded, though Kempka's testimony subsequently turned out to be entirely unreliable, for he was temporarily blinded by the explosion and did not actually see what happened to Bormann. 'On these facts,' concluded the report, 'there is a probability – but no certainty – that Bormann is dead.'[54]

The interrogation of the Hitler Youth leader Artur Axmann, who broke out with Bormann, was not yet available for the report. His was the fullest account, and when it was received in February the official verdict on Bormann's probable fate was modified. On Axmann's account Bormann left the Chancellery on foot, not in a tank; he was not wounded or killed when a shell exploded near a tank where they had sought shelter, but blown onto the ground. He remembered finding the bodies of Bormann and another fugitive from the bunker in the early hours of 2 May, lying sprawled on the Invalidenstrasse. He assumed they had been shot in the back, though he later claimed that they had committed suicide.[55] In the absence of this more certain testimony, the prosecutors' meeting on 17 November concluded that Bormann could be tried *in absentia*; the law for conspiracy allowed for one or more absentees. Counsel was appointed on Bormann's behalf. His attempt to have the proceedings against his invisible client set aside was rejected by the Tribunal on 22 November.[56]

The file on Bormann was never closed. Sightings were reported from all over Germany. In March 1946 came a more solid lead. A man fitting Bormann's description had been interrogated in October 1945 by Major Tilley, a member of the British team working with the FIAT organization. Few people knew what Bormann actually looked like, but when Tilley saw a picture of the absent defendant later in the year he saw a striking resemblance. He extracted the physical description of Bormann from the files:

Medium dark hair, is about 5ft 11ins. in height [Bormann was in fact much shorter than Hitler, who was 5ft 9ins.], has a peculiar hump on his nose, and has definitely one or two duelling scars on the left side of his chin, or the lower part of his left cheek, also a slight cast in one eye.

A second description, supplied through the interrogation of Speer's deputy, Karl-Otto Saur, added more particulars. Bormann had hard eyes ('narrows them frequently in conversation') and a hard stare. His build was broad-shouldered and stocky, his posture erect. In conversation he alternated between crisp, abrupt answers and lengthy monologues. The man interrogated by Tilley, a chemist named Dr Karl Peter Rath, resembled this description save for the fact that he had a beard and lacked a stocky build. Tilley was not put off by these obvious discrepancies. The beard in itself, thought Tilley, 'would make one suspicious'.[57]

When he turned his mind back to the interview with Rath, Tilley could recall other grounds for suspicion. Rath may not have had a cast in his eye, but his eyes flickered unusually, a fact he attributed to his wartime experiments with poison gas. However, when Tilley quizzed him on chemistry he seemed poorly informed; his general behaviour was out of the ordinary, and plans were made to arrest him on a subsequent visit. In the end he was allowed to go free, but Tilley now recommended that American counter-intelligence investigate Rath. Nothing apparently came of the new lead. Bormann was not discovered until some workmen digging up a road in Berlin in 1972 found a skeleton that was positively identified as Bormann's from the dental records, though the exact cause of death could not be determined. Even this discovery provoked scepticism, and not until 1999, with the DNA testing of the remains at the request of his family, was Bormann's death on 2 May 1945 in war-torn Berlin finally confirmed.[58] Bormann, like Hitler, Himmler and Goebbels, likely chose suicide rather than face the consequences of defeat.

Selective Amnesia?
The Case of Hess

The loss of memory by Hess in not the result of some kind of mental disease but represents hysterical amnesia, the basis of which is a sub-conscious inclination towards self-defense as well as a deliberate and conscious tendency toward it. Such behaviour often terminates when the hysterical person is faced with an unavoidable necessity of con-ducting himself correctly. Therefore, the amnesia of Hess may end upon his being brought to trial.

Record of examination of Hess by the Soviet Delegation,
17 November 1945[1]

A rare picture of interrogation. Colonel Amen interviews Rudolf Hess at Nuremberg. Hess wears the flying clothes in which he made his flight to Scotland in May 1941. Despite all Amen's efforts, Hess main-tained a complete amnesia about his time as Hitler's deputy.

On 10 May 1941 Rudolf Hess, Hitler's deputy, flew to Scotland from Augsburg in Bavaria to try to broker a peace deal with the British. He was caught, interrogated and imprisoned by the British authorities for more than four years before he was transferred to Nuremberg prison in October 1945 to stand trial. His was a difficult case. The British had no doubt that he should suffer the same fate as other German leaders when they were finally in Allied hands. He was a regular name on the list of major war criminals. When Churchill suggested summary execution in November 1943, he was reminded by the Foreign Office that Hess posed an embarrassing dilemma. Soviet leaders had already pressed the British government about putting Hess on trial before the war had ended. If Stalin accepted execution the Soviet side might call Churchill's bluff and publicly demand that Hess be 'summarily disposed of at once, which the British did not want.[2] Stalin never called for Hess's death, but the Soviet authorities did demand a trial. In their view the failure to deal with Hess left deep suspicions about British intent towards not just Hess, but the whole Nazi leadership. At the Potsdam Conference Stalin asked the British for a specific pledge that Hess would be delivered for trial.[3]

The British took the position that Hess should only be dealt with when the other major war criminals were in Allied hands and a decision had been taken about their collective fate. He was interrogated about his flight and about the German war effort when he arrived in 1941, but no thought was given then to the kind of charges he might have to answer as a potential war criminal. Hess's part in whatever judicial process was eventually adopted was uncertain, since he was clearly not directly responsible for any of the crimes committed after his flight. In July 1945 a Foreign Office study on Hess concluded that Hess could be charged with 'general responsibility for the main Nazi conspiracy', which pre-dated 1941, but Jackson had strong reservations about including Hess, and had to bow to British and Soviet pressure. However, it was the mental state of Hess that gave serious grounds to doubt whether he would ever be capable of sustaining interrogation and trial. On 4 October 1943 Hess began to display symptoms of total amnesia, which ended just as abruptly on 4 February 1945. Between that date

and 12 July the same year Hess recovered his memory and confessed
that the amnesiac state had been simulated. Faced with the prospect
of a major trial, Hess fell back into a state of complete amnesia in July
which lasted throughout the period when he might have been subjected
to interrogation. This state did not prevent Amen from trying to
force Hess to remember, but he sustained his amnesia throughout the
pre-trial period.[4]

Rudolf Hess was an oddity even among the cohort of enthusiasts
who surrounded Hitler. His tall gangling frame, bushy black eyebrows
and intense, staring eyes enhanced his reputation as a distant, prickly,
self-absorbed disciple – 'one of the great cranks of the Third Reich',
as Speer put it.[5] During the First World War Hess served as an officer
in Hitler's regiment. After the war he studied geopolitics under the
distinguished Munich academic Karl Haushofer and joined in the
activities of the infant National Socialist Party. He marched with Hitler
in the *Putsch* of November 1923, and was incarcerated with his leader
in Landsberg Castle, where he took down a great part of Hitler's
dictated autobiography, *Mein Kampf*. He became Hitler's private
secretary and his most devoted follower. In April 1933 Hitler rewarded
Hess by appointing him his deputy. Lacking the political instincts
and crude ambitions of many other leading National Socialists, Hess
became a marginal figure. Hitler remained true to his old companion
by naming him in 1939 as the man who would succeed as Fuehrer
after Goering, but to most Party bosses Hess was a political lightweight,
whose influence on the major decisions of state was slight. At some
point in late 1940 Hess conceived the idea of flying to Britain to try to
negotiate a peace settlement before the attack on the Soviet Union in
June 1941. A skilled pilot, Hess took a Messerschmitt Me-110 fighter
aircraft and on 10 May 1941 flew to Scotland with a letter, written in
English, explaining that he was on a mission of peace between the two
countries.

The motives for Hess's flight have never been established with
certainty. He was influenced by secret but misleading intelligence from
Britain which suggested that a powerful peace party existed in the
British establishment keen to reach agreement with Germany.[6] He was
almost certainly genuine in his belief that peace could be negotiated
and his beloved Fuehrer saved from the folly of a two-front war. When
Speer was asked under interrogation to explain why Hess had made

the flight he replied that Hess was 'deeply concerned about the repercussions of a war with Russia upon Western Europe', and was strongly
influenced by Haushofer to try to avert it. Hess's secretary, Laura
Schroedl, later confirmed that Hess hoped to construct a 'western bloc'
to meet 'the possible attack of an eastern bloc', making him among
the first of the Cold Warriors.[7] On the question whether Hess flew
with Hitler's knowledge and approval, the interrogation testimony
produced only negatives. Schroedl claimed that no one except Hess's
adjutant knew of the plan. Speer was at Hitler's retreat at Berchtesgaden the day of the flight, and could remember clearly that when
news arrived of Hess's departure Hitler was thrown into a flurry of
angry activity. He summoned Goebbels, Ribbentrop, Goering and
Himmler and announced an immediate communiqué condemning
Hess and denying any intention of a peace feeler. Hess undertook the
flight, Speer concluded, because he was 'very sore and embittered
at having been side-tracked by Hitler'.[8] Despite all the subsequent
historical speculation about the flight, there seems little reason to
doubt that Hess did act on his own and for comprehensible motives.

Hess was delivered to Nuremberg prison on 8 October, dressed in
flying boots and the German air force uniform he had been wearing
for his flight four years before. Andrus made him hand over everything
he brought with him, which included a collection of small packages of
food that Hess wanted chemically analysed to prove that the British
had been trying to poison him.[9] He gave these up with great reluctance,
but finally agreed to watch Andrus lock them away securely in his
presence. Amen began the interrogations on 9 October. The object
was to confront Hess with a number of his closest associates in the
hope that the sudden confrontation might jolt him out of amnesia.
Amen interviewed Hess in the morning, but found him unable to recall
anything, though he did know that a trial was to take place ('I have
seen it in the newspapers').[10] In the second session, which lasted for
forty minutes after lunch, Hess was introduced first to Hermann Goering, then to the geopolitician Professor Karl Haushofer, a long-time
friend and confidant, next to von Papen, and finally to Ernst Bohle,
who had translated into English the letter proposing peace that Hess
carried with him on his flight. The result was theatrical rather than
therapeutic. Goering was nonplussed by Hess who seemed on the
surface both articulate and co-operative, but refused point blank to

recollect anything about him. As the conversation continued, Goering's wounded vanity got the better of him:

GOERING Listen, Hess, I was the Supreme Commander of the Luftwaffe, and you flew to England in one of my planes. Don't you remember that I was Supreme Commander of the Luftwaffe? First I was a Field Marshal, and later a Reichsmarshal; don't you remember?
HESS No.
GOERING Don't you remember I was made a Reichsmarshal at a meeting of the Reichstag while you were present; don't you remember that?
HESS No.
GOERING Do you remember that the Fuehrer, at a meeting of the Reichstag, announced in the Reichstag that if something happened to him, that I would be his successor, and if something happened to me, you were to be my successor? Don't you remember that?
HESS No.
GOERING You don't remember that? We two discussed that very long afterwards.
HESS This is terrible. If the doctors wouldn't assure me time and time again that my memory would return some day, I would be driven to desperation.

Goering tried other key dates and events, but got the same response every time, even on the flight to Britain. 'No: that is all black,' Hess responded. 'That is all black. That is all blacked out.' After a few more questions Goering gave up: 'I have come to the end. I cannot ask him any more.' Hess repeated the same performance with each of Amen's prisoners. The most he could do, he said, was dimly recollect the previous fourteen days. Goering told his interrogator later that day that Hess struck him as 'completely crazy'.[11]

A few weeks later Amen tried the same tactic again, this time using two secretaries who had worked for Hess for seven years up to the time of his flight, Hildegarde Fath and Ingeborg Sperr. Amen asked them privately if they were willing to co-operate with him in trying to get Hess to regain his memory, and both agreed. Amen went to the interrogation room where Hess was already seated, manacled to a guard. Three other observers, including Kelley, the prison psychiatrist, came in, followed shortly afterwards by Hildegarde Fath. She was introduced to Hess, and showed him some photographs. They spoke in German, but the interpreter was not under instructions to provide the stenographer with a translation. Amen then fetched Ingeborg Sperr, who greeted the other two warmly. From their conversation the stenographer could only distinguish the German words 'thirty-four'. Amen then sat down to interrogate Hess directly. Again, he was faced with a blank wall. Hess had not the slightest knowledge of either secretary. The photographs gave Amen an opening, for Hess, perhaps inadvertently, did own up to knowing that they were snapshots of his family. But when Amen asked him how he could know that, Hess countered, 'The ladies told me that.' When Amen asked him if he believed what the ladies told him, Hess trumped him again: 'I have not the least cause to think that Germans do not tell me the truth.'[12]

The transcript of this final pre-trial confrontation shows that Hess had a quick mind under interrogation, in spite of the amnesia. When Amen asked him how he knew that the 'ladies' were German at all, Hess retorted, 'I have got the impression that they are not Americans'; when he was asked if his secretaries had done any work for him, Hess replied, 'I hope so.' He then told Amen that he had invited one of the secretaries to work for him in the future, when he was once more a high-ranking official of the Nazi state. Amen objected that Hess could never be Deputy Fuehrer as there was no longer any Fuehrer, but Hess assured him that he was not after his old job, just 'a high position in the German Nationalist State'. The interrogation gave Amen just one last chance. When he mentioned Goering's name, Hess could recall that he was a war criminal. Amen shouted at Hess that he could not possibly know this about someone he did not even recognize in the flesh. 'I cannot be provoked,' Hess said smugly. The brief final exchange that followed also went Hess's way:

Q. I am not trying to provoke you. What I want to know is, if you have no memory, which is what you claim, how can you possibly know that Goering is not a pickpocket or a thief or some other kind of criminal?
A. Perhaps it is known to the gentleman that I have over there an indictment in which Goering, myself and other people are named.

After half an hour, Amen had had enough. He ordered the guards to take Hess out. He parted from the two women with the words 'Heil, euch', which the interpreter told Amen meant 'Hail to you'. What it also conveyed was a surprising degree of intimacy. 'Euch' is the familiar expression for 'you', used only with family or close friends and col-leagues.[13]

From a close reading of the interrogations it is possible to argue that Hess knew a good deal more than he was prepared to tell his captors, and that Amen strongly suspected as much. The interrogation team tried to sound out other defendants on their reaction to Hess, but few additional clues were forthcoming. Alfred Rosenberg, who was the last senior Nazi to talk with Hess before his flight, was noncommittal. Hess, he said, looked at him with a 'tense, hard glare' when they passed each other in the exercise yard, which might or might not express recognition. To the question whether Hess held himself the way that Rosenberg remembered, he replied that it was difficult to tell with someone in shackles.[14] None of the defendants who were asked about Hess could confirm that there seemed anything odd about his behaviour in 1941, before his mission to Britain. Ribben-trop thought Hess had chosen some 'queer people' to have around him, 'star lookers' and 'people who prayed about health', which might have made Hess 'not quite normal'. Rosenberg also recalled that Hess relied on doctors who treated him 'with magic healing, magnetism and massaging', but he regarded Hess as a quiet, reserved but normal individual, who showed no signs of his later condition in the conduct of official business. Another Hess secretary, Laura Schroedl, interrogated about her employer after the trial had begun, answered 'no' when she was asked if Hess manifested any physical or mental abnormality or any sign 'of his "going mad"'.[15]

The question of Hess's sanity had to be demonstrated conclusively before he could take his part in the forthcoming Tribunal. The prison psychiatrist, Douglas Kelley, who arrived at Nuremberg on 10 October, shortly after Hess, was at once put to work to arrive at a clinical judgement. He spent hours with Hess, who spoke in excellent English, though he used German in front of Amen. Kelley wrote an interim report on 16 October, after discussions with the British psychiatrist flown in with Hess the week before. Hess had a history of unstable behaviour in British hands. He attempted suicide twice, and developed severe delusions about British attempts to poison him. The British psychiatrists who examined him in 1941 found pronounced paranoid tendencies which indicated a decline into permanent psychosis. 'Hess may be a mental patient on our hands permanently,' concluded one report.[16] The British government did not want his state widely known. If he were certified insane, Eden informed Churchill in May 1942, he could be repatriated under the terms of the Hague Convention.[17] Shortly before he was returned to Germany in 1945 a British army doctor examined Hess and found him still to be in a paranoid state, distinguished by severe delusions of persecution. The prognosis was pronounced bad, and care was recommended appropriate for a person 'of unsound mind with suicidal tendencies'.[18]

Yet Kelley found him in general in good mental health. The paranoia was not serious and the delusional states brief and disconnected. Most other mental functions were normal, with the exception of what Kelley called 'a spotty amnesia'. Some things he could remember very clearly, principally connected with the delusions of attempted murder, but even recent facts which a conventional amnesiac should have been able to remember, Hess appeared to lose within days. Kelley diagnosed a personality with a propensity to 'hysterical and obsessive' behaviour. It was this that induced the severe stomach pains which had plagued Hess persistently both before and after 1941. The amnesia might readily be explained as one that was self-induced, or conscious, but the power of hysterical auto-suggestion in such a mind made the memory loss none the less real for the individual experiencing it, just as the stomach cramps produced a genuine sensation of pain. Kelley recommended the use of intravenous drugs to create a chemical hypnosis which would undermine the suggestive factors in Hess's psychological make-up. He pronounced Hess both sane and responsible; appropriate treatment of the hysterical symptoms of amnesia ought to result in total recovery.[19]

This initial judgement was taken by the prosecuting counsel as evidence that Hess was a malingerer. He refused any of the chemical treatments proposed by Kelley, which suggested that he recognized that effective treatment would unmask the conscious element of his amnesiac state. Unsigned notes on Hess in Jackson's files, almost certainly written by Jackson himself, show that the judgement on Hess as sane and psychologically devious suited the prosecution case: 'At most fails to remember – the failure most complete where to remember would be most inconvenient. Loss of memory even if genuine is never an excuse from being tried' (and added in pencil, but crossed out, was a more cynical remark, 'Few defendants who could not make a good case of forgetting').[20] The Tribunal decided to establish a scientific commission, to be staffed by doctors and psychiatrists, whose task it would be to ascertain the exact mental state of Hess and to recommend whether or not he was fit to stand trial. Ten medical experts from the four prosecuting states were charged with examining and reporting on Hess, before the Tribunal pronounced a final judgement on 30 November, ten days after the scheduled start of the trial.

The reports arrived at a remarkable degree of unanimity in their assessments of Hess. So similar were the conclusions that one of those involved thought it provided solid proof 'that the science of psychiatry is sound'. At the least it confirmed that Hess's ability to frustrate Amen did not extend to those who knew what they were dealing with. No one dissented from the view that Hess was at least unstable, but that scarcely disqualified him from the courtroom, any more than it excluded other, more evidently dysfunctional personalities among the group of defendants. The Soviet report, produced following examination of Hess on 14 November, observed what Kelley had seen in October. Hess manifested a high degree of normal behaviour, knew he was in prison, and why, talked 'with precision and correctness', expressed emotion and moved naturally. His paranoid delusions while in prison in Britain were not diagnosed as a product of schizophrenia, but as the psychologically comprehensible reaction of an unstable personality to failure and incarceration. The amnesia was hysterically induced and not the product of mental disease. Hess was not, in Soviet eyes, insane.[21]

The American, French and British experts did not differ from this analysis in any important ways, though they amplified its conclusions. Hess was judged to be a voluntary amnesiac, who deliberately used memory loss as a defence mechanism in British hands until the behaviour became to some extent 'habitual'. It was considered that Hess would not abandon this most acute form of psychological defence while he remained under threat of punishment or exposure. The British doctors, who included among their number Lord Moran, Churchill's personal physician, regarded Hess as an opportunistic amnesiac, whose symptoms would disappear when Hess found himself in different circumstances. Unlike most amnesiacs, Hess showed no desire to recover his memory, and it was this unusual feature of his behaviour that confirmed the conscious part of his loss of memory. 'I can get my memory back by experiments after the trial,' he was reported as saying. 'It is not so important to get cured before the trial.'[22] The psychiatrists did not believe that his condition would interfere with his ability to comprehend the trial proceedings, but it would inhibit his capacity to mount a defence, or to understand the details of his past which would be used in evidence against him.[23] Hess was judged by all the medical teams not to be insane, but the issue of whether he was fit to stand trial was to be decided by the Tribunal.

On 29 November, the four prosecuting counsels signed the following statement: 'It is our position that the defendant Rudolf Hess is fit to stand trial.' His defence counsel had applied for an independent psychiatric assessment of Hess's mental state, but on the same day the court rejected the application on the ground that Hess had already been studied by a commission of experts and pronounced sane. The following day Hess was led into court to hear his fate. The psychiatric evidence was presented first. Then Hess was invited to speak. To the consternation of his lawyer he calmly announced that he had recovered from his amnesia:

My memory is again in order. The reason why I simulated loss of memory was tactical. In fact it is only that my power of concentration is slightly reduced but in conflict [sic] to that my capacity to follow the trial, my capacity to defend myself, to put questions to witnesses or even to answer questions – in these my capacities are not influenced. I emphasize that I bear full responsibility for everything that I have done . . .[24]

The declaration shocked the court; the following morning Hess was formally declared fit to stand trial.

His revival surprised the experts less. For the first few days of the trial Hess had paid little attention, his head bowed over a copy of *Grimms' Fairy Tales*.[25] There had been signs of recovery during the preceding days in the dock, as Hess, despite himself, had begun to take a greater interest in proceedings. When Hess returned to his cell later in the afternoon of his declaration he was interviewed by Kelley. 'How did I do? Good, wasn't it? I really surprised everybody, don't you think,' Hess asked. Kelley told him that he had by no means surprised everyone.[26] The sudden recovery of memory is common in hysterical amnesia. The Soviet psychiatric team had predicted it two weeks before. Colonel Andrus later claimed that he had triggered recovery, for the day before he had bluntly told Hess that he was a charlatan and like a man should own up to it.[27] Psychiatric observers took the view that Hess had suddenly realized that he might be excluded from the proceedings altogether and could not bear to lose the limelight.

Whatever the exact mechanism that jolted Hess out of amnesia, his claim that memory loss was merely tactical was misleading. A substantial part of the amnesia was not feigned. Hess unintentionally revealed that he had indeed suffered from a self-induced amnesia when he said in his statement that his memory was 'again' in order. In fact Hess took weeks to recover his memory, and then never fully. As the trial proceeded he began once more to manifest serious neurotic behaviour and in early March 1946 almost complete memory loss returned. His memory span was little more than half a day.[28] He continued to sit through the trial and was condemned to life imprisonment on counts of conspiracy and crimes against peace.

The Helpful Speer

Speer explained to me the plan he had evolved. He intended to throw into the ventilators of the ARP [air raid precautions] bunkers in the Reich Chancery some poison gas shells (or containers) and asked me how these poison gas containers worked and what their effect was. Speer spoke of solid poison gases which in his opinion achieved the best results. I understood from Speer that he wanted to throw filled poison gas containers into the ARP ventilators of the Hitler bunker on the assumption that these containers burst open during the descent and that the escaping gas would penetrate the bunkers with the fresh air.

Interrogation report on Dietrich Stahl, 15 November 1945[1]

Albert Speer eats a hasty meal at Nuremberg under the amused stare of an American military policeman. Speer made considerable efforts to cultivate the image of the apolitical technocrat, while denying complicity with major crimes.

Albert Speer was the only defendant at Nuremberg to consider assassinating Hitler. For his own reasons he only told his interrogators the details of his plot in October, though he had mentioned it in May when he was first questioned. There is now no secret about Speer's flirtation with murder; it is described in detail in his memoir of life in the Third Reich. Those details, however, differ in important ways from the testimony of the Armaments Ministry official, Dietrich Stahl, who was drawn into the plot by Speer because of his function as chief of the Main Committee for Munitions. Speer mentioned Stahl as a corroborating witness when he told the interrogators at 'Dustbin' on the day before he was taken off to Nuremberg that he had once been prepared to kill Hitler. Since Speer was given no opportunity to elaborate, Stahl was interviewed twice to see if Speer had been telling the truth.

Stahl confirmed Speer's story. He had been summoned one day in the middle of February 1945 to Speer's office (though Speer later claimed the meeting was by chance). An air raid interrupted the meeting and the two men adjourned to the bunker in the Armaments Ministry building on the Pariser Platz in Berlin. Here Speer discussed official business for a while and then launched into a blunt denunciation of the plans for scorched earth which Hitler had insisted upon, and the impossibility of making Hitler any longer see sense. Stahl remembered that Speer was in a highly emotional state. He recalled the rough sense of what Speer then said:

'I simply cannot stand it any longer and be witness to a government by lunatics. The nation will perish completely if nothing decisive is done about these insane plans for destruction. I finally have come to the decision to end this state of affairs, if necessary by force. However, there is no use removing only one, the most dangerous and closest of his entourage must be removed.'[2]

Speer then asked him to find out about solid poison gases (the gas was 'tabun', a deadly nerve gas), which he planned to insert into the air vents of Hitler's bunker, after first sealing up the entrance doors. Stahl knew nothing about solid gas, but went away and consulted a ministry expert, Colonel Soika, who explained that solid poison gas only split into fine airborne particles through the explosion of the shell. Liquid gases evaporated or formed smoke. He reported to Speer that solid gases would not work. By this time, as Speer later wrote, the air vents had been modified with the addition of a ten-foot-high chimney because Hitler was worried (rightly, it seems) about the possibility of poison gas entering the bunker, and Speer abandoned the plan.

Stahl, however, recalled a second plot, which Speer did not mention either under interrogation or during the trial or in his memoirs, though Stahl did later tell the court that Speer had had in mind other 'violent measures'. Speer told Stahl that he considered Bormann, Himmler and Goebbels as the three most dangerous and radical men in Germany. In the middle of March (Stahl could not recall the exact date) Speer summoned him once again. This time he had dreamed up a plot straight out of fiction. He wanted to assassinate all three of his colleagues in an ambush outside the Chancellery building. He told Stahl that he had found 'a few brave men' capable of using firearms. They would position themselves outside the Chancellery on an evening when all three men were inside with Hitler 'hatching their fiendish plans'. Their habit was to leave for the suburbs in three separate cars when the evening air raid sirens sounded. This was the point at which the brave men and Speer, who intended to take part in the killings himself, would leap out of hiding and gun down the occupants in their vehicles. He asked Stahl for machine carbines, a dozen pistols, ammunition and Verey-light cartridges, which he wanted for two purposes, to simulate a bombing raid in order to bring the cars to a halt, and to blind the victims. When pressed Stahl became hazy about the precise details of the ambush, but he could recollect that the brave men were recruited from among officers of the German air force. He did furnish Speer with weapons on two separate occasions, once on the day following the meeting in March, and again in April.[3]

Speer was an unlikely assassin and neither plot materialized. He carried a gun at all times in the last months of the war, but whether he was capable of using it to kill in cold blood was never tested. The image of the respectable middle-aged minister wrestling in the dark of an air raid to open the doors of a heavily armoured car in order to gun down one or other of the chosen victims defies credibility. In his memoirs Speer referred to the possibility of eliminating Bormann, Goebbels and Ley (but not, as Stahl reported, the more plausible target Himmler) as well as Hitler, but the existence of a second plot, or the supply of pistols and ammunition to sustain it, Speer overlooked.[4] Stahl did not know during his interrogation whether Speer had indeed been responsible for Hitler's death at the end of April. When he was told about the debris in the bunker and the charred bodies found there, Stahl exclaimed excitedly, 'I don't know if Speer got this stuff or not and whether he chucked it in.' He seemed in little doubt about his chief's will to act: 'I never doubted his intentions as I considered very genuine Speer's indignation . . ., an indignation shared by every responsible German.' He did not know that Speer abandoned in March all thought of assassination 'as quickly as it had come'.[5] Speer explained to his interrogators that he wanted at all costs to avoid an assassination 'which could be interpreted as another "stab-in-the-back"', like the myth of betrayal in 1918. 'The German mentality could be purged of Nazi nonsense,' Speer claimed, 'only by the bitter experience of defeat and subsequent disillusionment.'[6]

Speer's motives for bringing up the details of this story so late in his interrogation can only be guessed at. By that point he had already established himself as a co-operative, pliant and sensible captive, whose powers of recall and analysis far exceeded those of any other senior figure in the Hitler government. Speer benefited from the fact that his name did not appear on many of the early lists of war criminals. He was never identified with the radical or baser leaders of the movement, though he was an enthusiastic National Socialist, who joined the party in 1931 as a young architect desperate for orders. It was Hitler's fascination with architecture that brought Speer into the inner circle of the regime. After completing work for Goebbels, Speer was invited to work on the new Reich Chancellery building. It was Speer who designed the circle of searchlights for the night-time party rallies. Speer was chosen to supervise Hitler's ambitious programme for the rebuilding of Germany's cities. He was a fast-rising star when he was appointed Armaments Minister in February 1942, a post he held until the end of the war, when he briefly became Economics Minister in Doenitz's short-lived government established at Flensburg in early May 1945. It was his function as armaments overlord that explains the special prominence he achieved with the Allied intelligence teams investigating German economic performance. The desire to extract technical information from Speer sheltered him from the much harsher regime imposed on the other senior political figures.

While still at large in Flensburg in mid-May, Speer was visited by two junior American officers of the United States Strategic Bombing Survey who grilled him on the effects of bombing on the economy. When it was realized how much he knew, the whole Survey team was flown to Flensburg to meet him. The city enclave was still run by the German authorities while the Allies argued over its future. Two Luftwaffe officers greeted the plane bringing the young economist J. K. Galbraith to the interrogations. When they drove out to see Speer in a nearby castle, an SS guard unit greeted them and ushered them in. Speer asked them to arrest him to end the state of limbo in which he found himself (like a 'Grade B Warner Brothers', he told his interrogators in English), but the team had no power to do so. For three days they asked him in detail about the performance of the war economy. On the last day, 22 May, they stayed up all night, riveted by Speer's account of the last days of the Reich, which Galbraith jotted down (and which did include a reference to the assassination). The following day Speer's castle was surrounded by British troops and anti-tank guns. He was arrested by a British sergeant and taken by lorry to a nearby airport.[7] He was taken first to 'Ashcan', but stayed there only briefly. He was transferred to Paris, where he was put under light guard in a room in Eisenhower's headquarters and interrogated repeatedly on German weapons and war production. When Eisenhower transferred to Frankfurt in June, Speer was transferred to the 'Dustbin' internment camp.

Speer was treated well throughout the summer months. He seems to have been well-regarded by everyone who came into contact with him. Tall, good-looking, well-mannered, articulate, Speer was very different from the other men around Hitler. He was assisted by his knowledge of English, and his evident helpfulness. He made no secret that he had become disillusioned with Hitler and the regime, but he also strove to assure all those who talked with him that he would not attempt to avoid his responsibility. At Nuremberg Airey Neave was struck by his 'charm and apparent integrity' which shone out 'in that sordid place', though he also detected a 'self-assurance and arrogance' which exposed a darker side to Speer.[8] Kelley, so acute in his diagnosis of Hess, was entirely taken in by Speer. Hitler's architect he found quiet and introverted, someone 'to be written off as an extremely intelligent, sensitive, creative, highly skilled architect, boyish in nature and concerned only with his work'.[9] Kelley thought Speer a dreamer and artist, indifferent to the trial and to his fate. Although Speer certainly displayed both detachment and imperturbability, he was far from indifferent to what might befall him.

Speer impressed all those who interviewed him in the early weeks of captivity. 'The one German,' wrote a Foreign Office official in June, 'who has shown possibilities of affording us assistance and inspiration . . . is Speer . . . he is head and shoulders above our other captives.'[10] Very soon his interrogators, drawn chiefly from the intelligence agencies, used Speer as their conduit for a better understanding of the nature of the Third Reich. During June and July Otto Hoeffding, an interrogator with the economic branch of FIAT, invited Speer to write lengthy summaries of the domestic and foreign policies of the Third Reich. Speer was not well informed about much of what he was asked, but he gave helpful answers to everything.[11] On the war economy he provided a clear overall analysis, which helped the Bombing Survey to arrive at its conclusion that bombing had a very limited effect on Germany's war effort because of the existence of a good deal of slack in the economy up until 1942. Speer took up and utilized this spare capacity to expand production to unexampled heights two years later. His willingness to explore German economic performance so readily can perhaps be explained by the evident success that had attended his efforts to increase armaments. He was never reticent about his achievements.

Speer was at his most helpful in offering advice on where the Allied air forces went wrong in the conduct of the bombing campaign. He explained that the area bombing carried out by the RAF had only limited effects on production. Its purpose he found 'incomprehensible'. The precision attacks carried out by the US Eighth Air Force were regarded as more serious, but even here Speer insisted that the wrong target systems had been attacked, and there had been long delays between attacks that allowed Germany time to recuperate. It was Speer's view that the Allies should not have attacked the armaments industry, but instead singled out the basic supply industries such as chemicals or steel ('it is much easier to dam up a river near the source than near the delta'), and the transport net.[12] His personal preference was for a systematic aerial assault on the electricity-generating industry, which Speer believed might quickly paralyse production. He offered both criticism and advice freely, and the reports of his interrogations, most of which were conducted in Paris, were widely circulated.

By the time Speer arrived at Nuremberg he had played an indispensable role in providing his captors with all the technical information he had at his disposal. He had become over the summer the leading light of the very large cohort of German officials, scientists and technicians whose expertise was meticulously scrutinized by the Allies to serve their own military and technical ends. Speer was not treated as a major war criminal, likely to be charged with the monstrous crimes set at the door of the Party hacks and bureaucrats collected for trial. When the list of major criminals was compiled in June it was recognized that it might be more problematic to prosecute 'a man like Spier [sic]', who was 'essentially an organizer'. When news arrived at 'Dustbin' that Speer was one of the major defendants, the British sergeant in charge of him increased his rations to build up his strength for the ordeal to come. The commandant of the camp took Speer out on a drive unguarded. They stopped to walk in the nearby Taunus woods and conversed like friends.[13] When Speer arrived at Nuremberg he found the atmosphere very different. Here he was not a technician, on morally neutral ground, but a man indicted for crimes against humanity.

The interrogators at Nuremberg were not interested in the technical details of German production. Speer was indicted on all four main charges, but the main issue was to establish the degree of his responsibility for the exploitation of foreign workers and concentration camp labour in German industry during the war. These accusations Speer resolutely rejected. He had already prepared the ground in his earlier technical interrogations in which he had made clear that camp labour was Himmler's responsibility, while the seizure and exploitation of foreign labour came under the Plenipotentiary for Labour Supply, Fritz Sauckel, an old Party comrade and Gauleiter of Thuringia.[14] In his first interrogation, on 9 October, he realized that Sauckel, who had been interrogated six times during September, had pre-empted him by explaining that ultimate responsibility for labour allocation belonged to Speer. He set the record straight at once. He did not deny that foreign workers were imported into Germany, nor did he accept that it was in principle criminal: 'I thought it quite right that if there were not sufficient workers that they should be brought in from the foreign countries.' But responsibility for the programme, Speer explained, was entirely Sauckel's. He insisted that he had not made a single request to Sauckel for foreign workers, a denial so categorical that it made Speer hostage to fortune should one document demonstrate the contrary.[15] During the trial the prosecution was able to show a great deal more than one.

Speer persisted with his claim that he had nothing to do with anything that might be construed as a war crime. When asked about the fate of Jewish labour in Berlin, he blamed their transfer eastwards on Goebbels. The decision to remove all Jews working in German industry he regarded as a 'political' decision made by Himmler, to be set against his efforts, as a mere technocrat, to keep as much German skilled labour for armaments production as possible. When he was questioned more closely on the mistreatment of Soviet workers and prisoners-of-war, he took the opportunity to point out that he only ordered workers from Sauckel without specifying whether they should be German or foreign. On the harsh conditions imposed on foreign labour, Speer bluntly replied, 'I don't know anything about it and it was not a concern of mine', though he was willing to explain most carefully whose concern he thought it was.[16]

Speer showed a remarkable moral detachment in all these discussions. His personal justification for obstructing the transfer of Jewish labour was not expressed as moral revulsion against antisemitism, but on grounds of expediency: 'this was natural for me in my position as Minister of Production, for it was in my interest to retain all skilled workers for production purposes'.[17] He did not condemn the use of foreign labour, but did regret the fact that its efficiency was so much poorer than German. He knew an increasing proportion of the labour he acquired was foreign, even if he had not specified it as such. Like that of a man who knowingly receives stolen goods, Speer's guilt was beyond doubt. Yet he deliberately hid behind the nature of his office. 'At that time,' he told his Soviet interrogator, 'I took interest only in my own responsibilities . . . In those days I considered my task as a technical task . . . In my activity I had only one chief concern. I made a sustained effort to minimize the effects of the bombings, and to maintain production in my industries at as high a level as possible.'[18] He did not deny that he shared collective responsibility with his colleagues in working for a regime that perpetrated crime. Instead he denied any specific crimes, casting himself as accessory but not perpetrator. The image of the unpolitical technocrat, first the architect and then the Minister for Armaments, working in blinkered isolation on the job in hand became Speer's strategy for defence from the point of his arrival at Nuremberg.

In early November Speer assumed a new tactic. He asked Airey Neave, one of the British representatives at the trial, to tell the interrogation team that he wished to make a special statement about the interrogations he had undergone in British hands. A day or so later he was given the opportunity to explain his statement to Major Monigan. He pointed out that he had given technical information to the western Allies 'without reserve' over a four-month period, and that he had told the Bombing Survey how to fight a better bombing war ('big mistakes have been made; it is possible to shut down any industry in two or three months if you use the proper means . . .') so that they would not make the same mistakes when they bombed Germany's former ally, Japan.[19] This was a remarkable claim, not least for Speer's willingness to recognize, without moral demur, that his advice may have doomed the Japanese population to the terrors of a more effective bombing campaign and ultimate defeat. The motive behind his statement was apparently to avoid any danger that the technical and military secrets he had revealed would fall into Soviet hands. He wanted to remind his western captors exactly what they owed him for passing on his technical experiences, and to ensure that they should remain 'on one side of the fence'. The record shows that the interrogator was puzzled by Speer's remarks, whose ostensible purpose seemed lost amidst Speer's prolonged and detailed recollection of everything he had freely committed to the western cause. Nevertheless, he was allowed to prepare his statement and to submit it to Justice Jackson for consideration.

Speer drafted a three-page letter in German, executed in pencil and spelt out in capital letters, seven words to a line, as the prison rules required, which he handed to his interrogator to pass on to Jackson on 17 November, three days before the trial. A translated version exists in Jackson's files. Speer amplified the remarks he had made under interrogation, but the nub was the same: he had been unusually candid in passing on to the British and Americans German technical developments and quite open in pressing equal candour on others:

I myself have during this period not only given every possible information, but further still calmly dispelled the objections of my former colleagues towards open information.[20]

Speer also reminded Jackson that he had willingly collaborated with the Bombing Survey. He did not want this information to reach the hands of any third party. He concluded the letter with the disingenuous claim that he had done none of this 'in order to create advantages for me for the future'. Included in the letter were the names of five individuals that Jackson was encouraged to contact for confirmation that Speer had been the decent confessor he claimed to be.[21]

It is possible that Speer made play with his technical assistance because he genuinely disliked the prospect of having to share any of his information with the Soviet side, or the ruder interrogation he might be subjected to in the Lubyanka. An alternative interpretation is to accept that Speer did try to use the goodwill he had built up since May to influence the approach that the tribunal made to his case, and that his disclaimer was mere rhetoric. The letter was oblique in its reference to a 'third party', where Speer had been explicit under interrogation that he meant the Russians. The main body of the letter was concerned with the open and unrestricted way in which Speer had made himself available to the west, and all the men Speer recommended Jackson to contact, including the members of the Bombing Survey team, could have corroborated the thorough and scrupulous way in which it was done. In the end Speer's tactics failed to save him from a twenty-year prison sentence for crimes against humanity and war crimes, but it may be the case, though there is no certain proof, that his behaviour throughout the months of interrogation contributed to the willingness of the British and American judges to argue successfully against the strong Soviet demand that Speer should hang with the rest.[22]

The Unrepentant Goering

Goering's mastery of the facts and persuasive manner were particularly noticeable. On the other hand apart from the questions of the Jewish persecutions Goering's story amounted almost to a plea of guilty and there was little if anything of importance for which he was not prepared to accept responsibility.

British War Crimes Executive, letter to the War Office, 14 March 1946[1]

When Goering came to give evidence the whole court wondered what was going to happen. He went on the offensive immediately. There was none of this craven 'I didn't do it, I'm terrible sorry, it wasn't my fault.' His attitude was, 'What the hell do you expect? We were fighting a war for our survival.'

Seaghan Maynes, journalist at the Nuremberg Trials[2]

One of the most famous photographs from the Nuremberg trials. Herman Goering consults with his defence lawyer in a picture taken by the celebrated Soviet photographer, Yevgeny Khaldei. Goering admitted most of the accusations, but he was keen for the record to be straight.

In Hitler's absence, Reich Marshal Hermann Goering became, by general agreement, chief among the cohort of prisoners awaiting trial. Imprisonment took a physical toll on Goering, but it did not dim his brutal ebullience and seldom constrained his overbearing egomania. He bullied and coaxed his flagging fellows, and chided them for disloyalty or cowardice. He had little if any sense of contrition. In Goering's case there was nothing to be gained by pretending that someone else had been responsible, and for a man with so inflated a view of his own importance, such a defence would no doubt have stuck in Goering's throat.

Goering was an old-fashioned nationalist with a radical personality. A career soldier-turned-airman in the First World War, he became one of thousands of rootless young officers angry at what they saw as Germany's betrayal in 1918, resentful of the 'dictated' peace settlement, deeply hostile to Communism and anti-semitic in the sense that they shared the general prejudice of their class and background against Jews. Goering gravitated to the infant Nazi Party in the early 1920s, stood side-by-side with Hitler during the Munich *Putsch*, became one of a handful of Nazi parliamentary deputies in 1928 and rose by 1932 to become President of the Reichstag and one of the key political playmakers of the movement. After 1933 he built up the German air force in six years, and became in 1936 Plenipotentiary of the Four Year Plan, responsible much more than Schacht had been for transforming the German economy for war. In 1939 he was appointed Hitler's successor and in July 1940 was honoured with the unique title of Reich Marshal, which made him the highest-ranking officer in the armed forces. He was ambitious, powerfully jealous of his position, an astute and ruthless political animal who hunted down and destroyed any weaker prey that strayed onto his territory. He was utterly loyal to Hitler, on whom he relied for everything he had become. In captivity in 1945 he retained that loyalty unblemished. Unlike Speer, who confessed his part in running the Third Reich with some humility, Goering relished what had been achieved. 'Goering seemed to think,' recalled one of the American prosecution team, 'that Hitler had the answers, and in the long run Germany would discover that he had the answers . . . there was no question that Adolf Hitler was right in what he did.'[3]

To the Allies Goering had become, in the words of an American official, 'one of the world's worst criminals'.[4] At the foot of the filing card on Goering in the British card index of criminals was the single word 'Swindler'. During the early preparations for the Tribunal in May and June, Goering was picked out as the number one target for investigation and an early trial; Maxwell-Fyfe went so far as to recommend that the first trial should consist simply of Goering's prosecution.[5] The OSS research report on Goering was prepared much faster than the others, and ran to more than 100 pages. So complicated was the range of offices that Goering held and so intricate the web of crime in which he was implicated that the OSS drew up a special fact sheet headed 'Goering as a War Criminal', which none of the other defendants merited. The crimes were, indeed, monumental in character – organized the Gestapo, created the air force for aggressive war, bombed civilians (a charge that was later quietly dropped on account of the Allied bombing of Germany), terrorized occupied Europe, looted Europe's economy and art collections, and on seven counts was instrumental in persecuting and dispossessing the Jews of Germany and Europe.[6]

Goering was never a fugitive like so many of his colleagues. He willingly sought out the American army under the mistaken impression that he would be treated as an emissary from a defeated people. He sat and chatted with the American soldiers of the 36th Division, 7th US Army who collected him from his temporary quarters in southern Bavaria. One American commander present, Brigadier-General Stack, shook Goering's hand when they met ('War is not a game, which ends with handshakes,' protested Lord Woolton in the British House of Lords when the news leaked out). Goering was then fed, and shown to comfortable quarters. As war correspondents flocked to the scene, an impromptu press conference was assembled. Goering sat and fielded questions on the war: 'Did you order the bombing of Coventry?' ('Yes. Coventry was an industrial centre'); 'What contributed most to the end [of the war]?' ('The uninterrupted air attacks'); 'Who ordered the attack on Russia?' ('Hitler himself'); 'What future do you expect for Germany?' ('I see a black future for Germany and the whole world').[7] The reporters could not use their scoop. The American censors, on

When Goering surrendered to units of the American 7th Army in May 1945 he hoped to be treated as a negotiator. Here he sits with American soldiers before holding an impromptu press conference. Hours later he was imprisoned as a war criminal.

Goering was an avid art collector. A trainload of valuables accompanied him when he fled to southern Germany at the end of the war. Here some of the vast collection is on display in a former air force headquarters at Königsee.

Eisenhower's instructions, placed a total embargo on all reports. One question asked of Goering before the press conference began did get past the censor. When he was asked if he knew he was on the list of war criminals, Goering replied: 'No. That's a big surprise to me, for I don't know why.'[8]

The press interview prompted the army chief-of-staff in Washington, General George C. Marshall, to remind Eisenhower bluntly that under no circumstances were any Germans suspected of war crimes to be allowed access to the media.[9] Goering was moved to 'Ashcan', where from the outset he imposed his imperial style on the other prisoners. Andrus put him on a special diet to reduce his corpulence. The prison guards none the less christened him 'Fat Stuff', and shouted it down the corridor, one to another, when he was summoned to interrogation. He was interrogated irregularly on military matters. One interrogator found him a difficult man to question: Goering spoke too rapidly, and said too much, and would not easily brook interruption. He refused to change his views even when the evidence was clearly against him. He talked in generalities. When he was asked if Germany could have defeated the Soviet Union without the invasion of Normandy, he replied that the Germans 'would have socked the Russians so hard that they would have seen the sun, the moon and the stars'.[10] When he was visited by four Soviet interrogators in late July, who arrived with 'grim, vengeful looks', Goering charmed them. Soon listeners could hear roars of laughter coming from the interview room. Two hours later the Soviet delegation re-emerged in evident good humour, and left amidst much guffawing and back-slapping.[11]

Goering's preliminary interrogations were largely technical in character. His military position made him a principal witness to the German war effort, and his views on German strategy and operations were expected to yield an insider's perspective. He enjoyed the attention his seniority afforded, though his knowledge of the military aspects of Hitler's war lacked detail and sophistication, except in those areas of the air war where he had retained an active interest. He was interviewed by the American Bombing Survey team in June 1945 on lines that gave no hint that he was regarded as the most unscrupulous and vicious of the senior prisoners in Allied hands. His views on bombing differed from those of Speer, because he was fighting an air campaign, not a battle for production. Goering did regard the Allied bombing offensive as a central factor in the defeat of the German air force. Bombing forced the dispersal of aircraft production and contributed to a cumulation of small but significant interruptions in the production and distribution of finished planes, many of which in 1944 were left inoperable because they were short of vital components or spares. The number of aircraft reported as produced did not remotely correspond to the much smaller number of aircraft available at any one time for operations. Bombing compelled a dispersion of German military effort away from the fighting fronts to the defence of the Reich, where, according to Goering, it met its nemesis in the menacing form of the Allied long-range fighter, introduced in 1944. High losses of German aircraft in German air space rendered impossible the reinforcement of the fighting fronts with adequate numbers of aircraft, exposing the exiguous air forces there to ever higher rates of attrition, and denying to German armies the air umbrella they had come to expect. Bombing for Goering was principally a military defeat, not an economic challenge.[12] By expressing the consequences of bombing in terms of German military strategy, Goering provided a historically plausible explanation of German defeat, but it was Speer's economic analysis which won over the Survey team, and has seduced historians ever since.

Goering was the dominant figure at 'Ashcan'. Once slimmed down and weaned away from his habit of pill-popping – small doses of paracodeine, rather than the cocktail of drugs in which it was widely assumed he indulged – Goering manifested a renewed physical and intellectual energy. At Nuremberg he had fewer opportunities to bully or cajole his former colleagues, but he earned without question the dubious sobriquet of chief war criminal. His guards and interrogators found him a difficult person to dislike, despite his fearsome reputation. He displayed a raw sense of humour, and was seldom disarmed or intimidated by those who questioned him. When he was able to, Goering liked to control the interview situation. On one occasion a hapless interrogator from Jackson's documents division received some frank advice from Goering after offering him a cigarette: 'Captain,' Goering was heard to say, 'you don't do this right. If we'd won, we wouldn't have done it this way – you'd be standing up, and you wouldn't have your uniform on, you'd have a black-and-white prisoner's suit, and there would be two SS men standing behind you, sticking you in the butt with bayonets . . . That's the way you ought to treat us.'[13]

At Nuremberg Goering was treated with a wary respect. Airey Neave, a British major who was chosen to present the Indictment to the war criminals, and had been held at one time in Colditz castle, the notorious German prisoner-of-war camp, took an instant dislike to Goering when he entered his cell on 19 October to deliver the document. The dangerous face, the twisted mouth, the 'small and greedy' eyes replete with an unfathomable menace, all of these Neave detected in his first nervous glances. But Neave conceded that Goering, set alongside 'his miserable companions', was the only man he met at Nuremberg who 'might have been capable of governing Germany'.[14] The prison psychiatrist, Douglas Kelley, spent hours in Goering's cell in order to study closely the personality of the only survivor of the central quartet of Nazi leaders, whose other players, Hitler, Himmler and Goebbels, were already dead. He formed the view that Goering was 'a brilliant, brave, ruthless, grasping, shrewd executive'.[15] He also found Goering charming, persuasive, intelligent and imaginative. The one characteristic that set Goering apart from the urbane personality he revealed to Kelley was his complete lack of moral discrimination, his absence of any sense 'of the value of human life'. In this Goering was as candid as in all else. When Kelley asked him why he had ordered the murder of his friend Ernst Röhm during the purge of the SA on 30 June 1934, Goering stared at him as if he were 'not quite bright', and replied, 'But he was in my way . . .'[16]

The Interrogation Division began work on Goering on 28 August. He was interviewed briefly in September, but the greater part of his interrogation was conducted in the three weeks before the presentation of the Indictment on 19 October. All the interrogations were conducted by Amen himself. Throughout this and subsequent sessions Goering was questioned about the Third Reich from every angle. He had been at or near the centre of Nazi affairs for more than twenty years, and was the only National Socialist to have held high state office throughout the period from 1933 to 1945. His reputation as Hitler's confidant, which he was prone to inflate, was believed by his interrogators to offer an entry-gate into the mind of the absent Fuehrer which no other prisoner could unlatch. Goering was for the most part an obliging interviewee. He made no pretence that he could recall everything perfectly (asked about the Hossbach conference he protested, 'Considering that it is eight years ago . . . it is almost impossible for me to pin down what the Fuehrer said in 1937'), but he was not unwilling to provide answers or to admit liability, often with a disarming candour.[17] When asked whether he meant what he said in a speech made in Vienna in 1938 after the Austrian Anschluss, 'The Jew must clearly understand one thing at once, he must get out!', Goering replied without evasion, 'Yes, approximately.'[18]

Goering's description of the politics of Nazi Germany inadvertently confirmed the charge of conspiracy. He made it clear that the gang-leader took many of the key decisions, but he also revealed how the gang discussed their differing responsibilities and shared in the action. For Goering this was a point of personal pride; he was too large a personality to admit that in everything he had slavishly followed his leader. The conspirators were a group, governed by common loyalties and a common ambition to revive German fortunes. They relied on their leader to hold the unruly gang together by the force of his will, but aggression, racism and spoliation were the fruits of a shared enterprise. In Goering's Reich, Hitler was the arbiter as often as the instigator, the man with the final word, not the first. One example may suffice. When asked about Hitler's decision to pass the Emergency Decree on 28 February 1933 following the Reichstag fire, which was used to justify the mass arrest of German Communists, Goering confessed that he had already authorized arrest lists for 'the destruction of the Communist Party' well before the fire, and insisted that 'they would have been arrested anyway' within a few days or 'a week later', regardless of Hitler's sudden intervention.[19] Asked whether he had started the fire deliberately, as was then generally believed, but has since been largely discredited, he denied any responsibility with charac-teristic gusto: 'If I started the fire, then I would have burned it for a completely different reason, because the big congress hall was so ugly.'[20]

Goering was at his most informative on the key turning-points in the regime's history (though he was not asked in detail about the Jewish genocide, despite the fact that the prosecution possessed an order to Heydrich in July 1941 over his signature that authorized the search for a 'final solution' to the Jewish question). Goering explained how Hitler was obsessed by the idea of reaching accommodation with

Britain throughout the 1930s: Germany to have a free hand in Europe to fulfil its legitimate imperial ambitions, Britain to have a free hand to bind her existing empire more closely. Hitler's curious ambivalence towards Britain is well known, but it has seldom appeared in an odder guise than it did in Goering's first interrogation. India was Hitler's passage to an agreement with Britain:

Hitler *thought* England could not defend its Indian colony by land attack (from Russia) and its far east colonies (from Japan) without outside help, whereupon Hitler's tentative plan was to put a few divisions at England's disposal and he would thus help his own plans. Hitler further *believed* the constitutional disputes in India could be used as a basis for negotiation with England and ultimately a weapon against it.[21]

Goering insisted throughout his interrogations that Hitler's judgement on Britain ('the cohesion of the British Empire was not strong') nourished a persistent conviction that Britain would not fight in the event of war in continental Europe.

On Goering's account, Hitler had always held to the opinion that war should be fought 'against one single enemy'. Rather than risk a war on two fronts, Hitler's 'main idea' or 'whole policy' was to keep the two main western powers, Britain and France, out of the war over Poland. Hitler never advocated 'that a simultaneous attack against the East and the West should be conducted'. As the crisis in the summer of 1939 deepened, Goering watched Hitler's conviction develop a pathological insistence:

At this time, he still rigidly held to his idea that he would be able to come to some kind of accord with England, and that he could clear up the situation. As we saw it he held much too rigidly to this.[22]

Despite Goering's own reservations about Hitler's strategy, he revealed to his interrogator that the very day war was declared, 3 September 1939, he offered to send the whole of the German air force against the main British naval base at Scapa Flow in the Orkney Islands. 'This,' Goering concluded, 'was absolutely forbidden.'[23]

Goering did not pretend that Hitler was infallible. The miscalculation over Poland in 1939 was one that Goering might have avoided. Goering claimed, according to Kelley's later account, that if Hitler had appointed him Chancellor after the Munich conference in 1938, 'I would never have made war ... Instead of invading, I would have crushed Poland economically until she were forced to yield.'[24] Goering did believe in Hitler's maxim about fighting one enemy at a time. The defeat of Britain from the air in the winter of 1940–41 was at the point of complete success, Goering complained, until Hitler ordered his air force units eastwards for the campaign against the Soviet Union.[25] In 1941 Goering would have preferred to defeat Britain first by seizing Gibraltar and co-operating with Italy in destroying Britain's imperial lifeline through the Mediterranean. The two-front war that resulted in 1941 was fatal for Germany. Even here, Goering suggested, something might have been salvaged by holding on to the Ukraine in 1942 and using Russian workers to build an 'East Wall' of fortifications which 'no Russian army will ever break through'.[26] Hitler was undone, Goering concluded, by an unbridled opportunism ('He always left himself open for these very wide possibilities') and an inconstancy of ambition: 'It very often happened that when the Fuehrer had a certain purpose in mind, he only reasoned according to that purpose, and a few weeks later, he would give some very different point of view, when that particular subject was not in his mind.'[27] Goering was as unschooled as Hitler for high command in war, but the few glimpses of his strategic grasp evidenced in his interrogations suggest that Goering would have steered Germany's course more prudently if Hitler had died in 1939 and Goering replaced him as Fuehrer.

Such an outcome had been one of the possibilities hoped for in western political circles in 1939. Goering was viewed as a more moderate Nazi, with whom it might be possible to do business. The case against Goering at Nuremberg revealed a man who was anything but moderate. Though he might have prosecuted the war with greater prudence, he never expressed any regret for Germany's expansionist policy, openly asserted Germany's right to pursue race discrimination, and revelled in the disregard of international agreements: 'Of course, we rearmed,' Kelley remembered him saying. 'We rearmed Germany until we bristled. I am only sorry we did not rearm more. Of course, I considered treaties as so much toilet paper.'[28] He never had any illusions about his fate, which perhaps explains his uncompromising defiance. He approached the trial and the prospect of execution with equanimity, even a certain relish. He did not accept the validity of the trial – on a copy of the Indictment he scribbled: 'The victor will always be the judge and the vanquished the accused'[29] – but he never tired of talking. On 19 October, after Major Neave had delivered the Indictment to him, Goering was one of the few defendants to express an 'absolute willingness' to continue interrogation.[30] He was interrogated twice more.

The Limits of Responsibility:
Strategies of Denial

THOMAS DODD It seems to me that when any institution, whether it be an institution of government, or any other kind of an institution, embarks on an evil course, a man has a moral responsibility to completely disassociate himself from it, at least that, and a greater responsibility not to assist it in any way, manner or fashion to carry out any part of its program. Now, therefore, I suggest that since you had reasons for not taking a stand against it, or for not disassociating yourself from it, or from not disavowing it, you still had the recourse of not serving it.
VON PAPEN Yes.

Interrogations of Franz von Papen, Nuremberg, 19 September 1945[1]

Prisoners on exercise in the yard of the Nuremberg prison. They were allowed twenty minutes of exercise a day, two at a time, but were not permitted to communicate in any way with each other.

At the heart of the case against the defendants at Nuremberg was a profound moral issue: what responsibility should an individual bear for serving an immoral regime whose central apparatus compelled complicity and penalized dissent? In a one-man dictatorship it is seductively simple for individuals to suspend conventional moral behaviour on the grounds that obedience to the leader's will absolves them of personal responsibility. This is an issue of more than contemporary significance. Since 1945 there have been many examples of corrupt regimes – South Africa under *apartheid*, Chile under Pinochet, Argentina under the generals – whose collapse has occasioned a great deal of national heart-searching over the treatment of the perpetrators, from policy-makers to policemen. For the victims of oppression there is the added difficulty of living afterwards side-by-side with those who stood by and did nothing, whose lack of civil courage or crude self-interest or political naïveté allowed them to tolerate without protest a regime whose actions were manifestly criminal.

The Allies were well aware of the moral dilemmas involved in allocating responsibility. Justice Jackson in his report to the President in June 1945 put this question first, before all others. He feared the possibility that a combination of two legal principles – the immunity accorded to a head of state and the right to plead obedience to orders – might produce the absurd conclusion that in the Third Reich 'nobody is responsible'.[2] By June the question of immunity for Hitler was no longer relevant, but the argument that individuals were only obeying the leader's will was not compromised by his death. Jackson's case rested on the belief that there usually exists an element of voluntary participation for which any criminal should be judged responsible, and that such a principle has clear limits. Jackson chose the example of a firing-squad. The soldiers selected bore no responsibility for the judgement they were made to execute – that was the responsibility of those who chose and condemned the victims – but if they had the right to refuse to participate in acts they believed immoral, or sufficient rank to have some discretion in accepting or rejecting the order, these were options that ought to be taken. Simple obedience to orders was not extenuation enough. For those who volunteered for service in the SS or a post in the Gestapo obeying orders was judged to have no validity as a defence at all.[3]

The notion that individuals bore personal criminal responsibility for atrocious acts carried out under orders was clearly established in British and American law, though less so in the European legal tradition. The Soviet authorities ordered a new draft of the Soviet Criminal Code in 1945 to try to accommodate the principle that 'The carrying out of an order or instruction whose criminality was manifest for the subordinate does not absolve him from criminal responsibility'. The new draft was never brought into force, perhaps because the implications for the Soviet regime of state terror were too obvious.[4] The differences between European and Anglo-American legal practice may well explain why the defendants at Nuremberg so readily resorted to the argument that loyalty to Hitler and obedience to orders constituted a sufficient explanation for their actions, and why the interrogators spent fruitless hours in interview rooms trying to extract an admission of responsibility from men who had either lost, or never possessed, the power of moral discrimination in their own actions. 'The whole crew,' recalled the chief of Amen's Interrogation Analysis Division, Joseph Maier, 'they all whined and insisted they were mere "executive organs" of the Fuehrer. Only Goering was occasionally willing to accept responsibility for the orders issued over his signature.'[5]

However, the refusal to acknowledge responsibility was not one-dimensional. Defendants reacted to their interrogators in ways that reflected their personalities and psychological predisposition. Hess blotted out reality almost entirely, but Ribbentrop and Funk both displayed severe memory lapse in efforts to escape from uncomfortable truths. The military prisoners refused to accept that the armed forces had systematically committed war crimes, or had done anything other than wage war as their enemies had done. Sauckel, Ley, Frick and Kaltenbrunner stoutly maintained that they were mere agents of administration, divorced from responsibility for any criminality that their official functions might have spawned among the thousands of their subordinates, or the other elements of the Nazi apparatus. Among the conservatives who accepted and worked with Hitler in 1933, Schacht, von Papen and von Neurath, there emerged a specious defence, common among fellow travellers, that their presence in

The aristocratic former Foreign Minister, Constantin von Neurath, finds himself seated in the courthouse canteen next to Julius Streicher, the anti-semitic rabble-rouser and former party *Gauleiter*, who was generally shunned by his fellow prisoners.

government gave them a moderating influence on a regime that might otherwise indulge its radical appetites unrestrained. Only Hans Frank, eventually hanged for his part in the rape of Poland, was willing to confess that he had served an evil cause willingly and now felt an overpowering regret, though even he refused to accept that he had personally done anything criminal. The common distinctions between right and wrong, apparently so simple, proved for many and complex reasons to be beyond the grasp of most of those interrogated.

The inability to remember is not a surprising response. Selective amnesia was a psychological device to ease the path to full denial. Funk and Ribbentrop were the two defendants most psychologically undermined by their imprisonment. Though Funk could recall with remarkable clarity some of his career after 1933, on any issue where there was evidence of criminality he demurred and denied. So frustrating was his testimony that Funk continued to be interrogated regularly in the weeks after the Indictment was served, when he was free to refuse co-operation. He was confronted on numerous occasions by interrogators who possessed in front of them the written transcript of meetings in which Funk had participated but of which he now refused all recollection. As the evidence against him accumulated Funk shifted tactics, at times accepting his presence but denying his participation, or limiting his participation to its least damaging aspects.

Finally, in November 1945, Funk began to admit to much that he had refused to recall about his role in anti-semitic policy, above all the legislation for driving Jews out of German economic life.[6] But even then he placed limits upon his own responsibility on the grounds that he was a tiny cog in a large machine. 'You keep saying that you knew nothing about high policy and that you were only a small man in effect,' his interrogator asked, armed with a secret decree on the planned exploitation of the Soviet Union only shown, according to the record, to Goering, Keitel and Funk. 'Yes, I was,' replied Funk.[7] When he later openly admitted that he had signed legislation to dispossess Jews in 1939 as Minister of Economics, he would only admit that there had been one law under his signature (there were in fact numerous decrees, laws, and directives on aryanization that passed through the Ministry), and that he had signed it 'against his conviction'. He refused to recall any other legislative act, and denied any knowledge of the camps or of genocide ('About that I knew nothing at all'), though there was witness evidence that Funk visited Dachau in 1943 where gold was extracted from the teeth of victims, melted down and sent to the Reichsbank, of which Funk was president.[8]

Ribbentrop's memory loss went the opposite way to Funk's. In an early interrogation conducted by two officials, one British, one American, attached to Eisenhower's headquarters in June 1945, Ribbentrop adopted a style that was 'affable and even jocular'. He was described as 'cool, self-possessed and well-mannered', qualities that had never been a part of his reputation either at home or abroad. His jauntiness was evident in the answers he gave to questions largely concerned with German foreign policy, and German–Soviet relations in particular. There was no sign of a faltering memory. Ribbentrop did not accept responsibility as such. He told his interviewers that the dictatorship left important decisions in Hitler's hands, not those of the competent minister, but he was not diffident about his own role and could recall a remarkable amount of detail about the key moments of his career.[9] The Ribbentrop who entered captivity in Nuremberg in August was a very different creature. Pale, thin, shabbily dressed, ill-at-ease, fearful, Ribbentrop was a broken man. Kelley visited him in a cell that was always in a 'chaotic mess', strewn with crumpled paper; he gave the impression of a child 'cut off completely from his parents'. His habitual greeting when the prison psychiatrist arrived was 'Doctor, what shall I do? What shall I do?'[10]

Joachim von Ribbentrop had been an unlikely Foreign Minister. He possessed none of the qualities necessary for one of the most demanding of the senior offices of state. Nevertheless the prosecution thought his role in the conspiracy was substantial. 'If Hitler himself had ever been asked before an impartial court of justice why he framed his foreign policy as he did,' ran the British report on Ribbentrop, published in June 1945, 'he would most likely have answered that he allowed himself to be guided in the main by the confidential advice of his Foreign Minister, Ribbentrop.'[11] This outlook explains British and American frustration with Ribbentrop's constant disclaimers that he was a novice when Hitler appointed him, and remained little more than a cypher when it came to decisions on foreign policy. When he was asked by Amen why Hitler chose him for the post, which he assumed in February 1938, Ribbentrop replied: 'I don't know why he put me in. He didn't tell me; never talked about that; it was not his habit.'[12] His predecessor found Ribbentrop's appointment inexplicable. Von Neurath told his interrogator that when he asked to be relieved of his post on 14 January 1938, Hitler told him, 'But I will never make this Ribbentrop Foreign Minister.' Two weeks later he did just that, a decision that von Neurath attributed to Hitler's preference for a 'yes-man'. This was certainly Ribbentrop's reputation among his former colleagues. 'Germany's No. ·1 parrot' was Goering's cheerful description.[13]

When Ribbentrop was interrogated about German foreign policy, he showed himself forgetful, poorly informed and devious. The image of a 'yes-man' suited his purposes. On the memorable occasion when Jackson himself interrogated Ribbentrop on 5 October, the following sour exchange took place:

Q. Do you mean to imply that you did not fully understand the foreign policy, and that the foreign policy was not fully imparted to you?

A. I must tell you quite frankly that apart from that . . . all the further aims of the Fuehrer which he might have had, and which I only heard through these interrogations here, the Fuehrer never disclosed to me any of his definite big policy, or the future formation of the Reich . . .

Q. Do you really want me to go to my associates at this meeting [to determine the terms of the Indictment] and tell them that it is your position that as foreign minister of the Reich you didn't know what the foreign policy was?

A. I am sorry. I must say so. I am very sorry. The Fuehrer never revealed his definite aims to anyone.[14]

Jackson's visit to Ribbentrop was prompted by a letter which the defendant had sent to him some days earlier. In it Ribbentrop included a curious proposal. He was willing to put himself forward, together with other unspecified 'co-workers of the Fuehrer', for the voluntary assumption of responsibility. The object was to prevent the necessity of a trial, by allowing a small number of prisoners to take upon themselves full 'political responsibility'. Ribbentrop did not specify what the responsibility would be for, nor, he later told Jackson, had he given any thought to what punishment might be meted out to him if his captors agreed. Jackson was keen, after weeks in which Ribbentrop had offered nothing but long-winded, rambling, self-justificatory responses to every question, to discover precisely what Ribbentrop was willing to accept as his part. He ran through the most obvious points. Ribbentrop baulked at 'war of aggression' ('I couldn't do that for the war of aggression'); on breaking treaties he hesitated ('I have not thought about these details'); on slave labour, the mishandling of prisoners-of-war, killing of hostages, plundering of property, the concentration camps, the Jewish genocide, the Gestapo, the SS, Ribbentrop had one answer: 'No, I couldn't', 'No, I can't.' Jackson weighed up these responses, which cover almost six pages of the stenographic report. 'Your offer to me does not include taking any responsibility for anything that is classed as a war crime, or a crime of any character,' Jackson asked. 'Is that right?' Ribbentrop confirmed it: 'That was my idea. No crime.'[15] When Amen interrogated Ribbentrop two days later about the letter he concluded that the only thing

Ribbentrop would actually accept responsibility for was the fact that he did hold the position of Foreign Minister: 'That is the one thing you can't say, "if", "and", or "but" about. But that is the only thing you admit so far.'[16]

Ribbentrop was an extreme case, but he was not alone in adopting tactics of evasion and pretending ignorance. His list of those willing to assume political responsibility would in all probability not have extended far beyond Goering and Speer. Rosenberg accepted very little of the evidence presented to him about conditions in the wartime eastern territories under his jurisdiction. He blamed the harsh measures imposed on Soviet civilians as a consequence of 'the conduct of our enemies', and refused throughout to accept any moral responsibility for German actions. In his last interrogation, on 5 November, he was offered one final chance by his interrogator to 'admit and judge the crimes committed' by the regime he served. He turned the question on its head: 'Why did not the world listen to the sufferings and complaints of the German people for twenty years, since 1919? ... Humanity should also have been practised in the treatment of the German people ... The fact that Germany's complaints were ignored led to the passionate attitude of the German people. If crimes were committed punishment must be meted out, not only to the Germans, but to all who were responsible for them.'[17]

Other defendants passed the buck with equal facility. Fritz Sauckel ascribed responsibility for the programme of forced foreign labour to Speer, with his insatiable demands for armaments workers, and to Hitler ('Each programme I can safely say ... has been approved by the Fuehrer' ... 'express orders from and by the Fuehrer'). Since under oath he also informed his interrogators that the two principles he observed in the exploitation of forced labour were that they 'were to be treated and paid in the same manner as the German workers', and offered 'fair, right and humane treatment', his testimony was of questionable value, and was treated as such by the court.[18] Ernst Kaltenbrunner engaged his interrogators in prolonged and desperate arguments about jurisdiction in his efforts to demonstrate that he was not, as head of the RSHA, responsible for the Gestapo (Department IV of the RSHA) or for the programme of genocide (Department IVB4 of the Gestapo). His refusal to accept responsibility was maintained in the face of every effort of the interrogators, with charts, documents and affidavits to prove beyond doubt that he was the responsible head of the apparatus of terror.[19] Robert Ley refused to accept that he had any responsibility for the charges set against him: 'I have nothing to do with them at all. I was not in charge.' The most he would own up to was membership of the Nazi Party. Ley was so convinced of his innocence that when the interrogator showed him a list of lawyers from among whom he might select his counsel, he asked for 'a respectable Jewish attorney'.[20]

Ley was deeply affected by his incarceration. A weak, bibulous character, he was the victim of the degeneration of the frontal lobes of the brain, a condition consistent with high levels of alcohol consumption, but in Ley's case probably exacerbated by the after-effects of a head injury sustained in an air crash in 1917. The injury left Ley with a permanent stammer, though it did not inhibit his capacity to rant in front of a crowd when he became a leading Nazi in the 1920s. He was blindly loyal to Hitler, and was rewarded in 1933 with the leadership of the newly-created German Labour Front, a vast national organization that absorbed the trade unions and employers' associations into a single labour corporation. He was little liked by the rest of the leadership corps. He was outspoken and rude; he had a reputation as a womanizer and boozer; his enthusiasm for National Socialism and for Hitler was sustained with extravagant displays of emotional enthusiasm. He retained that devotion unalloyed through his imprisonment. His brain condition, according to the prison psychiatrist, did not seriously impair his intellectual capabilities, but his powers of judgement, lodged in the decrepit portion of his cranium, were seriously weakened, leaving him in a condition of exaggerated emotional instability.[21]

Ley deteriorated in prison. He hated confinement and was horrified that he was to be subject to investigation and trial like a common criminal. He left behind him a rough prison diary, scrawled on the back of four pages of the text of a paper he wrote titled 'Thoughts about the Fuehrer', which covers the period of his confinement at Nuremberg, from 12 August. The diary records the date, day and the same time, eight o'clock, next to each entry. Beside each entry Ley scribbled brief, sometimes cryptic notes: 'three months imprisoned'; 'tobacco'; 'peace in God'; 'bad'. He noted down the day of the intelligence testing, 8 October, but his name did not appear in Gilbert's list of rankings. On 16 October he noted 'Saw Hess', but did not refer to any of the other prisoners throughout the diary. While he kept his brief journal, Ley occupied himself by writing long and fantastical letters to his wife, who had killed herself almost three years before after a drunken tiff with her husband.[22]

The first of these 'dialogues', as Ley called them, was dated 14 August. Ley's description of the morbid but imaginary conversation with his wife gives a rare glimpse into the mind of a man grappling to come to terms with the trauma of defeat and loss and his own growing psychosis:

When catastrophe came over us, I was near despair. There I tempted God, I really did everything, in painful grief for my people, in memory of my dead Fuehrer and in presentiment of my fate, to finish my life. You know how seriously I meant it. You were also with me that time. And yet, I didn't succeed . . . Everything is so unreal and sounds like a novel. And, nevertheless, everything is so true. You know, my Inge, that I took everything extremely seriously. But God did not accept my life. He saved me miraculously, in order to send me then – into captivity – fate.[23]

Ley appealed to God often, in the dialogues and in his other prison writings, in the hope that an answer would come to explain his imprisonment and the accusations of crime. Inge comes to him again: 'Are you quarrelling with God, with your fate? Don't do it, everything has a purpose, even your grief and the grief of the millions of German people.'[24] Ley's uncritical enthusiasm for the cause is revealed in a lyrical passage where he recalls, as if waking from a dream, what the Nazi utopia might have been like:

Germany would have become so beautiful, strength through joy [the name of the recreational division of the Labour Front], spare time and recreation, new dwellings, the most beautiful cities and villages have been planned, service and just wages, a great, unique health-program, social security for the aged and incapacitated, roads construction and traffic lanes, ports and settlements, – how beautiful Germany could have been, if, if, if and always again, if.[25]

The dialogue ends with Inge's return to offer Ley words of comfort for having been brave enough to retain undiminished loyalty to Hitler: 'You have courageously portrayed the Fuehrer as he really is: *The greatest German of all time* . . . What enormously *positive things* National Socialism has achieved and yet suffered.'[26]

These were achievements bought at a terrible cost, for which Ley expressed an equivocal remorse, but from which he expressly absolved Hitler of any responsibility. Ley penned other documents during September and October in which he suggested world solutions to the problems exposed by the war – a council of reconciliation between German anti-semites and Jewish leaders ('hatred and love live in close proximity,' observed Ley), and, even more improbably, an alliance between Germany and the United States based on a revived National Socialism (shorn of the anti-semitism) led by the Party bosses ('they were and are *the best* representatives ... The most respected and active citizens').[27] The most curious document of all was a letter written to Henry Ford – whom Ley addressed with singular inappropriateness as Sir Henry Ford – in mid-August. Ley explained his position and his achievements in building up the Volkswagen works, which had been organized under the auspices of the Labour Front, and then complained that he was in prison for doing no more than Ford himself had done, 'to have written articles and books against the Jews' and to be responsible for 'no other crime'. He ended the letter with an appeal for reconciliation in the interests of the German people, 'even with the Jews'.[28] The letter, like all Ley's others, was never sent.

It was in this deluded state of mind that Ley received his copy of the Indictment. As the party entered his cell with the documents he shouted, 'Stand us against the wall and shoot us! You are the victors!' So strident and uncontrolled seemed Ley's behaviour that his 'unstable mental condition' was reported to the General Secretary of the International Military Tribunal five days later.[29] The same day, 24 October, Ley wrote a long letter to a doctor rejecting the Indictment in its entirety. It is the only written commentary on the charges by any of the defendants, and it reveals a sharper intellect than might have been suspected from Ley's recent history. Ley's concerns rested on the issues of jurisprudence about which American and British legal experts had already expressed reservations. He rejected the legal basis of the trial on the grounds that the law used to indict them had been made up after the crimes had been committed. He rejected the notion of conspiracy on the grounds that if such a thing existed, then all senior Nazi figures, all ministers and all of the General Staff should be arraigned, and not simply a representative of each element. The idea that there were organizations that could be indicted as collectively criminal Ley considered 'absurd'.[30]

The charges laid at Ley's own door – he was indicted on all four counts – he rejected categorically. The common plan or conspiracy to wage war was a fiction. Ley claimed to know nothing of foreign policy: 'The war fitted into my plans like hail in a cornfield.' Crimes against peace he also denied on the same ground. On war crimes, Count III, Ley was confident of his innocence. He did not regard the waging of total war as an adequate basis for demonstrating criminality. On the final count, crimes against humanity, Ley would accept no responsibility for any criminal act against the Jews, though he freely admitted his racism. 'I was anti-semitic, I admit, but is this a crime?' He concluded the letter with a defiant flourish: '*I am a German and a National Socialist but I am no criminal.*'[31]

These were almost the last words he wrote. For three days he had made no entry in his diary; the dates were only written in up to 25 October. In the evening of the 24th Ley hanged himself in his cell. For all the precautions taken by Andrus to ensure almost constant surveillance, and to remove any objects that might constitute a risk in the hands of a determined suicide, Ley carefully prepared his own death. He left a suicide note explaining that he could no longer bear the shame of his criminal status. He removed the hem of his towel, knotted it and soaked it in water to prevent the knots slipping. He attached the improvised rope to the water pipe of his toilet cistern, placed a noose constructed from the sodden towel around his neck, gagged himself with his own underwear to prevent anyone from hearing his moans and then sat down on the toilet in such a way that the weight of his own body might slowly strangle him. The guard patrolling outside found it difficult to see Ley clearly through the window of his cell door, but only after a gap of five or ten minutes, long enough for the suicide to be successful, did the guard finally alert his superior. The two rushed into the cell and cut Ley down. The prison doctor tried to revive him with drugs and heart massage without success. He pronounced Ley dead a few minutes later. The body was removed to allow Kelley to perform an autopsy, which confirmed the degenerative condition of his brain. The naked corpse was hurriedly buried, wrapped in a piece of butcher's paper, in an unmarked grave. Andrus changed the prison routine thereafter. A guard was posted on each door, instructed to look at the prisoner every minute of the day.[32]

Forgetfulness, denial, suicide: these were the chief weapons in the armoury of psychological defence against the accusations of monstrous crime. They were wielded chiefly by the men of the Party, whose responsibility was in little doubt but would not be admitted. For those defendants who had aided and abetted the Party, but were not themselves Nazis – Schacht, von Papen, von Neurath, and the military defendants, Keitel, Jodl, Raeder and Doenitz – the issue of responsibility was less clear-cut. They represented a conservative Germany which had little liking for the post-war Weimar Republic or for mass politics, which deeply loathed Communism and harboured a profound resentment at Germany's treatment by the other major powers after 1919. Conservatives collaborated with the Hitler government after 1933 in the belief that this was a movement whose radicalism, fanned by its plebeian following, could be tempered and exploited in the conservative interest. Much of what the Nazi regime stood for was congenial to conservative opinion: the political muzzling of the trade unions, the stamping-out of party politics in favour of a national reawakening, the rejection of the Versailles peace settlement of 1919. The alliance with Nazism became strained only when Hitler began to pursue a more active, expansionist foreign policy in 1937, and Nazi placemen were brought in to key areas of government which had hitherto been the preserve of the conservative elites. By this stage the capacity of conservative opinion to restrain the Nazi programme was greatly diminished. Conservatives were not immune from the pressures of the apparatus of police terror and surveillance; nor was there any united conservative front. Some conservatives came to identify much more closely with the regime and to serve it with enthusiasm; others baulked at further collaboration; a small minority toyed with the idea of active resistance.

The difficulty faced by the prosecution case at Nuremberg was to define conservative collaboration in terms which fitted the responsibility for criminal conspiracy. Jackson's formula – voluntary participation in institutions defined by their activities as criminal – was taken as a rough yardstick to establish responsibility. Conservatives, as outsiders to the Party, had a choice which most Nazis could not be expected to exercise so easily: they could resign their post. The interrogation team focused on this issue when they questioned the senior conservative defendants. The result was to raise more fundamental points about the nature of complicity and dissent under dictatorship. Those conservatives questioned about their failure to quit the Nazi ship took as their first line of defence the argument that they remained in office in order to prevent anything worse from happening. This was the argument used by Franz von Papen when he paved the way for a Hitler government in January 1933: '... we hoped to oppose radical tendencies,' von Papen wrote in his memoirs, 'by the application of Christian principles'.[33] Von Neurath justified to his interrogator his willingness to take on the office of Reich Protector of Bohemia in 1939, a year after his resignation as Foreign Minister, on the ground that he might 'restrain the extremists of the Party'.[34] The Finance Minister, Count Schwerin von Krosigk, who remained at his post throughout the twelve years of the Third Reich, and was fortunate indeed to avoid joining the list of major war criminals, was reported at 'Ashcan' offering the same apology: 'To have resigned ... would have been to make way for an extremist.' To have resigned during the war, von Krosigk continued, 'would have been tantamount to desertion'.[35]

There is no way of discovering the truth behind such sentiments. They may well represent the state of mind of senior officials alarmed at the decay in public political morality and the inexorable drift towards the cataract of war and genocide. It is not difficult to accept that men of conservative instinct in high office, conscious of the pressures of respectability and public example, patriotic and loyal, will explain collaboration with dictatorship in terms that allow them to set service to the nation or the people above their practical objections. The fact that they signally failed in this case to stem the tide of Party radicalism, and on the example of the armed forces, actively furthered it, weakens the argument. To American interrogators the idea that responsibility could be side-stepped because individuals chose to work from within to moderate the system rather than to confront it was ultimately unconvincing, because service to a criminal regime, of whatever kind, still furthered the objects of those crimes. The moral dilemmas exposed by the tension between acquiescence and detachment were explored in the lengthy conversations between Franz von Papen and Justice Thomas Dodd.

Von Papen was a conservative aristocrat, a senior member of the Catholic Centre Party in the 1920s, Chancellor of Germany briefly between June and December 1932, and the man popularly regarded as the chief instigator of the backroom negotiations that led to Hitler's appointment as Chancellor on 30 January 1933. Von Papen served as Vice-Chancellor until 1934, when the office was terminated. He then became successively German ambassador in Austria, then Turkey, where he remained until August 1944. He was arrested on 10 April 1945 by a platoon of American soldiers from the invasion armies sweeping through the Ruhr. He was not an obvious candidate for the status of major war criminal, and featured on none of the existing lists of wanted men. He agreed to be interrogated shortly after his capture only on the understanding that he was not a war criminal. Once armed with that assurance, he gave a number of interviews, distinguished by their frank hostility to the regime he had served. The Allied mood changed, however, over the summer. His OSS profile was not produced until late August 1945, but he was now described as a 'Nazi collaborationist of the highest order', responsible above all for easing Hitler's path to power. Colonel Andrus took a strong dislike to von Papen, following a number of angry exchanges in the early weeks at 'Ashcan'. When von Papen's wife asked the prison authorities at Nuremberg to allow a German Catholic priest to visit her husband, Andrus wrote personally to Eisenhower voicing his objections: 'As von Papen is one of the very worst of the war criminals and a dangerous, schemeing [sic] old man anyone associated with him should be viewed with suspicion.'[36] He was allowed instead to see the American Catholic chaplain, Sixtus O'Connor.

When Thomas Dodd began questioning von Papen on 3 September he concentrated on the extent to which von Papen had deliberately sought Hitler's appointment in January 1933. Although von Papen was open in admitting that he had already realized in the course of 1932 that Hitler would have to be included in government in some way, he refused to admit to Dodd that he had influenced the aged president, Field Marshal Paul von Hindenburg, to make the decision to appoint him Chancellor. When asked if he had recommended Hitler as a political solution he answered 'Probably', but on the question of the decision to appoint Hitler, von Papen insisted that both he and Hindenburg 'came to the same conclusion at the same time' only by chance.[37] Dodd continued to press von Papen on his motives for recommending Nazi participation in government, and elicited from him an explanation which captured much of the conservative outlook on the events of 1933:

> . . . there was no other way out. May I just say this: in our parliamentary life, the taking in of a Party growing stronger every day is the ordinary way, but keeping the Party out is the extraordinary way and so why shouldn't we try? I mean as I told you, the program of Hitler had some good points in our eyes and the people who adhered to his Party came from all walks of life, not all bad elements.[38]

The honeymoon with Hitler did not last long. Von Papen became disillusioned with his inability to control Hitler, and the thrust of Nazi policy against the Churches. Nevertheless he remained in office.

It was von Papen's failure to break openly with Hitler that perplexed Dodd. 'Maybe I don't see this thing in its proper perspective,' Dodd told him, 'but I have been asking myself since I first talked to you . . . why it was that you didn't disavow these people?' The verbal fencing match that followed contained within its delicate thrusts and parries the answer to that central question of responsibility. Dodd implied that emigration was an option, but von Papen countered it as unworthy: 'I think to emigrate and to leave your country is the worst thing you could do. I went the other way, and the other way is, certainly in my mind, not less courageous . . . living in Switzerland would have been much more comfortable to me.'[39] Dodd lunged again: von Papen should have taken 'an active and positive stand against' Nazism once he realized that the government he served was embarked upon a course of 'murder, arson and dishonesty'. Von Papen reminded Dodd that he did eventually resign in 1934, but did not resist Hitler more because he could work to greater effect by trying to impress upon Hitler at every opportunity 'that his way was wrong'. Dodd challenged him to explain why he did not cut all ties, instead of taking on a diplomatic role, but von Papen defended himself with the argument that the embassies gave him continuous opportunity to obstruct Nazi policy whenever his conscience pricked him to do so.[40]

For Dodd, there existed an inexplicable gap between von Papen's evident disillusionment with the Nazi regime and his willingness to continue to serve it, a paradox shared by a great many Germans after

1933. Dodd resolved the paradox with an analogy which is worth reproducing in full, for it brought a palpable hit:

Q. I don't quite know how to phrase it, but I have the feeling that a man in your position and with your sources of information and with your practical background and experience, would have been so shocked at the kind of government that was operating in Germany that you couldn't just have had anything to do with it. Let me put it this way: I feel confident that if in my own country, any administration with which I was officially and intimately connected, premeditatedly, murdered a dozen or half a dozen prominent well-known men in Washington; burned the Congress . . . and a few weeks later distorted and concealed and lied to the people; and then asked me to go to Argentina on a mission; that no matter what the consequences, I'd say, 'No' . . .

A. All right. In the first place, you can't compare the situation that rose in Germany with the United States. It is impossible to compare those.

Q. I know, it isn't exactly the same. But evil things do not differ too much the world over.

A. Now, let me say this: if you have been offered the position of an Ambassador to Argentina, you would say, 'No.' You took your stand . . . Then you disassociated yourself completely, and sat in your home waiting to find out what was going on; or perhaps going to another country . . .

Q. Stayed at home, or stayed in jail, or was executed, or any number of things.

A. Yes, that you certainly – I mean, it would have been honourable if I stepped out and founded an underground movement against Hitler, and was caught by the Gestapo and executed. You are right, that is the viewpoint. I could have done that.[41]

Dodd's morality was simple, the question one of black-and-white, where for von Papen and thousands who served the regime it was clothed in many shades of grey. The interrogations revealed a variety of ways in which responsibility might be avoided, or transferred, or ignored, or rejected, but on the great issues of political morality, as von Papen finally conceded, responsibility has no limits.

Confessing to Genocide

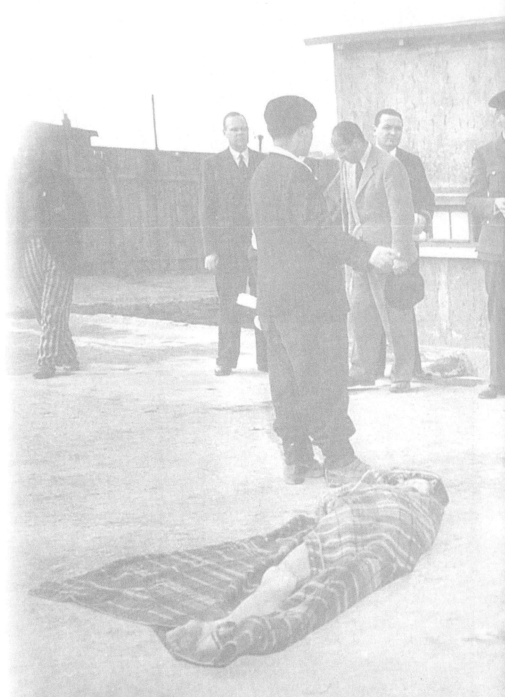

A delegation from the United Nations War Crimes Commission, founded in 1944, visits the concentration camp at Buchenwald shortly after its liberation in April 1945 by the American army.

Interpreter: (Reading) 'Poland 3,500,000; Germany, 180,000; Hungary, 500,000 plus. The plus sign means that these figures are positively known to me. In these I was involved personally, and I know about these from personal experience. Slovakia, 52,000; for the first period 14,000 plus sign, and the second period 38,000. Bohemia and Moravia together, 200,000; Greece, 60,000 with a plus sign; Bulgaria, 6,000, plus sign; Croatia, 3,000 plus sign; Italy, 14,000; Denmark and Norway together, 6,000 with a question mark; France, 220,000, question mark; Holland, 40,000; Belgium, 20,000. Grand total, 4,817,700.'

Interrogation of Dieter Wisliceny, Eichmann's deputy,
15 November 1945[1]

'The entire German governmental authority, part of which is now accused, knew from the beginning what was the course of action. Of course, the man Himmler is dead. They knew that, and they also knew he could not defend himself, therefore their tactic is to blame everything on Himmler, and thus exonerate themselves.'

Erich von dem Bach-Zelewski, interrogation of 25 March 1946[2]

Nothing was denied more vehemently in the interrogation rooms at Nuremberg than the persecution of the Jews. The prosecution teams knew that an almost unimaginable crime had been perpetrated against the Jews of Europe somewhere in the thick undergrowth of the Nazi terror, but the exact origin and scale of what is now historically familiar as the Holocaust lay largely concealed. The whole issue was complicated by the refusal of the Soviet authorities to accept that anti-Jewish atrocities were anything other than a part of the general campaign of murder and terror practised by the Nazi regime. This left the onus of proof on the western Allies, but the main sites of the genocide on Soviet-controlled territory in the east.[3] The chief perpetrators of genocide, Heinrich Himmler, Adolf Eichmann, and the Gestapo chief, Heinrich Müller, were dead or missing. Hitler's role was uncertain. Although his interrogators refused to believe it, the chief defendant selected to represent Nazi anti-semitism, Julius Streicher, played almost no role in carrying out the genocide and could furnish no account of it. In August the interrogation team was invited to ask more searching questions about Jewish policy to make concerted sense of the disparate strands of Nazi racism. The Indictment included the charge of 'systematic genocide' against 'Jews, Poles, and Gypsies and others', but even in October 1945, when the Indictment was drafted, much remained to be learned about who had carried out genocide, and upon whose orders.[4]

The major war criminals all denied that they had been involved directly in the persecution of the Jews. Many of them admitted openly that they had been anti-semitic, though few were willing to confess that they were still convinced anti-semites once the evidence of grotesque atrocities began to pile up. The surviving prejudice was difficult to conceal. One British diplomat came away from a visit to 'Ashcan' with the strong impression that the prisoners wanted it 'tacitly understood' that Germany's Jews had been all but annihilated 'and were good riddance'.[5] But even those who remained loyal to the racist sentiments of the movement denied all knowledge of or responsibility for the policy of extermination. Alfred Rosenberg, whose Ministry for the Occupied Eastern Territories embraced geographically some of the chief locations of the Holocaust, was typical. Interrogated about his views on the Jewish question, Rosenberg admitted that he had always advocated a comprehensive anti-semitic policy. A speech made at Frankfurt during the war was quoted to Rosenberg: 'Germany's answer to the Jewish problem will be solved as soon as the last Jew has left the Great-German area . . . Germany's determination to rid the whole of the continent of Jewish parasitism.' Asked by his interrogator, Thomas Hinkel, if these were his words, Rosenberg said, 'I don't deny it'; to the further question 'And you agree with the sentiments expressed by those words?', Rosenberg replied impatiently, 'Yes, yes.'[6] But when it was suggested to him a few minutes later that he bore some responsibility for the atrocities committed in the east, he refused not only to accept that he had anything to do with a policy which was 'in the hands of the police', but denied almost any knowledge of what the police were doing. The most he would admit to was having heard rumours that Jews were persecuted by the native Soviet population and 'that certain Germans had shot some Jews'. He denied all knowledge of the system of camps; he claimed to learn about the extermination of the Jews only from listening to foreign radio broadcasts.[7]

The other defendants sang the same refrain. Hans Frank, a lawyer and Party legal expert, who became Governor of rump Poland, was prepared to blame Hitler and Himmler for the perversion of racial policy, but would admit no crime on his part for abetting the murder of millions of Poles and Polish Jews under his jurisdiction: 'The orders were forced upon us,' Frank complained, 'against our will.' Funk 'knew nothing at all' about the camps or about the genocide. Baldur von Schirach was willing to concede that he had supported Hitler's aim for a 'Jew-free' Vienna, but on the movement of Viennese Jews out of the city he had no responsibility. Ribbentrop claimed to know so little about the camps and German race policy that he, like Rosenberg, relied on the foreign media (though two documents had already been found in the first of which Ribbentrop told King Boris of Bulgaria in 1942 that Germany favoured a 'most radical solution' to the Jewish question; in the second document, from 1943, Ribbentrop suggested to Admiral Horthy, the Hungarian head-of-state, that Hungarian Jews 'should be extirpated or imprisoned').[8] Among the key witnesses, chosen because of their evident proximity to the apparatus of racial oppression organized by Himmler, the same excuses could be heard.

Hans Frank, the National Socialist legal expert, and former governor of the Polish Government-General, the rump area of conquered Poland not incorporated into the German Reich. At Nuremberg Frank returned to Catholicism, reading the Bible in his cell for consolation.

Erich von dem Bach-Zelewski, the SS general responsible for organiz-ing anti-partisan warfare on the Eastern Front, and for smashing the Warsaw uprising in 1944, engaged in a bizarre act of denial under interrogation by insisting that he had tried to warn Jewish leaders in the Ukraine of their impending fate, and urged his interrogator to search out the rabbis who would corroborate his claim. Even though the Allies had secret wartime decrypts of Bach-Zelewski's murderous activities on the eastern front, he succeeded in persuading his captors of his good faith and was presented as a prosecution witness during the trial. The SS General Karl Wolff, who was part of the central SS apparatus in the late 1930s, proved willing enough to say what he knew about the camp system, but challenged the credulity of his interrogator by insisting that he knew little about that system after 1939, and learned of the extermination programmes only from the films and documents shown to those in Allied captivity.[9] Even this evidence Wolff described as 'propaganda'. He was not alone in finding the reality of the regime he served hard to accept.

The interrogators were sceptical about this response, but also puzzled. They assumed that the senior prisoners knew not only as much as they did, but considerably more. They took the view that knowledge of the camps was general in Germany; they assumed that extermination might be less widely understood, but could not see how men in high office, responsible for important elements of anti-semitic policy, could pretend ignorance with such conviction. At one point in Wolff's examination, his interrogator tried to establish just why on this point there existed such a wall of silence:

Q. Well, I can imagine that people would know about things and be ashamed to admit it, but I cannot imagine people not knowing about it ... I want you to understand that I am not talking about you personally. I am talking about the people of Germany. My opinion is that nobody seems to know anything about the operation of the concentration camps.
A. I can understand the disbelieving of the outstanding persons that are suddenly confronted with the facts ...
Q. There can be no defense, but I am wondering why the leaders of government don't come in and say, 'Yes, we knew these things were going on in these camps, but there was nothing we could do about it.'

Visitors to the Bergen–Belsen concentration camp in September 1945. The British army liberated the camp in mid-April 1945. Here they found thousands of starving prisoners, many of whom died in the weeks that followed from disease and the consequences of malnutrition. In June the British army burned the camp down.

Instead of that, they come in and say, 'We didn't know anything about what was going on in those camps until we saw the pictures.'[10]

Wolff had no further explanation to offer, save to suggest that Himmler and Hitler had sworn themselves to secrecy, a scarcely credible view in the light of Wolff's own revelations about the occasional visits made to the camps by prominent men from Party and government.

Any explanation can only be speculative in the absence of a clear body of individual testimony on the motives of the defendants. It was understandable that the defendants, once they were aware how much the atrocities revealed in the camps and ghettos repelled Allied opinion more than any other aspect of the Third Reich, would seek to distance themselves from any hint of complicity or responsibility. The armed forces had their own motives for refusing to accept any participation in atrocities, from fear that the honour and reputation of the services would be besmirched. When General Guderian, the hero of modern tank warfare, was interrogated in early November 1945 about the Eastern Front, he gave a blunt denial: 'I have not heard that any criminal actions on the part of the armed forces were committed.' He was content, like so many others, to pass the buck to Himmler: 'I did hear rumours about very undesirable activities on the part of police forces in rear areas.'[11] There was almost certainly collusion between the prisoners about the stand that should be taken against the grosser accusations. Secret microphones set in the lavatory cubicles at 'Ashcan' recorded the furtive discussions between prisoners on their prospects.[12] No sophisticated psychology is needed to understand that none of those indicted wanted to hang for monstrous crimes in which many of them were accessories after the fact rather than prime movers.

Yet the question of how much or how little Germans knew about the vicious face of the system they operated and inhabited has never been fully resolved by the subsequent history of the Reich. There is no doubt that the central apparatus for state terror and race policy, absorbed under the umbrella of the RSHA in 1939, did screen its activities from the rest of the government machine and from the population. The central role of Hitler in Nazi Jewish policy was disguised by the absence of written orders. Von Schirach told his interrogator that Hitler chose to talk to him in the open, away from others, about his plans for Vienna's Jews. After he had made clear what he wanted he went in to lunch, taking von Schirach with him: 'As was usually the case with Hitler,' von Schirach concluded, 'these instructions were given *en passant* and nothing was said about it afterwards.'[13]

The extermination of the Jews was, it is well known, shrouded in secrecy and veiled by an ambiguously innocent vocabulary. Those intimately involved in the genocide were sworn to secrecy by Himmler, barred even from discussing policy with their immediate superiors. Some of those working at the heart of the programme only knew the camps by their initials ('A' for Auschwitz, and so on). The central record of the programme, kept under lock and key in Eichmann's Gestapo office, was marked, one witness recalled, 'top secret' and

'highly secret', though this could hardly have surprised his interviewer.[14] The file of documents on the Holocaust was kept sealed in a
safe. The term 'Final Solution' used to identify the Jewish genocide,
distinct from the racial policies directed at gypsies and Slavs, was taken
by the prosecution from a document in Allied hands, the order on
Jewish policy sent in July 1941 by Goering to Reinhard Heydrich,
Kaltenbrunner's predecessor as head of the RSHA.[15] The ambiguous
nature of the term was exploited by those who organized the genocide.
The commandant of the extermination camp at Auschwitz, Rudolf
Hoess, told his interrogator that 'Final Solution' meant 'extermination'
of the Jews and was understood by all those working for Eichmann
in those terms; but when Eichmann hosted a meeting of ministry
representatives in Berlin in 1943 he told them that the final solution
meant the sterilization and evacuation of the Jews.[16] When Eichmann
was eventually caught and interrogated by the Israelis in 1960, he
insisted that the term 'Final Solution' shifted its meaning: in 1940 it
meant emigration and expulsion, but from the summer of 1941 it came
to mean 'physical destruction'.[17]

Some case can be made that the secretive habits and compartmental-
ized structure of the Hitler regime did make it both difficult and
dangerous for those not included in the immediate circle of perpetrators to find out more. The further away from the epicentre of
racial murder, the more subdued the tremors of discrimination and
violence. Many of those indicted at Nuremberg did have, as they
claimed, only the scantiest, word-of-mouth, knowledge of the details
of genocide and terror. Most defendants did, without question, know
more than they were willing to reveal. If, as Eichmann claimed, the
ministries in Berlin were told that Jewish policy amounted to no more
than sterilization and evacuation, this was still an exceptional act of
persecution. If knowledge of the camps was confined to a brief, carefully orchestrated visit, like Wilhelm Frick's visit to Oranienburg in
1937 ('I must say everything was in perfect shape and order'),[18] it
continues to defy belief that the senior defendants at Nuremberg were
all so wilfully ill-informed about one of the central features of the
entire system.

Once the interrogators began to probe beneath the surface, it was
soon discovered that some of the defendants were not just poorly
informed observers of a distant cataclysm, but were deeply implicated:

Funk was identified as one of the chief recipients of the gold and valuables seized from doomed Jewish families, or torn from the mouths of dead Jews by dental technicians; Speer, for all his protests, was identified by Hoess as the man who constantly badgered the Gestapo for more concentration camp labour for the armaments industry;[19] Kaltenbrunner was placed in his rightful position, at the head of the apparatus of destruction. Hans Frank, who adopted at Nuremberg the role of a pious penitent returned to the Catholic fold after supping briefly with the devil, was undone by the representations of Polish experts who catalogued his crimes for the Tribunal.[20] The attempt to separate the German army from the barbarisms in the east was undone by the testimony, among others, of Otto Ohlendorf, who detailed the close links between army and security forces denied by the professional soldiers.[21] Much of the defendants' mendacity has been exposed by the subsequent history of the German genocide, though the case of Speer, who stoutly maintained his distance from Jewish policy in the years following his release in 1966, has still not been settled beyond all doubt.

The odd man out in all this was the defendant widely regarded both inside and outside Germany as the Party's principal Jew-baiter, Julius Streicher. He was chosen as a defendant precisely on account of his unsavoury reputation. Of all the major war criminals, he was the one who generated the most loathing not only among his captors, but among his co-defendants. He was a singularly unprepossessing individual. Short, bull-necked, bald, Streicher was the very caricature of the strutting Nazi bully. He was ill-tempered, foul-mouthed, obsessed with sex, and above all possessed of a visceral, pornographic hatred of the Jews. There were doubts about his sanity long before his sojourn in Nuremberg. In 1940 Hitler removed him as Gauleiter of Franconia, following investigation for tax evasion, and he sat out the war spewing forth his diet of deranged racist journalism in the anti-semitic tabloid *Der Stürmer*, which he had edited since the 1920s. The other defendants refused to consort with him, and at 'Ashcan' he was forced to eat at a separate table. Only Robert Ley would talk to him. His loathing for the Jews absorbed his whole being. Kelley judged him to be a classic paranoid, whose beliefs were a product of his own emotionally charged delusions, utterly unrelated to the real world. His lurid, lascivious personality generated all manner of crude rumours at Nuremberg. A brief note passed from Amen to one of the American prosecution team in the courthouse survives in Jackson's files: 'The Marshall says that Stryker [*sic*] washes his face and brushes his teeth in the toilet.'[22]

He seized every opportunity at Nuremberg to parade his paranoia. He saw Jewish conspiracy all about him. He told Airey Neave that the list of prospective defence lawyers contained only Jewish names (the list, which included names like Bock, Weber, Fritz, Kramer, Schaffer and Schmidt, was entirely non-Jewish); he was convinced that the trial judges were all Jews; he complained to his first interrogator, Howard Brundage, that he and thousands of arrested and incarcerated National Socialists were being treated no better than Jews.[23] He told Kelley that he welcomed the trial as a platform to warn the world of the 'outstanding menace' posed by international Jewry. Under interrogation he adopted a more modest tone; he refused to accept that his years of anti-Jewish abuse could actually cause the racial atrocities of which he stood accused, and insisted that he had never advocated the destruction or extermination of the Jews until the year 1942, when he began to write 'more severe articles' in reaction to Jewish threats from abroad. On the camps he was able to claim, truthfully, that he had nothing to do with them. The interrogators spent fruitless hours trying to get Streicher to see that there might be a connection between his racist journalism and the vicious reality of German racism, but he persisted in maintaining that his attitude towards the Jews was more metaphorical than real. He was able to lure the interrogators onto his own ground time and again, forcing them to argue with him about the nature of Zionism or the character of his journalism, but in terms of hard facts on anti-semitic policy he provided not a single clue.

Streicher demonstrated not a shred of remorse. 'You are not ashamed of anything that you preached or wrote?' asked his interrogator. 'Basically, no,' replied Streicher. 'Whatever I have written, basically, I am convinced about.'[24] Asked later whether he accepted any responsibility for the killing of Jews in the camps as a result of his teachings, he gave an oblique denial: 'Only such a person can testify to a thing like that, who is paid to falsify the truth.' When passages were read to him from wartime articles in *Der Stürmer* calling for the extermination of the Jews, he made semantic play with the word 'exterminate' to argue that he had only advocated the expulsion of Jews so that they could form their own national state and no longer interfere, politically or biologically, with the nations that had hosted them hitherto. 'You are going to have a difficult time,' his interrogator concluded, 'trying to convince any reasonable man that your interpretation of that article was the correct one.'[25] His defence lawyer shared that concern. On 15 November he applied to the court for a psychiatric examination of his client. The Soviet prosecutors favoured it on the tenuous ground that Streicher had told a Soviet interrogator a few days before that he was in favour of Zionism. In Soviet eyes this was mad enough 'to order a mental examination', and three experts were appointed by the court to report on Streicher's psychological state. They concluded that he was sane, fit to plead and able to stand trial. On 22 November Lord Justice Lawrence, the president of the court, ruled that Streicher could be tried.[26]

The hard detail on the Holocaust was supplied not by the chief defendants but by more junior officials and security officers who did have direct experience and knowledge of the programme. Some of them were taken to Nuremberg both as witnesses to the main Tribunal, and as war criminals destined for future trials. Two of them, Dieter Wisliceny, a young SS officer attached to Eichmann's office in the Gestapo, and Otto Ohlendorf, commander of Einsatzgruppe D, and later an SS expert in the Economics Ministry, gave under interrogation during October and November 1945 the first full and unguarded accounts of the German genocide. The contrast with their seniors was striking. It might well be thought that they were keen to make a full confession so that their bosses would not get away with persistent denial. Yet the interrogations give little indication that this was their object. The major defendants were usually discussed only after they had been introduced into the questioning by the interrogator; moreover there was no way that the witnesses, held in a different part of the jail, could know whether the men they might incriminate had or had not spoken plainly and honestly about their responsibilities.

The most significant difference between the two cohorts of prisoners was their degree of knowledge. The defendants were, for the most part, distant from the apparatus of terror and race, and genuinely ill-informed about its practices; the witnesses were perpetrators of the first rank, with an insider's understanding. Such a contrast does not altogether explain the degree of candour with which the genocide was described. The interrogations have about them a matter-of-fact quality that belies their terrible content, as if the questions related not to mass murder, but to some more tranquil occupation. The occasional arguments between interrogator and subject over the number of dead possess a macabre air of unreality. The confessors wanted their record of crime to be as accurate as they could make it. Their bureaucratic punctiliousness perhaps explains the willingness to tell all; the interrogations show an unexpected degree of detachment from the murders that they catalogue.

The most important task for the prosecution was to establish clearly when the order for the extermination of the Jews was given, and by whom. The first evidence was given by Ohlendorf, whose Einsatzgruppe undertook the mass murder of Jews and Communist officials in the early months of the German–Soviet war. In answer to the question, 'To what extent did you get orders directly from Hitler?' he replied:

'Twice, and in each case with regard to the execution of the Jews; the first time this order was made known to all chiefs of groups and to all leaders of commands. The first time this order was passed through channels, but the second time Himmler repeated this order personally in Nikolayev, and he told the assembled personnel that he alone, in connection with Hitler, was responsible and would assume responsibility for these actions.'

The interrogator then asked him when these two orders were given and received the reply: 'The first one must have been in May 1941, and the second one approximately in September 1941.' The orders were given orally, but Ohlendorf remembered them with great clarity. The assembled men were ordered to carry out 'the execution of Jews and political functionaries of the Communist Party with severity, but also chivalry', as a command direct from the Fuehrer. 'Was this to be absolute and complete extermination of all Jews in this theatre?' ventured the interrogator, to which Ohlendorf replied simply, 'Yes.'[27]

When Wisliceny was interviewed a month later in mid-November, shortly before the start of the trial, the interrogation team came close to the central order for the Holocaust, which has eluded historians to this day. In the first interrogation the prisoner mentioned an order from Himmler authorizing the Final Solution, but the interrogator failed to follow it up. That same afternoon, 15 November, he mentioned it again, but had to prompt the interrogator, Colonel Brookhart, to be allowed to elaborate. In late July or very early August 1942, he had visited Eichmann in his office in Berlin to discuss the fate of Slovakian Jews, who were being transported to Poland. Eichmann told Wisliceny that there existed a written order from Himmler, on Hitler's authority, ordering the physical extermination of the Jews. He went to a safe and took out a thick folder of documents on Jewish policy. From it he extracted a red-rimmed page which he showed to his visitor. It was the original copy of the order, signed by Himmler but based on a decision by Hitler, to begin the 'final disposition' (as the interpreter rendered it) of the Jewish question. Wisliceny was impressed by the gravity of the moment. He recalled saying to Eichmann, 'May God prevent that our enemies should ever do anything similar to the German people.' Eichmann put the document back in the safe and told his subordinate not to be sentimental: 'this was a Fuehrer Order'. The order dated, Wisliceny believed, from April 1942, but he could not be exact. Eichmann confirmed the story when it was read out to him by his Israeli interrogator fifteen years later.[28]

The existence of an order for the Final Solution has always been in doubt among historians. Eichmann's thick folder must be assumed destroyed, deliberately or otherwise, along with countless other Gestapo records. Yet there is no reason to reject Wisliceny's account. He made no attempt to hide his part in serving a genocidal programme. The only question remains the date. Ohlendorf dated the first decisions over extermination to the spring and autumn of 1941, which conformed with the information in Allied hands on the so-called 'criminal orders' (the murder of commissars and Jewish Communist officials and partisans) issued from Hitler's headquarters for the conduct of the campaign against the Soviet Union. Ohlendorf was, on the evidence now available, wrong to assume that the orders from Hitler were for the extermination of all Jews, but it is significant that he recalled them in that light, when his own prospective fate might have counselled greater caution. It is also significant that Adolf Eichmann in his interrogation in 1960 recalled that about two or three months after the onset of the Barbarossa campaign in June 1941 (he could not be more precise), he was summoned to see Heydrich, who explained to him with a self-conscious sense of theatre that 'The Fuehrer has ordered the physical destruction of the Jews.' When he was confronted with Wisliceny's Nuremberg testimony that extermination only began in the spring of 1942, Eichmann replied tersely: '. . . that's not right. It should say, already in the autumn of 1941.'[29] What the Nuremberg interrogations revealed was the clear evidence that Hitler had a direct hand in authorizing the Holocaust, and that he initially ordered the systematic murder of some categories of Jews in the east in the summer or early autumn of 1941. At some time during the following six months he followed up this order with a personal directive to Himmler to undertake, in Wisliceny's words, 'the biological extermination of the Jews'.[30]

This summary represents the majority view among historians today, but arguments persist about timing (was the decision made in the first flush of victory against the Soviet Union, or in the first pallor of defeat before Moscow?), and about the degree of responsibility to ascribe to the chief perpetrators (was Himmler the architect of genocide, and Hitler his willing client? Were they both pressured into genocide by the radical racists who worked on the building site?). But in the light of the many core decisions exposed in 1945, along with ample testimony on the conduct of the genocide, the degree of uncertainty and instability in the historical picture of genocide which has been exploited for years by Holocaust deniers is less easy to understand. The same might be said of the perennial arguments over the number exterminated. The interrogations of lower-level officials very soon confirmed the strong rumours current since the middle of the war that the murder of Jews ran into millions. The World Jewish Congress supplied the tentative figure of 5.7 million dead, and this was used by the prosecuting teams in drawing up the Indictment. There was talk at Nuremberg about the possibility of nine million Jewish deaths, but there remained a good deal of uncertainty until more verifiable figures could be extracted from the prisoners themselves.[31]

The prosecution unearthed very precise figures on the numbers killed by the Einsatzgruppen. These four groups were made up of security forces drawn from the SS and the German police. They followed the army into the Soviet Union with specific orders to murder Jews, Communists and other potential dissidents. They organized mass shootings on a pattern which is now well known – graves dug by the victims, the machine guns turned against stripped and defenceless prisoners, the officers moving among the dead and dying to dispatch survivors with revolvers, the local workers rounded up to sprinkle quicklime over the corpses and fill in the trench. Group A killed 135,567; Ohlendorf told his interrogator that his section, group D, killed approximately 90,000 in a year, most of them shot, but a small number killed by mobile 'gas vans' supplied by the RSHA, where victims would be killed by carbon monoxide poisoning. Ohlendorf added that he had issued orders to ease the strain on both executioners and victims by forbidding the practice of individual execution. When asked why, he gave the following reply:

A. Because this type of execution caused a serious emotion, not only on the part of those who were carrying out the executions, but also on the part of those who were shot, and out of these executions I can explain a number of mistreatments of which I have heard.
Q. Such as?
A. Namely, that such persons who had to carry out these shootings lost any feeling and respect for human life, and when those people who had to be shot were emotionally affected or excited, then beatings would result as a matter of course.[32]

There is in this exchange a chilling insensitivity to the reality of mass murder. Ohlendorf's priority was efficient, swift killing. This requirement was met by the system of extermination camps which during 1942 replaced the butchery in the east with a 'rationalized' means of racial cleansing: handicraft killing was superseded by industrialized death.

The new locations of racial murder handled very much larger numbers. Dieter Wisliceny was an agent of the new system. He was responsible for arranging the transport of Jews from central Europe to the camps in Poland, and was uniquely positioned to give a more general picture of the processes involved in orchestrating the genocide. In 1944 he helped to draw up a document estimating the total numbers of Jews transported from all over Europe to the death camps. He listed the numbers to his interrogator through the hapless interpreter. Some figures were underestimates, he conceded, some overestimates. The total figure of 4,817,000 transported did not include Jews from the Soviet Union, the great bulk of whom were killed where they lived in the wave of Einsatzgruppen killings in 1941-2. Wisliceny pointed out that the numbers were for those transported to the extermination centres, not those actually killed. Since a fraction – he estimated one-fifth – were allocated to work, he believed the total of those who actually died was less than the number of those transported. However, Wisliceny also remembered a conversation with Eichmann in February 1945 about what would happen to them when the war was over. He recalled Eichmann's chilling reply: 'I laugh when I jump into the grave because of the feeling that I have killed 5,000,000 Jews. That gives me great satisfaction.'[33]

When pressed further on his sources, Wisliceny gave detailed references for each country. Most of the figures he obtained from co-workers, with more detailed knowledge of conditions in particular countries. In most cases the statistics covered only the period up to late 1943 or early 1944, and did not include all those transported. The figure of 3.5 million Polish Jews came from Eichmann himself, though the interrogator thought it too high. The figure for France, 220,000 transported, Wisliceny had most doubts about; the best current estimate suggests 83,000 deaths. His figure for the Netherlands was far too low, which suggests that in the transport statistics Wisliceny confused Dutch and French Jews. There was a similar confusion over Jews from Denmark and Norway. Instead of his figure of 6,000, almost all were saved or escaped. The mistake is likely to have arisen when Werner Best, responsible for occupied Denmark, reported to the RSHA that Denmark no longer had any Jews. If Wisliceny heard this report, he would have assumed that Best was talking about their transportation and liquidation, not their disappearance.

To flesh out his estimates, Wisliceny provided a detailed chart with numbers, destinations, dates, and estimates for those executed at once (Wisliceny confirmed that these included 'women, women with children, old people, and those who had an affliction of some kind'), and those allocated to labour camps.[34] He pointed out that the figure for Bulgaria, whose own Jews escaped the genocide, was composed of Greek Jews living in the areas of Thrace and Macedonia handed over to Bulgaria following the Greek defeat in May 1941.[35] Although Smith Brookhart, who conducted all Wisliceny's interrogations, thought the aggregate figure too high, the final total of those transported to the camps is close to the best recent estimates of those killed in the genocide, either murdered, worked to death, or victims of disease and malnutrition. In Wisliceny the interrogators had found a witness who could confirm that the genocide extended Europe-wide, and that upwards of five million Jews, taking together those killed in the Soviet Union and in the camps, had been murdered systematically.

There remained important gaps in the testimony, though the general shape of the genocide was now evident. The most important witness evaded capture until the spring of 1946, when Rudolf Hoess, the commandant of the extermination and labour camp complex at Auschwitz-Birkenau in southern Poland, was captured, disguised as a farmhand, by British military police on 11 March. The prosecutors asked immediately that he be brought to Nuremberg for interrogation, where he arrived in April, unwashed and unshaven since his arrest. After police custody, Nuremberg was like 'a rest in a sanatorium', confided Hoess in a brief autobiography, written as he awaited trial in Poland later in the year. He was interrogated extensively over the first ten days of April.[36] The timing was unfortunate: the prosecution had rested their case and could not introduce new evidence into the record. Hoess's interrogations were never used in court, but by chance Kaltenbrunner's defence counsel, under the illusion that his client's claim to have nothing to do with the camps would be confirmed, decided not only to call Hoess as a witness for the defence, but to use as a defence document an affidavit signed by Hoess during one of the interrogations. The core of what he had to say thus entered the Tribunal proceedings. His testimony gave solid corroboration to Wisliceny's account. He was commandant of Auschwitz from 1941 until December 1943, having worked in the concentration camp system since 1934. His interrogations reveal the same detached, methodical approach to genocide evident in earlier testimonies. Like the other middle managers of the apparatus, he was meticulous in supplying the details of the system. The absence of any sign of remorse or regret has often been remarked upon. Hoess saw himself as a bare functionary, whose function happened to be the mass liquidation of an entire people.

Hoess confirmed that the numbers involved in the genocide were, as Wisliceny had indicated, reckoned in many millions. Under interrogation he was asked to provide a global figure. He indicated that all statistical detail on the executions at Auschwitz had to be destroyed immediately on Himmler's orders; no records of the numbers executed were to be kept. The figure he cited was taken from Eichmann, who informed him that 2.5 million had been turned over for extermination. A further half million died from disease, hunger and overwork.[37] He confirmed an early date for the genocide. He claimed that Himmler ordered him in June 1941 to construct extermination facilities at Auschwitz. The instruction was given orally, and no document has yet been found. It is now known that the mass gassing of Jews did not begin in Auschwitz until the spring of 1942; the extermination facilities set up in the late summer of 1941 at Auschwitz, using hydrocyanide gas (Zyklon B) experimentally, were first used on Soviet prisoners-of-war, and Himmler's intention may have been simply to extend and rationalize the facilities available at Auschwitz to deal with prisoners of all kinds, not just Jews. Hoess was right to assert that 'Mass executions by gassing commenced during the summer of 1941', but wrong to suggest that the victims might be Jewish.[38]

Hoess was also able to fill in the unbearable details of camp operations at Auschwitz, which he did in the same flat, colourless tones with which he had outlined the number of camp victims. His account of camp life was not the first taken at Nuremberg, nor the first account of Auschwitz. Detailed information was available from November 1942, thanks to the courage of the Polish resistance worker Jan Karski, though the western Allies found it hard to believe. After the end of the war it was possible to interview survivors from the camp itself. The Allies received a long report from the New Zealand legation in Moscow in early May 1945 following a visit arranged by the Soviet authorities to Maidanek and Auschwitz. A French survivor supplied the visitors with details of life in Auschwitz so horrifying that it seemed 'like the invention of an insane mind'.[39] Similar accounts reached the western Allies from camps in Germany. A Czech doctor, Franz Blaha, first interrogated in May 1945 following his liberation from Dachau, supplied an affidavit in January 1946 on conditions in the camp, where he had been sent in April 1941. He worked in the autopsy room of the camp where he prepared 7,000 autopsies and supervised a further 5,000 during the course of the war. He supplied extensive evidence on the conduct of medical experiments, and confirmed the scarcely credible story that human skin was removed from corpses:

It was common practice to remove the skin from dead prisoners. I was directed to do this on many occasions . . . It was chemically treated and placed in the sun to dry. After that it was cut into shapes for use as saddles, riding breeches, gloves, house slippers and ladies' handbags. Tattooed skin was especially

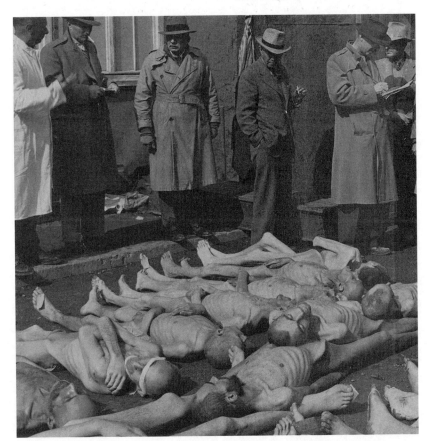

Journalists are invited to view the dead at the Dachau concentration camp. Rumours spread after the main Nuremberg trial suggested that the bodies of the major war criminals were burned in a crematorium oven at Dachau, but they were cremated in an undertaker's in Munich.

valued by SS men. Russians, Poles and other inmates were used in this way, but it was forbidden to cut out the skin of a German. This skin had to be from healthy prisoners and free from defects. Sometimes we did not have enough bodies with good skin and Rascher would say, 'All right, you will get the bodies.' The next day we would receive 20 or 30 bodies of young people. They would have been shot in the neck or struck on the head so that the skin would be uninjured.[40]

Blaha was also made to extract the gold from the teeth of dead prisoners before they were thrown into the crematorium.

Hoess, too, willingly supplied extensive details on the disposal of valuables, clothing and gold teeth, which were melted down by the camp dentist after he had collected each day's haul from large wooden boxes. The gold was turned into bars, locked in a safe, and taken to the SS Medical Office in Berlin once a month. When the interrogator challenged Hoess to admit that he had helped himself to Jewish valuables during these procedures, he responded with an indignant rebuttal: 'I could not do it, but it would have been against my principles to make myself rich on those things . . . it would not have been honest.'[41] The chasm between monstrous crime and petty morality was marked in Hoess. When Gustave Gilbert, the prison psychiatrist, talked to Hoess shortly after his capture, he was intrigued by the fact that the murder of more than two million people could have been perpetrated by someone who seemed so ordinary. After one psychiatric test, Gilbert later recalled, Hoess asked him: 'I suppose you want to know in this way if my thoughts and habits are normal.' Gilbert asked him whether he was. 'I am entirely normal,' Hoess replied.[42] However, his prison autobiography, written a few months later, reveals Hoess in a rather different light, for in it he complained of the psychological pressure he had had to bear under interrogation by men 'who were all Jews' and of psychiatric assessment by doctors, 'also Jews'. Hoess's normality was, unsurprisingly, only relative.[43]

A few days later Gilbert tried to find out why Hoess felt no guilt or responsibility for his prominent part in the genocide, by asking him what was the root of his anti-semitism. Hoess gave a reply that explained his prejudice in simple, but none the less plausible terms:

'For me as an old fanatic National Socialist, I took it all as fact – just as a Catholic believed in his Church dogma. It was just truth without question; I had no doubt about that. I was absolutely convinced that the Jews were at the opposite pole from the German people, and sooner or later there would have to be a clash between National Socialism and World Jewry . . . But *everybody* was convinced of this; that was all you could hear or read.'[44]

There were remarkably few examples where prisoners either offered or were asked to give an explanation for genocide rather than a description of it. The interrogators were instructed to find out the details of the crimes and to allocate responsibility, but it was not their role to ascribe motives or to suggest wider explanations for what happened. The interrogations surrounding genocide and the camps have about them a routine, passionless aspect, as though both parties to the bleak discourse wished to remain detached from their sordid subject-matter. If the interrogation transcripts reveal anything it is the unwritten assumption on the part of the interrogators that anti-semitic sentiment is a sufficient explanation for racial murder.

The current debate on the causes of the Holocaust revolves about the validity of this assumption. On the one side stands a history which embraces German anti-semitism at face value by assuming that a political movement and ideology which expressly commits itself to the exclusion and persecution of the Jewish community can encompass genocide, given the right circumstances. On the other is a history that sees anti-semitism as an insufficient cause separated from the other circumstances and historical forces capable of turning prejudice into mass murder. The evidence from the interrogations does not favour one approach over the other, but it suggests two things. First, the role of anti-semitic propaganda and language was significant in creating a mindset in Germany in the 1930s that predisposed acceptance of racial policy even in its most radical forms. The constant repetition of anti-semitic sentiment, whether fanatical Party propaganda or the casual racial aside, lodged in the collective psyche in ways that reduced the ability and willingness of a great many Germans to question race policy and encouraged them to endorse it. In his last letter Robert Ley wrote, 'We ended up seeing everything through anti-semitic eyes. It became a complex . . . We National Socialists saw in the struggles which now lie behind us, a war solely against the Jews – not against the French, English, Americans or Russians. We believed that they were all only *tools* of the Jew . . .'[45] Such sentiments are difficult to take at face value, but where they are held with the kind of religious fervour confessed by Hoess, they must play a central part in explaining the radical development of German racial policy.

Second, the pre-trial material shows the extent to which those who worked within the confines of the security apparatus and the camps, with their culture of secrecy and strict obedience, and their habits of physical and verbal violence, became inured to the harsh consequences of policy, however uncongenial. Such institutions display an inherent tendency to moral degeneration wherever they are established. In such an atmosphere the journey from physical abuse to murder was brief and unremarkable. The moral blunting that this cruel environment produced was widely evident: '. . . we SS men were not supposed to think about these things; it never even occurred to us,' Hoess told Gilbert, '. . . it was something taken for granted that the Jews were to blame for everything'.[46] This deadly cocktail of uncritical prejudice, moral abdication and reflexive violence produced a casual indifference to suffering and an easy familiarity with the pervasive morbidity of the camps.

The evidence for casual brutalization was widespread from the transcripts in Allied hands. Two examples may suffice here. In May 1945 came a report from a German prisoner, used by the British army as a secret *agent provocateur* in a POW camp in occupied Germany, of a conversation with an SS soldier who had served on the Eastern Front:

Amongst other stories he told how he shot 180 odd civilians, men, women and children with the pistol. He emphasized particularly a case of an old couple both of about 70 years of age. He did not bother, he said, first he killed off the old one and then whilst she was screaming he aimed at the old woman and shot her. He mentioned also that he repeatedly violated and raped Russian girls at the point of the pistol and that he had to shoot two girls afterwards to keep them quiet. The Battalion commander gave orders not to take Russians under 1000 men prisoners. When it happened once that they had a batch of under 700 he volunteered for the job because he got cigarettes and schnapps for it. The Russians were led to a sand-pit, shot at with machine guns and covered with earth.[47]

The same characteristic features are revealed in a conversation between two prisoners secretly tape-recorded early in November 1945 by British security men at one of the smaller interrogation centres run by the British army. The two officials came from the apparatus of oppression. Eugen Horak was an interpreter from the RSHA, who ended up on a guard detail in Auschwitz; Ernst von Gottstein was a technical director of the construction agency Organisation Todt, which used foreign forced labour on its wartime projects. Their discussion was recorded in the hope that it would intimate the whereabouts of other wanted war criminals, but its content reveals a great deal about how and why the barbarous, genocidal war was possible:

HORAK I was once present in Vienna when they were loading up people for one of those mass evacuations. Hundreds were crammed into the waggons, which normally took a couple of cows. And they were thoroughly beaten up as well. I went up to a young SS man and asked if the beating up was really necessary. He laughed and said they were only scum anyway ... What was the purpose of that beating up? I have nothing against the gas chamber. A time can come when it is useful for the race to eliminate certain elements. Extermination is one thing, but there is no need to torture your victims beforehand.

I saw some incredible things at Auschwitz. Some SS guard personnel could not stand it any longer and had to be sent to a nerve clinic in Giessen ... One SS coy. [company] actually mutinied and tried to get themselves posted to the front. But they had to carry out their orders ... When the serjeant [sic] major came along for volunteers for a firing squad, the majority of us did not wish to go. Then he gave us orders, 'You, you and you,' and the men had no alternative. It's quite right too that they had no chance of examining the moral implications of the order. Orders must be carried out ... Those people lose all feeling. Roschke for example once told me quite callously that he had volunteered for duty in the crematorium [at Auschwitz] because they got so much time off afterwards. This duty was absolutely repulsive ... There was a horrible smell of lime and burning flesh, smelling like a strong smell of urine ... (both laughing) But you get so used to it that you eat your sandwiches in there too ...

VON GOTTSTEIN *The only really good thing about the whole affair is that a few million Jews no longer exist.*

HORAK But those who are responsible are now in the soup.[48]*

One of the British officials who read the report wrote in red pencil under von Gottstein's observation the comment, 'The opinion of many non-Germans, among the Allies I have heard similar remarks.'

---

* The full document is represented below, pages 371–4.

'I hope they hang *all*': Final Retribution

'. . . we are trying to get a record here for the benefit of the children of Germany, so that when another time comes and a gang like this gets control of the government, they will have something to look back on and be warned in advance . . . we are anxious to make a record here that will be a lesson to the German people. I find that most of these people who come in here are very evasive, and they are trying to dodge their responsibility for things that happened within their own jurisdiction. Some of them claim to be still loyal to the Fuehrer, but I don't find any of them who seem to acknowledge that they have a duty to the German people.'

Howard Brundage, interrogating Fritz Wiedemann, 18 October 1945[1]

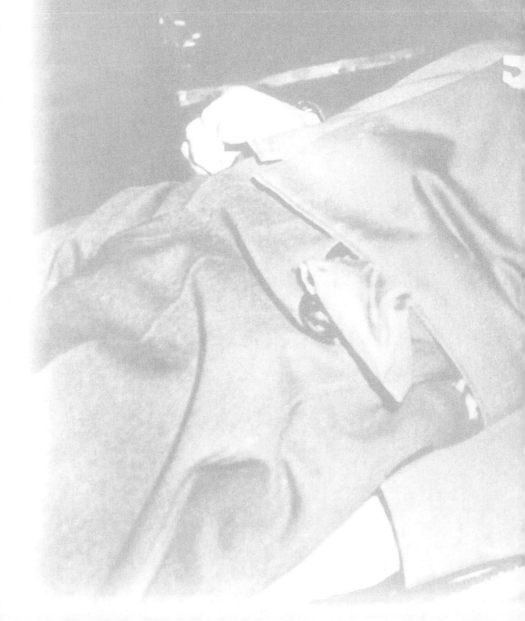

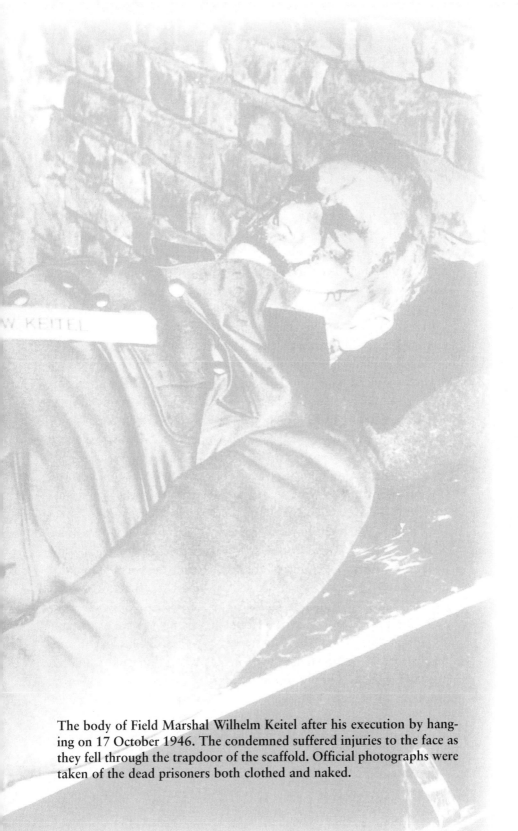

The body of Field Marshal Wilhelm Keitel after his execution by hanging on 17 October 1946. The condemned suffered injuries to the face as they fell through the trapdoor of the scaffold. Official photographs were taken of the dead prisoners both clothed and naked.

Few, if any, of those engaged in interrogating the Nazi elite expected them to avoid execution. Very occasionally the prisoners alluded to their probable fate. Only Hjalmar Schacht remained confident that he would be acquitted once the facts were known. When Thomas Hinkel asked him whether he would consent to further interrogation after the Indictment was served on 19 October, Schacht replied: 'I have no objection. My interests will be protected by further interrogation.'[2] Hans Frank convinced himself, though not those who interviewed him, that he was innocent of every charge and expected his return to the faith to protect him ('I want to point out that I am a believing Christian,' he assured his interrogator).[3] Goering was worried by the wording of the Indictment, which seemed to him to suggest that the defendants would be dragged through subsequent trials at the hands of each wronged nation, to be hanged only at the end of a gruelling process of public scrutiny. 'That may be possible,' Amen told him.[4]

The expectation that the major war criminals would be found guilty and condemned to death was revealed in inter-Allied discussions about the disposal of the corpses, which began in the very first weeks of what proved to be a ten-month trial. Early in December 1945 the Control Commission for Germany, seated in Berlin, warned the war crimes authorities in Nuremberg that the war criminals' bodies should, under German law, be given up to their relatives within twenty-four hours of their execution. The Commission suggested suspending the law under a Military Government directive, so that the corpses could be buried secretly in the prison precincts.[5] The main aim was to avoid any risk that the dead leaders should become the object of a revived Nazi cult. The British section of the Control Commission were unhappy about burial, from fear that Nuremberg prison might become in later years a place of 'national hero worship'. They suggested as an alternative taking the bodies out into the North Sea in police launches and dropping them over the side.[6] Burial won the day. It was decided that the corpses would be buried 'without publicity or ceremony and without any signs to indicate the position of their graves' within the walls of Nuremberg jail.[7]

In March the whole issue was revived when the American Legal

Division of the Control Commission suddenly announced that the war criminals should be executed in Berlin to avoid any accusation from the Soviet delegation that the American zone of occupation, in which Nuremberg was located, had been specially favoured. The British argued against the move since it promised serious security problems among desperate men 'who would go to almost any lengths to avoid hanging', and would make execution a far more public affair than had been expected. The American side agreed a compromise. All the Allies agreed to execution at Nuremberg. The bodies were driven out of the prison in American uniforms, incinerated in a crematorium in Munich, and the ashes scattered to oblivion on the river Isar.[8]

During the pre-trial and trial period Justice Jackson received a number of personal letters from the public asking him to allow them to view the executions. Ernest Schoenfeld, an American pepper merchant, asked if he could not only watch Julius Streicher die, 'but participate in it', thoughtfully adding that if Jackson agreed he would pay his own round-trip fare to the site of execution.[9] A distraught Dutch woman wrote in November 1945 asking Jackson to make every effort to see that all twenty-two defendants received the ultimate punishment:

I inform you that on the 24th November 1943 at Oranienburg was shot down my pretty beloved daughter at the age of 21 *year*! . . . The order was given by SS *Erich Kaltenbrunner* one of the 24 War criminals . . . Reading the newspapers concerning the proces Bergen-Belsen, I am afraid the murder[er]s of my beloved daughter shall be fondled and protected! It is necessary all those murder[er]s shall be hanged, not at once, but *slowly*! . . . you can see those Nazy's are devils and I hope you will do your best to let them hang *all*.[10]

They did not all hang. Twelve of the twenty-two defendants were condemned to death – Goering, Frick, Frank, Sauckel, Keitel, Jodl, Seyss-Inquart, Streicher, Ribbentrop, Kaltenbrunner, Rosenberg, and Bormann *in absentia*. Three were acquitted – Schacht, von Papen and Fritzsche – and the remainder given long prison sentences. Goering escaped the noose by swallowing cyanide (either hidden in his cell, or supplied by a friendly guard – there is no certainty) on the night of his execution. The others were hanged one after the other on the morning of 16 October. As Julius Streicher stepped forward to the gallows he shouted 'Heil Hitler'. Colonel Andrus, a martinet to the last, was heard to call out, 'Take that man's name.'[11]

The interrogators at Nuremberg knew that punishment of the accused was not the only purpose of the trial. In the early stages of preparing the tribunal John McCloy explained that its object was to 'raise international standards of conduct' and to preserve 'the moral force behind the Allied cause'.[12] The western Allies set out self-consciously to undertake what was grandly called by the Control Commission 'the moral rehabilitation of the German people'. The trial of the major war criminals was a part of that process of weaning Germany away from what was termed 'the spirit of totalitarianism'. The fear remained that the German people might once again turn to political extremism. 'No national pride remains,' ran a report on moral revival in February 1946, 'but if left to her own devices, [Germany] will, sooner or later, find a source of pride. The last time she did this, a source was found in Nazism and the leader was Hitler.'[13] The interrogations bear out this judgement. Most of those prisoners asked to explain their enthusiasm for National Socialism justified it in terms of the humiliations and suffering imposed on Germany, unjustly so it seemed to them, in 1919. Few interrogations point towards the future. Only once, in conversation with Fritz Wiedemann, Hitler's adjutant from 1935 to 1939, did the discussion turn to the wider purpose of the trial. Howard Brundage told Wiedemann that the work they were engaged upon was to establish a historical record which the German people could learn from, to be 'warned in advance' next time around. 'This terrible disaster that has come to Germany,' Brundage continued, 'has been entirely unnecessary.' The interrogations were part of that effort 'to find out who was responsible for it'.[14]

The record of the pre-trial examinations shows how difficult it was to allocate responsibility. The failure of most of the defendants to find it within themselves to accept that responsibility served Allied purposes as completely as a confession, for it revealed a true poverty of spirit among the survivors of the elite thrown up by the Third Reich. The reaction of the German public to the trial was mixed, but, as one British official put it, 'nobody in the present state of opinion in Germany is going to regard any condemned war criminal as a martyr'.[15] There was also another Germany dimly visible at Nuremberg beneath the mask of apathy and defeat, one that was not animated only by the spirit of totalitarianism. In August 1945, shortly after her husband had been transferred to Nuremberg, Luise Jodl wrote to Jackson, asking for an

Luise Jodl, the wife of defendant Colonel-General Alfred Jodl, in the courthouse at Nuremberg. Frau Jodl wrote to Jackson asking him not to forget the millions of Germans committed to western values 'and the family of the democratic people'.

audience in order to discuss the issues facing her husband and the German people:

Perhaps some day [she wrote], when you Americans have come to know Germany for longer, you will find out, that millions of us are ready to give their best to the western Allies. I won't mention those who seek contakt [*sic*] mainly for personal advantage, they may do their job in business affairs. I am speaking of those who perhaps are to[o] proud or to[o] shy, to be the first to knock at the door, but whose belief in western culture is firm and whose readiness to work and to help in the family of the democratic people is deep, carried by their love to their unhappy torn country.[16]

Jackson scribbled at the top of the letter, 'file, no answer'.

Part II

Interrogations: the Transcripts

Note on the Transcripts

The original transcripts of the documents and interrogations reproduced in Part II contained a great many internal inconsistencies of spelling and presentation. In some cases a change from an American to a British typist working on the same document is shown by the differing spelling conventions employed. Proper names were often spelt two, or sometimes three, different ways in the same document. Punctuation was also inserted inconsistently, as typists tried to make sense of the translator's version of events. All obvious errors and inconsistencies have been removed in order to make the text easier to read. Proper names had to be given in upper case throughout – for example HITLER, GERMANY; this convention has been abandoned in the printed text. Emphasis in the original has been kept, usually expressed in the documents by underlining the relevant passage or words. Occasionally a mistake has been retained and [*sic* (= thus)] placed in brackets, together with the word actually intended. Some unconventional translations have been retained (for example, 'final disposition' instead of the more usual 'final solution' has been kept because it is historically significant that the translator was not yet familiar with the term now currently used to translate *Endlösung*). No change has been made where to do so would compromise the historical importance of a particular formulation or mode of presentation.

Perspectives on the Fuehrer

'Hitler was the type of the half-educated. He had read a tremendous lot but had interpreted all that he had read according to his own lights and views of the world without improving his knowledge. He could not carry on a normal discussion . . . Hitler was never open to factual argument. Every decision was made from the viewpoint of Party tactics. In innumerable cases he did the exact opposite to what he had said before and did not consider himself tied by any promises or agreement. He was not only immoral but completely amoral. He pronounced death sentences with the greatest calm and without a trace of sentiment.'

Interrogation of Hjalmar Schacht at 'Dustbin', 1 September 1945[1]

[The following transcripts throw light on different aspects of Hitler's dictatorship. The first, and longest, was supplied by Albert Speer who gave three very full interrogation reports during July and August 1945, one on the personality of Hitler, another on 'Politicians and Politics in Nazi Germany', and a third on 'Nazi Foreign Policy and Military Leadership'.[2] The first of these is reproduced in its entirety; the third appears under the heading 'Waging War'. The reports were written out as questionnaires, based on a list of queries given to Speer by the interrogator, and then translated. Speer's report is a full assessment of how the personal dictatorship worked and with what consequences, and paints a remarkable portrait of Hitler's personality as he wrestled with the decline of his empire and then certain defeat. The other documents throw further light on Hitler as dictator. The report on the women around Hitler was commissioned at 'Dustbin' from one of Hitler's close associates, the doctor Karl Brandt, who was heavily implicated in the so-called 'euthanasia' campaign (the murder of the physically and mentally handicapped) between 1939 and 1941. It shows how Hitler used his long bachelorhood as a political weapon, to demonstrate that he was wedded only to Germany's fate, while holding out the promise to millions of German women that he might one day be theirs.[3] The third transcript exposes the quasi-feudal practice of granting gifts and land to faithful military and administrative servants. The sums involved were very large indeed (bonuses of 1 million marks in an economy where skilled workers could expect to earn an average of 3,000 marks a year). Many of the estates were seized from non-German owners or from Jews as part of the systematic Germanization of the areas conquered in the east. The final transcript provides a frank assessment of Hitler's military leadership by Colonel-General Alfred Jodl, his Chief of Operations. Jodl was a strong critic of Hitler's sometimes erratic intervention in military planning, but his final conclusion that on the whole 'he was a great military leader' should not be dismissed as mere sycophancy. Jodl, the shrewd professional soldier, was impressed by many aspects of Hitler's military leadership. Like almost all other military leaders asked to assess the reasons for German defeat, Jodl picked out the failure of the German air force as the primary explanation, a view with which Hitler concurred.[4]]

Document 1 'the driving force'

Interrogation of Albert Speer, undertaken by O. Hoeffding:
FIAT Intelligence Report, EF/Min/3, 19 October 1945

Speer Ministry Report No. 19, Part III: Adolf Hitler

Introduction

In accordance with the questioning, the previous analysis of the various personalities has concentrated on the emergence and background of the various personalities in the Hitler regime, and has attempted to define in general terms the characteristic features of the various individuals. It has been found again that the selection of these individuals, and the general trend which favored promotion of negative values, had their origins in the regime itself, and in the last analysis in Hitler's own person.

In the study of Hitler's personality I have again concentrated on the attempt to isolate the basic characteristics, without attempting to complete the picture by describing many more concrete incidents. Therefore, the present study is just as imperfect an account of Hitler's personality as the previous analyses of his collaborators. A perfect account can only be based on the great mass of material that is being brought together by your investigating agencies.

It is a particular weakness of this study that it does not describe in detail the atmosphere and the mood which, during the final phase of the war, dominated the entire nation, including Hitler and his collaborators. This factor is essential for a full understanding of events. It is intended to supply this background in a later study which will give a chronological account of my own experiences since the end of 1943, and will help towards understanding events and moods. This 'subjective analysis' will complete the picture given below.

The present account completely lacks a description of the attitude

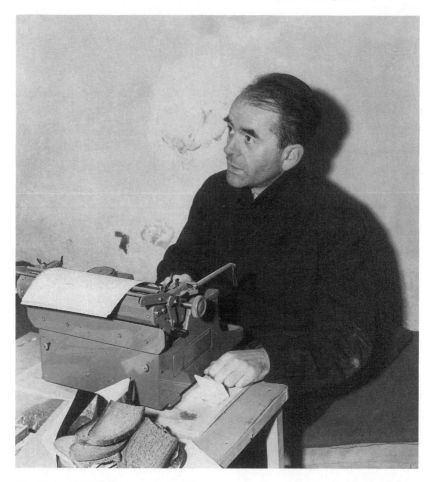

The former Minister of Armaments, Albert Speer, in his cell at Nuremberg. Speer wrote many long and detailed reports for his captors on the German war economy and military technology, and managed to persuade the western Allies that he was an apolitical technocrat.

of the people as a whole, of the helplessness combined with faith which gripped the nation when it saw its inexorable fate approaching, the paralyzing fear which preceded the 'twilight of the Gods' and cast its spell over almost everyone, the hopefulness with which many clung to the slightest chance, but also the fatalism and numbness to which the people were driven by the destruction of their cities, by lack of sleep and fear for their lives.

The present study attempts, in the first place, to show the many individual factors which combined to cause the sinister and inevitable course of our destiny; and in particular to demonstrate the consequences which resulted from the fact that all the power was concentrated in one man who used it to the detriment of the people.

In spite of the events discussed, which are tragic for Germany and the world, the study has come out rather sober and dispassionate. I am not a writer who is able to disclose his own feelings. It is the first time that I have tried to prepare a comprehensive study of this kind. Until now, my activities as an 'author' had never gone beyond a few memoranda.

It is not so difficult to analyze these events in retrospect as it was to keep a clear head when they were in progress. Many of the leaders, who in those days were confused in the extreme and failed, should now be able to arrive at similar conclusions. It is certain that in a year's time I would have a better and clearer judgment on things. Only three months have expired since the end of the war. This study itself was prepared in three weeks, and has not been revised. Therefore, it will contain many subjective judgments, in spite of my endeavor to be objective, and to suppress my personal criticisms based on the experiences of the last few months of the war.

I Choice of Colleagues, and Relations with Them

Q. We are anxious to obtain as comprehensive a picture as possible of Hitler's personality, his influence on his collaborators, working methods, etc. Our previous studies have given us the impression that there must have been a dominant will holding together divergent forces and personalities. Is this true and was that Hitler personally?
A. Up to now I have been obliged to criticize most of the political personalities whom we have discussed as inadequate. Nevertheless, betwen 1933 and 1942 there were surprising achievements, which could certainly not have been accomplished under an 'absentee' government and Party leadership. Also, our power to resist up to 1945 is a factor which cannot be lightly disregarded, although it was a fundamental mistake.

Of course the people in the widest sense – including the intellectuals – were fully behind the war effort, the Wehrmacht [armed forces] contributed all its traditional efficiency, and industry, to the extent that it remained intact, also did everything to avoid defeat.

However, there must have been a strong coordinating and driving force, particularly during the last two years. Such a force could only be, and actually was, provided by Hitler alone.

Q. How did Hitler proceed in choosing his principal collaborators?

A. Most of his important collaborators had been known to him since the period of his early activities and were already at hand. Their previous activities often determined their later employment. In the early days of his struggle he had a good deal of knowledge of their capabilities since he was with them a great deal. Later on he continued to view them from that perspective and placed them accordingly.

He acted very independently in choosing important collaborators. He never asked anybody seriously for advice. His new appointments were mostly surprises. He liked to appoint outsiders. The circle, however, from which he chose them, was preferably that of his old Party members. He forgot that they had aged in the meantime and had lived a life of luxury which was not conducive to hard and efficient work.

In a book on Napoleon's Field Marshals I once read how modest, energetic and unprejudiced they were at the outset, and how spoiled, sybaritic, and unsoldierly they became towards the end of their careers. Napoleon, too, was not able to part with his old guard. Though it won his first battles for him, it certainly later contributed to his losing the decisive ones in his career. Hitler also failed to accomplish the necessary changes in his entourage. As he grew older and more tired he ought to have refreshed and rejuvenated his surroundings . . .

Q. What were the personal relationships of Hitler with his close associates?

A. As long as they did not belong to his private circle he trusted them more or less impersonally. Even though he pretended to be greatly interested in their personal affairs, he made no attempt to establish intimate personal relations with them. He knew how to keep the necessary distance, even with associates who had been with him for long periods of time. In spite of all his friendliness, he was inaccessible and unpredictable.

Q. How did Hitler decide in whom to put his confidence?

A. I had the impression that he chose his collaborators as quickly and 'intuitively' as he made all his decisions. The word 'intuition' was altogether in great vogue with us. It is a capital word, too, and can so well cover up a lack of logic.

This 'intuition' made itself apparent in my own advancement. In 1934, when I was twenty-nine, I was a building manager in his Reich Chancellery, i.e. in a subordinate position. Professor Troost[5] was then his architect. Though up to that time I was completely unknown, after a few conversations Hitler included me in his intimate circle, invited me to lunch and took great interest in me. He had 'intuitively' taken a liking to me. My career as an architect was assured: he had 'discovered' me.

The day when Dr Todt[6] was killed I happened to be at Headquarters. Hitler got the news at about 9 a.m.; at 11 he summoned me and disclosed to me that I was to be Todt's successor. My protests had no effect. They were altogether well founded, since I knew nothing about either constructional engineering or armaments. He assured me that 'I would manage', and that he had confidence in me. I was a typical outsider; in this case with the soldiers as well as with the Party and industry.

What risks and what irresponsibility were involved in this 'intuition'! Other cases of 'outsiders' like me were in the last analysis Ribbentrop, the former champagne dealer, first as ambassador, later as Minister of Foreign Affairs, and Rosenberg, the philosopher, as Minister for the Occupied Eastern Territories. I suspect that in his early days Hitler also selected his associates irrationally, and irrespective of their qualifications.

Q. I understand that in your view Hitler's old political colleagues originally were forceful personalities. How do you then explain their later unconditional dependence on Hitler?

A. This question is closely related to the one I asked myself time and again: How strong was his power of suggestion?

One thing is certain: all his associates who had worked closely with him for a long time were entirely dependent on and obedient to him. However forceful their behavior in their own sphere of influence, in his presence they were insignificant and timid. This timidity, particularly on the part of his old colleagues, has always been beyond my comprehension. They did not have the courage to say the least thing that might displease him. Cowardice alone could not account for this. As a result of their long co-operation, they not only developed an uncanny faith in him, but also completely fell under his influence. They considered everything coming from him as above all criticism. Thus, when the Gauleiters, who visited him once or twice a year, heard him talking about the inevitability of a favorable outcome to the war, they would be deeply convinced and would never tolerate any doubts, let alone a discussion on the subject. That was so even in 1944.

Most of the leading men in his immediate entourage were even more dependent on his judgment and his opinion, since he could impress his opinions on them daily. They, too, were completely under his influence, and but pawns in his hands. One day, when the shorthand notes on the Fuehrer conferences have been fully evaluated, this picture will emerge very clearly. They were under his spell, blindly obedient to him and with no will of their own, whatever the medical term for this phenomenon may be. I noticed during my activities as architect that being in his presence for any length of time made me tired, exhausted and void. Capacity for independent work was paralyzed.

Bearing this experience in mind, while acting as Minister for Armaments I made a point of having discussions with Hitler only once every two or three weeks, and tried in that way to preserve my independence.

Doenitz, too, was of the opinion that it was impossible to work continuously in his immediate presence.

Q. How is it to be explained that he managed to put people who were strangers to him under his 'spell' after a short discussion?

A. Without doubt, there must have been some suggestive power of persuasion. On the other hand, one must not lose sight of the fact that there existed in the minds of the people a very powerful general conviction of Hitler's greatness and mission. One must therefore bear in mind the feelings of reverence for his historical magnitude with which most visitors approached him, and the significance which they therefore attached to each word of his. This attitude unquestionably provides an exceptionally good foundation for the intensive influence which he exercised as well as the persuasive power of his arguments.

In addition to that his technical knowledge and memory for figures always made an extraordinary impression, as these faculties seemed beyond people's comprehension. However, whenever technical subjects were discussed, he always allowed the experts to talk first and only afterwards formulated his opinion.

Q. You said just now that he preferred to have insignificant people in his entourage?

A. He aimed at having strong and tenacious co-operators. His choice was certainly originally inclined in that direction. Those who had been with him in his early struggle had once been tough and vigorous – the Gauleiters as well as his early collaborators, such as Goering, Goebbels, Ley, Himmler, Bormann, etc. However, they were corrupted by their mode of living and in that way became insignificant. Besides, the development of his peculiar working methods contributed to the fact that only people who put up with his eccentricities could work in his proximity. I do not know whether in earlier days he had been more tolerant of contradictions; in 1942, any contradiction had to be very carefully phrased – no 'frontal attack' was ever possible.

Q. What was his method of working with them?

A. He always attempted to persuade. If possible he talked in generalities. In case of any opposition he would only very seldom give his opponent a chance to get in a word in order to prove his point. He seldom began a discussion without a preconceived opinion.

As a rule a conference would only be called when Hitler had something to communicate. He was seldom loud or excited. When his relationship with any one of his collaborators reached the stage when Hitler lost his temper, one could be sure that a speedy dismissal or side-tracking was on the way. He seldom gave clear orders. His decisions in the military sphere too were roughly outlined and often given as 'an opinion' only. Yet he expected them to be executed as orders. A soldier had first to get used to that; the politicians were well acquainted with this indefinite type of order, which had its advantages for them.

Q. How did he react to good or bad events?

A. He kept complete self-control up to the end. The worst news could not make him lose his composure. When the news of Badoglio's[7] defection came quite suddenly I was with him. Very shortly afterwards he resumed our unimportant discussion on weapons with perfect composure.

His entourage particularly admired the way he always retained his self-control. It gave them the feeling that they were in the presence of a man who stood above and was able to handle any situation. This manner undoubtedly contributed to everybody's confidence in all his decisions.

One could detect no sign of emotion when he did not want to show it. Towards the end, his eyes often filled with tears when any event moved him emotionally. In spite of his bad state of health, he held himself well in hand right up to the end. This self-control was an essential factor in the influence exercised by him and was an extraordinary achievement of his unsurpassed energy. With so many eyes watching him for years, what waves of discouragement would have spread had he lost his control but once when a critical event was announced.

Q. When he was displeased with his collaborators, what was his method of replacing them?

A. He was not decisive in the exchange of collaborators whom he considered unsuitable. That was a great fault, which after the Roehm affair made itself apparent again and again. He preferred to 'freeze' them out by imperceptible degrees. Actually, with his authority there was no need for that. For weeks and months on end he would go on finding fault with, and sharply criticizing, some of his collaborators, thereby rendering them incapable of work, and yet in spite of that he would hold on to them. What is more, he would do so even if the rest of his entourage shared his opinion. It was due to this same habit of indecision that he criticized and ridiculed the ideology of the SS, Rosenberg's mystics, Bormann's church policy, and Goebbels' women (before 1939), yet drew no consequences and took no action.

Owing to this he had a great number of collaborators he did not think much of, who therefore had no authority, and yet had to remain in office. It was only seldom that a direct criticism could be extracted from him, in spite of the fact that everybody would have welcomed it. Many therefore developed a system of espionage by way of adjutants, so that they could obtain information on Adolf Hitler's real opinion after an important discussion.

If he summoned somebody to communicate his displeasure, it was usually an official occasion and resulted in speedy replacement of the individual. But even such replacements were seldom clearly formulated. He usually gave the person leave of absence, or else chose some other unobtrusive way of dismissal.

One of the most typical examples of this type of action was the appointment of Backe[8] as Reich Food Minister. Darré was merely given 'leave of absence', and not dismissed. To begin with, Backe was put in charge of the Ministry as *Staatssekretaer* [State Secretary]. When

Backe had to be made Reich Minister to strengthen his authority, it was made clear that Darré remained in office as Minister while 'on leave', and Backe was therefore appointed Reich Minister without Portfolio and at the same time 'put in charge of the management of the Food Ministry'. This was perhaps the most complicated of all solutions thought up by Lammers, the 'Reich Notary', who had to formalize all these arrangements.

At the same time Hitler always attempted to have two or three competitors for each important position, all of whom he directed immediately, even when they originated from the same agency.

Q. Was this double or treble commission part of a systematic policy, or did it happen by chance?

A. Outwardly there was no apparent system. But there was hardly a field which was not divided into two or three parts. He liked going over the heads of his immediate collaborators and conferring with their subordinates himself, giving them directions without their superior's knowledge. In cases of this sort the superiors were more or less dependent on the decency of their subordinates. That seldom worked out because the fact of a direct approach by Hitler had a tremendous effect on the subordinates' vanity. For instance, he established a direct relationship with Saur[9] and Dorsch[10] in my Ministry, which I could not have broken up even if I tried very hard. His old and experienced colleagues therefore carefully avoided introducing their best subordinates to him. As a result, his entourage contained a lot of second-raters, out of whom he often picked new collaborators.

Q. Could one attribute to Hitler the faculty of being a good judge of human nature?

A. That is a difficult question to answer. He made some good choices. On the other hand he sometimes appointed completely unsuitable people and kept them on. At any rate he could always be easily bluffed. He did not see through people who were merely acting a part with him. He was actually too trustful where his political colleagues were concerned. He would not willingly admit that some of them were false creatures who deliberately deceived him. His attitude towards his military officers, even before 20 July, was completely the opposite. He had a profound mistrust of them.

At all events he was definitely not a good judge of men. This bad judgment certainly became apparent in the choice of his successor designate. In this respect he failed completely. In a discussion in March 1945 he frankly and despairingly admitted to his secretaries that Hess had gone mad in his role of deputy; that Goering, owing to his mode of living and the defeat of his Luftwaffe, was rejected by the people; while Himmler, who appeared to him as a possible third heir, was on hostile terms with the Party and also useless since he was completely unartistic. He did not know whom else he could choose. That he considered Himmler an enemy of the Party was the fruit of the labors of Bormann, who took his place in Hitler's confidence by this insinuation.

Q. Did Hitler have any long-term policy for finding political replacements?

A. There was an indication of a clear outline. The scheme, though originating with Ley, had been accepted by Hitler. Through the building of the Adolf Hitler Schools and the elite training camps (*Ordensburgen*),[11] intensive training for leadership from earliest youth was to be provided. However, selection for and education in these schools was only suitable for building up a bureaucratic Party administration, and the scheme was doomed to be a failure.

Q. You have made it clear that Hitler was not forceful in his decisions and often hesitated. Do you think he had a clear conception of the results of his domestic policies? Did he realize to what extent Germany had been turned into a police state?

A. Very likely not. In Obersalzburg there were many instances when his immediate circle informed him of cases of incredible stupidity in the administrative offices, as for instance when, without any reason whatsoever, the people of Munich were forbidden to use bicycles in a certain area, or else were forbidden to ski in winter. On these occasions he would get very excited and would proclaim his constant and unsuccessful fight with this stupidity and bureaucracy. Bormann would be instructed to follow up these incidents.

Neither he nor his entourage knew anything about what life was really like outside, because they had become completely estranged from reality. He drew no sound conclusions from such isolated incidents. In all these things he was extraordinarily undecided.

To the imagination of the outsider Hitler was a keen, quick, brutally governing dictator. It is difficult to realize that in reality he edged along hesitantly, almost fearfully. But that was the case.

Q. Have you any explanation for this hesitancy?

A. Long before the war, it was known that with the exception of his architecture, he was interested in nothing but foreign policy and the Wehrmacht. Therefore the hope of all those who realized these critical conditions was that he would later concentrate again on internal politics and do away with the corrupt practices which, in contrast to his own mode of life, had been firmly entrenched.

Q. Did he then more or less leave internal politics to others?

A. He had certainly lost his grip on internal politics. They were in the end governed by Bormann, who knew how to present things in such a way that Hitler had the impression that he was still conducting them himself. This field however could at any time have been taken over again by Hitler. He had carried out the old principle of 'divide and rule'. There were political groups who were always ready and only too willing to do away with others. A few critical words from Hitler about Bormann, and all his enemies would have jumped at his throat.

Q. Can you tell us how information and opinions were reported to him, and altogether how he was advised about the foreign political situation?

A. Partly, of course, through Ribbentrop, the Minister of Foreign Affairs, who reported current information through Hewel.[12] Possibly even more influential, however, were the press reports which Dr Dietrich delivered to him two or three times daily. Here he could hear the voices of the press of the world. Dietrich was a soft and accommodating man. He followed the path of least resistance. A good many things are being written in the world. Hitler was always extraordinarily pleased when he had news which suited his course of action. His joy at hearing news of this sort, and his anger at news which crossed him, led to the temptation of bringing him the right kind of news. I sometimes had that impression.

At any rate, this daily information service was one of the most essential factors in shaping Hitler's moods and placating him. No doubt Dr Dietrich did not intentionally color them, but Hitler's influence and his daily intercourse with him probably led to Dietrich's becoming unconsciously biased in his selection. To be confronted with as strong a personality as Hitler's and to avoid being influenced by it is a problem which has often in the course of history produced negative consequences.

Q. How would you sum up your opinion of Hitler's ways of choosing his collaborators and his employment of them?

A. His methods of necessity led to weak collaborators, for his arbitrary method of choice brought no men with proper qualifications to the right positions, while in Hitler's proximity men of lesser character, who, then, because of their dissolute ways of living, had no powers of resistance, advanced. They were afraid of him and were incapable of defending any opinion, particularly as they themselves were laden with guilt. On this fertile ground, intrigues and 'back door politics' thrived.

The weaker and more frightened these intriguers were in Hitler's presence, the more brutal and egocentric they were in their interpretation of the concept of 'state authority' toward their subordinates. Subconsciously aware of their weakness, they deliberately collected subservient creatures around themselves, who were alike in their conception of law and morals, and with their mental outlook. Anyone who did not spend his nights drinking with them and carrying on filthy conversations with them was considered impossible and a 'philistine'. He had no possibility of making a career for himself.

So the inferiority of some leading personalities had a far-reaching effect on the quality of their subordinates. As this process had already been in operation for over ten years, it had in parts become deeply rooted. When the last phase of the war came, this corrupt and outworn section of the leading class was no longer capable of foreseeing the coming developments or of acting in the interests of the people. On the contrary, they betrayed the people, from whom they had already separated themselves long ago, putting their own interests before those of the people.

A system which makes the selection of the leading personalities dependent solely on the judgment, arbitrary discretion, and whims of the dictators inevitably leads to such results. There have been other historical examples of that type. Had we even to a modest degree been allowed frank criticism, resulting in some control over leading personalities and new appointments, a better selection would have been the result. As it was, the most flattering comment that could have been made about any of the leaders by the people was: 'He lives a decent life, he is a decent person.'

There is nothing more humiliating for German leadership than that in the end, this commonplace fact of decent behavior should have ranked as the highest praise that could come from the people.

II Hitler's Methods of Working

Q. How did Hitler's personal characteristics develop during the war?

A. Serious changes in his personality and his working methods undoubtedly took place during the course of the years. The Hitler of 1945 was not the one of 1938. On this, by the way, all his colleagues agreed. It was only the nature of this change about which opinions differed. Some regarded it as a spiritual derangement, while others based it on disorders of health. It appears to me to be an important problem, which should be here thoroughly gone into.

In my opinion one can take it as a leading thesis that he was a 'genius'. In connection with this I would also like to stress the negative characteristics which are usually taken for granted in a genius. They may be forgiven in an artist, but politicians with sound and rational working and thinking methods are surely of more use. But he wanted to be a genius. We often say that genius and insanity are closely related. That could have been applied to Hitler at a pretty early stage, not in a psychiatric sense but in respect of the strange ideas which he conceived.

For instance, he often asserted that his political, artistic and military world of ideas was a unit which he built up in all details while between the ages of 30 and 40 years. That, he said, had been his most productive period. All that he was now creating was the realization of his ideas at the time. He hinted that he had laid them down in his unpublished second volume of the book *Mein Kampf*. This second volume must have been written about 1925. Perhaps it shows up all that was fantastic in his make-up. It was at the same time that he had sketched his plans for Berlin, which were on a vast scale and probably should have been interpreted in connection with his political plans.

Q. I would like to go into his working methods. What can you tell me about those?

A. His working methods give an insight into his inner being; they also, in my opinion, serve as the key to the changes in his personality during the course of the war.

Many in Hitler's immediate entourage were shaken during the last two years by the rigid line he took in his decisions and the obstinacy with which he followed it. Whereas before, constant variations and entirely new ways continually occurred to him, elegantly extricating him from what looked like blind alleys; whereas earlier, from the time of the occupation of Austria and up to the Russian pact, he constantly offered both his entourage and the world new surprises, he completely lacked this gift from 1942 onwards.

Q. What possibilities are you thinking of?

A. I am not a politician and cannot judge what possibilities were still open. However, in earlier days, he could at least have made some sort of attempts. In 1940, or 1941, France and other occupied countries would have still offered opportunity for such considerations. A generous policy in occupied Russia might have been one of the ways of winning successes. He could have tried to mitigate the effects of his retreats and setbacks by political means. He could have taken stock of his general position. And finally, it certainly would not have been inevitable for him to prepare a 'heroic end' for the people.

In his book, *Mein Kampf*, there are certain ideas in connection with the loss of a war which make sense. Many of his closest colleagues were astounded in the last months to see how he himself ignored these precepts.

Q. Can you explain this change in his personality? What factors contributed to it?

A. For this it is necessary to first describe his working methods before the war, in order to understand the big changes that occurred after the beginning of the war.

Before the war, his working methods were those of an 'artist', in his undisciplined allocation of time. He had no definite time schedule for work; weeks were given to subsidiary problems; there was slow pondering over the crucial issues followed by a sudden 'intuition' on their correct solution; then a certain amount of abrupt, quick work in order to systematize and consolidate this solution – and consequently some very intensive working days – followed again by a period comparatively free from visible working efforts.

Q. He then had no regular and disciplined working methods?

A. Before the war, Hitler's time schedule was extremely informal. But many definite engagements were made, and even those were not often adhered to. He never allowed himself to be rushed into work; he practically always had time to spare. Many problems were discussed at dinner in the Reich Chancellery in the midst of his political circle. He in that way currently influenced his colleagues. The dinner table was everybody's big opportunity for obtaining information. Without it everything would have lacked orientation. This or that important politician could, after dinner, initiate an improvised discussion of his particular problem, so that during that particular period of three or four hours daily Hitler would, in fact, give most of his directives. After that, there might be one or two long discussions on military matters with high officers or else with Goering on some weighty problems of the Four Year Plan;[13] before supper there were mostly discussions with architects, who presented their plans to him, or else the time was taken up with his own work on architectural projects. Supper was taken in a smaller, not so exclusively political, circle as dinner, again without any women. Following that, one or two films, and after that, up to two o'clock in the morning, conversations in which he doubtlessly tried to 'relax'. He spoke of his career and of his youth, in order to remind himself of his mission.

He particularly liked, from time to time, to undertake motor tours of two or three days' duration. These were connected with big meetings, visits to building sites of the Autobahn and other projects, with outdoor picnics and an informal mode of life. Such tours were, on principle (mainly for security reasons), neither prepared nor announced.

Whenever he had to make big decisions, he went to Obersalzburg. Here his life was completely private. Fraulein Braun, who up to last year or two, never appeared in Berlin, kept him company; and the circle was otherwise, as already mentioned, also completely unpolitical.

There were hours of pacing up and down with his military adjutants and recapitulating their problems, often in endless and repetitive discussions, in order to clear up in his own mind all the details from every angle. There were walks in the vicinity of the Obersalzburg which included visits to small inns, and which brought him, so he said, the inner calm and assurance which he needed for his world-shattering decisions. There was more intensive occupation with artistic things, with architecture, and viewing numerous films. In view of his extraordinary intake of two films daily, many had to be shown two or three times over.

Q. How did he come to such decisions; were they the result of the so-called 'intuition'?

A. The whole picture of his pre-war activity was not, as I see it, a formation of opinions diligently worked out with the help of many individual observations, but one of emotional judgments influenced by many factors, often, as it appeared to me, with an attempt at rationalization after the event.

The 'intuition' which, according to his own remarks, played such a big part in his work, required a certain environment and this apparently unbalanced working method for its basis. It also needed a lot of self-assurance, which he derived entirely from the confidence of the people and his own immediate followers at the time. In his 'good days', he unquestionably had a 'nose' for coming events which was astonishing. He appeared to have an 'antenna'.

Every mass meeting, with its enthusiasm; every trip across the country, with people mobbing his car and almost making movement impossible; his entourage, awed and devoted, – all that was needed in order to give him assurance for his decisions. It was his spiritual food, which even under circumstances involving difficult decisions, endowed him with a certain light-heartedness and lack of constraint. His life before the war was not such as people imagined. Out of long experience he had evolved the working methods which fitted his nature.

Q. Did these working methods undergo any change after the beginning of the war?

A. At the time, changes, which had a decisive influence on further developments, were effected by him and his entourage in his time schedule and the general course of his life.

After the beginning of the war, he on principle gave up all amusements, being of the opinion that, in view of the sacrifices that had to be made by the soldiers, he was not entitled to them. He saw no more films, he at first completely refused to pursue any of his artistic inclinations, and cut himself off to a great extent from his intimate circle. His new entourage consisted of officers of the OKW and of the General Staff, his personal doctors (Professor Brandt and Professor Morell), and his personal adjutants. From year to year, his work became more severe and therefore more alien to his personality.

Whereas formerly he would not allow himself to be overwhelmed by work, he now became work's slave, as it seemed to him that he had to get through most of it personally. Before the war he had known very well how to delegate work to others, which worked out to his advantage. Now, however, as his problems began to accumulate, he would increasingly concern himself with details with which he would never have bothered before. He forced himself to become a diligent, methodical worker, and that neither suited his personality, nor bene- fited his decisions.

Q. What effect did this change in his routine have on his person?

A. Every active sportsman knows the condition of 'overtraining'. One gets into it unawares, and if the trainer does not check it in time, the sportsman, or the team, is ruined for a long time and must break off its training. Mental overstrain too can produce mental 'overtraining'. As I had occasion to observe in myself during the difficult period of the war, this mental stress expresses itself in an almost mechanical functioning of the mind, shutting out new and fresh impressions and decisions which would spring from them.

In the case of people who are not methodical workers, but arrive at their decisions intuitively, the advantages which they may derive from this intuitive method, and the almost irresponsible self-assurance that goes with it, will be reversed by overstrain and turned into uncertainty and tortured indecision. They suddenly lose the inner meaning of their personality and no more arrive at their decisions through automatic functioning of their mind, but must, as it were, squeeze them out of their tortured brain.

The instinct gives an early indication as to when a rest must be taken, in order that fresh mental energies can be developed. Excessive will-power easily extinguishes this instinct. After that, it is difficult to diagnose one's own condition – as it is with overtraining in sport.

At the appearance of mental overstrain, I used to turn to other activities – went on visits to factories or to the front – and in doing so, I also completely changed my time schedule. Or else I would rest completely for two or three days at a time. Thus, in spite of your bombing, owing to these instinctively taken precautions, I succeeded in remaining relatively fresh up to the end of the war.

Q. And had Adolf Hitler taken no measures to combat this mental overstrain? Did he not take a holiday, or in any other way try to divert himself?

A. One cannot consider days spent at Obersalzburg as periods of either rest or holiday. The work went on; he had no deputy and did not want to have one. Owing to that, many minor matters were currently put up for his decision by Bormann or by his adjutants. His entourage took no notice of his overstrain, and claimed his attention and exploited him as much as possible. He often stressed that he was unable to take a holiday.

At the beginning of the war, Hitler had from time to time put in some journeys to the front. However, when events at the Russian front began to take a tragic turn, which undoubtedly he did not fail to notice, his mental 'overtraining' grew even more pronounced; it had by that time already created physical difficulties, and often made him appear very tired. One had the impression that it was merely his will-power that kept him going.

Next to his emotional 'artistic' working methods, he doubtlessly had a naturally strong will, which was unique in his entourage. By means of that will-power he carried his mental overstrain much too far, thereby physically and mentally laying the foundation for the subsequent deterioration of his health. For purely physical reasons, no doubt most other people would have occasionally broken down under such stress, and after an enforced relaxation would have again been capable of new and fresh work after a while. Or else nature would have come to aid with an illness. Hitler's physician Morell, however, managed to cover up his exhaustion by means of artificial stimulants – a method which, as is well known, eventually completely ruins the individual. But Hitler got used to these means of keeping up his powers of endurance and kept on demanding them. He admired Morell and his craft, and was in a certain sense dependent on him and his remedies.

Q. Did this mental exhaustion become apparent only during the war, or was there any evidence of it earlier, possibly in another form?

A. Already before the war, in Berlin, Hitler had periods of such mental exhaustion, which expressed themselves in unwillingness to make clear decisions, in a certain absentmindedness or in discussions which were embarrassing for the other party. For it was impossible to make out whether he was at the time following the discussion or was thinking of something else. He was often completely silent. But later on, it often became apparent that he had attentively followed the conversation, though at the time he had hardly said anything, or else had merely reacted with a 'yes' or a 'no'. This state of exhaustion, however, did not last long. It would pass after a few weeks' stay at the Obersalzburg. His eyes would again be brighter, his capacity for reaction quicker, and his enthusiasm for making decisions would revive. While before the war he was overstrained only at times, during the war his working methods, his over-working, and his worries drove him relentlessly into a permanent condition of overstrain. As the predicament brought about by the situation at the front grew increasingly serious, his suspicions of his military entourage were intensified, prompting him continually to enlarge his volume of work and making his condition of overstrain worse and increasingly pathological. Even at the end, however, it did not, in my opinion, amount to mental derangement.

I believe that everybody who does a great deal of intellectual work can understand this condition of mental over-exertion. However, there is hardly another person who has endured a comparable, ever-increasing strain during the course of so many years, and who in addition has found himself a physician who tried out completely new drugs on him, in order to keep him capable of work and at the same time to carry out a unique medical experiment on him. It will be important to analyze his handwriting during the last months. It had the uncertainty of an old man. By his stubborn ways, his sustained outbursts of anger, he anyway often reminded me of a senile man. This condition became permanent after 1944 and was only seldom interrupted. Days on which, as in former times, he made quick and clear-cut decisions, on which he was tolerant of counter-arguments, were conspicuous occasions which excited much subsequent comment.

It is true that he liked to attend to numerous minor matters. But he failed to go into the heart of the problems. He no longer worked 'intuitively', but would arrive at his conclusions rationally, a method for which he was not mentally well-equipped or trained. What had been the main part of his being appeared to be switched off and extinguished.

Q. Did not Hitler have serious worries during the period of his 'early struggle' and did he not mentally and physically exert himself then at least as much as he did during the war?

A. As I heard later, he at that time too doubtless had periods of extraordinary strain. Even if not of such long duration, they were at least as hopeless and as worrying. At the time, however, there existed a powerful counteracting influence which was absent during the war – the constant change of environment, which continually renewed his faith and self-reliance; the meetings, from which he probably derived more energy and courage than he expended of his own strength to the audiences. Though at the time he communicated to his entourage and his intimate circle his own power of persuasion, he himself 'accumulated' from personalities and daily events new strength, which made him capable of taking on new tasks. It is only in this way that I can explain his endurance during the years of his 'early struggle', apart of course from the fact that he was younger at the time.

Q. And you think that this was not the case during the war in his relations with his military entourage?

A. During the war, there was nothing more soul-destroying than his entourage. Always the same dreary faces, not susceptible to broader interests, completely uninterested in cultural matters; officers, whose private discussions never involved anything but hunting, their own careers and those of their colleagues, family gossip, and technical military topics. This entourage, which influenced the course of his life, was not qualified to give him anything in return for the power of persuasion which he expended upon it. During that long period of time, it hardly changed at all. He therefore withdrew more and more from this circle. At the beginning of the war, as a sequence to his pre-war Reich Chancellery lunch parties, he went on for a time taking his meals with his officers and his more intimate followers. This custom was later abolished in consequence of an insignificant incident. From then he took his meals by himself, and only occasionally invited guests from the outside.

This self-inflicted isolation became more severe from early 1944 onwards. The meals which I occasionally attended became more monotonous and lacking in conversation, for here too, he merely invited his secretaries, his doctor (Morell), and others who really could not contribute anything new.

I had the feeling that in this phase, from autumn of 1944 onwards, he simply did not want any more discussions. All that was said was very flat, irrelevant and on a deliberately low intellectual level. It seemed as if that circle was specially chosen so as not to remind him of his grave and by then insoluble problems. He came to despise people and often said as much. As he would put it, only Fraulein Braun[14] and his Alsatian belonged to him and were loyal to him!

Q. Did his entourage put up with this isolation? Did it not see any danger in it?

A. It suited Bormann very well. He encouraged Hitler's new ways of life, as he wanted to be the only one in a position to make decisions. Besides, Hitler would tolerate no criticism of his ways of living. In any case, only a few clearly realized this development, as the process was so slow. An outsider could not, from his occasional visits, get the right impression of this isolation. There was general talk of a 'leadership crisis' while definitely it was a 'leader crisis'.

Q. How much were his decisions influenced by rational arguments and thinking?

A. He knew how to rationalize his intuitive decisions. I often had the impression that the rational basis was something he arrived at only after the intuitive decision had been made, in order to support it. When he tried to work out rationally and logically he was often incapable of coming to a final conclusion. He would try to evade rational arguments, however weighty. Whenever both his reason and his intuition spoke against the line to which he was committed, he would invoke his 'faith' in the road prescribed to him by fate.

Q. Was he then so sure of his infallible course, his lucky star, that his decisions were determined by his conception of it?

A. Yes. And the more so the more difficult the situation became. Out of innumerable isolated incidents, he had pieced together a firm conviction that his whole career, with its many unfavorable events and setbacks, was predestined by providence to take him to the goal which it had set him. In all difficult situations and decisions this belief of his served as a primary argument. The more his overworked condition caused him to lose his original gift of detaching himself in his thinking from the pressure of current events, and the more he was cornered by the course of events, the more emphasis he would place on this argument of his 'predestined fate'.

The incomprehensible fact that he escaped injury on the 20 July gave him new foundation for this belief. Dr Goebbels' press campaign about Frederick the Great and the course of the Seven Years War confirmed him in this belief and gave it a new incentive. Towards the end he even saw in Roosevelt's unexpected death[15] a parallel to

Frederick the Great's history; – the Empress Elizabeth had died shortly before the end of the Seven Years War, thus rescuing Frederick the Great out of a seemingly hopeless situation.

It is true that he cited this parallel in his first moment of elation on receipt of the news. Afterwards his reaction gave way to a calmer appraisal of the position.

Roosevelt's death, at any rate, helped to restrain him and his fanatical followers, who also believed in his destiny, from committing even more disastrous acts of despair which otherwise probably would have befallen Germany; for this event now gave them new courage and made them postpone their plans for destruction, as they now again believed in their own further existence.

Hitler must, up to the last few weeks, have believed in his mission and the inevitably successful conclusion of his destiny. To my mind, the opinion which he forcefully expressed in his conferences, that the war could not be lost, stemmed from his inner conviction and was not just a lie intended to drive others to further efforts.

He quite realized the difficult and hopeless aspects of the situation, yet he motivated his optimism by reasoning that so often before in his life he had been in difficult situations, which in the end always had turned to his advantage, and that this time, too, something would happen, somehow or other, at the 'last minute' to turn events in his favor.

If there was anything pathological in his ideas during the last few years, it was this unshakable faith in his lucky star. In my view, it must have been a case of auto-suggestion.

Three basic factors were responsible, in my view, for his thinking and actions: Owing to his self-imposed mental isolation and because he was acutely over-worked, he had lost the gift of working intuitively which had been his main asset. Furthermore, formerly he had the habit of reasoning out his problems only up to a certain point, after which he would rely on his intuition. After he had lost this capacity, he increasingly resorted instead to his abnormal faith in his lucky destiny, which was based on self-persuasion, relying on it as on an incontrovertible argument.

That was how he formulated his decisions. The longer and more difficult the war, the more pronounced became this process. The deterioration of Hitler's mental and physical condition had adverse repercussions on his important decisions, and thus on the course of the war, accelerating in reciprocal action the deterioration of his personal condition, as well as the unavoidable military defeat.

The result of this was the extraordinary condition of the petrification and hardening of his character and his mind, his shutting himself off from all problems, his severity, injustice and obstinacy.

One can definitely establish the following:

From earlier conversations we have seen that his selection of colleagues was on the whole a bad one, as in the case of all dictators. This inevitable process of negative selection of his colleagues prevented the creation of an entourage which, through its steadfastness or its intelligence, could have prevented this tragic development. In his happier times he could, in spite of that, rule alone; in the days of his misfortune, however, he had nobody around him.

Jealousies and discords, which are always bound to arise in the entourage of dictators, completely obstructed his every action. This is a feature inherent in all dictatorships, and not due to any peculiarity of Hitler's. Have not in the course of history similar systems broken down under as tragic circumstances for the people? Because there was nobody at hand to avert or mitigate the disaster.

That does not relieve Hitler of the responsibility for his inexcusably tragic effect on humanity. He built up the most radical of all dictatorial systems, thereby opening the door to the most serious faults and bringing about the biggest collapse that has ever been the lot of any nation.

III Private Life

Q. What sort of picture can you give us of Hitler's character?

A. It is impossible for me to obtain a clear picture of his character, his methods and his views. I have thought a great deal on this subject, but without any result. While all other people in Hitler's circle are more or less simple and comprehensible, his personality, to me at least, is a puzzle full of contradictions and opposites. I will try to draw his different characteristics. The attempt may miscarry, for there are contradictory answers to a great many questions. They all depend on what particular period, or what particular mood is under discussion.

Q. You have then the impression that he was illogical and unsteady?

A. There were certainly a combination of great opposites in him. He could be kind and make his circle enthusiastic about himself; in spite of that, however, he was merciless and unjust. And that not only towards his political and ideological enemies, but also towards his immediate circle. He could be loyal and honest and yet was amoral in his basic conceptions. He was extraordinarily generous to his artists and co-operators, tolerant towards their human weaknesses – unfortunately too tolerant – and yet in a great many things he had the mentality of a petty bourgeois, which may possibly be explained by his descent.

He wanted to be a politician, yet his working methods and his characteristics were those of an artist rather than a politician, let alone a warlord. He was neither stable and balanced nor detached; on the contrary he was in constant inner agitation, and always ready to rush into decisions. On the other hand, important decisions would hang over his head for months without his being able to make up his mind, even if it was imperative that he should do so.

Q. How can you characterize him further? What can you add to this?

A. He seldom showed himself as a 'human being' to his official collaborators. In this circle he was an impenetrable personality, and gave no clue to his personal existence. As an artist, I had the opportunity to get to know him in his private life. There he had a 'heart' (*Gemuet*) like every other human being. Here his conception of life was almost bourgeois. He tried to act as a good 'house father', good-natured, jocular, receptive to harmless jokes of others, even humorous and with a good deal of irony at his own expense. The simple life, petty bourgeois in relation to the otherwise prevailing standards, came to him easily; it was natural for him and entailed no sacrifice. It won him many sympathies and was much discussed by the people. The credit it gave him made up in the eyes of the people for other unpopular decisions. For the rest, his simplicity was also a conscious political line. He often said: 'While I am simple, my entourage must be covered with medals and splendidly equipped. My simplicity stands out all the better in those surroundings.' For that reason he was not interested in the 'tin shops' that Goering and others covered themselves with.

A useful gift was his ability to talk with the man in the street and to draw him out. After a few minutes' conversation, timidity was overcome and discussion proceeded with amazing freedom and often even humor.

I suspect that he was not happy with his 'mission'; that he would have rather been an architect than a politician. He often clearly expressed his aversion from politics, and even more from military matters. He disclosed his intention of withdrawing after the war from state affairs to build a large house in Linz, and there to finish his days. He was of expressed opinion that he would then completely retire. He did not want to influence his successor in any way. He would then be soon forgotten and left to himself. Possibly someone or other of his former colleagues would visit him occasionally, but he would not count on that. Outside of Fraulein Braun he could take no one with him. Nor would anybody stand living with him of his own free will for any length of time.

Q. When did he have such thoughts?

A. That was about 1939, but also during the war. He still wanted to busy himself with rebuilding Linz and to give it a theater, an art gallery, and many other buildings. Moreover, his art collections, which you have found, or at least its very best pieces, were destined for Linz. Even in the difficult days of the war, when there was no more talk of the building up of other cities, he busied his thoughts with Linz and its new buildings. I am describing this as an example to illustrate once more how fundamentally unbalanced he was after all. The tension and the pressure under which he labored produced the most various and unexpected effects.

Q. Did he choose Linz because of his early life in that town? Did he think and speak much of his youth?

A. His youth played a prominent part in his narrations. He described his father as an official of modest means, who brought him up with extraordinary severity, and his mother as good-natured and conciliatory. He preferred his mother and resented his father's opposition to his artistic tendencies. He asserted that the severity and rigor of his bringing up in his parents' house had been of great value to him.

He said that as a boy he had been prone to much mischief, and had always been the most active in carrying through some 'enterprise' with his school fellows, and that he had been a bad pupil. He was conscious for the first time of the problem of Austrian nationality in Linz in his early youth. He said that the many Czech residents were a problem in the city and that the attitude of everyone, including the school children, was unanimous against these immigrants. He said that his professor of German and geography, from whom he learned a great deal, had a far-reaching influence over him and promoted his first political conceptions; I do not know in what way. For the rest he much respected the Bishop of Linz at that time, who built the Cathedral of Linz from the people's contributions, and was a great man in every respect.

Q. Did he give any other facts from his youth concerning elements which influenced his later political attitude?

A. According to him he became anti-semitic in Vienna. There he had seen and recognized the Jewish danger. There was a strong anti-semitic attitude among the workmen also. He did not go into the exact causes in his own case. He earned his living as a builder's laborer. At the time he already rejected the Social Democratic views, nor did he join the trade unions, and thus got into his first 'political' difficulties.

Vienna does not appear to have left a favorable impression on him, in contrast to Munich, where he lived shortly before the war.

Q. Did his experiences during the world war have a far-reaching influence on his later development?

A. As far as I can remember, his accounts of his experiences during the world war were all in connection with his life as a soldier and had no political tendencies. Later on, during the war, he stressed that his experiences in the trenches had given him more insight into many details of military activity than all his military advisors. Therefore he felt superior to them. That no doubt was true in some respects, but his experience gathered in that way was of no use for real leadership. According to many officers in his circle this 'trench perspective' gave him the wrong outlook when it came to making decisions as a leader. This knowledge of details stood in his way rather than helped him.

Q. Did Hitler consider himself an 'artist', or was his preoccupation with art merely a hobby?

A. Architecture and political aims were closely connected in his case. He felt himself to be a thwarted artist. In his opinion, only three worthwhile professions existed: 'Architect, soldier or peasant, but never a politician.' He believed that in different circumstances of life he would have become a good and famous architect.

As a politician he did not treat building as a hobby, but – not unlike some of the former kings – as a means of his own aggrandizement. In his opinion, the greatness of a period was not measured by political achievements alone. With these, cultural achievements must go hand in hand. Architecture and the plastic arts would survive many generations.

Q. What were Hitler's architectural tastes?

A. He favored the classical style exclusively. His standards were the buildings of the 19th century in Vienna; his favorite architects Hansen and Semper, both of whom lived in the 19th century and erected many of Vienna's buildings.[16] He had a weakness for over-decorated, rich architecture – a line for which the decaying classical style of the 19th century had a marked tendency. Later he came into close contact with the architect Troost, who influenced him in favor of a calmer, more severe classical style.

In his spare time, in former days, sometime between 1925 and 1930, he occupied himself with fanciful architectural projects, which he sketched, fitting them into his future political frame.

His plans were much influenced by the city of Paris. He knew Paris well from illustrations and architectural works, and when it was occupied in 1940, he went there on a short visit with some of his artists. It was amazing how well he knew his way, even inside some of the buildings, purely owing to his study of the plans.

Q. Considering himself an architect, did he himself have much to do with the plans?

A. Even later on he sketched a great deal, and often in that way gave his architects a clear idea of what the building should look like. The sketches were technically correct. However, he always allowed the architects, whom he trusted, to carry out their own ideas. They were not to be guided by these sketches. The artist was the only one who could carry responsibility for his work. He therefore gave no 'orders', only suggestions.

Q. His artists, then, were quite favored by him?

A. They had a privileged place. They were envied by his politicians and his other collaborators, because they had such a free hand in their work. Though as a rule extremely aloof, his relationship with artists working for him was frank and unhampered. He discussed things with them as among 'colleagues'. Here one could converse and criticize quite frankly, even where his own opinions were concerned.

Q. Did you have the impression that he turned to art in order to escape temporarily from his political burdens?

A. His concern with architecture was doubtless a rest and a relaxation for him. He often said so himself. But to judge this activity in that light only would be to underestimate it.

Before the war he took this side of his work very much more seriously, and looked at it as an important part of the self-appointed tasks of his life. He described his desire to see his buildings erected as his life's greatest wish. These buildings were indeed so large, that even with strenuous activity, five to ten years would have been needed to realize them. Their combined cost, however, was less than that of our war expenditure for a few months.

Q. What was his attitude towards the other branches of art: painting, theater, etc.?

A. These, where he was concerned, were of little importance. Here he merely tried to rest and relax.

Remarkable was his preference for the 19th century and its creations in all spheres. He considered the 19th century the greatest cultural epoch. It lacked proper recognition, according to him, because it is so near to us. He was a passionate collector of 19th century painters.

Q. His activity in collecting pictures and other objects of art, was, as we have established, very intense. What was the reason for his collecting?

A. In contrast to Goering and many others, it was actually for the public. He intended after the war to found galleries in Linz, Koenigsberg, Breslau, and other eastern cities. He was annoyed about the private collections of Goering and others which, owing to their value, they had no right to keep from the public. But even here he came to no decision. His own art collections, in relation to his opportunities, were modest, and were mostly assembled before 1939.

Many art dealers were working for him, and in competition with each other they drove the prices, and consequently their profits, very high.

Q. What about his passion for music and the theater?

A. Where the theater is concerned, he privately favored the operettas, which he often visited for relaxation. It was nothing unusual for him to see a show he liked two or three times at intervals. He visited the Bayreuth Festival annually. That however sufficed for him for the whole year. He thought much of Wagner. Of the symphonies, he preferred those of Bruckner, who lived and worked in his native country. During the war he would often like to listen to gramophone records, again preferably passages out of operas and operettas – only very occasionally one of Bruckner's symphonies. These gramophone evenings were long and tiring. Only the biggest hypocrites could pretend to enjoy them. Of such, however, there were plenty. Once out of Hitler's circle they were about as fond of music as they were of being vegetarians.

Q. Did he have other pleasures and passions in his private life?

A. He condemned the gentlemanly sports of his 'important' colleagues, such as hunting and horse racing. In his opinion they were the remnants of the 'feudal rule' of the princes. He made fun of them in every possible way. He personally did not go in for sport. Nor was he in favor of it where his collaborators were concerned, as he was afraid of losing their services through accidents. But he was all in favor of youth's being trained for sport, and was an enthusiastic visitor of the Berlin Olympic Games. In sport he saw the 'Hellenic interpretation of life' partly realized.

Q. What was his conception of that?

A. Hitler regarded the Greek culture and interpretation of life in every sphere as absolutely perfect. In his view, they were the highest ideal to which youth could aspire. This was also the reason for his exclusive taste in architecture and sculpture. These conceptions of his were not founded in any profound historical studies.

Q. What were his relations with women?

A. Rumors that like many of his collaborators he was a ladies' man are untrue. Before the war, it is true, he enjoyed the company of women whom he considered beautiful, who were usually connected with the films or the stage. Their 'selection' was usually arranged by Goebbels. He appears, however, to have always remained true to the woman he loved, Fraulein Eva Braun. Her love was very significant for him; he spoke of her with great respect and deep reverence. He knew that he could have had any number of women; this he rejected, for, as he jokingly said, he did not know whether they would prefer him as 'Reich Chancellor' or as Adolf Hitler. 'Clever' women he would not have near him.

Q. Who was Fraulein Braun and what was her influence?

A. She was a modest woman. One must imagine the opportunities she had and how she could have exploited them as Hitler's prominent collaborators did. She did not do so. In this otherwise inadequate circle, she was a gain. She was no politician, though she had good common sense. She did not like Bormann. She did not, however, try seriously to influence Hitler, who would not have put up with it either. For all writers of history she is going to be a disappointment. She loved sport and was a good skier and mountain climber. Outwardly she often appeared conceited and haughty. That, however, was due to her inferiority complex; for her social position at Obersalzburg was not clearly defined. As the war was nearing its end, she flew to Berlin against Hitler's will. She resisted his efforts to send her back to Munich.

Of all those who during the last weeks lived together in the Berlin shelter, she was one of the bravest, and probably also the most intelligent. She wanted to stay in Berlin and die with Hitler.

In my opinion she carried out this plan. When I was there for the last time on 24 April 1945, she had detached herself from life. She was calm and determined and, at this time, one of the few who were faithful to Adolf Hitler – perhaps the only one. Earlier, Hitler had already asserted with resignation that he had only one friend who would remain loyal to the end in his decisive hour, and that was Eva Braun. We would never believe it. This time, however, his intuition had not failed him.

IV Hitler as Supreme Commander of the Wehrmacht and as Field Commander

Q. How did Hitler come to the conclusion that he alone was capable of leading the Wehrmacht and the army?

A. He attached vital importance to the military sphere. In his opinion, military leadership was a matter of intellect, tenacity, and nerves of iron. He felt that he possessed these qualities to a much higher degree than any of his generals. He was convinced that he alone could carry through this war. He felt that he alone was tough enough and inflexible enough to meet the blows of fate.

Owing to this conviction he felt justified in insisting on giving orders himself. His most intimate military circle did not dare to question his genius in this sphere; on the contrary, it did everything to strengthen him in his conviction.

Q. Did he go through any supplementary training?

A. No. He had undoubtedly read some books on military matters, but with emphasis on those concerned with the technical aspects of armaments. He had no thorough knowledge derived from experience of the sequence of actions which are released by a military order and which have to be considered in advance. Nor was he able later to improve his knowledge, as after 20 July 1944 the leading men in his military circle were definitely frightened.

Q. How did he make his decisions? In a general way, or taking in all the details?

A. Down to the last detail. The movement of every division was discussed with him. At the daily conferences on the situation even the most irrelevant details had to be reported.

While making up his mind, he was amenable to objections if they were put forward cleverly. But on the whole, his military circle would agree with everything in the end. Goering as well as Keitel played an unfortunate part in this respect. Both would accept Hitler's point of view unconditionally and uncritically, and would support him as strongly as possible. Even at the conferences on the situation in the East, where Zeitzler and later Guderian reported to Hitler, these two, in opposition to the reporting chief-of-staff, would support Hitler's optimistic point of view, thereby preventing many a sensible decision.

The shorthand reports dealing with the fate of Stalingrad will one day serve as tragic documentary evidence for the German people. Goering played a very unfortunate part in these discussions.

Q. Were decisions ever made on a long-term basis? How were they prepared and discussed?

A. By no means to the extent to which it was necessary, and not in the way you probably think. Hitler had little inclination for long-term studies. Besides, since 1942, such studies could only have arrived at conclusions most unwelcome to him. However, basic political questions apart, the military decisions would naturally have benefited from such general surveys. But the chief of the Wehrmachtfuehrungsstab hardly ever attempted to have such studies prepared and to force them upon Hitler.

Q. Did he take himself to be so much of a military leader and so infallible in his military decisions that such a procedure was possible?

A. He thought himself to be the best qualified of all to make the right decisions. His field marshals were only summoned 'in an advisory capacity'. He usually had a preconceived notion of what his decision would be. I do not know whether this was a result of his experiences of the first winter in Russia. At any rate he often repeated with much emphasis how his generals lost their nerve and their wits at the time, and insisted that it was merely due to his tenacity that the misfortune had not been greater. I think that in this case he was not altogether wrong. It was this period which confirmed him in his view that all his generals were inept.

The more difficult the situation became, the more he insisted that his orders were to be unconditionally obeyed. His order for the offensive of the 6th SS-Panzer Army in Hungary, issued in February 1945, provides an example.

His reaction to 20 July was indicative of the high opinion he had of himself as a military leader. He stressed the fact that the occurrence on 20 July historically justified him in his military decisions, in spite of the fact that during the last few years he had nothing but setbacks. These, however, he ascribed to the continuous treachery and intentional misinterpretation of his orders.

He issued an order that all the daily conferences on the situation should be taken down in shorthand verbatim, as he wanted to prove to posterity that he had always judged the position currently and given the right orders. Actually these documents are devastating for him and his entourage.[17]

Q. Hitler then, according to this, deemed himself to be a strategic genius, who kept to his preconceived opinions and plans, even when actual facts had overtaken them?

A. Yes, that was so. Then, when they turned out to be mistakes, he often did not want to admit that the orders had emanated from him. That was unjust and helped to bring about 20 July. In order to achieve his object, he sometimes tried to deceive his military entourage by false reports in order to make them accept his own line. Thus he tried to convince his field commanders that an immediate loss of the war would ensue from the abandonment of the manganese deposits in the Ukraine and later the nickel deposits in Finland, – in spite of the fact that, as he well knew, stocks were available for many months to come.

Q. What was the opinion of the high officers of Hitler's ability? Did they consider him an amateur who interfered with their business, or did they recognize him [sic]?

A. Our first set of high officers was very self-confident. Fritsch[18] was typical. They had to go. The officers after that became more cautious. The General Staff still had good officers, who however did not try to obtain any influence. Their disappointment and disillusionment were stored up for 20 July.

The second set, which received rapid promotion because it was adjusted to Hitler's surroundings, consisted of ambitious officers who would never openly express any unwelcome judgment even though they had formed it in their own minds.

Q. How is it possible that the German General Staff and the German generals put up with this situation, when they were otherwise so confident in themselves?

A. The answer to this question lies in the basic defect of all totalitarian systems, namely the bad selection of leaders. The unfortunate tendency towards the advancement of mediocre [individuals] began with Keitel himself. He brought with him colleagues of his own mental caliber, if only out of the instinct of self-preservation. In the military, as in the political sphere, Hitler became surrounded by anything but persons of character. They could only last if, right at the start, they had the subservient characteristics in their personalities which Hitler's old political henchmen had gradually acquired throughout the years. Keitel, Jodl, Warlimont, Winter, Buhler, Scherff were such types.[19] Zeitzler and Guderian tried to contradict, and had to go.[20] Krebs, Guderian's successor, was a smooth type, who could survive. Hitler's 'young field marshals', such as Rommel, Model, Schoerner, Kesselring, Hube, Dietl,[21] etc., in Hitler's presence always submitted to the laws of his entourage and only occasionally and 'tentatively' spoke their minds. They, too, took careful account of Hitler's peculiarities.

Q. Do you consider that the quality of the army was very much affected by this advancement of men who adapted themselves to Hitler?

A. In my opinion, this development was responsible for one basic fact. The right of criticism from below had been an important feature in the German army. A system based on authority, as typified by the army, can only survive if the subordinate can freely state his views to his superior. Therefore, I understand, criticism had always been encouraged in the German army, in order to avoid possible mistakes and so as to assure the contact of the leadership with the actual events. This system of criticism had always been difficult to maintain, for obvious reasons. The manner in which Hitler and his entourage governed and commanded was bound to stifle gradually every free opinion. Nobody in his surroundings had the courage to put forward his opinions, let alone stand up for them.

On the contrary, those who criticized lost their positions, or else fell into disgrace. In that way, command of the Army Groups gradually passed to officers who did not transmit criticisms to the High Command, but kept them to themselves, in that way also killing the criticism coming from their subordinates.

At the end of the war most senseless orders were not rejected and criticized, as they would have been before, but were accepted without protests. Some field commanders would only pretend to carry them out, while the less reasonable ones did and suffered heavy losses.

Q. When did the gradual abolition of criticism become an accomplished fact?

A. In 1942 it was already abolished to a great extent. In the spring of 1944 there was hardly any criticism in existence, and after 20 July all criticism ceased. From then onwards only 'blind obedience' existed. This was one of the disadvantages of Hitler's unfortunate policy for selection of military personnel, which in its turn was the direct result of Hitler's personality and of the totalitarian system.

Q. Do you believe that Hitler enjoyed the same authority among the mass of the army as in his immediate circle? Did they believe in his military genius, or was there personal criticism of him?

A. The officer corps of the field army definitely did not think of him as a great military leader. The private soldier was not in a position to see clearly in these matters. He would feel the inadequacy of orders from personal bitter experience, but he could not know who had issued those orders. I believe that the fact that the military decisions were dictated by Hitler to such an extent was not known either by the people or by the soldiers. They thought that the basic directives came from Hitler, but that Keitel and other high officers were responsible for the details.

Q. What were Hitler's other shortcomings as a military leader?

A. Many operations were either ordered or cancelled too late. He hesitated in his decisions and put them off from day to day, even when every hour was vital. As a result, great disasters were often only barely avoided in the East. 'Hedgehogs' were created unintentionally, merely because the retreat proposed by the General Staff had not been ordered in time. At the beginning of the invasion in the West, many days were lost in order to establish whether it was a feint, or a real invasion, and only then were the necessary orders given to Rommel.[22] No troops could be moved or sent into action without Hitler's approval. Army Group commanders lacked independence and only served as executive agents, even in minor matters. From experience they had learned always to secure orders from higher commands in order to be covered in case of casualties and defeats.

Q. In what form were orders given by Hitler?

A. OKW orders were usually issued as 'immediate Fuehrer orders'. These came out in great numbers and reduced the significance which should mark an order by the head of state and supreme commander. That was intentional. If possible Hitler was always to be made responsible for the consequences of such orders. As, however, numerous 'Fuehrer orders' came out which were not the result of Hitler's obstinacy, but had been put forward and proposed by the OKW, it was not a fair procedure.

Zeitzler, on the other hand, would give out Hitler's orders as his own even though he had been the only one to oppose them during the daily conferences and had been overruled. He was decent and did not want to hide behind Hitler's back. In his opinion he had to take responsibility for such orders, because he, in spite of being overruled by Hitler, had not resigned his post and in that way had acknowledged the order.

Q. Do you think that Hitler's decision to assume command of the army did in the long run make his influence even more unfortunate, or was it merely a formality?

A. That was the most unfortunate decision taken in this war, because, in consequence, the army was left without a commander-in-chief. A commander-in-chief is expected to defend the interests of his force and to have contact with his troops. He must currently make endless specific rulings – including matters of personnel – must iron out the differences between the army at home and the army at the front, and make decisions on questions of supply. Hitler of course had no time for this and no expert knowledge, so that actually the post of commander-in-chief of the army had been abolished.

Hitler did not bother about these specific questions, because he lacked technical knowledge. This part was more or less managed by Keitel, while the man who should have advocated the interests of the army vis-à-vis the head of state was missing. In consequence the army was gravely handicapped by the fact that the head of state himself was also its commander-in-chief, strange as the fact might seem.

Q. He however took particular interest in the army's equipment?

A. Yes. Yet here he apparently had accumulated knowledge which was superior to that of his military staff. He was better informed than they about the characteristics of specific weapons and tanks, ammunition types and innovations. Actually he knew more than was good for one in his high position.

He was closely familiar with the achievements of the First World War and his comparisons with performance in that war were at times embarrassing for us. He revelled in showing off what he knew.

Q. As Supreme Commander of the Wehrmacht as a whole, did he take interest also in armaments problems of the Luftwaffe and the navy?

A. He kept away from Luftwaffe matters up to the summer of 1944, in order not to offend Goering, who was very touchy about it. He very occasionally asked for reports on naval equipment.

Q. Did Hitler, then, have competent technical knowledge?

A. Yes, undoubtedly. Ever since 1930 he had shown interest in technical details, e.g. of automobile construction, and could easily acquire a grasp of technical questions. He could intelligently follow complicated reports, better certainly than his entourage. After my experiences as his architect, I introduced to him industrial technical experts and ordnance board officers. He was amenable to their arguments, and was even prepared to revise preconceived opinions of his own. I found that he readily accepted the judgments of qualified technical experts.

Had his military entourage realized that in time, and had it given the experienced officers of the front a chance to speak to him as 'experts', his judgments would have been sounder in many cases. But they were afraid that such a procedure would only have revealed their own lack of knowledge.

It often seemed that Hitler took refuge from his military responsibilities in long discussions of armaments and war production. He engaged in them for relaxation, as he had in architecture before the war. He would often say so himself. Thus, I was responsible, as before the war, in a sphere which engaged his personal as well as official interest.

IVa Hitler as Field Commander

Q. To what extent did Hitler's attitude to the Wehrmacht contribute to the 20 July plot?

A. The 20 July 1944 did not have its origins exclusively in the war situation. Its instigators had of course a clear picture of our future prospects in the war, and no doubt wanted to finish it, without actually knowing how they could do so. Without the conditions in the Fuehrer Headquarters itself, however, the conspiracy could never have assumed such proportions.

After the autumn of 1943, Hitler had expressed more and more outspokenly his discontent with the army officers. He was completely unrestrained in his remarks. Blunt statements that the officers were without honor, without intelligence, that they were liars, that he was dealing with nothing but a bunch of crooks, were often made by him in the presence of numerous army officers. Not one in his higher military circle ever protested against these statements, or tried to take any kind of action.

Doenitz would no doubt promptly have done so if the navy had been similarly attacked, just as I would have spoken up on behalf of armaments production.

High officers were sharply condemned by Hitler after they had saved soldiers out of impossible situations.

All the factors which have been discussed above exercised an aggravating influence. The army's hatred was directed more and more against Keitel, who was described as a complete failure, but to an increasing extent also against Hitler personally. Hitler could not be moved to adopt a more conciliatory tone. On the contrary he became even more aggressive. Owing to that the opposition movement acquired more and more followers. I am convinced that 20 July would not have occurred if Hitler had adopted a more decent attitude, and if there had been a real commander-in-chief of the army, even if the military and political situation had been just the same.

Q. How did Hitler come to the opinion that he was being deceived?

A. The basic reason was his lack of first-hand knowledge of conditions at the front. From 1942 onwards Hitler and his military collaborators only very seldom went to the front. He himself refused to undertake trips to the front and discouraged his principal collaborators from doing so. Before 1940 he had been courageous and ignored all security precautions on his journeys, entering restaurants and cafés, for instance, unannounced. After the outbreak of the war, however, his concern for his own life became more and more obvious.

It was his point of view – even in his conversations in 1942 – that he was the only one who had the toughness to see this war through. He asserted that anybody else was bound to fail in this task. He would drop hints that even more difficult situations were yet to come, adding that then he would show how steadfast he was, how good his nerves were. 'It was a good thing that this decisive war [was] waged under his leadership.' This conviction, dictated by his belief in his predestined fate, made him believe in his indispensability for Germany and induced him to adopt all the measures taken for the protection of his own person and his collaborators. As the bombing became more intense he counted on heavy raids on his headquarters and ordered the construction of vast shelters and whole underground cities in various parts of Germany, in order to be able to work in safety. It was understandable that, in this state of mind, he did not want to expose his life to the risks, however slight, of visits to the front.

It is completely incomprehensible, however, why his military leaders did not visit the front either. It is true that Hitler warned them against doing so, but in spite of that warning they could have gone. Lack of time could not have been the reason, for the front was often only at two or three hours' distance from the Fuehrer's headquarters.

I suspect that the reasons which kept them from the front were their guilty consciences, fear of justified reproaches, lack of knowledge of front-line conditions, and the impossibility of answering the questions about the eventual outcome of the war which were bound to be asked of them at the front – all that apart from considerations of personal safety, from the trifling dangers of strafing and other importunities. I felt embarrassed when, on my visits to the front, I was cordially received, but was also told that a visit from Keitel, Jodl, Buhle, Leeb, Zeitzler, or Guderian would have been of much greater importance and more appropriate. I was envious of the fact that these things were so different on the side of our enemy at the time. Make a point, in your investigations, of establishing what journeys to the front actually were made by Hitler's most important military collaborators. You will be astounded.

Hitler and his military colleagues thought themselves capable of conducting operations entirely from their situation maps. They knew nothing of the Russian winter, with its road conditions, or of the hardships of the soldiers who, inadequately equipped, had to be quartered in the open for weeks at a time. This undermined their powers of resistance. They were overtired and worn out. At the conference at the Fuehrer's headquarters, however, such units were regarded as fully operational and disposed of accordingly by Hitler. They knew nothing of the heavy air attacks in the West and the resultant inadequacy and difficulty of supplies, of the poor equipment of the troops, and of the lack of motor fuel and ammunition.

They never saw the bomb damage caused by the enemy in the towns and did not realize the immediate threat to armaments production, which was so vital for the prosecution of the war. During the entire war Hitler had never visited a bombed city.[23] Owing to this ignorance, the picture of the situation presented during the daily conferences became ever more inaccurate, and Hitler's most important decisions were based on false promises. They became completely unrealistic. Divisions exhausted with fighting, completely lacking weapons and ammunition, were disposed of and shifted to and fro on the map.

At the front, the division commanders were at a loss as to what to do with such orders. The time limits fixed for troop movements could not be adhered to in the circumstances. As a result the leading elements, without being able to form an organized force, were sent into battle in small sections and were dispersed and annihilated piecemeal.

Units without weapons, the so-called March Battalions, were sent into action. The Luftwaffe field divisions, consisting of totally inexperienced air corps officers and men, suffered heavy casualties, for no other reason than that the commander-in-chief of the Luftwaffe had the ambition to keep his formations, and because Hitler approved of this for political reasons.

New divisions were formed in great numbers, equipped with new weapons and sent to the front without any experience or training, while at the same time the good battle-hardened units bled to death because they were given no replacements of weapons and personnel. In that way, weapons and valuable lives were wasted. The best young recruits were allocated to the Waffen SS,[24] which thus acquired a surplus of valuable candidates for officers and non-commissioned officers. They were here available in such numbers that they could not all be put to proper use, and remained in subordinate positions. The army and Luftwaffe, by contrast, lacked such men, and the standard and numbers of its non-commissioned officers declined steadily, while in the Waffen SS great numbers of suitable men met their death as ordinary soldiers. The 'Hitler Youth' Division of the Waffen SS consisted of the cream of German youth. Without having a skeleton staff of old soldiers experienced at the front, they were relentlessly sent into action, which meant a steady blood-letting of the best German youth, without any military advantage.

Q. Should not Hitler's military entourage have kept Hitler informed of such matters, and was it not therefore responsible for these mistakes?

A. His entourage certainly shared in the responsibility for this. In spite of that, however, the heaviest share of the guilt for the conditions which caused the unnecessary death of many soldiers was to be borne by Hitler, as he was the commander-in-chief of the army. As the head of state he would not have been expected repeatedly to visit the front. The troops however were entitled to expect it from the commander-in-chief of the army, particularly in view of his system of making personal decisions on all details. History will not absolve him of the blame for not having done so. If he was too ill, he should have delegated the responsibility to somebody else. If he was too concerned about his life, he should not have been commander-in-chief.

The basic mistakes, which resulted in so much bloodshed and caused so much worry to all senior field commanders, could have been easily recognized and corrected after a few trips to the front by Hitler and his staff. Owing to the inadequate information on the actual situation at the front, virtually no GHQ orders could be carried out towards the end. Owing to lack of criticism from below, orders were executed either really or in appearance only, but mostly without achieving the intended results.

Add to that the negative characteristics, which made Hitler impossible as a Supreme Commander: his inadequate training, his lack of contact with the front and with the troops, his treatment of officers, his disastrous hesitation on the one hand, and on the other his conscious gambling on the strength of his 'luck'; his wilful sacrifice of soldiers' lives and fundamentally amoral conceptions, all the more apparent in the last stages. These characteristics, viewed in the light of the many battles they lost, will compel the historians of this war to pass a harsh judgment on him. The full extent of Hitler's inadequacy as a military leader is yet unknown to the German people, just as it does not realize how thoughtlessly he threw away the lives of German soldiers in the last phases of the war. Churchill's remark that as leader of military operations Hitler was the best ally of the United Nations is unfortunately only too true.

As during the war the entire emphasis of his work was concentrated on military matters, his complete failure in this sphere is an essential component of his career, more important in fact than were the successes which made him respected by and popular with the people. His positive achievements, such as his successes in the social sphere, were impressed on the people by powerful propaganda; but the fatal part which he played in the conduct of the war is as yet known to a small circle only.

That the war was inevitably lost from the beginning, the German people now know full well.

Through his obstinacy and his mistakes, however, he brought misery to innumerable people, needlessly surrendered many soldiers to a sad fate or death, and through the Volkssturm[25] he tried to drag the entire population into the whirlpool of events. In the end, when he saw himself doomed he consciously wanted to annihilate the German people, and to destroy the last foundations of its existence.

Thereby he more than outbalanced, he completely obliterated all the good that he originally wanted to do for the people.

Conclusion

Up to the beginning of the war, my relations with Hitler were marked by the fanatical enthusiasm which he was bound to inspire in any artist working for him. He was an ideal patron, and I was his architect in whom he had full confidence. This resulted in an intimate contact.

Although from 1942 onwards, as Minister, I retained the privilege of belonging to his 'private circle', our relations lost their previous informality as a result of my new task, and other circumstances created serious friction in our relations.

After the beginning of 1944 the intrigue conducted against me from outside began to meet with success,[26] and on the other hand my own attitude towards Hitler, and developments in general, gradually became clearer, until finally, in January 1945, it changed to active resistance against the policy which he had laid down. From then on, and not only within my official jurisdiction, I had to plan, initiate and execute many acts which were directed against his course of action, or against himself.

The erratic path which he followed led to terrible consequences. He deliberately attempted to let the people perish with himself. He no longer knew any moral boundaries, a man to whom the end of his own life meant the end of everything.

Although he was aware of my negative attitude, he kept me by his side. I, on my part, distinguished during that period between my duty towards the people and my personal relations with Hitler. It was this distinction, and also my desire to help him in cutting short his final struggle, which made me fly to Berlin on 24 April 1945, one of the last to do so, in order to bid him farewell, or to stay with him if he demanded it.

Although inwardly I had broken with him by that time, it has been difficult for me even now to write this study. I feel it to be my duty to help in exploring his faults, which were at the bottom of his disastrous influence, equally tragic for ourselves and for the world. Even if sometimes I had to speak in blunt terms, I should not like to be counted among those who malign him in order to exonerate themselves.

Was Hitler, as a historic phenomenon, a product of the aftermath of the First World War, was he a [con]sequence of the Versailles Treaty, the revolution, and the events which followed? Was he a figure which these events would inevitably have produced?

It is true that without these events he would never have found the soil on which his activity could bear fruit so rapidly and on such a scale. His whole demonic figure, however, can never be explained as just a product of those events. They could have just as well expressed themselves in a national leader of mediocre stature. He was one of those inexplicable historic phenomena of nature which emerge in mankind at rare intervals. His person determined the fate of the nation. He alone placed it and kept it on a path which now has found its end in a gloomy future. The nation was spellbound by him as a people had rarely been before in history.

The meaning of such unique historic events, whether they be called French Revolution, Spanish Inquisition, Napoleon, Hitler or Stalin, cannot be explained, like so many things in this world. It was the fate of mankind to produce four formidable men simultaneously who settled their differences with a consistency which had not seen its equal before.[27] It may be that the disaster will be followed by the calm which we are all longing for. Perhaps it has paved the way for sounder solutions.

Everyone who has gone through the tragedy of the past year on our side must shudder before the tragic and inexorable fate which has befallen us.

The possibility of a repetition of the absolute rule by one man, surrounded by weaklings, must be prevented for all time to come. On this question there should not even be the opportunity for a free choice. Never again must the path of a nation be allowed to depend so exclusively on one pair of eyes; or to be determined to such an extent by the mind and the abilities of a single man, as was the case in the era of Adolf Hitler.

Document 2 Hitler's Women

'Women around Hitler':
report written at 'Dustbin' by Dr Karl Brandt (n.d.), sent to interrogator
Major E. Tilley on 6 February 1946

Whenever Hitler graced his mountain retreat the Berghof with his presence, it meant for him a break in his normal duty routine, and it enabled him to lead the life of a private individual.

Apart from the normal retinue of adjutants and officials, other guests were commodiously accommodated either in single or double bedrooms at the Berghof. As much as possible was done to separate the guests proper from Hitler's own officials and it was only on rare occasions that they ever met. In this way Hitler was able to enjoy to the full the company and confidence of his guests in complete privacy. Not only did the prominent personages such as Heinrich Hoffmann,[28] Esser[29] and other high party officials play an important part in Hitler's life, but so also did other lesser men and women who were around him. For example his host of women secretaries shared in part the intoxicating atmosphere of the Berghof.

The Berghof was managed by an SS man and his wife, who, apart from their duties, were comparatively unimportant. The couple was accommodated in a side wing of the building. The notorious Eva Braun was lavishly installed in the main building. She had never before played the role of the 'housewife'.

It was only in later years that Eva aspired to becoming, and successfully became, the leading lady of the Berghof. She charmed all guests and her convincing personality won her esteem and respect. It was not an easy task for Eva to please Hitler. To my knowledge Hitler first met Eva in 1932 when he was introduced to her by Heinrich Hoffmann, in whose employ she was at that time.

It would appear that at this period Hitler was still very much under the influence of his niece, Geli Raubal,[30] the daughter of his sister Angelika. Moreover, Hitler was deeply indebted to his niece for her loyalty and comfort during the early years of his struggle.

I have heard it said that Geli was a woman of high and noble character, and her influence over all those whom she met was that of a spell. Geli died in 1928 and it is said that it was suicide. Hereafter Hitler never mentioned her name nor was the episode ever discussed, but I remember that the emotion with which Hitler spoke of her in earlier years amounted to the worship of a Madonna. Her room in Hitler's Munich flat has been preserved and left untouched ever since, and moreover Hitler requested that an exact replica of this room be built in his new home in Munich.

It is odd that Hitler, feeling the deep devotion that he did for Geli, should have been influenced by the entirely different personality of Eva Braun. Perhaps it is a tragic perception hiding Hitler's subconscious belief when he once exclaimed in 1934 that 'the greater the man the more insignificant should be the woman'. By saying this it seems that Hitler was giving expression to the emotion that great men with all their responsibilities had no right to bind themselves to intelligent women, not even in matrimony.

A marriage where an intelligent woman must remain in the background of affairs must inevitably fail; the happier union would be therefore with a woman of modest homely gifts who is satisfied with the normal everyday fundamentals of home life and yet is ever prepared to welcome her partner.

In the case of Eva Braun, it appears that her assured charm and intelligence embodied just those qualities which formed a contented alliance between herself and Hitler.

It is all the more astonishing that in spite of the unfavourable influence of relatives and friends, Eva underwent a complete change for the better whilst with Hitler, a change which, however, did not make a 'great woman' but certainly transformed her into a 'lady'.

Eva was the daughter of a university teacher and in consequence she acquired a thoroughly sound education. Until her teens she visited [sic] a convent school. My first impression of Eva was that she was a woman who had suddenly been transplanted into the whirl and scurry of world society – with it went the fine clothes, luxury and jewels and her changing moods under which certain guests had to suffer. As years went by, particularly during the early war years, Eva's character seemed to undergo a complete change, she grew more serious, and busied herself more with the domestic affairs at the Berghof and the Fuehrer's flat in Munich. At this period, she tried to understand and perhaps to share the mind and thoughts of the Fuehrer. To attain this object, Eva began studiously to read and to improve her knowledge and general educational outlook.

A stranger meeting Eva at this period would have undoubtedly gained the impression of a young, slightly spoiled lady, who although not a 'great' personality was certainly gifted with exceeding charm of manner, and vitality. At first glance it would seem astonishing that this gentle person could possess such a strong character – rather would one have expected to find a kind and obliging woman.

There can be no doubt that Eva was deeply in love with Hitler whom, until recent years, she addressed as 'Mein Fuehrer'.

True, in all, Hitler was not the complete lover pictured in Eva's romantic young heart, but he was the man to comfort her and care for her like a father. Hitler always tried to make life for her with him as pleasant and happy as possible.

He showered upon her every charm and kindness and allowed her to enjoy any of the small daily luxuries which life at the Berghof could offer. Indubitably, it must have been difficult for Eva to fit with Hitler's daily routine. Hitler's day was mostly taken up in conferences one after the other lasting until late evening.

It was only after dinner that the small exclusive party had time for private conversation where they remained until the early hours of the morning.

Even from that Hitler would retire to his work room to study the latest news and reports.

It seems very doubtful whether or not Eva played any part in the political scheme of things or whether she had any political influence whatsoever.

Here and there perhaps she may have used her influence over Hitler to help or speak for one or other friend, but she herself did not plan out any particular ambitious career.

To ask whether Hitler remained true to Eva is ludicrous. For a man of such prominence as Hitler, whose every move was known to the public, it would have been impossible for him to have done otherwise. Eva Braun herself would not have been justified in doubting Hitler's loyalty, for so long as she remained the chosen one at his side, she had very little to fear. After all, Hitler had done much for Eva in discovering her as an almost nonentity and placing her in prominence by his side.

Hitler and his Eva were certainly bound together by a deep emotional understanding and this is surely proved by the fact that he did eventually go through the ceremony of marriage with her during their last hours on 30 April 1945. (This was reported by the Press.)

It is quite natural that Hitler enjoyed the company of other women around him, but this had no special significance. One of these women was Leni Riefenstahl.[31] There are two reasons why Hitler insisted on remaining a bachelor and these he often confirmed in his own words.

The first is that Hitler perhaps felt that Eva Braun was not quite the proper personage to be presented to the nation as the wife of the head of the state.

The second and certainly the most preponderant reason was that Hitler wished to keep the mystic legend alive in the hearts of the German people that so long as he remained a bachelor, there was always the chance that any out of the millions of German women might possibly attain the high distinction of being at Hitler's side. Hitler believed this to be very sound psychology and he even spoke of this in Eva's presence.

According to the Press, Hitler was the father of two children by Eva. But she never had any children, and Hitler was often heard to say that the children of famous men had all the disadvantages in life.

The two children said to be Eva's were possibly those of a Mrs Schneider, a friend of Eva's who had resided at the Berghof for many years.

Eva Braun has two sisters, one of whom is Gretel Braun, who married Gruppenfuehrer Fegelein last year and the other, Ilse Braun, who married in Breslau. The latter played no prominent part in Eva's life and saw her only on rare occasions. Gretel, however, saw much of her sister both at the Berghof and also when they shared a small villa in Munich, Wasserburgerstrasse. Eva made great use of her younger sister, who served her almost like a personal maid. Even in the close circle of her own family, Eva played the role of the 'great lady'. Her parents were modest people who led a secluded life and were never much in the foreground of Eva's affairs.

At the beginning of the war Eva's father volunteered to join up in the services although he was an old man already in retirement. Finally, he was given the post of a paymaster in the German army.

In character Gretel Braun was generous and good-natured, but was far too easily influenced by others. Her marriage was thus very possibly contracted in a mood of fancy rather than governed by the principle of love.

Hitler was fond of Gretel and liked her company. He would often converse with her alone and enjoyed a certain 'mother-wit' which characterized her. Among the guests who frequented the Berghof was one Frau Marion Schoenmann. Her husband was an architect in Munich and was only seen at the Berghof on rare occasions. Marion was acquainted with Hoffmann and was also friends with Eva Braun. She was of Austrian origin and closely associated with the Vienna Opera circles through a certain 'Auntie Lu'. There were mutual recollections from the time of Hitler's youth which gave Frau Schoenmann the opportunity of having many talks with Hitler. They never mentioned her parents. She combined a very developed understanding of art with an unusually thorough knowledge of its history. With her remarkable cleverness and an intelligence far above the average she gave the tone to the women's conversation when she was present at the Berghof. She was typically Viennese with all its lively and spirited character. This woman in her forties, Hitler would have said 'hardly forty', possessed infinite experience of life and had the rare gift of being able to influence Hitler. She was a talented conversationalist and was always able to make her point in argument with well-chosen words even if the discussion was against the known beliefs of Hitler. She never hesitated to criticize the shortcomings of any of the prominent Party leaders. And it is natural that she showed a specific interest in the conditions prevailing in Vienna (Schirach)[32] and Munich. When these discussions grew too serious it was Hitler's custom to lead the conversation into lighter channels and to defend the interests of his men. Sometimes the discussions became extremely heated, but Hitler showed great tact in handling the matter, and Frau Marion did not overstep the bounds of good manners. A certain friction between Hitler and Eva became evident of recent times, and here Heinrich Hoffmann played a part.

It must be emphasized that Hitler's relation to Marion seemed not to be the cause of any jealousy on Eva's part. However, to avoid any further ill-feeling Marion stayed away from the Berghof except for a few occasional visits. It would appear that the discussions were somewhat unpleasing to Hitler because he did not ask for her presence.

Other womenfolk at the Berghof were not so much an influence on Hitler's life; they were solely to be near their respective husbands, for it was Hitler's wish that man and wife where possible should live together. For this purpose, the necessary rooms had been added when the Berghof was rebuilt so that the adjutants etc. were able to find room for their wives.

To this end ample accommodation for Hitler's adjutants and deputies and their wives was made available when the new Berghof building was constructed. My wife Anni Brandt belonged to this circle. She had known Hitler since 1925 and incidentally was a German swimming champion for several years in succession. Hitler always treated my wife in a friendly manner but she was never of her own accord much in the limelight. Frau Speer was in a somewhat similar position. She never played any political part and was noticeable for her intentional reserve. Both Frau Speer and my wife became more friendly towards Eva Braun in later years than was the case when they first met. Professor Morell and his wife joined Hitler's circle of friends in 1935. The Professor and in particular his wife strived to be in the good graces of Eva Braun, and unlike other guests they showered presents upon her (handbags, jewel-cases, etc.). This was not the custom at the Berghof until then. Frau Morell, whose past was not all that could be desired, found little in common with the other guests at the Berghof and perhaps it was for this reason that she clung to Eva Braun. It is probable that through this connection Mrs M. tried to help her husband in his effort to become the director of a pharmaceutical firm. As a woman and a human being, Mrs M. did not impress me very much. The wife of Reich leader Bormann came to the Berghof only occasionally. Hers was such a modest character that she kept in the background. Moreover, her husband would have forbidden her to show any spirit of independence. She lived in a house with her eight children only a few minutes away from the Berghof.

No prominent part was played by any other feminine visitors. Frau v. Buelow, who was a most active and cheerful person, was a very popular visitor. On the whole, however, there were no personal ties between these ladies on the one hand, and Eva Braun and Hitler on the other.

Hitler's lady secretaries played their own special part. This was due to the fact that they not only alternatively [sic] accompanied Hitler on his journeys, and were therefore present during important events, but they also belonged to the private circle and so were allowed to share the social life at the Berghof. Being the oldest, Hitler's personal secretary was Miss Johanna Wolf, former secretary of Dietrich Eckart.[33] She has peculiarly human qualities. Though placed in a high position, Frl. Wolf lived a very modest life and whenever time allowed she would stay with her 80-year-old mother. Frl. Wolf proved helpful at all times and showed the greatest tact in settling arbitrarily occasional disputes. Though of a somewhat melancholy character, she could show a great sense of humour.

To Hitler she proved a most loyal assistant, giving of her best, regardless of her own health. Owing to heart trouble and a chronic gall bladder complaint, she was somewhat pushed into the background by younger secretaries not always in a very nice way. Hitler, however, took a 'keen' interest in the well-being of Frl. Wolf and arranged for her current medical supervision, treatment and cures. It seemed that Frl. Wolf's quiet and gentle manner brought about somewhat sentimental ties between Hitler and herself. Also her extraordinary true and open character contributed to the happy relation of Hitler and his secretary. At the beginning of the war, Hitler employed two secretaries, one of which was Frl. Wolf (senior) and the other Frl. Christa Schroeder. Only on rare occasions were they replaced by Frl. Daranowski.

Miss Schroeder was not only highly intelligent but showed the rare gift of handling people skilfully. She also was a most critical person. She was of enormous perseverance and to quote one example I remember how she took dictation for several days and nights without a pause. Up to the very last day (of her secretarial work) she would not hesitate to express her views, even though they may have been against the beliefs of Hitler. At times this would lead to controversy, and Frl. Schroeder would choose herself to stay away from the Berghof, or be made to stay away. Though she suffered greatly under this state of affairs, she would not give up her right to criticize Hitler to an extent that brought her into danger.

As a human being or indeed as a woman she did not achieve any close communion with Hitler. In latter years, Frl. Schroeder was frequently under medical treatment. She had trouble with hormones, which necessitated long and continuous curative treatment at different health resorts. Frl. Schroeder was popular with her colleagues and with Hitler's close associates.

She had acquired a somewhat peasant servility due to the mode of working during the war period.

Frl. G. Daranowski, who married General Christian, one of Hitler's recent air force adjutants, played a special role in the circle of secretaries. She was an up-to-date woman with an enormous amount of vitality. The desire to ingratiate was evident. She was professionally efficient and her patience matched that of Frl. Schroeder but her character was directly the opposite. In her conversation with Hitler she was invariably in agreement with his views and avoided the slightest conflict of opinion. She certainly exercised feminine influence over him.

She did everything to heighten these sentiments. This was certainly not prompted by altruistic motives, but was connected with a resolve to play a definite role around Hitler or to obtain some kind of privilege for herself. Here may be mentioned her marriage to the General-to-be Christian, who was appointed Chief of the Operational Department of the air force on Hitler's orders and against the wishes and interests of Goering. One cannot but assume that Frl. Daranowski, who remained Hitler's secretary even after her marriage to the General, played a decisive role in this appointment.

The relations between Frl. Daranowski and Eva Braun – and vice versa – were naturally tense. Hitler knew it. This fact, however, exerted no influence during all those years, and during these times when Hitler was at his headquarters, no matter where the lady secretaries were, Frl. Daranowski was always the centre of attraction at the nightly tea-table talks. It must certainly also be attributed to her influence that Hitler – possibly as the result of strong hints, regarding the poor state of health of Frl. Wolf and later also of Frl. Schroeder – kept these two ladies absent from his surroundings and made him insist on lengthy visits to health resorts for them both.

Frau Christian appeared to have no particular affectionate relationship to her husband. (Obviously, one can be mistaken on this point.) She never bothered actively about the three children of his first marriage. After a few days these children were sent to their grandparents, where they remained. It was just a case of Frau Christian coquetting with the idea of being 'mother' to three children and with the arduous duties that lay before her.

A former servant of Hitler's, Junge, very soon married a secretary who had come from the Fuehrer's secretariat as helper. Frau Junge, a native of Munich, who was very young to find herself in this privileged position, at once blossomed forth in her new surroundings. With her amiability and charm she found the right thing to say to everyone. Very soon she became one of those in Hitler's circle who would have been most missed. She combined a naivety – possibly assumed – with the freshness and unaffectedness of youth. She was clever, not to say 'sly'. Wishing to somehow play a role herself, yet she was far from getting herself up against her colleagues or discrediting them. Hitler was fond of her, although he treated her in a somewhat fatherly manner. He often pointed out how like Frl. Braun, Frau Junge would become.

Frl. Martiali was a native of Innsbruck. Her father was Greek, her mother Tyrolese. She had been at a domestic economy school and was temporarily with Prof. Zabel in Berchtesgaden. He had in the previous year prescribed the vegetarian diet for Hitler which he used to send to the Berghof from his sanatorium. So Frl. Martiali sometimes visited the kitchen there to prepare the meals. At this time, Hitler was suffering increasingly from intestinal troubles and as the dietary assistant (a half-Jewess) who had come from Marshall [sic] Antonescu[34] was leaving, the choice fell on Frl. Martiali. Her appearance was quite plain and she would have passed unperceived wherever she went. She was unbelievably humble and unobtrusive but now and then she was present at the evening teas at headquarters. She really only spoke when an answer was required of her. She took trouble to make Hitler's meals nourishing and varied which with the scant possibilities open to [her] was doubtless very difficult. For instance she prepared sweets for Hitler with immense care. He appreciated and gratefully accepted this care for his person. Probably not a day passed without his referring to it, and he often spoke of the coming meal and the surprises Frl. Martiali had in store for him. It would almost appear as though the well-known phrase 'Love enters through the stomach' was true in this case. Hitler, who nearly always ate alone, often invited Frl. Martiali to share his meals on the pretext that she must taste her own dishes. This went so far that even in Berlin – when Frl. Braun was there – she had to take second place and had to eat alone whilst Hitler lunched or dined with Frl. Martiali or sometimes with one or other of the lady secretaries.

Frl. Martiali, quite alive to her position, thereupon tried to play a decisive role. How far this succeeded it is impossible to say. It is a fact, however, that from time to time differences would arise between Hitler and Frl. Braun, on this subject, without their occasioning any change on Hitler's part.

The ladies mentioned above such as Frl. Wolf, Frl. Schroeder, etc. all played different roles during the war to those they had played in peacetime. The fact that they joined in the war as women meant that they had to become accustomed to a rougher way of living. From another point of view – looked at with a masculine eye – they also played a special role. Even for Hitler himself they provided pleasant entertainment, especially in the evenings. After talks on the situation had finished at midnight or even at 2 a.m. then began the so-called 'tea'. All the ladies came to it, or attended it alternatively [*sic*]. Some of them had already slept so they came to the tea-table fresh and lively. Certain of Hitler's personal staff and his army adjutants also attended, but no other soldiers. Surrounding a round table there were about eight armchairs in which the single guests sat. Frl. Daranowski almost always sat on Hitler's left and on his right one of the other ladies, latterly Frl. Martiali. The subjects discussed naturally varied. Occasionally some critical happening was discussed, but more often trivialities were the order of the day. It may be mentioned that meanwhile Hitler's wolf-dog played a perfectly unbearable role at these teas.

Hitler's flat in Munich – in the Prinzregentenstrasse – was looked after by a married couple named Winter. The husband attended to all details, repairs, etc. in the house. The main work was done, however, by Frau Winter herself, whose position was that of housekeeper. She had known Hitler for many years. She came from modest surroundings. She kept the flat – consisting of five rooms – in order and looked after Hitler – where it was not the duty of the men-servants – whilst he was in Munich. She cooked simple meals for him which consisted principally of eggs, vegetables and salads. Over and above this she played a certain role owing to the fact that she recounted all the Munich gossip to Hitler and laid before him many appeals and questions which were addressed to him. Vital things she naturally passed on to the secretariat. All this undoubtedly gave her a key position, even if only a small one, from which she was able to influence Hitler regarding certain persons or their activities. One gained the impression that Hitler attached importance to her views and that he himself often asked her for her opinion. When this became more widely known it was evident that this not quite simple woman was treated with remarkable politeness and consideration by influential people. Gauleiter Wagner,[35] for instance, kept her supplied with theatre tickets, etc. She tried to pose as a lady moving in the highest circles; but she was good-natured and enabled many humble people to get certain facilities and to obtain interviews – even with Hitler. Her relations with Frl. Braun, whom she also looked after – were good. She answered the telephone, and this alone made her position a very confidential one. Frau Winter was fairly well known in Munich; where this was not the case, she soon remedied it herself.

There were a number of women who were often mentioned by Hitler in conversation and who attracted his attention owing to their peculiarities or their personalities. If, first of all, one mentions Frau Hess, it is because of Hitler's aversion to this woman. If any opportunity arose to express an adverse judgement then she was the object of it. He characterized her as a type of 'man-woman' whose ambition made her strive to dominate the man and therefore almost lose her own femininity. Her preoccupation with handicrafts – which he did not share – is interesting but not important. When Frau Hess after many years of married life had a child to whom she was devotedly attached, Hitler described her feelings as 'theatrical'.

She was the first to call Hitler 'Chief', by which name he was known for many years in his immediate working entourage. Whether there were other personal reasons for the unhappy relations between Hitler and the family of his former deputy is not known. It is probably that this clever woman with her sober outlook could never have had any affinity with a man of the type of Hitler.

There was in Munich another woman, Frau Troost, on whom Hitler had conferred the title of 'Professor'. She was the wife of the architect Troost[36] who had designed the Party buildings and the Haus der Kunst (Art Institute) in Munich. Frau Troost, whilst lacking any outward charm, had intelligence far above the average. Ambitious and clever, she understood how, through her mutual intellectual interests with Hitler, to play a leading role, if not the leading role, in the art circles in Munich. It was of course natural that she should be feared in those circles and harshly criticized in her turn. She has a remarkably developed sense of colour and in the development of her dead husband's work she has influenced the whole colour scheme of the new public buildings in Munich, and their interior architecture. She understood how to demonstrate to Hitler the effects of colour gradations and as she cared both for the heavy colours of the Makart period and also for finer shades of colour, it was easy for her to find complete agreement with Hitler. When he went to Munich, if it was possible he always visited the 'Atelier Troost' within the first few hours of his arrival, and there he spent hours talking and discussing with Frau Troost and her colleague Prof. Gall, matters in general, but especially subjects connected with art. It is natural that Frau Troost was almost always one of the guests invited to be present at the simple midday meals at the Osteria Bavaria in the Briennerstrasse. As she was usually the only woman present she sat on Hitler's right hand and from there she and Hitler led the conversation.

Two elderly ladies were also members of the Munich circle. One was Frau Bruckmann, widow of the art publisher, whom Hitler sometimes visited. The hours spent with this witty woman, who was well on to the seventies, always meant something special to Hitler. Although the subject of their talks was doubtless mainly recollections, yet the way of looking at things shown by this woman was so prized by Hitler that he talked about it long afterwards, and often referred to it even weeks later.

The same applies to a Frau Hoffmann who in spite of her age of more than eighty years had remained robust and who cherished a special loving regard for Hitler. He thought nothing of travelling from Berlin to Munich to present his birthday wishes to her in person. She was one of the first Party members in Munich and in Hitler's eyes was part of it. Neither of these two ladies played any political role.

The eight-day visit to Bayreuth for the Wagner Festival provided a special interruption of the year's activities. Hitler stayed in an annexe of the Haus Wahnfried, usually alone with his adjutant Schaub – or Brueckner – and a servant. There was on the ground floor of this annexe a fairly large dining-room for twenty-five to thirty persons, a correspondingly large lounge and open verandah which overlooked the old garden. A covered way led to Haus Wahnfried where the Wagner family lived. This festival time was for Hitler – apart from the musical impressions made on him by the operas – a proof of his friendship with the Wagner family. He had been on terms of friendship with them ever since the children were quite small. As the children grew up he was drawn more intimately into the family circle. He was always ready to help Frau Wagner[37] with word and deed. A strong intellectual friendship had long existed between Hitler and this wise and highly intelligent woman. Possibly the independent attitude towards life and its purpose which existed in the Haus Wahnfried played a certain role in all this. Above all, however, it was the personality of Frau Wagner herself which exerted the decisive influence. It is difficult to describe how these two highly developed characters were complementary to one another. Both had the same deep reverence for Richard Wagner[38] and his music. This had perhaps been the decisive factor in her marriage with Siegfried Wagner. She was at that time very young and doubtless very much under the influence of the great Richard Wagner. One may also assume with some certainty that the presence of Frau Cosima Wagner, so lively right up to a very advanced age, was of significance in this circle. On social evenings in Haus Wahnfried, the most gifted theatre folk were guests, constituting to a quite unusual degree all that was most brilliant in the artistic life of Germany. It is important to emphasize this artistic atmosphere in order to understand how it was bound to attract Hitler. It was of course natural that Frau Wagner dominated this circle, for she had had to fight in very difficult conditions in order to succeed in restoring the Bayreuth Festival[39] to its original conception. Whether the relations of Frau Wagner to Hitler were consciously fostered by her in order to attain to the fulfilment of her object, it is hard to say. If that were the case, it would be indicative of Frau Wagner's cleverness rather than of the nobility of her character. She did try to influence the political views of the Fuehrer. But as she seldom saw Hitler her influence was but slight – especially during critical times. As she had a large circle of acquaintances petitions were often forwarded by her. As they had mostly to pass through my hands, I know that the majority of them were concerned with political oppression to persons of half-Jewish blood, etc. In such cases Hitler always tried to settle the matter in the sense she desired. Rumours that the relationship between Hitler and Frau Wagner was an intimate one have no foundation whatsoever.

Frau Wagner's children were, with the exception of the oldest daughter, Mouse, devoted to Hitler. The elder daughter, although just as intelligent as her brothers and sisters, had been rather put in the shade by her charming sister, Verena. Hitler, who must have been aware of this, increased the tension instead of avoiding or decreasing it. This reached a point that the oldest daughter – no doubt hurt by certain special happenings – went to Switzerland and there often openly criticized Hitler. Publications in the press show how far she went. She referred to her origin which, she claimed, justified her attitude. As her mother was an Englishwoman, she regarded herself just as much English as her brothers and sisters regarded themselves German. This matter was never alluded to in Haus Wahnfried in the presence of others. Hitler undoubtedly saw a kind of high treason in this attitude of the oldest daughter and condemned it accordingly. He also never discussed this matter in wider circles, but he occasionally criticized it most severely.

With his own relatives, Hitler hardly had any contact. During the years 1932, '33 and '34, his sister Angelika[40] kept house for him in Haus Wachenfeld – later turned into the Berghof. In this little house she was looked on as the housekeeper and she did everything possible to make life agreeable for her brother whom she adored. She looked after him with a motherly care and he must have appreciated it very much. Owing to some tension, the origin of which is not known but which certainly disappeared in later years, she left Haus Wachenfeld which at about the same time became uninhabitable owing to its being rebuilt. Frau Raubal then married a Prof. Hamitsch of the Technical High School in Dresden and remained estranged from Hitler for a long time. He, however, often spoke of her and of her 'gift' for running his household. He also often mentioned his mother to whom he was devoted. He described her as a simple and unbelievably good woman who had brought up her children with great trouble and patience and always tried to help them. 'How unhappy my Mother would have been could she have seen her son in this position and with this responsibility; probably this little woman would hardly have dared to come to see her son.' He wished to express his adoration of his mother by a visible sign and intended to have erected at Linz[41] on the Danube by the architect Giessler a tall tower hung with bells, the base to form a mausoleum for the bodies of the mother and father.

Sgd. Dr Karl Brandt

Document 3 The New Feudalism

'State Bonuses':
paper written by Dr Hans Lammers at Nuremberg, 24 October 1945
(translation of handwritten document)

A practice already established in Germany in former centuries (under Frederick the Great, under Frederick William III and under Kaiser William I) which the Fuehrer again took over deliberately, was that of bestowing bonuses on deserving men. His purpose in doing this was to provide men who had rendered service to state and Party with a standard of living in keeping with their position, and to free them of financial worries after they had retired and to keep their families from having to lower the standard of living they were used to. In his opinion the relatively low incomes and pensions, subject as they were to all kinds of deductions, were inadequate for this purpose. The bonus recipients should be put in the position to somehow or other settle down as property owners, according to the amount of bonus by means of acquiring a smaller or larger estate or residence where they could settle down with their families. Bonuses were granted in land and property, chiefly however in cash. Cash payments were intended to enable the recipient to acquire property, but there was no compulsion brought to bear to use the money for this purpose. The money or the equivalent property bonus was paid out of the Fuehrer's 'Disposition' fund which was under my administration.

In individual cases Party funds were also probably used. Category of bonus eligibles whom the Fuehrer personally designated: Minister, State Secretaries, General of the Army, Generals, Reichsleiters, Gauleiters, etc. Usual amount of the bonus in these cases: Between 100,000 Reichsmark and a million Reichsmark. Occasion for granting the bonus: Birthdays (50th, 55th, 60th, etc.), special anniversaries, retirement from work, etc. In addition, bonuses of lesser value (perhaps between 10,000 and 100,000 Reichsmark) were also given to persons closer to the Fuehrer for birthdays, weddings, etc. and in larger numbers to persons in industry (factory directors, engineers, down to the section heads and foremen) based on lists given the Fuehrer by

Hans Lammers, a career bureaucrat, was chief-of-staff of the Reich Chancellery. From this vantage point he could watch the operation of Hitler's state. The Allies exploited this knowledge to revise their view that the Third Reich was a tightly controlled dictatorship centred on Hitler alone.

Reichsminister Speer. A bonus award was not subject to either income or gift tax. The bonuses were however subject to property tax, and the revenues of the bonus (interest, dividends) were also subject to income tax. Real estate was subject to property tax and the returns received from real estate were subject to income tax. I was concerned with the bonuses only to the extent that I had to make the payments and that I carried on certain negotiations in property acquisition. In the interest of justice I also made an effort to bring a certain system to the bonus recipients. In this, I achieved only partial success. However, I did manage to have the Fuehrer make a ruling that only he alone as Supreme State Chief should have the right to bestow the bonuses as discussed here, not just any other officials, as for instance the Reichsminister. However, an exception to this was Reichsminister Dr Goebbels. The latter frequently gave out considerable sums of money to big-name artists as tax-exempt gifts, and in fact in various instances gave repeatedly from year to year to the same artists. The Fuehrer also gave bonuses now and then to artists, for example rather high bonuses went to the sculptors Thorak and Breker.[42]

Regarding the details of the bonuses lacking all records, I am not able to give any exhaustive or any approximately accurate information. Better facts can be obtained in the Reichshauptkasse (Main Reich Savings Bank) [the German Treasury] as well as at the authorized finance offices of the bonus recipients. My former reviewers in the Reichschancellery (Reich Cabinet Counsel Dr Killy, and Senior State Counsels Haensel and Kaiser) probably can recall more cases of bonus awards than I. I remember the following significant awards:

Bonus for Reichspresident von Hindenburg: estate Neudeck (East Prussia) and neighbouring estates. I cannot recall the value now.

General of the Army von Mackensen:[43] estate Bruessov (Pomerania). Value unknown to me.

Reichsleiter Dr Ley: one million Reichsmark to buy, that is to enlarge, the family estate close to Waldbroehl.

Reich Minister von Ribbentrop: one million Reichsmark in two parts of 500,000 Reichsmark each.

General of the Army Keitel: land purchase amounting to about one million Reichsmark which was to be added to his estate Herscherede (Braunschweig) [Brunswick].

Reich Minister Funk: 500,000 Reichsmark in cash with which he established a foundation for the next-of-kin of those employed in his Ministry and in the Reich Bank who had died in action.

General Guderian:[44] a rather large estate in Warthegau. Value unknown to us.

General of the Army von Kleist:[45] a rather large estate in Silesia for the enlargement of his estate there. Value I do not recall.

General of the Army (Knight) Ritter von Leeb:[46] an estate in the woods of Bavaria. Value approximately 600,000 Reichsmark according to my recollection.

General of the Police Daluege:[47] an estate in the protectorate to which, as I believe, he had not as yet taken official title. I do not recall the value.

Family of the deceased General of the Army von Reichenau:[48] large estate in the province of Saxony. Value about one million and 200,000 Reichsmark.

Family of the deceased SS Obergruppenfuehrer Heydrich:[49] large estate Jungfrau, Breschau in the Protectorate.

General of the Army von Rundstedt:[50] 250,000 Reichsmark and a rather large estate in Silesia near Breslau, the latter through Reichs Marshal Goering.

Grand Admiral Raeder, the deceased chief-of-staff of the SA Lutze,[51] the deceased Corps Commander (leader) of the NSKK. Huchslein, SS Obergruppenfuehrer Sepp Dietrich,[52] the State Secretaries Schlegberger and Pfundtner, who were made available [sic], and the Fuehrer's personal doctor Professor Morell, also received many bonuses – the exact amount of which I cannot state. On my 66th birthday 27/5/1944 I received a cash bonus of 600,000 Reichsmark, which I invested in Reich Bonds.

As I was given to understand, the largeness of the amount was due to the following facts:

1. that the Fuehrer believed he had to consider that I had received only the usual small bonus at my 55th, at my 60th birthdays and at my 40th anniversary of my service. This due to the lack of a suggestion submitted to the Fuehrer.

2. that I was one of the few leading figures (people) of the state and of the Party who had failed to acquire any land or real estate whatsoever.

3. that through bombings in November 1943 and January 1944, I had practically lost my entire belongings.

The Fuehrer had generally ordered that land bought for bonus uses, whether from private hands or from state property, would have to be purchased without any force or pressure and an acceptable price would have to be paid. This as well as the low value of the money and the higher value of real estate were for him the determining factors of the size of bonuses.

Dr Lammers

I certify that the above is a true, correct and complete translation from German into English of the original document.

Document 4 Hitler the Warlord

United States Strategic Bombing Survey, Interview No. 62, Colonel General
Alfred Jodl, 29 June 1945, published 7 July 1945
(extract from pp. 2–3, 6–8)

II Meetings of German High Command – Procedure and Records

Q. Did the General Staff have periodical conferences with Hitler?
A. Yes, every day at least once, and often twice a day. Especially during the days of great activity. During the lulls, maybe the air force or the navy would not come in for days. But, during the times of some important happenings, everybody would come and there were conferences with all, or in a small circle if it was dealing with preparations not affecting everybody. It varied, of course, according to circumstances. In general, the conferences were always on a large scale and included the three Supreme Commanders (army, navy, and air force) and their chiefs-of-staff. All major matters were decided upon in conferences with the Fuehrer, where everything was concentrated. Naturally, the chiefs-of-staff would frequently come individually to see me, or I would go to see them, in order to discuss details.
Q. Who were the chiefs-of-staff of the three armed forces during the war?

Colonel-General Alfred Jodl was Chief of Operations at Hitler's Supreme Headquarters. He was a military technician who remained convinced at Nuremberg that Hitler had been 'a great military leader'.

A. At the beginning of the war, Colonel General Halder[53] in the army, Jeschonnek[54] in the air force, who succeeded Kesselring,[55] and in the navy it was Admiral Giesse.[56] The Supreme Commanders were Brauchitsch, Goering, and Raeder.

Q. Were there regular conferences between the three Supreme Commanders and Hitler alone?

A. The four alone, very seldom. I do not think there would ever be such a conference, without General Keitel or myself. Now and then the Fuehrer would talk alone with Brauchitsch if he had something personal, and very often with Goering, but if there was a regular conference, we were always present.

Q. Were these daily conferences held at any particular time?

A. Yes, but this time has changed in the course of the years. Towards the end, that is from February 1944 up until July 1944, as we were in Berchtesgaden, they began at 12 or 12:30 and lasted until 3 or 4 o'clock. Later in the evening I would send one of my general staff officers up there again, or go myself to see if something important had happened. The same time of conferences was observed when we were in East Prussia from July 1944 until December, but after that we moved to Berlin and the conferences would begin at 4 or 5 in the afternoon and last until late in the evening. But even there, I would send one of my officers or go myself to the Reichs Chancellery once more at midnight or 1:00 a.m.

Q. Was everything that was said taken down in shorthand?

A. Not at the beginning. I had one of my general staff officers take notes about the most important things. These notes were, of course, in longhand and whatever I found important in them I would have typed up and kept in my file, but we did not keep stenographic records until the end of August or the beginning of September 1942.

Q. Where are the copies of these stenographic notes from these conferences?

A. I have no idea, because we had not control over them. I must add, and it is important for you to know, that these stenographic transcripts were introduced as a result of a rather violent disagreement which I had with the Fuehrer in August 1942. As far as I know, these transcripts were made in three copies. One went to the Reichs Chancellery; the second went to the Berghof; and the third to General Scherff, who was in charge of writing the history of the war for the Fuehrer.

Q. Did Lammers have a copy of the stenographic transcripts?

A. I don't think so. There was a copy kept in the Reichs Chancellery in Berlin, but in that part of the Chancellery controlled by Reichsleiter Bormann. There was also a copy, I think, in the Reichs Chancellery in Berchtesgaden, also under Bormann's control. The third set, I think, went to General Scherff, and he most likely brought them to Berchtesgaden, that is to the Obersalzburg. You must realize that those transcripts were kept to use against us, not for us. We of the military were not even given a single copy. Bormann had complete jurisdiction over the stenographers and over the distribution of their notes . . .

[There followed a detailed discussion of the possible whereabouts of the stenographic records.]

III Personal Influence of Hitler in German Military Decisions

Q. Did Hitler make military decisions in these conferences?

A. From the very first day on. All decisions that were of any importance were made by him, himself.

Q. Do you believe that Hitler's decisions were good and contributed to the success of the war?

A. I cannot generalize on that. There is no doubt that many of the major decisions made by the Fuehrer himself prevented us from losing the war sooner. One of his biggest leadership achievements was the decision to occupy Norway. Another of his great personal accomplishments was the decision for the attack on France through Sedan, which he decided entirely on his own, and against the advice of his staff who had all urged him to follow the so-called 'Schlieffen-Plan' for an envelopment attack through Holland along the coast. That was also an outstanding personal accomplishment, but perhaps his greatest military achievement was the way he personally intervened to stop the retreat of the German army in the east in November 1941. Nobody else could have accomplished that. A panic had already started there. It might easily have led to the same kind of disaster that overtook the French army in the campaign of 1812.

Q. Were there any decisions by Hitler in the military field which you as a soldier considered bad?

A. Not at the beginning of the war. In 1942, however, during the summer campaign in Russia, I personally became convinced that the Fuehrer was not making sound decisions. I believe that the reason for it was the hot continental climate which he could not stand. He complained of constant headaches, and so it occurred that he would give orders and the next day, after they were carried out to the letter, he would bawl out the General Staff for having done what he had ordered. This went so far that I had Scherff write down what he ordered every day and what the General Staff carried out, so as to prove that all that happened through my decisions was exactly what he had ordered. That led to conflicts between him and myself up until August 1942, when he decided to call in the stenographers in order to have a proof on his side of what he had ordered. I do believe that at that time his leadership was bad.

Q. Do you regard as one of Hitler's mistakes the fact that he did not order the invasion of England in 1940?

A. I cannot consider that a mistake because at that time I gave him a situation appraisal in which I advised against it. This document is with the others in Flensburg.[57]

Q. If you take the good and bad decisions together, would you say that Hitler's military leadership, in general, was fortunate or unfortunate for Germany?

A. In the course of the latter years, there were naturally decisions taken in the East which are hard to understand, and which cannot be justified from a purely military point of view. It had been proved in the early years of the war that he had frequently been right when the General Staff was wrong, and this served to increase his mistrust of our advice later on. When the retreat from the East was suggested by the OKW, he opposed it because he believed that it was just another sign of weakness and excessive conservatism. He had too little immediate contact with the troops, and so some of his decisions in the latter period were not based on military reality. But, looking at the whole picture, I am convinced that he was a great military leader. Certainly, no historian could say that Hannibal was a poor general just because in the end Carthage was destroyed.

Q. Would you perhaps say that Hitler was a good general on the offensive, but fell down when he was forced to retreat?

A. Actually, it was clear from the moment he took over the Supreme Command that what he most lacked was the experience of a long military career through all the grades up to the top. You can learn only by experience. He took part in the trench warfare in the last war and he mastered that form of warfare outstandingly, but he had had no real experience with mobile warfare and all the difficulties that are caused in communications with the uncertain conditions of mobile warfare. He, therefore, tended to overlook the difficulties of executing some of the operations which he had planned . . .

[There followed a discussion about the level of German military casualties, which Jodl suggested totalled 2 million dead and 6 million wounded, with 400,000 killed in bomb attacks.]

V Other Effects of Allied Air Operations

Q. Let us talk more directly about the air warfare. In what manner has the Anglo-American air force contributed to the decision of the war?
A. Not taking into consideration the Russian air force, which was of no great importance, I would say in general that in the end the winning of the complete air superiority in the whole area of the war has altogether decided the war. I would go as far as to say that our power on the land was numerically and, from the point of armament, sufficiently strong, if not to win, at least to hold our own on all fronts, if our own air force had kept up on the same level.
Q. As far as the aerial warfare goes, which of the different kinds of air attack was the most decisive?
A. I cannot give any one clear answer to that. It was a series of events. In the long run, the most effective thing was after all the strategic bombing against the Zone of the Interior, because there the root and the basis for all armament and war potential was hit and the effect increased from one attack to the other. Even if the Luftwaffe had remained strong enough so that we could have temporarily carried on successful operations at the front, it would have done us no good if in the meantime the foundations of our armament industry were being destroyed, and the transport as well, and the hydrogenation plants. So I would say that the decisive factor was not so much the very unpleasant effect of your air attacks at the front, as the destruction of the home-land, almost without resistance.

Q. Was there any shortage of supplies or equipment at the front as a result of the bombing?

A. The first that became noticeable was the decrease in ammunition. Of the equipment, tanks were also short towards the end. There were also times when we had enough equipment, but could not transport it to the front with the necessary speed.

Q. What else did you lack at the front?

A. The most serious was artillery ammunition. In course of time, large production centers were destroyed in that field, and then the production of light howitzers was greatly affected by the destruction of one plant which was heavily hit . . .

Q. Were you hindered operationally through any of these shortages?

A. We were hindered in 1943, through a drop in manpower, probably less in numbers than in quality. Only the younger age groups were any good any more. We were also hindered as of 1943 through a continuously decreasing mobility caused by the reduced production of motor vehicles. That went continuously down from 1943 on.

Q. What else besides motor vehicles?

A. Maybe not yet in 1943, but towards the end of 1943, or beginning of 1944, ammunition was not quite sufficient. At the same time, I remember Field Marshal Keitel told me that the front was short of fuel, so that he did not know any more how to make it go around. Then came the destruction of the transportation system which was a decisive point for me. We were unable to carry out fast troop movements any more. Then came the decline of the Luftwaffe, not so much in the number or quality of the aircraft, but through the catastrophe there was no fighter which could stand up against the Anglo-American fighters.

Q. What other reasons were there for the decline of the Luftwaffe?

A. I am of the opinion that the Luftwaffe did not recognize the time at which their aircraft were getting obsolete. They should have recognized that at the time of Rommel's withdrawal from El Alamein. At that time, we had for the first time seen the doubtless superiority of the enemy air force. Even though they may have recognized the tremendous offensive power of the four-engined bomber, they were inclined to underestimate this bomber and regard it as welcome prey for the ME-109. I have probably forgotten to speak about the basic difficulty of the Russian campaign. In the Russian campaign there was very heavy fighting because the Russians would keep on fighting even when their situation seemed hopeless, in isolated pockets. Then, of course, the Luftwaffe was called in and the Fuehrer became accustomed to employing the whole air force tactically. It was certainly well equipped for tactical operations and made a very good account of itself. As a result, however, we probably lost sight a little of the strategic air warfare. There were also heavy losses of planes and crews in the Russian campaign. At the time when the Russians were surrounding large bodies of our troops, the Luftwaffe was made responsible for their supply. We then lost the cream of our pilots because the supply planes to these German pockets were flown by our best instructors, and we suffered great loss of excellent manpower there, which led to a decline in our pilot training. Then there were two more reasons which the Fuehrer fully recognized. The first one was the neglect of technical development in the Luftwaffe, because the Luftwaffe High Command was very little technically inclined. The neglect of high frequency, etc. As the Fuehrer used to say, the typical fighter pilots who had practically assumed the leadership of the air force had very little understanding of the technical things. The Fuehrer towards the end was of the opinion that the technical development inside the Luftwaffe had got very strongly into the background through the pure fighter spirit of the leaders. Towards the end, the Fuehrer believed that the organization inside the Luftwaffe was bad, so that he himself took a hand more strongly, but at a time when it was already too late.

Q. Was it the desire of the General Staff of the OKW to have the Luftwaffe operate primarily in support of ground operations?

A. It was not so. We fully recognized the importance of the independent operation of the air war, for instance the war against England. On the contrary, I was of the opinion that we also needed an independent Navy Air Arm.

Q. When you talked about the deterioration of technique, did you mean that technical questions had been transferred to Speer?

A. On the contrary, a turn to the better occurred then.

Q. When Hitler personally took a hand in the affairs of the Luftwaffe, was this followed by an improvement in the technique?

A. That was too late to have any effect. He did not take a hand directly until after the 20th of July 1944. It may perhaps be maintained by the Luftwaffe that he made utopian demands, demands for engines which could not be constructed. This may be the case, but it is certain that he himself ascertained what had been overlooked in past years. Whether he would have been in a position to change this, I do not know; whether he had as many technical prerequisites for this branch of the service as he had for the ground forces, I do not know either. It is, however, certain that, through his conferences with the leaders of the aircraft industry, he ascertained certain facts that led him to the conviction that unbelievable slip-ups had occurred.

Q. To what extent were military operations affected through the bombing of German cities?

A. First of all, the psychological effect on the front-line soldier was very great. That is something that is frequently overlooked, but it was of first importance in my opinion. While previously the soldier believed that by fighting at the front he was protecting his native land, his wife, and his children, this factor was completely eliminated and replaced by the realization, 'I may hold on as much as I please, but still my wife and children go to the dogs.'

Q. Did this interfere with his fighting ability at the front?

A. Absolutely. This could be gathered from a lot of reports from the front. For instance, there was a division from Hamburg. Suddenly, in 1943, the report of the heavy attacks[58] arrived and created great unrest.

Q. How did the troops evidence this concern?

A. Through a diminishing will to resist. They fought well and the number of deserters was always very small, but they were no longer as enthusiastic as before. The feeling was there 'What am I fighting for? I can be as courageous as possible and still at home everything is smashed to bits.' This certainly was a strong reaction which weakened the fighting spirit of the troops. Parallel thereto, there was an effect on the working capacity of the armament workers . . .

'The world's worth criminal':
Goering in the Third Reich

'I've talked to Mrs Goering a lot. I was interested in finding out whether she knows that she has been married to one of the world's worst criminals. She definitely is not aware of this.'

Curt Reiss, 3 August 1945[1]

Reichsmarschall Hermann Goering is by no means the comical figure he has been depicted so many times in newspaper reports. He is neither stupid nor a fool in the Shakespearean sense, but generally cool and calculating. He is able to grasp the fundamental issues under discussion immediately. He is certainly not a man to be underrated . . . Goering is at all times an actor who does not disappoint his audience. His vanity extends into the field of the pathological . . .

BWCE, Special Report No. 10, 'Hermann Goering', 1 June 1945[2]

[Hermann Goering was regarded by the Allied prosecutors as their most important prisoner following the suicides of Hitler, Goebbels and Himmler. When the British prosecution met with Jackson on 29 May they agreed that the 'first target' was the trial of Goering by September 1945 at the very latest; a month later the British Attorney-General was still in favour of a speedy process against Goering on his own.[3] The decision was finally made in mid-June to proceed against a number of major war criminals simultaneously, but Goering always remained the key figure in Allied eyes. He was interrogated regularly on a whole range of subjects. At Nuremberg he was interrogated on twenty-four days between 27 August and 20 October. No other defendant was involved in so many areas of potential crime. The three interrogations reproduced below reflect the many sides of Goering's role in the Third Reich. The first examines Goering as art collector, connoisseur, and looter. The second displays Goering in the role of a senior wartime commander and the highest-ranking officer in the Wehrmacht. Goering's remarks on the problems facing the German air force reveal a sophisticated level of awareness on his part of the deficiencies which finally crippled German air power. His grasp of technical and tactical detail belies his reputation as an indolent commander. The absence of a German long-range fighter to match the Mustangs, Thunderbolts and Spitfires of the long-range Allied fighter force Goering regarded as the most telling deficiency (though he did not confess to his interrogators that when the first long-range fighters were shot down over Germany he told his staff they had drifted there with the assistance of strong winds).[4] Goering was at his most informative and entertaining on issues of foreign policy. The third document explores Goering's role in the annexation of Austria in March 1938, when he spent a day on the telephone trying to broker an agreement with the embattled Austrian Chancellor, Kurt Schuschnigg, to get the Austrian government to invite German forces in to help maintain 'order'. The success of his efforts opened the way to the Anschluss or 'joining on' of Austria to her powerful German neighbour. A plebiscite was organized on 10 April in which 99.08 per cent of those voting on union with Germany gave their assent. The

Herman Goering, widely regarded as the leading figure in the cohort of major war criminals, photographed in his cell at Nuremberg. He made no effort to disguise his responsibility or to deny the many accusations laid at his door by the prosecution.

conditions under which those ballots were cast were exposed in an interrogation of Goering's brother, Albert, who was living in Austria. Albert did not share his brother's political convictions and was saved from the Gestapo on a number of occasions by the intervention of his influential sibling. His account of the plebiscite is appended to his brother's interrogation.]

Document 5 A Souvenir from Monte Cassino

Testimony of Hermann Goering, taken at Nuremberg on 8 October 1945
by Colonel John H. Amen

COLONEL AMEN TO THE WITNESS THROUGH THE
INTERPRETER IN GERMAN:

Q. What were the names of your principal agents for the purchase of art objects?
A. If I may, I would like to explain to you how this whole matter was handled. Since it had been known for a long time that I was very interested in art objects, I used to get offers from several countries. For instance, partly these offers came from art dealers say in Switzerland, Italy, or other countries near there, and they would inform me an auction would be held, and they would actually send me the auction list. Also, it happened very many times that private people would contact me if they had art objects that they wished to place on sale. Moreover, there were several men that were interested in the subject generally, and I told them just what my wishes and interests were . . .
Q. Frequently, you and Rosenberg[5] and the government were all trying to get the same objects for yourselves, were you not?
A. Yes. It is very unfortunate that this happened. Many times we did not know about it, and thus the prices went very high with the art dealers. Colonel, if I may make the remark, I want to tell you, for instance, that if I went to Holland, or Paris, or Rome, I would always find a huge stack of letters awaiting me. There would be letters from private people, princes and princesses, and anything that you want, and there were many genuine offers, and many fake offers, and the prices were anywhere from good to improbable, and everybody offered me this stuff to buy.
Q. Some of the objects which you got were confiscated objects of art, were they not?
A. We must differentiate here between two separate cases. Firstly, those objects that were bought in free trade, so to speak. The second case are those that were collected by the organization of Rosenberg. Those were articles that had been confiscated from people who had left the

country. I would like to make a short remark here about this Rosenberg commission. They collected and registered all their art objects, and they were destined to either go to the Fuehrer's gallery in Linz,[6] that was to be built, or to the Hohe Schule that Rosenberg was going to build at the Chiemsee. It was my intention that not all of these art objects should go to southern Germany, and I had the intention to buy some of them for my gallery. I bought these things and they were estimated, not by German art experts, but by French experts, and then it happened very often that after I made all the arrangements, the Fuehrer would see a photo of the objects and I would have to return things to him because he wanted them.

Q. What confiscated objects did you get from Poland?

A. Personally, I did not get any confiscated objects from Poland. There is one portrait with my collection which, however, was not destined for my gallery. It was the first intention that this would go to the Kaiser Frederick Museum in Berlin. It was merely stored with the objects that belonged to me because the shelter that I had was especially safe and suitable. There are a number of other objects down there which do not belong to me, which were merely stored because it was considered a safe place for such objects. It was the intention of the Fuehrer that all art treasures that were confiscated in Poland were to be transferred into a museum that was to be erected in Koenigsberg, with the exception of four or five portraits that were to go to the Kaiser Frederick Museum in Berlin. This collection in Berlin was executed by Dr Muehlmann.[7] Not for me, however, but for the German government, officially. As far as those Polish art treasures are concerned, they were first stored at Krakow, under Governor General Frank, and then later, at the request of the Fuehrer, I wrote a letter to Frank that those articles were to be transferred to Koenigsberg, with the exception of the four or five pictures I mentioned before. However, this did not happen and they were put in a safe place somewhere in southern Germany.

Q. How about the confiscated objects from Monte Cassino?[8]

A. As far as these art treasures at Monte Cassino go, at first we didn't even know about them, but it was later evident that they had come from a museum in Naples. It so happened that a parachute division and another division of mine were fighting near there, and when the fighting got heavy, it was decided that it would be necessary to save those art treasures from destruction. There were several there that belonged to the monastery, and they were transferred to the Pope in Rome, and the Abbey [Abbot] of the monastery wrote us a long letter in Latin to thank us for this. The others were transferred to the Fascist Italian government in Northern Italy,[9] and with the exception of fifteen portraits and some statues that were taken to Germany. Then, when my division returned, they brought many of these objects from Italy. However, I did not like that very much and I did not think it was fitting to the circumstances. I traveled to see the Fuehrer about two days later and asked him what was to be done with these objects. He said he would like to have them transferred to him. Then they remained in my shelter for a few months, and then later were transferred to the Reichs Chancellery against receipt. In order to stay on the safe side, I want to say here I only have one object that came from Monte Cassino. This was the statue of a saint that was found in the ruins of Cassino and when the division came back, they gave me this as a souvenir from Cassino. This thing is completely insignificant and at most it is worth between fifty and sixty marks and it is no art object.

Q. You had agents operating in France?

A. I don't want to say agents – art dealers; I had those. As far as private circles, and purchases from private sources are concerned, they were principally Bunjes and Lohse who met these people socially, and they would hear of possibilities to buy from them. Just in order to give you an example of how this thing works, just before the war with America broke out I got an offer from America, through either Spain, or Portugal, or Switzerland, offering me some art objects from New York. I just want to explain to you that after it was known I collected these things, I did receive offers from all over the world, as all the art dealers in the world naturally had connections with each other.

Q. What objects were there in New York?

A. They were portraits from the school of Fontainebleau, and they were painted in the 15th century, and it was especially well known I had a particular interest in them.

Q. Who had them in New York?

A. I don't know. It came through some art dealers, and I don't know just what the connections were.

Q. And there were art dealers operating on your behalf in Holland?

A. Possibly it will be the efficient way for me to answer the question in this way. You are asking me about Holland. Well, I can say that after it had become well known I was interested in objects of art, there was no art dealer of any repute in either Holland, Belgium, Switzerland, Sweden, France or England, before the war, and also Czechoslovakia, who would not make me their offers, because they were interested, naturally, to sell their art objects. However, of course, they did not make these offers to me alone. They would write to all people who were interested – to the Fuehrer, for instance, and other personalities, and they would inform me of any auctions to be held. I, at various times, visited them in order to get the feel of the market and find out just what was happening.

Q. The same is true in Belgium and Italy?

A. Yes. If I may, I would like to correct myself about the interrogation of Saturday morning. The question was put to me, whether I knelt in front of the altar. I understood the question in such a manner that you meant whether out of respect or reverence I knelt in front of the altar. I remember now that the altar was on a low stool, and the inscription was underneath, and so naturally I knelt down to look at the inscription. There was hardly an art object where I wouldn't get down on my knees and take a magnifying glass and inspect it. In that sense it was true.

Q. But the kneeling had no religious connotation?

A. No.

Q. What about the Sterzing altarpiece?[10] Is that the same altar that we spoke of Saturday?

A. No. It is not. The Sterzing altar was a present of the Duce, that is, of the Italian government, to me personally. The altarpiece of Sterzing, as Sterzing itself, is a purely German thing. Sterzing is a little town in the South Tyrol and belonged to Italy. The altar was made by an old master from Ulm, and his name was Gulfi (?), and one day I heard the church in Sterzing was interested in selling this altarpiece because they needed money, and I wrote to them concerning this, and then the Italian government heard about it, and they bought that altar for me and gave it to me as a surprise present for my birthday.

Q. In addition to the purchases which you made from time to time, and the gifts which you received, there were also a number of exchanges which you worked out.

A. Yes. If you intend to build up a gallery, you just have to exchange objects just like you would if you were collecting stamps. Just to give you an example here. If, for instance, you want to have an altar in your gallery, it is very likely that the centerpiece is owned by a museum, the right wing and left wing by some others, and maybe an upper or lower piece from the same altar by yet another agency. If you want to have the whole piece, the only choice you have got is to offer them exchanges and ask them what they want in return for these objects. I mentioned before that with my collection there were many portraits, for instance, which did not belong to me. There were many that were sent to me merely for inspection and for an exchange, and no final agreement was ever reached on them.

Q. Did you, from time to time, sell some of the confiscated objects which you had obtained?
A. Exchanged?
Q. No, sold.
A. As far as the confiscated objects are concerned, I only exchanged them.
Q. But you sold, from time to time, some of the objects which you had purchased on the open market?
A. This happened only once, really. I bought a great collection *in toto* and then I asked Hofer to sell those pictures in which we were not interested, with the instructions to use the money that he received for them, for the purchase of new pictures. I want to say here that there was no money ever used, that came from the sale of art objects, for anything else, except the purchase of other art objects. For instance, we once discovered a very precious picture and, in exchange, we had to give 175 other pictures for it.
Q. What was the Kunstfond [art fund]?
A. The Kunstfond was an art fund which I had instituted for the purchase of art objects.
Q. Where did the money come from that went into that fund?
A. It was partly made up by private contributions which I received to build up my gallery. At one time I also received a large amount from the Fuehrer, and then I, myself, would give to this fund. The fund did not contain any money that came from state sources.
Q. Who was authorized to deposit and withdraw from that account?
A. To deposit or withdraw money in there?
Q. Yes.

A. That was me.

Q. Exclusively?

A. Yes. Only me.

Q. Were all of your purchases and sales cleared through that account?

A. No. This fund was instituted only very much later, by me. Here is something else I want to draw to your attention. I inherited a certain amount of art treasures.

Q. Did you employ various people to work on this art collecting business?

A. Does the Colonel mean in the acquisition of these art treasures, or after the acquisition, to work on them?

Q. Both.

A. In the case of who I employed before the acquisition of the objects, I think I explained how they were offered to me from all sides, in all countries. After the acquisition, there were two things that were mainly done with them. The first thing was to classify them, and second to conserve them; that is, to prevent them from blistering, or the paint from peeling, or what have you. All those things that are required to keep them in good condition. This was handled at first by my secretariat, and later on by Hofer and his staff.

Q. Most of these objects were kept in Berlin, were they not?

A. Yes. Almost all of them. Only when the Russians were approaching were they moved.

Q. When and how were they moved?

A. They were moved from the end of January 1945, through February and March 1945, by rail.

Q. Where are they now?

A. They were moved to Berchtesgaden.

Q. All of them?

A. Since I, myself, was arrested by Hitler,[11] I don't know whether all of them ever did get there, but I am sure that the greater amount of them did get there. I would say at least 90 percent. Over 90 percent. I have something to say else here; that I had a number of art objects which were not destined to go into the gallery. They were art objects, but in themselves they were not so precious or good enough to be in a gallery. They were merely something I would like to call glorified furniture, and it is quite possible that they were left in Berlin and that they were not treated as carefully, and moved as carefully, as the others.

Q. What would you estimate the entire collection to be worth?

A. That is almost impossible to determine. That depends very much on the market, and that is why it is never estimated. The only thing that was ever estimated was the value of some certain pieces. Just to give you an idea about that. Once a picture was offered to me in Holland for 3,000 guilders. In the course of the years it was offered to me a total of seven times, and the last time it was offered to me the price was 45,000 guilders. That is because other people would offer prices for the same picture. It is impossible to even estimate the value of some of the pieces I had. For instance, the Sterzing altar could never have been estimated. It depended very much on who was interested in it, and at what time. Just to give you an example, if I wanted to sell something by Lucas Cranach the first man might offer 50,000 marks; the next man might have Lucas Cranach as his particular hobby, and he might offer 100,000 marks. Then somebody else would be interested in the object as such, but not to a greater extent than 10,000 marks, and that is why it is impossible for me to estimate the value of the total collection. I really don't even know the extent of my collection any more. I only remember the most important objects.

Q. I think you testified on Saturday that none of these objects were ever in fact turned over to the government? Is that correct?

A. Yes. That is correct. I couldn't hand it over to the government, because who was there to act as a representative of the government? According to our Constitution it was quite sufficient if I informed the Fuehrer of the fact that I had certain objects and gave the Minister of Finance notice to the same effect. As it was, the gallery, as such, was never intended to be handed over to the government after it was built. It was my intention to hand it over to the people, and the way this would have been effected is that at a certain date it would have been said in a communiqué, 'Goering, on such and such a date, has decided to hand over this gallery as a gift to the German people.' If you look at it this way, I was the government myself . . .

Q. But in point of fact, none of these objects were ever given to the German people?

A. Well, how could this be done. The gallery had never been built yet, and all this was to happen after the war.

Q. But, I say, it never happened.

A. That is quite clear. That is quite impossible.

Q. Do you remember a box of jewels, belonging to a Jewish woman, that was turned over for safekeeping to one of the ministries?

A. Yes. These were objects that had been found by the Devisen Fahn-dungs Stelle. That is an office which does police work, as far as foreign currency is concerned. They had found these objects when a Jewish woman tried to cross the border, and I remember when my train came back from Berlin, these objects were handed over to me. They had been given to the Secret Service man on the train for reasons of safety, and it was merely an accident. They were taken to the Prussian State Ministry [Goering's political headquarters in Berlin] and they were opened by an expert under oath, to be estimated. Then a part of them were kept in the State Ministry, and another part were sent to the Central Tax Collector's Office in Berlin.

Q. Do you recall the name of the Jewish woman?

A. No. I was told that this had come from more sources than one. They had collected this over a period of time.

Q. Up to the end of the war, what would you estimate your total personal income to have been?

A. You mean my monthly income?

Q. Yes. Monthly, or yearly.

A. My income was made up first by my salary; second it stemmed from the especial fund that I received as a Reich National [Reich Marshal?].

Q. How much did you receive for each of these?

A. The two of them together amounted to about 28,000 marks a month.[12] In addition to this came free residence, and all representative functions and matters were being paid for; and this, of course, was variable. Then, I derived income from books and articles that I had written. Of course, this was variable, but I would estimate the total sum that I had derived in such a manner, throughout the war, as about one million, and maybe one and one half million marks.

Q. What other sources of income did you have? Income from securities?

A. I had other income derived from interest on my capital and securities.

Q. How much do you estimate that to have been?

A. I am sorry that I really can't tell you, because I can't check it. Unfortunately I did not take very much interest in the administration of my own finances. They were left to the secretary, and I don't think that she had enough perspective to do the thing right, and I found out very much later that I had lost a great amount.

Q. How about income from industries in which you were financially interested?

A. I had no financial interest in industry except shares that I had bought as a private person, and I only had those in state factories.

Q. Such as?

A. For instance, there were the Hydrier Works.[13] Any factories that belonged to the state, that is what I am talking about. We were allowed to have shares, that represented a financial interest in it.

Q. Then let me ask you again, at what fee you would estimate your total monthly income?

A. That is very difficult for me to say, because so many of these things were distributed over so many years. As I mentioned before, I received 28,000 marks in currency, per month, and then I would say possibly five to seven thousand marks would be added to that from interest and annuities, and so on, and I would say that I received a total of 35,000 marks in currency each month. The sum I mentioned before that I had received as an author, of course, was distributed over many years. This income which I mentioned as a million, and a million and a half marks, has been distributed over this period of time . . .

Document 6 The Commander-in-Chief

United States Strategic Bombing Survey Interview No. 56,
Reichsmarschall Hermann Goering, 29 June 1945, distributed 6 July 1945

I Organization and Planning for German Aircraft Production.
Effects of Allied Air Attacks on Aircraft Production

Q. Was the production of aircraft under the control of the Luftwaffe until the spring of 1944?

A. Yes, until about May or June, 1944.[14]

Q. Up until that time, were you satisfied with the quality and quantity of the aircraft produced?

A. No. The quantity was far short of what it was aimed to be and increased only after Speer took over.

Q. Why did the quantity remain below par prior to the time Speer took over?

A. Because the Luftwaffe was dependent on them for the allocation of raw materials and stood alone in this respect. After the Minister of War Production (Speer) took over, he included the air force armament in the whole picture, where, up until then, we stood alone. I have been asked very often in the last few months about these production questions and I had to answer them without being able to think it over properly. All these things are so deep-rooted that you would have to go back some ten or fifteen years. The more I have been asked about them, the clearer they become. I am drawing your attention to this so that you don't blame me for having said something else some six weeks ago. I am sure you will understand this and I want to make it very clear.

Q. Were you satisfied with the aircraft production after Speer had taken control?

A. The production was marked by the fact that the biggest priority was given to the manufacture of fighters, and the bombers fell back so that, toward the end, they were hardly worthwhile mentioning.

Q. It has been said that as much as 55 percent of German war production went toward production for the Luftwaffe. Is this correct?

A. That is probably figured a little too high, but undoubtedly the air force has swallowed up a large part of it, because our air force included the flak[15] and the signals, which are permanent installations. Then there are ground organizations, machine tools for aircraft and so on.

Q. Do you think that even more than 55 percent should have been put into that part of your total war effort – as distinguished, for example, from your land effort?

A. I would not say that. But I do believe very definitely that in the years 1940 to 1943, we should have invested even more in the air force.

Q. What were the effects of our bombing attacks on aircraft assembly plants? Did they cause any substantial loss in production?

A. The effects were not so detrimental because the main attacks concentrated on the assembly plants, which were separated from the manufacture of the individual parts. In that manner you have, for example, destroyed at one time Marienburg, but in spite of that, in a comparatively short time, the assembly was on in some other place, while the production of the different parts themselves was not hit, so that the whole thing could keep running. Therefore, you can see that the attacks on the industry producing these parts were very disagreeable, but the American air force attacked assembly plants at first.

Q. Did we destroy many finished aircraft in those attacks on the assembly plants?

A. That depended on the circumstances. If a certain accumulation occurred in these plants, then naturally a lot were destroyed. When the weather was favorable and we were able to fly away all the machines, then the losses were comparatively small.

Q. Did the dispersal of the assembly plants cause any substantial loss in production or decrease in quality?

A. Basically, I can say that the widespread dispersal caused considerable delays due to the bad transportation, but generally speaking, it functioned all right, although the quality suffered considerably. It happened, for instance, that the fittings at the assembly were not accurate enough, and similar things. Sometimes it was just that the fittings of the wing section were rough, in other cases the two landing wheels were different. It was, therefore, decided to concentrate production again and an order was issued that everything would be concentrated in one subterranean plant with the exception of the prime components.[16]

Q. In 1944, a lot of the German pilots complained about the quality of their planes? Were these complaints valid and were they the result of dispersal?

A. Absolutely. In the first place, the transportation situation was bad and the components did not get through it all. It would have finally ruined us if we had not started changing over to concentration. It was the one and only reason.

Q. Do you think that the increase of quantity of aircraft had anything to do with the decrease in quality?

A. It had as well. I can talk here quite freely. Production was transferred to the Speer Ministry. The man responsible for the production there was Saur.[17] Saur was a man completely sold on figures. All he wanted was a pat on the shoulder when he managed to increase the number of aircraft from 2,000 to 2,500. Then the Luftwaffe was blamed that we had received so-and-so many aircraft and where were they. We said they would have to see those aircraft of which a large part was immediately destroyed. Secondly, spare parts were never made because spare parts would have cut down the number of aircraft produced, and so there was a continuous fight between the Luftwaffe and the Speer Ministry, in which Speer himself would stand up for us, but Saur lived only for his numbers, numbers, and numbers. The 262,[18] for instance, was one of the most delicate machines, where we always had to keep changing the engine, or at least overhaul it, and we just simply could not even get a fraction of engines in the reserve because they were needed for the manufacture of new airplanes. A Group would have 80 machines – the 262 – of which only 20 would be operational. There would be some 40 aircraft idle, which were intact except that they required an engine change, and when we demanded extra engines, we were told that we could not have them because new airplanes had to be built. Then we would get 40 new aircraft. This would then in turn increase the inventory to 120 aircraft, but the ones already used were still grounded because they were without engines. Consequently, the number of operational aircraft was not increased at all.

Q. Do you believe that Speer did a good job?

A. Yes. Speer was positively a genius.

Q. Why did you not have Saur removed from office?

A. He was not in my command at all. He was Speer's man, but practically he was responsible to the Fuehrer and had a lot of influence with him. I never had the slightest influence in these matters. The Fuehrer had appointed him personally. But even though Saur caused us great difficulties in this field, it is without doubt that in other fields he brought about a tremendous increase in production. He had the whole armament problem on his hands, and if you weigh his bad qualities against the good ones, you still must say that all in all he was a good man.

II Reasons for Discrepancy between Numbers of Aircraft Produced and Operational Strength of Luftwaffe

Q. Did the production provide the Luftwaffe with all the aircraft which it needed for operational purposes? Production records indicate fairly large quantities of aircraft while the aircraft in operation is a much lower figure.

A. As long as we had enough fuel, there was no particular difference.

Q. When did you first cut the use of planes operationally because of shortages of gasoline?

A. To quite an extent already in June 1944, when we finally managed to get the 'bugs' out of the He-177,[19] which gave us a little trouble. This aircraft was put in operation on the Russian front after it had been used against England. I had to ground that aircraft because it consumed too much gasoline and we just didn't have enough of it.

Q. Normally, how long did it take for a plane to be ready operationally after delivery by the plant to the Luftwaffe?

A. After it was finished in the factory, there was only the question of slow-timing it. After this was completed, it was immediately put on the way to the Groups, namely, by the ferrying squadrons. Toward the last, when the needs increased, the aircraft were ferried by the combat pilots themselves.

Q. Did any of these planes have to go through a modification center?

A. Yes. We had those in order not to disturb the current production. A number of changes were agreed on and these were not accomplished in the factory, but rather in the modification center.

Q. How long did the airplanes stay there?

A. That varied according to how many changes were necessary and how heavily the modification center was taxed. There were cases when too many machines would pile up and that slowed down the modifications. It also depended on the weather because during the bad spells, the modified aircraft were not able to take off which again caused the modification centers to fill up. Later, we tried to cut these modifications to a minimum and to deliver them to the air force already completed.

Q. In 1944, did you send planes directly from the factory to the front instead of to a modification center?

A. Not necessarily, but only when there was very little to change on them. It happened later that we distributed the machines directly to the Air Divisions. Sometimes it happened that a wing would be up to its strength as far as pilots were concerned, but was lacking in aircraft, while at the same time, something big was expected in their sector. In a case like that, we would send aircraft to the front directly, by-passing the Air Division.

Q. What percentage of the, say, 30,000-odd planes built in 1944 went into actual operation?

A. Our losses at that time were very heavy so that, generally speaking, all of these fighters were used in operations. The consumption and the losses of aircraft were very heavy, so that only during the winter months was it possible to build up the reserve, thanks to the decrease in the number of sorties. At one time, we had increased the operational aircraft from 2,500 to 6,000 fighters, and I would like to mention that this is the highest point of all. This amount was reached approximately in January 1945.[20] If their availability was good, it came up to 75 percent of operational aircraft. During the bad spells, it went down to 50 percent. In other words, we had 30,000 machines produced in 1944,[21] out of which, on the average, 2,400 to 2,600 were produced each month. This number is in fighters, fighter-bombers and light bombers. I do not include other bombers and transport aircraft, because we were not able to use them any more. These operational aircraft were divided among all of the theaters of operation.

Q. What is the greatest number of operational planes you ever had at any one time?

A. On all fronts? That is hard to say. I only knew the exact number in the West. There I had over 3,000 fighters ready. 2,500 to 3,000 in actual flying. That was in the West only.

Q. Why were not more of the 30,000 fighters produced in 1944 put into operation?

A. They all became operational as long as the lack of gasoline did not become noticeable. One of the main difficulties was the bad transport situation. It was impossible to take back the damaged aircraft so that new aircraft had to be supplied. Toward the end, we were short of well-trained pilots as well.

Q. Did you have many more planes than you were able to operate?

A. If we consider the bombers, we had a lot more planes. But in the fighters, the losses were very high. Back in 1942, when an airplane was forced down in a foreign country [an occupied territory], it was just picked up or repaired on the spot, and came back immediately into circulation on its own. Later, this became impossible and the machine was lost forever. Toward the end, we were not in the position at all to undertake the repair of such machines.

Q. Were the attacks on repair facilities and hangars at airfields important in defeating the Luftwaffe?

A. I could not say that they were a major factor, but they naturally did contribute, as you can see when you look at the German airfields as they are today.

Q. In other words, the wastage was so great in 1944 and 1945 that production could not keep up with it?

A. The new pilots were much worse trained than the old ones and the losses were considerably higher.

Q. What were the causes of wastage? How does the amount of wastage in the air compare to the wastage on the ground?

A. I would like to put it differently. After the last strong attack on England, which was made by the 9th Corps and their bombers,[22] this Corps had to be withdrawn because of the lack of aircraft. We had to ground all the bombers and reorientate completely to fighters. As far as I can remember, five wings were affected by that. Thus, of course, those people needed a lot of aircraft for their retraining. Consequently at that time the bombers were grounded and a part of the fighters, which I would normally have given to the fighter squadrons as a very strong replacement, had to be used for retraining. But I would like to add that the situation would have greatly changed if the war had continued, because in April, the ME-262 became the airplane which again could attack the bombers disregarding the enemy fighter cover. The manufacture of the 262 was supposed to be dispersed into subterranean workshops in Kahla which were to produce 1,000 completed aircraft per month. There was also a large factory near Kaufering which had considerable concrete cover which was to produce another 1,000 planes per month, and we were building a tunnel at Garmisch. All that was for the 262 which already must have had a monthly production of 1,500 machines. This was then to be increased to 2,500 and 3,000. We have to consider further that jet planes did not need any high-quality gasoline, and that as hydrogenation plants for this work had to be underground by Autumn, we had decided to completely change the production to jet planes, even the bombers. The Do-335[23] had two props, one puller and one pusher type. I gave the orders to retain the puller-type propellor, but to replace the pusher type by a jet engine. In this way, we would have achieved what we were lacking most in the fight against the American airplanes, namely the long-range fighter. The FW-190 and the ME-109 are, of course, comparatively short-range ships.

Q. Were substantial losses sustained in ferrying aircraft?

A. Sometimes, when, for instance, through bad luck a ferrying flight would hit the enemy planes, and very often when we had to ferry aircraft under pressure during bad weather. Toward the end we had some very bad weather in Germany.

Q. Did you lose much on account of machine flaws in ferrying?

A. No.

Q. On account of inexperience of pilots?

A. Especially through the inexperienced pilots, especially in fighters. During the ferrying of bombers, the ferry losses were within bearable limits.

Q. We have read that you have said that for every four aircraft lost in combat, about forty would crash on the way home. What did you mean by that?

A. That is the old song again. That statement was never meant that way. It was meant to refer to the ratio of combat and non-combat losses, and was made at a time when we had the upper hand. The Americans were not in the war and we were very strong in comparison to the English air force.

Q. How do combat losses compare with losses by other causes?

A. If you include in combat losses all losses in fights, both direct and indirect, they would be just about the same. Toward the end, the combat losses became larger. At the beginning, the total of losses from other causes was in my opinion higher. The percentage of pilots lost per plane was changing. In case of a heavy-scale Allied penetration, we would lose through weather, enemy action, crash, etc., 40, 50, or 50 percent [sic] of the machines and the pilots lost were 12 or 15 percent.

III Principal Reasons for Luftwaffe Defeat

Q. In your opinion, what were the reasons for the failure of the German Luftwaffe against the Allied forces?

A. I most firmly believe that the reason was the success of the American air force in putting out a long-range escort fighter airplane, which enabled the bombers to penetrate deep into the Reich territory and still have a constant and strong fighter cover. Without this escort, the air offensive would never have succeeded. Nobody thought such long-range fighter escort was possible.

Q. As a result of such operations, was the Luftwaffe defeated primarily because of the attacks upon the aircraft industry, or the attacks upon the Luftwaffe in the air?

A. By far the greater damage resulted in the industry. The kills in the air were naturally only a fraction of what was reported by your pilots. But the decisive thing was that you did manage to get the fighter cover.

Q. Notwithstanding the bombing of the factories, there are records which indicate that the total production in 1944 was very much higher than in any previous time. Is this correct, and if so, how do you reconcile it with what you have just said about the effects of attacks on aircraft production?

A. If you consider the production purely quantitatively, then that is correct. But you have to consider that I can always build four or five fighters instead of a four-engined bomber. You don't want to take purely the numbers of aircraft but you want to compare the types. For instance, what was the drop in production of heavy and medium bombers as compared to the increase in small fighters. The expenditure of material for one HE-177 is the same as for four fighters. The production increase in 1944 was in fighters only. Added to that was the fact that more raw materials were made available to the Luftwaffe after Minister Speer took the whole thing in his hands. And one more point, in the spring, 1944, you attacked the aircraft industry very heavily, especially air frames. Following that the Jägerstab[24] was established and a large-scale dispersal followed, so that the main factories were able to continue their work. Had the air force of the US attacked the engine industry at that time, the further building of fighter planes would have been very difficult.

Q. Referring to the invasion of Normandy, why did the Luftwaffe prove so ineffective?

A. The largest amount of fighters was stationed in the homeland for the protection against the bomber attacks. These should have been used as soon as the invasion started, but the attacks of the American air force on the French bases were so heavy that we were unable to place and maintain anywhere any large units. Therefore, we had to fly them into the battle zone from away back, and not having a long-range fighter, we were at a disadvantage.

IV Selection of Industrial Target System for Allied Air Attack

Q. From our point of view, should we have attacked the electric power system in Germany?

A. We were very much afraid of that. We had ourselves contemplated such an attack in which we were to destroy twenty-one power plants in Russia.

Q. What do you think about attacks on explosive plants? Would they have been effective?

A. Ammunition factories were built with a special security system against accidents, but nevertheless I believe that an ammunition factory can easily be destroyed.

Q. Generally speaking, did you ever have any shortage of ammunition?

A. Artillery ammunition, yes. But it was not caused through air raids, but through the lack of allocations, etc. We had never a shortage of flak ammunition. Toward the end a certain shortage appeared in some places, but when a large-scale attack came, we always had enough ammunition. The point is that ammunition cannot always be properly distributed. The Fuehrer considered flak as an extraordinarily important part of the air defense and, therefore, increased its production considerably.

V Luftwaffe Commanders

Q. Who was the best operational commander of the Luftwaffe during the whole war period?

A. At one time it was Field Marshal von Richthofen,[25] and then Kesselring.[26]

Q. How about General Galland?[27]

A. Galland was only a fighter man, and had a tremendous experience in this field, but came in conflict with the Fuehrer's conception for the operational usage of the ME-262.

Q. Was the use of these young commanders in staff positions successful, generally, in the operation of the Luftwaffe?

A. Galland was never a General Staff officer, but with the young General Staff officers we had very good luck, because they had practical experience. One of the best men was General Pelz,[28] who was as courageous as he was gifted.

VI Production of Messerschmitt 262

Q. It has been said that some 1,400 ME-262s were built. How many went into operation and why did they not all go in?

A. This probably includes everything from the first machines until the end. The first aircraft were primarily experimental ships and their engines had a lifetime of about four or five hours. Then again, they were completely new machines of which a great number had to be used for the training of pilots. Furthermore, we had to shake out the 'bugs' from the engines. So that a lot of the first machines were lost through forced landings. Another thing, the ship had a kind of brake which had to be applied very carefully, otherwise it would roll off the runway and until we had corrected that, we lost a number of machines this way. It was hard to throttle it back because it was very fast. A lot of other things came into it. It just was a completely new ship and a completely new type of engine. But toward the end, everything was under control, and what was needed was a little more experience for the pilots, so that they might know how to fly this ship at its high speeds.

Q. When was it decided to produce the ME-262 as a fighter-bomber instead of a fighter?

A. That was in May, 1944. The Fuehrer had originally directed that it be produced as a fighter, but in May, 1944, he ordered that it be converted into a fighter-bomber. This conversion was one of the main reasons for the delay in getting this plane into action in any quantity.

Q. That's all – our time is up.

Document 7 Conquest by Telephone

Extract from the interrogation of Hermann Goering taken at Nuremberg
on 3 October 1945 by Colonel J. H. Amen (from pp. 15–23 of the
original transcript)

Q. Now, do you remember in March 1938, 11 March, to be specific,
you had some telephone conversations with Seyss-Inquart[29] and Glaise
Horstenau?
A. Yes, certainly.
Q. And those conversations were monitored?
A. Certainly. I knew that they were. I knew that they were being
monitored, and that is why I held them the way that I did.
Q. And what was the substance of those conversations?
A. If I remember correctly, – you mean the conversations that took
place the day before the Anschluss?
Q. Yes.
A. I made a number of telephone calls to Vienna on that day. On that
day, the whole thing started to slide, and if I remember correctly,
Schuschnigg[30] went so far as to say that there would not be any
elections. I said that it would be too late; and I talked to Seyss-Inquart,
and told him that this was not sufficient. Things really started to slide
then, and I felt that this was the decisive hour. In other words, it was
to be decided now whether we would achieve the Anschluss without
any difficulties, and without paying too high a price. Then, when
Schuschnigg went a little farther, I demanded the next thing; and so it
went on. I don't want to deny that I possibly was the most active man
in Berlin on that day. I might have been even more active than the
Fuehrer himself. I just felt that it was the only decision.
Q. Well, what was the substance of what you said in these telephone
conversations? With particular reference to invading Austria, the first
call was about ten o'clock in the morning.
A. As far as I can remember the telephone conversation, the whole
conversation took place in the morning, and was about the mission
that Glaise Horstenau received from us in Berlin. It was his mission to
talk to Schuschnigg on the one side, and to Seyss-Inquart on the other;

to tell them that things were critical now; and it was his mission to go with Seyss-Inquart to stop the elections and to force further compromises from Schuschnigg. I remember when Glaise Horstenau took off in a plane from Berlin, he did not look very courageous, and he was worried about what would happen. Also I knew that Seyss-Inquart – I am sorry, I made a mistake here – that Glaise Horstenau was a very jovial gentleman, but he was not very energetic, and I just was worried about what had happened to his mission. I wanted to make sure that things were working all right.

Q. Well, the election had been proposed for 9 March?

A. Well, the election was not to take place.

Q. Well, that is the substance of what you were saying, that the election should be called off, or else Germany would invade Austria, right?

A. Yes.

Q. And is this the substance of the conversation: 'Goering asks me (Seyss-Inquart) to tell the Chancellor immediately that he has one hour to revoke the Plebiscite, and to answer publicly that the Plebiscite should be revoked; and that in three or four weeks Austria would make the Plebiscite, concerning the Anschluss with Germany, conform to the rules of the former Saar Plebiscite,[31] held by Germany in that area?'

A. This was the immediate opinion of the Fuehrer. It was his opinion that it should be handled in such a manner. As I said before, in the course of the day, events started to slide so fast, that towards the evening there was a completely different development, from which then followed the occurrences which subsequently took place.

Q. Well, when Seyss-Inquart had been informed by Schuschnigg that the latter was willing to delay the election but would not agree to the application of the rules of the Saar area election, Seyss-Inquart then found you and informed you of the Chancellor's decision?

A. Yes, we were in continual conversation by telephone.

Q. And then at one o'clock in the afternoon, there was a second phone call from you to Seyss-Inquart and Glaise Horstenau which went as follows: 'Reichsmarshal Goering says that the situation in Austria can only be saved when Chancellor Schuschnigg resigns within two hours from now.'

A. I wasn't the Reichsmarshal at the time. I was only a Field Marshal. I was only a Field Marshal at the time.

Q. 'And the situation in Austria can only be saved if Chancellor Schuschnigg resigns within two hours from now, and when Seyss-Inquart is nominated as his successor, as next Chancellor of Austria. When you (Seyss-Inquart) don't give me any reply by phone within those two hours, I know that you are hindered by force.'

A. Yes, as far as I can remember, this was at four o'clock.

Q. 'Know that you are hindered by force from doing so, and we will begin to march against Austria.'

The Chancellor resigned at 3:30.

A. Well, the hours really don't matter, but in substance this is just about what happened, and I believe I said it before, that by the time Schuschnigg would agree to some compromise, it was so late already that some other developments had taken place; and the events just kept on sliding; and they were temporarily accelerated then. We were informed that the people of Vienna were already on the streets, and the people of Graz and Styria, in general, had declared their independence a few days before, and declared their willingness to go with Germany. As I said before, I considered this the most favorable hour for a rapid and cheap way to gain the Anschluss; and I will not deny that at all times I have been for the Anschluss of Austria, which has a purely German population with the Reich.

Q. Well, late in the afternoon of that day, do you recall making another telephone call to Seyss-Inquart, demanding that he immediately send a telegram to you which would ask for the assistance of German troops in Austria, because the internal conditions in Austria were such at that time that the Austrian government could no longer cope with them?

A. Yes, this was desired by the Fuehrer, and I wished for the same thing.

Q. And isn't it a fact that this telegram, in effect, was a pretext to get German troops inside of Austria under the guise that you needed them to control the internal situation?

A. Yes, that is so. The true reason behind that was that we were not so much afraid of finding any resistance in Austria, as we wanted to have troops in Austria as quickly as possible, for fear that some outside influence, say, the Little Entente [Czechoslovakia, Yugoslavia, Romania], would make an occupation of their own, say, of the Burgenland, or some other part, say, Southern Styria.[32] This was in effect to guarantee that none of the other neighbors would come in and take their little parts, so to speak. The Fuehrer had misgivings about this, and that is why he wanted troops in there. The telegram was made the internal reason for it.

Q. But isn't it also a fact, that prior to 4:00 p.m. on 11 March 1938, you had sent Keppler[33] to Vienna; and that after arriving there, Keppler gained admittance to the Chancellery, set up a German office inside, called Schuschnigg and told him, in effect, the following –

A. I want to say something here about the dispatch of Keppler. He was dispatched by the Fuehrer. I would have sent somebody else. Of course, that doesn't matter here. At any rate, he was dispatched by the Fuehrer, and he received his information from the Fuehrer; and I was there when he received it; and I added my own remarks to him.

Q. What was Keppler? How did Keppler happen to come there?

A. We used Keppler for missions of high diplomatic nature, so to speak. As far as my own opinion of him goes, he was competent for certain economic matters. However, personally, I would have never trusted him in such a task. He did not carry out the power of his convictions, and he was not hard-hitting enough to carry out something like that. At least, that was my opinion of him. He was a little slow, and I thought at the time that somebody else might have been better used for that.

Q. Now, was he instructed, or did he, in effect, tell Schuschnigg: 'You see, now, that what I told you two weeks ago is correct. You should have followed my advice. Are there any wishes which you have?'

A. This is correct; but of course, this is from the Fuehrer. I never talked with Schuschnigg before. The Fuehrer is referring to the conversation which he had with Schuschnigg, two weeks prior.

Q. Now, where were you when these various telephone calls were made?

A. I was in the Reichs Chancellery, together with the Fuehrer, in one room.

Q. And how did you know that the conversations were being monitored?

A. That is self-understood. Which state does not monitor official conversations? I wanted Schuschnigg to hear all that.

Q. What instructions did you or the Fuehrer give to Keppler?

A. The Fuehrer gave him this instruction, and he furthermore gave him instructions to support Seyss-Inquart; and at that time, that is in the afternoon, the exact manner of the Anschluss had not been fixed, and that was only fixed later when Hitler talked at Linz. My instructions were the following – to be frank, at that time I knew Seyss-Inquart very little, and also his new entourage. However, the idea that I had of them, or let's say, the suspicion that I had of them, was that they were very willing to kick out Schuschnigg, and that they wished for a close relation with Germany. However, they did expect to get something out of this for their own personalities, and it was their wish to remain as independent as possible. I didn't want this whole thing to have the effect that the government of Schuschnigg would be kicked out, and that merely a camouflage Nazi government of Austria would be instituted under them. But I told Keppler to keep a sharp lookout that they should not take things into their own hands, and that the Anschluss was to be effected in such a manner as the Austrian people had wanted it in 1918.[34] And just that was the reason, that I had misgivings in sending such a soft man as Keppler.

Here is something that I want to say by way of explanation; I can only emphasize again that I spent a great deal of my youth in Austria, and therefore was very familiar with everything that went on in Austria. Moreover, my father, at the time of the Kaiser, in Austria, had the following ideological concept of the Anschluss. This is only by way of explanation of how I came to have this opinion. So to speak, I spent half my youth in Germany, and half my youth in Austria.

Q. Was the Fuehrer present during all of these telephone conversations, to which you have testified?

A. He was present at 80 percent of them at least – no, I remember now, there was only one conversation which I did not make from that phone; that was later in the evening.

Q. And everything which you did on that day was done with the knowledge, approval, and at the direction of the Fuehrer?

A. Yes, he partly directed the conversations, or he heard them and consented to what I said. I can only say again, that on this afternoon perhaps, I was more driving than he was. However, he consented to all these things. Of course, I couldn't do any of those things without the Fuehrer's approval.

Q. Do you think the Fuehrer is dead?

A. Absolutely, no doubt about it.

Q. What makes you think so?

A. Well, this is quite out of the question. We always knew that the Fuehrer would kill himself if things were coming to an end. We always knew that. There is not the least doubt about it.

Q. Well, was there any understanding or agreement to that effect?

A. Yes, he said this only too clearly and too explicitly to different people, and we all knew about this exactly.

Q. What about Bormann?

A. (Throwing hands into the air) If I had my say in it, I hope he is frying in Hell, but I don't know about it . . .

Document 7b Vote 'No' if you dare

Extract from the interrogation of Albert Goering taken at Nuremberg on
25 September 1945 by William Jackson (from pp. 23–4 of the
original transcript)

Q. I just want to identify those 'fake elections' you talked about. When and where were they?

A. I am talking about the elections now, after the Anschluss of Austria. That is, the elections when the population of Austria agreed to the incorporation of Austria into Germany. I personally, I voted 'No', but it was terribly difficult because even the voting itself was faked, and under the most trying of circumstances. It was fixed so that it was almost impossible to vote 'No'.

Q. Well, did you have a choice, a 'Yes' or 'No' choice?

A. May I make a sketch of the thing?

(Witness draws a diagram.)

The whole thing took place in a rather large hall. There was an entrance, and when you came in there was a round table at which sat several officials, and they registered you. They would hand you an envelope which had a sheet of paper in it; and there were two circles in it, a large circle and a small circle, and you were supposed to make a cross in one of the circles, the larger circle meaning 'Yes', and the smaller circle meaning 'No'. Then at the other end of this hall was a telephone booth, and you were supposed to go in there, and make your cross, put the ballot in the envelope, return, and drop it into a box which was provided at the end of the table. It was handled in this manner. However, when somebody came in, the officials would greet him with 'Heil Hitler', and then give him the ballot and they said, 'You are voting "Yes", there is no reason to go into the booth at the end of the hall'; and everybody would make a cross in the larger circle. Then they would give the ballot to the official, and he would put it in the envelope, and put it in the box. Nobody dared to go to the booth in order to vote secretly. Well, I came into this place, and I was the only one among hundreds of people who dared to go into this booth. The official gave me the paper and said I could fill it out right there, and I told him that law and order must be kept, and I proceeded to the booth, and I made my cross in the 'No', then sealed the envelope and dropped it in the box. This is the way that voting was handled at that time.

ENSIGN JACKSON I ask to have this drawing marked as Exhibit 'A', for identification, 25 September 1945 (Albert Goering) . . .

Waging War

'In August, 1938, I was together with Hitler and other people present at the maneuver in East Prussia. When he returned from the maneuver to his train, he said to his military adjutant, later General Schmundt, and to me – we were standing in a group of three – "I can see now that Clausewitz is right: War is the father of all things; every generation has to go into war once."'[1]

Interrogation of Fritz Wiedemann, Nuremberg, 9 October 1945

[At Nuremberg the waging of aggressive war was the central charge, from which the other crimes outlined in the Indictment were a direct consequence. Most of those interrogated about war preparations and the conduct of the war showed a ready willingness to explain, however impressionistically, what they saw as the motives for the key decisions of the war – the attack on Poland in 1939, war with the USSR two years later, the declaration of war on the United States: and so on. The prisoners who were asked specifically about war and foreign policy showed a remarkable consistency in their testimony. Without exception they asserted that Hitler did not expect the two western powers, Britain and France, to declare war in September 1939. Fritz Wiedemann, until 1939 Hitler's adjutant, told interrogator John Martin that he was 'convinced that Hitler would not have started the war against Poland in '39 if he had known at the time that it would mean England's entry into the war'.[2] According to Wiedemann, it was fear of Britain that prevented Hitler from ordering his war against Czechoslovakia in September 1938. Emerging from a meeting in October 1938 with Hitler, Goering told Wiedemann that he now knew why Hitler had backed down from war and accepted the Munich compromise: 'You see, Goering, at the last moment I thought the British fleet would shoot.'[3]

The interrogations also confirmed the eastern orientation of Hitler's foreign policy outlook. 'It is a fact,' Goering told Amen, 'that he [Hitler] always said German politics would finally lead towards expansion towards the East.'[4] Yet when the confrontation with the USSR came in 1941 almost all of the testimonies taken during the pre-trial period pointed out that the plans for Barbarossa arose in response to changing diplomatic and military circumstances: the apparent threat posed by Soviet forces along the western Soviet frontier; Soviet territorial expansion into the Baltic states and the Romanian provinces of Bukovina and Bessarabia in the summer of 1940; and above all the negotiations with the Soviet Foreign Minister, Molotov, in November 1940, which exposed the Soviet ambition to become a major player in the Balkans and eastern Mediterranean. Despite the efforts of the Soviet interrogators to expose a long-held plan of conquest in the east, the short-term crisis in Soviet–German relations was what German politicians and soldiers remembered. Such short-term circumstances are a major part of current historical explanations for the decision to launch Barbarossa in 1941.[5]

These perspectives emerge clearly in Documents 8–10. The first interrogation of Foreign Minister Joachim von Ribbentrop was taken early in his captivity, before his psychological decline. In it he supplied explanations for the major decisions for war, including a historically plausible account of the reasoning behind the German declaration of war on the United States. The second document gives Albert Speer's account, produced at 'Dustbin', of his impressions of German foreign policy and war-making. Here, too, he records Hitler's dismissal of American soldiers as 'poor fighters', incapable of mounting a serious threat in Europe. The third interrogation is the most historically valuable. Field Marshal Wilhelm Keitel, chief-of-staff of Hitler's supreme headquarters (OKW), was at the centre of the German war effort throughout the entire war period. He was not interrogated a great deal, and the document reproduced here, in effect an account of the entire course of the war, has been ignored since. Yet Keitel, widely regarded by his contemporaries as a 'yes-man' (one of those, according to Speer, 'who blindly and without dignity followed their chief's opinion'),[6] was the key figure between Hitler and the Wehrmacht. Directives from OKW, including the 'criminal orders' of 1941, came under Keitel's signature. Keitel confirmed in his interrogation that Hitler was serious about the invasion of Britain in 1940; he took the view that Hitler decided definitely for war against the USSR only in November 1940, when diplomatic efforts to attach the USSR to the Tripartite Pact of Germany, Italy and Japan (signed in September 1940) faltered. 'Only if such efforts should fail altogether,' ran a report on Keitel's interrogations, 'then there would be the need for military clarification of the issue.'[7] Keitel believed that there was little coherence to Hitler's war planning ('Things developed from episode to episode . . .'); he also thought his chief made 'incredible exaggerations to impress his staff'. He recalled a principle confessed to him once by Hitler: 'Keitel, one must demand the impossible, because then one perhaps obtains the possible.'[8]]

Document 8 Ribbentrop, Hitler and War

Memorandum for Justice Jackson, report by two political officers of SHAEF
on an interview with Joachim von Ribbentrop, June 1945

Throughout the conversation Ribbentrop voluntarily spoke in nearly flawless English. It will be recalled that even before the war began Ribbentrop had refused to speak English with American and British diplomatic representatives and spoke to Sumner Welles[9] only through an interpreter during the latter's visit in 1940. It may also be mentioned that the cold austere manner which Ribbentrop put on with his assumption of the Foreign Ministry is now completely absent and throughout the interview he tried to appear affable and even jocular.

In the discussion of Foreign Office personnel the name of Schulenburg,[10] the last German ambassador to Moscow, came up. Ribbentrop remarked that Schulenburg had once been a 'fine fellow, a great friend', but that he had gone 'senile'. He would have tried to save him from being executed for complicity with the 20 July plot against Hitler's life if Schulenburg had answered frankly when Ribbentrop had asked him if he were involved. Schulenburg had replied that he had no connection with the plot. Ribbentrop said his execution was regrettable but that Schulenburg had been guilty of 'treachery' against him since he had lied to him and furthermore expected to become Ribbentrop's successor as Foreign Minister.

Asked why Germany had invaded Russia, Ribbentrop answered that it was 'the greatest mistake in history' and was a complete reversal of his 'fundamental foreign policy'. He had never been able to determine precisely why and when the Fuehrer had decided on the invasion. There were various elements in his decision – ideological grounds and Party and army influences. It was also provoked by certain incidents such, for example, as the report that some twenty-one or twenty-two Russian divisions were massed along the border of East Prussia. There was the fact that the Soviet Trade Delegation had shown more interest in obtaining offensive than defensive armament. Military fears were also stirred by the fact that the Russian Purchasing Commission had turned down certain items of armament the Germans were offering on the grounds that Russia was already producing superior equipment of the same type. The old Party members had grumbled against the rapprochement with Russia on the ground that it was against basic 'grundsaetze' (principles). Ribbentrop said that he was 'sick of hearing the word "grundsaetze"'. The army feared, of course, that Russia was quite steadily and dangerously becoming stronger and might ultimately attack Germany if the latter weakened from a long war. One incident that had angered the Fuehrer was Russia's 'ultimate announcement' of its occupation of Bessarabia[11] at the very moment the Fuehrer was waiting at Compiègne for the French surrender plus the fact that the occupation did not stop at Bessarabia but included Bukovina[12] where there was a large German population. Of course, Ribbentrop said, German arrangements with Russia had included the 'usual agreements about spheres of influence'.

To the question whether his 'arrangements' with Russia had not in fact contemplated the latter's occupying Bessarabia, he answered with a smile and an expression of mock embarrassment 'Must I answer that question? After all Russia is one of your Allies.'

Ribbentrop went on to say 'of course we had to act very quickly to counter the Russian move'. (Presumably he referred to German infiltration into Romania.)[13] There was no doubt, he said, that Russia had ambitions to extend its influence through the Balkans and the army feared that if war went on in the West and greater Russian support became necessary, it would be given only at the price of extension of Russian control over areas necessary to German security.

Hitler was a man, Ribbentrop stated, who never changed his fundamental ideas. He was 'starr-sinnig' (obstinate) in maintaining them. He thought only in terms of 'historical periods' and applied this concept to every problem. Proceeding with the discussion of incidents that had determined the invasion of Russia, Ribbentrop referred to Hitler's dispute over Finland with Molotov during the latter's visit to Berlin in 1940. Ribbentrop remarked with a severely 'righteous' expression Germany was 'definitely in the wrong' in having any dispute with Russia about Finland. In the winter of 1940–41 Hitler had suddenly summoned Ribbentrop and excitedly presented him with reports from the police that 960 Russians were attached to the Russian Trade Delegation in the Kurfurstenstrasse and that parties of five or ten Russian officials were in fact organizing communism in the factories.

When the decision to attack Russia had finally hardened, Ribbentrop had delivered a 'strong warning' against such action to Hitler, but he said ruefully, Hitler was a 'very strong personality who could not be changed'. The Nazi system was very different from the American. It was a dictatorship in which final responsibility for important decisions did not rest with the competent minister.

Ribbentrop then launched into an exposition of his Russian policy. He had long felt that there were common elements in communism and the Nazi system which made a rapprochement possible between the two countries despite their different political systems. When he had first broached the idea of rapprochement to the Fuehrer, the latter abruptly dismissed it with the statement that he had 'fought communism all my life. You know nothing about it.' Ribbentrop persevered, however, and quoting Bismarck, finally obtained permission to endeavor to negotiate a trade treaty. He immediately sent Gesandter [envoy] Schnurre to Moscow who in a mere eight or ten days had concluded a satisfactory trade agreement. It sounded 'fantastic' Ribbentrop said laughingly but the incident which apparently decided the Fuehrer to attempt a political rapprochement with Russia [in 1939] was a motion picture of Stalin reviewing a military parade – a May Day parade he thought. The film had been sent by the German military attaché at Moscow and was shown at the Berghof. Hitler 'took a fancy to Stalin's face' and remarked emphatically he 'looks like a man one could do business with'. Promptly thereafter he gave Ribbentrop permission to try to come to a political understanding with Russia. At first negotiations were started with the Russian chargé d'affaires in Berlin but progress was unsatisfactory. 'One never knew what Russian official had plenipotentiary powers.' Ribbentrop suggested to Hitler that it would be necessary to send someone to Moscow. Hitler agreed and sent a direct telegram to Stalin asking him to receive Ribbentrop. Stalin's acceptance was immediate.

At his first meeting with Stalin, not quite knowing what the situation was or the latter's reaction would be, Ribbentrop indulged in a long 'diplomatic speech'. Stalin, however, came right to the point and said that while the two countries had been pouring filth 'over each other's heads' (the word actually used, according to Ribbentrop, was a Russian expression for liquid manure) there was no reason why they should not come to agreement and before midnight of the day of his arrival he had drafted and signed a non-aggression pact with Stalin. Ribbentrop said the timing of this was very important because 'of the difficulties he was having with Poland'. He, Ribbentrop, flattered himself that Stalin had confidence in him. He remarked it was perhaps exaggerated to say that Stalin who indisputedly was one of the great historical figures had confidence in him but that was his feeling. Ribbentrop proceeded unctuously to say that his policy of rapprochement with Russia was designed to establish peace in Europe and to enable Germany to come to an alliance with the British Empire on a basis [of] equality and carry out Hitler's plans 'to get nearly all Germans into one Reich'. His policy and that of Hitler had been to come to an understanding with England. Hitler had not wanted to invade England. They had talked about it at Compiègne after the fall of France and Ribbentrop had written down briefly three or four main points of an agreement which made clear that neither British prestige nor the Empire was to suffer. Hitler had said that he would present the offer immediately and personally and 'did so in his Reichstag speech in July 1940'. The offer was 'turned down by Chamberlain [sic]', Ribbentrop said, and Hitler thereupon 'reluctantly' decided on an alliance with Japan, as previously, he had 'reluctantly' made an alliance with Italy when Eden and Sir John Simon had refused the arrangement with the Empire which he had offered during their visit to Germany in 1936.[14]

Ribbentrop went on to allege that the 'defensive' alliance with Japan was made 'for the sake of Peace to neutralize the United States and prevent its entry into the war'. He, Ribbentrop, had never wanted war with the United States. In the few five or six speeches he had made he had clearly brought out that Germany and the United States had no 'divergencies'. He had refused to allow the German press to reply to American newspaper attacks.

The Japanese attack on Pearl Harbor had come as a 'disagreeable surprise' to Hitler and to him. To the question why if this development was 'disagreeable' he had declared war, he denied there had been a 'formal' declaration of war in the note he had handed[15] the American chargé d'affaires. He argued confusedly that no such statement was in the note, regretted that he did not have a copy of it at hand for consultation, and went on confusedly to say that possibly Hitler may have made some declaration in a speech he delivered a day or two after the Pearl Harbor attack.[16] Hitler had discussed with him the question of declaring war on the United States. Ribbentrop implied that, but did not specifically assert, he had argued against war with America but that Hitler had said that Germany was already, in effect, at war with the United States since American warships were firing on German naval units and that if Germany did not take a 'stellung' [position] that the pact with Japan, while it provided only for a defensive alliance, would be 'politically dead'.

Hitler never changed his ideas, Ribbentrop stated. Even in the last days of the war he talked about coming to an understanding with the British Empire. Ribbentrop had taken leave of Hitler on 22 April. He had been directed by Hitler to go to the wireless station at Nauen to get in touch with German diplomatic agents abroad but he found, on nearing the place, it was already in Russian hands. He then went to Wenk's (?) division whose mission was to relieve Berlin. From there he communicated with the Fuehrer asking whether he should join those forces as a soldier or return to Berlin. The answer came back that he was not to stay in the army but to await further instructions which would be forthcoming the next day. The next day he had the announcement of Hitler's death . . .

He asserted that he had done 'what everyone tried to do in this war – do the best one could for one's own country'. On being told the interview was at an end he said that he had never thought that the war would come to such 'proportions that government[s] were placed under arrest'. He had always been loyal to the Fuehrer and had stayed by him to the end, 'that was the Germanic way'.

When I made no reply to these remarks, but merely said goodbye, that we would probably talk to him again before long and turned away, Ribbentrop's expression was one of rather nervous consternation and his exit was less assured than his entrance.

Document 9 Hitler's 'chess game of power politics'

FIAT Intelligence Report No. 19, Part II, examination of Speer by
Mr O. Hoeffding on 'Nazi Foreign Policy and Military Leadership',
7 September 1945

Nazi Foreign Policy and Military Leadership
1 Foreign Policy

Q. I am particularly interested in the political preparations for this war. I realize that you consider yourself more or less an outsider in the political events before 1939, but I should like to hear your views on this subject. Was it your impression that German foreign policy was largely determined by Hitler personally?

SPEER Yes, exclusively by Hitler. He made up for his lack of interest in domestic politics by being the driving power behind foreign policy and military affairs – insofar as I can judge in retrospect.

Q. Do you think that in the middle thirties Hitler had a clear conception of his long-range objectives in foreign policy?

SPEER He had a clear conception, in my view, but it was different from the subsequent actual course of events. I can well remember the time before the outbreak of the Abyssinian war – 1935 or so. When I was at the Obersalzburg, he said that he had to make a final decision whether to side with the Italians or the English. He considered this a fundamental decision. Even then he emphasized, as he frequently repeated later on, that he was ready to place the Reich with its Wehrmacht [armed forces] at the disposal of the British Empire as a 'guarantee', if England would give him a 'free hand' in the East. He was much preoccupied with this question at the time, especially since he realized the inadequacy of Italy as an ally. He said that it was part of the political testament which Hindenburg had left him before he died, that Germany should never again join forces with Italy. In the days of the Abyssinian conflict, therefore, he was distressed by the fact that the situation as he saw it called for German–Italian co-operation directed against England. I am not familiar with the details of this situation.

Q. What was Hitler's conception of a 'free hand in the East'?

SPEER I assume that, in the long run, he had aggressive intentions. In our phraseology, expansionist plans with a view to providing a foundation for the further development of the German people. Hitler did not think much of colonies, whose fate would be determined by the British navy. His expansionist plans were probably directed eastward because he regarded the development of a great German land power as the most promising long-range policy.

Q. Did you ever hear anything from Hitler on the connections with Germany alleged at the Moscow purge trials in 1936/37?[17]

SPEER At the time he regarded the trials as a fake staged entirely for the purposes of domestic politics. Later on, after 20 July 1944, he often posed the question whether, after all, there might not have been some truth in those allegations.[18] Although, as he said, he still had no positive indication of a conspiracy between the German and Russian General Staffs, he thought – after 20 July – that such collusion might have been quite possible, without his knowledge. This seems to show that at the time of the trials Hitler knew nothing of any secret connections. Incidentally, he often stressed that Stalin had done absolutely the right thing – the trials and their consequences for the Russian General Staff had been a move which decisively contributed to the military success of the Russians later on. By liquidating his General Staff, Stalin had introduced a new and more active element into his army, and had laid the foundation for selecting new military leaders.

Hitler, even before 20 July, used to express his regrets that we did not take similar action at the same time, but he said that it was too late to do this in wartime.

Q. So you have no reason to believe that at that time there was a German plan for eliminating Soviet Russia without war, through internal penetration?

SPEER If such a plan had existed it would certainly have been discussed in Hitler's circle after 20 July, when there was a lot of agitated discussion on the background to the plot.

Q. Do you think that Hitler had planned a systematic campaign for undermining other foreign countries internally through fifth column activities, and to achieve his aims without war?

SPEER I do not think that Hitler thought much of such methods. He knew the difficulties of his own career up to 1933, and in his view there were no propagandists in other countries who could repeat what he had achieved. He often criticized politicians like Mussert[19] and Mosley,[20] describing them as plagiarists without any original ideas which might be effective in their own countries. He thought more of Degrelle,[21] but he did not expect anything from any of them.

Q. What about his policy towards Western Europe: do you think he was subjectively sincere in his assertions that he was not interested in regaining Alsace-Lorraine for Germany?

SPEER Undoubtedly, if he had been given a 'free hand' in the East as his 'sphere of interest'. He did not think of a *revanche*, and did not want to resume the war of 1918. He said that it was not worth while to wage war for an insignificant strip of territory like Alsace-Lorraine, whose population, in his words, had become 'worthless' through the frequent changes in their national allegiance, which had made them a doubtful asset for either side. They should be left wherever they were.

Q. To what extent did the passivity of the Western Powers towards his 'peaceful conquests' of the Rhineland, Austria and Czechoslovakia encourage Hitler to undertake further acts of aggression?

SPEER He regarded the re-militarization of the Rhineland[22] as the most dangerous of all his military enterprises. I happened to be on his train en route for Munich when the Rhineland occupation started. I could observe how everybody was worrying about a possible military counter-action. We would not have been able to do anything if at that time France or England had made the slightest protest and backed it up by military pressure. Hitler said later on that our own forces were negligible and could not have offered resistance. He described the Rhineland occupation as the most daring of all his enterprises, much more bold than all his later moves. Our rearmament was then at its very beginning. I can recall that in Hitler's entourage the 'peaceful' conclusion of that operation was attributed to the influence of the King of England (Edward VIII). Hitler placed hopes upon him.

Q. Was not his intervention in Spain incompatible with the intention which you attribute to Hitler of staying on good terms with the West if he was given a free hand in the East?

SPEER I must emphasize that Hitler and the most important people around him had been able for years to deceive all the others by spreading misleading opinions. Therefore, all that I am saying here may be quite wrong as regards facts. I am only quoting what I heard in conversations with Hitler and his entourage. It may be that some of this talk was intentionally misleading.

Intervention in Spain was decided upon and initiated during the Bayreuth Festival in August 1936. It was said that an alarming call for aid had come in from Franco and required an immediate decision. Goering should be able to tell you more about this, since he was in on the discussions with Hitler. The war in Spain was presented to us as a conflict with the 'Reds', and later with the Russian expeditionary forces in Spain. Hitler did not want a Soviet Spain, and was afraid of similar repercussions in France after Spain had gone Soviet. He did not want to be encircled by Soviet states in East and West. This is how Hitler explained the situation to us. He could not understand why the Catholic church failed to react favorably to his intervention, especially since the church was being restored in the 'liberated' parts of Spain. According to the reports which he was getting, the 'Reds' were cruelly and violently persecuting religion. I had the impression that Hitler hoped to improve his relations with the Vatican as a result of this intervention, or at least expected the Catholic church to show some appreciation of his action.

Q. Did the intervention set the seal on the German–Italian alliance?

SPEER That had started with the Abyssinian war, when he had committed himself to co-operation with Italy to defeat the Sanctions. This was the turning point at which friendship with Italy was established. Hitler and his military advisors were over-estimating Italian military power at that time. The Italian fleet with its up-to-date units and numerous U-boats was taken at face value. Only during the war did it emerge that the Italians were anything but sailors and could do nothing with their fleet. The same applied to the Italian air force, which impressed us at a time when we had no planes ourselves. Not enough attention was paid to the fact that the Italians are no soldiers. Mussolini's influence upon the nation and its 'warlike spirit' were also much overrated. This was the first instance of our falling victims to our own propaganda, as often happened later on. However, England, too, seems to have had an erroneous picture of Italy's power at that time.

Q. Was it a deliberate policy of Hitler's to give support to movements abroad which ideologically were akin to Nazism in order to bring them to power in their own countries?

SPEER No, as far as I was able to observe he did not care. His relations with foreign states were purely a chess game of power politics. He was indifferent to the political structure of any country. In his intimate circle he often emphasized that it would be a mistake to export National Socialism abroad. This, in his opinion, would only result in an undesirable national invigoration of these countries, while democracy would tend to weaken their fighting power.

His attitude in foreign policy was comparable to his tactics in domestic politics before 1933, when he repeatedly conducted secret negotiations with the Communists, the Center Party and the German National Party, all at the same time, just in order to promote his own rise to power. The ideological positions of the various parties did not bother him at that time either.

He did not show such 'largesse' in the final stages of his career. Then he was running on a narrow-gauge track, and bluntly refused any kind of peace feelers or parleys with the Russians or with the West.

Q. Do you know if the Austrian Anschluss was also considered a risky move?

SPEER No. Not to a great extent. He considered that German–Italian collaboration was assured in this case, and that Germany and Italy would for some time form such a powerful group that the other powers would not do anything serious about Austria. He always was very grateful for the political aid which he then received from Italy, and regarded it as a sacrifice on Mussolini's part, since Germany's union with Austria created serious frontier problems for Italy. In Hitler's view the German troops on the Brenner created a political problem for Mussolini, who would have preferred to have Austria between Germany and Italy. If, later on, anybody criticized Mussolini, Hitler would retort that on this occasion Mussolini had rendered him a valuable and unselfish service, for which he owed him gratitude. Unfortunately, he really kept an alliance in this case, but it was the most unfavorable commitment which we could have.

Q. What were Hitler's reactions to the Munich agreement?

SPEER As far as we could see at the time he was very favorably impressed. We did not have the impression that he regarded the agreement as only a stepping-stone. He seemed to think that Czechoslovakia would have to come to terms with him in any case, since the agreement had given him the Czech fortifications which at that time were practically impregnable, and thus had opened the Czech river valleys to him.

He dropped hints to the effect that he now could include Czechoslovakia as part of his sphere of influence even if it remained independent.

Q. What, then, caused his next move against Czechoslovakia?

SPEER I could not understand it at the time. But afterwards I thought of one incident: One day, in March 1938 or so, Hitler asked me very pointedly how soon I could complete a large-scale expansion of the Reich Chancellery building. He said that it was absolutely essential for him to have his project completed in the shortest possible time. The existence of an impressive building was essential for his political program. He hinted at some very special events which would be forthcoming. His demand was presented in a very peremptory manner, quite different from his usual way with me. I was to give him the earliest date of completion within 24 hours, and I promised to have it ready in 9–10 months. He was satisfied with this proposal and gave me full powers to expedite construction, and I actually did complete it on time, in January 1939. When the building was finished, Hitler commented on how extremely useful it would be. When the 'little nations' came to him, they would have to be received in grand style, in order to be profoundly impressed, and the building would fully serve this purpose. One of the first conferences in the Reichskanzlei [Reich Chancellery] was Hacha's[23] visit, and later the visit of Prince-Regent Paul of Yugoslavia.[24]

In retrospect, I also believe that his ambitious plans for rebuilding Berlin have to be regarded as part of his program of power politics. For obvious reasons, he never talked about this directly, but various apparently insignificant remarks have since come back to me. Thus, he motivated his project of building a stadium at Nuremberg for 350,000 spectators by saying that in future all the Olympic Games would be held there. For an architect, of course, all these projects were very fascinating tasks.

Another incident which occurs to me: at one of the Nuremberg Party rallies, probably that in 1938, Hitler concluded his speech by proclaiming 'the Germanic Reich of the German Nation' as his future aim. There was a great deal of discussion of this passage, which was interpreted as an opening to an important chapter in his policy, in which many things might happen which small fry like ourselves could not as yet realize.

The Reichskanzlei building, the re-planning of Berlin, and the speech must be connected politically as well as chronologically. Great decisions must have been made about that time.

Q. Do you think that the economic policy which Germany then applied in south-east Europe was primarily designed to make the Balkan states economically and politically dependent on Germany?

SPEER I cannot say anything on this. All that I have said before is only the vague impression of a man who was on the periphery of the complex of foreign policy. By carefully sorting out these impressions I can reconstruct a coherent picture, but I cannot give any details.

Q. It was your impression, then, that Hitler regarded the Munich agreement as a permanent solution?

SPEER I had the feeling that this was his opinion. I also believe that Ribbentrop's mission to Paris [December 1938] was a serious undertaking.[25] I am convinced that if instead of Ribbentrop a more agile and attractive personality had been dispatched, some positive results could have been attained.

Q. When, do you think, did Hitler realize that war in the West was inevitable?

SPEER I am unable to answer this. When the Polish problem came up, he and his political entourage apparently once again assumed that they could expect the West to adopt a detached attitude, as in the case of Czechoslovakia.

I do not think that Hitler's intentions were confined only to getting the Corridor and Danzig[26] from Poland. You should be able to find documentary evidence on this. But he was not conscious of the fact that in the case of Poland the West would live up to its commitments. I remember that a few days before the attack on Poland Attolico[27] appeared in the Reichskanzlei, greatly excited. Later on I heard that the day and hour for the attack on Poland had been definitely fixed. Attolico, two or three days before the intended attack, brought the news that Italy would not join in if the Western powers declared war – that is, would not keep to the terms of its alliance. Thereupon, the attack on Poland was postponed for a few days. The officers responsible declared that it was virtually impossible to transmit the postponement orders to all units in time, and refused to accept responsibility for a possible outbreak of hostilities on parts of the frontier. This postponement was due to the shock which Italy's refusal gave Hitler. He had thought that Italian participation would discourage the Western powers from declaring war, while a declaration of war was much more likely if Germany was on her own. I do not know what kind of optimism induced him to invade Poland after all. Those were very nervous days, and at all events a war in the West was considered a possibility, but not a certainty.

Q. Do you know anything about the connection between the non-aggression pact with Russia and the invasion of Poland?

SPEER The pact was certainly a decisive event. Hitler and his private circle were on the Obersalzburg during the Moscow negotiations. Vague rumors were current that something was afoot concerning Russia. We were at supper when a slip of paper was handed to Hitler, who on reading it became extremely agitated. He jumped to his feet, banged the table and shouted 'I've got it, I've got it.' This emotional outbreak, caused by such a decisive event, was quite in contrast to his usual self-controlled manner. Only afterwards, when telegrams were exchanged with Stalin, did he tell us that that evening's news had been Ribbentrop's message on the conclusion of the pact.

Q. Were you able to observe later on whether Hitler considered this pact as a permanent solution, or as merely an expedient to gain time, for the duration of the war in the West?

SPEER I cannot say for certain. In my view it was clearly a long-term policy, but not for an unlimited period.

Q. Would you say then that when Hitler invaded Poland, he did not expect a declaration of war from the Western powers?

SPEER That was the case in my view. I can recall that he did not consider war as inevitable. He, and Goering too I believe, said at the time that England would declare war but only nominally, in order to keep its treaty of alliance.[28] Afterwards, the English would soon settle things by political methods, and would yield again. The hope that the declaration of war was merely a political gesture was abandoned only when it became known that Churchill had an influential post in the British war cabinet. This, it was said, really meant war. This may have been the background of Hitler's peace offer after the Polish campaign.[29]

According to a report which had reached us a little earlier, a British General Staff officer had been in Poland in order to assess its military strength, and his report was said to have been very unfavorable.[30] The British General Staff was expected to advise strongly against a participation in the war, since Poland would quickly collapse. As far as I remember, it was rumored that such a recommendation was about to be made by this officer to the General Staff. This, again, gave rise to hopes that England would not take an active part in this conflict.

Q. You believe, then, that Hitler did not realize in September 1939 that he had started a World War?

SPEER From what I observed, I had to assume that this was not his intention. He intended to carry his plans one step further, as with Czechoslovakia. This is borne out by the status of our rearmament at that time. If we had prepared for a full-scale war in 1939, we would not have engaged on programs like the construction of battleships and the Wilhelmshaven locks. All this planning must have been based on much later dates. The Four Year Plan[31] also, as far as I know, was carried on normally without any revisions in 1939. If 1939 had been the date, the Four Year Plan would have had to be concluded by this date, at least in certain parts. The entire armaments program was running according to a long-term schedule: it was not adjusted to any specific date. A study of this question will probably confirm my impression, although my own knowledge of this period is not complete enough to arrive at definite conclusions.

On the other hand, there is this consideration. From the standpoint of the balance of military power, 1939 must have been the best year to start a war, better than two or three years later, for this reason: before the war, we undoubtedly were ahead in our rearmament, for example in the case of the Luftwaffe, as regards quality as well as numbers. If we assume hypothetically that the ratio then was 5 to 1, this was due to the fact that your rearmament was only just getting under way. Once you had reached full production, our relative superiority would have rapidly decreased, since we could never think of multiplying our production indefinitely.

Q. Goering has said that it would have been better for Germany to wait another two years. What is your view?

SPEER No, this is an error of judgment. The favorable ratio of strength which was revealed in Poland and France – to our surprise, for we outsiders had not been informed on the situation – would never have been attained again. Nevertheless, I do not think that this was the time when Hitler wanted to have a large-scale conflict. On the whole, I don't think Hitler wanted a conflict with the Western powers. He wanted a partial settlement with Poland, which would strengthen him to the extent that the Western powers would no longer be able to interfere in further developments in the East. I think that in the end he wanted to come back to his basic idea of collaborating with England. He assumed that England, at last, would realize that his power could no longer be broken. He probably considered the Eastern space, and the suppression of Bolshevism, as his great objectives. It is my personal belief that this was the approximate general line of his policy.

Q. What do you know about Hitler's views on Japan at that time? Did he then have any definite policy?

SPEER The rapprochement with Japan was an addition to his power which he did not exactly reject on the basis of his own principles, but which he judged undesirable in the long run. In conversations he repeatedly touched upon the problem of whether he ought to side with the 'yellow' against the 'white' race, and he always discussed this with an undertone of regret. He emphasized, however, that he did not have to reproach himself, since after all in the first World War England had fought against us with Japan, and therefore given this opportunity, we had no reason to act differently. He considered it necessary for attaining his objectives, but I do not believe that he intended it to be a merger of German and Japanese interests 'for eternity'. Hitler regarded Japan as his only ally which was a really great power, while Italy was turning out to be more and more of an impossibility as time went on.

Q. What was the part of the United States in pre-war German plans and speculations?

SPEER There were no men capable of world-wide thinking in the Reichskanzlei. The group which gathered there had never got beyond Germany. It counted for something if one of them had been on a vacation trip to Italy. Hitler himself had seen nothing of the world and had no first-hand knowledge of foreign countries. He thought of England in terms of an island state. He underestimated the power of the Empire, and much more that of the USA.

There were two men who attempted to influence Hitler, one of them being his second Adjutant, Wiedemann, who would insist on starting political discussions about America, urging that it should be possible to establish connections there. Hitler got so annoyed with him that he sent him as Consul-General to San Francisco – a kind of punitive transfer – and told him that he should cure himself of his ideas. Hitler was convinced that there was no possibility of collaboration with

America. Incidentally, he would never believe that there was a unified American nation, a new people such as we have come to know it now. He regarded America as a mass of individual immigrants as yet not fully consolidated.

Q. Didn't he draw any conclusions from America's entry into the First World War?

SPEER He did not think much of that. He said that the Americans had not been particularly prominent then, and had made no great sacrifices in blood. They were not a tough nation, and if put to the test, they would be found not to be a closely-knit nation in the European sense. He retained this view during the war, when assessing the military valor of the Americans. He predicted that they would turn out to be poor fighters who could not stand up to a serious test. This, of course, was the basic idea behind the Ardennes offensive,[32] and the hopes which Hitler placed upon it. He also expected that any great sacrifices demanded from the Americans would result in serious domestic political complications.

The other man who attempted to influence Hitler was Ambassador Hewel, often at the price of serious reproaches from Hitler. Hewel had been ambassador in Batavia [Jakarta] for a long time. He must have been with Hitler in 1923/24. He pointed out again and again that Hitler was underrating America and England, that they were much tougher than he thought. Hitler always contradicted him – not, I believe, to improve our morale, but out of his own conviction.

The first few months of 1938 brought developments which must have been crucial in the history of this war: Ribbentrop's appointment as Foreign Minister, and later, in February, the replacement of Blomberg[33] by Keitel, of Wehrmacht-Adjutant Hossbach by Schmundt,[34] and Goering's promotion to the highest rank in the Wehrmacht. These were very exciting days, and one had to assume that some decisions had been made which required these changes in personalities. I am convinced that an analysis of the events which led up to those days will clear up many points. In any case, Hitler then decided to create a group of men who were active, aggressive, and obedient to him.

a. Ribbentrop

Q. Do you know from personal observation to what extent Hitler's conduct of foreign policy was influenced by Ribbentrop?

SPEER I think it is an established fact that in matters of foreign policy, just as in the military sphere, Hitler used very stubbornly to cling to his own standpoint. This will be shown by all the minutes which you may find. Nevertheless, a good advisor might have made him revise his decisions, at least up to a point, if he had known how to handle him. Ribbentrop was an unfortunate figure in this respect. Just as he failed to make himself popular in England, he was unable to work with Hitler smoothly, as a real diplomat should. He was just as clumsy and heavy with him as he had been in England. I always regarded Ribbentrop as the man who would carry out Hitler's decisions unquestioningly and drastically. We often heard that Hitler was pleased with Ribbentrop because he adopted a peremptory tone in his negotiations with the small powers and knew how to enforce Hitler's policy line in the resulting agreements.

Q. Did Hitler have a high opinion of Ribbentrop's talents?

SPEER Goebbels was a determined opponent of Ribbentrop and did his utmost to push him aside. He once discussed the matter with Hitler on the Obersalzburg, probably in 1944, and was told that he completely misunderstood Ribbentrop, who was 'a second Bismarck'. Goebbels was much shaken by this retort, and so were we when he told us about it.

Q. How did Ribbentrop succeed in bluffing Hitler to that extent?

SPEER It is incomprehensible to me. On the other hand, Hitler very often criticized Ribbentrop's shortcomings in conversations. He particularly objected to Ribbentrop's manner of stubbornly defending his point of view, which Hitler found most inconvenient. He complained that his conferences with Ribbentrop usually went on for hours. Most of these discussions, however, concerned jurisdictional matters, on which Ribbentrop was exceedingly sensitive.

I do not know how Hitler could have had such a high opinion of Ribbentrop. We were all much shaken by it. There was no other man in the entire Reich government who was so unanimously condemned during the last few years as a disastrous influence for Germany. Saying this means a lot, as otherwise everybody disagreed on everything. Especially during the period when our military situation was favorable, he made no attempt whatever to exploit our successes politically. The United Nations probably could not have wished for a better partner . . .

[The transcript contains a further nine pages on issues of military leadership and personnel selection.]

Document 10 OKW at War

United States Strategic Bombing Survey, Interview No. 55, Field Marshal Wilhelm Keitel, 27 June 1945, distributed on 5 July 1945 (pp. 8–19 of transcript)

III The Campaign in the West

Q. After the campaign in Poland had been finished, what was the plan of action against France and England?
A. I have gained the personal opinion from the Reichstag speech at that time that the Fuehrer hoped that the Polish campaign would not lead to another war. One was of the opinion that another war could be avoided. That was also my opinion when I left the Reichstag after the speech.
Q. But the OKW must have had a plan for a campaign against England even if Hitler felt that way?
A. Those were plans which were already created during the preparations for war against France. First in the winter of 1939–1940, in other words, after the Polish campaign had been concluded, we switched from a careful defense on the Siegfried Line to the massing of troops in order to prepare for an attack in the spring of 1940. In 1939 we had only a few divisions in the West and those were stationed from Basle to Aix-la-Chapelle, and north of Aix-la-Chapelle we only had territorials and reserve battalions. The soldiers thought that because they had not been attacked during all that time, both France and England were not very determined to [make] war against us. One

Field Marshal Wilhelm Keitel was chief-of-staff of Hitler's Supreme Headquarters, responsible for representing Hitler's views and wishes to the whole armed forces. Generally regarded as a weak personality, Keitel put his signature to the notorious 'criminal orders' in 1941 permitting German soldiers to murder thousands of commissars, partisans and Jews.

had to say that if they had attacked in the West with sixty divisions they would have torn this veil to shreds.

Q. Could you name us the time when you switched from the defensive to the offensive?

A. Against France we could attack on firm soil. We knew that English troops had landed in Northern France. I had thought, however, that the British Expeditionary Force was much stronger than it actually was.

Q. When did you decide on the offensive in the West?

A. Well, it's like this. When the Polish campaign was finished with such rapidity most of the people were of the opinion that we should immediately attack in the West. As a soldier, I always believed that time was always against us and never in our favor. Therefore, it was my idea to immediately replace casualties, to put the equipment in shape, and to transport them to the West rapidly, inasmuch as there was an attack to be expected there any day.

Q. Why was this plan not carried out?

A. Partly because transportation was delayed, and partly because a great amount of units, particularly tank units, had to be re-equipped. Engines had to be exchanged, etc. Finally, in November, bad weather set in and this made it impossible to attack. All this I had to consider, as a soldier. We then approached Hitler and he said that the enemy would be stronger in the spring than now, and with great stubbornness insisted that we should attack in the Fall of 1939.

Q. Was the plan to start the offensive in France along the Dutch coast or through Sedan?

A. The General Staff of the army, of course, had considered where it would be best to attack and had arrived at two alternatives. One was to violate Dutch neutrality and the other was to attack the Maginot Line.[35] The General Staff was of the opinion that the attack should be made according to the old Schlieffen plan. In October 1939, the Fuehrer said that he was not in agreement with this plan. I remember this very well and he said that he would think it over and call the Supreme Commanders in a few days and then give his orders. This ended with his order that a breakthrough should be made through Sedan and Luxemburg and in the general direction of Abbeville.

Q. Was the final aim of this plan to eliminate the French from the war and to attack the English?

A. The aim of the campaign was, of course, to destroy the French army and at the same time to eliminate the British Expeditionary Force. The opinion was to the very last that the English were not successful in their Dunkirk evacuation, inasmuch as they only saved lives, but lost all their equipment.

Q. Is it your opinion that the British would not have been able to evacuate their troops if you had employed the Schlieffen plan?

A. On the contrary. You can only answer this question if you know Flanders and know that in Northern Belgium or Western Belgium or Northern France you can only operate on a small coastal stretch. In addition, you cannot operate the tanks in this territory. We had two or three tank divisions driving towards the coast which would have met with another two tank divisions, but which couldn't meet on account of the geographical situation.[36]

Q. Was the consumption of equipment greater than anticipated?

A. No. It was unexpectedly low with regard to ammunition. However, as far as motor vehicles were concerned, the loss was more considerable than anticipated. This was particularly the case because we had so many types of motor vehicles that we were lacking in spare parts.

Q. Do you believe that the ease with which the campaign in France was proceeding was due to the effect of the Luftwaffe?

A. It was excellent in its attacks on French airdromes in paralyzing the French air force in the first few weeks of the campaign.

Q. How was the support by the Luftwaffe of the ground forces?

A. It functioned very well. Liaison between Luftwaffe and ground troops had been fully exploited during the Polish campaign and he who was well-versed in this liaison had, of course, superiority. In the beginning of the Western campaign, we were definitely superior in experience and in the method of employment. That could be gathered very well from the fact that the French had to ask the English for help in furnishing them fighter planes because the French realized that with their own means they could no longer master the situation.

Q. After the defeat of France, what was your plan to win against England?

A. Well, the armed forces more or less thought that the war had come to an end, but I remember that a directive was issued that nobody was to be demobilized and that the training had to be carried on with the greatest vigor. The Fuehrer said in his Reichstag speech on 22 July

[July 19] that we did not want to conquer any British territory, that we left the French their entire fleet. We also allowed the French to keep their colonies with only the exception of those that were formerly German, and we let them have their own government and we hoped that discussions for peace would result. On the other hand, we realized that the English continued to mobilize and we didn't forget for a moment that the United States bolstered the morale of England to say the least. Then again, we knew of the efforts of Cripps in Russia.[37] We tried to extend the Axis Pact by getting Yugoslavia into our sphere of influence. However, there was a certain feeling of uncertainty because one was sure that the massing of troops on the Russian border meant something and we finally realized that the mutual distrust was increasing. Finally, in the late summer, the question arose 'Will there be any war with Russia?'[38]

Q. In the meantime, what was the plan of the armed forces to beat England?

A. England could only be attacked by crossing the Channel or by increasing the U-boat warfare as was done in 1914 to 1918 – the blockade. England, as is known, depends in more or less everything on imports from overseas.

Q. Was anything done to put the plan of invasion into effect?

A. Yes. After we had become masters on the coasts, we immediately considered that we could perhaps bring the war to a speedy conclusion by crossing the Channel and attacking England. Three points have to be taken into consideration. First of all, the British navy which would play an important role in such an enterprise. Could it be neutralized or could it be held in check so that we could chance such an enterprise. Secondly, was the necessary shipping space available not only for the troops, but also for the supplies. Thirdly, was the Luftwaffe strong enough to put an umbrella over this enterprise inasmuch as we had to figure on strong English counter-action. Shipping space as such was not available in the required quantity. At least, not immediately. It was attempted to find this shipping space in the French canals, in the French harbors and in the German harbors. However, this would have taken considerable time due to the damages inflicted on the German waterways. No day could be set and besides it depended upon the capability of the German navy and how long we could cross the Channel on calm seas. This was only possible until August or the beginning of September inasmuch as gales start in September and nothing could be done thereafter.

Q. Had Hitler himself accepted this plan?

A. Yes, he did. He was very much urged to follow this plan because the general opinion was that the time was very favorable. Then came the question as to who should assume responsibility for this stroke. The navy had to be listened to, and the air force, of course, as well; because it could have been clearly assumed that during this stroke the English navy had to be regarded as an important factor. The navy had certain doubts and the air force added a few to that. Therefore, the decision could have been taken only by an office that was above the three armed forces. All preparations and necessary measures were taken. The invasion itself could then not be carried out. That was the beginning of September, 1940. The next order said that the invasion was to be postponed until a different time of the year, but that all orders and directives were to continue in their validity.[39]

Q. Do you know why Hitler ordered that?

A. That is difficult to answer. There were not only political but also realistic reasons. We had dominated the air, but we could not have known at what time we could expect a more favorable ratio between the two navies. We had started, for instance, the expedition in the Atlantic, and the cruiser warfare. Later, during the Bismarck trip,[40] the whole English fleet had gone out into action. The first thing that was stopping us was the respect for the English fleet, because we had to count on the English throwing in their whole fleet, with the destroyers, cruisers, battleships, as well as their carriers – we did not have a single carrier – and we had to understand clearly that against such a formidable fleet there must be sufficient protection from the air, and secondly that those ships are very difficult to hit with a bomb dropped from 4–5000 meters, and therefore, the situation in general was very problematic. There was, therefore, a possibility that the English fleet might be lured away some place.

Q. What was your personal attitude towards this decision?

A. On the one hand, I believed that with the invasion of England, the whole war could have come to an end probably in a few weeks under certain circumstances. On the other hand, although I was considered an optimist by nature, I was very much worried. I fully realized that we would have to undertake this invasion with small boats that were not seaworthy. Therefore, at that time I had fully agreed with the decision of the Fuehrer. You could even feel quite obviously that each one of the three parts of the armed forces was trying to pass the responsibility on to the other one. The army people told me: 'It doesn't depend on us; we are ready, but can the navy go through with it?' The navy passed the responsibility on to the air force, and in the end, one must realize that one cannot after all sail to England with what are practically unseaworthy rowboats.

Q. Of what opinion was the air force?

A. They were very positive, until they were pinned down to answer the question, 'Can you guarantee that the English fleet will be kept away?' On this they said: 'Well, of course, we cannot guarantee that.' Then the navy would say: 'In that case, we can't, of course, cross the Channel.' In the army, they would say: 'Well, if something goes wrong, it is hard for us to disembark along the way.'

Q. How could you avoid making the decision yourself?

A. The Fuehrer always made the important decisions himself. He asked me, and he had talked with the different Supreme Commanders [Commanders-in-Chief], both individually and jointly. He also asked General Jodl, and then he would always make the decision himself, quite independently. He would often say, 'I want to think this over for twenty-four hours', and then he would come out with a decision that was final. I said then that under those circumstances, and considering the English fleet and the fact that we did not have a sufficient bomber force, I personally would not undertake it. In these circumstances, Hitler always made the final decisions himself. It was all the same to him whether Goering shared his opinion or whether Brauchitsch or Raeder were of the same opinion. He took their viewpoints or sometimes he even asked them to give him the arguments in writing, but then there was no more discussion. Discussions took place only when he asked for them. When he decided the Generals concerned were called and none of them knew what the results would be. Neither did I . . . Then he would appear and say: 'I have come to this decision and no more discussion will follow.'

IV Air Attacks and Blockade Operations

Q. What was the connection between the invasion plan and the heavy bombardment attacks on England?

A. I believe that the bomber warfare did not begin until later, and that the beginning of the heavy bombardment was actually marked by the indisputable fact that it was not us who started bombing the cities but the English.[41] We had seen the first attacks on Berlin, and at that time nobody thought of an attack on London. There is a certain connection between the invasion and the bombardment insofar as we were not able to carry out the invasion and the war had to be continued by warfare against the English armament industry and especially against the English harbors. Furthermore, in the harbors you not only knocked out the cargo, but you also destroyed by the sinking of a ship so many tons of carrying capacity. The harbor installations were also hit and through that, the war potential of England was hit heaviest. The large warehouses and docks were also severely damaged.

Q. At that time, did you personally agree to the bombing of England?

A. I had considered it militarily correct, but I had to criticize it insofar as we had not remained consistent enough as far as the fight against the harbors was concerned. Every command pilot should have been obliged to report why he attacked any other target except the harbor. But the OKW did not exercise a command function over the air force, but issued only general directives. In a large number of the harbors, there was a considerable amount of construction going on and the completion of these vessels would have been made impossible. Finally, there was the possibility of preventing or making it very difficult to enter those harbors through the laying of mines either from the air or from the water. I was of the personal opinion that the fight against the harbors with mine and bomb was the strongest means of warfare after the invasion did not come off.

Q. You said that there were two plans? Invasion or blockade. Was this bomber offensive part of this blockade?

A. Yes. It was a considerable part of the blockade.

Q. What were the other steps taken?

A. Submarine warfare and cruiser warfare. One must consider these three. The submarine warfare, the blockade and the cruiser warfare (both with real and auxiliary cruisers), the mines from the sea and from the air and the aerial warfare against harbors and sea strong-points.

Q. Do you mean attacks against English ships?

A. Yes, but on the whole, these were with a limited success. We believed the pilots when they said that they had sunk this or that cruiser. We thought this or that battleship was sunk by us and after a certain time, that battleship would appear on the sea after an overhaul in an American harbor. That was not a falsified claim, but that happens in a fast-moving airplane. I, personally, as a non-flyer, believed that the level bombing against battleships is to say the least very problematic.

Q. What measures were taken in foreign countries to carry out the blockade through economic warfare?

A. I believe that the success of our economic warfare was very limited. The only thing that we could do was that we could, for instance, buy all the sardines in one country and pay for them with guns, and therefore prevent them from going to England. We could try to buy goods in Spain in exchange for war equipment. We could buy mercury or lead in Spain. In such manner we have tried to buy up things that looked also very valuable to us.[42] Outside of that, we had no means and we have never used any pressure. Anyway, decisions in these questions were to be up to the Foreign Ministry and the execution up to the Ministry of Economics and it was only the delivery of arms in payment, which was the job of the Wehrmacht. I did have an Admiral in the OKW who dealt with it, and continuously followed the questions of economic warfare. This was Admiral Gross.[43] Gross was very active when it came to the blockade runners. We had a limited traffic through blockade runners with Japan. We had exchanged arms for quinine and rubber. That stopped in the spring of 1943.

V Russian Campaign

Q. You must have had a certain plan in mind when you started the campaign against Russia? How long did you expect the campaign to last?

A. The opinions on this question vary. My personal idea was that if we succeeded to beat Russia in a short campaign, say by the winter of 1941, we would have been able to see clearly. Later on we realized that this was to be a long war. When we attacked Moscow we could still maintain that the balance was in our favor. Later on, however, it was realized that unless we could finish the war by winter, a new military power would arise in Russia and would oppose us.

Q. When were the first discussions held in the OKW with regard to the campaign in Russia?

A. I have thought this question over several times. The first thought of an impending campaign against Russia arose in November 1940 on the occasion of Molotoff's visit to Berlin. At that time, very lengthy and very far-reaching political discussions took place with regard to demands by Russia on the Fuehrer. They concerned the Baltic, Finland, Romania, the Bukovina and similar questions.[44] In connection with this, there was employment of many Russian divisions on our eastern border and the Fuehrer told us then 'I believe that it will come to blows with Russia because I cannot give in to their demands.' I was not present at these discussions, but I was informed of these discussions later on.

Q. Did the Yugoslav campaign[45] disarrange your time schedule?

A. This campaign came as a complete surprise. We had invited Yugoslavia to join the Axis Pact, but the attitude of Stalin, who had told them that they shouldn't worry about anything and should not give in to our demands, killed all that. But you see all these things in a historical light today and, therefore, slightly tinted.

Q. Was the Fuehrer aware of the fact that the war might last a long time?

A. After the decisive battles at Bryansk, which was a terrific beating for the Russians, or perhaps, after the siege of Moscow and Leningrad, or after the battles on the Donetz Basin, one had to realize that it would come to a long war. I don't know when the Fuehrer became aware of this. The Fuehrer always kept to himself. I believe, however, that already in the winter of 1941–1942, the Fuehrer was well aware that this war could not be brought to a rapid conclusion.

Q. Was it contemplated to bring it to a decision then?

A. Yes, in the year 1942. The winter of 1941 brought for us as well as for the German Eastern Army a crisis and then a counter-attack out of the territory of Moscow,[46] which, however, was paralyzed in the snow and ice. If the German army had then started a retreat, it could very well have become a catastrophe.

To elaborate on the above question, the preparations for the Russian campaign were under way prior to the Yugoslav campaign. The exact time was not determined. It was only in the Fuehrer's mind. However, the strategic and operational plans had been prepared by the General Staff. It is our firm and decided conviction that the Russians started this war by putting division after division at our eastern border. The Fuehrer had set a day, but it was not made known to us until March or April. At that time, the first concrete orders were given, with respect to the fact that we had to figure on a Russian attack. The construction by the Russians of airdromes from Lithuania to Romania of a size which was completely unknown to us pointed this out the stronger. These airdromes had two runways made of concrete whereas our airdromes were made of meadows. In addition, we had to deliver weapons to Russia in exchange for oil and other goods. We delivered naval guns which we could hardly spare, such as the 20.3 cm naval gun, which, although we couldn't admit it, was hard for us to manufacture.

Q. You had a non-aggression pact [with the USSR] and somebody must have broken it?

A. I can't tell you that. This is purely political. It was one of the most remarkable traits of the Fuehrer that he drew a line between political and military affairs. He told Ribbentrop to take care of his political affairs and to keep off military affairs. He told his soldiers: 'Don't discuss politics, this isn't what you are here for, but do what I tell you.' In other words, don't put your fingers into every pie. Nobody was supposed to know more of any matter than was absolutely necessary for his task. This was one of our sacred things and there were posters in every barracks stating this. We only had five divisions at the Russian front during the French campaign and when the Russians massed their troops at the eastern border, the all-round opinion was that something was bound to happen. In addition, there was a demarcation line between Poland and Russia, but the Russians sent reconnaissance units across the line and there were prisoners taken and soldiers killed. There was a permanent guerilla warfare at this line.

VI North African Campaign

Q. Did the General Staff have prior knowledge of the projected scale of American and British operations in North Africa?

A. In North Africa we had seen for the first time the strength of the Allied air force and its effective operations during the battle of El Alamein. It was there for the first time that we felt the effect of an air force upon ground operations. That strength was not expected. It came as a surprise.

Q. What reasons lie behind the failure of Rommel to achieve success in Cyrenaica and Libya? What prevented adequate supplies from reaching Rommel?

A. It was the breakdown of the supply system. The reason for it was that the Italians did not live up to the minimum expectations as far as transportation and the security of transport was concerned. Therefore, they were not able to bring up the bare necessities of supplies. The quantity needed was about 80,000 tons monthly and the actual achievement was between 20,000 and 30,000 tons. We figured that was due to the lack of skill and lack of will by the Italians. It should have been possible to keep up a channel of supply despite all the difficulties with the utmost use of fast warships and destroyers, which could travel quickly without a convoy and load and unload in a hurry.

Q. How did the Allied air force affect you there?

A. The air force had not only crippled the transport, but the disembarkation point of Tripoli as well. All those things could have been prevented if sufficient fast, small boats had been used. As it was, we had large steamers that had to dock for some five days, which gave your observation planes a lot of time to see them and they became easy prey for your bombers.

Q. Was it intended to occupy Tunis and Bizerte in order to shorten the supply lines?

A. Yes, but not until after the American attack on the coast of North Africa. If these had been occupied, our situation would have been much more comfortable. I advocated the occupation before, but Hitler insisted on abiding by the treaty with France. The necessity of occupying Tunis was clearly visible after the American attack in North Africa.

Q. Why was the assault on Malta never pushed through to a conclusion?

A. That again was a mistake in that we did not drive the aerial campaign to a conclusion. There again, the lack of skill and lack of will on the part of the Italians made it impossible to support this attack from the sea. It could not have been done without battleships and we did not have any in the Mediterranean. It was planned, but Rommel's campaign was given priority by the Fuehrer.

Q. Did the loss of oil after the low-level Ploesti attack[47] affect the German military machine in south-west Russia?

A. For a short period, but hardly at all. The one attack in 1943 was very disagreeable for a short period of time. It had no direct effect on the Russian front. Economy in oil was steered in such a manner that an equalization was possible.

VII Allied Invasion and Subsequent Campaigns in Western Europe

Q. What was the importance of air force operations in the preparation for the invasion of Normandy, the subsequent French campaign, and the crossing of the Rhine?

A. The Allied air force has played the most decisive part in the battle of Normandy. It is my belief that the invasion succeeded only due to our inability to bring up our reserves at the proper time to bear pressure on the beach-heads. On 6 June, von Rundstedt[48] asked me by telephone if I would give him full command of all the armored forces in the sector, which I gave him. Later on, I was reprimanded by Hitler for giving him this privilege. All our tank divisions were rather far back. Nobody can ever prove to me that we could not have repelled the invasion had not the superiority of the enemy air force in bombers and fighters made it impossible to throw these divisions in the fight; and then we had no bombers of our own with which we could have fought the landings.

Q. What should have been the role of the Luftwaffe?

A. They should have kept away the enemy air force over the landing territory with their fighters, and with their bombers should have brought immediate pressure on the landings themselves. That did not succeed to a sufficient extent. Naturally, it is quite possible that the viewpoints of the Luftwaffe, those of Goering, Field Marshal Sperrle,[49] and also the view of Field Marshal von Rundstedt do not coincide with mine.

Q. Did the place of the invasion come as a tactical surprise?

A. Only partly. In general, perhaps yes, and yet not quite. We have always figured that the invasion would come either by an attempt to cut off the Cherbourg peninsula from the east and from the west simultaneously in the shortest way possible in order to get possession of Cherbourg harbor and therefore gain a departure place for further operations, or by cutting off all of Brittany through a landing in the south. In other words, to get a good foothold in Brittany and simultaneously neutralizing Brest, St Nazaire and Lorient. The third possibility was the shortest possible route, that is an attack in the general direction of Calais. That's where we had very strong forces, and more reserves, while due to the shape of the coast itself, the other reserves were placed north-west of Paris in such a manner that they could be utilized either against a Cherbourg [Calais?] or a Brittany attack. As a consequence, they proved to be too far back.

Q. Did 'spoofing' attacks on the Pas de Calais cause a surprise?

A. We have never decided that an attack would definitely come in that region, but we did not decide until too late to withdraw the reserves from the Pas de Calais. That was caused by the fact that nobody knew exactly where the attack would come and we were unable to be sure that more landings would not follow. We even called on divisions from Marseilles and Boulogne before we drew on those in the Pas de Calais. We could easily calculate how many divisions had landed and how many were still in England.[50] The Normandy invasion could well have been a diversionary attack, although in tremendous size. The divisions in England were still numerous and the Pas de Calais was the natural place for them to land.

Q. Did you ever figure on the possibility of an airborne operation against Bremen?

A. No. The reason is that we always believed that all airborne operations and parachute operations can only be successful if they can be followed up in the shortest time by ground forces action. The Fuehrer himself kept command in all of the battle of Normandy so that von Rundstedt did not have a free hand as far as the reserves were concerned. I am mentioning this because when you ask von Rundstedt, his opinion will probably be different.

Q. What are the most important reasons why the Luftwaffe did not have any success during the invasion?

A. I am of the opinion that we were not able to compete with the Anglo-Americans as far as the fighter and bomber aircraft were concerned. We had dropped back in technical achievements. We had not preserved our technical superiority. We did not have a fighter with a sufficient radius. As you know, we were on the way to make up this deficiency through new types, which did not make their appearance in time. I feel sure that the force as such, especially its personnel, officers, non-commissioned officers, and enlisted men, were not as courageous and anxious to fight as at the beginning of the war. I refuse to say that the Luftwaffe has deteriorated. I only feel that our means of fighting have not technically remained on the top.

Q. Was any German manpower diverted from the West Wall for the repair of air raid damage?

A. No. No manpower has been diverted but a lot of industries came to a standstill. There was sufficient labor to take care of all emergencies. It took too long to get them where they were needed. You can easily imagine that, if you only take a look at a bombed-out railroad yard. We have never used manpower from the Wehrmacht or the armament industry for that. It was all controlled centrally, inasmuch as Speer steered the war production as well as the utilization of labor for the building of streets and for the repair of railroads. All of the coal territory around Aachen was lost in late summer of 1944. The industrial workers in the territory around Aachen were out of a job and the same went for the Saar. All this made extra manpower available.

Q. Was the High Command surprised by the strength of the Allied air force immediately preceding, during, and after the invasion?

A. We were pretty well informed about your strength. We had a pretty good view of your air force preceding the invasion, during your daily attacks on Germany, and it was easy to see that all of it would be concentrated at invasion time. Our assumption as to your procedures has proved to be correct. We figured on four phases: (1) An attack on the coastal defenses and the destruction of batteries, especially those which could not have sufficient concrete cover, in other words, the immediate defenses of the coastline; (2) Attacks on the possible concentrations of the reserves along the whole front on the Cherbourg peninsula as well as in the Pas de Calais; (3) Destruction of transport bridges over the Seine and of all traffic points leading towards the invasion coast; (4) Attacks on the zone around the West Wall so as to disturb the cushion of our forward forces. We did not know the exact date of the invasion. We could have guessed it by the study of the tides. If we had fully believed our radio intelligence interception, we would have even known the exact time of the invasion through the radio communications that you had with the French.[51]

Q. Did the accumulation of fuel reserves for the invasion have any effect on the training of pilots?

A. By all means. The training was the thing that has suffered most. After the loss of Romania, our oil situation became very difficult and after the systematic attacks against hydrogenation works, the production dropped considerably, so that strict saving measures had to be ordered. The training program of the Luftwaffe took the largest cut.

Q. When did you begin to cut down the training of pilots?

A. After the first loss of hydrogenation plants.[52] That began already in May 1944.

Q. How effective was the patrolling of automobile roads by fighter-bombers in stopping the movement of troops and supplies?

A. I have already pointed this out in talking about the crossing of the Rhine near Remagen and why this crossing succeeded.[53] The only answer was that the withdrawal of German forces was not technically possible any more so as to prevent the crossing. Especially, because we could move on the roads only at night or during bad weather, while all the time, the night was about ten hours long. Ten hours for us against twenty-four hours for you.

Q. What were the main causes for the delays in re-equipping Panzer divisions?

A. Just because the consumption of tanks on all fronts in Italy, Russia, and in the West was so large that the production could not compensate for the losses and sometimes, although the necessary tank replacements were available, they could not be transported to the front. Every 50 or 100 km that a tank has to run on the road under its own power to the zone of operations, constitutes needless wear and tear. We, therefore, used rail transport to bring them up as far as possible. Due to the large destruction of our transport need, the whole train of tanks were often 'lost'; nobody knew where they were and, consequently, they did not reach the front. In the east, we were able to move the tank on the railroad to within twenty miles of the front.

Q. What were the effects of air force attacks in the Ardennes offensive?

A. The time of the Ardennes offensive was so chosen that we could expect a series of days during which the Anglo-American air force was unable to play a decisive part. We were clear in our own minds that an offensive was entirely impossible in those days if the enemy fighter-bombers and the rest of the air force were permitted to bear full pressure. Our air force had a large reserve of fighter aircraft piled up, but these were hampered through unfavorable weather conditions as well.

Q. What was the aim of the offensive?

A. The reaching of the region around Liège and the high ground around the river sector, and if any strength remained, to push on as far as possible.

Q. Who made the decision for this?

A. Hitler himself.

Q. Were you personally in agreement?

A. The place and the general direction of the attack all originated in the head of the Fuehrer. Through the army, and the mobilization of the Volkssturm Divisions in the rear, and through the calling in of the best reserves, he took care of assembling this offensive strength.

Q. Do you believe today that it was a mistake?

A. If we wanted to do it at all, this was the only time to go through with it. Purely from the soldier's point of view, I say that the reason the success was so limited was due to the insufficient training of the troops, who were not at all trained for this type of warfare. But something had to be done to prevent the threat of a break-through from Aachen in the direction of Cologne. I believe I belong to the school of thought that this break-through could not have been stopped by throwing in more new divisions around Aachen, where you were extremely strong, and our men were plainly being slaughtered. It is no use to get your troops killed and still retreat mile by mile. I am sure in the terms of the military situation in the Aachen sector, it was high time something should happen. We completely succeeded in surprising the Allied troops both strategically and operationally. The offensive did not succeed because among other reasons the leadership of armored troops was not in competent hands.[54] It is probably the responsibility of the OKW that the place of the leadership was not given proper weight. Good technical equipment and goodwill alone can't make it.

That is a lesson and not a blame. And to that I would like to add that if I had had more influence on that, the leadership would have been different. That was the wish and the command of the Fuehrer, which in the long last we obeyed.

VIII The Possibilities of German Strategic Withdrawal

Q. What were the reasons for hanging on to territory in Russia, the Balkans, Mediterranean, etc., when shortening of the lines might have been a more fruitful policy?

A. That is a very complicated problem. In general, we have defended the viewpoint that the further we can keep the fighting away from the heart of the country, the less the danger to this heart. There was talk about the Rhine in the west, the Alps in Italy, the River Weichsel in the south-east, and the Danube. If we had withdrawn to those fronts, then there would have been no distance for aerial warfare at all. The thing to do is to keep the enemy from the heart of the country as far as possible. That's the only way to protect the heart of the country from actual warfare . . .

Q. Were there many discussions as to how the lines in Russia could be shortened?

A. Yes, of course. The question, whether at a certain given time the front should not have been retracted, is a problem which the war scientists will debate for a long time to come. Personally, I advocated the idea of shortening the lines in order to win time. That process was begun very early on the Balkan front. We also evacuated Greece and Albania and took five or six divisions from there and sent them to the Western Front.

Q. Were there discussions in OKW about the possibility of a withdrawal from Russia?

A. The OKW had very little influence on that. The Fuehrer took care of all these questions . . .

Genocide

Q. Can you state absolutely definitely, what did the word 'Endloesung', final solution, stand for?
A. I can only tell you what I understand by it, as I understood it from the Reichsfuehrer [Himmler].
Q. And what did it mean?
A. It meant, extermination.
Q. Of whom?
A. Of the Jews.

From the interrogation of Rudolf Hoess at Nuremberg, 2 April 1945[1]

[The dimensions of the genocide of the Jews and of the camp system and security apparatus that accomplished it had to be reconstructed by the Allies in the summer and autumn of 1945 more from oral testimony than from documentary evidence, for a large part of the central archive on the genocide had been deliberately destroyed. Many of those interrogated at Nuremberg refused to accept that a genocide had taken place. Wilhelm Frick, the Interior Minister, responded to the information from his interrogator that nine million may have died in the camps by suggesting that the number was 'too high by two zeros', i.e. only 90,000. Frick continued: 'Even this number is terribly high and highly improbable.'[2] The prosecution got no reliable and detailed information on the genocide from any of the major war criminals, who confessed not only ignorance, but in many cases incredulity. There were witnesses at Nuremberg who could recall those details. An SS doctor, Werner Kirchert, interrogated in early November 1945, discovered the existence of a policy of extermination during the war 'in the course of conversation with my comrades'. Kirchert remembered in 1943 a doctor from Mauthausen who, at the time of a visit to Berlin to request a transfer from the camp on psychiatric grounds, told him about 'Human extermination', the selection of Jews for labour or destruction, and the incineration of the bodies of those chosen for death. Kirchert also recalled that he talked freely about who had ordered extermination. He thought Himmler was responsible, but 'it was the opinion among my colleagues that also Hitler himself had known about this program'.[3] Kirchert was not unwilling to confirm the existence of the genocide, but he knew too few details of the extermination centres or the scale of deportations. The chief pre-trial witness was Dieter Wisliceny, and two of his interrogations are reproduced below. Wisliceny, an Eichmann deputy responsible for Jewish affairs in Slovakia and then Greece, described the entire genocidal programme, though he was not a witness to the slaughter in the camps. That evidence was forthcoming from the testimony of lower officials and camp guards, or from former prisoners. Two of these accounts follow the Wisliceny interrogations. The Allies might have learned much more from the forensic evidence then being assembled by a Polish prosecution team in Cracow, but it was not sent to Nuremberg. Soviet contributions to the case were few, since the official line from Moscow denied that a genocide of the Jews, distinct from the general slaughter of civilians in the east, had been German policy.[4]

Documents and interrogations provided the Allies with sufficient material to justify the inclusion of the Jewish genocide in the Indictment issued in October 1945. In the absence of Adolf Eichmann, the Gestapo official responsible for the transportation of Jews to the camps, or Heinrich Müller, the head of the Gestapo, there were still uncertainties in the record about the scale and nature of the genocide. The fullest account of the terrible mechanics of mass murder came with the arrest of the former commandant of Auschwitz, Rudolf Hoess, in March 1946. Two of his interrogations complete the document selection. The second recalls a bizarre confrontation between one of Hoess's guard detail leaders at Auschwitz, Otto Moll, and Hoess himself. The interrogators agreed to allow Moll to be questioned in the same room as Hoess in order to establish quite clearly what Moll had, and had not, been responsible for in the camp. In the course of the discussion Moll's own criminal responsibility was not only confirmed, but enlarged. Both Moll and Hoess were executed. Moll was tried by an American military court in May 1946 at Dachau and sentenced to death. Hoess was tried in Warsaw and executed at Auschwitz in March 1947.][5]

Document 11 The Fuehrer Order

Extract from the interrogation of Dieter Wisliceny, taken at Nuremberg on 15 November 1945 by Lieut.-Colonel Smith W. Brookhart and Mr Sender Jaari, pp. 1–9

Q. You are the same Dieter Wisliceny who appeared this morning, and you understand you are speaking under oath.
A. Yes.
Q. Referring to your statement of this morning, as to the number of Jews estimated to have been affected by actions of the RSHA since

1941, what are you able to say as to the number in each of the designated areas who died or were executed or disappeared?

A. Since 1942, by order of Himmler, Jews were only valued as workers. All other Jews, who were not used in that capacity, were to be executed by order of Himmler.

Q. Do you mean all those other than the able-bodied were to be executed?

A. I mean specifically women, women with children, old people, and those who had an affliction of some kind.

Q. Were all to be executed?

A. Yes. At one time, Eichmann told me that the percentage of Jews who did (this) work, amounted to something like 20 to 25 percent.

Q. Did you say 20 or 25 percent were able to work, or 20 to 25 percent were unable to work?

A. Were able to work.

Q. Did the 25 percent considered able to work include any women or children?

A. Yes, in those 20 to 25 percent women and children were included that were considered fit to live.

Q. For the children, what age was chosen to determine whether they were of value and therefore fit to live?

A. I can't say it exactly but I believe from twelve to thirteen years upwards.

Q. Who made the determination as to the fitness of the Jews to survive?

A. That came from the inspector of concentration camps. The whole question of the annihilation of the Jews was brought about in closed camps.

Q. You are speaking now of the camps that were closed, as distinguished from those labor and factory areas that you described yesterday?

A. Yes. I came to know about a number of such extermination camps.

Q. Their names?

A. The largest one was Auschwitz, Maidanek, near Lublin. In the immediate vicinity of Lublin there were several such camps.

Q. Do you remember their names?

A. No, because the designations for these transports always went by the name of Lublin. Maidanek, too, was never mentioned by name, but was always referred to in the record by Camp M. It was only by accident that I learned one time that this Camp M was Maidanek.

Q. How did that come about?

A. When the Russians took over the camp at Maidanek, with all of its devices, Eichmann once mentioned that this camp, Maidanek, was our Camp M.[6]

Q. He said that to you in conversation?

A. Yes.

Q. What designation did Auschwitz have?

A. Auschwitz was commonly known as Camp A.

Q. What was Camp T?

A. If I correctly recollect, that belonged to the complex Lublin system. I remember having heard the designation Camp T.

Q. Was that also an annihilation camp?

A. Yes, sir.

Q. Were there others?

A. As far as I can remember now, there were none. Later on, when everything was concentrated in Auschwitz, certainly in the period 1943–1944.

Q. How do you classify camps Mauthausen, Dachau and Buchenwald?

A. They were normal concentration camps from the point of view of the department of Eichmann.

Q. When you referred to Auschwitz and the several camps at Lublin as being annihilation camps, were you speaking primarily from the standpoint of the annihilation of the Jews?

A. Only the extermination of the Jews. About other things I cannot say anything as I don't know anything exactly.

Q. When in 1942 did Himmler issue the order that you have already described?

A. It must have been in the spring of 1942. May I say how I got to know about this order?

Q. Anything you know.

A. In the spring of 1942 I received the assignment from Eichmann to demand of the Slovak government, the furnishing of between 15,000 to 20,000 single Jews for labor purposes. These Jews were supposed to work in the armament industry. This contingent of 15,000 to 20,000 Jews was supposed to be accredited to the Slovak government on its regular quota of workers which they were supposed to furnish. The Slovak government had offered, of its own accord, to furnish Jewish workers for the German armament industry. This proposal was then accepted, and I received the assignment to request 15,000 to 20,000 Jewish workers from the Minister of the Interior. That took place in March or April of 1942. These labor forces were transported by rail, and their destination was Auschwitz and Lublin. Auschwitz was at that time in the process of construction. This labor contingent was not exterminated but was actually used for labor purposes. In May 1942 the Slovak government asked whether the families of these workers could not be transferred to the Reich, because they were depending on the support of the Slovak state, as their providers were in Germany. No arrangements had been made for the transfer of funds back to Slovakia, for the maintenance of dependants there. At that time Eichmann was in Bratislava [the Slovakian capital]. He visited Minister Mach and the Prime Minister Tuka,[7] accompanied by me. During this visit, this question was discussed. Eichmann declared himself prepared to accept these families into the Reich area, specifically into Poland. He gave Minister Mach and Prime Minister Tuka the assurance that these Jewish families would be assembled in the area of Lublin in the towns and villages which had been evacuated by the Polish civilian population. He gave the same assurance to Ambassador Ludin, and he left even me in [no?] doubt as to what disposition was going to be made of the families.

I want to add to this that this was made so much easier because during my work in Bratislava, I only came to Berlin very seldom at that time. The first contingent of workers – that is the single men – were 17,000 and the families which were there in May and June 1942 amounted to 32,000 to 33,000 people. They were sent by the Slovak government. Then a pause took place between the transports.

In July, Prime Minister Tuka summoned me to him and asked for an explanation as to what had happened to the Jewish families in Poland. In particular, he was concerned about the fate [of] those Jews who had been christened, and he asked for permission that these people might have the right to follow their Christian religion. He also requested that a Slovak commission be permitted to travel in these areas that were occupied by Jews in order to ascertain the well-being of these people. This action of a Slovak government was based upon the diplomatic action of the Papal Nuncio, Monsignor Bursio. The request of Prime Minister Tuka was then given verbally to the German embassy.

The ambassador then dispatched me to Berlin to talk matters over with Eichmann and requested that the wish of the Slovak government be granted. I then went to Berlin. That was July, 1942, the end of July or the beginning of August 1942. During this time no further transports went from Slovakia into Poland. I then had a very serious talk with Eichmann and also supported this point and told him the wish of the Slovak government should be granted because otherwise our international prestige would suffer very seriously. I referred him to the statement of the Pope and the state secretary, Maglione.[8] They had been made in public and in addition to that, to the Slovak ambassador in Rome, at the Vatican.

I further pointed out that the President, Dr Tiso,[9] was himself a Catholic priest, and that the Slovak government had only agreed to the deportation of Jews, to Poland, on condition that they would be treated humanely.

Eichmann then stated that a visit by a Slovak commission in the area of Lublin would be impossible. When I asked him why, he said, after much delay and a great deal of discussion, that there was an order of Himmler according to which all Jews were to be exterminated. When I asked him who was going to assume responsibility for this order, he said he was prepared to show me this order in writing which had been signed by Himmler. I then requested that he show me this order. This order was under the classification of Top Secret. This discussion took place in his study in Berlin. He was sitting at his desk, and I was in the same position, opposite him, as I am now opposite the Colonel. He took this order from his safe. It was a thick file. He then searched and took out this order. It was directed to the Chief of the Security Police and the Security Service [Heydrich].

The contents of this order went something like this. I cannot give it precisely since I am under oath, but it is approximately as follows. The Fuehrer has decided that the final disposition of the Jewish question is to start immediately. By the code word, 'final disposition' was meant the biological extermination of the Jews. Himmler had put the limitation on this order that at the present time able-bodied Jews who could be used for work were to be excluded.

Q. Did Himmler put that order into the Hitler order, or was it included in the text of the order?

A. 'I designate the Chief of the Security Police and Security Service and the Inspector of Concentration Camps with the execution of this order.' Excepted from this order were those few in concentration camps who were needed within the framework of the labor program. The particulars of this program were to be agreed between the Chief of the SD and the Security Police and the Inspector of Concentration Camps. 'I am to be informed currently about the execution of this order.' I saw with my own eyes the signature of Himmler under this order.

Q. What was the date of the order?

A. I can't say exactly, but it must have been from the end of April or the beginning of May 1942.

Q. Do you know whether it was addressed to Heydrich or not?

A. Yes, it was addressed to Heydrich.

Q. In other words, it was issued before Heydrich's death [June 1942]?

A. Yes.

Q. Did Eichmann have the original letter?

A. Yes.

Q. You saw the original letter in Eichmann's office?

A. Yes, I saw the original order.

Q. It was addressed to whom?

A. It was addressed to the Chief of the Security Service and the Police. The second title was to the head of the WVHA [SS Wirtschafts- und Verwaltungshauptamt (SS Economic and Administrative Main Office)], to whom the Inspector of the Concentration Camps was subordinated. It was an official decree, with an official title.

There were also other letters from Himmler to Heydrich and Kaltenbrunner, which were addressed, 'Dear Heydrich' or 'Dear Kaltenbrunner'. In this case it was an official decree. It was surrounded by a red border as a special delivery document.

Q. An immediate action document?

A. Yes, urgent document. I was very much impressed by this document which gave him as much power to use as he saw fit, and to which Eichmann gave me explanatory comments. I believe I said at the time, 'May God prevent that our enemies should ever do anything similar to the German people.'

Q. What did Eichmann say?

A. That I shouldn't get sentimental, this was a Fuehrer Order. I realized that this meant the death warrant for millions of people . . .

Document 12 A Morbid Accounting

Extract from the interrogations of Dieter Wisliceny taken at Nuremberg
on 17 November 1945 and 23 November 1945 by Lieut.-Colonel
Smith W. Brookhart

[17 November 1945, pp. 4–11 of the original transcript]

Q. In your list, Exhibit A, you have included several figures as positive although many appear to be out of your area, Slovakia.

A. I was myself in Hungary in 1944. Slovakia was my working area. I was myself in Greece in 1943. Dannecker[10] was in Bulgaria in 1943. I visited him in Sofia and he gave me the information himself. At that time this matter was on the carpet. In Croatia was Abromeit. He was my personal good friend. He was in Croatia until 1944 when he was sent to Hungary.

Q. When did you confirm the Croatian figures from Abromeit?

A. In 1944.

Q. Now let us go back to your chart on those countries about which you had some doubts as to the accuracy of the figures. Take Poland – what is the basis for your information?

A. A remark made by Eichmann concerning three and one half million.

Q. When?

A. This was in Hungary in 1944.

Q. And the figure for Germany?

A. A remark by Novak also in Hungary in 1944.

Q. What was Novak's position?

A. Novak worked on all transportation matters. An example if you permit; when evacuations had to be made, a request was to be made to the Reichs Minister of Transportation. That was his work.

Q. Did Novak handle all transportation for IV A 4 6 [IV B 4 6, Gestapo Jewish Office]?

A. Yes, he must have detailed knowledge of all Jewish evacuations.

Q. Throughout the entire period from 1939 on?

A. Yes, from 1939 to the end. No, correction, from 1940.

Q. All right, let's go ahead with Bohemia and Moravia.

A. This figure I learned during a visit to Prague. I had matters to arrange in Prague because my driver was paid by the Central Department for Regulation of the Jewish Question in Bohemia and Moravia. This department was handled by Hans Guenther who, by the way, was a brother of Eichmann's deputy, Ralph Guenther. Hans Guenther mentioned this figure to me during our conversation.

Q. When?

A. September 1943.

Q. Now, take up Italy.

A. In Italy was Dannecker again. This figure I learned also in 1944 during a conversation in Hungary. With the exception of Brunner, all those people mentioned in the lower right hand corner on my chart, Exhibit B, were present. On top of this, Hunsche, Novak, Kryshak and Hartenberger,[11] all those last names also are to be found on my Chart B. Therefore, it was possible to get an understanding of the whole matter. I did it intentionally for I inquired into this problem intentionally because Dr Kastner had asked me to ascertain how many people had been deported from the different places.

Q. Next, take Holland and Belgium.

A. I once reported to Eichmann in Berlin. It was the beginning of September 1943. There I met a certain Asche who worked upon these matters in Brussels as the Commander of the Security Police and he mentioned these figures.

Q. That is, the number of deportees?

A. Yes, it may be possible that both these figures are too low.

Q. Take now the two areas about which you have a question. First, Denmark and second, Norway.

A. This information originates from Hartenberger.

Q. What date?

A. Also summer of 1944 in Budapest. Hartenberger was together with Guenther, the Deputy of Eichmann, in Copenhagen.

Q. Why do you put the question mark behind 6,000?

A. Because Hartenberger himself was not quite sure of the figure.

Q. Where did you get the information pertaining to France?

A. To obtain this figure was very difficult and I believe that this figure is the most uncertain of all the figures. The man who sat in Paris [was] Hauptsturmfuehrer Brunner. He was an opponent of mine. Between Brunner and me there hardly existed any personal or official connections but before Brunner was appointed to Paris, Dannecker was there.

Q. Is Brunner the same Hauptsturmfuehrer shown on the chart line leading down from IV A 4 B?

A. Yes, he is the same but this section was under process of dissolution since 1943. Therefore, in summer of 1944 in Budapest I asked Dannecker who was fairly well informed about figures concerning France, and Dannecker mentioned this figure of about 220,000 but as said before regarding the French figure, I am most in doubt.

Q. Let's take your new chart now. Explain the caption headings.

A. First column, country and figure. Second column, time. Third column, concentration camps, that is, to which concentration camp they were sent. Fourth column, labor allocation. Fifth column, executed. Sixth column, remained alive. Seventh column, remarks.

Q. Take the various categories by countries and make such explanations as you think necessary to fill out our understanding of the chart.

A. Slovakia is the first. The first evacuation was March–April 1942. The transports went to Lublin and Auschwitz. It concerned 17,000 men and women for labor allocation.

Q. Were the 17,000 single Jews?

A. It concerned 17,000 single male and female Jews. They were not executed. I assume that they remained alive.

Q. You have already said that mail from this group continued to be received for two years.

A. Yes.

Q. That is why you think they may have escaped execution?

A. No – I know it from the fact that the Commander of the Auschwitz camp, Hoess, mentioned it during a conversation in Budapest. He stated that the labor which he had received then or at that time from Slovakia had grown to be his most expert workers. Furthermore, they were specially selected.

Second evacuation, May–June 1942. These transports went solely to Auschwitz. In this case the evacuated were complete families. These were treated in accordance with the so-called 'final solution' which I got acquainted with through Eichmann. These were people about whom the Slovakian government made inquiries on which I went to see Eichmann. I don't know how many of them remained alive.

Q. What did Eichmann say as to their disposition?

A. 'Not too many of them are alive.'

The third evacuation was in October 1944. The transports went to

Auschwitz. I assumed that the 14,000, which was the number of the transport, were executed.

Q. Why do you assume so?

A. Because Auschwitz at that time was working full time in executions. Shortly thereafter Himmler prohibited executions in general and the extermination facilities were blown up.[12] This was the result of the discussions between Dr Kastner and the representative of Himmler, Sturmbahnfuehrer Becker.[13] Therefore it is possible that at least a part of these 14,000 remained alive because the interval between the transports and the order prohibiting executions was very short. It is a question of days.

Q. What did Hoess, the Commandant of Auschwitz, tell you about the 35,000 and 14,000 shipments?

A. Hoess did not tell me anything about the 14,000 because they were sent to Auschwitz in August and I saw Hoess in July. He did not make any mention of the 35,000. He only mentioned the 17,000, the first transport.

In February 1945, there was just a little handful of 800 human beings left in Sered, a collecting camp in Slovakia, and Brunner sent this group to Theresienstadt[14] – the Russian troops approached Slovakia at that time.

Q. Let's take the next country of which you have direct knowledge.

A. The next country – Greece. In February 1943, Brunner and I were sent to Saloniki. Brunner was not personally subordinated to me. He was to work on the technical problems, I was to get in touch with the German military authorities and the German ambassador in Athens. I was to take special interest in Jews of foreign citizenship in Greece. There existed in Greece a great number of Spanish and Italian Jews. The goal of my negotiations was to make the Italian and Spanish diplomatic authorities accept the return of the Spanish and Italian Jews to their original countries. It was also to be investigated if the Jews of Saloniki could be fitted into the framework of the organization Todt. Brunner, however, had other directives. He was to technically prepare the evacuation of the Jews from Saloniki . . . In March, Brunner received a cable that the evacuation of the Jews from Saloniki and Macedonia was to start at once . . . Brunner carried out the action . . . From March to May 1943, 55,000 Jews then were transported from Saloniki and Macedonia to Auschwitz.

Q. How were they handled?

A. By train by way of Marawska-Ostrawa and then Auschwitz. Here is a remark in the last column – of the number of Greek Jews very few can have remained alive according to a remark by Hoess to Eichmann. This remark was made in connection with the remark about the 17,000 Slovak Jews because Hoess said the Greek Jews had no labor value at all, and that he made the remark that the best workers he had were those 17,000 Slovak Jews.

Q. Do you have any other reason to think that these 55,000 were executed?

A. The value of Jewish lives was only calculated by Hoess and Eichmann in relationship to their ability to work. Nothing else mattered.

Q. The second evacuation?

A. The second evacuation from Greece took place in July 1944. This action was carried out by Burger who came to Athens from Theresienstadt.

Q. Where were the 5,000 sent?

A. In the first column there is a remark that these 5,000 Jews of the second evacuation originated from Athens, Epirus, in northern Greece, from islands and from south and middle Greece. They went to Auschwitz. In the column headed remarks, the following remark is found: 700 Jews with Spanish citizenship were transported in August 1943 to Bergen-Belsen and later in December shipped to Spain.

Q. Out of this 5,000 group?

A. No, on top of these 5,000. The 5,000 are in the column for executed.

Q. How was this group of 700 identified as Spanish Jews?

A. They had Spanish passports or other proof of having Spanish citizenship. The Jews who belonged to the 55,000 from Saloniki and Macedonia were the so-called Spaniels [Spaniards] who originally had come to Greece from Spain. The richest of these families had obtained Spanish citizenship during the last century while Greece still belonged to Turkey. All Jews in Greece had arrived from Spain in the 15th century.

The next country is Bulgaria. In the first column the figure of 8,000 is mentioned plus the remark that these 8,000 all came from Thrace and Macedonia.

Q. What happened to them?

A. They were transported to Auschwitz in March–April 1943. I want to point out that these Jews all were originally Greek citizens and lived in the part of Greece which Bulgaria took over from Greece. They were all sent to Auschwitz and all are to be found in the column marked executed. If any one of these remained alive, I don't know.

Q. What did Dannecker tell you about their disposition?

A. Do you with your question mean the political history or what happened politically before it was decided to evacuate these people or what happened to these people after evacuation and upon arrival in Auschwitz?

Q. What made you include this group in your table about which you say you are sure that these actions were taken?

A. When I called upon Dannecker in Sofia the evacuation of Jews in Bulgaria, Thrace and Macedonia was just going on. Therefore I know this figure for certain.

Q. What do you know about their ultimate execution?

A. All were executed or, may I express myself the following way – Auschwitz was considered as kind of a filter or screening place. Everything arrived there which had not beforehand been explicitly declared as labor slaves and what was pressed through this filter and remained alive, that of course I don't know. That was only decided upon at Auschwitz.

Q. You referred to this camp during the last session as an 'annihilation camp'.

A. Yes, this name I have heard often from Eichmann himself. This was also brought forward in the letter which I mentioned. Only that which was needed for current labor use remained alive. Everything else was annihilated . . .

[23 November, pp. 3–7 and 21–5 of the original transcript]

Q. In connection with some of your figures on the total number of Jews affected by measures in several countries, there has been some question raised as to their accuracy, particularly on Poland. Whereas you show a total of $3\frac{1}{2}$ million in the category of those affected by these various police actions, the total Jewish population, according to the statistics that have been submitted, was less than that.[15]

A. I have stated that this figure is not known to me, but that Eichmann always operated with the figure of 3½ million. It was his conception that it was 3½ million. I have made this chart without having any statistics or figures at my disposal, only from my memory. I only mentioned the figures which were always mentioned to me.

Q. Examine the table which is in this book before you, purporting to cover from September 1939 to September 1943, which shows a gross loss to Poland of 1,900,000 out of a total of 3,300,000, and Table 2 showing 1,600,000 killed. What do you have to say about those figures?

A. First, as to Germany, to my estimation the figure of 5,000 left in Germany in 1943 is far too small. In Theresienstadt there lived a great number. In 1943 at least 25,000 German Jews were alive in Theresienstadt.

Q. What do you base that on?

A. In January 1944 I was summoned to Berlin by Eichmann. Up until December 1943 I had been in Athens. Since, despite the explicit order of Eichmann, I had not arranged evacuation of Jews from Greece, he called me back in December.

Q. This was 1943?

A. This was December 1943. As I mentioned before, I then was in Berlin in January 1944, in his office. He told me that I evidently was unsuitable for the practical work and he intended to appoint me commandant of Theresienstadt. There I would be able to give my philanthropical sentiments – that was his expression – free rein.

In this connection we discussed Theresienstadt in detail. At that time, there were between 35,000 and 40,000 Jews in Theresienstadt.

Q. How do you know?

A. Eichmann mentioned that.

The individual figures were then discussed, and I believe I can recall that Eichmann mentioned 25,000 as the number of German Jews. But, of course, this figure is not quite reliable as the figures were often confused in Eichmann's mind.

Q. Go on with that table and comment on the other figures on the basis of your information and knowledge.

A. On Table 3, the figure mentioned, 1,600,000 dead, is absolutely too low.

Q. But remember this is 1943.

A. Then in that case, it is possible that the figure is right.

Q. What was the final figure?

A. I am convinced that with the exception of the few thousands of Polish Jews found alive in concentration camps, every single Polish Jewish individual has been killed.

Q. What about those that moved east into Russian territory?[16]

A. As far as those Jews required to go with the Russian army are concerned, I am, of course, unable to make any statement. However, the Jews who remained in German-occupied territory which had been under Russian rule were certainly exterminated by the Einsatz Groups.

Furthermore, in order to support my conviction, I would like to refer to a conversation I had with Eichmann in Budapest in the summer of 1944. At that time he said:

'The biological power source of Jewry is the Polish Jewry. These Polish Jews have been exterminated up until the last person. From this blow, Jewry will never recover.'

Those were Eichmann's words.

Q. What was the total number that you understood had been affected in Poland?

A. In case the figure mentioned in this table, 3,300,000 is correct, I am absolutely convinced that by October 1944, every single one had been exterminated.

Q. But 300,000, according to this table, fled into Russia.

A. I would like to know if these 300,000 were transported far into the interior of Russia or if some of them were left in Kiev or Kharkhov or some other Russian towns more to the west.

Q. The 300,000 figure appears only as the number removed or deported to USSR.

A. Even 300,000 seems somewhat too high.

Q. Examine the table where it speaks of Austria and tell us about that figure.

A. The 8,000 figure mentioned under Austria as Jews alive in Austria is far too low. In Vienna alone at that time there lived more than 8,000 Austrian Jews. The Hungarian Jews had not arrived in 1943.

Q. Consider Romania and examine the figure 850,000; loss of 420,000.

A. I gave the figure of around 200,000 deported and mentioned at that time that that probably was too low a figure because from Cernauti alone, around 80,000 were deported, but please take into consideration that these figures end in September 1943. Certainly more than 92,500 were deported from Romania.

I assume that the figure of 125,000 killed is somewhat too high. A greater number were deported than mentioned in the table and fewer were killed on the spot, according to my personal opinion . . .

Q. Turning now to the second page of your table on which you show 200,000 Jews evacuated from Bohemia and Moravia, a question has been raised on the ground that that is a gross exaggeration, that there were never more than 90,000 Jews in that territory.[17]

A. When you look down at the next figure, the figure for Slovakia, that is absolutely wrong.

Q. Let's deal with Bohemia and Moravia. Tell us what support you have for your figure of 200,000.

A. This figure of 200,000 was mentioned to me by Hans Guenther who was in charge in Prague.

Q. Is that the only information you have on that area?

A. That is the only source of information I have. I didn't concern myself very much with Bohemia and Moravia, if the figure mentioned in Table 1 is as correct as the figure which is shown for Slovakia, namely 135,000, which is 45,000 too much, then you can understand that these figures are of no value.

Q. But I wish to draw your attention to the fact that in this figure concerning Slovakia 45,000 are included who lived under the administrative unit of Slovakia before the independent Slovakia was founded and a part of Slovakia was ceded to Hungary, namely, Western Slovakia, and those 45,000 lived in Western Slovakia.

A. The official statistics showed 89,000 Jews in 1940.

Q. What official statistics?

A. The official Slovakian statistics.

Q. Tell us how the Hungarian figure is made up. Do you know the composition?

A. Yes, Hungary as it was after the peace of Trianon,[18] then Siebenbuergen, which came back to Hungary from Romania after the Vienna agreement.[19] Carpatho-Russia was included in Hungary in the spring of 1939 after the Vienna agreement, and Western Slovakia also in the spring of 1939 after the Vienna agreement, and Batschka in 1941 from Jugoslavia.

The evacuation of Jews from Hungary took place in many stages.

It started with Carpatho-Russia and Siebenbuergen. From Carpatho-Russia alone, more than 200,000 Jews were evacuated. From Siebenbuergen, the previous Romanian area, it was almost 100,000 including the Jews from Nagyvarad.

The second stage was northern Hungary, including the parts ceded by Slovakia. Here the number of Jews evacuated was about 40,000.

I want to draw your attention to the fact that in the first phase the number was not 300,000 but 320,000.

The third phase was southern Hungary, including Seged, but exclusive of Batschka. I believe 46,000 Jews were evacuated from there.

Then, the next step was the whole of western Hungary. There were also about 40,000 Jews evacuated. Before the action in western Hungary, and starting at the end of the first action and continuing during the second, in northern Hungary a special rounding up of Jews took place in Batschka. There were about 10,000. Adding those, we get the result of 456,000. Of course, I can be wrong by one or two thousand.

Q. You mean that your figure as shown on your chart for the first evacuation includes the 456,000?

A. Yes, these are the 456,000 as shown on my chart.

Q. There were an additional 40,000, approximately, that were dealt with later?

A. There were then about 40,000 who were handled by the later actions.

Q. Turn now to Belgium. You have given a figure of 20,000. This is questioned on the grounds of being an underestimate.

A. Yes, I told you, too, when I received this information, that was already 1943. After that time I have no information about Belgium or Holland.

Q. What is your opinion of the figure that is stated in this book on Table 1, showing a total of 100,000, of which there was an 80,000 loss, of which 30,000 were reported as dead?

A. You will certainly remember that I mentioned in my first interrogation that I was of the opinion that the figures mentioned by me in connection with Holland and Belgium were too low. I consider that the figures mentioned in the tables of the book you show me are possible. As you can see from my chart, I have put question marks both in the column referring to Holland and that referring to Belgium because the information I had was old and not sure.

Q. In Holland there is a question of whether you weren't grossly underestimating the number of Jews. You show 40,000 whereas there were 170,000 in that country.

A. The actions in Holland did not start before 1943, practically at the same time as I received my information. In 1942 only some few Jews were selected for labor, Jews like the 17,000 in Slovakia. It is absolutely impossible that the number of Jews involved in Holland and Belgium was considerably higher.

Q. On the other hand, you apparently overstate the number in Denmark that were affected by RSHA activities. You show 6,000, whereas only 2,000 are purportedly affected.

A. In both countries?

Q. Yes.

A. These figures I received from Hartenberger, who was in Denmark himself in 1944, together with Guenther. I cannot state anything more about it. I don't have any other material at my disposal.

Q. Now, turning to France, where you show 220,000, that is questioned as being about 100,000 too high.

A. My only answer is that this is '43.

Q. I am not necessarily relying on the table.

A. I can only refer you to my first chart in which I expressly stressed that the figures concerning France are probably unreliable. I only have them from Dannecker. Just because Dannecker was known for exaggeration and liked to build himself up, I doubted the figures and questioned them myself.

Document 13 'incredible things at Auschwitz'

HQ BAOR, interrogation reports from No. 1 Sub-Centre, 10 December 1945.
(D) Taped conversation held on 3 November 1945 between Ernst von Gottstein and Eugen Horak

ERNST VON GOTTSTEIN Hauptbauleiter OT, Gauamtsleiter für Technik, Gau Karnten
EUGEN HORAK Interpreter in Gruppe VI/C of the RSHA

HORAK I was present in Vienna when they were loading up people for one of those mass evacuations. Hundreds were crammed into wagons, which normally took a couple of cows. And they were thoroughly beaten up as well. I went up to a young SS man and asked if the beating up was really necessary. He laughed and said they were only scum anyway. You know the whole thing was so unnecessary and one could well have got along without it . . . what was the purpose of all that beating up? I have nothing at all against the gas chambers. A time can come when it is useful to the race to eliminate certain elements. Extermination is one thing, but there is no need to torture your victims beforehand.

I saw some incredible things at Auschwitz. Some SS guard personnel could not stand it any longer and had to be sent to a nerve clinic in Giessen. When my party arrived we were divided into two sections, those who were really keen on the whole affair, and those like myself who were continually asking for something to distract us. Lieben, Boehme and I were always having good books sent, and used to listen to good music. One SS Coy. [company] actually mutinied and tried to get themselves posted to the front. But they had to carry out their orders. It was just at the time that Ogruf [sic] Dix gave the orders to increase the death rate.

VON GOTTSTEIN The motto of the SS ought to have been 'Meine Ehre ist Gehorsam' ('My honour is obedience').

HORAK You are quite right. When the serjeant [sic] major came along for volunteers for a firing squad, the majority of us did not wish to go. Then he gave an order, 'You, you and you,' all the men had no alternative. It's quite right too that they had no chance of examining the moral implications of the order. Orders must be carried out. But those empowered to give them should have been properly selected beforehand. I have seen for myself all that has been revealed in the Belsen trial. These people lose all feeling. Roschke for example once told me quite callously that he had volunteered for duty in the crematorium because they got so much time off afterwards. This duty was absolutely repulsive. One had to stand the whole night in the crematorium. There was only one door and no windows. The two sentries had to go in, lock the door on the inside, and pass the key through the peep-hole to the officer outside. They were just connected with the outside world by telephone. An NCO and a private were normally on duty, but in a concentration camp experience counts a good deal more than rank. The one with more experience generally had a pistol and the other a rifle. There were nine people on duty in the crematorium, themselves certain candidates for the gas chamber. They knew too much or they were eventually exterminated as opportunity arose. There were four ovens on the left side of the crematorium, and the gas chamber was on the right, a normal size room with a narrow door and no windows. They did not use gas but a powder which they heated to a certain temperature and which gave off poisonous fumes. It must have been quite agreeable because the people never made a mess. The sentries had to see that the nine people on duty did not escape through the ventilators. And they watched them pulling the bones and pieces of flesh that had not been burned out of the ovens, or dragging the corpses from the gas chamber and cramming them into the ovens. There was only room for one body in each oven. There was a horrible smell of lime and burning flesh, something like a strong smell of urine . . . (both laughing). But you get so used to it that you could eat your sandwiches in there too.

VON GOTTSTEIN It's a wonder that the guards were not exterminated as well.

HORAK They always had one foot in the grave. After the wildest excesses the old SS people demanded that they should be 'racially examined'. What a circus it was! There was a Flamand who had volunteered for the SS, was wounded at the front and posted for guard duties at Auschwitz. I think his father was a Belgian minister and he had a row with him because he went to the SS. He was eventually sent away and got a vacancy at the SS Cadet School with the help of my brother. He went to Berlin, had another row, was flung out and returned to Belgium. That was the kind of guard troop we got. What a crowd they were! If I saw Meister I would hand him over to the next soldier. He was a serjeant [sic] with the Bavarian Gendarmerie and came to the Waffen SS as an Oberscharfuehrer, a broad, thick-set beer swiller and a real swine. He was like death incarnate, always thinking out new methods. In June '41 I saw him chasing a Jew behind a dray until he was exhausted. Then he asked him if he would like some water. So he made him kneel down in front of a bucket and when he bent down to drink he pushed his head down under water with his foot and held him until he drowned. What a swine he was. Everybody knew about him. I can't prove all I heard about him, but I actually saw this. Then there was Untersturmfuehrer Mueller, or some quite ordinary name, a grey-haired elderly man, who used to practise the most incredible obscenities on the corpses when he was drunk. He was generally known as the 'crematorium clown'. Another of them, Emmerich, if he didn't like anybody's face, just ordered the guard to eliminate them. One couldn't bear the cries and the screams very long, and the smell used to remain in your nostrils for days.

VON GOTTSTEIN The only really good thing about the whole affair is that a few million Jews no longer exist.

HORAK But those who were responsible are now in the soup . . .

Document 14 A Doctor at Dachau

Affidavit of F R A N Z B L A H A, Nürnberg, Germany, 9 January 1946

I, FRANZ BLAHA, being duly sworn, depose and state as follows:

1. I studied medicine in Prague, Vienna, Strassburg and Paris and received my diploma in 1920. From 1920 to 1926 I was a clinical assistant. In 1926 I became chief physician of the Iglau Hospital in Moravia, Czechoslovakia. I held this position until 1939 when the Germans entered Czechoslovakia and I was seized as a hostage and held a prisoner for cooperating with the Czech Government. I was sent as a prisoner to the Dachau Concentration Camp in April 1941 and remained there until the liberation of the camp in April 1945. Until July 1941 I worked in a Punishment Company. After that I was sent to the hospital and subjected to the experiments in typhoid being conducted by Dr Muermelstadt. After that I was to be made the subject of an experimental operation and only succeeded in avoiding this by admitting that I was a physician. If this had been known before I would have suffered because intellectuals were treated harshly in the Punishment Company. In October 1941 I was sent to work in the herb plantation and later in the laboratory for processing herbs. In June 1942 I was taken into the hospital as a surgeon. Shortly afterwards I was directed to conduct a stomach operation on 20 healthy prisoners.

Because I would not do this I was put in the autopsy room where I stayed until April 1945. While there I performed approximately 7,000 autopsies. In all 12,000 autopsies were performed under my direction.

2. From mid 1941 to the end of 1942 some 500 operations on healthy prisoners were performed. These were for the instruction of the SS medical students and doctors and included operations on the stomach, gall bladder, spleen and throat. These were performed by students and doctors of only two years' training although they were very dangerous and difficult. Ordinarily they would not have been done except by surgeons with at least four years' surgical experience. Many prisoners died on the operating table and many others later from complications. I autopsied all of these bodies. The doctors who supervised these operations were Lang, Muermelstadt, Wolter, Ramsauer and Kahr. Standartenfuehrer Dr Lolling frequently witnessed these operations.

3. During my time at Dachau I was familiar with the many kinds of medical experiments carried on there with human victims. These persons were never volunteers but were forced to submit to such acts. Malaria experiments on about 1,200 people were conducted by Dr Klaus Schilling between 1941 and 1945. Schilling was personally asked by Himmler to conduct these experiments. The victims were either bitten by mosquitoes or given injections of malaria sporozoits taken from mosquitoes. Different kinds of treatment were applied including quinine, pyrifer, neosalvarsan, antipyrin, pyramidon and a drug called 2516 Bohring. I autopsied the bodies of those who died from these malaria experiments. 30 to 40 died from the malaria itself. 300 to 400 died later from diseases which were fatal because of the physical condition resulting from the malaria attacks. In addition there were deaths resulting from poisoning due to overdoses of neosalvarsan and pyramidon. Dr Schilling was present at the time of my autopsies on the bodies of his patients.

4. In 1942 and 1943 experiments on human beings were conducted by Dr Sigismund Rascher to determine the effects of changing air pressure. As many as 25 persons were put at one time into a specially constructed van in which pressure could be increased and decreased as required. The purpose was to find out the effects of high altitude and of rapid descents by parachutists. I have seen the people lying unconscious on the floor of the van through a window in the van.

Most of the prisoners used died from these experiments from internal hemorrhages of the lungs or brain. The rest coughed blood when taken out. It was my job to take the bodies out and to send the internal organs to Munich for study as soon as they were found to be dead. About 400 to 500 prisoners were experimented on. Those not dead went to invalid blocks and [were] liquidated shortly afterwards. Only a few escaped.

5. Rascher also conducted experiments on the effect of cold water on humans. This was done to find a way for reviving aviators who had fallen into the ocean. The subject was placed in icecold water and kept there until he was unconscious. Blood was taken from his neck and tested each time his body temperature dropped one degree. This drop was determined by a rectal thermometer. Urine was also periodically tested. Some men lasted as long as 24 to 36 hours. The lowest body temperature reached was 19 degrees C, but most men died at 25 degrees C or 26 degrees C. When the men were removed from the ice water attempts were made to revive them by artificial warmth from the sun, from hot water, from electro-therapy or by animal warmth. For this last experiment prostitutes were used and the body of the unconscious man was placed between the bodies of two women. Himmler was present at one such experiment. I could see him from one of the windows in the street between the blocks. I have personally been present at some of these cold water experiments when Rascher was absent and I have seen notes and diagrams on them in Rascher's laboratory. About 300 persons were used in these experiments. The majority died. Of those who lived many were mentally deranged. Those not killed were sent to invalid blocks and were killed just as with the victims of the air pressure experiments. I only know two who survived – a Jugoslav and a Pole, both of whom are mental cases.

6. Liver puncture experiments were performed by Dr Brachtl on healthy people and on people who had diseases of the stomach and gall bladder. For this purpose a needle was jabbed into the liver of a person and a small piece of the liver was extracted. No anaesthetic was used. The experiment is very painful and often had serious results as the stomach or large blood vessels were often punctured resulting in hemorrhage. Many persons died of these tests for which Polish, Russian, Czech and German prisoners were employed. Altogether these experiments were conducted on about 175 people.

7. Phlegmone experiments were conducted by Dr Schutz, Dr Sabor, Dr Kieselwetter and Professor Lauer. 40 healthy men were used at a time of which 20 were given intra-muscular and 20 intravenous injections of pus from diseased persons. All treatment was forbidden for three days by which time serious inflammation and in many cases general blood poisoning had occurred. Then each group was divided again into groups of 10. Half were given chemical treatment with liquid and special pills every ten minutes for 24 hours. The rest were treated with sulfanamide and surgery. In some cases all the limbs were amputated. My autopsy also showed that the chemical treatment had been harmful and had even caused perforations of the stomach wall. For these experiments Polish, Czech and Dutch priests were ordinarily used. Pain was intense in such experiments. Most of the 600 to 800 persons who were used finally died. Most of the others became permanent invalids and were later killed.

8. In the fall of 1944 there were 60 to 80 persons who were subjected to salt water experiments. They were locked in a room and for five days were given nothing to eat but salt water. During this time their urine, blood and excrement were tested. None of these prisoners died, possibly because they received smuggled food from other prisoners. Hungarians and Gypsies were used for these experiments.

9. It was common practice to remove the skin from dead prisoners. I was directed to do this on many occasions. Dr Rascher and Dr Wolter in particular asked for this human skin from human backs and chests. It was chemically treated and placed in the sun to dry. After that it was cut into shapes for use as saddles, riding breeches, gloves, house slippers and ladies' handbags. Tattooed skin was especially valued by SS men. Russians, Poles and other inmates were used in this way, but it was forbidden to cut out the skin of a German. This skin had to be from healthy prisoners and free from defects. Sometimes we did not have enough bodies with good skin and Rascher would say, 'All right, you will get the bodies.' The next day we would receive 20 or 30 bodies of young people. They would have been shot in the neck or struck on the head so that the skin would be uninjured. Also we frequently got requests for the skulls or skeletons of prisoners. In those cases we boiled the skull or the body. Then the soft parts were removed and the bones were bleached, dried and reassembled. In the case of skulls it was important to have a good set of teeth. When we got an

order for skulls from Oranienburg the SS men would say, 'We will try to get you some with good teeth.' So it was dangerous to have a good skin or good teeth.

10. Transports arrived frequently in Dachau from Studthof, Belsen, Auschwitz, Mauthausen and other camps. Many of these were 10 to 14 days on the way without water or food. On one transport which arrived in November 1942 I found evidence of cannibalism. The living persons had eaten the flesh from the dead bodies. Another transport arrived from Compiègne in France. Professor Limousin of Clermont Ferrand who was later my assistant told me that there had been 2,000 persons on this transport when it started. There was food available but no water. 800 died on the way and were thrown out. When it arrived after 12 days more than 500 persons were dead on the train. Of the remainder most died shortly after arrival. I investigated this transport because the International Red Cross complained and the SS men wanted a report that the deaths had been caused by fighting and rioting on the way. I dissected a number of bodies and found that they had died from suffocation and lack of water. It was mid summer and 120 people had been packed into each car.

11. In 1941 and 1942 we had in the camp what we called invalid transports. These were made up of people who were sick or for some reason incapable of working. We called them Himmelfahrt [journey to heaven] Commandos. About 100 or 120 were ordered each week to go to the shower baths. There four people gave injections of phenol evipan or benzine which soon caused death. After 1943 these invalids were sent to other camps for liquidation. I know that they were killed because I saw the records and they were marked with a cross and the date that they left which was the way deaths were ordinarily recorded. This was shown on both the card index and the records in the town of Dachau. 1,000 to 2,000 went away every three months so there were about 5,000 sent to death in 1943 and the same in 1944. In April 1945 a Jewish transport was loaded at Dachau and was left standing on the railroad siding. The railroad was destroyed by bombing and they could not leave. So they were just left there to die from starvation. They were not allowed to get off. When the camp was liberated they were all dead.

12. Many executions by gas or shooting or injections took place right in the camp. The gas chamber was completed in 1944 and I was

called by Dr Rascher to examine the first victims. Of the 8 or 9 persons in the chamber there were still three alive and the remainder appeared to be dead. Their eyes were red and their faces were swollen. Many prisoners were later killed in this way. Afterwards they were removed to the crematorium where I had to examine their teeth for gold. Teeth containing gold were extracted. Many prisoners who were sick were killed by injections while in hospital. Some prisoners killed in the hospital came through the autopsy room with no name or number on the tag which was usually tied to their big toe. Instead the tag said 'Do not dissect'. I autopsied some of these and found that they were perfectly healthy but had died from injections. Sometimes prisoners were killed only because they had dysentery or vomited and gave the nurse too much trouble. Mental patients were liquidated by being led to the gas chamber and injected there or shot. Shooting was a common method of execution. Prisoners could be shot just outside the crematorium and carried in. I have seen people pushed into the ovens while they were still breathing and making sounds although if they were too much alive they were usually hit on the head first.

13. The principal executions about which I know from having examined the victims or supervised such examinations are as follows:

In 1942 there were 5,000 to 6,000 Russians held in a separate camp inside Dachau. They were taken on foot to the Military Rifle Range near the camp in groups of 500 or 600 and shot. These groups left the camp about three times a week. At night they would bring them back in carts drawn by prisoners and we would examine them. In February 1944 about 40 Russian students arrived from Moosburg. I knew a few of the boys in the hospital. I examined them after they were shot outside the crematory. – In September 1944 a group of 94 high-ranking Russians were shot including two military doctors who had been working with me in the hospital. I examined their bodies. – In April 1945 a number of prominent people were shot who had been kept in the bunker. They included two French generals whose names I cannot remember. But I recognized them from their uniform. I examined them after they were shot. – In 1944 and 1945 a number of women were killed by hanging, shooting and injections. I examined them and found that in certain cases they were pregnant. – In 1945 just before the camp was liberated all 'Nacht und Nebel'[20] prisoners were executed. These were prisoners who were forbidden to have any contact with the outside world. They were kept in a special enclosure and were allowed no mail. There were 30 or 40, some of whom were sick. These were carried to the crematory on stretchers. I examined them and found they had all been shot in the neck.

14. The rooms could not be cleaned because they were too crowded and there was no cleansing material. No baths were available for months at a time. Latrine facilities were completely inadequate. Medicine was almost non-existent. But I found after the camp was liberated that there was plenty of medicine in the SS hospital for all the camp if it had been given to us to use. New arrivals at the camp were lined up out of doors entirely naked for hours at a time. Sometimes they stood there from morning until night. It did not matter whether this was in the winter or in the summer. This occurred all through 1943, 1944 and the first quarter of 1945. I could see these formations from the window of the autopsy room. Many of the people who had to stand in the cold in this way became ill from pneumonia and died. I had several acquaintances who were killed in this manner during 1944 and 1945. In October 1944 a transport of Hungarians brought spotted fever into the camp and an epidemic began. I examined many of the corpses from this transport and reported the situation to Dr Hintermayer but was forbidden on penalty of being shot to mention that there was an epidemic in the camp. No preventative measures were taken at all. New healthy arrivals were put into blocks where an epidemic was already present. Also infected persons were put into these blocks. So the 30th Block for instance died out completely three times. Only at Christmas when the epidemic spread into the SS camp was a quarantine established. Nevertheless transports continued to arrive. We had 200 to 300 new typhus cases a day and 100 deaths caused by typhus a day. In all we had 28,000 cases and 15,000 deaths. In addition to those that died from the disease my autopsies showed that many deaths were caused solely by malnutrition. Such deaths occurred in all the years from 1941 to 1945. They were mostly Italians, Russians and Frenchmen. These people were just starved to death. At the time of death they weighed 50 to 60 pounds. Autopsies showed that their internal organs had often shrunk to one third of their normal size.

The facts stated above are true: this declaration is made by me voluntarily and without compulsion: after reading over the statement I have signed and executed the same at Nürnberg/Germany this 9th day of January 1946.

s/Dr Franz Blaha

Document 15 Auschwitz-Birkenau

Extract from the interrogation of Rudolf Hoess, Commandant of Auschwitz, taken at Nuremberg on 2 April 1946 by Mr Sender Jaari (from pp. 11–19, describing the procedures at Auschwitz from October 1942 following the completion of the main crematorium)

Q. Now, when the train arrived the prisoners were unloaded just as they were unloaded during the previous executions?
A. Yes.
Q. Then where did they march?
A. Then those who were fit for labor were selected, and the others marched to this newly erected crematorium.
Q. Did the selecting of the able-bodied Jews take place in the building, or outside?
A. Outside as before mentioned when the train arrived.
Q. That is, the Jews marched past the two SS doctors?
A. Yes.
Q. So, when a train with two thousand persons arrived, two thousand marched past the two doctors, and they just nodded, this one to labor and this one to the plant.
A. Yes.
Q. What kind of examination was that. Was that a sufficient examination?
A. Yes, the doctors said that was sufficient.
Q. Were they real high-classed doctors?
A. Not all of them. There were a lot of doctors around.
Q. They must have been exceedingly clever, just to look at persons dressed up and still being able to say, 'He is good and this other one is a bad one.'

Rudolf Hoess, the commandant of the Auschwitz extermination camp from 1941 to 1943, responsible for the murder of more than one million Jews and thousands of Soviet POWs. He was hanged at Auschwitz by the Polish authorities in 1947.

A. Yes, that is the way in which it was done.

Q. Have you ever been examined by a doctor for military duty?

A. Yes.

Q. Did he just take a glance at you, and then say that you were OK?

A. No.

Q. What did he do to examine you?

A. I had to undress, and was closely examined, my heart, lungs and other organs.

Q. Did not it ever enter your mind that the people that you were to employ in your war industries and in your factories should be perfect specimens of manhood, physically strong and able-bodied persons?

A. Only those who appeared at first glance to be strong and healthy were selected.

Q. How long did a laborer last, on average?

A. That depended where he worked and at what he worked.

Q. How many hours a day did he work?

A. In an armament industry, ten hours. It also depended on the route of march from the place where they were housed. Also whether they did outside or inside work, and also whether they worked in subterranean rooms.

Q. And how much food did a worker receive?

A. Those who worked in permanent industries received a normal food ration from the economic office, and they also received an additional supply of bread rations.

Q. Did they receive the same food as the guards?

A. No, the guards were fed according to military rations, and the prisoners were fed civilian rations.

Q. But the prisoners quota was so large that it did not matter whether or not the workers survived?

A. No, that is not correct. No, I was reprimanded repeatedly by my superior authority, who complained that not enough workers or men fit for labor were selected and used for labor purposes.

Q. But on the other hand you received complaints from Mueller and Eichmann that not enough were being executed, didn't you?

A. Yes, that is correct, that was the opposition, or contrast.

Q. Which point of view won?

A. Pohl[21] won, because the armament industry needed so many men that it was made a duty of every camp commandant, no matter where he was, to preserve as many laborers as possible for purposes of labor.

Q. But still Auschwitz succeeded in exterminating quite a number, something like in the millions, didn't they?

A. Yes.

Q. How many millions?

A. I again refer back to the statement made to me by Eichmann in March or April, 1944, when he had to go and report to the Reichsfuehrer [Himmler] that his offices had turned over two and one-half million to the camp.[22]

Q. To the Auschwitz area?

A. Yes.

Q. Only in the Auschwitz area?

A. Yes.

Q. Two and one-half million, you say?

A. Yes.

Q. Are you a little confused just now?

A. The reasons why I remember the number, two and one-half million is because it was repeatedly told to me that Auschwitz was to have exterminated four or five million, but that was not so. We had an order from the Reichsfuehrer of SS to destroy all materials in [on] numbers immediately, and not to preserve any records of the executions that were being carried out.

Q. The two and one-half million were people delivered to Auschwitz, were they the ones executed?

A. Executed and exterminated.

Q. Then quite a number more were delivered to the camp of Auschwitz?

A. Yes. According to the percentage that I have already mentioned, you would have to add 20 to 30 percent, who were used for labor purposes.

Q. Were these two and one-half million people gassed?

A. Yes.

Q. And how about the half million which were put to death by other means?

A. They were those who died from diseases, and who perished by other sicknesses in the camp . . .

Q. The people who were to be gassed in the permanent plants undressed in the free outside these large buildings, didn't they?

A. No, there was a special room.

Q. Just a moment ago you said they were undressed in the free outside?

A. No. The train was unloaded, they deposited their baggage, they were sorted out according to those fit for labor, and then the ones who had been selected marched away, and all the others undressed in an undressing room.

Q. What was told would happen to them there?

A. They were told that they were going to be conditioned to take a bath, and to be deloused and disinfected, and the signs were there corresponding to these institutions.

Q. They undressed and put their things away just the same way you told me yesterday, as it would happen in the farm houses?[23]

A. Yes.

Q. How many people could be gassed at the same time in one of the chambers in a permanent plant?

A. In one chamber, two thousand.

Q. A whole train load?

A. Yes.

Q. And how did the gassing take place?

A. It was all below ground. In the ceiling of these gas chambers, there were three or four openings that were fenced around with a grating that reached to the floor of the gas chamber, and through these openings the gas was poured into the gas chambers.

Q. And then what happened?

A. The same thing happened as I already told you happened in the farm houses. It depended on the weather conditions. If it were dry and a lot of people were in the gas chambers, it was comparatively fast.

Q. How long a time did the gassing take?

A. As I already stated, from three or five minutes to fifteen minutes.

Q. And how would you know when they were all dead?

A. There was an aperture, or vision slit through which one could look.

Q. And did you hear any noises from the outside?

A. Yes, but only muffled, because the walls were very thick cement, so that it was almost impossible to hear anything.

Q. And after how long a time were the doors opened?

A. After half an hour, as in the case of the other places.

Q. And who went in to remove the bodies?

A. The detail of prisoners who were working there. I might add that in the installations of the plants electrical ventilators were added which removed the gas fumes.

Q. But was it not quite dangerous work for those inmates to go into these chambers and work among the bodies and among the gas fumes?
A. No.
Q. Did they carry gas masks?
A. They had some, but they did not need them, as nothing ever happened.
Q. Then the bodies were removed to where?
A. Into the crematorium that was situated above.
Q. Did they have elevators?
A. Yes.
Q. Where were the rings removed. Was it in the gas chamber itself?
A. No, there was an anti-chamber [*sic*] outside the gas chamber just before the elevator where the rings were removed.
Q. And where they pulled out the gold teeth?
A. Yes.
Q. How were the crematoriums arranged?
A. There were four crematoriums. The first two larger ones had five double furnaces, and they could burn two thousand human beings in twelve hours.
Q. What kind of fuel did you use?
A. Coke.
Q. And the bodies were just shoved in, were they?
A. There were little barrels as used in the crematoriums in towns and the bodies were pushed up to the opening and slid in.
Q. How many bodies could one oven take or hold?
A. This double furnace could take in three corpses at one time.
Q. How many minutes would it take before the body was reduced to ashes?
A. It was difficult to say. When the full burning power of this furnace was still available, the process took place comparatively fast, but later on after a lot of bodies had been burned, it was more slowly, but then it also depended on the body composition of the corpse.
Q. What kind of bodies burned faster?
A. The heavy set fat persons.
Q. Did you get any fat persons, or strong persons into the ovens?
A. I do not mean strong bodies, but heavy fat persons.
Q. Were you often present at these executions and burnings?
A. Yes.

Q. Why?

A. Because I had to do this. I had to supervise these proceedings.

Q. Why did you have to supervise these proceedings?

A. To see that everything was carried out in an orderly manner . . .

Document 16 Demarcation Dispute

Extract from the interrogation of Otto Moll and Rudolf Hoess taken at
Nuremberg on 16 April 1946, 14:15 to 16:15, by Lieut.-Colonel
Smith W. Brookhart (the interrogation was conducted in English
and German)

Q. You are the same Otto Moll who appeared here this morning and you understand that your statements here are made under oath?

A. Yes. May I make a request please?

Q. Yes.

A. In Landsberg I made the request that I be confronted with Rudolf Hoess, the commandant of the Auschwitz Camp, so that I may testify in front of Hoess and Hoess may testify in front of me. I request you now that this may be granted. I would like to have Hoess testify in my presence, as I would like to see him make the statements in my presence and I can testify as to the truth.

Q. Assuming that you are confronted by Hoess, are you going to tell the truth, or are you going to continue to give us the same kind of a story that you gave us this morning?

A. No. I want Hoess to come here and state just what orders he gave me and I can say 'yes' or 'no' as to what is true and what is not true. Hoess should come here and say what orders he gave me, what duties I fulfilled and in what manner I accomplished them and then I can deny or confirm what he says.

Q. We will conduct the interrogation in the manner we wish and on the basis of the subjects in which we are interested. You are to listen carefully, you are not to interrupt or make any sound whatsoever until you are requested. Do you understand that?

A. I will remain silent and I will listen to him.

Q. You will be given the opportunity to speak at the proper time.

A. Please approve this request that Hoess may come in here and repeat his incriminating testimony against me. It hurts me to see that he, the commandant, is running around free, when I have to go around shackled to a guard.

Q. We are not interested whatsoever in your feelings in this matter.

(Rudolf Hoess, commandant of the Auschwitz Camp, enters room)

Q. Are you the same Rudolf Hoess that has appeared here on numerous occasions and given testimony?

A. Yes.

Q. Do you understand that the statements you make here this afternoon are made under oath?

A. Yes.

Q. Do you know this person sitting to your right that is shackled to the guard?

A. Yes.

Q. What is his name?

A. Otto Moll.

Q. Where did you know him?

A. First at Sachsenhausen[24] and later at Auschwitz.

Q. What did this Otto Moll do at Sachsenhausen and later at Auschwitz?

A. In Sachsenhausen he was a gardener and later at Auschwitz he was used as a leader of a work detail and later on he was used as a supervisor during the various actions.

Q. You mean the actions whereby people were executed and later cremated?

A. Yes.

Q. You told us this morning about his first assignment in 1941 when farm buildings were converted into an extermination plant. Will you restate what you said about that?

A. At first he worked on the farm and then later I moved him into the farm house, which was used as a professional extermination plant.

Questions directed to Otto Moll

Q. Otto Moll, is what the witness has just said true?

A. First, I was used in work in connection with the excavation of the mass graves. Hoess must know that. He is in error if he said that I worked in the buildings where the gassing was carried out. At first I was used for the excavation of the mass graves and he must remember that. Hoess, do you remember Swosten, Blank, Omen, Hatford and Garduck [*sic*]? Those are the people who worked in the building at the time when you alleged I worked there and I was working on excavations. Surely Hoess remembers that.

Question directed to Rudolf Hoess

Q. Is that right?

A. Moll is correct insofar as he says he was first used in the excavations – that was before he was being used for the executions.

Question directed to Otto Moll

Q. What is being said here, as I told you this morning, is that you are responsible for this operation, namely for killing and destruction of the bodies in the first improvised slaughter house.

A. I was responsible to see that the corpses were burned after the people were killed. I was never responsible for the actual supervision of the killing. It was always the officers or the physicians who were present at the time. As my commandant, at the time, Hoess should be able to confirm this.

Questions directed to Rudolf Hoess

Q. What do you say about this?

A. As I said this morning, Moll is only partly correct. As I explained, the gas was actually thrown into the chamber by the medical personnel and Moll was not responsible for supervising the entire process, beginning with the arrival of the transport and the burning of the corpses, he was only responsible for a part of this process, at least initially.

Q. You did say that he was responsible for seeing that these people were exterminated.

A. I could have been misunderstood. What I said, or meant to say, was that Moll was responsible in the buildings where he worked. At first, to see that the people were undressed in orderly fashion, and after they were killed, to see that the bodies were disposed of in an orderly fashion, later on when the extensive extermination plant was completed, he was responsible for the entire plant.

Q. Just what operations in the plant was he responsible for?

A. He was responsible for everything up to and including the actual leading into the gas chambers of the people and after that, to remove the bodies to burn them.

Q. Will you please repeat about Moll shooting people through the neck.

A. As I explained this morning, those that were too weak to be moved to the gas chamber, or who could not be moved for some other reason, were shot through the neck by him or . . . some of the other fellows around, with small caliber arms.

Questions directed to Otto Moll

Q. Well, what do you say about that?

A. It may be possible that some of them were shot by me, but it was a comparatively small number and I would like to know if Hoess ever saw me do it.

Q. I told you this morning that Hoess said he saw you do it many times and so did many others.

Questions directed to Rudolf Hoess

Q. Hoess, isn't that right?

A. Yes, it is true. I mentioned this morning that there were comparatively few killed in that manner.

Q. You could not tell if it was a few dozen or a few hundred. That was your problem.

A. I cannot quote you an exact number – that is impossible for so many years; there were many. Sometimes there were a few out of each incoming transport and sometimes there were none. That is why I cannot tell you the exact number.

Questions addressed to Otto Moll

Q. Well, this is the first thing you have admitted, now you are telling the truth about which you lied this morning. Are you ready to tell us the truth regarding your responsibility about other operations?
A. Yes, I will tell you the truth as long as my Commandant is present. Let my Commandant tell you what I did and what my duties were.
Q. We know what Hoess said. What we want to know is your story. You are asking us for the opportunity to tell your story and that caused us to bring Hoess in here.
A. No, I asked that I be interrogated in the presence of Hoess.

Question addressed to Rudolf Hoess

Q. You told us this morning that Moll was considered the best man for exterminations because he handled the teams of prisoners and guards better than your other subordinates. Is that right?
A. Yes.

Question addressed to Otto Moll

Q. Moll, suppose you tell us what was your method of selection of foremen from the Capos[25] and just what you found to be the best method of handling the guards that had charge of the transports after they came in.
A. When I was ordered to do this work, the work details had already been selected. My Oberfuehrers had already selected the Capos or foremen, whatever you call them. I carried out correctly the work in all kinds of weather. I was never drunk on duty, or when I was with the prisoners, and I never mistreated any of the prisoners. I achieved good success in the work of the prisoners because I, myself, helped them with their work with my own hands. The prisoners had respect for me because I always behaved as an exemplary soldier toward them, therefore, I was designated for any kind of difficult work that came up. May I ask Hoess to confirm that?

Question addressed to Rudolf Hoess

Q. Is that correct?

A. Yes, that is what I stated this morning.

Questions addressed to Otto Moll

Q. You were decorated for your work, were you not?

A. I received a decoration for my services. Almost all of them who served for a number of years in the whole of Germany received these decorations. I did not receive any decoration for special work that I had done like this work. I would not have wanted to receive a decoration for this kind of work.

Q. Why?

A. Because I did not look upon this work as honorable work.

Q. Did you ever protest?

A. I asked many times why those things had to be done, why they could not be stopped. I even asked Hoess and he answered that he himself did not like this, but he himself had strict orders and nothing could be done about it. He, like the rest of us, suffered by this work and none of us were really sane anymore.

Questions addressed to Rudolf Hoess

Q. Is that right, Hoess?

A. Yes, others also said that and already testified to that in the Reich.

Q. When do you think you lost your sanity, Hoess?

A. I think you mean that: just when our nerves started to crack. I can testify that I was not healthy in 1942. I told you about my leave in 1943, however, I had to do those things as there was no one there who would do it for us. There were strict orders and they had to be followed. Many of the others felt as I did and subordinate leaders came to me in the same manner as Moll did and discussed it and they had the same feeling.

Q. Do you think that Moll is crazy?

A. No.

Questions addressed to Otto Moll

Q. How long do you think you have been without your sanity?
A. I did not mean to say that I was insane or I have been insane, what I mean is that my nerves have cracked and have cracked repeatedly. They were very bad after the accident I described in 1937, later, they were very bad after I had an attack of typhus and I was in the hospital and was granted a leave of absence by the doctors for the conditions of my nerves. I was never declared unfit for duty on account of bad nerve, or because of the so-called paragraph 51.
Q. How many people do you estimate went through the operation, which you were responsible for – how many victims?
A. When you use the words – 'you were responsible' – I want to emphasize again that I do not wish to have that word applied in any way to the actual killing of the people, as I was not responsible for the actual physical ending of their lives and I will not admit that as it is not the fact.
Q. You did not pull the trigger, but you caused someone else to do it. Is that your position?
A. I do not understand the question.
Q. How many victims were exterminated in the camp from 1941 on?
A. I don't know the number and I don't think I would be able to give you any number at all as far as the total number of victims goes. I believe Hoess might know that.
Q. The only thing we are interested in is what you have knowledge of.
A. When I was in charge of these excavations, as I told you about before, together with another comrade, which was confirmed by Hoess today, we put between 30,000 and 40,000 people in these mass graves. It was the most terrible work that could be carried out by any human being.
Q. Stick to the figures.
A. I don't know who those people were or how they got there. I only excavated the mass graves. I was responsible for burning the bodies right there.

Question addressed to Rudolf Hoess

Q. How does that figure strike you, Hoess?
A. It is impossible for him to know the exact figures, but they appear to me to be much too small as far as I can remember today. The people buried in the two big mass graves of the so-called dugouts one and two, amounted to 106,000 or 107,000 people.

Questions addressed to Otto Moll

A. I could not complete the excavation detail, which I mentioned before, I then got the attack of typhus.
Q. What do you estimate was the number of bodies you handled?
A. It was later they went through my crematory plant and I would say between 40,000 and 50,000, that is at the crematory where I was responsible. I was not responsible for the two large crematories, as they were two SS corps [members] Nussfeld and also Foss, who were responsible for the two large cremations and Hoess will remember that.
Q. You tell us about the figures you know.
A. I told you the number, maybe 50,000 and possibly there were more.
Q. Is that for all times from 1941 clear to the end?
A. Yes, that is from 1941 for the entire length of my service when I had anything to do with the matter.
Q. Don't you think you are much too modest? You had the reputation of being the biggest killer in Auschwitz. The figures there run into millions. Won't you change your answer?
A. It is not true that I was the greatest killer in Auschwitz.
Q. You were the greatest cremator.
A. That is not true either. The number is not right and is probably brought up by the men who want me to be punished by death.

Questions addressed to Rudolf Hoess

Q. Hoess, what do you think would be the correct figures?
A. Moll, in my opinion, cannot possibly have any idea of the number of killings in the dugouts where he was working and responsible. At any rate, they were far, far too low – that is, Moll's figure.

Q. What figure would you attribute to Moll's responsibility?

A. It is impossible for me to quote the exact, or even a very rough figure, of the number of corpses that were handled by Moll. As the use of the extermination plant varied at all times, I do not know how many corpses I would have to attribute to Moll and how many to Nussfeld and the others.

Questions addressed to Otto Moll

Q. Moll, how many women and children do you estimate were among the bodies you handled?

A. Men and women were there in about equal numbers and the ratio of children to the other people was about one child in one hundred people brought in. Sometimes transports arrived without children. I would also like to say that I was not constantly working with these transports and of course, I cannot tell you what happened during my absence when I was not there, as I was away on leave of absence, etc.

Q. We have heard that there were more children than that. Do you want to change your statement?

A. As I told you, it may be one child in a hundred or it may be more. I cannot remember that exactly.

Questions addressed to Rudolf Hoess

Q. What do you say to that Hoess?

A. My estimate is that one-third of all the victims would be men and two-thirds women and children. I am not able to quote the exact ratio between women and children, as that depended or/and [*sic*] varied greatly with the transports that came in, however, I do remember that in the transports that came in from the Ukraine and Hungary the proportion of children was particularly high.[26]

Q. In what year was that?

A. That was particularly in 1943, or it may have been early in the year 1944.

Questions addressed to Otto Moll

Q. Moll, yesterday, you told us you had two installations and spoke of the furnace in which there were twelve large ovens and two additional with two ovens each, making a total of twenty-eight separate burning units. How many human beings could you cremate at one time?

A. Two to three corpses could be burned in one furnace at one time. The furnaces were built large enough for that.

Q. Did you operate at full capacity often?

A. I would like to emphasize that I had no responsibility at all with the cremation in the stoves. What I was responsible for was the burning of the corpses out in the open. Corporals Nussfeld and Foss were responsible for the cremation in the furnaces.

Questions addressed to Rudolf Hoess

Q. Is that right, Hoess?

A. First of all, Moll is slightly wrong in regard to the figures he quoted on the furnaces. The two large units were made up of five double furnaces each and the others of four double furnaces each. It is true that Nussfeld and Foss were responsible for the furnace details, each had a large and a small one and Moll was responsible for the bodies out in the open. Moll was responsible for the disposition of the ashes, but later on I put Moll in charge of the entire cremation. This was in the year 1944.

Q. Was that in the two months you were back at Auschwitz after you were away?

A. Yes, that is when I was transferred back to Auschwitz.

Q. How often were the crematoria detail of prisoners exterminated?

A. As far as I can remember, it was twice before I left for the first time and they were exterminated again after the action against the Hungarians was completed.

Q. On whose orders were the prisoners exterminated?

A. I received that order from Eichmann and he ordered in particular that the furnace commandoes should be shot every three months, however, I failed to comply with these orders as I did not think it was right.

Questions addressed to Otto Moll

Q. You have said that your detail was never exterminated. What do you say now?

A. No, that is not true. The work detail with which I worked was never exterminated as long as I was there and as long as I worked. As regard to the first work detail I had for the excavation of mass graves, which I had to leave because of my attack of typhus, they may have been exterminated when I returned to duty. The only thing that I know of is when I left, the last work detail I worked with, was still alive and that is, every member of the detail was alive when I left. Sometime later when I left mutiny broke out in the camp. I know that the entire guard company at the camp was used to suppress this mutiny. I was not there, I was at Gleiwitz at the time. I do not know anything about this, but Hoess can tell you that.

Q. Did you ever cremate any of your crematorium detail?

A. No.

Q. You mentioned that in the killing of the people in the gas chambers that it took only one half minute. On what do you base that?

A. The gas was poured in through an opening. About one half minute after the gas was poured in, of course I am merely estimating this time as we never had a stop-watch to clock it and we were not interested, at any rate, after one half minute there were no more heavy sounds and no sounds at all that could be heard from the gas chamber.

Q. What kind of sounds were heard before that?

A. The people wept and screeched.

Q. You observed all of this and heard the sounds?

A. Yes, I had to hear this because I was near there with my work detail. There is nothing that I could do against this as I had no possibility of changing this in any way.

Q. We are not interested in your opinions on that. You helped make the arrangements to put them in the gas chamber and burned them afterwards when they were killed. The only thing you failed to do personally was pour in the gas. Is that it?

A. I was not responsible for the preparations as there were no special preparations. The victims were led to the gas chamber by the duty officer and then there was a work detail from the administrator, they told them to undress, there was a further detail from the proper administration [*sic*], which were responsible to collect all the valuables from the people. The whole thing happened very correctly and in no instance was there any reason to interfere. I had no right to interfere, always a doctor supervised the entire thing.

Q. You recall yesterday, you said you were told that if any prisoners coming off of new transports detailed for the gas chambers would escape, you would be court-martialled.

A. I was talking about the work detail, not about the transports.

Q. This came at the time you were testifying about your responsibilities at the crematorium.

A. No, I only say as far as the work detail is concerned for which I was responsible.

Q. We will not argue about it, as the notes show otherwise.

Questions addressed to Rudolf Hoess

Q. What do you say of the detail of Moll.

A. Moll is not looking at this the right way. It actually is true and I have explained this before, that the officer was responsible for the entire transport, that is he was responsible to see that all were unloaded from each transport, the doctors were responsible for the phase of work to see that the people were killed and all the bodies disposed of. It was the responsibility of the subordinate, like Moll, to see that the people actually got into the gas chambers under the doctors and then to see that their bodies were burned. As far as the subordinate leader was concerned, it was his responsibility to see that none of his work detail escaped and he would be responsible to see that none got away. In the last analysis I was responsible for the entire matter, that is for the entire situation dealing with these transports.

Q. You have told us about some of the problems of making sure that everyone was exterminated. For instance, that mothers hid their children under their clothing after they undressed. Who was the person that gathered up the children, searched them out and put them into the gas chamber?

A. I think that this thing has been slightly misunderstood. The way this thing happened is that mothers had babies with them, who would be wrapped in blankets or cloth. The people had been told that they were going to take a bath, they had no idea that they were going to be killed.

It was not the idea, the mothers did not want to take the children in with them to the bath and they left them outside. Later on, the work detail from the administration, which was responsible for them, would pick up the babies and put them in the gas chamber then.

Q. Was it Moll's responsibility to see that the children were disposed of?

A. Yes, but it would not mean on the other hand that Moll would have the particular task of picking out the babies from under the blankets. I did not tell any one of the officers or non-coms [NCOs] that they would be responsible for any particular thing, but the entire team was responsible for the extermination. It was to be done and all of them carried out the orders smoothly and properly.

Questions addressed to Otto Moll

Q. You, Moll, said that your team respected you because you gave them a hand. Was this job of picking up small children and gassing them a part of the hand you loaned them?

A. Possibly this was not expressed correctly by Hoess. I had nothing to do with the searching of the clothes because that was not my duty. As I said, the officers that had charge of the duty when the transport came in was responsible for them until the moment they entered the gas chamber. I had nothing to do with that, I never touched the babies or had anything to do with it.

Q. Did any of your men have anything to do with that? Anyone under you?

A. Yes, the prisoners were responsible for that. They had to clean up the room after it had been cleared of people, they would then take the babies and throw them into the gas chamber. There was a strict order against any SS men touching any of this property.

Q. We are not talking about property. We are talking of people. Did you have a special operation to kill these babies or were they thrown into the room where people were still alive and all were gassed together?

A. Such a thing only happened rarely and I cannot remember a case where a baby was found, but if they were found they were thrown into the gas chamber.

Q. How do you know?

A. Well, that was an order for the officer responsible for the transport and if any children were found they were to be disposed of like all the rest in the gas chamber.

Q. You carried out your orders?

A. I emphasize again that I myself did not find any children, but if I did find any, I would have to do it too.

Q. Did you shoot any babies in the neck, like you did the other victims?

A. Such a thing never happened.

Q. That is what you said about shooting other people this morning, then we proved you a liar. Are you sure you are telling the truth this time? . . .

The Hess Case

At times I have been doubtful of [Hess's] mental stability. I have formed the impression that he is controlled in some degree by some form of mental influence. He is cunning, shrewd and self-centred . . . He is very temperamental and will need careful handling if he is to be outwitted . . . I believe by the very nature of his make-up, which reflects cruelty, bestiality, deceit, conceit, arrogance and a yellow streak, that he has lost his soul and has willingly permitted himself to become plastic in the hands of a more powerful and compelling personality. My personal view is that he has lost favour and in order to rehabilitate himself he has cunningly conceived the idea of appearing as a Peace Envoy to enable him to justify his action . . .

Report on Hess by Major Sheppard, 21 May 1941[1]

Hitler's deputy from 1933 to 1941, Rudolf Hess, reads a copy of Ernst Glaes's *Jugend* while the trial proceedings get under way. Ten days into the trial Hess shed the amnesia that had prevented effective interrogation, but memory loss returned later.

[Rudolf Hess was the odd-man-out at Nuremberg. He had strong psychotic tendencies, suffered from hysterical amnesia, and could not be effectively interrogated. His only systematic interrogation took place in Britain in the early summer of 1941, following his flight to Scotland.[2] These interviews showed that Hess was the victim of a profound delusion about the nature of British politics and society. He had expected an official reception and the chance to talk peace; instead he was treated first as a criminal, then, following his transfer to a secure location in Wales, as a mental patient. At Nuremberg he was unable to recognize his erstwhile colleagues, and they, in return, doubted his sanity. Albert Speer, asked at 'Dustbin' to describe the major players of the Third Reich, gave a frank account of Hess. Speer confessed that he had rather liked Hess, because he was honest. Hess was none the less a feeble character, sensitive, indecisive, unable 'to keep his feet on the ground'[3]. Speer thought Hess's flight was prompted by his fear that only the Soviet Union would benefit from the war between Britain and Germany: 'Hess was worried about the prospect of Western Europe's bleeding itself white in internecine war, which would make it easier for Russia afterwards to overwhelm not only Germany but all of Europe . . .'[4] Hess himself was unable to communicate any of this to his Allied captors. He was interrogated several times in the presence of others whom Amen thought might trigger recollection. The confrontation with Goering and the meeting with two of Hess's secretaries reproduced here give a rare moment of theatre in the routine of interrogation. The interrogations are followed by the assessment of the psychiatric experts assigned to the Hess case to review his mental state. It concurs with all the reports produced before the trial. The committee of experts appointed by the Tribunal judged that Hess indulged in 'a conscious exaggeration of his loss of memory'.[5] Colonel Andrus, who guarded Hess at Nuremberg, thought Hess was a complete sham and told him so repeatedly. He was tried, in the end, regardless of his true mental state.]

Document 17 'I have lost my memory'

Extract from the interrogation of Rudolf Hess, taken at Nuremberg on
9 October 1945, 14:30 to 15:10, by Colonel John H. Amen

COL. AMEN Your name is Rudolf Hess?

RUDOLF HESS Yes.

COL. AMEN Will you look over here to the right to this gentleman here.

RUDOLF HESS At him? (pointing to Hermann Goering)

COL. AMEN Yes.

HERMANN GOERING Don't you know me?

RUDOLF HESS Who are you?

HERMANN GOERING You ought to know me. We have been together for years.

RUDOLF HESS That must have been the same time as the book that was submitted to me this morning. I have lost my memory for some time, especially now before the trial. It is terrible, and the doctor tells me that it is going to come back.

HERMANN GOERING Don't you know me? You don't recognize me?

RUDOLF HESS Not personally, but I remember your name.

HERMANN GOERING But we talked a lot together.

RUDOLF HESS We were together; that must have been the case. That must have been so. As the Deputy of the Fuehrer all the time in that position, I must have met the other high personalities like you, but I cannot remember anyone, to the best of my will.

HERMANN GOERING Listen, Hess, I was the Supreme Commander of the Luftwaffe, and you flew to England in one of my planes. Don't you remember that I was Supreme Commander of the Luftwaffe. First I was a Field Marshal, and later a Reichsmarshal; don't you remember?

RUDOLF HESS No.

HERMANN GOERING Don't you remember I was made a Reichsmarshal at a meeting of the Reichstag while you were present; don't you remember that?

RUDOLF HESS No.

HERMANN GOERING Do you remember that the Fuehrer, at a meeting of the Reichstag, announced in the Reichstag that if anything happened to him, that I would be his successor, and if anything happened to me, you were to be my successor? Don't you remember that?

RUDOLF HESS No.

HERMANN GOERING You don't remember that? We two discussed that very long afterwards.

RUDOLF HESS This is terrible. If the doctors wouldn't assure me time and time again that my memory would return some day, I would be driven to desperation.

HERMANN GOERING Don't you remember that I visited your family and your wife? I saw you and your wife together repeatedly. You also visited my family with your wife.

RUDOLF HESS This is all a fog, behind which everything has disappeared; everything that happened in that time.

HERMANN GOERING Do you remember that I lived just outside Berlin, in a great house in the forest, at Carin Hall; don't you remember that you came there many times? Do you remember that we were together at Obersalzburg with the Fuehrer, where you have been for years, near Berchtesgaden?

RUDOLF HESS I have been there for years?

HERMANN GOERING Yes; for years, even before the acquisition of power.

RUDOLF HESS That means nothing to me.

HERMANN GOERING Hess, remember all the way back to 1923, at that time when I was the leader of the SA, that you led one of my SA troops in Munich already for me before 1923? Do you remember that we together made the putsch in Munich?

RUDOLF HESS The putsch in Munich was already mentioned this morning.

HERMANN GOERING Do you remember that you arrested the Minister?[6]

RUDOLF HESS I arrested the Minister?

HERMANN GOERING Yes.

RUDOLF HESS I seem to have a pretty involved past, according to that.

HERMANN GOERING I am just calling the most glaring things to your attention. Do you remember the beginning of the year 1933, and that we took over the government then, and that you got the central political office from the Fuehrer, and that we discussed it for a long time?

RUDOLF HESS No.

HERMANN GOERING You also told me that you wanted to become a member of the government, and I told you that I would try to help you. Do you remember that you moved to the Wilhelmstrasse, into the palace, which really belonged to me, as the Prime Minister of Prussia, but I enabled you to live there?

RUDOLF HESS I don't know.

HERMANN GOERING I visited you many times, and I handed it to you so you would have a house in Berlin. I turned the house over to you for your benefit.

RUDOLF HESS I have been told that everything will come back at one time by a shock.

HERMANN GOERING Just a moment. Do you remember Mr Messerschmidt.[7] You were well acquainted with him. He constructed all our fighter planes, and he also gave you a plane that I refused to give you, the plane with which you flew to England. Mr Messerschmidt gave that to you behind my back.

RUDOLF HESS No; that is all black. That is all black. That is all blacked out. It is all beyond fourteen days, and everything then I have a slight memory, and nothing exact. They told me that people who suffered heavily in the war would get attacks like that.

HERMANN GOERING Do you remember that the war started?

RUDOLF HESS I know that there was a war, but I don't know how it came about.

HERMANN GOERING Do you remember that you flew in a plane, you yourself, in this war, flew to England?

RUDOLF HESS No.

HERMANN GOERING You used a Messerschmidt plane. Do you remember that you wrote a long letter to the Fuehrer?

RUDOLF HESS About what?

HERMANN GOERING What you were going to do in England, that you were going to bring about peace.

RUDOLF HESS I have no idea of it.

HERMANN GOERING I have come to the end. I cannot ask him any more.

COL. AMEN(to Hermann Goering) All right. You move over here. (At this point Dr Karl Haushofer enters the room).

COL. AMEN(to Rudolf Hess) Do you know this man?

RUDOLF HESS (to Dr Karl Haushofer) Pardon me, but I really don't know who you are.

DR KARL HAUSHOFER Rudolf, don't you know me any more?

RUDOLF HESS I don't know you.

DR KARL HAUSHOFER I am Haushofer.

RUDOLF HESS Are we calling each other by our own first names?

DR KARL HAUSHOFER We have called each other by our first names for twenty years.

[After Haushofer, Franz von Papen and Ernst Bohle were both introduced to Hess, and received the same blank reaction. The interrogation was terminated by Amen after forty fruitless minutes.]

Document 18 The Young Ladies

Extract from the interrogation of Rudolf Hess, Miss Ingeborg Sperr and
Miss Hildegarde Fath taken at Nuremberg on 16 November 1945 by
Colonel John H. Amen

(In a hearing room at the end of the Interrogation Corridor, in the Palace of Justice, the following transpired between Miss Ingeborg Sperr and Colonel Amen, with the reporter and interpreter present. Miss Sperr was not sworn.)

Colonel Amen to Miss Sperr:

Q. You are Miss Sperr, are you?
A. Ja.
Q. Do you speak English?
A. (through the interpreter) No.
Q. You are Fraulein Sperr?
A. Sperr.
Q. And you were Mr Hess's secretary?
A. Ja.
Q. For what period of time?
A. From 1 May 1934, until the end.
Q. And was Miss Fath there at the same time as you were?
A. Yes.
Q. Did you work together or separately?
A. We also worked together, partially.

Q. Would you have any objection to talking to Hess and seeing whether you can do anything to help him remember?
A. I do not understand that question?
Q. Have you any objection to talking to him and helping him to see if he can bring back his memory about any of the things he used to know, as to which he now hasn't any memory?
A. No: if I can help him, of course.

COLONEL AMEN (to the interpreter) Tell her that Miss Fath is going in first and as soon as they get through we will have her go in.
THE INTERPRETER Yes.

Q. And you might be thinking in the meanwhile, of anything you could say to him which might help to bring back anything.
A. I shall try.

(Colonel Amen then proceeded – accompanied by court reporter and interpreter – to the hearing room in which Mr Hess was already seated, manacled to a guard. It was in this room that Colonel Schroeder, Major Kelley and Senator Pepper also came in upon the proceeding. This took place at 14:55 hours.

A few minutes transpired and then a woman entered the room. As she approached Hess, to this reporter she showed unmistakable signs of recognition. Hess and the woman greeted each other and proceeded to converse in German with each other. The woman, who by this time was identified to the reporter as Miss Hildegarde Fath, showed some snapshots to the prisoner. The prisoner showed definite signs of recognizing the pictures.

At this point Colonel Amen, in answer to Miss Fath's question, told her that Hess might keep the photographs.)

MISS FATH Except that I would like to keep this one (indicating a larger snapshot).

(Further conversation ensued, in which the reporter caught a reference to some medical doctor in Freiburg.

At this point, at 15:03, Colonel Amen left the room. The conversation between Miss Fath and the prisoner continued.)

MISS FATH I write, yes.
MAJOR KELLEY Do you want to write the address? Yes, you may.

(Some more conversation took place between the two. At this point Colonel Amen came into the room, accompanied by Miss Sperr. Miss Sperr warmly greeted Miss Fath. Miss Sperr and the prisoner met; to this reporter there were obvious signs of recognition.

The conversation ensued among the three persons, during which this reporter caught the expression '34'.)

MISS FATH (addressing Colonel Amen) Can't we afterwards speak together?
COLONEL AMEN Yes, you two women.
MISS FATH Yes, she is not kept in our prison.
COLONEL AMEN You can talk together, in another room, while the guards are there.
MISS FATH Yes, for a while.

(These questions to Miss Fath were put by the Colonel directly in English.)

Formal questions directed to Hess by Colonel Amen

Q. You remember these young ladies, don't you?
A. No, no; I do not remember them.
Q. You never saw either of them before?
A. As it is stated to me, it seems to be so.
Q. What seems to be so?
A. It has just been stated in the conversation with these two young ladies that I have seen them before.
Q. They worked for you for years?
A. Yes.
Q. But you say you don't remember?
A. No.
Q. And you don't remember any of the pictures that were shown to you?
A. No.
Q. Are you glad to see them?
A. Yes. I am always glad to see Germans, Germans who tell me of my family.
Q. What makes you think those are pictures of your family?
A. The ladies told me that, and besides, I have a picture of my son in my cell.

Q. Well, it is not the same as that one.

A. No, no; he is younger in that picture.

Q. You believe what the young ladies say, don't you?

A. I have not the least cause to think that Germans do not tell the truth.

Q. But you can't tell the difference between either of these young ladies and any other young ladies, is that right?

A. Not as a matter of course, but these two young ladies told me they were working for long years with me, in which case they are distinguished from other young ladies.

Q. Except that you don't know if it is true or not.

A. I repeat that I have no cause to doubt that Germans do not tell me the truth.

Q. Do you think all Germans will tell you the truth?

A. Yes, with all Germans with whom I am closely acquainted. Of course, there are some in all countries that do not tell the truth and who are not honorable.

Q. How do you know they are German young ladies?

A. According to the language, I have got the impression that they are not Americans.

Q. Well, there are other people besides Americans in Germany, aren't there?

A. Yes, I acknowledge that fact.

Q. When was it that this young lady worked for you? (indicating Miss Fath)

A. I do not know that.

Q. She just told you, didn't she?

A. But this has not left such an impression that I could repeat it by heart. But, at any rate, she was with me before I took off from Germany.

Q. Well, how about the other young lady? (referring to Miss Sperr)

A. The same way.

Q. Were they with you at the same time?

A. I do not know that.

Q. Did they do the same kind of work?

A. I do not know that.

Q. Did they do any work?

A. I hope so.

Q. Do you think so?

A. I have the impression.

Q. Where did you get the impression from?

A. I don't know how a scientist would express that. I can't express that in any other way.

Q. A scientist?

A. I assume that there are scientific definitions for this, that I do not know, but I believe it, that they were working for me.

Q. Did you tell one of these women that she could work for you again, later on?

A. Yes, yes: she was to rely on the fact that at one time she would be able to work for me again.

Q. What do you have in mind about that?

A. I consider that it has been told me that formerly I had a high position in the National Socialist State and that at one time that will again be the case.

Q. You mean you are going to have a high position in the Nazi State again?

A. Yes.

Q. The same position?

A. I do not know exactly what that position was, and in the same way I cannot know about the future position, what that will be.

Q. You have those plans for after the trial, is that it?

A. Yes.

Q. And what kind of work do you expect her to do for you?

A. That I do not know. I somehow think that work will correspond to the same type of work made before.

Q. What was that?

A. That I do not know. I know merely that they were working for me and that they will be similarly occupied again.

Q. What makes you think you can give them the same kind of work, if you don't know what kind of work they did before?

A. I merely said that one cannot express that in a literal way. I merely assume that they will be again working for me as they have been, as they have done before.

Q. Your previous work was that of being Deputy Fuehrer, wasn't it?

A. Yes.

Q. But now there isn't any Fuehrer.

A. It does not necessarily mean that I will be again Deputy to the Fuehrer. I merely want to say it will be again a high position in the German Nationalist State.

Q. How will you obtain that position?

A. I cannot say that at this time, but I have the impression that it will be again such – not impression, but the feeling.

Q. And where do you get that feeling from?

A. I do not know that. That is a matter for scientists and professional people to find out, where one gets such a feeling.

Q. But in any event you are perfectly willing to employ both of these girls again, and you believe that everything they have said to you is true, is that right?

A. Yes, of course.

Q. And yet you have never seen either one of them before?

A. I have already stated that I cannot recall having seen them before, but according to what the ladies have told me, I must have seen them before.

Q. You mean if they are telling the truth.

A. I do not know how often I should repeat that I have the conviction that Germans tell me the truth. But perhaps the gentleman might take cognizance of that fact.

Q. I could bring a lot of Germans in here that won't tell you the truth.

A. Yes, especially out of a prison where usually there are criminals kept.

Q. Such as Goering, for example?

A. No; this man did not understand me correctly. I said especially out of a prison where, as a matter of course, criminals are kept.

Q. And I said 'Such as Goering'?

A. That is quite evident that I did not mean that.

Q. Well, is Goering a criminal?

A. Yes, but an honorable criminal, a war criminal.

Q. How do you know what kind of criminal he is?

A. Because he is the same type of criminal that I am.

Q. But you don't know anything else about him, do you? You don't even know he is Goering, do you? That is what you told the gentlemen who were here yesterday.[8]

A. Even by raising your voice you cannot say that I did not say yesterday that I knew Goering from this time, and from the fact that I walked with him every day.

Q. I am asking you, how do you know he is not a criminal? How do you know he isn't a pickpocket or a thief?

A. I assume that the gentleman is trying to provoke me, but I cannot be provoked.

Q. I am only asking you how you know that it [he] is. I am not trying to provoke you. What I want to know is, if you have no memory, which is what you claim, how can you possibly know that Goering is not a pickpocket or a thief or some other kind of criminal?

A. Perhaps it is known to the gentleman that I have over there an indictment in which Goering, myself and other people are named.

Q. Well, forget about his being a war criminal. I am not talking about that. I am talking about how you know he isn't some other kind of criminal, like a thief, or a pickpocket or a murderer?

A. I am convinced of the fact that in Germany no pickpockets and thieves and people of that type are elevated to high ranks – at least in Germany.

COLONEL AMEN All right, that is all.

(To the guards) You can take him out and leave the girls.

(At this point, 15:32 hours, the two women bid goodbye to Hess and gave him a photograph and a book. Hess left the room. The two women remained.)

MISS FATH Is he not allowed to stay?

COLONEL AMEN No, but you can talk here for a while, if you want to.

(Here the official interpreter announced that this expression was used by Hess when the two women said goodbye to him, 'You can be proud of the fact that you are prisoners. I am not going to write.'

The interpreter also stated that the other girl said, 'Well, I will ask for permission.' Hess, on parting with the two women, the interpreter stated, said, 'Heil, euch.' This expression means 'Hail to you', which is a corruption of the formal greeting.)

Document 19 'the science of psychiatry is sound'

Justice Jackson files, report of the American experts (n.d.: December
1945?), 'Additional psychiatric comment on the Rudolph Hess case'

The role of the psychiatrist in the trial of the leading Axis war criminals
attained historical significance. This significance was derived in large
measure from the fact that the psychiatric panel was appointed by the
International Military Tribunal and reported its findings directly to
that body. This at one stroke obviated the distressing spectacle of
scientific experts being pitted against each other so common in civilian
criminal trials. This was in sharp contrast to universal practice of
civilian courts in which the medical expert finds himself appointed
either to the defense or prosecution and his impartiality brought into
question by the very fact that he is made a party to a contest. He is
denied access to information which permits him to be impartial.

The nature of the charges against the defendants are such as to
arouse the keenest interest of all students of human behavior. In at least
three of the defendants, namely: Hess, Streicher and Krupp definite
question was raised as to their sanity and as to their ability to defend
themselves against the charges.

The Tribunal took cognizance of these questions to request the
examination of these defendants by representative psychiatrists of
four of the victorious countries. Thus these scientists were permitted to make their study as impartial workers utilizing scientific
methods. It removed the restriction imposed upon the expert witness
in civilian courts in both criminal and civil trials in that they served
neither prosecution nor defense. It is therefore unique in criminal
jurisprudent [sic] and hence of tremendous historical interest. It sets a
precedent which should be followed in all civilian criminal court
proceedings.

The appointment of psychiatrists from four geographically widely
separated countries, speaking three different languages, and coming
from other cultures assured a diversity of viewpoint and breadth of
approach in the studies made. It served also as a severe and critical test
of the science of psychiatry and the ability of professional workers

unaware of the methods used by one another to come to similar conclusions in spite of language and other barriers. That the ten designated scientists came to unanimous conclusions on the main issues involved in the case is proof that the science of psychiatry is sound and that these representatives were independent in their work and free from political influences.

The Tribunal raised specific questions of a legal nature some of which required interpretation unfamiliar to the psychiatrist. However the Tribunal did not limit the psychiatrist to direct categorical replies and authorized a report made in the form which commended itself to the examiners. This is unique in court practice.

This psychiatrist as an expert witness in the court is not qualified to pass on legal matters. To attempt to do so would be stultifying and would confuse scientific method and legal practice. For example, the expert witness does not appreciate all the legal implications of the question 'can the defendant plead to the indictment'. He may inform himself but in so doing he must depart from the practice of medicine and enter the sphere of the profession of the law and specifically the field of criminal jurisprudence.

Likewise his concept of insanity differs from that of the judge. To the psychiatrist the word insanity means the existence of unsoundness of mind of such a nature and degree as to prevent him from distinguishing between right and wrong and from adhering to the right. To some others it is synonymous with psychosis.

Although, in general, insanity means the same thing to the court it has however other implications as well. These have to do with such questions as were raised in defendant Hess' case, namely: is 'the defendant (Hess) of sufficient intellect to comprehend the course of the proceedings of the trial, to challenge a witness to whom he might wish to object and to understand the details of the evidence'. The interest of the court in the defendant's intellect is understandable but it is not consistent with the psychiatrist's conception of insanity. Two fundamental principles were established in this examination. Firstly, the psychiatrist serves science and the purpose of the criminal court best when he is free as an impartial witness to utilize the scientific method in his examination. Secondly, his report is of greatest value when his findings are reported in definite understandable medical language. This was made possible by the International Military

Tribunal by their instructions to the psychiatrists and by their request concerning the form of the reports.

Our examination revealed that Hess is not insane, has no disorder of consciousness, understands perfectly everything that is said to him and therefore understands the nature of the proceedings against him. He asserted that he had suffered a loss of memory for the past, but it was the definite impression that what he interpreted as depending upon memory was not available to an examiner, but what he did not understand as depending on memory as such was reproduced.

He claimed that he had no recollection or mental image of his parents yet he answered some other questions about his family without utilizing his usual phrase 'I don't know'. Moreover, he carried on the various mental and physical activities of his daily life despite the alleged loss of memory for the time when he learned them. The titles of some of the books he has been reading indicate that he must have, in order to understand their significance, retained some of the background of his education and training, although he says he does not remember what studies he undertook in his early years and has no memory of his tutors. However when asked if he had ever studied astrology he replied emphatically '*No*' instead of 'I don't remember'.

These among other phenomena suggest that a part of the memory loss is simulated and it is probable that the hysterical or unconscious part is rather superficial. He adhered quite consistently to the patter of saying 'I don't know', 'I don't remember' to questions relating to his past life. It is probable that this type of response was originally developed consciously as a protective measure during a period of stress; that it has become habitual and therefore has become unconscious in part.

Detailed studies by means of special techniques that could have been made to determine the extent of the unconscious elements in his memory loss were resisted by him. His refusal was explained in such phrases as 'My memory has nothing to do with my responsibility' . . . 'I can get my memory back by experiments after the trial . . . It is not so important to get cured before the trial . . . There is no possibility of doing it in a natural way'. He obviously wanted to retain the amnesia.

His behavior was dissimilar to that of the usual amnesic as evidenced by the lack of any attempt to recover his memory. His behavior during the early sessions of the trial, his apparent inattention to the proceedings and his reading of books including novels in the court room when matters which should have been of vital interest to him were under discussion must be interpreted as abnormal reactions.

It is now the consensus among psychiatrists that only an unstable person can or does use this method of dealing with the major issues of life, and there is a sufficient amount of evidence in his personal history to indicate that he has been an unstable personality and has a neurotic character which has expressed itself in hysterical symptoms from time to time. His present claim to a loss of memory is one of these hysterical reactions developed in connection with the dilemma in which he found himself in England. The British record states that he had a loss of memory from November 1943 to June 1944, at which time it was recovered. His present amnesia started in February 1945 and now serves the psychological purpose of complicating the examination proceedings.

He therefore has a selective amnesia, hysterical in type, utilizing defense mechanisms of an emotional neurotic nature. He has no brain disease as such as [and] his capacity for thinking is basically intact. His difficulty being emotionally determined he is not wholly aware or entirely conscious of the significance of his symptoms, and although his ability is unimpaired he does not use it in the examinations and may not during the trial proceedings.

The hearing of the Tribunal on 30 November 1945 concerning the mental state of the defendant Hess was noteworthy on several counts. First among these is the remarkable degree of accord revealed in the reports of the groups of psychiatric experts representing the four countries responsible for the trial. While there can be no doubt that the fortunate fact that the experts were appointed by the Tribunal itself rather than by the prosecution and defense separately contributed to this agreement, the extent of concurrence as to diagnosis, as to sanity and as to fitness to plead was remarkable. This was the more so since there has been a considerable curtailment of exchange of scientific information between the various countries during the war period and the normal transfer of ideas, technics and procedures has been limited.

This essential agreement between the groups whose examinations, with the exception of that of the French who participated in all three, were carried out separately strengthens the conclusions of the psychiatric panel.

Of equal note is the fact that all four prosecutors, and so far as could be determined, the counsel for the defense, also accepted the findings although some degree of difference as between the prosecution and defense was voiced, this being based upon the unanimous agreement of the psychiatric panel that the defendant's amnesia, while it would not interfere with his grasp of what was said, would result in his making a less adequate defense.

It may be noted that the methods of treatment which were at one time proposed to Hess, which he refused and which his counsel referred to as 'forceful', are by no means so. They consist very simply in the administration of sedatives such as sodium amytal or pentothol which are in daily use in general hospitals of large and small cities throughout the country. They have also been used with conspicuous success in the treatment of those who have suffered from temporary impairment of memory as a consequence of battle experiences. They are pleasant to take and their immediate effects are to reduce anxiety and apprehension which may be present and there are no undesirable after effects.

When the defendant was called upon to speak there ensued an episode which while apparently startling, is actually quite common in this type of condition. Hess announced that his memory was 'again in order', that he had simulated his loss of memory for tactical reasons while in England but he had intended to reserve his declaration for a later period in the trial and that his attorney was not a party to this deception. He qualified his statement by saying that his powers of concentration were still somewhat impaired but that he felt that he could grasp what was said and that he accepted the entire responsibility for the acts for which he was being tried though he denied the competence of the Tribunal to try him.

Analyzing these statements, one notes first the theatrical and dramatic nature of his declarations and of his pose, and related to this the lack of contact which the audience seemed to feel with him during the declaration as contrasted with that which they had evinced when Goering made his attempt to address the Tribunal on being asked to plead to the indictment.

From his statement there appeared an interesting doubt as to whether he himself considered that he had always maintained full control of his memory, this being manifested in the statement that his memory was *again* in order though his concentration was still impaired.

The reports of all four expert groups had stressed the fact that while Hess suffered from a degree of hysterical amnesia, he consciously simulated a still greater degree of memory loss than he actually had and that he used it precisely as indeed the defendant admitted he did to protect himself against inquiry and examination.

A further point which throws considerable light upon the instability of his personality is the very fact that having maintained this degree of simulation over a long period he discarded it at the very time when he might have hoped that it would save his life.

In the absence of further direct examination, no definite explanation can be given for this throwing away of his carefully built up protection. Certain conjectures however seem reasonable. Among these is that the association with the other defendants after a long period of practical isolation, the reviving by the prosecution of a great train of happenings and incidents in which Hess had taken part in earlier years and amazing though it may be to ordinary folk, the very possibility that he might be adjudged incompetent to plead and hence thrown out of the limelight, resulted in the overcoming of the hysterical amnesia, and then in a determination to drop his simulation. Incidentally, it had been noted over the last few days prior to 30 November 1945 that he was taking progressively more interest in the trial, was wearing his earphones and had almost dropped reading his novels.

It is difficult for those not acquainted with the defendants to realize how extraordinarily important prestige and the limelight are to them.

With regard to the further unfolding of Hess' behavior, we feel that it is essential to stress his great instability. Within a period of four years there has been a great variety of symptoms, delusions of persecution, two suicidal attempts, at least two periods of hysterical amnesia, various bodily symptoms such as abdominal cramps which apparently are of neurotic origin and finally this last dramatic outburst. These abnormalities of behavior have appeared and vanished as the pressures to which he has been subjected since he broke away from his established position in the Nazi hierarchy have waxed and waned. At present it can only be stated that as the psychological stresses of the trial mount, further evidences of his instability may well appear either in the form of his previous symptoms or in ways which differ from those which he has as yet shown.

D. Ewen Cameron, Professor of Psychiatry, McGill University

Nolan D. C. Lewis, Professor [of] Psychiatry, Columbia University Director of the New York State Psychiatric Institute and Hospital

Colonel Paul L. Schroeder, MC, Professor [of] Psychiatry, University of Illinois, Director of the Institute for Juvenile Research

The von Papen Case:
Resistance and Compliance

Q. Will you continue, Herr von Papen?
A. Up to the Munich agreement, the world, the English and British government, Mr Chamberlain, the French government and Mussolini, they all believed that it was possible to come then, to an understanding, the main wishes of Germany fulfilled, and to have a reasonable and peaceful government established after all in Germany. If these people could hope so, why shouldn't a good patriot, and a man, in the first place, who is responsible for all these goings-on, have the same hopes, and the same convictions, and the same fervent hope that it may become so. That explains my doing, I may say.

**From the interrogation of Franz von Papen at Nuremberg,
12 October 1945**[1]

Former Chancellor of Germany, Franz von Papen, at work in his cell. Von Papen was not initially on the list of war criminals, but was added because of his alleged role in bringing Hitler to power in 1933 and assisting the *Anschluss* of Austria with Germany in 1938.

[The transcripts of the interrogations of Franz von Papen, former Chancellor of Germany from June to December 1932, were among the longest conducted at Nuremberg. This can largely be explained by von Papen's willingness to speak English, which approximately doubled the time actually available for discussion in any two-hour interview. There was also the interest that Judge Thomas Dodd showed in the von Papen case. He did not consider von Papen to be like the rest of the defendants. He was quite unable to grasp why men like von Papen, respectable, educated public servants, did not reject Hitler and the NSDAP uncompromisingly. His predecessor as Chancellor, Heinrich Brüning, also a Catholic politician, left Germany and settled in the United States.[2] General Kurt Schleicher, Chancellor from December 1932 until Hitler's appointment in January 1933, withdrew from public life, and was assassinated by SS men on 30 June 1934, the 'Night of the Long Knives'. Von Papen stayed on despite his growing disillusionment. When he was first caught in April 1945 he spoke off the record to his interrogators about his hostility to Hitler, but did not want it broadcast in case he became a victim of German retaliation.[3] At Nuremberg six months later he told Dodd that he now considered Hitler 'the greatest crook I have ever seen in my life', and dated that view to the outbreak of war in 1939.[4] The two extracts from von Papen's interrogation, Documents 20 and 21, show Dodd trying to understand why von Papen first supported the idea of a Hitler government in 1933, and then, when it was manifest what a Hitler government meant in reality, why he continued to serve the regime until shortly before the end of the war. Von Papen's own explanation stands for the complicity of a wide circle of conservative Germans, who were slowly disabused of their early illusions about Hitler, but too patriotic and too prudent to pull away from the system. It is now known that von Papen, as ambassador to Turkey during the war, passed on to the Turkish government gold that had been looted from the victims of genocide.[5] For those who served the regime, even from love of the fatherland rather than of Hitler, accessory to crime was hard to avoid.]

Document 20 'a way out of the mess':
von Papen and Hitler in 1933

Extract from the interrogation of Franz von Papen taken at Nuremberg on
3 September 1945 [p.m.] by Mr Thomas J. Dodd (no interpreter present)

Mr Dodd to the Witness:

Q. Mr Von Papen, we were discussing, I think, at noontime the events of January, 1933, as I remember?
A. Yes.
Q. Let me ask you this question and maybe we can get started. Isn't it a fact that Field Marshal von Hindenburg was very much opposed to the idea of having Hitler become Chancellor of the Reich?
A. Yes, certainly. He refused. We tried to get Hitler into the government, and he refused.
Q. When did you first try?
A. After the first election of the Reichstag under my Chancellorship [July 1932].
Q. Would you tell us, if you now recall, what you said to von Hindenburg on that occasion and what he said to you about Hitler?
A. At what time?
Q. At the time after the election of the Reichstag under your Chancellorship.
A. My government was made – I must say first that I had been very much surprised at the offer to me to become Chancellor. I didn't know anything about that, but the idea of his [Hindenburg's] government – of such a government apart from the parties, independent of the parties has been much discussed in all political circles.
Q. Much discussed?
A. Discussed, yes, of forming such a government. Hindenburg said to this party, 'I want to go on independently of you and not to take such ministers as you will impose upon me. I want to take technical people.' It was the idea to make a more authoritative government, a stronger government. Now, then, at the beginning, certainly there was not the idea – it was not Hindenburg's idea to take Hitler in.
Q. Did you urge him to take him in?

A. No, but after the elections when he came out with his party even stronger [July 1932], then we tried to get him in, to get the majority with him, because we thought the object of the forming of a new reform of the constitution could certainly be made much easier with the majority of the Reichstag than without it. But he refused.

Q. Hindenburg?

A. Hindenburg refused, and Hitler refused too. And that was repeated after the second time, after the second election [November 1932]. But the second time the position of Hitler was less strong because he took only about 40 [196] seats in the Reichstag, and I think therefore Hindenburg seemed to be inclined – what I told to you of the negotiations of 2 December[6] – to reform the constitution without the majority because we couldn't find one and send the Reichstag home for a couple of months –

Q. And in the meantime govern himself, is that so?

A. Yes, it was the same state of affairs that we had – the Reichstag was always adjourned; it was not in session. But then you wanted to know why Hindenburg was so strongly opposed to making Hitler Chancellor. He was not opposed to take his government [take him into government], but to make him the Chancellor. That he was opposed to, but then between 2 December and the end of January very much had changed. Schleicher, who tried to split the [National Socialist] Party, had failed completely, and the result of that failure was certainly to strengthen the National Socialists. And then there was the outcome of the second election, small as they were, but they were taken as the sign that the party was always growing bigger and bigger [regional election in Lippe, January 1933]; so that if at the end of January he wanted to repeat the order he gave to me on the 2nd, that is to say to form a new government and to reform the constitution, the risk was certainly much bigger then because of the growth of the National Socialists. That was the difference between the two dates.

Q. I have the impression from what you have said that von Hindenburg was always opposed to Hitler. He didn't think that he was the kind of man that should be heading up the government, isn't that so?

A. Yes.

Q. And therefore it must be that someone or more than one person in conversation with him urged him at the proper time to change his mind, do you understand?

A. Maybe. It is quite possible –

Q. Didn't you think that he should take Hitler on 30 January? What did you think about it?

A. Well, when he charged me to form the government, I talked it over, talked over the situation, and I must confess I did not see that outcome. At the end of January the risk was much greater, and Schleicher said to me that there would be civil war and revolution and uproar in the country; and since he [Hitler] had grown up these two months in the country, if we wanted or not to have him at the top of the government, there was no other way. All we could do was to limit him with as many securities as would be possible, and that we tried to do. Then you will remember that in forming this government I was made president [of Prussia] and Goering the very important post of Interior. That was the only condition of the Nazis, and we couldn't prevent that, but at that time we thought it would be possible for me as the president of the Prussian government[7] to get in and stop him eventually. Apart from that the members of the government were the same as my government, trustful men Hindenburg knew and I knew and we had confidence in them.[8] The only new one was von Blomberg,[9] who as a special wish of Hindenburg took the place of War Minister . . .

Q. Getting back again to how it was that Hindenburg came to accept Hitler, I think your explanation is overly simple. Do you understand what I mean?

A. Yes.

Q. Because I am reminded that the Nazis called von Hindenburg names during the campaign and they vilified him, isn't that so? They abused him?

A. Yes.

Q. He knew that?

A. Certainly.

Q. He knew about the notorious character of Roehm?[10]

A. I don't think he knew particularly about that. The man's name at the time was unknown.

Q. Weren't those things pretty public knowledge about that time, in January of 1933, about Roehm?

A. No, I think it was a year later. I never heard his name or his activities at that time. You must consider the time not under the results we see today.

Q. I am aware of that, but that is what makes it difficult to understand your simple explanation of Hindenburg's acceptance of Hitler because of what I recall and understand about those times. Do you agree that Hindenburg was very much opposed to the 'Kleine Corporal' as he called him on more than one occasion?

A. Yes. You said there may be some persons that advised him to do it. It may be.

Q. Didn't you advise him to do it?

A. No, certainly not. I can swear upon it that I didn't . . .

Q. Well, man to man, isn't it a fact that you had become convinced for a number of reasons that the thing to do was to permit Hitler to become Chancellor of the Reich? That's so, isn't it?

A. Yes.

Q. And Hindenburg was opposed to that view, isn't that so?

A. Not at that time.

Q. But he had been opposed?

A. No, no. The time when Hindenburg asked me to become the mediator to form the government with Hitler on top, it was the first time I heard of the idea to take him in.

Q. But that wasn't the same thing as making him Chancellor?

A. That was the sole and only condition to have the Nazis in the government, to make Hitler Chancellor. Since one year there was only that talk.

Q. My proposition is that von Hindenburg was at one time ready to accept Hitler as Vice-Chancellor with considerable doubt in his mind?

A. Yes.

Q. He was continually opposed to taking him as Chancellor right up to the date of 30 January 1933?

A. He didn't want him, but he didn't see any other way.

Q. And isn't it also a fact that you had also become convinced that he had to be taken as Chancellor?

A. Yes, after I heard of the failure of Schleicher and the decision of Hindenburg not to entrust Schleicher with the same post as on 2 December [i.e. as Chancellor].

Q. Very well, we are faced with this situation with which we both agree, that Hindenburg didn't want Hitler and that you had become convinced that he had to take Hitler?

A. Yes.

Q. Now, what I want to know is what did you do, what part did you play in changing the old Field Marshal's mind?

A. I had nothing to change. The moment he was convinced there was no other way – he wanted to work longer with Schleicher, and there was no other way for him.

Q. Herr von Papen, you are a man of great experience, I know, and you know German politics very well. I am sure you will understand when I say to you that a man in your position in those days must have counseled with and advised the Field Marshal von Hindenburg about such an important matter.

A. Certainly.

Q. As to the acceptance or refusal of Hitler as Chancellor of the Reich?

A. Yes. When he told me about the situation, I completely agreed with him then there was no other way than to try to take the party in with Hitler on top and try to have as many securities around him as possible for this experiment.

Q. I understand that, but my point is that you have said to me this morning and again this afternoon, if I understood you correctly, you have made it appear to me that you intended to convey the impression that it was von Hindenburg who suggested Hitler to you.

A. Yes.

Q. Well, the facts are to the contrary, isn't that right? Von Hindenburg didn't want Hitler and you and others who had become convinced of the necessity of taking Hitler suggested Hitler to von Hindenburg?

A. At the time he didn't want him, but the old man had no other chance [choice].

Q. There was a chance –

A. Which way do you suggest we should have gone?

Q. I am not prepared to make that suggestion.

A. That was the only way which we could have gone.

Q. What I am interested in now is establishing this question of fact: That you and others suggested Hitler to von Hindenburg rather than von Hindenburg suggested Hitler to you, and I think that is so, is it not, as a matter of history?

A. No.

Q. How can you deny it on the record?

A. Because I am taking into consideration all the possibilities. I am not saying anything that is not true.

Q. I am not trying to mislead you, but as a matter of history in that period in Germany, I do not see how you can say that it was von Hindenburg who suggested to you the taking of Hitler when the whole history of the situation as given by so many is that Hindenburg didn't want Hitler.

A. You misunderstand. He had at that time suggested to me – he said, 'I have now decided to make that government. Would you be good enough to be Chancellor.' [Von Papen here meant Vice-Chancellor.]

Q. I understand, but that was the last period. There must have been an intervening period of time when he was still opposed and he was becoming less opposed and less opposed and finally not opposed at all.

A. There were discussions between Meissner[11] and Hindenburg and Oscar Hindenburg and Hindenburg and Schleicher and Hindenburg that made Hindenburg decide to leave all resistance and go the other way . . .

Q. And you want me to understand that during that thirty days from 1 January to 30 January, when you were convinced on 1 January about Hitler, you want to tell me that you didn't tell Hindenburg in that time that Hitler was the best way out with what you understood him to represent?

A. In my mind the first of January and consecutive days, I stood on my old conviction that Schleicher should see other people and try to split the [Nazi] Party and try to make the best of it, but I remember even as I learned of the failure of his endeavors the Marshal's refusal to empower him. I didn't see any other way to do it.

Q. But you are not answering my question.

A. You mean if I influenced the Marshal?

Q. Well, to some extent you were one of his advisers. He had great confidence in you.

A. Certainly.

Q. And he must have talked to you about it.

A. Well, probably, but I don't remember all the details of these days, but the substance of our discussion has been for a way out of this mess.

Q. Yes, he was looking for a way out of this mess, and you were convinced that the only way out was to take Hitler, isn't that so?

A. Yes.

Q. And you must have told him so.

A. Probably.

Q. You don't have any serious doubt about it, have you, sir?

A. I don't remember that I had any political discussions with him before the date of Schleicher's dismissal. I don't think I had.

Q. I am not trying to mislead you. I am merely trying to explore what to me seems perfectly clear as the only logical sequence of events, the only fair deduction I can draw from what you said this morning and this afternoon.

A. Public opinion was thinking that I managed the Hitler government –

Q. Well, I am not concerned about that today. We will talk about that later on. My concern now is to establish or disestablish the fact that in those crucial days in January 1933, you on the one hand and those who were associated with you had come to the conclusion that there was only one way for you to go, and that was to take Hitler even though you may have done it reluctantly, and that once you came to that conclusion, you did your best to get von Hindenburg to accept him.

A. But that wasn't necessary. I mean at the same time I came to the conclusion, he came to the conclusion too. I mean it was a concordance of chance. He came to the conclusion after the failure of the dismissal of Schleicher and I too.

Q. You had come to that conclusion before that day?

A. Certainly not. Why should I, as long as I had hopes I could split the Party and go along. Why should I?

Q. Do you want to have me understand that you had not reached a decision about naming Hitler as Chancellor until the very period that Hindenburg did it?

A. I can't say that very day, but certainly after the fact of the failure of Schleicher and Hindenburg's refusal to deal with him any further, that's absolutely true . . .

Q. And when had Hindenburg decided to take Hitler?

A. Well, I can't say, a few days earlier.

Q. It was 30 January, wasn't it, when the final decision was made?

A. It was 30 January when we formed the government, but the decision was made a few days earlier . . . I don't want to minimize my part, understand. I am responsible for everything I did in my life, but I don't think I did anything to convince him to go that way. I said this: 'It seems to me it is the only outcome,' but I did nothing to get him in that direction . . . But none of us, Hindenburg nor the German people, knew at that time how, if these people were put in responsibility, how they should work. In any democratic state we should try to have them put in to show what they could do, and if after a certain time of experience they proved to be good enough and trustful – I mean it is easy enough today to know, to come to a conclusion, but at that time there was no way to tell. It was a mass movement which had a great part of the German youth and it might even become strong enough to sweep through the leftist or Communist parties at one time. You never could tell what it would grasp in together [sic]. It would be in my mind, it would have been a good thing to try it.

Document 21 'this problem of responsibility'

Extract from the interrogation of Franz von Papen taken at Nuremberg on
12 October 1945 by Mr Thomas J. Dodd (no interpreter present)
(pp. 12–17 of transcript)

Q. How widespread would you say the knowledge was in Germany, from 1934 on, about what was going on in the concentration camps?
A. Oh, I don't think anybody hasn't had an idea what was going on. We knew of the concentration camps, but we always believed that the people were treated honestly there, kept in prisonship, yes, but well treated.
Q. How do you account for this disgraceful, to put it mildly, the disgraceful affairs that went on in there? How do you account for that?
A. I have very often tried to explain it to myself how this could come about.
Q. You know, there isn't any doubt about it. Those aren't fabricated stories. I think in the beginning it was so shocking that even some of us doubted the truthfulness of it, in the beginning.
A. In the beginning.
Q. Well, when these discoveries were first made –
A. Yes.

Q. I think even some of us found it hard to believe that any such thing could be going on.

A. So you must trust that we had been out of belief to think it possible. I mean, everybody who knows something of the German people, knows that the average German person is a mild and decent man. I mean, I couldn't imagine that such gangs ever should be created.

Q. That is why I asked. I have often wondered what the explanation was for it?

A. The only explanation I have, and I wrote it down in my recollections – perhaps you have read it – is the idea of totalitarianism on both sides, say, destroying whole cities with hundreds and thousands of women and children one day, got up the feeling on the other side that the war should be conducted unreservedly, and every crime committed to extinguish lives, whenever it was necessary, or when it was thought useful. That is the only explanation I have about that. I don't find another one.

Q. Well, you can see that it isn't complete, because many of these things went on before the war period.

A. You think so?

Q. Oh, I think so. I think some of them did. I think it got worse as it went along.

A. I never heard of that.

Q. Well, I think that is pretty well established. I don't say to the same extent. I think it did get worse, but I think that some of the beginnings of it were there; but it is pretty clear that some of it went on even before the war had started. Of course, it is hard for us to understand the whole principle of a concentration camp. We don't have any political prisons, you know.

A. I know.

Q. And therefore, we find it hard to understand at all the principle of locking men up just because you disagree with them politically. You know that.

A. Yes, certainly, we didn't know that in Germany. I mean, as far as we had established right in Germany, then after being arrested for some charge, twenty-five hours later, you must be before the judge, and it should be said to you what you are charged with, and you couldn't be held back a second day. Now, we didn't know that [the camps]. I mean, that is an invention of dictatorship.

Q. Well, of course, in the so-called 'Emergency Law' of July of 1934,[12] I think it was the beginning of the power – do you recall, after the Reichstag fire, Hitler asked for and received power to suspend civil rights?

A. Suspend the constitution and parliamentary rights.

Q. And most of these things that were done thereafter were done in the name of that statute, of that emergency power?

A. Certainly, that was the legal act with which we then created a new right, but I have never known that, I mean, we knew about concentration camps, and political prisoners were kept there, and that even before the war some were killed there, but these treatments, these butcheries, we had no idea that was going on in the camps.

Q. It is probably one of the most shocking things in the whole history of civilization, I expect. I don't mean to shock you, but I assume you know that one of the colonels who is here was in Dachau the day it was taken, and to hear his eye-witness accounts – and he is an honest man – on what he saw, there, was incredible.

A. I believe all of that. The question is how it could be possible, and I think that at the end of the war – for instance, I have seen these things, that there was no food in the concentration camps, I think that was certainly in some cases due to the complete destruction of railway and other facilities, that real food couldn't be produced. That may be an excuse for that, but not for the cruelties and outrages of the other kinds; but the only explanation I have is this: that mental disease of humanity, that everything is allowed in war. I mean, it is difficult to understand that ourselves. For instance, let's take the case of the bombardment of Dresden. We say that the Allies must have known that there were hundreds, and hundreds of thousands of people thrown there, in Dresden. It was the only town that was not bombarded. Then it was bombarded in the morning, the complete town. The buildings were destroyed, and the people flew to the public gardens, the wives and the children; and in the afternoon the public gardens were bombed, so I understand, where 300 to 350,000 people were killed [in] one day.[13] We didn't understand that, too. It wasn't necessary to win the war. So I mean, I don't blame anyone. Just to make up my mind how other people came to the conclusion that it might be right to kill people in the concentration camps, I have no other explanation for that.

Q. Well, I think you will agree though, that there is quite a difference between that and even an outrageous bombing incident.

A. Sure, I do. One is warfare, and the other is murder.

Q. Yes, I think there is a great distinction.

A. Yes, but psychologically, it might have –

Q. Yes, some connection, but very slight, I think you will agree, a very slight connection.

You have told me that, in your opinion, Hitler was one of the greatest crooks in history.

A. After all that turned out, yes.

Q. I mean, your present opinion?

A. Yes.

Q. I wonder what you think, or if you care to express the thought. Don't you feel that there are men now living, whoever they are, who were responsible to some extent for not only the war, but the events which led up to it, and some of the things that took place during it? Do you understand what I mean? Do you think there are such men?

A. I am one of them, certainly, in the big sense of your question. I mean, I had a part in his rising to power. I had a part in creating his government, and certainly I have a responsibility about all the historical developments thereafter.

Q. Well, I understand what you said about that, but do you feel that you are responsible to an extent that justifies your being declared to be responsible? What would you say to that? I don't want to mislead you in any respect. I am not trying to frame a cautious question.

A. I know, but it should be to history to decide, to weigh the motives and the acts. Certainly, in human life, there is a saying, 'Nothing succeeds like success', and in that way I certainly had a great failure. I think, in the judgment of God, the motives have a better place and the ideas one had, and He doesn't judge so much of the success or of the effect of it, but the ideas or the motives.

Q. Well, as between men, knowing the history of your own career better than anyone else, and knowing the part, whatever it was, that you may have played, and knowing the results of all the play, what is your judgment on yourself?

A. I don't think, Mr Dodd, that from the human point of view, you could say, or could the German people say that I am guilty of all this disaster.

Q. I don't say guilty of all of it, but I mean, guilty of some of it, or a part of it.

A. If you say responsible for it, I must say responsible for all of it, because when I stepped in with the Hitler government, then I had the responsibility. When I stepped out later on, the second, third acts in my life, being in Vienna and Turkey, it was only done, as I explained to you, in the will to do some good, and to get Germany out of this mess, to help her; and I am quite sure that in the opinion of most of the Germans, this is recognized.

Q. Well, as I see it, from having talked with you, and having given some thought to it, I should suppose that the question of your responsibility would first center in whatever you feel you had to do with the helping of Hitler and his people to power, if that is the right terminology; is that a fair statement?

A. The helping of the people to get in power.

Q. The helping of the Hitler people.

A. I mean, not the Hitler people. It has never been my design to have National Socialism reign in Germany. I wanted to have a normal life for Germany. You know my ideas about Germany, and what I hoped and strived for in my life for Germany. That couldn't conform to having National Socialism being a decisive power in Germany, never. You know, I am a conservative man.

Q. Well, not in its full flower, as we rather knew it, but in its development, it was acceptable; was it not?

A. Yes, at this point. I mean, I saw good points of the National Socialist program, the social points, the getting away from class hatred. One of the serious things in Germany was the growing of class hatred, as it was then, and getting away from that was a great relief to us all, and it resulted in a great progress; so we were certain that we could fight Bolshevism. That has ever been his idea, his words. He fascinated the people with those words. Now, that was worthwhile to do, and I think it was legitimate, and I was entitled to do it at that moment . . .

[p. 19 of the interrogation transcript]

Q. Well, to this extent do you feel any responsibility, that being a prominent figure in Germany, you didn't take any active or positive stand against it? Do you feel any responsibility for not stepping forth and declaring that you, as an individual, would not have anything to do with the government that was, in your judgment, guilty of murder on 30 June; guilty of arson in February, in the burning of the Reichstag; and guilty of dishonesty in its purposes, through the enactment of these infamous laws? Do you feel any responsibility for not standing up and making known your position as a prominent statesman of Germany? Do you feel any moral responsibility?

A. Well, I ceased to be what you call a 'prominent statesman' in Germany when I left the Hitler government.

Q. Well, by 'prominent statesman' I mean only this: I think the name of Franz von Papen meant something in Germany. You were a man that a great number of people must have considered an able patriot and a leading figure in the country. You were for a number of years. And it has always seemed to me that a man who occupies that position, I don't care whether it's in Germany or the United States, has some great responsibility to stand up and make a stand when one's government embarks upon a course of murder, arson and dishonesty; do you understand what I mean?

A. Yes, certainly I felt that, Mr Dodd, and I think I acted upon this responsibility when I told Hitler, that not a minute longer could I be a member of his government; and I urged him to make it public to the German people. He wanted me to assist in the Reichstag session, and I said: 'Under no means would I keep that seat again, because the German people would perhaps believe that I am still a member of your government.' He refused it to be published, but I think many people knew, or it was told around, and I left. In what way could I act again, say, against the Nürnberg Law,[14] or against the cessation of rights, and so on?

Q. I don't know, but it would seem to me there must have been some way that you could have made your influence felt. It might have called for great sacrifice on your part that perhaps you were not prepared to make.

A. I could act in two ways. In one way I acted to impress upon Hitler, whenever I had the opportunity to talk to him, that his way was wrong; that all these persecutions of Jews and churches and all this, would inevitably lead to destruction of all trust in Germany outside [in] the world.

Q. I know.

A. I said that very often. I very often have impressed that upon him.

Q. There was a second –

A. Yes, there was a second course. I could emigrate and publish a book.

Q. Well, I am just rather suggesting these things. It seems to me that when any institution, whether it be an institution of government, or any other kind of institution, embarks upon an evil course, a man has a moral responsibility to completely disassociate himself from it, at least that, and a greater responsibility not to assist it in any way, manner or fashion to carry out any part of its program. Now, therefore, I suggest that since you had reasons for not taking a stand against it, or for not disassociating yourself from it, or from not disavowing it, you still had the recourse of not serving it.

A. Yes.

Q. And so I understand the record, I think you did serve, at least in Austria and Turkey. I say that, I hope, not offensively, but I mean informatively.

A. I don't think so. I mean, as I told you this morning of the part of my activities in Austria, always when the Jewish question was put there, I made the strongest resistance, and the church question, too; and whenever something was suggested to me that was against my conscience, I acted in conformity with that.

Q. As an individual, I am sure you did. I make no suggestions that you did not. I have never suggested that you personally engaged in any of these persecutions. I am not suggesting that.

A. I mean, but even if an order was given to me, say, for instance, in Turkey, to get the German scientists who were Jews, and so on, I said, 'No, I won't'; or suppress the Catholic schools, I said 'No, I won't.' I have always acted against that, I mean, in my domain, in my resort.

Q. I don't know just how to phrase it, but I have the inherent feeling that a man in your position and with your sources of information and with your practical background and experience, would have been so shocked at the kind of government that was operating in Germany that you couldn't just have had anything to do with it. Let me put it this way: I feel confident that if in my own country, any administration with which I was officially and intimately connected, premeditatedly, murdered a dozen or a half a dozen prominent well-known men in Washington; burned the Congress or the building that houses

Congress; and a few weeks later distorted and concealed and lied to the people; and then asked me to go to Argentina on a mission; that no matter what the consequences, I'd say, 'No.' I am sure I wouldn't be in a position to be invited by August, because I would have already taken my stand, with whomsoever would stand with me against such administration of our country's affairs.

A. All right. In the first place, you can't compare the situation that rose in Germany with the United States. It is impossible to compare those.

Q. I know, it isn't exactly the same. But evil things do not differ too much the world over.

A. Now, let me say this; if you have been offered the position of an ambassador to Argentina, you would say, 'No.' You took your stand. That is to say, nothing could be published in the United States papers about it, and you remained at home. Now, what was done by you, I mean, if you have been responsible in the origin of such a government? Then you disassociated yourself completely, and sat in your home waiting to find out what was going on; or perhaps going to another country.

Q. Or organizing an underground, if I had to, opposition to the administration.

A. Now, if you were to organize an underground opposition –

Q. However I could form it, underground, overground, or on the ground.

A. I mean, all that, under the conditions in Germany, was impossible, so to speak. Opposition – there was certainly a great opposition against Hitler.

Q. Let me go a step further with my analogy. If I went to Argentina, and if I was instructed beforehand by the then head of government, that I should do all in my power while there to bring about a 'better relationship', to use your own expression,[15] between the two countries, with an ultimate view towards annexation of Argentina, I would say, 'How can I do that in the face of what I know to [of] your record? How can I lend you a helping hand to do even the smallest job, because you illustrated to me that you are a man of evil intentions, and I would rather suffer than do your handiwork.'

A. Yes, and you stayed at home and did nothing.

Q. Stayed at home, or stayed in jail, or was executed, or any number of things.

A. Yes, that you certainly – I mean, it would have been honorable if I stepped out and founded an underground movement against Hitler, and was caught by the Gestapo and executed. You are right, that is the viewpoint. I could have done that.

Q. But I only mention this not to say that I would do this or that, and it is certainly not a good choice to put one's self in a position of courage and another in a position of lack of it. I am not suggesting that, but in order to point out the difficulty that I am having in my own mind, I merely cite that as an example of what would seem to me to be an analogy.

A. An analogy. If ever there was a situation in the United States similar to that that has been in Germany after the first war, after the revolution, after the starving of the country, after the twelve or thirteen millions of unemployed or half-employed people, and the striving of many people, many honest people, to better this, and you couldn't come to a result, because the surrounding powers wouldn't let you; you said, 'Well let's go,' and then you came in power yourself and tried to get your country out, and you had no result, and the only way out was to take the then strongest power with a fairly good program, I should say, in power, to have these people reunited, having got away this class hatred, having exteriorly [*sic*] and territorially united and prosperous again, I am sure you would have gone the same way, I am sure.

Q. Well, let me make this interruption: Certainly you are not suggesting here that Hitler had abolished class hatred; in effect, he had raised up religious hatred.

A. To a great extent, naturally.

Q. Well, he had substituted something worse for it.

A. No question about it, but I mean in the beginning of his career, I am certain he did, because many people felt that was a man of theirs. The working class had no confidence in ours, and they must have a man of theirs, who felt how they felt, and who understood their ideas, and who understood what was poverty, and what was suffering, and how it was good to restore people, and to get them to work again. There was a lot of good feeling about it, and I told you about my own experience, after these two stages, when I was Chancellor myself, and when I was being Vice-Chancellor.

Q. Yes, I know you did, and all of this part of my conversation and my thinking has to do with this problem of responsibility.

A. Yes, certainly, you are right. I could have chosen that way, to say 'No, stop,' and instead of staying at home, make myself a martyr.

Q. Or done something effective.

A. That would mean the same, I mean there was no other way. If I acted then, I was shot. That was clear.

Q. Then, of course, the next category that comes to my mind, is that beginning with 1938, probably with March, 1938, from that time on, the Sudeten situation, and the swallowing up of all of Czechoslovakia; the repudiation of the commitment of Munich, up to 1 September 1939, and in that year, or a little more than a year, the history is a history of aggression, and the repudiation of promises and commitments. It seems to me that you must feel that at least during these years, added to what had gone before, your continuous service gives you some responsibility . . .

A. Up to that point, I think if the European powers believed they could do good negotiating with Hitler, and having a treaty between England and Germany, it was done at Munich. Up to that point, I think, I was entitled, as a German patriot, to believe myself the same, that that would be possible, and you agreed with me when you said that he changed completely his tactics and his policy after Munich. It would have been a great achievement. Now then, for the first time, Hitler held a world that was internationally given, in the agreement with England. That was certainly the worst he could do, because that destroyed the rest of the confidence of the outer world in Germany. Now, it was not necessary to denounce him publicly, and say that a German statesman in my position should stand up and say – the world knew that all had been in vain, and that a word that he publicly and honestly had given was broken. The world knew. The question was now only, could we save Germany from a war or could we not? Would he go to the worst?

Q. So you would say that that was your reason for continuing after up until September 1939?

A. Yes.

Q. And I just suggest to you, not to reiterate too much, but to make clear what is in my mind, that added to the incidents of murder, dishonesty, oppression and persecution at home, we now have the fact of dishonesty abroad in dealings with other nations; don't you think that is a fair statement, after the breach of the commitments made at Munich?

A. Yes.

Q. And you say that you were aware of that, of course, as everyone was, you were aware of this new instance of bad faith, which is a mild term, but that you continued in the hope that you could do something to prevent what appeared to be the inevitability of war.

A. Yes.

Q. Well then, we come to September of 1939, and we have the final factor of war, the concluding factor of war, after all of these other demonstrations of evil, and so I ask you then, understanding perhaps, or accepting for purposes of this discussion, all of your explanations for the other periods, how could you then again serve this regime as an ambassador to an important country [Turkey], important in its geographical location, and knowing the case, how could you serve such a regime as an ambassador to Turkey in the war years?[16]

A. The situation was in my mind, simple: either I had to resign my post and go home –

Q. Yes?

A. And go to the army where I was destined to lead a regiment, or a battalion, and go to war; or I had to stay in my post, one of these two possibilities.

Q. Well, certainly, you didn't believe in the war, did you, as a matter of moral judgment?

A. I didn't believe in what?

Q. In the war.

A. I was disgusted with the war, certainly.

Q. In the war that Hitler started with this invasion of Poland, you didn't believe in that as a righteous cause for Germany's sake?

A. I certainly did not.

Q. Well, how can you explain your conduct in serving such a regime as that, serving as an ambassador to an important country, and an important country because of its location and because of other facts?

A. Yes, the same consequences of my mind, as I explained to you before, was the idea, 'What can I do? Can I serve my country better in going as a battalion commander to the Polish Front or Italian Front[17] or could I better serve my country in staying at this point here?' which you say was an important point; and I was of the opinion, that way there, I did serve firstly, my country, because it kept one prominent state out of war, and it gave me the opportunity to restore peace, if possible, to have a finger in the business, a very small one, but one possibility, to have peace again; and in the third way, I think my activities in that country served the interests of yours, because I always had in mind, that after starting this criminal war, we should do everything to save the rest of this poor old continent; and when we come to explain my activities in Turkey, I will tell you in more detail, especially of my ideas there, what they were; so I think, if I may say, this, my son, who has been in Argentina, when war broke out, as a business man; who didn't need to come back, and certainly in a country with all the papers available he knew what was going on; he was judging the German government as well as I was judging it, if he took the pains to come back at the risk of his life, to fight for his country, because he thought, 'Right or wrong, it is my country, and I have a post in the army. I must go to fill it,' and as millions of other Germans said, what would be the use of an ambassador, accredited, appointed to an important post, what would be the use of his saying, 'No.' In this post, I served the aims of the Hitler government, but if I had better go to the battalion, I am fighting there, and I don't serve the aims of the Hitler government. I don't see the logic of it.

Q. I discern a distinction between the responsibility of a man of military age taking up arms when his country is at war, and the responsibility of a man of your background and your then age, in taking up a new mission in the interests of a particular government.

A. I had taken that mission prior to the war, in the hope to avoid war, Mr Dodd.

Q. Yes, I know you had taken it prior to the war, but not long prior to the war.

A. No.

Q. Only a few months.

A. That I could do something to maintain peace, I mean, in that time, otherwise I certainly wouldn't have accepted. If I had heard in March, when Ribbentrop asked me to go down there, if I knew I couldn't do anything good to prevent war, I certainly wouldn't have gone. I, three times, rejected his idea to go there.

Q. You see, it would be much simpler, and I am sure for many others, if Herr von Papen said, 'Well, I did contribute to some extent to the rise of the Hitler people to power, because I felt they represented something worthwhile for Germany, and I continued to support the government, to some extent, both by way of my mission to Austria, and later on by way of mission to Turkey, because I continued to have some faith in the fundamental decency of the government.' Then I might disagree with Franz von Papen about his judgment as to the fundamental decency of such a government, but I would have to allow for a difference of judgement; but as the record now stands, I understand Franz von Papen to have said that soon after the Hitler people came to power, he became disgusted with them; he knew they committed murder; he knew that they committed arson; and he knew that they persecuted people, that they violated his Concordat with the Holy See;[18] and [that] they persecuted the Jews, and that they victimized the Catholics; that they were rash and violent in their treatment of Austria; that they repudiated their agreement to the world with respect to Czechoslovakia, and they pulled Germany, and ultimately the world, into a terrible conflict in which he had no faith and no belief. Thus, I say, that it is very difficult for us to understand, in view of that position, how you could continue to cooperate even to the slightest extent with such an administration of the affairs of your country.

A. Would you have a better judgment of me if I did not continue after the declaration of war, and went into the field as a battalion commander?

Q. Well, I don't know. That is a very hard question for me to answer, but what I was trying to point out in my rather lengthy question or statement – it was more in the form of a rhetorical question – was the difficulty that your own position presents, in order for me to accept your explanation, since you didn't believe in the administration and since you didn't believe in its works and in its conduct.

A. But I mean, I think it is proven by lots of facts in Austria and in Turkey, that I certainly was not a National Socialist, and I didn't try to perform their ideas.

Q. Well, you certainly furthered their cause.

A. Indirectly, yes, by serving them, but undoubtedly, and on many occasions, and you began with the Marburg speech[19] this morning –

Q. Yes?

A. And my dismissal, and seeing the murder of my people later on, and getting my papers to Switzerland, and the murder of Kettler[20] –

Q. All of these.

A. All this. I mean, if I was a man who intended to serve the cause of

Hitler, and Hitlerism, and National Socialism, I could have a life much easier.

Q. Well, will you understand this statement when I say that I think you are going to find that the world and history will have great trouble in accepting your explanation. I say that to you quite frankly. I may be mistaken.

A. Maybe, but up to now, history, public opinion knows me by propaganda. I have been made responsible for everything that happened.

Q. Well, not everything.

A. Well almost. I have been in all capitals of Europe. There was a treaty made here. I was there. I made a treaty with Russia, and –

Q. I never heard that.

A. Yes, certainly, I made a treaty with the Russian ambassador, on the Bosporus.

Q. Yes, I understood you had some conversations with the Russian ambassador.

A. But there are many people who have known me and my work, if I may say so, be it in Austria and be it in Turkey, and many people, independent and objective people, who say – the Netherlands minister in Ankara, or the Swiss minister, or the Portuguese minister, many of the people, who have – ask the Turks, for instance. Ask the man who knows exactly about me, what I have done in those five years in Turkey. Ask the man who is an ambassador in Paris now, Newmann, who conducted the foreign policy of his country as the General Secretary. He was one of the greatest brains of that country. He knew exactly what I thought of my government, and everything. Ask him about it. Ask him about his opinion about me.

Q. Well, I do not suggest that there are not those who are your friends and who understand, but I am simply suggesting that you have given me your explanation –

A. For instance, a man –

Q. And your reasoning about the thing.

A. For instance, there is a man, he is here now, Herr Horthy.[21] I have known him intimately whenever I have been in Austria, and we have often talked about the Anschluss and Hungary all the time. Now, you may believe he is a bitter enemy of Hitler, who wanted to kill him, himself.

Q. I should think he would be.

A. Ask him what he thinks of me, of my activities there. He will give you an objective answer. He is an old man and he is –

Q. Well, I shall be interested in talking to him. I will talk to him.

A. Yes, I see my position, I see my situation. It is very serious, and even before an international court, where in fact these events that took place in the last years, last two years, all of these outrages and terrible things, it is awfully difficult for me, but –

Q. I had had the hope and the idea that from one like yourself, understanding your background, and the distinguished positions you occupied, your cultural background – and I don't say that fulsomely or flatteringly, I say that as a matter of fact – that now that we are at this point, you could be among the most helpful in telling us just how this thing developed, and what its real purposes were, and how it really operated. I am not suggesting that you have concealed it. I am suggesting that it is unfortunate that we can't get that help from a man like you, because I think it would be of great assistance, not only to Germany but to the rest of the world.

Albert Speer: True Confessions?

He [Speer] says that his predecessors failed to achieve full industrial mobilization for war, the extent reached being much less than that achieved in 1914–18. Economic mobilization had been almost entirely in the hands of Wehrmacht officers who lacked industrial experience. Two thirds of these were regular army officers. Gen. Thomas had a staff of over 1,000 in the OKW and there was a staff of 2000–3000 in the Army Ordnance Directorate (HWA) in the OKH (High Command of the Army). Speer says these staffs were far too large, inexperienced and inefficient. People fought for priorities . . . Development was haphazard, research uncontrolled, and lack of coordination between the competing requirements resulted in hopeless confusion.

M.I. 14 report on German war production, based on interrogations of Albert Speer, 25–28 June 1945[1]

[Albert Speer was interrogated more times than any other of the major war criminals. This close attention reflected not only the Allies' interest in his areas of competence as Armaments Minister from 1942 to 1945, but the fact that he gave full, thoughtful and helpful replies to most of the technical inquiries he was invited to consider. He was almost certainly the most articulate and intelligent of all the defendants, bar the former Economics Minister, Hjalmar Schacht. Moreover Speer made it clear that he disagreed fundamentally with Hitler's decision to pursue a scorched-earth policy in 1945, and hinted not only at his 'treasonable' efforts to obstruct demolitions and destruction, but his brief flirtation with the idea of assassinating Hitler. The first three documents that follow show Speer as the expert, the assassin and the traitor. At Nuremberg he became less co-operative, if only because he now recognized that he had to defend himself against accusations that he had not expected. He accepted a general responsibility for serving an evil regime, but would not admit specific crimes. The final two interrogations show Speer first in his efforts to get the Americans to recognize the great value of what he had freely contributed in terms of technical advice and information, and second his refusal, in the face of a limp Soviet interrogation, to accept his responsibility for anything not immediately connected with his technical functions as Armaments Minister. Throughout, Speer, though willing to accept a general responsibility, seldom confronted the moral implications of the individual acts in which he was directly involved – a psychological tactic that he openly displayed when he was interrogated more gently later in life by the journalist Gitta Sereny.[2] On one occasion he was asked about the transfer of gun production to the Mauthausen concentration camp by the Austrian Steyr company. 'This situation was not agreeable to me,' he retorted, not from any pangs of conscience, but because 'I did not have control about how many guns were produced and whether all the guns were dedicated to the right purpose'.[3] Speer's capacity for stripping issues down to their technical core permitted him to avoid confronting the more thorny issues of the rights and wrongs of producing weapons with camp labour. By this stage of the war the imperatives of rationalization had long extinguished what moral imperatives the technocrats might once have possessed.]

Document 22 Speer the Expert

SHAEF report, interrogation of Albert Speer, 5th Session, 30 May 1945

1. Due to the activities of the Four Year Plan, Germany had by 1936 reached a state of economic mobilization which was exceptional for a country not yet at war. In Speer's view, however, the extent of this mobilization was insufficient, and after September 1939 for quite some time the tempo of mobilization was not accelerated. The government aimed at a very gradual transition towards a full war economy. No drastic measures were taken, with a few exceptions such as the stoppage of peacetime building activities. It was the policy of the Reichswirtschaftsministerium [Economics Ministry] not to cut civilian standards below a certain level, which in Speer's view had been fixed much too high.[4] Measures which he considered necessary at that stage, such as the tapping of female labor resources, were not attempted.[5] Speer considers the record of German war production during the first two years of war as 'tragically' inadequate. He blames this on the inefficient and irresponsible way in which the Four Year Plan mobilization plans were made. However, he still preferred this agency to another plan which the OKW had wanted to enforce at the outbreak of war, which would have placed the entire economy under military direction. Speer's personal opposition to this plan derived from the fact that building, his special field, was to have been placed under an inexpert colonel. Speer cites General Thomas, and Staatssekretaere Landfried[6] and Koerner[7] as the best sources on the history of German economic mobilization in the early phase of the war.

2. The expansion of industrial capacity for armaments purposes was effected before the war to a considerable extent by the construction of state-financed shadow factories owned by OKW, which as a rule were attached to existing private firms. These were to take over their

operation on the outbreak of war. This was adopted especially in ammunition manufacture . . .

5. Speer does not know of any national income statistics kept during the war; if they were prepared it would have been by Wagenfuehr.[8] Speer suggested that the Planungsamt [Planning Office] iron allocation tables, which he had described earlier, would furnish the division of total production between the armaments sector and other production. These tables, when he took over [February 1942], showed 40 percent of the steel going into 'immediate armaments' and 60 percent into 'indirect armaments' including a very small civilian consumption. At the end of his tenure of office, the ratio had been reversed. Speer admitted, however, that this breakdown understated the share of consumers' goods, and entirely left out agriculture.[9]

6. There was no policy of neglecting capital equipment in industry and basic services through excessive concentration on armaments end products, and a policy of allocations which enabled long-term maintenance of capital resources was pursued until December 1944 when the decline of steel production enforced a reversal of this policy. In the conversion of textiles and other non-essential industries to war production there had been no large-scale scrapping of machinery. The usual rule was to store the machinery, but to some extent deterioration ensued from lack of storage space which necessitated storing in the open air.

7. In the latter phases of the war, labor shortage prevented the working of multiple shifts on an optimal scale. Excessive working hours were frequently kept, e.g. in the Jaegerprogramm [Fighter Programme], where seventy-two hours a week was the rule after March 1944. The strain was particularly great on the depleted force of skilled labor, which had continuously not only to do its own work, but also to train new recruits who were replacing called-up workers.[10] The only exception where this difficulty was not encountered was the few plants organized along modern mass-production lines and equipped entirely with specialized machine tools which could be operated by unskilled workers, e.g. BMW at Allach.[11] Direktor Werner[12] had attempted to expand the use of such methods since late 1943.

There was no deliberate policy of creating capacity reserves in the aircraft industry by single-shift operation of plants. In effect, however, most plants in the aircraft and aero-engine industry were working below capacity. Speer attributes this largely to the Luftwaffe's policy of continuous modifications of equipment in production, which militated against efficient serial production. As a flagrant example of waste of capacity Speer cited Flugmotorenwerke Ostmark [Austrian Aero-engine Works], the buildings of which he had rushed to completion in six months in 1942 (after he had been told that the British had built a big aero-engine plant in the same period) but which did not produce a single engine until mid-1944. The first cause of delay was difficulties in getting machine tools, which Speer attributes to the generally inefficient machine-tool allocation system of the Luftwaffe. Further delays ensued because the Luftwaffe could not make up its mind what type of engine to produce at Ostmark. Originally the plant had been intended for Junkers, then it was assigned to Daimler-Benz, and finally turned over to Steyr.[13]

8. There was virtually no planned relocation of industry *before* air attacks, chiefly because Allied intentions were unpredictable and decisions as to what to relocate were difficult and risky. Speer confirmed that in the early war period an initial dispersal of certain products (e.g. fuel injection pumps) was followed by concentration in fewer plants. He explained, however, that the initial dispersal had been due to the unsystematic placing of war contracts, which enabled the firms to follow their desire of taking on the greatest possible variety of manufactures as a re-insurance to obtain steady production, and to the detriment of efficiency. The subsequent concentration – in 1942 – had been due to Speer's rationalization policy and efforts to limit production in each plant to as few items as possible. Considerations of air-raid precautions did not enter into either process . . .

9. Asked to what extent German military strategy, at various stages, had been influenced by economic considerations, Speer replied that in the case of the attack on Russia the need for oil certainly was a prime motive. Soon after the outbreak of the Eastern war Goering had called Speer and Krauch[14] to a meeting to discuss the conversion of German hydrogenation plants from coal to crude oil feedstocks,[15] and to calculate the advantages which were to be gained from this. In the case of the Balkans campaign, the ferro-alloy resources were apparently not a major factor, but their desirability was appreciated. The formulation of such economic considerations was the responsibility of the Wehrwirtschaftsamt [Defence Economy Office], OKW. According to

Speer, the broad economic factors involved were generally known and discussed, but no detailed analyses were called for or prepared for high-level planning. Economic warfare specialists were not prominent on the military staffs, and no civilian experts were employed or consulted. To remedy this defect, Speer in 1942 created an informal Beirat für Wirtschaftskriegführung [Advisory Council for Economic Warfare], for which he selected industrialists like Voegler, Krauch and Roechling[16] and some power experts. The discussions soon showed that at that time already the Luftwaffe stood no chance in attacks on economic objectives in England, and the council's work concentrated on a scheme, apparently thought up by Speer himself, for an attack on the power plants in Russia to be conducted by Mistel composite aircraft developed by Bambach,[17] known as 'Operation Eisenhammer'. This was a 'private scheme' of Speer's which was not taken seriously by Hitler, the Luftwaffe and the OKH. He considers the subsequent employment of the Korps Meister, a unit which he apparently had coveted for this purpose, on tactical operations against Russian railroad junctions as a typical example of the Luftwaffe Generalstab's [General Staff's] lack of appreciation of economic warfare.

In the German air attack on Britain no economic strategy had been followed. It was purely designed as an attack on civilian morale and for publicity effect in Germany.[18] In Speer's view, the attack should have been directed either against ports or against coal mining, and preferably against the latter, in order to paralyze transport and power. When asked whether he changed his mind on this after observing the small effects of Allied bombing on Ruhr coal output, Speer retorted that he had never been aware of the Ruhr attack having been aimed at coal output, but was unable to formulate his views on the proper method for a more specific attack on coal mining.

10. Economic considerations were very influential in forming German strategy in its defensive phase. Hitler personally attached great importance to defending the economic resources gained in the East, especially Nikopol. On this issue, however, Speer backed the army General Staff, which wanted to abandon Nikopol as at the time Germany had 2½ years' stocks of manganese, and Speer estimated that it could get by with Romanian production alone. The winter offensive in Hungary in 1945 was again Hitler's idea, which was condemned by both Speer and the Generalstab. Speer did not consider that the

Hungarian oilfields were immediately threatened; he would have preferred an offensive to regain Upper Silesia.[19]

11. Speer was not directly concerned with countering Allied economic warfare measures directed against German trade with Neutrals,
as such operations were the responsibility of the Auswaertiges Amt
[Foreign Office], which was in complete control in this sphere. Speer
assumed that the German diplomats acted stupidly according to their
tradition . . .

Document 23 Sixty Acts of Treason

SHAEF report, interrogation of Albert Speer, 7th Session, 1 June 1945,

Part I, section 2

Last Days of the Third Reich

5. Asked to give an account of the political background of his role,
and economic developments during the final phases of the war, Speer
began with a description of Saur's[20] part in this connection, which
Speer considered important. Differences of opinion between the two
began to arise in summer 1943, when the series of attacks on Hamburg
had shaken Speer's confidence in Germany's ability to win the war.
Saur, on the other hand, remained optimistic, and persisted in this
attitude almost to the very end.

Speer, up to mid-1943, could consider himself a 'strong man'. He
had direct access to Hitler, reported to him verbally at frequent intervals and his views carried weight with the Fuehrer. When his reports
started getting pessimistic, Hitler's readiness to listen to Speer began
to fall off, and gradually Saur, always the optimist, became more and
more popular with Hitler, and was frequently summoned to report to
him directly. Speer stressed that Saur, unlike Dorsch, never used his
favored position for intriguing against Speer, and personal relations
between them remained good. Speer's personal interviews with the
Fuehrer became more infrequent, and Hitler would pay no attention
to Speer's warnings about Germany's difficulties. Speer finally decided

that these interviews were a waste of time, so he started reporting in writing, and soon found that his reports were read by Hitler and sometimes were acted upon. (Speer's principal reports dating from this period were in his personal files and have been secured.) Speer noted that the frank tone which he adopted in his correspondence could only be appreciated if one knew the moderation of language that was the custom in reporting difficulties to Hitler. When Speer, in a memorandum on the effects of the oil offensive, said that the consequences were 'tragic' he was saying in effect that the war was lost. Speer repeatedly thought of resigning his post. However, he refrained from doing so, because owing to his personal standing with Hitler, he had developed into an unofficial spokesman for all Ministers in charge of specialized fields, e.g. Food and Agriculture. They urged him not to leave, because he was the only one who had access to Hitler, and could go against Bormann. Speer had first wanted to resign in spring 1944 when during his illness Dorsch started an intrigue against him, attempting to set himself up as controller of building independent of Speer. On this occasion Speer sent Fraenk[21] to the Obersalzburg to warn Hitler of his intention to leave, but Goering and others persuaded him to change his mind. His position with Hitler, however, remained weak, and Hitler's conferences with Saur became more and more frequent. Speer was glad in a way to be out of these meetings, because Hitler would usually go into endless detail which taxed Speer's memory to the limit. He suggests that a search should be made for the minutes of the Hitler–Saur conferences.[22]

6. On 30 January 1945, after the loss of Silesia, Speer decided that Hitler must be told that the war was lost economically. He wrote a memorandum (said to be in our hands) setting out his arguments which he was going to submit to Hitler at a conference in Saur's presence. Speer had briefed Saur not to intervene until he had presented all his arguments. During the conference, however, Saur forgot all about the briefing and indulged in his customary rosy optimism, carrying Hitler with him, so that Speer did not get anywhere. A similar incident occurred later in February, after six Hauptauschussleiter [Main Committee Chairmen][23] had presented an ultimatum to Saur, trying to force him to go to Hitler and tell him that the game was up. Saur agreed to do so, but changed his mind again while talking to Hitler, and ended up by consoling Hitler with the prospect of a four-

engined jet bomber soon coming into service.[24] Actually, according to Speer, this bomber was not expected to mature for another two years. Speer thought it was very likely that (as Gauleiter Hofer[25] had said under interrogation) Saur deliberately exaggerated production figures when reporting to Hitler. Speer admitted that in the final phase of the war he had adopted the same policy, not only towards Hitler, but especially towards the Gauleiters. Speer instructed his regional commissioners, Rohland[26] in the West, Wolff in the East and Saur in the South, to spread the story that German armaments production was going well. His reason for doing so was the fact that the Gauleiters started getting 'hysterical' towards the end of March, and were about to carry out a drastic scorched earth policy. Speer's move was part of his campaign to frustrate this policy, and to get the Gauleiters to postpone demolitions. His idea was to build up their sagging morale through false tales of production successes. Speer then proceeded to a detailed account of his campaign.

Speer's Sabotage of the Scorched Earth Program

7. When he saw that defeat was inevitable, Speer decided that it was essential to save as much as possible of German industrial capacity, transport services and public utilities so that there would be possibilities of employment for the common people after defeat and to avoid conditions of chaos. Acting under orders from Hitler, passed on and strongly backed by Bormann, the Gauleiters in the threatened areas were getting ready to carry out widespread demolitions. In the Ruhr and elsewhere these were aimed primarily at the power plants. Speer claimed that on his instructions the Germans had carried out no scorched earth policy when retreating from France, Belgium and Holland, the Balkans and the Government-General [Poland]. He had the necessary authority to issue orders to this effect, and any scorching that may have been done was performed by the troops on their own initiative. His refusal to scorch the earth there was due to a desire to save the French, Belgians, etc., etc. from unemployment, and he did not see why the German workers should be deprived of the same favor. Yet, in the words of an article by Suendermann in the V.B. [*Völkischer Beobachter*] inspired by Bormann, Germany was to be 'turned into a

desert'. Speer first tried to counteract these intentions in September 1944, when he sent Bormann a draft decree to the effect that no destruction measures (*Zerstoerungen*), but only immobilization (*Laehmungen*) should be carried out in threatened Reich territory. '*Laehmung*' was usually effected by removing vital machinery parts and burying them. In order to get this proposal accepted Speer requested Bormann to ask Hitler whether the latter intended to reconquer the territory then lost (Saar, Aachen, Luxemburg), as it was vital to Speer to have it back for economic reasons. Hitler, as Speer had expected, promptly replied that, of course, he was planning a reconquest. As a second move, Speer got Hitler to agree with his view that in this case a scorched earth policy would only harm the Germans and not the Allies, and asked him to inform the Gauleiters accordingly, which Hitler did. Thus, Speer was covered for the time being, and he issued a supplementary decree to his regional representatives, informing them that he would punish those who carried out immobiliz-ation measures too early, but not those who carried them out too late, or not at all. He had a conference with Kesselring on the same subject, who also subscribed to Speer's view.

8. When the loss of the Rhineland and Upper Silesia caused growing unrest among the Gauleiters, who knew that their own lives were forfeit, and did not care what happened to the rest of Germany, Speer realized that he would have to renew his campaign. Out of their fear, Speer claimed, the Gauleiters pretended to be optimistic till the very last, 'clutching at any straw of hope'. Speer was afraid, however, that when war came close to their Gaue they would 'run amok' in scorching the earth. In particular, Speer had a row with Florian,[27] in the Ruhr, who argued that if Germany lost the war, both himself and the people were lost in any case, a 'terrible view to take' according to Speer. To meet these tendencies, which he knew were also strong in Hitler's surroundings, Speer wrote his memorandum of 15 March 1945 (said to be in our hands) in which he said that total collapse would take place within four to eight weeks. In such a case, Speer continued, he was in favor of concentrating on saving the factories, etc., on which the German people depended for its livelihood, and the personal fate of the leaders should be of no importance. He did not know Allied intentions. If they intended to destroy German industry, he wanted them to take the blame for destroying the existence of a 'brave and

decent people'. It was at this time that he formed the Verkehrsstab [Transport Staff], which was to concentrate on maintaining transport services. He also urged that measures should be taken to insure food supplies. He summarized his program in four points:

a) There should be no destruction, only temporary '*Laehmung*'. He drafted a decree by which the exclusive right to instruct Gauleiters on such measures should rest with him.
b) Bridges were to be destroyed only for operational reasons, i.e. chiefly in order to protect planned lines of resistance.
c) Stocks of food and consumers' goods, including Wehrmacht stocks, should be distributed to the population. (He did not know the Allies' intentions as regards such stocks.)
d) Food production was to be given priority over armaments production.

9. Speer presented these arguments in very blunt terms in a meeting with Hitler (Saur warned him that he would be arrested if he was not more careful). Hitler asked for time to think it over and promised a written reply by the evening. The reply was negative. Hitler argued that if Germany lost this war, its people would have no right to live (*keine Existenzberechtigung*); the 'eastern race' was too powerful and would destroy Germany in any case. Speer was much shaken by this reply, which provided the basis for the scorched earth decree (*Zerstoerungserlass*) of 19 March, signed by Hitler. The argument was that it was useless to hand anything over intact to the enemy, who would destroy it in any case. Everything of direct or indirect value to the enemy was to be destroyed, all bridges to be blown, etc. Speer said he kept this decree in order to expose the authors of this policy later. The decree was implemented in orders to the Wehrmacht from the Chef des Wehrmachtstransportwesens [Chief of the Armed Forces Transport], who ordered the creation of a 'transportation desert' (*Transportwueste*) in Germany and the Chef des Nachrichtenwesens [Chief of Communications] issued a similar decree for the destruction of all transformer stations, telephone exchanges and cables. All records which might assist in restoring such services were to be burnt. Speer hurried to Berlin in order to try to get this decree revoked, but had to leave for the Ruhr immediately because he heard that the Gauleiters were getting ready for blowing up power plants and flooding coal

mines. (This was the day of the airborne landings across the Rhine.) Speer found that the demolition parties were standing by and went to work without delay. He found 'many courageous men in industry' who were also determined to frustrate this plan. After a late conference with these industrialists, it was decided to prevent the demolitions by hiding all detonators and fuses in the coal mines by throwing them down the mine shafts. Speer obtained fifty machine-pistols with ammunition and had them distributed, via Rohland, to trustworthy workers in key installations, with orders to open fire even on Gauleiters personally if required. The next day Speer got to work on the Gauleiters, most of whom finally yielded to his arguments, and agreed that Hitler's decree 'could be interpreted in Speer's sense'. Florian alone was recalcitrant, and wanted to go as far as ordering the population of towns in his Gau, all heavily bombed, to set fire to the surviving houses. Florian read out this decree to Speer, who advised him to publish it without delay by the most prominent means (e.g. posters in the towns), which Speer considered the best way of sabotaging it, as the people would have revolted on seeing it. He also called up the Party Chancellery asking them to stop Florian . . .

11. On his return to Berlin, he was informed by Seebauer, who had just been talking to Saur, that a 'queer' situation had arisen in the capital. Himmler was to be made War Minister, and Saur his Plenipotentiary for Armaments. Speer rushed to the Reichskanzlei [Reich Chancellery] where he encountered a frigid atmosphere. On the 'Fuehrer's stock exchange' (*Fuehrerboerse*) he could always sense how his shares stood before even having seen Hitler. This day they were very low. Finally he was officially summoned to the Fuehrer (usually he was informally invited) and had a talk with him which was conducted in a decent manner, but in which Hitler informed Speer that he wanted him to go on sick leave. Speer refused to accept such a solution, and said that he would prefer a straight dismissal. Hitler argued with him that he had no use for a Minister who did not 'radiate faith' in a critical situation. It was obvious to Speer that the Gauleiters had reported to Hitler on his activities. After a lengthy argument Hitler finally explained that for reasons of foreign and domestic policy, he could not afford an outright dismissal at this moment. Speer took this for an opportunity to arrive at a face-saving compromise, saying that if the Fuehrer wanted him to accept the sick-leave solution for 'reasons

of state' he could not but accept. However, at this point he brought in the rumor he had heard from Seebauer, and, as his own suggestion, proposed the Himmler–Saur arrangement, and also suggested that deputies should be appointed for all the various jobs held by Speer. Hitler refused to consider this proposal, and started arguing again. He re-told Speer all his biography with its many difficulties and crises which he had successfully overcome. Worn out by this tirade, Speer finally shut up 'so as not to have to insult the Fuehrer' and the meeting was concluded after two hours without any result. It took place on 26, 27 or 28 March.

12. Speer then wrote a letter to Hitler, speaking in purely personal terms which, for this reason, he had intended to withhold from the Allies (who found it nevertheless). He urged Hitler once again not to 'destroy the existence of the people'. He repeated what he had told Hitler at their meeting – that he had neither hope nor faith in German victory, that it was time to realize that the war was lost, and that the German leaders personally had to face what a just Providence had in store for them. Twenty-four hours later Speer received a telephone call from Hitler and was invited to his presence. Once again Hitler pressed Speer to declare that he had faith, or at least hope, in a German victory, but Speer would only go as far as assuring Hitler that he backed him unconditionally. Hitler finally had to be content with this; they shook hands and after some more arguing Speer persuaded Hitler to repeal his Scorched Earth Decree. An order to this effect, which also reinstated Speer in full control of scorched earth decisions, was signed at 6 a.m. and Speer had it immediately distributed by couriers.

13. Speer proceeded to organize a special campaign to prevent bridge demolitions. After Remagen and the executions which followed it, the engineer troops had 'become nervous' and blew bridges on the slightest provocation. Speer made use of a sudden resurgence of optimism in Hitler and his generals which was due to a plan to attack the southern flank of the US forces which then had reached Erfurt and Weimar, to press them back as far as Suhl and possibly to effect a juncture between the Wenck and Model Army Groups. Hitler told Speer and Saur of the great hopes which he pinned upon this attack. Speer retorted that the area to be reconquered would be useless to him if the earlier demolition orders had been carried out, but Hitler assured him that there had been no time for this as the US advance had been

so rapid. Speer's comment on this was that it was better not to issue demolition orders in the first instance, rather than rely on their not being carried out. He finally got Hitler to sign an order on the bridge demolition question, to the effect that OKW was to have powers only to order the blowing-up of operationally important bridges, and engineer troops alone would be held responsible for the execution of such orders. All other bridges were to be destroyed only after consultation with the Gauleiters, in their capacity as Reich Defense Commissars, the Chairmen of Armaments Commissions, and the Reichsbahn [National Railway] authorities. Speer was confident that the bad state of communications would make such consultations impossible, which would save the bridges and absolve the troops of their responsibility. This was only one of his 'illoyal tricks'; others included six or eight orders which he forged on behalf of the Wehrmachtfuehrungsstab [Armed Forces Operational Staff] ordering the non-destruction of specific bridges. Speer said that he normally preferred more honest methods, but had no choice in this case. He would have considered it as the most satisfactory end of his activities if he had been called to account for them and sentenced. It was still a puzzle to him how he had escaped such a fate, as he counted up all the acts of high treason which he had committed from the end of January onwards, and he arrived at a total of over sixty.

Document 24 Speer the Assassin

FIAT report EP 254–82 (Stahl–Speer) based on two interrogations of
Dietrich Stahl, 10 November 1945

Confirmation of Speer's plot to kill Hitler with solid poison gas, and Himmler, Goebbels and Bormann by other means

20. After a brief discussion, during which Stahl gave more or less the same versions as Speer of the Hitler plot, but added Speer's further plans for the destruction of Nazi leaders, a report was written which is given below. Most statements not directly relevant to this plot

have been omitted and notes are added especially where Stahl gave additional facts during the verbal account. The first written statement contained some obscure points and after a second interrogation Stahl explained in writing the kind of ammunition issued by him to Speer and their purpose. This additional report is inserted in the appropriate places in the statement. The reasons for choosing solid poison gas he claims not to know. He, like Speer and many others, disclaims any knowledge of Kampstoffe and has been unable to throw any light on the reasons for Speer's choice of this method which, if applied wholesale by any underground organization, might prove unpleasant to the troops of occupation.

The headings are not by Stahl.

21. First discussion of plot to kill Hitler

'Approximately in the middle of February this year – I cannot recall the exact date – I was called to Speer's office during the forenoon because he wanted some information on the imminent issue of ammunition. I arrived at his office about noon when an air raid alarm sounded. Herr Speer took me with him into the ARP bunker and there I stayed alone with him for an hour or an hour and a half in one of the ARP cabins.'

22. (*Note*: The ARP bunker was in the Speer Ministry at the Pariser Platz in Berlin.)

23. Speer's motives

'After completing purely official business Speer described to me in detail his struggle against the insane measures for destruction (*Zerstorungsmassnahmen* or Scorched Earth Policy), against the defense of towns and villages which were worthless from a strategical viewpoint, against the Volkssturm, etc., and he expressed his great sorrow that nothing sensible or serious was done to terminate this lost war. I shared his views and sorrows and asked him if he could not convince Hitler of his viewpoint. Herr Speer told me that he was only seldom admitted into Hitler's presence and never alone, furthermore that Hitler always cut his talk short as soon as he (Speer) started it. For those reasons he had chosen the method of written communications because Hitler did read them. When he had pointed out at the end of his technical (*Note*: written) report that the war could not be continued, if for no other reasons than war production, Hitler, when he next saw him, replied: "You could have saved yourself your final sentence. I know that myself."'

24. Reasons for killing the triumvirate

'Furthermore, Herr Speer thought that Bormann, Himmler and Goebbels were the most radical and dangerous members of Hitler's entourage.'

25. (*Note*: In his first verbal account of the plots Stahl said that Speer did not mention his plans for killing these three men until *after* experts decided against the use of solid poison gas – See para. 39.)

26. Reasons for Speer's decision

'In the course of this fairly long discussion Herr Speer, who was emotionally very upset, said approximately the following (I am here giving the sense though not the exact words): "I simply cannot stand it any longer and be witness to a government by lunatics. The nation will perish completely if nothing decisive is done about these insane plans for destruction. I finally have come to the decision to end this state of affairs, if necessary by force. However, there is no use removing only one, the most dangerous and closest of his entourage must be removed."'

27. Poison gas for Hitler-bunker

'Speer explained to me the plan which he had evolved. He intended to throw into the ventilators of the ARP bunkers in the Reich Chancery some poison gas shells (or containers) and asked me how these poison gas containers worked and what their effect was.'

28. Solid poison gas (Taken from Stahl's second written report)

'Speer spoke of solid (*kompakte* or *feste*) poison gases (*Gasstoffe*), which in his opinion achieved the best results. I understood from Speer that he wanted to throw filled poison gas containers into the ARP ventilators of the Hitler-bunker on the assumption that these containers burst open during the descent and that the escaping gas would penetrate the bunkers with the fresh air.'

29. (*Note*: Stahl added orally that he had understood Speer to say that before throwing the poison gas containers into the air shafts of the bunker he would have had the bunker doors locked so that no escape was possible.)

30. Stahl's ignorance of C.W. [chemical weapons] (First Report)

'I was unable to give him any information because I never knew the existing poison gases nor their effect and the mode of application. Very much impressed by all that he had described to me I promised to obtain detailed information through my liaison officer in the Amtsgruppe Munition [Working Group for Munitions] of HWA (Army Ordnance) and to let him have the results immediately.'

31. Speer's reasons for revealing plot to Stahl (Second Report)

'Probably in order to gain a clearer picture of the possibilities and of the effectiveness of solid Kampfstoff he told me of his plan, in the hope that I should be able to give him details. However, I myself know absolutely nothing about the effectiveness and the functions of such poison gas shells and, therefore, I obtained information discreetly from the relevant military office (Amtsgruppe Munition) as I have described in detail before.'

32. Lieut.-Colonel Soika consults General Henrici

'I turned to Lieut.-Colonel, Diplom-Ingenieur Soika for information on the existing poison gases and poison gas shells (or containers), explaining to him that I knew nothing about them and that I really should be in the picture. He was unable to give me any definite information because he, too, lacked precise information. The entire Kampfstoff field was a strict secret. Soika made inquiries and a few days later he explained to me that solid poison gas was only split up into fine particles through the explosion of the shell (or container) and did not evaporate or form smoke like liquid Kampfstoff.'

33. (*Note*: In this paragraph Stahl gives an opinion based on a mis-understanding of a brief discussion with him of the rumors concerning the state of the Hitler-bunker when the Russians first arrived there. No mention had been made of remnants of poison gas or containers but Stahl was asked if he had any explanation for the charred condition of the bodies and the heavy debris found in the bunker according to early reports. At the time of the discussion he exclaimed rather excitedly 'I don't know if Speer got this stuff or not and whether he chucked it in.')

37. Speer's indignation was genuine

'I never doubted his intentions as I considered very genuine Speer's indignation at the senseless continuation of the war, the insane orders for destruction, etc., an indignation which was shared by every responsible German.'

38. Stahl offers proof that he obtained information on solid poison gas in February 1945 (Second Report)

'Whether the information I asked for and transmitted (to Speer), concerning the use and effect of poison gas shells, was factually and technically correct I am unable to judge because I know nothing about Kampfstoff shells (or containers). The fact that I obtained the information as described by me may be ascertained if this is considered important.'

39. Speer's plot to kill Himmler, Goebbels and Bormann in March 1945 (First Report)

'I believe it was in the second half of March, after Hitler's official order for destruction (*Zerstorungsbefehl*), when I was once more called to Herr Speer. The general situation had meanwhile become still more hopeless. He explained to me that he had now thought of a different plan. Himmler, Goebbels and Bormann, the three most dangerous and mischievous, gathered almost every evening in the Reich Chancery for the purpose of hatching their fiendish plans and imposing the most terrible death sentences, etc. During night air raids all three drove in their cars from the Reich Chancery to the suburbs of Berlin and such a moment was to be used for an ambush. He (Speer) said that he had found a few brave men experienced in the use of arms and that he himself would take on one of the three cars.'

40. Arms and ammunition for killing the Big Three

'Herr Speer ordered me to supply him with machine carbines, pistols (I believe it was a dozen) and the required ammunition. Furthermore, for blinding them (*zu Blendungszwecken*), he demanded Verey-light cartridges similar to those dropped from aircraft for marking a target.'

41. Type of light signals demanded by Speer (Second Report)

'The Verey-light cartridges (*Leuchtpatronen*) which I placed at his disposal were normal Verey-light and signal cartridges (*Leucht und Signalzeichen*), which are fired from Verey-light pistols to mark targets. Apparently Speer wanted to imitate the marker-flares of the enemy aircraft in order to simulate the dropping of bombs in the area and thus to force the cars to stop.'

42. (*Note*: Here Stahl changed his original verbal statement slightly. At first he had said that Speer planned to shoot down the three most dangerous Nazis, i.e. Himmler, Goebbels and Bormann, in front of the Reich Chancery as they hastened through the front entrance to drive off in their three cars to a nearby bunker. When asked to explain, at the next meeting, why he issued Verey-light cartridges for the purpose of blinding the three leading Nazis and whether he had not meant 'Rochling Patronen' as described by Speer, for use against tanks in order to blind their drivers, he explained that Speer had asked for Verey-light cartridges. Stahl could not state why such lights or flares should not have attracted the attention of the enemy bombers which by that time would have presumably reached Berlin, for Speer envisaged the shooting of the three leading Nazis during an air raid or at a time when an air raid was impending. Stahl was also asked if the purpose of these Verey-lights was to indicate to the enemy aircraft the exact position of the Reich Chancery. He then gave his new version, i.e. that Speer, in some vague manner, intended to waylay these three men at three separate places on their way to the suburbs. Stahl was told that this explanation was still more unsatisfactory than his previous one for in that case he was almost certain that at least one if not two of the three leading Nazis would be missed as an ambush might be prepared at the wrong places. Stahl said that he himself had observed Goebbels on a number of occasions driving hurriedly in his heavily armored car to or through Bernau, to his nearby suburban villa. Stahl had a small factory in this suburb of Berlin. He presumed that Speer had similar information on Bormann's and Himmler's destination. In the end Stahl said that he really knew nothing of the details of the plan and that we had better ask Speer just what he had intended to do.)

43. Speer's other collaborators (Second Report)

'I do not know which collaborators Speer had chosen. He merely remarked that he had made an appointment with some officers of the Luftwaffe and also mentioned that he was taking charge of one car himself. I objected that his position would be hopeless if his plan did not succeed completely. Speer replied that this was completely immaterial to him.'

44. Lieut.-Colonel of the Luftwaffe (Second Report)

'When I delivered the indent for the ammunition in Speer's ante-room on the following day (*Note*: on the day after Speer told him of his second plot to kill the "Big Three") a Lieut.-Colonel of the Luftwaffe, unknown to me, stood there and telephoned. I assume that he was one of these gentlemen. I had not seen this officer previously nor did I see him again later.'

45. (*Note*: At first Stahl said that this officer was in the army and that he was to lead Speer's second group, to take care of the second car or man, presumably Goebbels. Unfortunately Stahl cannot remember the name of the officer but he thinks Speer will be able to give us the name and other details. – Stahl dismissed the inquiry why the plot was never carried out with the answer that events moved too fast and that Speer had too many other worries at the time.)

46. Alleged Gestapo interference (First Report)

'We were living in a restless and turbulent period; no one was secure and Herr Speer too from that time on always carried a loaded pistol on his body. I myself had barely escaped, with Speer's intervention, a Gestapo trial for defeatist utterances.' . . .

49. Further issue of arms to Speer in April 1945

'In April of this year I personally delivered to Herr Speer further machine carbines, pistols and large quantities of ammunition. There was no further opportunity, however, to talk to him alone and, there-fore, I cannot state in detail what he actually did.' . . .

5 October 1945

(signed) Dietrich Stahl

Document 25 Special Pleading

Extract from the interrogation of Albert Speer taken at Nuremberg on
2 November 1945 by Major John J. Monigan (pp. 1–6 of the transcript)

To the Interpreter by Major Monigan

Q. Do you swear that you will truly and correctly translate from German into English, and from English into German, the testimony to be given here today, so help you God?
A. I do.

To the Witness, through the Interpreter

Q. I understand that you have talked with a British officer, Major Neve [Neave], about some statement or subjects that you wanted to discuss. That has been considered by the British and by the Americans, and it is our wish that you prepare a statement concerning the matters which you wish to discuss, and we will work out the procedure to follow thereafter.
A. That concerns my work in the last four months; that is the theme of it.
Q. Yes.
A. Yes, that is right.
Q. And it is those subjects that you wanted to talk with the British about?
A. I wanted to talk with the English Colonel, Colonel Lawrenz [Lawrence], who led the discussion about this matter. I would like to state briefly what is concerned here.
Q. Yes, go ahead.
A. I have stated that in the last four months I was in this camp where scientific and technical matters were discussed ['Dustbin']. It mainly concerned making use of our war technical experience on a long-range view. At the same time, several people came over from Wimbledon[28] and told us what had been discussed there. Because of my former experience and because they told me what had been discussed, I have a pretty good idea of what is wanted in this case. I was the only one

who was in this camp from the beginning to the end. I strived, by talking to several people in this camp, to make the discussions very clear and concise. Besides that, I have offered my services without reserve, which has also been recognized in writing from there to your office.

I do not think it good – and I have already told the British officer this – if, in case of a jail sentence at the time of the trials, I should get into the hands of the Russians, which, on the occasion of a radio speech, I heard while I was in the British camp.

I do not want to create a wrong impression. I personally know that the foundation of the trial – the total responsibility of everyone concerned – is contained as a matter of justice. So that, according to my opinion, the decision will be made.

In case no death penalty should result, I want to point out that I possess these pieces of information. I want to give you one example.

When the discussions between the British and Americans were on about the Thuringian and Saxonian [sic] Districts, I had drawn up lists showing where scientific and technical installations and persons were located, who had to be evacuated from these areas; and I noted that at a later date these persons were evacuated by trucks and surrendered to the British–American authorities.

I want to emphasize again in this case that I do not want to say here that I have done such and such, but I have noticed in the last months that the soldiers are different from the pacifists [civilians?]; they always try to adopt the latest points of view. That is their profession; they are always anxious to know what happened on the other side.

That is one subject.

Colonel Lawrenz can give the information about this. As far as I know, he has offices in London, the Economic Warfare office. If this is to be contemplated, it would be good if I could be given a chance to talk this matter over with him, because he knows about this.

The second point is my knowledge about the effects of the air war in Germany. Even before the final termination of the war, when I was still at liberty, President d'Ollier,[29] who, as far as I know is at the office of Economic Warfare in America, visited me after his co-workers in the United States Strategic Bombing Survey had found out about my knowledge of this subject.

Besides that, at that time, in order to emphasize the importance of these discussions, General Anderson[30] of the Eighth American Air Force, was with me. He was a three-star general.

I believe I am the only one in Germany who has knowledge about the mistakes that have been made in the air war against Germany. Undoubtedly, big mistakes have been made; it is possible to shut down any industry in two or three months if you use the proper means and if you avoid the mistakes that have been made in this case. This war was an economic war which was led, for the first time, in this manner.

I have given all of these pieces of information to the American authorities with all my comments. It was necessary because my concentrated experiences were possibly to be used in the war against Japan.

Because of these experiences, I think it would be wrong if I were to disclose these pieces of information to anybody except the American authorities, because it has already been presented by me that the armament production was destroyed in the most prompt manner by air.

If, during the trial, the war should be discussed, then naturally I am resolved to present the prompt destruction of the German industry. Although it would be a reason for my defense to cite the long function of German industry, however, I suppose that that will not be a matter of discussion at the trial.

I would only recommend that they ask President d'Ollier or the people of the United States Bombing Survey about this matter, and whether it is good that these experiences which I have, should get into other people's hands.

In conclusion I want to say that I have given my experiences at the time in the West, and that I was active in transporting the most important members, persons, and plans from the East to the West.

I hope to play a good part in the trial by having been here, since, and that should be all of my task.

Q. Was it your wish, then, to discuss further these matters which you have talked over with Colonel Lawrenz and Mr d'Ollier on the effect of the American and English bombing on German production? Or was it just to point out the duties which might arise if such experiences were told in general that you talked about to Major Neve?

A. I don't understand the question.

Q. Perhaps we can simplify the question. Is it your wish to talk over further the items that you discussed with Colonel Lawrenz and President d'Ollier? You feel that those subjects were covered in your discussions with them previously?

A. In general, yes.

Q. But the purpose of your discussion with Major Neve was to point out what you have just told us here concerning the undesirability of those experiences being published in general?

A. Yes; to point out especially that I have knowledge of these things which should stay on one side of the fence. I feel that it is my duty to say that. I do not want to give the details here of what I know; I would like to state that to Colonel Lawrenz. That is, as to technical matters.

Q. Yes. Well, do you wish to talk to Colonel Lawrenz about these matters?

A. If you think it necessary, yes.

Q. I see.

A. I do not know if such a course is contemplated. As long as there is no danger, it is not necessary.

Q. I see. However, the purpose of talking to Colonel Lawrenz would be to consider what information might be disclosed, which it might be undesirable to disclose, and not for the purpose of giving Colonel Lawrenz any other information which you haven't already covered? Is that right?

A. Yes, that is right.

Q. I think that clears that up; I think we understand what it is . . .

Document 26 'not a concern of mine'

Interrogation of Albert Speer taken at Nuremberg on 14 November 1945 by
Colonel Rosenblit of the USSR, assisted by members of the delegation.
Also present: Lieut. Daniel Margolies

Note: The interrogation was conducted in Russian. The questions were translated into German and the answers into Russian by a member of the USSR delegation. Simultaneously questions and answers were translated into English for information purposes only.

Colonel Rosenblit

Q. You are about to be interrogated by a representative of the Soviet delegation, Colonel Rosenblit. The interpreter has been informed that he is responsible for an accurate translation.

What is your full name?

A. Albert Speer.

Q. What was your position with the German government?

A. Beginning with 8 February, 1942, I was Reichsminister for Armaments and Munitions. I also took over all the positions previously held by Dr Todt. Dr Todt died in a crash on 8 April [February] 1942. Later on I became Inspector General of the highway system in Germany.

Q. Will you please enumerate these functions that you took over as the successor of Dr Todt.

A. As I said, I was Inspector General of the highway system in Germany. Also Inspector General of Waterways and Waterpower. Chief of the organization of Dr Todt, and Chief of the Head Office for Technical Developments of the NSDAP, in the framework of the Four Year Plan. I was also plenipotentiary for construction activities.

Q. Since when had you been a member of the National Socialist Party?

A. It must have been either 1931 or 1932 [in fact 1 March 1931].

Q. Are you familiar with Hitler's programmatic publication, *Mein Kampf*?

A. I read it only superficially, but I am not saying this as an excuse.

Q. As a member of the National Socialist Party, did you share Hitler's opinions as laid down in his book, *Mein Kampf*?

A. Only partly at that time. I mean, in 1932 the Party was more civilized than it had been at the time when it started its activities.

Q. Do you admit that Hitler stated very clearly in his book *Mein Kampf* that he had aggressive intentions against the countries in the West and in the East, and particularly against the Soviet Union.

A. Yes, he did.

Q. Do you admit that the subsequent application of the original ideas and intentions was the principal cause of the later violation of the international treaties, and of the aggressions against the Soviet Union, Czechoslovakia, and other countries which were subsequently occupied by Germany? Do you agree that this was the main reason for the start of the Second World War?

A. I had nothing to do with the development of these plans. I was an architect.

Q. But you were Reichsminister, and as such you occupied a very important position.

A. This was true only beginning with 1942.

Q. Well, then what is your present opinion regarding the start of the second imperialistic war; don't you think that it was a result of the program that Hitler had developed in *Mein Kampf*?

A. Well, Hitler had a dual personality. He had two passions. One of them was his political passion and the other was his passion for building, and the pursuit of his passion for warfare would interfere with his construction activities. It should be considered as self-evident that I as an architect, who had many orders for the construction of tremendous buildings, was not interested in a war which would prevent me from executing these orders. Personally, I am still convinced regardless of my present status that it would have been better for humanity if the war had been avoided.

Q. Is that all? Now, I have a number of other questions. Weren't Russian prisoners-of-war employed in the armament industry?

A. There is no doubt that Russian prisoners-of-war were employed in German war industries. However, it should be known to you that employment of manpower including that of all prisoners-of-war was not handled through my ministry.

Q. I know that. How many prisoners-of-war were employed in German war industries at the end of the war?

A. An approximate figure must have been, including prisoners-of-war of all nationalities, seven or eight hundred thousand. However, this figure includes those who were employed in all fields of production, not only in war industries.

Q. Where did the prisoners-of-war who were employed in munition and armament industries come from? What office furnished them?

A. These prisoners-of-war would be supplied to the factories by the Labor Department, which received them directly from the Stalags.

Q. When you speak of Labor Office, is that Sauckel's?

A. Yes, it is a sub-department of Sauckel's department.

Q. Inasmuch as the prisoners-of-war were assigned to factories, Sauckel's office would get in touch with the Stalag and receive prisoners-of-war from them. In your capacity as Minister for Armament and Munition industries, did you not have direct dealings with the Stalag in connection with the procurement of prisoners-of-war as manpower?

A. No, I had no direct dealings with them.

Q. Where were the Soviet workmen employed, in the armament and munition industries?

A. Yes, of course.

Q. How many?

A. I could not tell. I do not know that.

Q. Approximately.

A. All I know is that the total figure of foreign workers whom we employed was approximately two and one half millions of all nationalities.[31] I don't know how many of these came from the East.

Q. Who supplied the Eastern workers and all the foreign workers?

A. Whenever I put in a requisition for labor, I did not distinguish between foreign workers or German workers. I just gave my figure that I required. It was up to Sauckel to decide how many of those he would supply to me should be German workers, and how many foreigners.

Q. It is not quite clear to me what the relations between your department and that of Sauckel were.

A. Sauckel was entirely independent by orders of Hitler; he had been established as an independent agent. He didn't permit me to interfere with the management of his affairs.

Q. Do I describe the situation correctly when I say that you were the one who ordered manpower and Sauckel was the one who supplied it?

A. Yes, but when I put in my order for manpower I didn't distinguish between foreign and native labor. I had no say about it [,] what proportion of Russian workers would be assigned to agriculture or to industry.

Q. Now I would like to know the following: were there any laws which standardized the treatment of foreign manpower in Germany?

A. Yes, there were such laws. The Ministry of Labor was responsible to enforce such laws.

Q. Were there in the armament and munition industries any workmen below the age of fifteen?

A. I could not tell you. They were, by Sauckel, assigned directly to the factories, and I had no supervision over social conditions or policies in the factories. I was concerned with production policies and not social policies. My department was a wartime creation, and it took on the task of streamlining wartime production in addition to the functions already performed by other departments. My department was not even concerned with the ordering or obtaining of goods and merchandise which entered into the production of our war industries.[32]

Q. But was it not known to you how foreign workers who got into your industries were treated, including prisoners-of-war?

A. No, I don't know anything about it and it was not a concern of mine.

Q. Whose concern was it?

A. It would have been the concern of various agencies. As far as prisoners-of-war were involved, they were the concern of the Stalags and of the administration of the OKW, and inasmuch as civilian workers were concerned, it should have been a matter that concerned Sauckel and his administration.

Q. Do you admit as a Reichsminister that the employment of prisoners-of-war and of foreign workers in the war industries was a violation of international law and regulations?

A. Sauckel emphasized in a conversation with me that the manpower which he supplied to me had been obtained legally.

Q. I don't care what Sauckel told you. What was your own idea?

A. I was just about to say I know now that the introduction of prisoners-of-war and of foreign workers into German war industries was a violation of the existing international laws.

Q. But before that, did you as an educated person not know that it was so?

A. At that time I took interest only in my own responsibilities, and did not care how Sauckel obtained the manpower which I needed. I can only repeat that I had no say about what manpower Sauckel supplied for our industries. In those days I considered my task as a technical task, and I didn't feel responsible for such matters.

Q. I am not satisfied with this reply. Do you have nothing else to say about this?

A. In my activity I had only one chief concern. I made a sustained effort to minimize the effects of the bombings, and to maintain production in my industries at as high a level as possible.

Q. It seems to me that your explanations avoid the subject . . .

[pp. 8–11 of the transcript cover issues of propaganda]

Robert Ley: Profile of a Suicide

His thick, stocky, sullen composition makes him appear brutal and repellent. Even after his world collapsed, he remains a fanatical Nazi. Compared with other Nazi bigwigs, his attitude to share of the blame is surprising. He says: 'Now they all want to picture Hitler as a sick man who was led by Bormann. Hitler is sick and Bormann is dead – a clever maneuver! No, all of us who had a leading position are responsible for everything.' He makes a theatrical impression, he might even be slightly demented.

7th US Army Interrogation Center report, Dr Robert Ley, 29 May 1945[1]

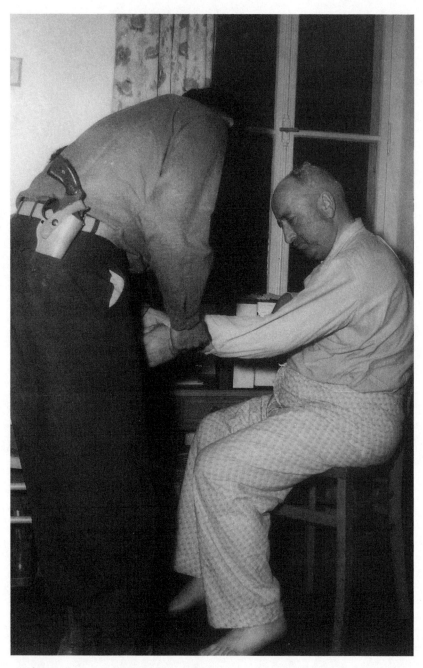

Robert Ley shortly after his arrest by American troops near Berchtesgaden in May 1945. Ley admitted his anti-semitism, but could not bear the shame of being treated as a 'common criminal'. On 24 October he committed suicide in his cell.

[Robert Ley was one of many suicides among the National Socialist elite, a phenomenon that deserves more attention than it has had so far. Ley became obsessed with the shame of incarceration, and his behaviour displayed pronounced indications of psychosis on his transfer to Nuremberg in August. His prison jottings suggest strongly a mind on the threshold of collapse. In addition to his political testament and his dialogue with his dead wife, both of which are reproduced here, he wrote other notes and letters, which are preserved among Jackson's files in Washington. 'Truth and Justice have never once created a world empire,' he observed in one entry on the coming reign of the Holy Ghost on earth. He asked his new young mistress, a seventeen-year-old Estonian named Madeleine Wanderer, to raise his children in the Catholic Church, 'for the best'. In very large letters on a heavily coffee-stained paper he scrawled 'community – comradeship – labour – nature – race – knowledge – belief – the Trinity – God – democracy . . .'.[2]

Those who had charge of Ley did not like him. His personality profile prepared at the 7th US Army Interrogation Center in late May 1945 described Ley unflatteringly as a drunkard and a womanizer. Ley denied the first charge vehemently ('I have been a teetotaler for the last ten years'); on the second he was more candid ('He admits that he appreciated women,' but 'needed diversion' following the death of his wife).[3] Later at Nuremberg his personal secretary, Hildegarde Brüninghoff, when asked about her employer's morals, did little to defend them. In an affidavit on 'The Private Life of Ley' sent to the Interrogation Division, she confirmed that Ley appeared often to exist in a world of sheer fantasy, that he exhibited a fierce temper, and was intolerant of any contrary opinion. She expatiated on his anti-semitism which was, like Streicher's, vulgar, strident and very public. On one point she begged to differ: after the death of his wife Inga, who was known to indulge heavily in drugs and drink, he no longer chased women. He had been a devoted husband and father.[4] Very shortly after her testimony Ley killed himself. Brüninghoff was among those allowed to see the body before it was buried. He left a long letter condemning the Indictment. This has been reproduced from a translated version in Jackson's files as Document 29.]

Document 27 The Testament of Robert Ley

Justice Robert Jackson, Main Files Box 3, Testament of Robert Ley, n.d.
[August 1945]

To my German People!
My political Testament:

Have I a right, after this unique catastrophe that befell the poor German people, to turn to this heroic people? For many – I do not delude myself – many will accuse me as one, sharing the responsibility. I am prepared to take this responsibility upon me. I am not trying to evade it cowardly. I belong to Hitler, not only in good but also in bad days. I have experienced the fight, I experienced victories, I shared in the years of fulfilment and in the foremost front participated in the rebuilding with personal great achievements; I was able to lead millions of workers in a heroic fight and in war. Therefore, I am prepared before all to go through this time of severest tests, valiantly and manly even unto death. So help me God.

I have learned to see the fateful way of providence in everything. My selfwilled obstinacy, my willpower are completely broken and so I commit myself unconditionally into the hands of my creator to await his decision. May what he decides, happen; he will give me strength to bear it. God led me to Adolf Hitler, God gave me the power of convincing speech and the ability to win people over, God let me build up such great works and organizations as the German Workers Front (DAF) and Strength through Joy (KdF) etc.,[5] God permitted my downfall and led me to this lonely, cold and bare cell, reduced me to a nobody, humiliated me as no man before was humiliated; he will take care of me also in future. Therefore, my German People, I believe that the Lord God inspired me in writing these lines, intended for you. They are the product of serious pondering, which led me to the brink of insanity and desperation. It is always the same question: Wherefore, why and where from. I have searched for faults and negligence, wrongs and the evil. I have examined myself and the others. The criticism of myself halted before nothing, not even before the memory of the dead

Fuehrer, the most sacred thing that I possess on this earth. I have literally racked and tormented myself and have – excepting human weaknesses which are pardonable – always come to the one conclusion: We deserted God and so God deserted us.

In place of His divine grace we substituted our own human will and in anti-semitism we violated one of the principal laws of his creation. Our will converted to obstinacy and our anti-semitic policy became our dominating force. Looking back upon all this today I know I could recount dozens of examples how paralyzing and actually disastrously these two factors influenced us. Consequently our aspect was wrong, we misjudged situations and missed opportunities that could have become our destiny. The anti-semitic spectacles upon the nose of defiant and bold men was a disaster. This must for once be courageously admitted. It is to no avail to evade the issue or to bury oneself even deeper in stubbornness or even apathy. There is a reason for everything, even for this catastrophe. If it is true, that success is the only proof for the soundness of an idea, then disaster holds proof, that somewhere mistakes were made. National Socialism, in all its positive aspects was correct, great and powerful and it will succeed in spite of all. On the negative side in anti-semitism it was correct only insofar as it was concerned with necessary protection against the flooding with Jews, especially from the East, and as long as it was necessary to fight the excesses. Also during the war this defense was necessary. Everything in addition was wrong and finally led up to those blinds [blinkers] which prevented us from seeing.

This is not to be considered as an exoneration of myself. My fate is small and unimportant. I am finished with the world. I no longer quarrel, I have accepted my fate. I bear my responsibility. This is no criticism of my dead Fuehrer. He is too great and too noble to be tainted by a passing mistake. That will be forgotten, his greatness will remain.

It is impossible to consider this as doubting our idea. Because all the positive [things], the People's Community (*Volksgemeinschaft*), true socialism, achievement as the standard for the new society, reason as the basis of all human being, all the great, beautiful and noble given to the German people by National Socialism can remain without anti-semitism and then, freed of it, will really develop and men will not have to wrest it from fate.

Certainly, it is bitter and hard to admit mistakes. There will be some who will accuse me of treason. But it is better to accept this accusation and to tell the truth than to keep fundamental knowledge stubbornly and defiantly. This concerns the substance of the German people. Political unity is shattered, a Reich of 1,000 years is lost, shall now the substance of Germany be lost too because we do not have the courage to free ourselves from the stubbornly followed policy of anti-semitism? We National Socialists must have this courage. Our youth does not believe our opponents. Should this wonderful German youth be lost as Carthage was lost? Never! Fate may demand my life but I will gladly bear the suffering if only it will be granted to me to prevent the horrible destruction of the German Folk substance by my courageous confession. Forms may break, men may fall, parties and systems perish, but the people must remain and must continue to live.

In order to be successful we must take this step completely. It is not enough to say, we will no longer talk about anti-semitism, we will tolerate the Jews, we are forced to do so. No, we must take the step completely, half steps are no good. We must eliminate suspicion and meet the Jew with an open heart and on a clear basis. We must purify our relations. Without reserve and without inhibitions the German and the Jew must find each other again, must make peace with each other and must agree on a new life together for future times on the basis of their advanced knowledge. This ideological clarification is more important than economic and cultural reconstruction. The quicker we shall find the courage [for] it and the clearer and bolder we take up this new position, the better for our people. Either we shall be exterminated or we are ready to take this step. Stubborn hesitation does not help, even less believing in miracles. Courageous advance on the road taken is the only salvation.

The Jew also should learn from this. At the moment he is triumphant. He is in a position to exterminate and destroy National Socialist leadership. But he cannot destroy 80 million Germans. He will not suddenly be able to conjure up a paradise in order to buy the Germans with it. The more the Jew acts out of revenge the more embittered enemies he will make for himself. For new suffering carries with it new thoughts of revenge into almost every German family. Already today almost all of Germany is affected. Does anyone believe that anti-semitism can be rooted out by that? It will only be strengthened and stirred up. And there is furthermore the national pride of the Germans. They will point to the grand achievements of National Socialism. For the lack of any ideals youth will all the more cling to the old ones. The expelled Jews will not be able to return unconcerned but will be met by a secret phalanx of defense and hatred. The occupation army will depart some day. New political constellations can bring new opportunities for Germany. Nothing is eternal on earth, the least of all peace alliances. And then anti-semitism will rise again and will rage more furiously than ever before.

Above all I predict something else. The Jewish question exists in every country. A wise Jew says: Wherever Jews go, anti-semitism will flame up also. An influential Jew said about North America: He knows that in 80 years the Jews will suffer great persecutions. Who can guarantee that in Bolshevistic Russia some day anti-semitism will not come to life again as it was in Czarist Russia. I am even deeply convinced of this. At any rate, in Western Europe where the Jewish question was carried into every village by our occupation armies, it will not cease to stir the people's minds. I am certain of it. To be an anti-semite is to occupy oneself with [the] Jewish question. The mystery of it already attracts all curious people and does not let them go any more.

Add to this the fact that millions of American, British, Russian, French a.o. [and other?] occupation soldiers are constantly encountering the Jewish question. They have to take sides, pro or contra. And this alone will make them think. They compare. Here and there they will find confirmed some of the things the anti-semite[s] assert. They become thoughtful. They will become anti-semites and thus bring anti-semitism into their homes, into their countries.

Do they believe to be able to root out anti-semitism by spectacular trials, even though they may be staged ever so cleverly. Just the contrary, they will only attain the opposite. The world attention is directed to a problem which can only be dealt with, if it remains in obscurity, or else, if one finds the courage to solve this Jewish problem by open discussion and enlightenment as a consequence of the catastrophe unequalled in history. One has to go on from where the wave of anti-semitism has started. One must not abruptly retard and stop by force and terror the surge, because then one will be drowned by it, it must be caught, controlled and made to run its course. Then the stirring sea will again calm down, and it will not have the devastating effect which I predicted for certain. The German anti-semites made the first step, they also have to make the second.

Jewry must make its peace with Germany and Germany must make its peace with Jewry in the interest of world peace and world prosperity.

They must not only conclude an armistice but a peace, based on reason, clear knowledge and clear rights and duties. The Jew has to make friends with Germany and Germany must make friends with the Jew. This will bring blessing to the rest of the world. It is time that one realizes that here we have to deal with a natural phenomenon. If humanity cannot control the aroused passions, it will be ruined by them. They can only be mastered again by starting the process of calming mind and passions from its point of origin, Germany. And here the outspoken anti-semites must be the pioneers for this new – and yet so close at hand – idea. They must find the courage, to conquer themselves and to advance courageously. The torch of conviction must burn brightly in their hands so that the people will go along on the same road. This God taught me in the prison cell at Nuremberg. And now: My plan:

1. Formation of a committee, where Jews and anti-semites, who are honestly determined to follow this road, meet in order to exchange their thoughts and to determine the conditions under which Jews and Germans want to live together.

2. An executive committee, again consisting of Jews and Germans, who will carry out these agreements.

3. An organization for education and propaganda to carry these thoughts into the tiniest village.

I will not say more at present, because more would only confuse the purpose. Certainly there is much to be discussed yet in order to assure the good co-operation and living together and to guarantee it. But all this would come about later.

German people! Many will judge me as insane because I write thus. They will say, he has lost his mind because of the catastrophe. Others will denounce me as a traitor, who would like to turn Germany over to the Jews. They prefer to stubbornly stand aside and perish, rather than admit a mistake. They do not recognize, that I am not at all admitting a mistake, but am drawing the consequences from the events, and consequently am going the way once taken clear to the end. They don't understand, that one must first have been an anti-semite in order to reach the next phase of this recognition. For this reason nobody has yet dared to think or act thus, because the foundation was lacking. Therefore only you, my German people, – do not be frightened by what I am going to say now – can dare to invite the Jew to make his home with you.

Is it not peculiar – one might almost believe in predestination – that almost all the Jews in the world speak German. Hatred and love dwell in close proximity.

Who, my German people, will help you economically as long as this question has not been solved. Reconstruction is a matter of confidence, but confidence may only be gained by being honest, open, and sensible. The solution of the Jewish question in Germany is and remains the predisposing factor. I beg of you, my German people, be a wise householder, soberly face your accounts:

You are totally defeated, but you are in possession of a magnificent idea and an excellent people.

God is showing you a way, learn from the catastrophe. Become reconciled with the Jew and invite him to find his home with you.

It would have to be the devil's doings if this work would not succeed, and a sensible 'modus vivendi' could not be found. I know the way, I declare it openly.

But will the Jew collaborate? If he is intelligent he will, should revenge obscure his reason, I cannot help this. Then at least I have done my duty, and have told humanity my insight given to me by God. If the Jew shuts his eyes to this, the world catastrophe, as I pictured it above, will run its pittyless [sic] course. But if Germany should find a solution to this question and recover its health from this solution, the whole world will recover its health and this most pressing of all questions would be solved the world over. Zionism in its present form will never lead to the goal, the Jews must find a home, Germany is ripe to grant this home within her, with her.

And what does America say to this Plan?

The age of nationalities is past, the age of races begins. Nations are no more factors, the continents will compete with one another. That is the certain – the only certain end of this war. America on one side,

Asia on the other. Between the two lies Europe. Therefore America has an elementary interest in Europe's recovery. But Europe can only recover its health if its heart, Germany, recovers. For this reason alone America is interested that Germany finds itself.

But America, as well as all peoples, is interested in the solution of the Jewish question. It knows that if no solution is found, one day it will face the same problems cropping up as in Germany. All this leads me to the conclusion that my plan is not opposed to American interests, on the contrary that it is in the best and highest interest of America. And not only in the interest of America but in the interest of all humanity.

I know that my proposals are daring and even bold. But I also know that in these great days timidity and despondency do not lead to the goal. And if a person asks me what will Hitler, your Fuehrer, say to that I answer him:

This Genius of unique greatness, equal to Hannibal as a military leader, certainly does not which [wish] that Germany should perish like Carthage.

I can only say: I dared it. Now do what you want. I leave it to God's hand from whom I believe to have received the inspiration and the revelation. Weeks ago I was terrified by these thoughts. Then I did not even dare to touch the subject of anti-semitism. Today it is as clear as sunlight to me. I should be able to speak of it for hours. Ever so many new more complete plans occur to me. I am actually possessed by these ideas. God must now help me, to deliver my plans to the right instances [authorities]. I trust in him, he will surely find the right thing.

Dr R. Ley

Document 28 Ley's Dialogue with the Dead

Justice Robert Jackson, Main Files, translation of 'Ein Zwiegespräch' by
Robert Ley, written 14 August 1945

Inga[6] *A dialogue* *14 August 1945*

My wife, how I am thinking of you. I know you are dead, lying under
the grass, already for 2¾ years, under the knotty oaks, birch-trees and
pines in the ancestors' forest at Rettland and yet you are bodily near
to me. I am feeling you. You are embracing me with your love, your
charm and your beauty. <u>Illegirl</u> how beautiful you were! Beautiful in
body, soul and spirit. One did not know, what more one should admire
about you, your tall figure, your noble face or your long blonde hair.
This external beauty was paired with a clean soul, a true character,
high intelligence and a wonderful voice. Your clear soprano enchanted
everybody. You were a rare creation of Our Lord. Sometimes one was
tempted to believe in a trick of nature, so ethereally transparent was
your white skin. And yet you were reality, for you gave me three
children who are your image. Are they still alive and how are they?
How I worry about them and yet I am completely helpless and unable
to protect them. Fate played terribly upon me[:] first it took the wife
from me and now it is taking my children. But I don't want to write
about that now.

   You are entering my cell again. You want to talk to me. I am willing.
What is life – you ask me – didn't I give it voluntarily, when I knew,
that I am incurably sick and only within a few years would languish
away in decay and pain. I wanted to die just as I was born, beautiful
and young. You were right, my girl, and yet it isn't always so. I too
tried it once. When catastrophe came over us, I was near despair. There
I tempted God, I really did everything, in painful grief for my people,
in memory of my dead Fuehrer and in presentiment of my fate, to
finish my life. You know, how seriously I meant it. You were also with
me that time. And yet, I didn't succeed. I do not want to continue with
the story, how I wandered over snow-fields on the 'Wilden' and the
'Zahmen Kaiser' 2,500 meters high, climbing steep slopes up and

down, without ever having climbed mountains before, I don't want to describe the tragic drama in the attic at Schleching.

Everything is so unreal and sounds like a novel. And, nevertheless, everything is so true. You know, my Inge, that I took everything extremely seriously. But God did not accept my life. He saved me miraculously, in order to send me then – into captivity – fate.

Dear girl, you are smiling, I see you in your beauty, standing in front of me. You smile kindly and knowingly, like the experienced mother to her boy. In spite of your youth, you always used to call me 'Bobsie'. You know what a calming effect this always had on me. You say you talked with God, and you also know why God-Father did not yet want my life in Schleching. Therefore tell it to me, that I understand God. For nothing is more terrible, than to become confused about Him. I admit it to you, I cursed God, when all that indescribable misery of disgrace and distress came over all of us, over Germany, and also over me. Do you know that the Fuehrer is dead, he who adored you so very much, and whom you loved so very much. Do you know that all of Germany is occupied, the Reich smashed, and many millions are in captivity; wives and children at home are crying and mourning for them. Do you know that the nation is penniless, all cities destroyed, and the beautiful, irreplaceable treasures of art and culture are totally destroyed. Do you know all that, and in spite of it, you continue to smile. Now your face is getting serious and full of dignity, now you are totally Inga, my wife. You speak: It is not true to believe that the devil created the world and God would only try now and then, to bring a little order into it. God created the world and everything happens according to his will, also the present time hardly to be understood by us Germans. First of all this world drama has not yet reached its end. The bolshevistic world revolution must necessarily go its way that it started. Even if Stalin, whom one must admire in his consequence [sic] and his energy, would like to bring to a standstill the course of events, he will not be more able to do so than Hitler was able to do so, when he took his first step into the National Socialist revolution with the proclamation of his program. Men believe that they themselves are acting and yet they are only the tools in the hand of a higher being. She is silent, I lose myself in meditation, and finally in a deep relaxing sleep and dream: Germany would have become so beautiful, strength through joy, spare time and recreation, new dwellings, the most beautiful cities and villages have been planned, service and just wages, a great, unique health-program, social security for the aged and incapacitated, roads construction and traffic lanes, ports and settlements, – how beautiful Germany could have been if, if, if and always again if. I am awaking, still quite confused from what I have seen. Where is my wife? Gone, and I alone in the dreary, bare and so cold cell. Why?

I do not know. I have not yet received the indictment, and I don't know why I should receive one. I have not committed murder and have not ordered any. I did not start a war, I had no power to do so, I did not even know about it. To the contrary, for me the war came at the most inopportune moment. I was in the midst of my social reconstruction, which I now had to interrupt. God in heaven, what have I done that I am treated under such conditions as a criminal. Lord God, give me an answer, I have a right to it. Here Inga, my dearly beloved wife, comes to me again and says:

Are you quarrelling with God, with your fate? Don't do it, every-thing has its purpose, even your grief and the grief of the millions of German people, but before I continue these thoughts, I would like to end my preceding dialogue, otherwise you will go to sleep over it again. I had begun with (1) Stalin cannot change the course he has already taken and I continue secondly: Stalin also does not want to change his course because Russia was never yet as close to the realization of the testament of Peter the Great as it is just now. This testament like all Russian thought is based on two – one would like to say tragic factors – once on the passion absolutely to become a naval power, secondly on the mystic belief that the East is called upon to bring the true belief in God (*Gottesglauben*) to the West, even with the opposite symbol of atheistic Bolshevism. Italy thinks in the same way as Peter the Great, Toilstoy (*sic!*), Dostrojewsky, and others. Stalin is Great Russian, he intends to go his way and he must. Will the new bomb – one calls it uranium bomb – not hinder him, I answer. My intelligent girl laughs at me. Did you not always keep repeating yourself, against every weapon there is a defense. That is right, I answer, however we were not able to resist any more the immense air superiority of our adversaries by using the jet fighters. A quarter of a year too late. There she becomes serious, very serious and says: that was bitter and pathetic at the same time, however Stalin now has jet fighters and the factories in addition.

Besides you know yourself, that with regard to research work in atomsmashing all belligerents were equally advanced; who tells you that Stalin does not have the same bomb. Or how is it with regard to the death rays? Whatever may be the case Stalin will follow his course, will have to and will want to do so. He cannot retrace his steps or he himself would be consumed by the fire of the revolution.

I become very thoughtful and look at her keenly and steadily and ask: Then we have misjudged Bolshevism and its bearer Stalin? Yes and no my Inge answers and with her beautiful voice continues, thus I come to your own personal fate and to the common fate of the entire German people. Now she smiles again and caresses me and looks questioningly upon me with her expressive eyes. Haven't you always said and maintained that success is the only proof of the soundness of an idea. To judge by the complete collapse, the unconditional surrender, the imprisonment of all German leaders and by your own fate, my dear Bobsie, National Socialism would have to be completely wrong, Hitler a fool and all of you bewitched. That, however, is incorrect. Few know you and the Fuehrer as I do. You yourself, my dear husband, have only recently set forth in a pamphlet 'Thoughts about the Fuehrer' that to the end the Fuehrer was completely master of himself, that all rumors of brain hemorrhages and hallucinations were untrue and founded on malicious reports. You have thus courageously portrayed the Fuehrer as he really is: The greatest German of all times, and just as persistent you stick to your idea to which you owe your great successes in the social-political sphere. You are quite correct in this and the same holds true in many other spheres.

What enormously positive things National Socialism has achieved and yet suffered.

Document 29 Confessions of an Anti-semite

Translation of a letter from Dr Robert Ley to Dr Flicker [Pflücker],
24 October 1945 (not sent)

Defense

I. Principles of Law

God himself instituted the law. First he gave us the ten Commandments and all moral principles and only thereafter meted out punishments. For that, he appointed independent judges in Israel, who were not permitted to make laws themselves.

The Inter-Allied Powers are violating those principles of law by not setting up a law until 8 August 1945, that is after all the crimes mentioned in the indictment, which they wish to judge, had been committed. In making the Tribunal itself the legislator, they are again fundamentally violating the principles of law which have been handed down.

In clause six, para. C, it says: 'for this the Tribunal is the competent authority . . .', or clause 8 'if this, in the opinion of the Tribunal, appears justified . . .', or clause 9 'In proceedings against a member of a Group or organization, the Tribunal can . . . rule that the Group . . . was a criminal organization.'

This tendency to assign legislative power to the Tribunal is continued in the next section. It is, therefore, not surprising that the rules for the proceedings are laid down by the Tribunal alone – clause 13 or 14 c. Therefore, it is not to be wondered at that the defense comes off badly – clauses 18 b, c, 19, 20, 21, 25. In clause 3, however, the charter protects itself by forbidding a priori any refusal on the part of the defendant. I understand that the victor thinks he has to exterminate and destroy his hated opponents. I am not defending myself against being shot or killed. I am defending myself, and with every right, against being branded as a criminal and against a procedure without any legal foundation based on pure caprice.

To proceed to the indictment itself.

It is so absurd and so based on propaganda that I cannot find words to describe a procedure of this kind. Even the choice of defendants is completely biased. The indictment strikes its own death-blow. If there really was a 'Nazi' conspiracy, *all* Reichsminister[s], *all* Reichsleiters, *all* the member[s] of the General Staff would have to be indicted, for one is as guilty as another. However, what I find most difficult to understand is what a man like Krupp von Bohlen und Halbach is doing amongst the defendants, an honorable old man who was concerned only with his business interests. What has this man to do with the 'Nazi conspiracy'? The indictment is also precarious in the definition of criminal organizations. It knows that this concerns <u>many millions</u> of the best German men and women who really cannot be branded as criminal even with the grossest of propaganda. The indictment therefore falls down in advising the Tribunal to what extent such an organization must be considered criminal. This is all so absurd that the indictment must collapse of itself.

And now to continue with the individual three counts of the indictment.

Count I

I. *Common plan or conspiracy.* I want here to talk only of myself. I was a member of a <u>legal</u> party whose program was decent and reasonable through and through, which, before the assumption of power, had over <u>a million</u> member[s] and 15 million voters. It was legally called into power by the Reich President of that time, von Hindenburg, who, repeatedly, was legally elected by the nation,[7] and it then legally (law of authorization (*Ermaechtigungsgesetz*)[8] and many others) reconstructed the State, economy, social organization, according to its principles. This was known to everybody in Germany. That is why we gained the majority; the <u>people</u> desired it. If this is a conspiracy, then all parties in all countries are conspirator parties. In America, the whole system changes with the victory of one party. In England, the Labour Party is at present trying to put their program through and the Bolshevik revolution in Russia cost infinitely more in blood than the Nazi Socialist one in Germany.

To give only one example: I am charged with having merged the trade unions and with having founded the German Labor Front. This action was perfectly legal; Hitler, as Reichschancellor, ordered it in pursuance of the law of authorization, von Hindenburg supported it as he was Reich President. No one turned a hair; a few dozen people were arrested for a few days for concealment and embezzlement and what the working man thought about it has been shown by the increasing confidence in the German Labor Front over twelve years. The property and financial conditions of the trades unions were in utter disorder, the bank had no more cash; subsidies [i.e. unemployment assistance] had not been paid for months; the members openly revolted against the leaders. The State had to act if it did not desire unrest.

And the result was: I took 5 million members over and the German Labor Front finally had 30 million members, of which 24 million were individual members and approximately 6 million collective members. The 24 million individual members had without exception joined voluntarily.[9] The contribution collected amounted to 95 percent – no expression of confidence can exceed this. The attitude and the achievements of the workers were so exemplary, that there must have been limitless confidence in the leader. Whoever, in the face of such facts, which were (recognized) even by our opponents – Sir Patrick, the American Commission in Mondorf, etc. – can therefore accuse me of being a criminal, is either completely ignorant or malicious. The wealth of the German Labor Front was multiple of what the trades unions possessed. This was naturally also the case with what the German Labor Front achieved for the workers. These were the results of the 'Nazi conspiracy' in the sphere of domestic politics. It was the same in almost every other sphere. If they are crimes, the world is all topsy turvy.

And in the sphere of foreign politics?

I never took part in any meeting at which the alleged 'criminal' plans were discussed or, as the indictment states, jointly planned. The indictment is accusing me of things of which I know nothing and it can never be proved I did.

And now a word about the 'criminal' organizations such as the 'Political Leaders',[10] 'SA', etc.: before our assumption of power, these organizations (existed) first in the Social Democratic Party, in the 'Reichsbanner' organization and in the Communist Party in the 'Rotfront' organization.[11] It was only when they attacked our meetings that the NSDAP founded the SA, called the Schutzstaffel (*sic*).[12] Furthermore the Bolshevik Party in Russia has similar organizations.

The same applies to the Fuehrer principle. Nowhere is the Fuehrer principle more rigidly laid down than under Bolshevism in Russia. Moreover, is it a crime to acknowledge the Fuehrer principle? If so, all the armies in the world would have to be 'criminal organizations'. In all this, the indictment is so absurd that it is evident, from this alone, that it does not desire to seek justice, rather a prejudiced basis for further assertions.

Anti-semitism

Whatever it is necessary to say on this subject, I have already said elsewhere. The quotations made in the indictment are torn entirely from their contexts, it is therefore necessary to present the facts of the case correctly.

We National Socialists, started by Hitler, saw in the struggles which now lie behind us, a war solely against the Jews – not against the French, English, Americans or Russians. We believed that they were all only the tools of the Jew and, when reading the indictment, one is almost inclined to believe that this was actually so. We were on the defensive. The disastrous end of the last war had already been attributed to the Jew. Then, particularly, the disintegration of Germany after the war, morally and economically, had to be ascribed to the increasing unhealthy influence of, above all, the Eastern Jews. There is a great deal of evidence to support this. During the war itself, we believed that the inhumane bombarding of our cities and even villages was due to Jewish influence on the enemy side. There is no lack of statements on the enemy side, such as those of the Jew, Kaufmann, Morgenthau,[13] Ehrenberg[14] etc., demanding the complete extermination, sterilization and destruction of Germany and of the German people. This intention was shown in increasingly gruesome detail. I would explain these statements [of German anti-semitic sentiment] thus. They were outbreaks of rage at the devilish treatment destined for the German people and at the gruesome bombing of which I was a daily witness. Today I regret these statements and I had [have] put down how I think the Jewish problem could be solved in a positive sense.

This Jewish problem exists and it would be better to assemble all forces which recognize it and are willing to help in solving it, better to tackle and solve the problem with courage, in the interests of the Jews and of all peoples, than to give the spirit of revenge free play and thereby pour down further misery on humanity. Now is the one opportunity; should humanity let this opportunity slip by, a much more horrible drama of wars, revolutions and the like will, in fifty years' time or perhaps sooner, be repeated. One must not think that National Socialism can be exterminated by such methods. Thus, hundreds and thousands will spring up to take the places of those struck down. An idea which gained such a complete hold of a people is neither a conspiracy nor can it be wiped out. The greatest Jew, Saul, as Paul, acted more wisely than his descendants apparently desire to act today. Revolutions are natural catastrophes which cannot be judged by standards of right or wrong, they come and go and men must learn from them. I have honestly and sincerely said what there is to be said on this subject.

Now back to Count I of the indictment. There is no truth to any of the charges that I had any part in the attacks on Austria, Czechoslovakia, Poland, Denmark, Norway, Belgium, Holland, Luxemburg, Yugoslavia, Greece, USSR, and USA. It would be more true to say that I neither knew anything about them, nor made any plans beforehand and was completely taken by surprise by the whole war. This was fitted into my plans like hail in a cornfield. Proof of this is that I was planning extensive 'strength through joy' trips and activities and that I was in the middle of my preparations for the 1939 Reich Party Rally in Nuremberg. There can be no question of a conspiracy or joint planning. Even afterwards, I was *never* consulted or included at conferences. There is, therefore, no need for me to go into the details of the indictment.

Count II of the indictment – 'Crimes against Peace' – says 'All the defendants . . .', during a period of years preceding 8 May 1945, [']participated in the planning, preparation, initiation and waging of wars of aggression, which were also . . .'. So far as I am concerned, this most certainly is <u>not true</u>. I have already said above what has to be said with regard to joint planning, that I never took part in any such meeting and that the Fuehrer, as was his wont, *never* spoke to anybody of anything which did not concern him. The first I heard about the beginning of any operation was in the newspapers or over the radio. I freely and openly admit that, during the war, I did my duty as a German in the position fate had put men in, so that the war might be won. If this is a crime, let me be sentenced.

The indictment lays down under Count III:
VIII. Statement of the Offence
'All the defendants committed war crimes between 1st September, 1939, and 8th May, 1945 in Germany and in all . . .' This is not true. I committed no war crime – not even what the indictment includes as such. The indictment continues: 'All the defendants, acting in concert with others, formulated and executed a common plan or conspiracy to commit war crimes . . .' This is equally untrue, for, as I explained above, I knew of nothing, and took no part in any plan or conspiracy.

Then the indictment refers to 'total war' as proof. We understood total war as the extreme effort, achievement and employment of all German men and women in the cause of victory. This was our sacred duty. Who has the right to accuse us of it?

And now there is another 'common plan and conspiracy' and, under it, I am now accused of things of which I have no idea, which I never ordered and never executed. This is a cheap way of offering evidence, but has, however, not the least connection with law and justice. Moreover, I emphatically dispute the fact that German soldiers committed crimes such as are mentioned here.

I therefore declare that I was not a participant in any of the so-called 'crimes' under VIII, A to J, and that I am not responsible for them, should they have been committed. I must decline collective responsibility for the following reasons: (1) because it contradicts all sense of justice; (2) because the indictment itself accuses us National Socialists of adhering to the *Fuehrer principle*. But it is nothing but the Fuehrer principle that *someone* is responsible in every sphere and for every deed. The indictment, here, contradicts itself.

In detail, the indictment charges me with having participated in recruiting labor for Germany because with the defendant Sauckel, I was president of the committee for the 'welfare of foreign workers'. This is correct but, as the word 'welfare' indicates, no crime was ever committed against these workers but was a blessing for them.

1) I never brought or deported a single foreigner into Germany.

2) Neither did I put a <u>single</u> foreigner <u>to work</u> in Germany, nor <u>supervise</u> or oppress any.

3) With my German Labor Front organization, I did all that was humanly possible to improve their billets, arrange for their food and clothing, complete their professional training, give them just treatment and just wages, in short, I looked after the interests of foreigners in just the same way as those of the German workers. All my orders, inspections made by myself or by the inspector Gohdes and his colleagues prove this fact. It is impossible to prove the contrary. If it is a crime to help men, I admit my guilt.

Now a word of a personal nature: The indictment wishes to defame us defendants also personally under Count III of the indictment, as if we enriched ourselves. I personally never touched anyone else's property, Jewish or not Jewish. If I bought small gifts in foreign countries, I paid the price demanded without haggling or making use of my name. I received no salary from the Labor Front, but, for my position, an almost ridiculous amount for my expenses. My income from the Party was 3,000 RM a month. I acquired my fortune by writing, at which I worked through the night. In addition, the Fuehrer once gave me a state donation in recognition of my work [see p. 274 above].

Count IV of the indictment, 'Crimes against Humanity'. The indictment states: 'All the defendants committed Crimes against Humanity during a period of years preceding 8th May, 1945 . . .' and continues 'All the defendants . . . formulated and executed a common plan or conspiracy to commit Crimes against Humanity as defined . . .' Where is this plan? Show it to me. Where is the protocol or the fact that only those here accused met and said a single word about what the indictment refers to so monstrously. Not a thing of it is true. Many of the defendants were never anti-semitic, let alone participating in a 'common plan'.

I was anti-semitic, I admit, but is this a crime? Millions are anti-semitic in the world, anti-semitic newspapers in America are printed in over a million copies. There is no people and no country on earth without anti-semitism. A well-known Jew himself said, wherever Jews go, anti-semitism goes. Christ himself was anti-semitic and, after him, the greatest Popes, Emperors, Kings, poets and artists. Who will accuse me on account of my conviction? Was this not one of the main war aims of America and England: the fight for freedom of opinion?

In detail, I must say:

I never persecuted, tortured, imprisoned nor dispossessed etc. <u>a single</u> Jew.

I had no influence with regard to concentration camps. I had no influence with Himmler. I did not appropriate any Jewish fortune – not a penny.

If I used aggressive language in my articles, I had reason for it and regret it today. However, who is the master of his emotions when all one's emotions break out. We ended up by seeing everything through anti-semitic eyes. It became a complex and so a disaster to ourselves. It was not, however, a conspiracy – I never had a preconceived plan with anybody, not even with Hitler.

They may kill me – may do whatever they like with me. I accept the victor. I do not suffer from peevish spite or any false illusions. I accept my fate.

<u>However, I am no criminal.</u>

If one wishes to prevent, once and for all, aggressive wars, and their consequences, or, better, any wars at all, one should make use of this great victory to establish an international Charter, an international, independent tribunal and legal procedure and to form an international army to guarantee this Charter. This would have been <u>Justice.</u>

It would have been better for the dignity of this system of law to consider and treat us as enemies – as England did with Napoleon – or to shoot us, than by hook or by crook to construct a system of law which is no system.

This will bring no blessing to humanity and it will not please the Lord God.

<u>I am a German and a National Socialist but I am no criminal.</u>

Obeying Orders: Complicity and Denial

Q. Did you know that there were hundreds of thousands of people killed in concentration camps?

A. No, I certainly did not.

Q. That also is an astounding thing to me.

A. I can absolutely say 100 per cent clear, that I did not . . .

Q. I grant you it is secret but you cannot have hundreds of thousands of people dying in concentration camps and not know.

A. Is that true, Colonel?

Q. I think it is conservative. I think millions is nearer.

A. I can't imagine that.

Q. There are lots of things you can't imagine. You have an education coming to you.

Interrogation of Joachim von Ribbentrop, 10 September 1945, taken by Howard Brundage[1]

[The typical behaviour of the major prisoners at Nuremberg was to pretend either that they were not responsible for the crimes of which they were accused, or that they were ignorant of the details of crimes perpetrated by others. Hans Frank, Wilhelm Frick, Walther Funk, Joachim von Ribbentrop, Alfred Rosenberg, Fritz Sauckel and Julius Streicher, all of them from the NSDAP, took an identical stand on the key issues of racism and terror on which they stood accused. There is in their testimony ample evidence that their abdication of responsibility to the will of the Fuehrer during the Third Reich ('I have no conscience; Adolf Hitler is my conscience,' claimed Hans Frank in 1935) was replicated in their persistent denial of responsibility at Nuremberg. The military defendants, including Goering, who was both Party leader and senior commander, were more prepared to accept responsibility where it was due, and to argue over detailed issues of evidence, as was their right. It is no doubt the case that some of the defendants were genuine in their ignorance of the details of policy; they were under no pressure before 1945 to insist that the veil of secrecy over the camps and the security services should be lifted, while they broadly approved their purposes. None the less, denial and professions of ignorance were regarded sceptically by the interrogators. Subsequent research has proved them generally to have been right. No area of the Third Reich was more difficult to break down than the army, whose leaders insisted that the Wehrmacht had not perpetrated crimes in the east and pointed the finger of blame at the security services and the police, or the barbarous behaviour of Soviet partisans, for which traditional Prussian military justice sanctioned harsh reprisals. The three documents presented here show the different faces of denial. The first comes from the numerous interrogations of Wilhelm Frick, Interior Minister from 1933 to 1943, and then Reich Protector of Bohemia following the assassination of Reinhard Heydrich. So convinced was Frick that he had done nothing contrary to international law that he asked his interrogator to investigate the possibility of his immediate release on his own surety. Ribbentrop was a different case. He knew that he could not avoid association with the preparation and waging of aggressive war, and he sheltered behind an evident confusion and loss of memory to shield himself from the uncomfortable truth. The efforts of the interrogators to extract testimony display a pathos largely absent from other interviews. The final example is drawn from the military elite. General Heinz Guderian, the famous tank commander in 1940 and 1941, who became chief-of-staff of the army in 1944, presented his interrogator with a standard view on army responsibility for atrocity, which came to be accepted widely in the 1950s as the reality: the army fought while the SS murdered. The success of the army in presenting itself as a functional force divorced from the racism and terror of the regime kept serious research on the eastern war at bay for a generation. More difficult to explain is why the long catalogue of crimes committed by the German armed forces in the western theatres of war, which was the mainstay of the United Nations War Crimes Commission from its formation in 1943, has failed to attract the same attention as the 'barbarization of warfare' in the east. The German armed forces in both theatres brought habits of rough justice against enemy soldier and civilian, and was known to have done so at Nuremberg.[2]]

Document 30 'not a dangerous person'

Extract from the interrogation of Wilhelm Frick taken at Nuremberg on
25 September 1945 by Henry R. Sackett (from pp.1–4, 22–7)

The Witness through the Interpreter

I would like to bring up one very essential point regarding the questions that the Colonel asked at the very end. Do you want it right now?

Questions by Mr Sackett to the Witness through the Interpreter

Q. All right.
A. The Colonel said that it seemed that the gentlemen of the government don't want to be responsible for the things that, according to their particular position or function, would be their responsibility. That is absolutely correct, because an outsider can hardly judge the way the

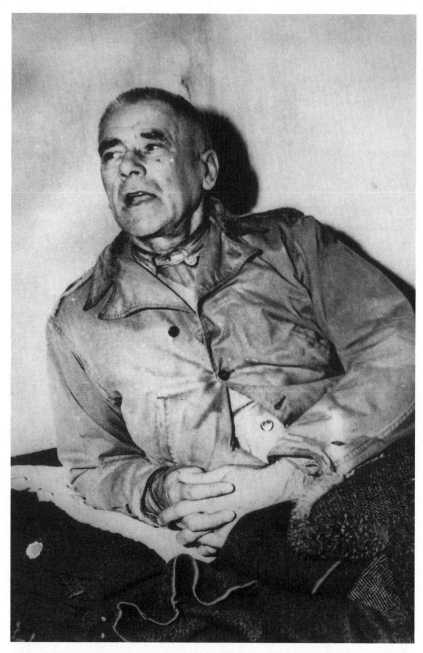

Wilhelm Frick was Interior Minister in Hitler's cabinet from 1933 to 1941. He denied any responsibility for the terror apparatus or for anti-semitism. He told interrogators that when he visited Sachsenhausen concentration camp in 1936 he found everything 'in perfect shape and order'.

authoritarian system developed. For instance, I, as Minister of the Interior, was responsible for all the matters of the police, but actually if I ever tried to interfere in the matter with the police, then I received through Mr Lammers an admonition from the Fuehrer that I was not supposed to interfere in these matters, that Himmler was perfectly capable of taking care of them alone.

Q. Assuming that it was true that there were many situations that you couldn't control, wasn't it a fact that you did receive information as to what was going on generally?

A. No. I was not informed. Just as I told you before during this morning's discussion, when Himmler was appointed Chief of all the Police, I asked him to give me a report at least every fortnight, so that I could be informed on the running business of the police, and yet he hasn't come even once.

Q. I didn't mean informed by Himmler. I meant didn't you receive information as to those arrests of Jews and so forth from Order Police and people in his organization?

A. No, for the actions of the Security Police were always so extremely secret and the personnel of the Security Police was sworn to discretion to such a high degree that normally the only way in which one would hear anything would be very doubtful unbased rumors.

Q. Isn't it true that as Minister of the Interior you were the State head of the Order Police?

A. Yes. Formally I was at the top. I was in charge of the police, but the thing was this: I, as Minister of Interior, had under me the Police Chief, who was Himmler, and Himmler's police were divided into two divisions, the uniformed police, Order Police, which was headed by Daluege, and the various branches of the not-uniformed Security Police under Heydrich, consisting of the Criminal Police, the Secret State Police and others.

Q. You were Minister of the Interior in 1938, were you not?

A. Yes, until 20 August 1943.

Q. In November of 1938 there were some 25 or 30,000 Jews arrested by someone and placed in concentration camps?

A. Yes. They were arrested, but they were not arrested by me and they were arrested without knowledge of me, for that was actually the way the authoritarian government degenerated, in as much as everything was done by a personal decree of the Fuehrer to one particular person, and very often the actual instance [office] of highest authority was bypassed, as in my case.

Q. I didn't say that you caused the arrest of the 25 or 30,000 Jews, but you were in favor of the suppression of Jewish peoples as a group in Germany, were you not?

A. No. I had not interest in the oppression of the Jewish people. My law of 1935 was not called the law on oppression of the Jewish people, but merely the law for the protection and the safeguarding of German blood.

Q. You have reference to the Nuremberg laws?

A. Yes. I am referring to the Nuremberg Law through which the Jews lost their rights of citizenship.

Q. Will you tell me what you had to do with the promulgation of the Nuremberg laws?

A. The laws were worked out in the Ministry of the Interior, more exactly in the Health Division, because it was a matter of race, and these laws were formulated in closest contact with the office of the representative of the Fuehrer, Hess.

Q. When did the idea of the master race, as distinguished from the inferior race, come into the Party thinking?

A. It was not a matter of superiority, but merely a question of retaining the peculiar quality of the race, for it is an absolutely scientific truth that the product of a mixed marriage has certain defects that show themselves in reproduction and so forth, and it is for the self-protection of the people that you have to think of the purity of the race. That sort of thing is perfectly justified; just as any other nation, let's say, the Japanese, could go ahead and try to retain the purity of the Japanese race. In fact, the Jews themselves have always adhered to a very elaborate race doctrine and provided very severe punishment for mixed marriage, and also, as I am informed, the American government in its immigration laws adheres to the idea of a very definite quota of people from Nordic countries that can be admitted at one time. At any rate, it seems that the American government adheres to a sort of race conception also.

Q. Well, wouldn't it have been possible to control the marriage of the various races without depriving the Jewish people of their personal and political rights?

A. That is a chapter in itself, but actually such measures have been taken and marriages between Jews and gentiles were eventually forbidden.

Q. Well, do you take the position that the Party program as to the Jewish people is predicated merely on a marriage proposition and health measures?

A. Yes, for no other reason because there couldn't be any other reason, but the fact remains that the Jews in Germany failed to assimilate themselves within the body of the German people, and thus, there have been persecutions even in earlier centuries, and eventually the matter was made a matter of law . . .

Q. Dachau was the first concentration camp that was built in Germany, wasn't it?

A. Yes. That was the camp that Himmler started to build right away in 1933.

Q. How many concentration camps were there in 1936 when Himmler came into your organization?

A. Well, I don't know. The only one that I have seen was the one at Oranienburg. I visited that with Himmler in 1937 and found it absolutely in perfect shape. It was a model institution.

Q. Well, I didn't ask how many you had visited. How many were there in 1936 in numbers, whether you visited them or not?

A. I could not say at all exactly how many there were, because they were not an institution of the State, but they were on the Party budget, and were partly financed by the SS budget, and I was always forbidden from taking any sort of interest in these institutions, but I do know that most of them were created after the [outbreak of] war.[3]

Q. Well, approximately how many were there in 1936?

A. Well, I couldn't really say, because, as I say, I had never got any information on that particular topic and the thing was always withheld from me. I do remember the one in Oranienburg and the one in Dachau and I think there was one in the province of Saxony,[4] but I do know that to the very end I was told, and I was extremely upset about it, that there were all of eighty-three concentration camps in Germany, but this was towards the very end. We did not have any insight into the matter, because the entire affair was handled by the SS, and they refused us access or any control of the institutions.

Q. Well, you knew that in November of 1938 a large number of Jews were arrested and put into concentration camps, did you not?

A. No. It is absolutely new to me. I never was informed of that, and that must have been handled directly from Himmler to the Fuehrer or vice versa.

Q. I don't mean that you were officially informed of it by any Party or government organization, but did you have personal knowledge from general conversation on the subject?

A. No. Even as far as my private information is concerned, I did not know anything about such large numbers. I knew that occasionally individual Jews had been transported to concentration camps, but anything about these mass arrests is entirely new to me.

Q. Well, didn't you know about the mass arrests after 1938, such as 1940 and '41?

A. Well, I had learned, for instance, that the manager of the firm Aschinger had been arrested. This man was married to a gentile woman who was a friend of my wife, and so my wife told me about it. I went to Heydrich and asked him, 'What is the reason for arresting this man who is perfectly innocent, the only crime that he has committed being that he is a Jew?' And in this particular instance I obtained his release, but, as I say, I am informed only about individual cases and know nothing about mass arrests.

Q. When did you learn there were some eighty concentration camps in Germany?

A. That I heard last spring in Augsburg through the State Secretary in the Finance Ministry, Reinhardt. That was in May 1945, and he told me then that he had heard there were eighty-three concentration camps, and none of them had been in any way financed by the budget of the Reich. As I say, in spite of the fact that the function of the concentration camp is a function of civil law, the running of the camps was entirely in the hands of the Party, and the guards were not police, but SS.

Q. Assuming that you didn't have any official knowledge of these camps, do you, as Minister of the Interior and as head at least of the Order Police of the Third Reich, mean to say that there could be some seventy-five or eighty concentration camps constructed without your knowledge?

A. Yes. It may sound very surprising, just as the Colonel has pointed out this noon, but the fact remains that we did not have any more sectional responsibilities in our Ministries in spite of the fact that it would have been one of our particular concern[s], as that concern was taken away from us. The secrecy of this particular institution was the more strictly kept, because all the members of the SS were not only sworn, but they were also threatened, because they knew perfectly well if they ever revealed any information on the camps, they would be slapped into the camps themselves.

Q. I understand it is your position that you didn't have official connection with the construction of these camps, but I can't understand how you could build seventy-five or eighty camps housing hundreds of thousands of people and an ordinary citizen, let alone a cabinet member and an original Party member, not know that they were in existence. Can you explain that to me?

A. That is exactly the position that is very difficult for a member of a democratic system to understand that, for instance, I, as Reich Minister of the Interior, made my last report to the Fuehrer, I think, in 1937. It just must be pointed out that eventually the only persons that had sort of influence on Hitler were Bormann and Himmler and occasionally Goebbels, and the fact remains that those people who had any sort of share in these camps, were not only bound to utmost secrecy, but there was no freedom of the press and no freedom of speech, and how could a person, even a Reich Minister, find out?

Q. Perhaps Hitler or Bormann or Himmler didn't tell you about the camps, but it was common knowledge amongst the citizenry that these camps were in existence. How could you keep from learning it?

A. Perhaps it was known in the immediate vicinity, but how could it be passed on? It would be merely by accident, perhaps, that such news would be passed on, and certainly it never received any publicity.

Q. I might say that the waiter who waits on my table down at the hotel had several friends that were in these camps and it came to his attention from numerous sources that they were in existence. If he knew that that situation went on, it is beyond me to understand that a Cabinet member wouldn't have sufficient friends to at least advise him of it.

A. That there were concentration camps, we knew, because it was published that Himmler was building Dachau, but how many there were and how many people there [were] in them, that was far beyond our knowledge. I thought that maybe there might be a dozen or two, but I was absolutely floored when I was informed there were eighty-three.

Q. Well, you knew that Jews were being put into concentration camps for no other reason than the fact that they were Jews, did you not?

A. Well, that individual Jews were at times transferred to concentration camps we knew, and we didn't know exactly for what reasons, but then also it must be said that most of the camps were not within Germany, but in the Eastern territories, and what went on there was not known to us.

Q. Did you know that thousands upon thousands of people were killed in these concentration camps?

A. I had heard about it. I had heard rumors, but everything was very vague, and one couldn't make any investigation of that, because then immediately somebody would have said, 'Oh, he is sticking his nose into our business', or 'He is trying to spy on us.' Then some repressive measures would have been taken.

Q. You not only heard that people were being killed in concentration camps, but you also heard that there was a lot of them being built, didn't you?

A. Well, yes, that during the war camps were being built we were informed, but officially we never had any evidence. We never had any files. We never had any proof.

Q. Well, I think we will quit for today. We will go into this some more later, and if you have some things that you would like to state at a later date, I will be glad to hear from you.

A. I would like to have, if possible, some information on what the plans are, as I have been here now in detention since the 2 May. This is the second or third time that I have been up here for interrogation, but I have been cut off completely from all the news and the press, and so forth and if it were possible to get some idea as to what plans were for us, I'd appreciate it.

Q. I can't answer that question, because I am not making these decisions and my only purpose here is to interrogate you to establish facts. I assume you are telling the truth, and I am trying to find out the story, and that is a question that I can't answer and honestly don't know myself.

A. I would only like to state that at my age of almost sixty-nine years I simply couldn't be considered a dangerous person, and wonder whether it would not be possible to consider my release as being at your disposal and at liberty.

Q. That is something I don't have charge of, but we will see what develops on it.

Document 31 'talking in a dream'

Extracts from the interrogations of Joachim von Ribbentrop on 5 October,
7 October and 8 October 1945

I Testimony taken at Nuremberg by Mr Justice Robert H. Jackson on
5 October 1945. Colonel John H. Amen, Colonel Howard Brundage also
present. [Conducted in English.]

To the Witness by Mr Justice Jackson, in English

Q. I am Justice Jackson, and I have a letter which you addressed to me under the date of 2 October 1945, in which you make certain proposals. I want to ask you some questions about various statements in the letter, and I will tell you frankly why. We are to meet within the coming week to determine what we will do as to the indictment of yourself and others as war criminals, and I want your proposal in as definite form at the time I get to the meeting as I can have it. There are some things I want to ask you about because I don't understand just what your proposition involves . . . In your letter to me you say you are ready to supply information and to present objectively the course of foreign policy followed by the Fuehrer, in so far as this policy was evident to you, as his Foreign Minister. Do you imply by that, that you were not familiar with his foreign policy, or that any part of it was concealed from you?

A. I was familiar only with a certain part of his foreign policy. I never knew or heard at all of [from] him, or of [about] his final conception which he really has as to the formation and how the Reich, the definite Reich, was to be formed and so on . . .

Q. Do you mean to imply in your letter that you did not fully understand the foreign policy, and that the foreign policy was not imparted to you?

Joachim von Ribbentrop, German Foreign Minister from 1938 to 1945, was one of the few prisoners to collapse psychologically waiting for trial at Nuremberg. He suffered conscious memory loss and insisted that foreign policy had been carried out by Hitler. The outbreak of war he blamed on the British.

A. I must tell you quite frankly that apart from that which I just told you now, all the further aims of the Fuehrer which he might have had, and which I only heard during the interrogations here, and all the documents which were supposed to be in there, the Fuehrer never disclosed to us any of his definite big policy, or the future formation of the Reich. There was the question occasionally – not often, but once or twice he mentioned it, the idea of creating the Germanic Reich, the Gross-Germanic Reich was the idea, but he never revealed to me, you know, what this conception really meant, or what he understood by this conception. And I may say I have had the feeling all along that he was during the war – he said that once or twice – the military timetable of the General Staff came up, and he was driven to one decision after another. His conception later on was a very much larger one.

Q. Do you really want me to go back to my associates at this meeting and tell them that it is your position that as Foreign Minister of the Reich you didn't know what the foreign policy was?

A. I am sorry. I must say so. I am very sorry. The Fuehrer never revealed his definite aims to anybody.

Q. You say to me, on page 5 of your letter, that 'My goal as a diplomat was to attain diplomatically the goals of Germany.' Yet, you say now you didn't know what the goals were.

A. I mean, the goals that the Fuehrer disclosed to me.

Q. You mean the first steps?

A. Yes. These goals.

Q. Further than that you had no knowledge of the foreign policy of the Reich?

A. I personally don't think the Fuehrer had a real conception of it . . .

Q. You have asked me to do something about preventing these trials because you say you think the German people would think that any verdict or decision as to war criminals would be directed at them. I am interested to know how the German people could think it was directed at them, as a whole, when you yourself say you disagreed with the policy but couldn't do anything about it?

A. I think this: I think that this war has been so terrible, and I want so much my people to come to reconciliation – the German people with the other nations – especially also with the American nation.

Q. When did this war become terrible, Ribbentrop? When did this war impress you as terrible?

A. It became to me terrible – I can tell you the exact moment. From the moment of the African landings – I mean the English-American forces.[5]
Q. That is just about when I thought it began to affect you that way, and up to that time, when the destruction was going on in other people's countries, this war never impressed you as being terrible, or having any terrible aspects. There is nothing that happened to Germany that Germany didn't inflict on Warsaw, and tried to inflict on London, is there?
A. I may say this, that in Warsaw, I think the Fuehrer tried five or six times to make them see he doesn't [Ribbentrop, who was speaking in English, clearly meant 'does' here] want to get the civilian population out, and everything else; and as far as London is concerned, I may tell you I was personally very much against the bombing of London because I knew the English people and knew it would affect them exactly the way it did;[6] but, of course, I had nothing to say in it.
Q. But Ribbentrop, when you knew all these things, you knew the bombing of London wouldn't do any good and it would do Germany harm, and you knew the attitude of the Vatican, and you knew the attitude of the United States, and in other words, on your own statements, you knew Germany was running a course that was going to bring the whole world against her, as it did, and you let the German people in for this out of what you say is loyalty to the Fuehrer. Now you say to me that the German people, if they knew these facts, will think it is against them. It seems to me if the German people knew these facts, they are the people who would want to deal with you, and with the other men who led them into this, and I would like to know what you think about that.
A. That may be so. That may be so for the moment, yes. But I wonder – don't you think that in the long run that Germans condemned before a court of not Germans, would in the long run stand between the countries, no matter what it was? That is the question I am asking myself.
Q. I am not being interrogated. I don't happen to think that. It seems to me that the one thing that the German people need, is to know how you fellows went on this reckless course and you never warned the German people what they were getting into. It seems to me, if I may say so, and I don't want to be unpleasant about it, but it seems to me you would have more difficulty squaring your accounts with the

German people, than you would with the American people, because after all, we take care of ourselves. You are in the position of a man who, on the basis of your statements, knew that this was running amuck [sic] . . .

Now let us get back to the letter. You say on page 5, 'If the necessity for finding responsibility can be satisfied by the voluntary assumption of such a responsibility by myself, and perhaps by other co-workers of the Fuehrer, and in this manner the proposed trial of the Germans can be prevented, I stand ready to take such a step, as the former Foreign Minister of the Fuehrer, who is taking over the political responsibility of the men and women of our regime who were imprisoned here.' Whom do you have in mind as perhaps to take responsibility with yourself?

A. It is a very difficult question, which I have already asked. I have already thought about it, but I have not come really to a definite conclusion yet about it. But I should think that a number should be found.

Q. What do you have in mind taking responsibility for? What is your proposal?

A. I can't take any responsibility for criminal matters, but I thought of a political responsibility.

Q. Do you take responsibility for the war of aggression?

A. I couldn't do that for war of aggression.

Q. Are you willing to take responsibility for waging war in violation of treaties?

A. That is very important. May I think these questions over. They are very important questions. I have not thought about these details. What was my conception was that one would simply say, 'Here. These people have declared themselves responsible for the consequences,' or something like that.

Q. Are you willing to take any responsibility for the killing of American airmen?

A. No. I couldn't.

Q. Are you willing to take any responsibility for the deportations of slave labor? Of course you knew of that policy?

A. Yes, I knew. What I knew of that policy, I mean, what we did in that part was, for instance, bringing people – I mean it was on agreements with the governments made in these countries. That was our part we took in it.

Q. You mean, with Laval?[7]

A. With Laval, and with the Balkan countries, and with the various countries, we made agreements.

Q. Then you think there is no responsibility for that?

A. I beg your pardon?

Q. Then you think there is no responsibility for that?

A. Well, as far as we were informed, the Strength through Joy and the German Labor Front (words 'Strength through Joy and the German Labor Front' furnished by the interpreter) were taking care of that, and we even put people in there to get them synchronized, and propaganda, and that they have through their own people, the French and so on; and we considered that – I don't know of any other details about this.

Q. You don't take any responsibility for the policy of deportation of slave labor?

A. Slave labor? No.

Q. And you don't take any responsibility, I suppose, for the killing, or branding, or other mistreatment of Russian prisoners-of-war?

A. No. I couldn't.

Q. Do you take any responsibility for the killing of hostages?

A. No, I couldn't.

Q. Do you take any responsibility for the plunder of property, such as this Rosenberg looting of cultural shrines?[8]

A. No. That I can't.

Q. You had nothing to do with that?

A. No.

Q. And you wouldn't take any responsibility for the destruction of the Warsaw ghetto?

A. No. I can't do that.

Q. Nor for the bombing of Rotterdam?

A. No.

Q. The destruction of Lidice.[9] You wouldn't take any responsibility for that?

A. No.

Q. And I suppose you take no responsibility for the concentration camps?

A. No. I can't.

Q. Nor for the extermination policy against Jews?

A. You mean for these criminal things? I can't.

Q. And you take no responsibility for the persecution of the churches?

A. No.

Q. How many Jews were exterminated, in your estimation?

A. I have not the slightest idea. I don't know at all. I only heard them, as I told you, the first time at Maidanek, and then after the breakdown, through the radio, when I was before being taken prisoner.

Q. Have you any idea whether it is a large number or a small number?

A. I don't know at all. I couldn't tell you. I have not the slightest idea.

Q. Would it surprise you to know that more than four and one-half million Jews were exterminated?

A. That is not possible.

Q. Why is it not possible?

A. That is not possible.

Q. What makes you say it is not possible?

A. That must have been propaganda. It is quite out of the question.

Q. If you are able to show me any reason why that is not true, I would like to know it. How many Jews were there in Germany at the time the program of extermination started?

A. I think we had in Germany altogether 400,000 Jews.

Q. How many are there left?

A. I don't know.

Q. You don't know of many, do you?

A. I can't tell you. I don't really know, I must say . . .

Q. Do you take any responsibility for the Gestapo, secret police, and their handling of prisoners?

A. No. I couldn't do that.

Q. What about the SS? Do you take any responsibility for what they did?

A. I don't know what you are hinting at? What you mean by that, I don't know?

Q. Their whole course of treatment of civilians in other countries, and their treatment of American prisoners?

A. Well I –

Q. In other words, you take no responsibility for any war crime, or crimes of any kind?

A. Crimes, I can't take. But may I say this. I mean I assure you that the Geneva Convention – we have held that Geneva Convention up as much as we possibly could.

Q. Ribbentrop, I am sorry to disagree with you because I would rather be pleasant than disagreeable, but unless all of the proof in this case, coming from your own people, is not to be believed, the Geneva Convention was flagrantly violated. But the point is, you take no responsibility for anything that is criminal. Aside from that you are willing to take responsibility. Is that the point?

A. (No answer)

Q. Your offer to me does not include taking any responsibility for anything that is classed as a war crime, or a crime of any character. Is that right?

A. That was my idea. No crime.

Q. So that, if we are in a position to prove crimes, your offer doesn't reach that situation at all, does it?

A. That, of course, is right. Yes. But I thought one could, perhaps, find some other way to prevent these proceedings, if a number of people declared themselves responsible, and say a statement being made about it, and not holding the proceedings then.

Q. And then the world would forget all that I have called your attention to, such as these concentration camps and deportations and killing of American prisoners? . . .

Q. If you took responsibility, as you propose, what was your idea of the penalty that should be imposed?

A. I have not thought about that. I don't know.

Q. What are you prepared to suggest as appropriate?

A. I would leave this entirely to the other side.

Q. I think that is all.

II Interrogation of Joachim von Ribbentrop taken at Nuremberg on
7 October 1945 by Colonel John H. Amen [also present Lord Wright,
President of the UNWCC]

Colonel Amen to the Witness in English

Q. Have you been thinking over the testimony which you gave before Mr Justice Jackson the other day?

A. Yes, I have been thinking about it, yes.

Q. Have you reached any conclusions, one way or the other, about any of the matters concerning which he questioned you?

A. Which ones are you referring to?

Q. None in particular. I just want to know if you have any comments to make, or any change of mind, or any thoughts based upon that conversation?

A. I have, so far, not come to any further conclusion. I have talked yesterday with Colonel Brundage about it, but I have not come to any further conclusion about it. I am still thinking about what might be done.

Q. You recall, do you not, that all of the matters which he mentioned, such as the concentration camps, and slave labor, and killing of the Russians, and killing of aviators, were all matters which were brought to your personal attention in one way or another?

A. You mean, he mentioned it?

Q. No. I say, do you now concede that all of those matters were brought to your attention at the time they were happening?

A. Oh, no. That is not right . . .

Q. Killing of Allied aviators?

A. No. No.

Q. You are not trying to say that was not brought to your attention, are you?

A. What do you mean exactly, please?

Q. The killing of Allied aviators that landed behind the lines. The orders that have been brought to your attention repeatedly, one day after another.

A. You mean, what you told me the other day?

Q. I don't tell you things. I show you orders. That is not telling you something. You saw the orders about the killing of aviators, didn't you?

A. Yes, I saw the order.

Q. Now, I say, you concede that they were brought to your attention, don't you?

A. No. I am sorry. I did not know.

Q. I showed you the correspondence about the Foreign Office having to approve them, did I not?

A. No, I am sorry. It is different. I could not speak very well the other day.

Q. What do you mean, you could not speak very well the other day?

A. Well, I wanted to explain, but I did not have the chance.

Q. I did not let you explain?

A. I did not have the chance.

Q. Did not I keep asking you if you had anything further to say about it, that was in answer to the question?

A. Well, I wanted to say –

Q. Have you got anything to say now, which I didn't let you say the other day?

A. I think I can explain it.

Q. All right, say it.

A. As far as – I am sorry, I don't recollect it exactly, but I can tell you the situation.

Q. How can you tell me it, if you don't recollect it?

A. I mean, I don't recollect this special meeting you were talking about.

Q. That is the trouble. You keep saying, 'I don't recollect, but I will tell you anyway', and that does not make any sense.

A. I can tell you, if I don't recollect, the way I think this whole thing –

Q. No. That is not very interesting to us, unless you can recall something specific. After all, you held a very important position.

A. I can recall one or two things.

Q. Tell us what you recall.

A. I will tell you exactly the way the situation was. The situation was that the Fuehrer had been pressing very hard on these aviation matters on us all here, for some time. I could explain the whole situation. It was that there were thousands of women and children killed every day by bombing.

Q. There have been, yes, through the war.

A. Yes. That was the whole situation and the Fuehrer was pressing very hard.

Q. What are you talking about? German women and children, or are you talking about other women and children?

A. No. German women and children.

Q. You don't think they are the only ones who were killed during this war, do you?

A. No. I know that, but I know one attack at Dresden, 40,000 women and children were killed.

Q. So the ratio the Germans worked out was that they would try to kill

50 to 1. You know that, don't you? Every time a German was killed, they said they were going to kill 50 Allies, is that right?

A. No.

Q. You never heard about this?

A. No. I am sorry.

Q. I have not shown you those letters yet?

A. No. I haven't seen them.

Q. I will show them to you tomorrow, but go ahead.

A. I wanted to tell you, that was the situation. Now, this matter – I have the whole time in this question been always for finding something of why wilful bombing on women and children should be done, but the Fuehrer was pressing hard, and he said I should think about something that should be acceptable under the Geneva Convention. That was the general idea which we – I, of the Foreign Office, had. Now, at this meeting of what I conceived probably happened – that was not a meeting but it was a casual meeting; we had not a real meeting; it was a State function of the Fuehrer. Then it was very probable I said something during this meeting.

Q. You say it is very probable. Did it happen? Are you telling me something that may have happened, or something that actually happened?

A. I cannot recollect it.

Q. Then don't tell me about it. Maybe the Lord Chancellor [Amen meant the President of the UNWCC] would like to ask you some questions about that?

A. I think, Colonel, it is very important that you should know –

Q. Yes, but not when you say 'probably'. The minute you say 'probably', it makes all your testimony worthless, because anything is probable, and anything is possible. I mean, I want you to talk facts. You always say, 'maybe', or 'possibly', or 'possible', and that makes it all worthless.

A. Yes, but what can I do if I don't remember exactly.

Q. You can stick to the things that you know about. Something that you are willing to say definitely; do you understand?

A. All right. I can say this, for instance. You see, if this casual – if this talk there – I must have said during this –

Q. You see. That is another point. That is of no interest to anybody, 'I must have said'. It is just like somebody talking in a dream.

A. Then I won't talk about that. One thing I can tell you. It was later on. All that went on at this meeting was not discussed with myself. I got probably Ritter and told him to get a report –

Q. 'Probably Ritter'; what good does that do anyone?

A. Yes, but it must have been so that Ritter got the order from me to make a written report on this whole matter in the sense that something legal shall be found, and announced probably about the wilful bombing of women and children. This matter, it was reported to me through this, in this letter which you showed me, and I thought it important enough, and it only struck me later, after the second thing you showed me, that evidently I did not want to take the responsibility, and I said, 'It must be shown to the Fuehrer.' Now I do recollect something. I think the Fuehrer – I was not quite sure whether it was this one, but one of these matters in aviation, the Fuehrer turned the whole thing down and said, 'It is absolutely nonsense, this legal thing.' That I do remember.

Q. He turned it down? The order was signed to kill on the spot all Allied aviators that landed behind the lines?

A. I never seen an order like that.

Q. 'I never seen'; you saw an order like that, and you know all about it, and you discussed it and communicated about it, and it is ridiculous for you to say you never knew it.

A. I never knew this.

By Lord Wright

Q. You say you never knew of orders to kill Allied aviators?

A. I never knew of an order.

Q. Did you think that such a thing was being done?

A. I heard once or twice that there have been lunchings [lynchings] once or twice. Once or twice I heard that, but other than that I knew nothing about it. Never.

By Colonel Amen

Q. Once or twice you heard about it?

A. About lunching [lynching], yes.

Q. When was the first time you heard about it? You know perfectly well you are just talking nonsense. All right, tell me the two times you heard about it. Tell me the two occasions, the 'once or twice' when you heard about it.

A. I don't know.

Q. You don't know anything about it? It may be somebody told you about it? Is that right?

A. How should I remember this.

Q. I don't know how you should remember it. You don't remember anything. That is obvious. But I am hoping that some day you will see how ridiculous it is to sit here and make all these 'ifs', 'ands', 'buts', and 'maybe's', and to say nothing, because it won't help you in the trial. You have got to find some kind of a story and stick to it. Your position now is that you don't know anything about anything, except what you heard through some third or fourth person.

A. That is correct.

Q. It could not be the truth. You could not occupy the position you occupied and have that true.

A. It was so. I was occupying it.

Q. It was not so, and you know it was not so.

A. I can assure you it was.

Q. I have the proof setting [sitting] right in my desk to show it was not true. Letters written by people you know. I can't show you everything we have. I ask you, to see if maybe some day you will tell the truth about something. You have not yet, and I hope you will begin soon, because if you don't, it will be too late. Then you write letters, and say you want to assume responsibility, and then when Justice Jackson asks you what you want to assume responsibility for, it turns out it is nothing except the fact that you held a political position which, obviously, you could not dismiss anyhow. Is that right? I mean, after all, you did occupy that position. That is the one thing you can't say, 'if', 'and', or 'but' about. But that is the only thing you admit so far. Is that true? Specifically, I mean. Everything else is purely conjecture. Is that right? Anyhow, that is all for today.

III Extract from the interrogation of Joachim von Ribbentrop taken at
Nuremberg on 8 October 1945 by Colonel Howard Brundage (from pp. 31–
41 of the original transcript)

Q. As you review the situation, don't you agree that what you call a
difficulty is merely that you bumped up against a proprietor, and when
you ask him for his land, he says no, then that was a justification for
invading? Doesn't that look like the record to you then?

A. Well, [I] can say one thing, Colonel: the original proposal of the
Fuehrer to the Poles was really very reasonable, the proposal with
Danzig and the Corridor; it was very reasonable.

Q. I am now trying to get your opinion after the fact. In other words,
you are now able to sit down and review the whole record and see
just what actually did happen. What you call negotiations merely
amounted to Germany making demands, and if there wasn't acceptance of those demands, then it meant invading the country.

A. Well, in Poland, for instance, we had lost, hadn't we? We had lost
all that through Versailles.[10]

Q. You say the Poles got stiff and said no. That was the reason you
invaded; Yugoslavia the same; Norway the same. You can go down
the whole list. In other words, here is a man with great power that
would call somebody in and tell him what he wanted and say 'We are
willing to negotiate', but if the other fellow didn't negotiate, that meant
war. Is not that the fact?

A. Well, I wouldn't put it that way, really.

Q. Well, you are able to see the record just as well as I am. How else
would you put it?

A. I think it was with Poland that the Fuehrer had made reasonable
offers and he saw that the Poles didn't go and didn't march at all, and
he saw that the English stood against it. You see, I will tell you
something. For instance, when I went to Russia, I personally had also
a certain hope that our Russian non-aggression pact [August 1939]
which we made with the Russians, you see having the alliance with
Italy, would bring Polish agreement diplomatically.

Q. Let's look at the record. You made a pact with Russia, and then you
broke it, because you said that they were massing troops on the border,
installing large supplies and materials, and having trouble with their

troops, so you attacked Russia. Is that not the constant record as you review it?

A. Well, the Fuehrer decided that. You know, I told you that I was at the beginning very much against that and afterwards also tried very hard to adjust things, but I could not disclose myself for the reasons that the Fuehrer also, of course –

Q. That isn't responsive. I want to know if, as you review all these separate instances where there were pacts made with countries, followed very soon by invasion and war, if you don't find that in every instance the war was started because of some intelligence that was brought in, or some rumor, and was what you might call a defensive war, but in fact it was a mere breaking of the treaties?

A. If the Fuehrer were here, he would answer you that all these steps which he had to take were in the interests of the people out of self-preservation.

Q. Irrespective of his treaties?

A. That he would answer, yes.

Q. What is your answer?

A. It is very difficult, you know.

Q. Well, it isn't so difficult.

A. The Polish question is really very simple.

Q. This is a case of what we call second guessing now, you know. This is after the game is over and you can sit back, and it is very easy to tell what mistakes were made. All I am trying to do is to develop whether or not you consider those things to be mistakes.

A. Well, the result is, of course, disastrous; there is no doubt about that. What would have happened, Colonel –

Q. Take every case where you made a treaty with a country, a non-aggression pact or a pact of co-operation, and in almost every case, shortly after the treaty was made, for one reason or another, the German army marched into that country. Now I want to find out from you whether or not you think that these moves that were made based upon mere rumor or intelligence of some kind were not a mistake in the handling of the policy of that government?

A. It is very difficult for me to answer that, Colonel, because one can't take – I think the Polish question was simply a question, you see – the moment –

Q. We have been over that. That is merely a question where you asked for something and the Poles said no.

A. They said no, yes.

Q. That is all that amounted to. Now let's take another instance. How about the Russian situation? You had a non-aggression pact with the Russians and still you attacked them.

A. Take the Russian situation. You see, there were these, not rumors, but they were not rumors, of course, but they were very, very clear reports about these Russian military displays. I think our military people can tell you about that. I mean, the Fuehrer told me then also already in the first conversation about his concern about it, you see. There were most definite reports, no doubt, about it. There were, of course, also most definite tendencies. I mean, there has been the question of Bukovina and Bessarabia.[11] Then, of course, something else which played a role was this: Communistic propaganda was being made in Germany, which agitated the Fuehrer very much. There was furthermore a pact made with the government of Serbia . . . Something very important which also came in there, and I don't know today, really, where the Fuehrer got this from, but you know that the Russian–English relations, of course, I mean the English will tell you more about this – I don't know, of course – they were never interrupted, since our non-aggression pact. There has been the visit of an English statesman in Moscow,[12] and I think what made the Fuehrer also dread and what made him decide, apart from all the military display and all that, to make a march was the idea that he might be confronted with an invasion from the West and at the same time an attack from Russia from the East.

Q. But didn't he make sure of that when he attacked Russia?

A. Pardon me?

Q. Didn't he make sure of that when he attacked Russia? He removed all doubt when he went to war with Russia that he was going to have a two-front war.

A. Yes . . .

Q. I want you to understand that these questions I am asking you have no particular importance, except that I would like to get from you, for the purposes of the historical record, just where you think these mistakes were made. First, of course, I am interested in the whole broad picture, which is the making of treaties and then very shortly thereafter invading the country on one pretext or another.

A. Well, I can only answer this, Colonel: the Fuehrer absolutely had made up his mind to settle the Polish question somehow. Troops were already marching. When I asked him, he stopped it again. We tried again to treat with Great Britain – do you remember that – afterwards to come [to] an arrangement, but Britain didn't do that. After the war started, I think it is the timetable of the General Staff, and one can't call it differently. What was the situation after Poland? France and England declared war on us. We were standing in the West. Then came this news that they were going to Norway. The Fuehrer was very much afraid of Norway and Denmark, you see, and here he said, 'This would be disastrous for us. We have no more Swedish iron and all that. We can't go on with this war.' I mean, that is one link after another, I think, that was made.

Q. Can you explain that after you got into those countries, that you took them over, lock, stock and barrel? You don't go in merely to keep the British out, you go in to get all the Germans in . . .

A. Well, of course, you mean using the country? Well, of course, then there was the idea of war potential. Using it for war purposes.

Q. Is that in your opinion good faith on the part of the sovereign state?

A. May I tell you something, Colonel?

Q. Don't tell me anything until I first get your opinion. I want to know what you think is the ethical situation, and let's take Norway as the subject. Do you think the treatment that the German sovereign state gave to Norway after it invaded it only because it thought the British were going into Norway, was that ethically proper treatment?

A. Ethically?

Q. Yes, from the standpoint of ethics.

A. Politics and ethics?

Q. I think a country should have some regard to ethics. Don't you think so?

A. Oh, yes.

Q. You are in a position now where you can review the situation.

A. War is a terrible thing, Colonel.

Q. Yes, I know that.

A. In Denmark we did, you see, for instance, in Denmark we went in. The Danes didn't resist. The Norwegians fought against us which was their good right; I don't blame them for it, because we went in there, but of course, we were at war with Norway. Denmark didn't resist. We went into the country. I didn't like it very much. It was not very pleasant to have to do it, you see, but we kept good relations with Denmark . . .

Q. However, what was the reason you went into Denmark?

A. The same reason, of course.

Q. What?

A. The fear of landing. The fear of landing, Denmark and Norway.

Q. Would you like to express an opinion as to whether that whole operation in its broad sense was a good one or a bad one?

A. (Pause.)

Q. Not from the standpoint of results, but from the standpoint of moral and ethical conduct.

A. I can't answer that question, you know, so simply, because there is such a lot of harm that had been done to us, of course, with Poland. I don't know whether you know the whole story of the German–Polish relations during the last twenty years, you see. That is where the whole thing started, isn't it?

Q. Yes, that is where it started.

A. And then England and France invaded – I mean not invaded – but they declared war on Germany. That is the way it all went.

Q. Well, let's talk about that for a minute. This is not too important, that we are talking about. You started an invasion on [of] Poland and you know, I told you about the border incidents where they sent four companies to the border and they injected poison into twelve inmates of concentration camps and dressed them in German uniforms and left them there. I also told you about the attack on the German radio station, where they left a dead body in civilian clothes with Polish identification papers on it, merely manufactured incidents so as to give some excuse for going to war against Poland. Now, that being the first important move, and admitting those facts to be true, don't you say that the operation was a bad one?

A. I most certainly don't like these details that you told me.

Q. Whether you like them or not, is that ethical conduct on the part of a sovereign state in your opinion.

A. Has that really been done? Is that proved?

Q. Oh, yes.

A. That seems to be so extraordinary.

Q. You know Mueller of the SS?

A. Whom?

Q. Mueller.

A. There was a Mueller there, I guess.

Q. He was Heydrich's man.

A. Yes, there was a Mueller there.

Q. They took twelve men out of concentration camps and the doctor gave them an injection and they used the bodies in connection with these incidents. That is true. That is the fact.

A. (Pause.)

Q. You would rather the record would show that after having a chance to think all these things over, that you don't care to express an opinion as to whether the conduct of Germany through the course of events that have taken place was proper or improper conduct?

A. Well, I am sure of one thing Colonel, that the Fuehrer did these things out of what he thought was out of self-preservation of his people. I mean that is what he thought.

Q. That is why a hold-up man goes out at night with a gun so as to take valuables away from somebody else; it is all in self-preservation. That isn't any reason.

Document 32 'very undesirable activities'

Interrogation of General Heinz Guderian taken at Nuremberg on
5 November 1945 by Major-General Alexandrov and a member of his staff

The Soviet Interpreter to the Witness

Q. You are informed that you are being interrogated by General Alexandrov, head of the Soviet Delegation. The Interpreter has been informed that she is responsible for a faithful translation, according to law.

What is your name?

A. Guderian.

Q. Your first name?

A. Heinz.

Q. What was your official position at the time when the war against the Soviet Union started?

Colonel-General Heinz Guderian became Chief-of-Staff of German forces on the eastern
front in 1944. He insisted with other military leaders that the army bore no responsibility
for atrocities, despite the massive evidence gathered by Soviet authorities to the contrary.

A. I was Commander of Panzer Group No. 2.

Q. In your statement of 11 September, 1945, you claimed no official
instructions had been issued to you as to the treatment of the Russian
population, and that you had already available to you an order by the
OKW dealing with this question –

A. That is not what I stated.

Q. What then was your statement?

A. I had an order from the OKW about the treatment of the civilian population and of prisoners-of-war. To this order by the OKW there was an annex from the OKH signed by Brauchitsch, and I did not pass on this order to my subordinate units.

Q. What was the date of this order and what were the instructions contained therein?

A. The date of the order is not known to me. I don't remember it any more; it is too long ago. This order had been received by us before the start of the operations.[13]

Q. What operations are you talking about?

A. I am referring to the operations against the Soviet Union. This order contained changes of the general policy concerning the treatment of civilian populations and would have led to considerable damage to discipline in the German army. This order granted German soldiers liberties which could easily have led to excesses.

Q. What changes are you talking about?

A. I am talking about the changes which ran counter to the provisions of the Geneva Convention. The supplement by Field Marshal Brauchitsch indicated that even the OKH did not like the new provisions, and it appeared that the OKH did not desire that the order be complied with. As a result I did not take the order with me into the field and did not distribute it. Therefore Panzer Group No. 2 treated the civilian population in conformance [sic] with the Geneva Convention and International Law.

Q. Can we say that throughout the entire activities of Panzer Group No. 2 under your command International Law and the provisions of the Geneva Convention were complied with?

A. I commanded the Second Panzer Group for six months. During these six months I learned of only about one case where two soldiers violated provisions of International Law. They were members of a service unit. I did not approve the sentence against these two soldiers, which was rather mild, and I ordered capital punishment against them. Otherwise, I had proof that the conduct of our Group was correct, and this was confirmed to me by the civilian population. During those six months I never learned about any excesses perpetrated by the civilian population; therefore I had no reason not to be correct in my policies.

Q. How do you know that Field Marshal Brauchitsch did not want this order passed on to the troops?

A. I inferred from the supplement by the OKH to OKW's order that Brauchitsch did not feel very happy about it.

Q. Would you tell us now what in particular in this order was not in conformance with International Law.

A. I could not give you the details any more. The gist of the order was that in case of any resistance on the part of the civil population or the prisoners-of-war this resistance should be broken without [with] armed might and without any consideration for the people who might be affected. The order was formulated in such a manner that excesses on the part of our own troops could not have been prevented. This is why I did not distribute the order.

Q. Did I understand you correctly that you did not approve of this order?

A. I considered this order as harmful and did not pass it on for that reason.

Q. Did you consider this order as criminal?

A. It could have led to criminal action.

Q. Was this order issued to the entire army and not just to you as Commander of Panzer Group No. 2?

A. I don't know. I don't know what the other armies did. As for my own command, I know the order never reached my troops.

Q. I am asking you whether the order of the OKW was addressed to the entire army or whether it was addressed particularly to you?

A. In any case it must have been addressed to all armies in the East.

Q. How was it possible, in view of the discipline in the German army, for you to refuse to pass on an order from the High Command?

A. That is correct. I wanted to maintain discipline in my army and I wanted to prevent any criminal excesses.

Q. Would you look at these orders of the OKW. I am calling your attention to the order of 13 May 1941,[14] concerning military jurisdiction in connection with the Plan Barbarossa –

A. (The witness examined the document.)

Q. I am also showing to you an OKW order of 16 September 1941, dealing with the Communist Resistance Movement[15] –

A. (Examining the document) – I don't recall this order (indicating the first document), and this (the second document) is the order to which my statements refer. This other order I do not recall. It is possible, in view of the war of movement in which we were engaged and in view of the isolation in which I found myself, that it did not reach me or that I did not read it.

Q. How do you evaluate these orders?

A. In reference to this order, I would say again, that it could only lead to actions which could make things worse instead of improving them, but I repeat again, that there was no trouble with the civilian population in my army and that therefore I had no occasion to apply any such instructions.

Q. Would you say then that such orders on the part of the OKW sanctioned criminal actions by German troops?

A. I could not imagine that any army chief with a sense of dignity would execute any such orders unless there were compelling reasons for his doing so, and I have never learned in conversations with my colleagues that any reprisals of this nature were ever applied.

Q. There were a number of commanders who not only complied with these orders but went even further.

A. I didn't hear of any such thing.

Q. There is ample evidence on bestiality and mass atrocities perpetrated by German troops in the occupied territories in the East. Don't you think that such orders made it possible for German troops to conduct themselves in this criminal way?

A. As I said, I have not heard that any criminal actions on the part of the armed forces were committed. I did hear rumors about very undesirable activities on the part of police forces in rear areas.

Q. Did you, yourself, at the front witness the senseless destruction of cities and villages?

A. I have already stated that throughout my activities I heard only about one such incident and there I enforced severe punishment. As far as I know, my troops were never guilty of any senseless destruction.

Q. If my memory is correct, your subsequent position was chief-of-staff of the OKH?

A. I became chief-of-staff of the OKH on 20 July 1944.

Q. And after that did you not receive reports on the conduct of the armed forces in occupied territory?

A. I did not receive any reports of any excesses on the part of the armed forces. If I had heard about them I would have seen to it that they were punished.

Q. In all of your statements you always confine yourself to the area of responsibility of your subordinate armies.

A. I answered the question about the order of 13 May 1941, in stating what effect it had on my Panzer Group No. 2 because I was in command there until the end of December, 1941. Then for fourteen months I did not hold any command.

Q. But your position in the German army, in which you later on acquired the position of chief-of-staff of OKH, should have given you access to information about the German armed forces in the occupied territory; your information should have gone beyond the activities of your own Panzer Group.

A. Subsequent to 20 July 1944, I did have access to all information on the armed forces in the East, but this was confined to the operational zones and did not include the rear areas. The rear areas were not under army control; they had a civil administration.[16]

Q. But orders are written in order to be complied with?

A. I did not understand this question.

Q. We are talking about orders of the OKW pertaining to the conduct of German armed forces in occupied territory; in this connection I am asking you, aren't orders written in order to be complied with?

A. That's right.

Q. And we have ample proof in the form of documents and other evidence, that these orders were executed by the German army.

A. But I have nothing to add to this, because I don't know any more.

Q. Who do you consider is responsible for the issuing of such criminal orders?

A. Hitler.

Q. Only Hitler?

A. Yes.

Q. How about the High Command of the armed forces?

A. There is no doubt but that in giving these orders the OKW was complying with Hitler's instructions. I don't know what discussions preceded these orders; I was not with the OKW.

Q. But you yourself felt that you should ignore these orders?

A. I considered it my duty.

Q. How about those who did not think it was their duty to ignore these orders?

A. Unfortunately I had no jurisdiction over them. I regret it.

Q. But don't you think that they are responsible together with Hitler?

A. It is not up to me to determine now who is responsible. If I were a President of a German Court I would do so.

Q. I want to know your opinion.

A. My opinion is revealed in my actions. I considered it as harmful to pass this order to my subordinate units, and I failed to pass on these orders in order to maintain discipline in my command.

Q. In view of the fact that these orders were issued by Generals Keitel and Jodl, I want to know how you feel about these Generals.

A. I have already informed the Tribunal of my opinion. General Keitel is basically a decent character. He was absolutely overpowered by Hitler's personality, and he considered it as his duty to approve of everything that Hitler said. I never had occasion to observe that he would oppose Hitler in anything. I think that these orders were issued because people did not have sufficient sense to realize what they would lead to. It was not meanness but lack of judgement. General Jodl was a very conscientious and hard-working General Staff officer. He was a very reserved personality. He kept very much to himself and did not have many contacts with other people. He was also very strongly under the influence of Hitler. He would maintain his own views and oppose Hitler only on rare occasions.

Q. What was your personal attitude toward the German aggression against the Soviet Union?

A. When I learned about the attack on the Soviet Union I felt it was the greatest misfortune that could befall Germany.

THE INTERPRETER That is all.

Germany's Future

Taking a long view there are definite possibilities for solving the German–European problem . . . I can envisage an economic solution of the social and economic problem of central Europe only as a systematic depopulation through colonial emigration. In order not to endanger natural sentiments of other states only the west coast of Africa can be considered as a possibility . . . It has the great advantage that it gives to the German people the hope of progress for their children. The western powers . . . have only this one possibility to incorporate in the western world the mass of German nationals. If this course is not followed the eastern world, which affords ample space and natural opportunities, will in time absorb the mass of the German nation.

Interrogation of Hjalmar Schacht, FIAT
Evaluation Report 241, 31 July 1945[1]

[During the summer of 1945 certain of the major criminals were sought out by the Allied interrogators for their views on the reconstruction and reform of post-war Germany. Given the sorry position in which the prisoners now found themselves, it is surprising how willing they were to present advice. The chief contributors were Albert Speer, Hjalmar Schacht, Walther Funk and Robert Ley, all of whom had experience in economic and social policy. Ley wrote a lengthy memorandum on house building in the ruined cities which is reproduced here. Though the document is highly technical in nature, it is of interest both as an example of just how willing former ministers were to maintain a semblance of their former responsibilities, and of their desire to salvage something from the wreckage of the Reich. Schacht wrote the longest and fullest accounts, ranging right across the many elements of the German problem as he saw it – the exaggerated militarism and xenophobia, the concentration of economic power in mammoth industrial trusts, the sacrifice of traditional social values, the stifling of individual initiative in the name of the state. The most important of Schacht's reports provides a fitting conclusion to the interrogations. Schacht was a conservative and a patriot. His interpretation of German ills was rooted in the past; his call for a shift of population back to the land, the revival of artisan trades and the resurrection of Christian values and a sound social order are echoes from the days of the Kaiser. Schacht believed that what had most aggravated German sensibilities was the absence of a colonial empire to match those of Britain and France. His solution to the German problem was simple: colonies in Africa. Here German technical energies could be diverted from 'thinking of military equipment and armament' to more harmless problems of 'tropical and sub-tropical traffic . . . fight against diseases, acclimatisation etc.'.[2] Schacht was apparently unaware of the extent to which the colonial empires were in terminal decline by 1945. Full admission to the club of imperial powers would, he argued, prevent post-war Germany from remaining 'a festering sore in Europe'.[3]

The Allies, too, were determined to avoid this prospect. They worried about the 'moral rehabilitation' of the German people and

devised worthy programmes of re-education. The censors in the occupied zones sent selected letters to the Allied authorities to illustrate the
latent threat of National Socialist revival. One letter, sent two years
after the end of the war, opens a remarkable window on to the
nature of the Third Reich and the millions of ordinary Germans who
supported it:

... we haven't deserved these blasts of fate ... But it is too late. The best
people are gone, above all those who should be the leaders of our young
people. Mutual trust is lacking. How those who wanted the best were betrayed
and deceived. Now, Alfried, we must show that the spirit of those days is not
dead. Trouble and want bind us closer together. We must go on living, for
our life's work for the young people has not yet succeeded and must be
carefully sifted. My boys are enthusiastic about the camp life of those days
and think wistfully of those times. There are thousands of different opinions
re A.H. here. I myself spoke to a U-boat sailor, who says that 2 boats of his
flotilla were set aside which took him to SP [Spain?]. One of the two, either
88 [code for Hitler] or M.B. [Bormann] is said to have lost a leg. Even English
people are of the opinion that both are alive. I can well believe that 88 was
mentally or physically broken. Is it surprising? ... But fanaticism will come
again. I too was despairing ... but today in spite of poverty, restrictions and
work I am very satisfied, when I feel my head will burst I go to the old,
faithful fighters and we give each other courage. My boys are with an old PG
[Parteigenosse = Party comrade] getting their bellies filled again. I myself go
once a week to a very good comrade to eat. It is the old true comradely spirit
of the SA. How I think back to that unity.[4]

These were by no means isolated sentiments. The British authorities
collected a whole album of such letters for circulation which they
titled *Aus deutschen Urkunden* [from German sources]. The British
programme of moral rehabilitation was targeted at youth. Those, like
the author of the letter, were part of the 'parents and older folk'
regarded by the Control Commission officials responsible for re-
education as the 'hard-bitten Germans'.[5] In March 1946 one British
official observed that what all Germans needed to adjust to the post-
war world was butter instead of guns: 'if we are to make war unpopular,
we have to give the Germans something to put in its place. To have
any value, a substitute has to be tangible and of day-to-day utility.
Things of day-to-day utility are connected with food, clothing, shelter

and transportation'.[6] Vengeance was far less in evidence. At the height of the Nuremberg Trial, in February 1946, it was recommended by the secretary of the Sub-Commission on Rehabilitation that 'Our policy must also be framed so that the Nazis in our midst can have a feeling of hope'.[7]]

Document 33   Rebuilding the Reich

Extracts from SHAEF Interrogation Report, 8 July 1945:
Dr Robert Ley, 'Ideas on the Reconstruction of Housing in Germany'.

SECRET
DR ROBERT LEY
IDEAS ON THE RECONSTRUCTION OF HOUSING
IN GERMANY

I Source

Name: Dr Ley, Robert
Rank: Reich Commissioner for Housing, Leader of DAF
Interned: 15 May 45
Interrogated: 7 July 45

II Preamble

Dr Robert Ley, during a recent interrogation, requested the permission to write up his ideas on a Reconstruction Program for Housing in Germany. The permission was granted on the basis that such a prepared paper could contain information of intelligence value, and at the same time be of vital interest to all persons and offices concerned with the reconstruction of Germany.

This report was written by Dr Ley, and then translated verbatim, and arranged in report form by 'Ashcan'.

III. Dr Ley's Reconstruction Program

A. General Considerations

1. Scope of Task

The volume of the task at hand is composed of three parts:
  Reconstruction of destroyed towns and villages
  Reconstruction of destroyed industrial installations
  Reconstruction of destroyed traffic lanes.
Only approximate estimates can be made in the absence of precise figures. According to the reference material available to me as Reich Commissioner for Housing just before my internment, about one third of all living quarters were destroyed completely, amounting to a damage of about RM 100 milliards [billion]; damage to industry: about RM 20 milliards; damage to traffic lanes: about RM 10 milliards. Thus the entire cost of reconstruction would be RM 130 milliards, not considering irreplaceable losses of cultural and art monuments. A comparison with the reconstruction of the German armed forces in 1933–39, for which RM 90 milliards[8] were spent in more than six years, encourages me to assert that the present reconstruction job can be amply accomplished in ten years. At that time (1933–39) the German people was [were] out of the habit of work because of the preceding unemployment, was [were] irritable, disunited, and unaccustomed to grand-scale jobs, hence listless. Today it has been educated to highest efficiency and to a long-range, communal outlook; no job is big enough to discourage it. As long as the German people is [are] properly led it will cause no disappointment. Hence my unlimited optimism even in today's catastrophe, which makes me foretell a reconstruction in a matter of ten years, although about a year ago I submitted a plan for only five years' duration to the Fuehrer.

2. Construction Prerequisites

I realize that my proposal must be executed on purely capitalistic basis, i.e. through investment of interest-bearing capital. I can see no more secure and profitable investment for the capital now undoubtedly becoming fluid, than mortgages on apartments and shares in industrial and other business enterprises. The security of material collateral, further guaranteed by German industry and know-how, is sufficient to allow even the small depositor to invest his money here without fear of losing it. The further consideration that an interest of 4 or 5 percent would still allow tolerable rents, shows that the investment would not only be safe, but even pretty profitable compared to the income usually attained in similar situations, e.g. in America. The volume of the job would give financial institutions a fair profit even at low brokerage rates, so that the business would be profitable for all concerned.

A necessary condition is rational construction. The reconstruction is a job for the entire nation and must be attacked with drive, enthusiasm, mass employment of men, highest technology, and most rational methods. Examples for such nationwide jobs are the abolishment of unemployment in 1933–35, the construction of the German super-highways, the realization of the Four Year Plan, the construction of the West Wall,[9] and at last the unimaginable achievements of German war production. What was possible when those problems were tackled, is still possible today. Outside of the Party or party-like groupings we had the necessary organizations – those of labor, of technology, of planning – and all of them are anxiously waiting to enlist in the reconstruction, even under American guidance or supervision. I am convinced that none will abuse the confidence put into them. Let us be isolated and guarded, etc., but only allow us to work, to the advantage of the entire world, and thereby also to the advantage of my poor nation.

The construction of the West Wall involved the use of more than a million cubic meters of concrete in little more than a year. This quantity was normally planned for use during eleven years, but time was pressing and the aid of sound organization and rational methods of work allowed the accomplishment in one tenth of the period. The strict technical supervision, planning, and execution were in the hands of Dr Todt; I handled manpower, quartering, feeding, and care of the workers. Work was portioned out to private firms, workers were treated as free workers, so that free initiative on both sides was preserved. This circumstance alone allowed hitherto unknown achievements which almost doubled the output of army engineers, who worked under otherwise equal conditions. Later on, the Organization Todt was created from this beginning in spite of my objections; it was nothing but one huge engineer construction battalion, and the output dropped considerably from the West Wall times. Therefore I believe fanatically in a free economy under strict central planning and guidance. Semi-military organizations such as the Organization Todt or the National Labor Service (*Reichsarbeitsdienst*)[10] are much too bureaucratic to achieve big results. With the strict organizational and technological management goes the financing. The procurement, transfer, and guarantee of funds must be handled by one central institution. I am no financial expert and leave this part of my plan to the decision of experts; but it should not be hard to devise a proper form.

3. New Methods of Construction

It will be much harder [i.e. more complex] to produce cheap yet durable and good homes, factories, and traffic installations, through rationalization in all fields of construction, i.e. through new methods of work, new machines, new standardization. The office of the Reich Commissioner for Housing and my Office of Homes (*Heimstaetten-amt*) have worked on precisely these problems for years. I daresay that all preparatory work is recorded there, and has already been practically tried in the construction of homes. Furthermore the membership of the Academy for Home Construction (*Akademie für Wohnungsbau*), whose head I was, included all leading experts who had anything at all to do with these questions. The following chapters may be completed and ready for use:

(a) *Standardization*

Standardization has been completed to the last for all products – bricks, concrete blocks, light concrete bricks, porous sand-stone, roofing tiles, rafters, cross sections and lengths of timbers, doors, windows, flooring, hardware, furniture, and all furnishings down to wooden spoons.[11] It has been examined and approved, and is recorded in technical papers. Some articles were already being produced by the industry.

(b) *Methods of Work*

Thoroughgoing prefabrication systems allowed us to have the majority of the work done in concrete block factories, and thereby to become almost independent of the weather. Far-reaching preparatory work in collaboration with steel and iron mills and with RR [?] car factories had led to the possibility of producing a finished steel house with a living area of about 30 square meters, including furniture, and reduced basement space for 2,000 RM. The same (degree of progress in preparation) applies to wooden buildings. The rate of construction on brick buildings had been increased through the use of new type scaffolding, centralized mixing of plaster, and other methods to a daily output per bricklayer of up to 3,000 bricks. This marks a huge progress, since bricklayers in some parts of Germany laid as few as 300 bricks a day early in the war. A steadily increasing number of apprentice shops for masons made sure that workers and architects became familiar with our methods.

(c) *Economy of Materials*

Centralized allocation of all building materials in co-operation with the merchants will prevent single firms or contractors from evading the central guidance and rationalization. This is necessary to guarantee the final result of cheap and yet good homes. It should be safe to say that homes can be built for half the previous cost, thus permitting tolerably low rents fitting the workers' income, provided that all possibilities for economy are exhausted, such as using transportation of the postal system for the transportation of workers, using the National Railways (*Reichsbahn*), rationalizing the manufacture of building materials in saw mills, hardware plants, etc.

4. City Planning

(a) *Reconstruction of Destroyed Cities*

In the emergency at hand existing road sites and existing structural bases must, no doubt, be used. This will save the cost of digging building foundations, establishing drainage and electric systems, etc.; but the cost of removing wreckage will make up for it. These considerations make a discussion of new zoning superfluous. The downright revolutionary conclusions reached in research conducted in my office, which had already far progressed, will thus have only theoretical value for us Germans. Perhaps they can be used in a more fortunate country.

(b) *Emergency Home Construction*

Practice has given us so much experience in this work, that I need only point to it here. This also applies to the repair of damaged apartments. Last year we furnished quarters for about 500,000 families in emergency housings and repaired houses.

5. Potential Difficulties

The only difficulties in this plan are political ones, since the plan is unusable without central management. Central management is made difficult by the mistrust which the occupying powers have towards the knowledgeable experts in the field, and it is to be expected that the powers wish to solve the problems without these experts. I declare that this [is] tantamount to squaring the circle. I declare in the interest of my people, that I am willing to undergo every personal restriction, even solitary confinement, and expect not the least improvement in my present situation; I merely want to work and to help my people with my knowledge and experience. Furthermore, I know that Germany is now divided into four political districts [zones of occupation], giving rise to almost insoluble difficulties. This, however, is not my problem, but purely one for the victorious powers whose total victory we Germans have acknowledged by our unconditional surrender.

[There follow details of organizations and individuals recommended by Ley as competent to assist in the reconstruction programme.]

6. Reconstruction Problems

(a) *Wreckage Removal*

Wreckage removal and baring of the existing walls (foundations) is a major part of the entire reconstruction job.[12] Most difficult will be the decision where to put the wreckage, and what to do with it. The first question becomes immaterial since there will be no space to put the huge masses of rubble. Therefore the only possibility will be to use them anew, to process them into new stones or plates, which can be used in new construction. This will not be an easy task either, first because stones to be used as such must be reasonably clear of plaster and lime, so that the cement will stick. Stones which are to be cast into plates, however, will have to be bound with foam or porous concrete, in order to make the plates light and maneuverable in spite of the required thickness. I am convinced that the entire prefabrication plan depends on the solution of this problem.

(b) *Use of New Building Material*

The handiest stone building material is still the brick, which can be put in place with one hand. If one man needs both hands to move a piece of building material, they may still pass; but if two or more men are needed, or even hoisting gears, then the saving effected by the size of the material is doubly or triply outweighed by the loss in time and energy. We have experimented on this with precise time study, and measured brickwall space. Thus there is only one way left open, to manufacture lightweight plates 50 × 50 × 10cm. The plates must be manufactured with foam or leavening. At a specific gravity of 1.5, then the weight is 27kg, which can still be handled by one man. I therefore planned to have brick rubble ground to small pieces, to mix it with even parts of foam or porous concrete, and to cast plates of the above dimensions; they were to be used in prefabricated construction, the girders being of like material, or of 100 percent concrete, or of cast iron or of wood. In Hamburg we had some practical experiments of this sort, but without porous concrete . . .

After further consideration it seems simpler and promises more practical results to pour the brick rubble with the cement on the building site as poured concrete (*Schuettbeton*), rather than to prefabricate it into standard size plates. To obtain *Schuettbeton* a one to eight or even a one to ten mixture will give sufficient firmness. We began work according to this system in almost all cities, most successfully in Hamburg. If the necessary scaffolding and machinery is available, tall structures can be erected in this manner. But in this case, the mixture will have to be at least 1:3 or 1:5. The greatest difficulty for this process is the necessity for planking, which on the other hand is balanced by the possibility of casting all parts, including beams and stairs from the rubble–cement mixture.

(c) *Construction Considerations*

Local conditions will indicate how far the installation of air raid shelters is possible or desirable. In my opinion this should be disregarded entirely or largely, anyway. If the intentions of the San Francisco Conference [May 1945, founding of the United Nations] are realized, there will be no more war, and if they are not, the present weapons and defense methods will undoubtedly be outdated in a future conflict, so that present-day measures would have no value.

But there are other improvements and innovations which I would suggest in spite of the necessity of using the existing base walls and layouts.

(i) In Berlin, Hamburg, and almost all big cities, 2, 3, 4, and even more courtyards have been built behind each other. Such courtyards lack light, wholesomeness, and cheer. I can see that a reinforcement of the base walls would make it possible to build taller houses, the height of which would compensate for a saving in horizontal space, thus making way for wider yards and streets, i.e. more light and sunshine.

(ii) Hospitals, administrative buildings, and shops must be fitted into the reconstruction. Whether buildings for cultural and recreational facilities are also planned depends only on the funds available to the various communities.

(iii) One of the more important aspects is intracity traffic. In spite of many drawbacks nothing has been able to take the place of street cars. To plan something new here is superfluous, as we Germans will lack the means for anything new in our catastrophic condition.

(iv) But one thing should by all means be considered. Every new building should contain garages, to make room for the people's car (*Volkswagen*), which is to come in spite of all past disappointments. A research series has been conducted in this field.

(d) *Farm Reconstruction*

Beside cities a huge number of villages and farms must also be rebuilt. Other principles apply to their planning and construction. In a farm the stables are most important. Water and electricity should by all means be supplied in every new building. I have a lot to say about the 'mobilization of the village' if I may call it that,[13] as I am a farmer myself, and a descendant of farmers. For that reason I was assigned the design and production of the people's tractor (*Volkstraktor*). The tractor's design had been completed, it had been tested for three years in various types of farms, factories had been planned, and the organization of its sale and employment had been planned. The people's tractor is a counterpart to the people's automobile; together they were to form a grand social project.

D. Conclusion

I believe this exhausts the problem of the reconstruction of destroyed cities and villages, as far as it can be treated without reference material. I will say nothing about the reconstruction of industry, trades, and traffic, as other agencies than the Reich Commissioner for Housing are competent for these problems.

I think these few lines prove how profoundly National Socialism was devoted to the problem of housing. But I would be able to do just as thorough and largely revolutionary a work on other great social projects which we had attacked, and with the execution of which I had been entrusted, e.g. Old Age security, public health, new wage scales, 'Strength through Joy', vocational training, efficiency increase (*Leistungsertuechtigung*),[14] labor initiative (*Betriebliches Vorschlagswesen*),[15] efficiency and trade competition, model plants, advancement plan for ordinary talents, reasonable [rational] organization of plants, people's cars and people's tractors, etc. This proves that much good was accomplished after all alongside with the quantity of ugly and damnable things of which we are accused. I have only one desire – to see all these successful projects used and/or taken up, so that they will be put to work for the benefit of mankind. If it is now impossible to let our unfortunate nation benefit from them, I would be happy and content to see them used anywhere or by anyone in Europe. The splendid bearing of domestic and foreign workers in Germany during this war proves how sound and positive the ideas were. Not only the absence of any strikes, but the increase in output which continued until the very last prove the confidence the workers had in their leaders. Thus I would like to make my contribution to the reconstruction of Europe, hoping that it will one day benefit Germany, too.

Signed: Dr R. Ley, Reich Commissioner for Housing

Document 34 Schacht's New Germany

FIAT Interrogation Report, 7 September 1945, 'Second Preliminary Report on Dr Hjalmar Schacht', enclosing three statements by Schacht in answer to Major Tilley's questions. Schacht's 'Third Report' is on German reconstruction and the international order

THIRD REPORT

69. Task

I have been asked to write down a few ideas on the reconstruction of Germany. This task Germany can only view from within the European framework. Only economic problems can be considered, not political or purely national. Nationalism I have always understood to mean that a nation must endeavour not to force its supremacy on others but to be a model to them in its cultural achievements.

70. Hesitations or Inhibitions

I hesitate for various reasons to undertake this task. Although I feel mentally and physically at the height of my power – late virility is hereditary in our family – I have no desire to re-enter public life. The fateful disappointment over my having been duped by Hitler in the beginning I have taken much to heart. If despite this I write here, it is merely with the wish that perhaps I can add my mite to the alleviation of distress which Hitler has brought to the German people. Furthermore, since the beginning of 1939 I have not studied any official statistics or documents, but I have had to obtain my intelligence solely from press reports which were severely restricted during the war. For one year I have been in prison and am not informed on conditions in the rest of the world.

Hjalmar Schacht was the 'economic magician' responsible for masterminding the German economic revival under Hitler. A staunch nationalist, he parted ways with Hitler in 1937 over excessive military spending, and ended up in 1945 in Dachau concentration camp.

71. Political Conditionality

The question is difficult to answer whilst there is no clarity about German political conditions. If, for instance, the various announcements in the press should be put into practice, reports about a partitioning of Germany or the expulsion of all Germans from the future Poland,[16] all these would naturally have a corresponding influence on any economic programme. However, I have no other choice than to disregard all these matters for the present. One thing is certain: the economies of other European countries is [are] largely dependent on the economic life of Germany. After the last world war it became obvious that, if Germany suffered economically, the other countries must suffer with it . . . After the Second World War it will be of great importance to all these countries to see to what extent Germany will remain their market. The lowered purchasing power of the German population will make itself felt for a long time to come in the world market, especially in the countries which are Germany's neighbours.

72. Political Shape of Germany

Thus it will be important to consider how large will be the surviving Germany (*Rest-Deutschland*), whether this Rest-Deutschland remains an integral economic unit or whether it is divided into territories separated from each other by currency and customs boundaries or whether it is united with other neighbouring countries in a customs union of a larger territory. There can be no doubt that the latter would be of importance in the re-establishment of its purchasing power. The smaller the economic areas the more difficult their economic reconstruction.

(See First Report, paras. 59–62, in which Schacht expressed the hope that Germany be incorporated in the British Empire!)

73. No General Plan

The premises stated above would preclude a uniform economic plan, but quite apart from that I must confess that I am opposed to the making of theoretical plans which do not face up to practical experience. Obviously all economy must be directed according to definite general principles, but the now fashionable setting up of four-year plans and similar plans, the creation of planning bureaux, etc., is propaganda rather than effective achievement . . .

74. Surveillance

From long experience we know that no one who works under foreign orders is as interested in the success of his or her affairs as when he deals with them according to his own lights. In view of the results of this war it is obvious that the sovereignty of Germany will remain restricted in many respects for a long period to come. The German people will resign themselves to this, but under foreign sovereignty they will undertake their economic and cultural tasks the more eagerly, the more the task of solving these problems is left to them. The foreign government should, therefore, limit itself, in the field of political economy, to the dictation of certain guiding principles and to their surveillance, and to leave the execution of the corresponding measures to the German administration. Obviously inspection and the right to veto at all times through liaison officers and liaison officials must remain the right of the foreign powers.

75. Economic Principles

The general principles, the observance of which should be demanded and controlled by the foreign powers, are in my opinion above all the following:
76. (a) *Currency*. The basis of all modern economics is monetary exchange. Therefore the first task will be the re-establishment of a

German currency. In view of the *monetary* and financial position of Germany the task is extremely difficult. Though I have no documents with figures available I estimate the currency in circulation at 70 to 75 billions and the public debts of all kinds at no less than 450 billions.[17] The German population is completely exhausted, much more so than in the first world war. Such figures and such depletion render very difficult the re-establishment of a stable currency. Nevertheless a stable currency is the most essential basis for any national economy.

Only the gold standard can be the basis. All that the German people have been told in propaganda talks and literature of the *Verrechnungsmark* [non-convertible mark] and of human labour as currency basis is complete nonsense. It is not by accident that gold with its manifold special properties, which I need not point out here, has established itself all over the world as basic currency. However, Germany cannot live without economic contacts with the rest of the world, and if for no other reason it must return to the gold standard.

77. (b) *Agricultural production.* While there is no doubt that the re-establishment of a gold currency will be successful, the same is not necessarily true of the next problem, the increase in German agricultural production. Agriculture is the most important factor in the maintenance of all peoples.

Statistics prove that Germany is the leader or one of the leaders of all countries in the agricultural production per acre. Only the future can tell whether and to what degree a further increase in production is possible. In any case Germany must above all orientate its chemical and technical science towards an increase in agricultural production . . .

78. An artificial extension of the small-holder settlements of the German peasants is inadvisable. We have had bad experiences with the settlements of small-holder peasants. The overhead expenditure of these peasants is comparatively high in relation to the agricultural return. Only to a little extent and only occasionally do they supply the free market, to a large extent they consume the harvest themselves. In contrast to that the allotment garden of the manual labourer has made a great contribution to the supplementary diet. Whereas the number of small-holder properties is limited by the requisite areas, there is sufficient land available for the allotments of the manual worker. On the other hand the allotments of the manual worker do not contribute

to the supply of the open market, but a large number of consumers are thus made independent of the open market by their home-grown supplies and in that manner the open market is freed for a more liberal supply to the non-agricultural part of the population. Workers' houses with $1/8$ to $1/4$ hectares of land, as well as suburban allotments, have achieved astounding results in the production of vegetables, potatoes and fruit, as well as the breeding of rabbits and goats. Therefore, in rebuilding German cities and especially German industry, special attention must be paid to the establishment of workers' homes with small gardens.

79. (c) *Rationing.* In view of the poverty inflicted on the German people by Hitler's war, it will be necessary, for a long time, to keep the German consumption of foodstuffs and clothing, as well as of housing, etc., on a low level. Compared with the liberal pre-war supplies the German people of all classes must accustom themselves to a modest and economic management of their households; this can only be done through state control. During the war it was surprising to see to what extent and for how long a period the consumption by the population could be reduced without noticeable direct ill-effects. The longer the war lasted, however, the more under-nourishment and 'under-consumption' became the rule of the day. But there is no doubt that compared with consumption in peacetime considerable savings can be effected by rationing. The diet will have to be confined to a certain quantity of calories, houses must be furnished as simply as possible, clothing will have to be worn longer, savings must be effected in all refuse and offals, there must be an avoidance of all peacetime extravagance . . .

82. (e) *Revolutionizing industrial thinking.* In the reconstruction of German industry I see greater difficulties in the intellectual atmosphere than on the purely technical side. The tendency to large concerns, the massing and concentration of production in a few all-comprising concerns, constitutes a social and possibly also a political danger because it directs the mentality to exorbitant goals which are not easily accessible to ordinary human intellect.

83. On the social side large industrial concerns cause a mechanization of the human mind and of human consciousness and thus deteriorate permanently humanitarian, moral and religious education. But without these factors peaceful living side by side of people is impossible . . .

84. Far be it from me to wish to fight technical progress which gives to mankind greater living comforts. But through intellectual and moral education the aggressive centre of gravity of technics must be kept within humanitarian bounds. Therefore, the supercharged big industrial concerns which are based on the ruthless exploitation of technical inventions and discoveries, must be subject to a certain control. The more this control is the result of the voluntary decision of the managers and technicians, the better.

85. (f) *Handicraft and trade.* A most unpleasant effect of the war has been the abnormal reduction, nay elimination of small artisans' workshops. Unfortunately there is no greater promoter of large technical concerns and of capitalism than war. Whoever has inscribed social freedom in politics on his banner must strive to the utmost to avoid war. One cannot preach 'freedom and bread' if one aims at war. War has taken from their workshops and placed in armament industry countless artisans who were spread over the entire country down to the smallest villages. This did not apply only to journeymen but also to the master artisans who were conscripted and had to close down their shops.

85(a). In the rural areas of Germany there is an insufficiency of artisans and handicraft workers, to a large extent they are non-existent. Villages and small towns are clamouring for artisans. Artisans who, during the war, were drawn into industry must not only be returned to rural areas but from industry master workers, foremen and other trained personnel must be brought to the country and the small towns, in order to re-start the handicraft shops in decentralized work . . .

86. (g) *Return to the land.* With the return and the re-employment of the artisans in the rural areas there will be a reverse movement to the land of agricultural workers.

87. Here, too, the armament industry has caused havoc during the war by drawing to the industrial cities masses of agricultural workers. At present these workers still have ties of friendship and family on the land. They will gladly accept any opportunity for work offered by trade but will also favourably consider that especially now, after the war, the country offers greater facilities for housing and food than the large bombed-out cities. When you get down to the bare necessities of nourishment and housing, the loss of cinemas, restaurants, theatres etc. does not seem so unbearable, especially since the wireless broad-

casts and cinemas of nearby small towns are a substitute for the pleasures of the large cities.

88. (h) *Reconstruction of industry.* With its large population Germany cannot possibly be brought back to the level of an agrarian state. We may also disregard the fact that an increase in agricultural production is dependent on progress in industrial technology. Basing myself on what I have said under (e) ('revolutionizing industrial thinking') the development of German technical science cannot be and must not be impeded. This applies, above all, to the retention and continuation of all technical schools and research institutes. On the other hand it would be advisable, nay necessary, to impart to technicians not only purely technical knowledge but to let them enjoy also a humanistic university education. The sharp separation of purely technical training from general intellectual knowledge is a great mistake.

88 (i). Furthermore, it should be possible to eliminate from technical science all that relates to purely military weapons and war methods. The forces thus liberated must be increasingly employed in civilian tasks, principally in the advancement of agriculture . . .

94. (m) *Simplification of administration.* The Hitler system brought a tremendous extension of the bureaucratic apparatus. Not only did the government tasks grow, but side by side with every government body an equivalent Party body was placed which dealt with the same problems. This bureaucratic apparatus resulted in a tremendous expenditure policy which must be reduced at all costs. The entire administrative apparatus must be limited and simplified on a large scale. For this purpose it is especially important that a large part of the paid work done under Hitler by officials and Party members should be taken over voluntarily by citizens who have the time and are financially able to do this . . . There are innumerable tasks which especially the middle classes can and must undertake in future in this field . . .

95. (n) *Moral education.* In this connection an important role will be played by the Church and by those employed in it. One of the greatest mistakes in the recent economic development of the German people has been the total neglect of spiritual and moral education in favour of purely technical and economical interests. But the economic activity of man, like every human activity, must have a moral foundation. Why leading personalities in Germany without exception had not the courage to oppose the excesses to which the Hitler system fell prey,

why they tolerated all the mischief done by charlatans, or why they covered it up, why they thought they had to assure the good will of Party bosses (*Parteibonzen*) through costly presents and contributions, why they did all this, may only be understood if one realizes to what extent the religious and moral education of the nation has been neglected during the period of seductive technical progress which is wholly orientated towards the materialistic side of life.

96. The future conduct of the State will have to correct this error by energetic measures and I hope that losing this war has brought the population to the realization that money and good living are meaningless if they destroy character and humaneness . . .

105. Guilt of the German Nation

This war has aroused unheard of passions in the entire world. No matter how rightly you look for the guilty on one side only – and I am the last to deny the guilt of Hitler and National Socialism and am far from maintaining that the German nation should not bear the consequences of its wrong decisions, its ignorance and its frivolity – (*Note:* Schacht's own incomplete sentence.) However, I wish to point out one mistake which has contributed to a large extent to this misfortune. In Versailles the German nation, which at that time, with clean hands and honourably, had entered a war not of its own making, had been morally maligned and had been treated as unworthy. Hitler profited by the feeling of despair which had the German nation in its grip. I beg and advise most earnestly that there be no repetition of this mistake. Let all really guilty men be punished; if the foreign powers should not do it the German nation, through its own courts, would condemn and punish the guilty. One may belittle and scold the German nation for its political stupidity and frivolity but one should refrain from the moral defamation of the entire nation. France, too, once had a revolution which, considering the period, was no less bloody and horrible than the crimes of Hitler and his followers. But at that time no one thought of morally outlawing the entire French nation . . .

108. I do not know the intentions of the western powers. I do not know what importance they attach to the question whether the German people are to be orientated towards the west or towards the east,

but two things I do know; the first is that the tearing asunder culturally of the German nation will create a permanent state of unrest in Europe. I emphasize the word culture (civilization; in German, *Kultur*) because I do not attach great importance to any national-political prestige. The second is that, if the German nation cannot find a place, i.e. peaceable social intercourse with the countries with western culture, it will be an easy prey for the east because the enormous Russian empire disposes of so many possibilities given to it by nature that it can by itself alone employ, nourish and absorb all surplus German population. I am not discussing the question whether this is fortunate or unfortunate for the world. Neither do I utter here any judgement on the value of the eastern culture but, to balance the possibilities for existence which Russia could offer, the western world can only offer the closer intertwining with Germany and the opening of equal opportunities for the German nation. I cherish the hope that the western powers may become convinced that the German nation in its material and spiritual culture is too valuable to become lost to the western world.

Notes

Preface

1. F. Genoud (ed.), *The Testament of Adolf Hitler* (London, 1961), p. 104, entry for 2 April 1945.
2. PRO, FO 371/46778, memorandum by J. D. Beam, 'Visit to Ashcan', p. 1.
3. PRO, FO 371/46778, Ivone Kirkpatrick (British Supreme HQ) to Anthony Eden, 21 June 1945, p 1.
4. PRO, FO 371/51025, SHAEF message to 21st Army Group, 2 June 1945.
5. IWM, FO 645, Box 155, testimony of Kurt Daluege, 2 November 1945, p. 2.
6. PRO, FO 1032/1860, Control Council for Germany, RDR Division memorandum 'The Problem of Germany – February 1946', p. 1.

Part I Interrogations: an Introduction

Outlaw Country

1. PRO, PREM 4/100/13, paper by Lord Simon, 'Outlawry and Hitler and Co.', 10 November 1943.
2. PRO, PREM 4/100/10, note by Prime Minister, 1 November 1943, pp. 1–4. Churchill used the term 'outlaw' in 1941, when discussing the possible fate of Rudolf Hess. See PREM 3/219/7, minute from Churchill to Eden, 13 May 1941: 'This man like the other Nazi leaders is potentially a war criminal and he and his confederates may well be declared outlaws at the close of the war.'
3. PRO, PREM 4/100/13, paper by Lord Simon, 10 November 1943. Outlawry was abolished in criminal cases by the Administration of Justice (Miscellaneous Provisions) Act 1938, chapter 63, clause 12. In civil cases it had already been abolished by the Civil Procedure Acts Repeal Act 1879, chapter 59, clause 3. Details of the legal status of the outlaw in Earl Jowitt and C.

Walsh, *Jowitt's Dictionary of English Law* (2nd edn., ed. J. Burke, London, 1972), p. 1297.

4. PRO, PREM 4/100/10, minute by the Foreign Secretary, 'Treatment of War Criminals', 22 June 1942, pp. 2–3.

5. PRO, PREM 4/100/10, note from Churchill to General Ismay, 23 August 1944.

6. PRO, PREM 4/100/10, Prime Minister's draft telegram for Marshal Stalin, 17 September 1942.

7. PRO, PREM 4/100/10, War Cabinet paper by the Deputy Prime Minister, 'Treatment of Major Enemy War Criminals', 26 June 1944.

8. PRO, TS 26/896, notes of a meeting with the Lord Chancellor, Lord Simon, 8 April 1945, p. 3; House of Lords debate in NA II, RG 107, McCloy papers, Box 3, telegram from ambassador John Winant to Edward Stettinius, State Department, 23 March 1945, p. 5.

9. PRO, PREM 4/100/10, Foreign Office to Washington Embassy, 22 October 1944, p. 2; W. S. Churchill, *The Second World War* (6 vols., London, 1948–54), VI, p. 211.

10. NA II, RG 107, Stimson papers, Box 5, memorandum to the President, 'Trial and Punishment of War Criminals', 22 January 1945, pp. 1–4.

11. NA II, RG 107, McCloy papers, Box 1, State Department to Stimson, 16 March 1945, enclosing article from *Pravda*, 'The Punishment of the War Criminals', p. 5.

12. M. Marrus, *The Nuremberg War Crimes Trial 1945–1946: A Documentary History* (New York, 1997), p. 25, memorandum from Morgenthau to the President, 5 September 1944.

13. NA II, RG 107, Stimson papers, Box 15, memorandum from Stimson to the President, 9 September 1944, pp. 1–2.

14. NA II, RG 107, McCloy papers, Box 1, UNWCC, report by Dr Ečer, 11 November 1944.

15. NA II, RG 107, Stimson papers, Box 5, memorandum from General Cramer, 'Trial of War Criminals', sent to McCloy, 9 October 1944, p. 2.

16. NA II, RG 107, McCloy papers, Box 1, memorandum to the President, draft of 28 November 1944, p. 5.

17. NA II, RG 107, McCloy papers, Box 1, Morgenthau to McCloy, 19 January 1945, enclosing 'memorandum re: the War Department Memorandum Concerning the Punishment of War Criminals', pp. 2–4.

18. PRO, TS 26/896, 'War Crimes: Notes of a meeting held in the Lord Chancellor's Room, 8 April 1945', pp. 2–3.

19. NA II, RG 107, McCloy papers, Box 2, notes for a meeting with Lord Simon, 16 April 1945, pp. 2–3; PRO, LCO 2/2980, notes of a meeting with the Lord Chancellor, 16 April 1945, p. 2.

20. NA II, RG 107, McCloy papers, Box 2, memorandum from the Lord Chancellor, 21 April 1945.

21. NA II, RG 107, McCloy papers, Box 3, memorandum from Stimson to McCloy, 26 April 1945; T. Taylor, *The Anatomy of the Nuremberg Trials* (London, 1993), p. 40.

22. NA II, RG 107, McCloy papers, President Truman, Executive Order 9547, 2 May 1945.

23. A. Neave, *Nuremberg: A Personal Record of the Trial of the Major Nazi War Criminals in 1945–6* (London, 1978), pp. 245–6.

24. H. S Truman, *Year of Decisions: 1945* (London, 1955), p. 206.

25. NA II, RG 107, McCloy papers, Box 3, Statement by the President, 2 May 1945.

26. PRO, PREM 4/100/13, instructions to the United Kingdom delegation in San Francisco (n.d.), pp. 1–2; TS 26/896, 'War Criminals', War Cabinet memorandum by the Lord Chancellor, 26 April 1945.

27. Taylor, *The Anatomy of the Nuremberg Trials*, pp. 32–3; PRO, PREM 4/100/13, minute by the Prime Minister, 3 May 1945.

28. NA II, RG 107, McCloy papers, Box 2, telegram from Rosenman to President Roosevelt, 3 May 1945; report from Jackson and Murray Bernays, 4 May 1945; telegram from Cutter to McCloy, 6 May 1945.

29. H. Gaskin (ed.), *Eyewitnesses at Nuremberg* (London, 1990), pp. 57–8, recollections of lawyer Whitney Harris. See also J. F. Murphy, 'Norms of Criminal Procedure at the International Military Tribunal', in G. Ginsburgs and V. N. Kudriavtsev (eds.), *The Nuremberg Trial and International Law* (London, 1990), pp. 61–73.

30. NA II, RG 107, McCloy papers, Box 2, memorandum by Justice Jackson, 1 May 1945.

31. PRO, TS 26/896, letter to Patrick Dean, Foreign Office, 12 April 1945, p. 2; see also LCO 2/2980, BWCE minutes of meeting, 15 June 1945: 'Sir Thomas Barnes stated that the object was to execute Goering & Co.'

32. PRO, LCO 2/2980, Tass Agency, *Soviet Monitor* for 12 and 13 June 1945, pp. 1–3.

33. NA II, RG 107, McCloy papers, Box 3, memorandum to McCloy, 1 May 1945, 'Personnel Recruitment, War Crimes Activities, European Theater of Operations'; PRO, TS 26/904, costs of trial at Nuremberg; FO 371/51072, BWCE memorandum on personnel, 8 September 1945.

34. A. Wieviorka, 'La France et le procès de Nuremberg', in *idem* (ed.), *Les procès de Nuremberg et de Tokyo* (Paris, 1996), pp. 70–71.

35. Taylor, *The Anatomy of the Nuremberg Trials*, p. 59; A. and J. Tusa, *The Nuremberg Trial* (London, 1983), pp. 78–9. Despite Jackson's reservations about the Soviet side, sentiments similar to those of Nikitchenko had been

aired at a meeting between the American and British prosecution teams in May. See PRO, LCO 2/2980, minutes of meeting of 29 May 1945 of prosecuting counsel, p. 1.

36. Gaskin, *Eyewitnesses*, p. 73, recollection of lawyer Bernard Meltzer.

37. NA II, RG 238, Box 26, memorandum to Jackson, 'An Educational Program in Connection with the Prosecution of the Major War Criminals', 30 May 1945.

38. PRO, TS 26/896, Patrick Dean (Foreign Office) to Maxwell-Fyfe, 9 June 1945; PREM 4/100/13, Eden to Churchill, 22 May 1945; NA II, RG 107, McCloy papers, Box 3, draft planning memorandum, 13 May 1945.

39. PRO, LCO 2/2980, 'Minutes of 2nd meeting of BWCE and the Representatives of the USA', 21 June 1945; 'Rough Notes Meeting with Russians', 29 June 1945; J. Heydecker and J. Leeb, *Der Nürnberger Prozess* (Cologne, 1979), p. 97.

40. NA II, RG 107, McCloy papers, Box 3, Bernays to Ammi Cutter, 9 July 1945, pp. 1–2.

41. PRO, FO 1019/82, Maxwell-Fyfe to Jackson, 21 September 1945, p. 2; FO 1019/98, memorandum to Jackson from Maxwell-Fyfe, 23 September 1945, p. 1.

42. PRO, WO 311/39, Cmd. 6668 (1945), Agreement for the Prosecution and Punishment of the Major War Criminals of the European Axis, London, 8 August 1945. On the Potsdam discussions see PRO, CAB 99/38, 'Terminal: Record of the Proceedings of the Berlin Conference 17 July to 1 August 1945', p. 252.

43. NA II, RG 238, Box 26, letter from William Green (publisher of *Fortune*) to Jackson, 29 November 1945, enclosing proof of 'The Nürnberg Novelty', pp. 1–2.

The Criminals

1. PRO, FO 1049/288, Political Division, Control Commission for Germany, 'Ashcan Report', Berlin, 1945, p. 17.

2. PRO, PREM 4/100/10, note by the Prime Minister, 1 November 1943, p. 2.

3. PRO, PREM 4/100/10, memorandum by Eden, 'Treatment of Major Enemy War Criminals', 16 June 1944, p. 2.

4. NA II, RG 107, McCloy papers, Box 1, State Department to H. L. Stimson, 16 March 1945, enclosing article from *Pravda* by Professor Borissov; Box 3, telephone conference, General John Weir and Lieut.-Colonel Joseph Hodgson, 17 May 1945.

5. PRO, PREM 4/100/10, memorandum by Eden, 'Treatment of Major Enemy War Criminals', 16 June 1944, Annex 1 and Annex II. Graziani was wanted in connection with the conduct of anti-partisan warfare during the period 1943–5 when he served as Minister of National Defence (and later Minister for the Armed Forces) in Mussolini's so-called 'Salo' Republic. See L. Ganapini, *La Repubblica della Camicie Nere* (Milan, 1999), p. 11.

6. NA II, RG 107, Stimson papers, Box 5, Bernays to Stimson, 'Memorandum: Report to the President', 7 June 1945, p. 5.

7. PRO, LCO 2/2980, Foreign Office Research Department, 'Marshal Rodolfo Graziani', 29 June 1945; on Italian war crimes in general see FO 371/51044, 'War Crimes: Charges against Italian War Criminals', file May 1945. On the Graziani trial, see *Processa Graziani: L'autodifesa dell' ex Maresciallo nel resoconto stenografico* (Rome, 1948). Graziani was sentenced to nineteen years in prison but served only three, dying shortly after his release in 1951. On Italian policy in 1945, see D. W. Ellwood, *Italy, 1943–1945* (Leicester, 1985), chapters 11, 12; A. Kochavi, *Prelude to Nuremberg. Allied War Crimes Policy and the Quest for Punishment* (Chapel Hill, NC, 1998), p. 77; M. Grindrod, *The Rebuilding of Italy: Politics and Economics 1945–1955* (London, 1955), chapters 1–3.

8. PRO, PREM 4/100/10, memorandum by Eden, 16 June 1944, Annex I.

9. PRO, PREM 4/100/10, memorandum by the Deputy Prime Minister, 'Treatment of Major Enemy War Criminals', 26 June 1944.

10. PRO, PREM 4/100/10, memorandum by the Lord Chancellor, 'Major War Criminals', 4 September 1944, p. 3.

11. PRO, TS 26/896, Patrick Dean (Foreign Office) to Maxwell-Fyfe, 19 June 1945, pp. 1–2.

12. T. Taylor, *The Anatomy of the Nuremberg Trials* (London, 1993), pp. 35–7; NA II, RG 107, Stimson papers, State Department to Stimson, 'Memorandum on War Crimes', 9 October 1944, pp. 1–5.

13. NA II, RG 107, Stimson papers, Box 5, memorandum to Roosevelt, 'Trial and Punishment of Nazi War Criminals', 22 January 1945, pp. 2–3; see also Stimson to Stettinius, 27 October 1944. The Soviet delegation later refused to try organizations on the ground that it was a principle inconsistent with Soviet jurisprudence; see RG 107, McCloy papers, Box 3, Colonel Telford Taylor to McCloy, 30 June 1945, p. 2.

14. PRO, WO 309/1420, 21st Army Group, Administrative Instruction 94, 'Organisation and Administration of Civilian Internment Camps in Germany' (n.d., but March 1945?), Appendix O; NA II, RG 107, McCloy papers, Box 1, file ASW 00052, detention report.

15. IWM, FO 645, Box 163, miscellaneous interrogations, 'Nazi Personalities in the Protectorate', 25 March 1945.

16. J. Heydecker and J. Leeb, *Der Nürnberger Prozess* (Cologne, 1979), pp. 60–61; on Neurath, see J. L. Heinemann, *Hitler's First Foreign Minister. Constantin von Neurath, Diplomat and Statesman* (Berkeley, Calif., 1979), pp. 220–21.

17. P. R. Black, *Ernst Kaltenbrunner: Ideological Soldier of the Third Reich* (Princeton, NJ, 1984), pp. 258–61.

18. NA II, RG 238, Box 39, Bernays to Jackson, 21 May 1945, enclosing report 'Press Reports of Captures' (this list also included 'Col. Count Claus von Stauffenberg, attempted assassin of Hitler', who had in fact been shot on the evening of 20 July 1944); Colonel B. Andrus to William Jackson, 24 April 1946, 'Information Concerning Capture of Defendants'. On Raeder's capture, see E. Raeder, *Mein Leben* (2 vols., Tübingen, 1957), II, pp. 303–4; for Fritzsche, see H. Fritzsche, *The Sword in the Scales*, as told to H. Springer (London, 1953), pp. 13–14.

19. PRO, LCO 2/2980, minutes of the second meeting between BWCE and representatives of the USA, 21 June 1945, p. 2.

20. PRO, TS 26/896, Patrick Dean (Foreign Office) to Maxwell-Fyfe, 19 June 1945, p. 2.

21. PRO, LCO 2/2980, BWCE minutes of meeting, on 15 June 1945, p. 3, on Russian figures; on American figures, see NA II, RG 238, Box 18, memorandum from Bernays to Colonels Amen and Storey, 25 June 1945, Appendix A, pp. 1–3.

22. PRO, WO 311/576, BWCE to War Office, 20 June 1945; War Office to SHAEF, 27 June 1945.

23. PRO, WO 311/576, War Office to Adjutant-General, 31 July 1945; BWCE to War Office, 'The First List of Defendants' (n.d., but *c.* 15 August 1945).

24. PRO, WO 311/576, War Office memorandum, 'Keitel, Donitz [*sic*], Schacht and Krupp as War Criminals', 15 August 1945, pp. 1–3; NA II, RG 238, Box 7, memorandum to Jackson from Lieut.-Commander John Bracken, 'Grand Admiral Karl Doenitz as a War Criminal', pp. 1, 6. Bracken reported the conclusion of the British Admiralty 'that there is insufficient evidence to sustain a charge against Doenitz'. On Potsdam, see PRO CAB 99/38, 'Terminal: Record of the Proceedings of the Berlin Conference', p. 252; K. Dönitz, *Mein wechselvolles Leben* (Göttingen, 1975), p. 210.

25. See P. Sudoplatov, *Special Tasks: the Memoirs of an Unwanted Witness – A Soviet Spymaster* (London, 1994), p. 169. Sudoplatov was a KGB agent deputed to look after Raeder in Moscow. He toyed with the idea of trying to recruit Raeder, who appeared co-operative, but claims that he had to hand him over for trial at Nuremberg in exchange for the White Russian general Pyotr Krasnov, who was in British hands. This claim is scarcely plausible.

Krasnov was handed over in late May 1945, when Raeder was still in Germany, easily available for an exchange.

26. NA II, RG 107, McCloy papers, Box 1, UNWCC, report by Dr Ečer, 11 November 1944, pp. 7–8.

27. NA II, RG 238, Box 6, 'Cartels and National Security', Report of the Subcommittee on War Mobilization, November 1944, Part I; Peter Drucker to Bernays, 13 June 1945, enclosing 'The Pattern of Nazi Economic Crimes'.

28. IWM, FO 645, Box 154, Foreign Office Research Department, Schacht personality profile, file 1, p. 2. On Schacht in general, see H. H. G. Schacht, *76 Jahre meines Lebens* (Bad Wörishofen, 1953); A. P. Simpson, *Hjalmar Schacht in Perspective* (The Hague, 1969). On Schacht's imprisonment by the Allies see PRO, WO 208/3155, personality file on Hjalmar Schacht.

29. PRO, WO 311/576, War Office memorandum, 15 August 1945, p. 2: 'Whatever the views of our American and Russian allies I should regard it as most inadvisable to indict Schacht with the others on the list . . . he is not a war criminal in the sense of this prosecution.'

30. IWM, FO 645, Box 152, minutes of meeting of chief prosecutors, 12 November 1945, pp. 3–4: 'Mr Justice Jackson,' ran the minutes, 'referred to the background in the United States which was that there was a drive against American munitions manufacturers'; memorandum by Maxwell-Fyfe, 'The situation arising on the Medical Report on Gustav Krupp', 10 November 1945; Foreign and Commonwealth Office Library, London, Krupp papers, War Crimes folder, H. Phillimore to Patrick Dean, 1 September 1945 (now deposited in the Imperial War Museum).

31. IWM, FO 645, Box 152, minutes of meeting of chief prosecutors, 12 November 1945, p. 1. On the original terms of the indictment against Krupp, see FO 1019/84, Major Airey Neave to BWCE, 2 October 1945, Indictment against Gustav Krupp. Jackson's views can be found in NA II, RG 238, Box 26, draft of press release (n.d).

32. NA II, RG 238, Box 18, memorandum by Bernays for all legal personnel, 'Prosecution of Major War Criminals', list B, 'Organizations'.

33. NA II, RG 238, Box 34, Indictment, first draft, p. 1 (this differed from the version sent to the British prosecutors in August by leaving out the name of Hitler: PRO, TS 26/896, draft Indictment, International Military Tribunal, No. 1).

The Charges

1. NA II, RG 107, Stimson papers, Box 5, Bernays to Stimson, 7 June 1945, 'Memorandum: Report to the President', p. 2.

2. PRO, TS 26/896, 'The US Draft Indictment, Part I' (n.d., but August 1945).

3. NA II, RG 107, McCloy papers, Box 1, UNWCC memorandum, 6 October 1944, Annex A.

4. NA II, RG 107, Stimson papers, Box 5, memorandum on war crimes by Colonel R. Ammi Cutter, 9 October 1944, p. 5: '*Conspiracy* theory. This theory is based on treating all racial and minority persecutions as essential parts of the great war crime – conspiracy to subjugate Europe, incidentally eliminating certain United Nations minority nationals in a barbarous manner – essentially all the membership of certain stated Nazi groups would be treated as part of the same conspiracy.' The advantage of this measure was that it allowed anti-semitism to be included among the indictable offences.

5. NA II, RG 107, Stimson papers, Box 5, Stimson to Stettinius, 27 October 1944, enclosing 'Trial of European War Criminals: *The General Problem*', pp. 1–5.

6. NA II, RG 107, McCloy papers, Box 1, 'Punishment of War Criminals: Agenda for Conference', 9 November 1944; 'Memorandum of Conference on War Crimes Procedure', War Department, 9 November 1944, pp. 1–6.

7. NA II, RG 107, McCloy papers, Box 1, draft memorandum for the President, 28 November 1944, pp. 3–5. See also S. Pomorski, 'Conspiracy and Criminal Organizations', in G. Ginsburgs and V. N. Kudriavtsev (eds.), *The Nuremberg Trial and International Law*, pp. 215–17.

8. NA II, RG 107, McCloy papers, Box 3, draft Planning Memorandum, 13 May 1945, p. 2.

9. NA II, RG 107, Stimson papers, Box 5, Bernays to Stimson, Memorandum: Report to the President, 7 June 1945, pp. 4–5.

10. NA II, RG 238, Box 18, Bernays to all legal personnel, 25 June 1945, enclosing memorandum 'Prosecution of Major War Criminals', pp. 4–6.

11. See for example PRO, WO 311/39, 'Draft Memorandum on the Jewish Case against Germany's Major War Criminals' (n. d., but July 1945); LCO 2/2978, minute of the Lord Chancellor, 30 January 1945, 'War Crimes: the Inter-departmental Committee', who noted the UNWCC conclusion that 'treatment of Jews *inside* Germany is outside the scope of their enquiries'; NA II, RG 107, Stimson papers, Box 5, Stimson to Stettinius, 27 October 1944, pp. 2–3 on Jewish lobbying.

12. NA II, RG 238, Judge Advocate General papers, memorandum to General John Weir from Rafael Lemkin, 14 July 1945, pp. 3–14; see also D. Lipstadt,

Denying the Holocaust: The Growing Assault on Truth and Memory (London, 1993), p. 63.

13. NA II, RG 107, McCloy papers, Box 2, War Department, 'Draft Directive on the Identification and Apprehension of Persons Suspected of War Crimes', draft 2, 14 June 1945, p. 1.

14. NA II, RG 107, McCloy papers, Box 3, Jackson to Lord Wright, UNWCC, 5 July 1945, pp. 1–4.

15. NA II, RG 107, McCloy papers, Box 1, UNWCC, report by Dr Ečer, pp. 4–5.

16. NA II, RG 107, McCloy papers, Box 3, memorandum 'Morgan's Opinion on Conspiracy Theory for Prosecution of War Crimes', 12 January 1945, pp. 2–4; see also the view expressed by H. A. Smith, Professor of International Law at London University, on 'The Great Experiment at Nuremberg': 'The high authorities of four great powers who have set up the court at Nuremberg have now decided that this is a very special case in which they are justified in departing from the principle that a man must not be punished for an act which did not constitute a crime at the time when it was committed. Only history and experience yet to come can decide whether this very serious decision is right or wrong . . .' (*Listener*, 34, 13 December 1945, p. 694).

17. NA II, RG 107, Stimson papers, Box 5, Bernays to Stimson, enclosing 'Memorandum: Report to the President', pp. 6–7. See also J. P. Kenny, *Moral Aspects of Nuremberg* (Washington, DC, 1949), p. 6; R. K. Woetzel, *The Nuremberg Trials in International Law* (2nd edn., New York, 1962), pp. 150–53.

18. PRO, TS 26/896 Foreign Office minute, 'The US Draft Indictment, Part I' (n.d., but August 1945), p. 1.

19. PRO, LCO 2/2900, Foreign Office Research Department memorandum, 'Nazism as a Conspiracy for the Domination of Europe: the Evidence of *Mein Kampf*', 22 June 1945, pp. 1–2.

20. NA II, RG 238, Box 30, 'Memorandum: Interrogation of Dr Hermann Rauschning', 19 July 1945, enclosure 2, 'informal conversation with Hermann Rauschning, 18 July 1945'.

21. R. M. W. Kempner, *Ankläger einer Epoche: Lebenserrinerungen* (Frankfurt/Main, 1983), p. 21.

22. A. Vaksberg, *The Prosecutor and the Prey: Vyshinsky and the 1930s Show Trials* (London, 1990), p. 259; S. Mironenko, 'La collection des documents sur le procès de Nuremberg dans les archives d'état de la fédération russe', in A. Wieviorka (ed.), *Les procès de Nuremberg et de Tokyo* (Paris, 1996), pp. 65–6.

23. T. Taylor, *The Anatomy of the Nuremberg Trials* (London, 1993), pp. 75–6, 80.

24. NA II, RG 107, McCloy papers, Box 3, General Cramer to McCloy, 5 May 1945, 'Memorandum: War Crimes Planning Group: Trial of Major Criminals', pp. 2–3, 6.

25. LHA, Hechler 1, 'The Enemy Side of the Hill: the 1945 Background and Interrogation of German Commanders', by Major K. W. Hechler, Historical Division, US State Department, 30 July 1949, p. 5.

26. NA II, RG 107, McCloy papers, Box 3, draft Planning Memorandum, 13 May 1945, pp. 3–5.

27. NA II, RG 107, McCloy papers, Box 3, Bernays to Cutter, 9 July 1945, pp. 2–3; Taylor, *The Anatomy of the Nuremberg Trials*, p. 57.

28. NA II, RG 238, Jackson papers, Box 16, Bernays to Jackson, 'Memo: Use of Wiener Library', 6 August 1945; see B. Barkow, *Alfred Wiener and the Making of the Holocaust Library* (London, 1999).

29. PRO, WO 311/39, War Office to 21st Army Group, 21 July 1945.

30. NA II, RG 238, Jackson papers, Box 32, Lieut.-Colonel Leonard Wheeler to Jackson, 2 August 1945; 'Summary of a report of a conference held in Reich Chancellery', 25 June 1945; PRO, FO 371/46749, Director of Military Intelligence to Foreign Office, 2 June 1945, enclosing translations of 'Case Green', the 'Hoszbach [*sic*] memorandum' and the meeting of 23 May 1939 when Hitler addressed the heads of the armed forces on the Polish crisis. See also R. E. Conot, *Justice at Nuremberg* (London, 1983), p. 37. On the story of the Hossbach Memorandum, see J. Wright and P. Stafford, 'Hitler, Britain, and the Hossbach Memorandum', *Militärgeschichtliche Mitteilungen*, 42 (1987).

31. NA II, RG 238, Box 32, translation of 'Secret Additional Protocol to the German–Soviet Pact of 23.8.39' (the word 'aggression' was fittingly inscribed in pencil across the top of the document). See also Vaksberg, *The Prosecutor and the Prey*, p. 259; Mironenko, 'La collection des documents sur le procès de Nuremberg', pp. 65–6. Soviet prosecutors were under instructions to shout down any witness during the trial who tried to raise the German–Soviet pact in the course of his testimony.

32. NA II, RG 238, Jackson papers, Box 14, Bernays to Amen, 4 August 1945; Box 21, memorandum to Jackson from Colonel Storey (Documentation Division), p. 2.

Asking the Questions

1. LHA, Hechler 1, 'The Enemy Side of the Hill: the 1945 Background and Interrogation of German Commanders', by Major K. W. Hechler, Historical Division, US State Department, 30 July 1949, p. 117.

2. NA II, RG 107, Stimson papers, Box 5, Bernays to Stimson, 'Memorandum: Report to the President', 7 June 1945, p. 2. On the issue of rights, see *European Convention for the Protection of Human Rights*, 1950, Article 6, 'Right to a Fair Trial', paragraphs 1, 3.

3. A. Speer, *Inside the Third Reich* (London, 1970), pp. 504–5; H. H. G. Schacht, *76 Jahre meines Lebens* (Bad Wörishofen, 1953), p. 565; PRO, FO 371/46777, SHAEF to British chiefs-of-staff, 28 May 1945, for details of the 'Ashcan' camp. Details on those held at 'Ashcan' in WO 208/3153, weekly roster of 'Ashcan', June–July 1945. Thirteen of the eventual twenty-two defendants were held there.

4. LHA, Hechler 1, 'The Enemy Side of the Hill', pp. 28–33; A. Neave, *Nuremberg* (London, 1978), pp. 61–2; information on calories from PRO, FO 371/51025, SHAEF message to 21st Army Group, 2 June 1945.

5. PRO, FO 371/46778, Ivone Kirkpatrick (Political Office, British Supreme HQ) to Eden, 21 June 1945.

6. LHA, Hechler 1, 'The Enemy Side of the Hill', p. 29.

7. IWM, FO 645, Box 161, testimony of Fritz Sauckel taken at Nuremberg, 13 September 1945, pp. 3–5.

8. See J. K. Galbraith, *A Life in Our Times: Memoirs* (London, 1981), pp. 212–19, 232–40; on the Bombing Survey, see D. McIsaac, *Strategic Bombing in World War Two* (vol. 1, New York, 1976).

9. LHA, Hechler 1, 'The Enemy Side of the Hill', p. 16.

10. PRO, LCO 2/2980, minutes of second meeting between BWCE and representatives of the USA, 21 June 1945, p. 2. The psychiatrists hoped that if 'the mental condition of some of the defendants was exposed to the world, they would be deflated and it would be more difficult to build a myth around them of being great men'.

11. NA II, RG 107. McCloy papers, Box 3, Bernays to Jackson, 9 May 1945, memorandum for the Chief of Counsel, p. 1.

12. A. and J. Tusa, *The Nuremberg Trial* (London, 1983), pp. 160–61; T. Taylor, *The Anatomy of the Nuremberg Trials* (London, 1993), pp. 40–41.

13. NA II, RG 238, Box 18, memorandum to Jackson, 'The Interrogation Division', 9 August 1945, p. 2.

14. PRO, WO 311/576, BWCE (Paris Section) to War Office, 8 August 1945.

15. PRO, WO 311/583, Office of US Chief of Counsel to War Office (n.d.); WO 208/3153, weekly roster of 'Ashcan' internees, 30 June 1945.

16. F. von Papen, *Memoirs* (London, 1952), pp. 543–5; B. Andrus, *The Infamous of Nuremberg* (London, 1969), p. 62.

17. NA II, RG 107, McCloy papers, Box 3, telegram from Office of Chief of Counsel to Secretary of State, 19 August 1945, p. 1; RG 238, Jackson

papers, Box 39, memorandum from Jackson to Storey, 5 November 1945, 'Disposition of Persons Held at Nuremberg', p. 1.

18. NA II, RG 238, Jackson papers, Box 39, Andrus to Jackson, 22 August, 1945, 'Present Custody of Certain German Prisoners'.

19. Schacht, *76 Jahre meines Lebens*, pp. 568–70.

20. Speer, *Inside the Third Reich*, pp. 505–7.

21. R. E. Conot, *Justice at Nuremberg* (London, 1983), p. 47; PRO, WO 208/4475, Foreign Office, Political Intelligence Department, Digest for Germany and Austria, 3 November 1945; H. Fritzsche, *The Sword in the Scales* (London, 1953), p. 13; E. Raeder, *Mein Leben* (2 vols., Tübingen, 1957), II, p. 305; J. L. Heinemann, *Hitler's First Foreign Minister: Constantin von Neurath* (Berkeley, Calif., 1979), pp. 220–21.

22. Raeder, *Mein Leben*, II, pp. 304–5; P. Sudoplatov, *Special Tasks* (London, 1994), p. 169; Fritzsche, *The Sword in the Scales*, pp. 16–19.

23. NA II, RG 107, McCloy papers, Box 3, Office of Chief of Counsel to Secretary of State, 19 August 1945, pp. 1–2; J. Stern, *The Hidden Damage* (London, 1990), pp. 260–62, 285–91; R. West, *A Train of Powder* (London, 1955), pp. 8–15, 25–8; H. Gaskin (ed.), *Eyewitnesses at Nuremberg*, pp. 102–3 (testimony of Mary Burns, Priscilla Belcher), pp. 114–15 (testimony of Jean Tull), p. 124 (testimony of Yvette Wilberforce).

24. PRO, FO 371/51035, 'Notes on a visit to Nuremberg with the Attorney General', 17/18 August 1945, pp. 1–3; NA II, RG 107, McCloy papers, Box 3, Office of Chief of Counsel to Secretary of State, 19 August 1945, p. 1; D. M. Kelley, *22 Cells in Nuremberg: A Psychiatrist Examines the Nazi Criminals* (New York, 1947), pp. 8–9.

25. NA II, RG 238, Jackson papers, Box 39, Colonel Andrus to Chief of Counsel, 29 September 1945.

26. NA II, RG 238, Jackson papers, Box 3, Internal Security Detachment, 'Rules for Prisoners', 11 September 1945, pp. 1–2; Box 15, HQ Internal Security Detachment, 'Rules for Prisoners', pp. 1–3. Witnesses kept at Nuremberg, as distinct from defendants, were allowed to talk to each other, and to enjoy complete freedom in the exercise yard (see Kelley, *22 Cells in Nuremberg*, pp. 8–11).

27. Gaskin, *Eyewitnesses at Nuremberg*, pp. 30–31 (testimony of prison guard Paul Graven).

28. NA II, RG 238, Jackson papers, Box 39, Kelley to Andrus, 2 October 1945; Andrus to Office of Chief of Counsel, 7 November 1945; RG 107, McCloy papers, Box 3, Office of Chief of Counsel to Secretary of State, 19 August 1945; on Kaltenbrunner, see P. R. Black, *Ernst Kaltenbrunner: Ideological Soldier of the Third Reich* (Princeton, NJ, 1984), p. 261.

29. Kelley, 22 *Cells in Nuremberg*, pp. viii, 12; G. M. Gilbert, *Nuremberg Diary* (London, 1948), p. 17.

30. PRO, WO 208/3136, Lieut.-Colonel H. V. Dicks, Directorate of Army Psychiatry, 'Psychological Reactions to Defeat: A discussion of probable modes of German behaviour', May 1945, p. 1.

31. ibid., p. 3.

32. ibid., pp. 4–8, 10–11.

33. NA II, RG 238, Jackson papers, Box 34, memorandum to Amen from Bernays, 8 August 1945.

34. NA II, RG 238, Jackson files, Box 33, collection of cards and charts, file 'Aggression'.

35. NA II, RG 238, Jackson papers, Box 18, memorandum to Justice Jackson, 'The Interrogation Division' by Colonel Amen, 9 August 1945, pp. 1–2, Exhibit A, Exhibit B; memorandum to Jackson from Bernays, 'Analysis of Evidence and Exchange of Information'; memorandum to Jackson from Storey (Documentation Division), 1 October 1945; memorandum from Bernays to Jackson, 10 July 1945, 'Preparation of Evidence'.

36. IWM, FO 645, Box 160, Ribbentrop interrogations, 4, 5, 6 October 1945.

37. NA II, RG 238, Jackson papers, Box 18, Amen to Jackson, 'The Interrogation Division', Exhibit B, for a full list of the staff of the Division. There were 42 in August 1945, with a further 33 prospective staff in the pipeline; see also Taylor, *The Anatomy of the Nuremberg Trials*, pp. 136–7.

38. B. M. Stave and M. Palmer (eds.), *Witnesses to Nuremberg: An Oral History of American Participants at the War Crimes Trials* (New York, 1998), p. 115 (testimony of Joseph Maier, Chief of the Interrogation Division Analysis Branch). On the administering of the oath, see the record of interrogations in the IWM, FO 645 collection. In subsequent trials the American Counsel insisted on interrogators who could speak German, and on the tape-recording of interviews. The experience of 1945, wrote Colonel Telford Taylor, one of Jackson's staff, made it 'difficult if not impossible to establish any *rapport* between the questioner and the subject . . .'. See T. Taylor, *Final Report to the Secretary of the Army on the Nuremberg War Crimes Trials under Control Council Law No. 10* (Washington, DC, 15 August 1949), pp. 59–60.

39. NA II, RG 238, Jackson papers, Box 2, 'Interrogation Notes, Albert Goering', 5 September 1945; Dupré Sassard, HQ USFET to Office of Chief of Counsel, 11 September 1945, enclosing USFET Special Interrogation Brief, 'Corruption in the Nazi Party'.

40. See IWM, FO 645, Box 161, testimony of Albert Speer taken at Nuremberg by Colonel Rosenblit, 14 November 1945, p. 1.

41. IWM, FO 645, Box 156, testimony of Hermann Goering taken at Nuremberg by General Alexandrov, 12 November 1945, p. 2; Box 161, testimony of Albert Speer taken at Nuremberg, 14 November 1945, p. 2.

42. IWM, FO 645, Box 158, testimony of Ernst Kaltenbrunner taken at Nuremberg, 12 November 1945, pp. 10–11.

43. S. Mironenko, 'La collection des documents sur le procès de Nuremberg dans les archives d'état de la fédération russe', in A. Wieviorka (ed.), *Les procès de Nuremberg et de Tokyo* (Paris, 1996), p. 67. At the meeting of the Vyshinsky Commission on the Nuremberg Trial, the deputy minister from the Ministry of State Security observed, 'one could often hear anti-Soviet declarations, and our interrogator Alexandrov does not refute them properly'.

44. NA II, RG 238, Jackson papers, Box 1, interrogation of Fritzsche by the Russians, 12 September 1945.

45. IWM, FO 645, Box 161, testimony of Albert Speer taken at Nuremberg, 14 November 1945, p. 3; see also Speer, *Inside the Third Reich*, p. 509.

46. IWM, FO 645, Box 158, testimony of Wilhelm Keppler taken at Nuremberg, 6 November 1945, p. 13.

47 LHA, Hechler 1, 'The Enemy Side of the Hill', p. 28.

48. Gaskin, *Eyewitnesses at Nuremberg*, pp. 30–31 (testimony of prison guard Paul Graven), p. 59 (testimony of lawyer Bernard Meltzer); LHA, Hechler 1, 'The Enemy Side of the Hill', pp. 36, 54–5; F. Gaiba, *The Origins of Simultaneous Interpretation: The Nuremberg Trial* (Ottawa, 1998), pp. 109–12.

49. IWM, FO 645, Box 160, von Papen interrogations at Nuremberg, 3, 19 September and 12 October 1945.

50. IWM, FO 645, Box 155, testimony of General Karl Bodenschatz taken at Nuremberg, 6 November 1945, p. 1.

51. IWM, FO 645, Box 160, testimony of Joachim von Ribbentrop taken at Nuremberg, 4 October 1945, pp. 4–5.

52. A. Neave, *Nuremberg: A Personal Record of the Trial of the Major Nazi War Criminals in 1945–6* (London, 1978), p. 117.

53. ibid., p. 116; Gaskin, *Eyewitnesses at Nuremberg*, p. 59 (testimony of Bernard Meltzer).

54. PRO, WO 311/15, Judge Advocate General's Office to Deputy Judge Advocate, BAOR, 12 December 1945; see also MI9 to Military Department, Judge Advocate General's Office, 6 July 1945; minute 'Interrogation Teams', 9 July 1945.

55. NA II, RG 238, Jackson papers, Box 39, letter from Peter Calvocoressi to Jackson, 12 October 1945; telegram from War Department to Jackson, 17 September 1945.

56. NA II, RG 238, Jackson papers, Box 16, Storey to Captain William

Ashcroft, 10 September 1945, about photostats; on Soviet problems, see Gaiba, *The Origins of Simultaneous Interpretation*, p. 44. By the end of October the Soviet and French delegations had not managed to supply a single interpreter at Nuremberg. See also PRO, FO 1019/93, Internal Administration with the Russians, memorandum by Major Hill, 27 October 1945; BWCE to Maxwell-Fyfe, 29 October 1945.

57. NA II, RG 238, Jackson papers, Box 27, Amen to Jackson, 23 July 1946: 'there remains only one set of interrogations; namely, the originals which have been, and continue to be, kept under lock and key in my office'; Box 16, Security Division, draft general order (n.d.).

58. PRO, FO 1049/288, Political Division, Control Commision for Germany, 'Ashcan Report' (n.d.), p. 3.

59. IWM, FO 645, Box 161, testimony of Albert Speer taken at Nuremberg, 14 November 1945, p. 8.

60. LHA, Hechler 1, 'The Enemy Side of the Hill', pp. 33, 36–7, 116–17.

61. von Papen, *Memoirs*, pp. 546–7.

62. Speer, *Inside the Third Reich*, pp. 508–9.

63. IWM, FO 645, Box 161, Sauckel interrogations at Nuremberg, 22–28 September 1945.

64. IWM, FO 645, Box 160, testimony of Joachim von Ribbentrop taken at Nuremberg by Justice Jackson, 5 October 1945, pp. 1–55.

65. IWM, FO 645, Box 160, testimony of Joachim von Ribbentrop taken at Nuremberg, 7 October 1945, pp. 5, 7.

The Absentees: Hitler, Himmler, Bormann

1. PRO, FO 1049/288, Political Division, Control Commission for Germany, 'Ashcan Report' (n.d.), p. 2.

2. IWM, Speer Collection, Box S 369, FIAT Report 19, Part III, 1 October 1945, exploitation of Albert Speer, 'The Character of Adolf Hitler', pp. 3–4.

3. PRO, FO 1049/288, 'Ashcan Report', pp. 19–20.

4. Hitler's trial lasted from 26 February to 1 April 1924. He was sentenced to five years in jail and a fine of 200 marks. He was released on 20 December 1924. See I. Kershaw, *Hitler* (London, 1991), p. 207.

5. NA II, RG 107, McCloy papers, Box 1, memorandum by Colonel W. Chanler, 'Can Hitler and the Nazi Leadership be Punished for their Acts of Lawless Aggression?', pp. 1–2, 5–6.

6. NA II, RG 107, Stimson papers, Box 5, Bernays to Stimson, 'Memorandum: Report to the President', 7 June 1945, p. 3.

7. NA II, RG 107, McCloy papers, Box 1, Chanler memorandum, p. 5 (see note 5 above).

8. PRO, TS 26/896, War Crimes, note of a meeting held in the Lord Chancellor's rooms, 8 April 1945, p. 2; see also LCO 2/2981, Attorney General to Lord Simon, 23 November 1944, 'Suggested Trial of Hitler and his Colleagues', pp. 1–2.

9. PRO, TS 26/896, Sir Thomas Barnes to Patrick Dean, Foreign Office, 12 April 1945, pp. 1–2.

10. NA II, RG 238, Box 34, *Free World*, vol. 9, April 1945, p. 38.

11. Details can be found in L. Bezymenski, *The Death of Adolf Hitler: Unknown Documents from Soviet Archives* (London, 1968); A. Petrova and P. Watson, *The Death of Hitler: The Final Words from Russia's Secret Archives* (London, 1995); D. M. McKale, *Hitler: The Survival Myth* (New York, 1981); H. Trevor-Roper, *The Last Days of Hitler* (7th edn., London, 1995). See also I. Kershaw, *Hitler, 1936–1945: Nemesis* (London, 2000), pp. 824–31, 1038–9.

12. PRO, FO 371/46748, telegram from Roberts, British Embassy, Moscow, 6 May 1945, reporting Soviet announcement of the death of Goebbels. Litvinov, Soviet wartime ambassador in Washington, told the British that in the Soviet view Hitler, Himmler and Goering had all 'gone to earth'. On Goebbels, see also H. Fritzsche, *The Sword in the Scales* (London, 1953), p. 10. On Hitler's jawbone, FO 371/46748, article from *The Times*, 7 June and 9 July 1945. On the argument that Hitler took poison, see Bezymenski, *The Death of Adolf Hitler*, pp. 70–75.

13. PRO, WO 288/4475, BBC monitoring service, 'Hitler in Ireland', 16 June 1945.

14. PRO, FO 371/46748, 'Hitler's Last Hours', *The Times*, 21 June 1945.

15. PRO, FO 371/46749, memorandum from Joint Intelligence Committee, SHAEF, 30 July 1945, 'Hitler's Last Days', pp. 3–4.

16. PRO, FO 371/46749, Moscow Embassy to Foreign Office, 12 September 1945, and additional Foreign Office minutes from Northern Department officials.

17. PRO, WO 208/3781, Intelligence Group, Control Commission for Germany, to Central Intelligence Bureau, October 1945, enclosing briefing document, 'The Death of Hitler'; WO 208/4475, SIS report, 31 October 1945, 'The Death of Hitler'. Based on the testimony of three eyewitnesses, Kempka, Karnau and Erich Mansfeld, the report concluded that Hitler did indeed shoot himself, that Eva Braun took poison, and the two bodies were then burnt. Additional testimony from the air force adjutant Nicholas von Below only became available in March 1946, confirming that Hitler had shot himself (WO 208/3781, Intelligence Bureau, Control Commission to Intelligence Bureau, Advanced HQ, Berlin, June 1946).

18. PRO, WO 208/3790, censorship civil communications, 10 January 1946, enclosing a letter to H. M. from his daughter.

19. IWM, FO 645, Box 160, testimony of Joachim von Ribbentrop before Justice Jackson at Nuremberg, 5 October 1945, p. 2; Box 156, testimony of Hermann Goering taken at Nuremberg, 3 October 1945, p. 23.

20. IWM, FO 645, Box 161, testimony of Wilhelm Scheidt taken at Nuremberg, 25 September 1945, pp. 7–8; Box 152, Keitel personality file, interrogation analysis, 10 October 1945. In his memoir written at Nuremberg Keitel recalled the birthday gathering but made no mention of the conversation about 'another task'. See W. Görlitz (ed.), *Generalfeldmarschall Keitel: Verbrecher oder Offizier? Erinnerungen, Briefe, Dokumente des Chefs OKW* (Göttingen, 1961), pp. 342–3.

21. IWM, FO 645, Box 151, note on Krupp (n.d., but November 1945), p. 1–2.

22. NA II, RG 238, Jackson papers, Box 34, Indictment first draft, p. 1; PRO, LCO 2/2980, rough notes of meeting with the Russians, 29 June 1945; FO 1019/98, Jackson to Maxwell-Fyfe, 22 September 1945, p. 2; memorandum to Jackson from Maxwell-Fyfe, 23 September 1945.

23. PRO, WO 311/39, report of BWCE Meeting, 26 September 1945, p. 5.

24. PRO, FO 1049/288, Political Division, Control Commission for Germany, 'Ashcan Report', pp. 12–13.

25. PRO, FO 1049/288, 'Ashcan Report', p. 8.

26. IWM, Speer Collection, Box S 369, FIAT Report 19, Part III, exploitation of Albert Speer, pp. 3–4. The recent biographies of Speer have overlooked this remarkable document. See J. Fest, *Speer: eine Biographie* (Berlin, 1999), p. 384: Fest uses only Speer's account of German politicians, not the account of Hitler. G. Sereny, *Albert Speer: His Battle with Truth* (London, 1995) makes little reference to the interrogation and exploitation material.

27. FIAT Report 19, Part III, p. 4. On the 'Führer myth' see I. Kershaw, *The 'Hitler Myth': Image and Reality in the Third Reich* (Oxford, 1987).

28. IWM, Speer Collection, Box S 369, FIAT Report 19, Part III, pp. 4–5.

29. ibid., p. 6.

30. ibid., pp. 9–10.

31. ibid., p. 12.

32. ibid., pp. 12–14.

33. ibid., p. 26.

34. LHA, Hechler 1, 'The Enemy Side of the Hill', pp. 93, 108.

35. ibid., p. 142.

36. IWM, FO 645, Box 155, testimony of Walther Brauchitsch taken at Nuremberg, 19 November 1945, p. 10.

37. IWM, FO 645, Box 157, testimony of Franz Halder taken at Nuremberg, 29 October 1945, pp. 6–7.

38. R. Smelser, *Robert Ley: Hitler's Labor Front Leader* (Oxford, 1988), p. 233.

39. IWM, FO 645, Box 159, testimony of Robert Ley taken at Nuremberg, 1 September 1945, p. 1; see Smelser, *Robert Ley*, p. 233.

40. IWM, FO 645, Box 160, testimony of Joachim von Ribbentrop taken at Nuremberg, 10 September 1945, pp. 20–21; testimony of 8 October 1945, p. 49.

41. IWM, Speer Collection, Box S 369, FIAT Report 19, Part III, exploitation of Albert Speer, p. 26.

42. IWM, FO 645, Box 161, testimony of Baldur von Schirach taken at Nuremberg, 3 November 1945, p. 2.

43. IWM, FO 645, Box 161, testimony of Baldur von Schirach taken at Nuremberg, 15 November 1945, p. 4.

44. IWM, FO 645, Box 161, testimony of Julius Schaub taken at Nuremberg, 27 September 1945, pp. 5, 19, 24–6.

45. IWM, FO 645, Box 161, testimony of Christa Schroeder taken at Nuremberg, 13 September 1945, pp. 5–6.

46. IWM, FO 645, Box 162, testimony of Fritz Wiedemann taken at Nuremberg, 9 October 1945, p. 13; later in the interrogation Wiedemann was asked if war had always been Hitler's intention from 1933. 'No, I don't think so,' he replied. When pressed further he pointed to the Ethiopian crisis of 1935–6 as the turning point, when Hitler 'got his ideas mostly from Mussolini' (p. 24).

47. NA II, RG 338, Box 81, 21st Army Group Interrogation Centre, interim report on Werner Grothmann, 25 June 1945, pp. 1–2, 8–9; see also P. Padfield, *Himmler: Reichsführer SS* (London, 1990), pp. 608–11.

48. NA II, RG 338, report on Grothmann, pp. 11–12.

49. IWM, FO 645, Box 157, testimony of Margaret Himmler taken at Nuremberg, 26 September 1945, p. 12.

50. NA II, RG 338, Box 81, 21st Army Group Interrogation Centre, report on Gebhard Himmler, 25 June 1945, pp. 1, 6–7.

51. NA II, RG 238, Jackson papers, Box 1, OSS Research and Analysis Branch, biographical report on Martin Bormann, 20 August 1945, p. 4. According to the Soviet authorities the charred remains of Bormann had been found and identified on 10 May. See also Donovan (OSS) to Jackson, 25 September 1945; PRO, WO 208/3155, telegram from General Eisenhower, SHAEF, to John Deane, Military Mission in Moscow, 17 June 1945; note, 21 June 1945, reporting Soviet statement 'that Bormann is not, and has not been in Soviet custody'.

52. NA II, RG 238, Jackson papers, Box 1, Donovan to Jackson, enclosing letter from Gibbs Baker to Donovan, 21 September 1945, from a 'knowledge-able' intelligence source.

53. NA II, RG 238, Jackson papers, Box 1, draft International Military Tribunal Order (n.d.); J. von Lang, *The Secretary: Martin Bormann. The Man who Manipulated Hitler* (Athens, Ohio, 1979), pp. 4–5.

54. IWM, FO 645, Box 151, Elywn Jones, BWCE, to Maxwell-Fyfe, 16 November 1945, 'Information re Bormann', pp. 1–2; PRO, LCO 2/2982, note on Bormann (n.d.); WO 208/4428, Hugh Trevor-Roper to Intelligence Bureau, Control Commission for Germany, 6 February 1946, on Kempka.

55. von Lang, *The Secretary*, pp. 334–5; PRO, WO 208/3790, letter from Trevor-Roper to Intelligence Bureau, BAOR, 7 March 1946, on Axmann's testimony.

56. NA II, RG 238, Jackson papers, Box 1, judgement by Lord Justice Lawrence, 22 November 1945.

57. PRO, FO 1031/63, FIAT report, Dr Karl Peter von Rath and Reichsleiter Martin Bormann, 1 March 1946, pp. 1–2; on numerous other sightings of Bormann, see WO 208/4428, Martin Bormann, personality file.

58. von Lang, *The Secretary*, pp. 347–69.

Selective Amnesia? The Case of Hess

1. IWM, FO 645, Box 151, 'Report of the Examination of Rudolf Hess by the Soviet Delegation', 17 November 1945, p. 2.

2. PRO, PREM 4/100/10, note by Sir Alexander Cadogan for the Prime Minister, 9 November 1943.

3. On Soviet pressure for a trial see PRO, PREM 3/219/7, Tass in English, No. 23, 19 October 1942, citing an article in *Pravda* of 15 October calling for Hess's trial 'by a special international tribunal'. See also Churchill minute to the Secretary of State for Air, 6 April 1945: 'The Russians are very suspicious of the Hess episode and I have had lengthy arguments with Marshal Stalin about it at Moscow in October [1944].' On the discussions at Potsdam, CAB 99/38, 'Record of the Proceedings of the Berlin Conference 17 July to 1 August 1945', p. 266, plenary session, 1 August 1945. The issue provoked a sharp exchange between the new British Prime Minister Clement Attlee and Stalin. According to Attlee's account Stalin asked for Hess to be sent to Germany to join the other war criminals. 'I want advance delivery,' Stalin told him. 'You've already got it on some of them,' retorted Attlee. 'What more do you want?' See F. Williams, *A Prime Minister Remembers: The War and Post-War Memoirs of the Rt. Hon. Earl Attlee* (London, 1961), p. 77.

4. IWM, FO 645, Box 151, Foreign Office Research Department, 'Rudolf Hess: Identity, Personal History and Place in the Nazi Machine', 7 July 1945, p. 2; HQ Internal Security Division to Jackson, 16 October 1945, report from Dr Kelley, 'Psychiatric Status of Internee', p. 1; PRO, LCO 2/2980, minutes of second meeting between BWCE and representatives of the USA, 21 June 1945, p. 1.

5. IWM, Speer Collection, Box S 369, FIAT Report 19, Part I, examination of Speer, 'Politicians and Politics in Nazi Germany', p. 7.

6. On this see P. Padfield, *Hess: Flight for the Führer* (London, 1991). There is still no evidence that the British secret service deliberately lured Hess to Britain to embarrass Hitler, or that such a ploy was condoned by Churchill.

7. IWM, Speer Collection, Box S 369, 'Politicians and Politics', p. 7; FO 645, Box 161, testimony of Laura Schroedl taken at Nuremberg, 4 March 1946, p. 13. Schroedl also claimed that she first discovered his plans to fly to England in September 1940, and that several others who worked for Hess were in on the secret.

8. IWM, Speer Collection, Box S 369, 'Politicians and Politics', pp. 7–8; this is the conclusion arrived at in R. F. Schmidt, *Rudolf Hess: 'Botengang eines Toren'? Der Flug nach Grossbritannien vom 10 Mai 1941* (Düsseldorf, 1997), p. 192. The argument that Hitler approved of and knew about the flight remains unconvincing.

9. D. M. Kelley, 22 *Cells in Nuremberg: A Psychiatrist Examines the Nazi Criminals* (New York, 1947), pp. 26–7; D. Irving, *Hess: The Missing Years 1941–1945* (London, 1987), p. 280; B. Andrus, *The Infamous of Nuremberg* (London, 1969), p. 73.

10. Padfield, *Hess*, p. 304.

11. IWM, FO 645, Box 157, interrogation of Rudolf Hess taken at Nuremberg, 9 October 1945, in the presence of Hermann Goering, pp. 1–5; Box 156, testimony of Hermann Goering taken at Nuremberg, 9 October 1945, p. 1.

12. IWM, FO 645, Box 157, testimony of Rudolf Hess, Ingeborg Sperr and Hildegarde Fath taken at Nuremberg, 16 November 1945, pp. 2–5.

13. ibid., pp. 9–10.

14. IWM, FO 645, Box 160, testimony of Alfred Rosenberg taken at Nuremberg, 16 November 1945, pp. 10–12.

15. IWM, FO 645, Box 160, testimony of Joachim von Ribbentrop taken at Nuremberg, 8 October 1945, pp. 47–8; testimony of Alfred Rosenberg, 16 November 1945, p. 13; Box 161, testimony of Laura Schroedl, 4 March 1945, p. 15.

16. PRO, PREM 3/219/3, report by Colonel M. Rees, 19 June 1941, p. 2.

17. PRO, PREM 3/219/7, Eden to Churchill, 20 May 1942, pp. 1–2.

18. PRO, PREM 3/219/2, Desmond Morton to Churchill, 11 August 1945, enclosing medical report on Hess by Captain M. Johnston.

19. IWM, FO 645, Box 151, HQ Internal Security Detachment, Kelley to Andrus, 16 October 1945.

20. NA II, RG 238, Jackson papers, Box 2, notes on Hess (n.d.).

21. IWM, FO 645, Box 151, 'Record of the Examination of Rudolf Hess by the Soviet Delegation', 17 November 1945, pp. 1–2.

22. NA II, RG 238, Jackson papers, Box 2, 'Additional Psychiatric Report on the Rudolph [sic] Hess Case', p. 4. British report in IWM, FO 645, Box 151, report on Rudolf Hess, 19 November 1945.

23. IWM, FO 645, Box 151, memorandum to General William Mitchell, General Secretary, IMT, 20 November 1945.

24. IWM, FO 645, Box 151, Defence Counsel von Rohrscheidt to General Secretary, IMT, 29 November 1945; Prosecuting Counsel to IMT, 'Matter of Rudolf Hess', 29 November 1945. Hess's statement is in NA II, RG 238, Jackson papers, Box 2, 'Hess Statement', 30 November 1945; German original in A. Seidl, *Der Fall Rudolf Hess 1941–1987* (Munich, 1988), p. 25: 'Ab nunmehr steht mein Gedächtnis auch nach aussen hin wieder zur Verfügung.'

25. H. Gaskin (ed.), *Eyewitnesses at Nuremberg* (London, 1990), p. 97, testimony of photographer Eddie Worth.

26. Kelley, *22 Cells in Nuremberg*, pp. 32–3.

27. Andrus, *The Infamous of Nuremberg*, pp. 121–2.

28. IWM, FO 645, Box 151, letter from IMT Court Contact Committee to all prosecutors, 21 August 1946, enclosing report from Dr G. M. Gilbert, 17 August 1946, 'Competence of Defendant Rudolf Hess'.

The Helpful Speer

1. IWM, Speer Collection, Box S 368, FD 3063/49, FIAT report 254–82, Stahl–Speer, p. 5.

2. ibid., pp. 2, 4–6.

3. ibid., pp. 7–9.

4. A. Speer, *Inside the Third Reich* (London, 1970), pp. 430–31; on the gun, see FIAT report 254–82, p. 7.

5. FIAT report 242–82, p. 6; Speer, *Inside the Third Reich*, p. 431. Speer seemed oblivious to the very considerable risk to which he had exposed his deputy.

6. PRO, WO 208/3152, MI14, 'Report on Speer Interrogations', 4 June 1945, p. 2.

7. J. K. Galbraith, *A Life in Our Times: Memoirs* (London, 1981), pp. 220–30.

8. A. Neave, *Nuremberg: A Personal Record of the Trial of the Major Nazi War Criminals in 1945–6* (London, 1978), p. 139.

9. D. M. Kelley, *22 Cells in Nuremberg: A Psychiatrist Examines the Nazi Criminals* (New York, 1947), pp. 193–4.

10. PRO, FO 371/46778, Kirkpatrick to Eden, 21 June 1945, with additional notes by Cavendish-Bentinck, 24 June 1945.

11. There were three main reports, which can be found in IWM, Speer Collection, Box S 369. The first report, numbered FIAT 19, Part I, on 'Politicians and Politics in Nazi Germany', was produced on 20 August 1945 and ran to 29 pages. The second, FIAT 19, Part II, entitled 'Nazi Foreign Policy and Military Leadership', was produced on 7 September 1945 and was 17 pages in length. The third, FIAT 19, Part III, on 'The Character of Adolf Hitler', was 27 pages long. Only the third was a full written report by Speer himself, the others being based on oral testimony. Hoeffding gave Speer directives about the third report, and Speer turned these into actual questions, to give it the same character as the first two. Hoeffding simplified or deleted some of the questions where they were redundant or too long.

12. IWM, Speer Collection, Box S 369, SHAEF G-2 report, interrogation of Albert Speer, 6th session, 30 May 1945, pp. 3–4.

13. PRO, LCO 2/2980, BWCE meeting, 15 June 1945, p. 2; Speer, *Inside the Third Reich*, p. 508.

14. IWM, Speer Collection, Box S 369, SHAEF G-2 report, interrogation of Albert Speer, 7th session, 6 June 1945, p. 1; SHAEF G-2 report, interrogation of Albert Speer, 20 August 1945, p. 19.

15. IWM, FO 645, Box 161, testimony of Albert Speer taken at Nuremberg, 9 October 1945, pp. 9, 12.

16. IWM, FO 645, Box 161, testimony of Albert Speer taken at Nuremberg by the Soviet delegation, 14 November 1945, pp. 6–7.

17. IWM, FO 645, Box 161, testimony of Albert Speer taken at Nuremberg, 11 October 1945, p. 10.

18. IWM, FO 645, Box 161, testimony of Albert Speer taken at Nuremberg, 14 November 1945, p. 7.

19. IWM, FO 645, Box 161, testimony of Albert Speer taken at Nuremberg, 2 November 1945, p. 4.

20. NA II, RG 238, Jackson papers, Box 6, letter from Speer to Jackson [n.d.], pp. 1–3; IWM, FO 645, Box 161, 'Request to withhold Technical Information', translation of letter from Speer to Jackson.

21. NA II, RG 238, Jackson papers, Box 6, letter to Jackson, pp. 2–3.

22. This view is suggested in M. Schmidt, *Albert Speer: the End of a Myth* (New York, 1982), p. 168. Joachim Fest, in *Speer: eine Biographie* (Berlin, 1999), pp. 386–91, argues that the approach to Jackson was the outcome of

a complex set of psychological pressures on Speer, including realization of the criminal character of the regime he had served. The letter is, none the less, hard to reconcile with any question of remorse or doubt. Speer added a postscript to the letter ('Further information about my activity from Mr Hoeffding (FIAT)') which suggests very strongly that he wanted Jackson to take into account his assistance to the Allies, not that he was trying to confront his past. Speer certainly did win the sympathy of some of those on the bench. When the British trial judge Lord Birkett was interviewed in 1959 by John Freeman in the first of the BBC's very successful 'Face to Face' series, Freeman asked him if he had warmed to any of the accused before him at Nuremberg. Birkett replied: 'The kind of man for whom I felt sympathy was a man like Speer, who was only brought in by Hitler towards the end, and was involved in all this, not in creating aggressive war or anything of that kind, but because he took part in the Sauckel policy, of bringing all these people from other satellite countries.' See H. Montgomery Hyde, *Norman Birkett: The Life of Lord Birkett of Ulverston* (London, 1964), pp. 576–7.

The Unrepentant Goering

1. PRO, WO 311/39, BWCE, Nuremberg to War Office, 14 March 1946.

2. H. Gaskin (ed.), *Eyewitnesses at Nuremberg* (London, 1990), p. 77, testimony of Seaghan Maynes.

3. B. M. Stave and M. Palmer, *Witnesses to Nuremberg: An Oral History of American Participants at the War Crimes Trials* (New York, 1998), pp. 170–71, testimony of Henry King, US prosecution staff.

4. NA II, RG 238, Jackson papers, Box 1, Carl Fritzsche, USFET, to Jackson, 14 August 1945, enclosing letter from Curt Reiss to Robert Murphy, US Political Adviser for Germany, 3 August 1945.

5. PRO, WO 208/3785, MI6, 'Hermann Goering: Personality File', Card 1 for 'swindler'. See also LCO 2/2980, minutes of 3rd meeting of BWCE, 5 June 1945, pp. 1, 4; minutes of BWCE meeting, 15 June 1945, p. 3.

6. NA II, RG 238, Jackson papers, Box 1, OSS Research and Analysis Branch, 'Hermann Goering as a War Criminal', second draft, 16 June 1945; Goering fact sheet, 'Goering as a War Criminal'.

7. J. Heydecker and J. Leeb, *Der Nürnberger Prozess* (Cologne, 1979), pp. 28–9.

8. ibid., *Der Nürnberger Prozess*, p. 30.

9. NA II, RG 107, McCloy papers, telegram from Marshall to Eisenhower, 12 May 1945.

10. LHA, Hechler 1, 'The Enemy Side of the Hill', pp. 55–9.

11. ibid., pp. 33–4.

12. NA II, RG 332, USSBS Interview 56, Hermann Goering, 29 June 1945, pp. 1–9.

13. Gaskin, *Eyewitnesses at Nuremberg*, pp. 79–80, testimony of Roger Barrett.

14. A. Neave, *Nuremberg: A Personal Record of the Trial of the Major Nazi War Criminals in 1945–6* (London, 1978), pp. 65, 69, 72.

15. D. M. Kelley, *22 Cells in Nuremberg: A Psychiatrist Examines the Nazi Criminals* (New York, 1947), p. 51.

16. ibid., p. 65.

17. IWM, FO 645, Box 151, Office of US Chief of Counsel, Interrogation Division summary, interrogation of Hermann Goering, 28 August 1945, p. 3.

18. IWM, FO 645, Box 156, testimony of Hermann Goering taken at Nuremberg, 20 October 1945, pp. 5–6.

19. IWM, FO 645, Box 156, testimony of Hermann Goering taken at Nuremberg, 13 October 1945, p. 2; see also testimony of 8 September 1945, p. 15.

20. IWM, FO 645, Box 156, testimony of Hermann Goering, 8 September 1945, p. 22.

21. IWM, FO 645, Box 151, Office of US Chief of Counsel, Interrogation Division summary, interrogation of Hermann Goering, 28 August 1945, pp. 3–4.

22. IWM, FO 645, Box 156, testimony of Hermann Goering taken at Nuremberg, 8 September 1945, pp. 2, 5; testimony of 24 September 1945, p. 6: 'The Fuehrer's main idea was to try to keep the Western powers out of the war, and he never advocated that a simultaneous attack against the East and West should be conducted.'

23. IWM, FO 645, Box 156, testimony of Hermann Goering taken at Nuremberg, 24 September 1945, p. 4.

24. Kelley, *22 Cells in Nuremberg*, p. 64.

25. PRO, FO 1049/288, Control Commission for Germany, Political Division, 'Ashcan Report' (n.d.), pp. 11–12.

26. PRO, WO 208/4463, Hermann Goering personality file, Scavenger Report No. 10, 1 June 1945, p. 4.

27. IWM, FO 645, Box 156, testimony of Hermann Goering taken at Nuremberg, 24 September 1945, pp. 3, 8.

28. Kelley, *22 Cells in Nuremberg*, p. 63.

29. Neave, *Nuremberg*, p. 74; Heydecker and Leeb, *Der Nürnberger Prozess*, p. 103: 'Der Sieger wird immer der Richter und der Besiegte stets der Angeklagte sein!'

30. IWM, FO 645, Box 156, testimony of Hermann Goering taken at Nuremberg, 19 October 1945, pp. 1–2.

The Limits of Responsibility: Strategies of Denial

1. IWM, FO 645, Box 160, testimony of Franz von Papen taken at Nuremberg, 19 September 1945, p. 21.

2. NA II, RG 107, Stimson papers, Box 5, Bernays to Stimson, 'Memorandum: Report to the President', 7 June 1945, p. 3.

3. ibid., pp. 3–4.

4. A. Vaksberg, *The Prosecutor and the Prey: Vyshinsky and the 1930s Show Trials* (London, 1990), p. 295.

5. B. M. Stave and M. Palmer, *Witnesses to Nuremberg: An Oral History of American Participants at the War Crimes Trials* (New York, 1998), p. 115, testimony of Joseph Maier, Interrogation Division.

6. NA II, RG 238, Jackson papers, Box 7, interrogation of Walther Funk, 12 November 1945. For the full text of Funk's interrogations see IWM, FO 645, Box 156, testimony of Walther Funk, 19 and 22 October, 8 and 10 November. Most of Funk's questioning occurred after the indictment had been served on 19 October. Funk made no objection to interrogation after indictment. See also B. Andrus, *The Infamous of Nuremberg* (London, 1969), pp. 55–6, who claims that Funk confessed to him voluntarily that he had known about the extraction of gold teeth from Jewish victims at the same time that he was denying all knowledge to his interrogators.

7. IWM, FO 645, Box 156, testimony of Walther Funk taken at Nuremberg, 22 October 1945, p. 8.

8. Funk testimony, 22 October, p. 40. On Dachau see NA II, RG 238, Jackson papers, Box 16, affidavit of Franz Blaha, 9 January 1946, introduction.

9. NA II, RG 238, Jackson papers, Box 4, memorandum for Jackson, 'Political Interrogation of von Ribbentrop' (n.d.), pp. 1–4; the same interview is reported in PRO, FO 371/46778, British Supreme HQ, Berlin, to Eden, 21 June 1945, enclosing 'Interview with Ribbentrop', conducted by representatives of the British and US Political Offices. The British version took the same view of Ribbentrop, but expressed in more colourful prose (p. 1): 'His attitude, or pose was one of a man who had nothing to be ashamed of, who had lost a good game through no fault of his own and who had the right to expect that, after giving three cheers for the winner, he should be allowed to go home for tea.'

10. D. M. Kelley, *22 Cells in Nuremberg: A Psychiatrist Examines the Nazi Criminals* (New York, 1947), pp. 93–4, 111.

11. IWM, FO 645, Box 153, Foreign Office Research Department, personality file, Ribbentrop, 25 June 1945, p. 1.

12. IWM, FO 645, Box 160, testimony of Joachim von Ribbentrop taken at Nuremberg, 4 October 1945, p. 46.

13. IWM, FO 645, Box 159, testimony of Constantin von Neurath taken at Nuremberg, 3 October 1945, p. 7; M. Muggeridge (ed.), *Ciano's Diary 1939–1943* (London, 1947), p. 342.

14. IWM, FO 645, Box 159, testimony of Joachim von Ribbentrop taken at Nuremberg, 5 October, 1945, p. 6.

15. von Ribbentrop testimony, 5 October 1945, p. 53; see also J. von Ribbentrop, *The Ribbentrop Memoirs*, introduced by A. Bullock (London, 1954), pp. 179–80 (these memoirs were constructed from the pages of notes written by Ribbentrop during his incarceration).

16. IWM, FO 645, Box 159, testimony of Joachim von Ribbentrop taken at Nuremberg, 7 October 1945, p. 8.

17. IWM, FO 645, Box 160, testimony of Alfred Rosenberg taken at Nuremberg, 5 November 1945, pp. 21–2.

18. IWM, FO 645, Box 161, testimony of Fritz Sauckel taken at Nuremberg, 12 September 1945, pp. 3–7, 12. See also Fritz Sauckel, 'Notes on function of Plenipotentiary General for Labor', Interrogation Division report, 22 September 1945, pp. 1–2.

19. IWM, FO 645, Box 158, testimony of Ernst Kaltenbrunner taken at Nuremberg, September–October 1945.

20. IWM, FO 645, Box 159, testimony of Robert Ley taken at Nuremberg, 18 October 1945, pp. 1–2.

21. Kelley, 22 *Cells in Nuremberg*, pp. 154–6; on Ley's personality see IWM, FO 645, Box 155, Hildegarde Brüninghoff, 'Private Life of Ley', Interrogation Division (n.d., but October 1945), pp. 2–6.

22. NA II, RG 238, Jackson papers, Box 3, Ley notes and diary, written on reverse of 'Gedanken um den Führer' (n.d.). The diary entries read from 12 August to 25 October. See also G.M. Gilbert, *Nuremberg Diary* (London, 1948), p. 19; R. Smelser, *Robert Ley: Hitler's Labor Front Leader* (Oxford, 1988), pp. 294–5.

23. NA II, RG 238, Jackson papers, Box 3, Robert Ley, 'A dialogue' (*Ein Zwiegespräch*), 14 August 1945, pp. 1–3.

24. ibid., p. 6.

25. ibid., p. 5.

26. ibid., p. 10.

27. NA II, RG 238, Jackson papers, Box 3, Robert Ley, 'To My German People! My Political Testament', pp. 4–5; Kelley, 22 *Cells in Nuremberg*, p. 165.

28. NA II, RG 238, Jackson papers, Box 3, letter from Ley to Henry Ford, 18 August 1945.

29. A. Neave, *Nuremberg: A Personal Record of the Trial of the Major Nazi War Criminals in 1945–6* (London, 1978), p. 131; PRO, LCO 2/2982,

memorandum for the IMT General Secretary from Major Neave, 24 October 1945, p. 4.

30. NA II, RG 238, Jackson papers, Box 3, Ley to Dr Flicker [this is a mistranscription; it should read Pflücker, the prison doctor], 24 October 1945, pp. 2–4.

31. Ley to Flicker [Pflücker], p. 9.

32. Neave, *Nuremberg*, pp. 131–2; H. Gaskin (ed.), *Eyewitnesses at Nuremberg* (London, 1990), pp. 30–31, testimony of Paul Graven, prison guard; Kelley, *22 Cells in Nuremberg*, pp. 171–2; J. Heydecker and J. Leeb, *Nürnberger Prozess* (Cologne, 1979), p. 105. Versions vary a little in the retelling, but agree substantially on the main elements of the story. This was not the only suicide. In early October Dr Leonardo Conti, implicated in the so-called 'euthanasia' policy, hanged himself from his window bars. See Andrus, *The Infamous of Nuremberg*, p. 87.

33. F. von Papen, *Memoirs* (London, 1952), p. 256.

34. IWM, FO 645, Box 159, testimony of Constantin von Neurath taken at Nuremberg, 2 October 1945, p. 3.

35. PRO, FO 1049/288, Control Commission for Germany, Political Division, 'Ashcan Report' (n.d.), pp. 1–2.

36. NA II, RG 238, Jackson papers, Box 39, Andrus to Eisenhower (USFET), 16 September 1945, p. 2; Box 4, OSS Research and Analysis Branch, biographical report on Franz von Papen, 30 August 1945, p. 10; Andrus, *The Infamous of Nuremberg*, p. 59, where he refers to him as the 'cunning and malicious von Papen'. On his capture see PRO, FO 371/46777, Foreign Office minute, 'Capture of von Papen', 11 April 1945; interrogation of von Papen, 16 April 1945. On British views see IWM, FO 645, Box 152, Foreign Office Research Department, Franz von Papen, 26 August 1945.

37. IWM, FO 645, Box 160, testimony of Franz von Papen taken at Nuremberg, 3 September 1945, p. 26.

38. IWM, FO 645, Box 160, testimony of Franz von Papen taken at Nuremberg, 19 September 1945, pp. 19–20.

39. IWM, FO 645, Box 160, testimony of Franz von Papen taken at Nuremberg, 12 October 1945, pp. 1–2.

40. ibid., p. 21.

41. ibid., pp. 21–3.

Confessing to Genocide

1. IWM, FO 645, Box 162, testimony of Dieter Wisliceny taken at Nuremberg, 15 November 1945, pp. 1–2.

2. IWM, FO 645, Box 155, testimony of Erich von dem Bach-Zelewski taken at Nuremberg, 25 March 1946, p. 4. On the use made of Bach-Zelewski's evidence see R. Breitman, *Official Secrets: What the Nazis Planned and what the British and Americans Knew* (London, 1998), pp. 222–3. Despite knowledge from intelligence intercepts during the war of Bach-Zelewski's role in mass murder on the Eastern Front, the authorities at Nuremberg had no idea how great a war criminal he was. His willingness to point an accusing finger at his colleagues turned him into a witness for the prosecution. Though later tried, he avoided hanging.

3. See Z. Gitelman, 'Politics and the Historiography of the Holocaust in the Soviet Union' in Z. Gitelman (ed.), *Bitter Legacy: Confronting the Holocaust in the USSR* (Bloomington, Indiana, 1997); see also J. Bridgman, *The End of the Holocaust: The Liberation of the Camps* (London, 1990), pp. 25–7; N. Levin, *The Jews in the Soviet Union since 1917* (2 vols., London, 1990), II, pp. 424–5.

4. IMT Indictment, 6 October 1945, Count 3, Clause VIII, reproduced in M. Marrus, *The Nuremberg War Crimes Trial 1945–1946: A Documentary History* (New York, 1997), p. 65.

5. PRO, FO 371/46778, memorandum 'Visit to Ashcan' by J. Beam, sent to Eden 21 June 1945 from Political Office, British Supreme HQ.

6. IWM, FO 645, Box 160, testimony of Alfred Rosenberg taken at Nuremberg, 22 September 1945, pp. 17–18.

7. ibid., pp. 21–2.

8. IWM, FO 645, Box 156, Office of US Chief of Counsel, Interrogation Division summary, interrogation of Hans Frank, 7 September 1945, pp. 1–2; Box 156, testimony of Walther Funk taken at Nuremberg, 8 November 1945, p. 34; Box 161, testimony of Baldur von Schirach taken at Nuremberg, 15 September 1945, p. 32; Box 153, Foreign Office Research Department, Ribbentrop personality file, 25 June 1945, digest of documents.

9. On Bach-Zelewski see IWM, FO 645, Box 155, testimony of Erich von dem Bach-Zelewski taken at Nuremberg, 25 March 1946: 'I wonder why it is,' Bach-Zelewski asked his interrogator, 'that of those tens of thousands of Jews that were saved in Eastern territories, none of them testified, and none of them have been interrogated. I am thinking particularly of the rabbis, and the chiefs of synagogues, who would make excellent witnesses . . . I told all the many rabbis with whom I talked that they should advise their congregations to

flee . . .' (pp. 2–3). On Woolf see Box 162, testimony of Karl Woolf taken at Nuremberg, 6 September 1945, pp. 16–17, 7 September 1945, p. 13.

10. IWM, FO 645, Box 162, testimony of Woolf, 6 September 1945, pp. 17–18.

11. IWM, FO 645, Box 156, testimony of Heinz Guderian taken at Nuremberg, 5 November 1945, p. 6.

12. B. Andrus, *The Infamous of Nuremberg* (London, 1969), pp. 59–60 on arrangements to eavesdrop on prisoners at 'Ashcan'.

13. IWM, FO 645, Box 161, testimony of Baldur von Schirach taken at Nuremberg, 15 September 1945, p. 5.

14. IWM, FO 645, Box 162, testimony of Dieter Wisliceny taken at Nuremberg, 15 November 1945, pp. 6–8.

15. International Military Tribunal, *Nazi Conspiracy and Aggression* (11 vols., Washington, DC, 1946–8), III, pp. 525–6, Doc 710-PS, Goering to Heydrich, 31 July 1941.

16. IWM, FO 645, Box 157, testimony of Rudolf Hoess taken at Nuremberg, 2 April 1945, pp. 23–4.

17. J. von Lang (ed.), *Das Eichmann-Protokoll: Tonbandaufzeichnungen der israelischen Verhöre* (Berlin, 1982), p. 67.

18. IWM, FO 645, Box 156, testimony of Wilhelm Frick taken at Nuremberg, 6 September 1945, p. 20; Box 155, testimony of Karl Doenitz taken at Nuremberg, 28 September 1945, pp. 6–7.

19. IWM, FO 645, Box 157, testimony of Rudolf Hoess taken at Nuremberg, 2 April 1945, p. 17.

20. NA II, RG 238, Jackson papers, Box 1, memorandum from the Polish delegation, 'Frank's Capital Crimes' (n.d.), pp. 1–13. The documents included the following comments by Frank in a government conference on 16 December 1941: 'As far as the Jews are concerned – and this I shall tell you quite openly – they must be done away with in one way or another . . . Gentlemen, I must ask you to arm yourselves against all considerations based on pity. We must destroy the Jews wherever we come across them and wherever this is possible . . . And the Jews are particularly harmful gluttons as far as we are concerned. We have at the moment about 2½ million Jews, we cannot poison them but will nevertheless be able to intervene in ways which will lead in some way to successful annihilation, and this in connection with the great measures to be discussed in the Reich' [a reference to the forthcoming conference at Wannsee, outside Berlin, where the genocide was announced by Heydrich] (pp. 10–11).

21. IWM, FO 645, Box 159, testimony of Otto Ohlendorf taken at Nuremberg, 26 November 1945, pp. 15, 17–24. There is now a very considerable literature on the role of the German armed forces in the atrocities perpetrated

on the Eastern Front. See in particular H. Heer, 'The Logic of the War of Extermination: The Wehrmacht and the Anti-Partisan War', in H. Heer and K. Naumann (eds.), *War of Extermination: The German Military in World War II 1941–1944* (Oxford, 2000), pp. 92–119; K.-H. Pohl (ed.), *Wehrmacht und Vernichtungspolitik: Militär im nationalsozialistischen System* (Göttingen, 1999), particularly the article by C. Gerlach, 'Verbrechen deutscher Fronttruppen in Weissrussland 1941–44', pp. 89–108.

22. NA II, RG 238, Jackson papers, Box 6, note from Amen to William Jackson, 30 April 1946. On Streicher's career see R. L. Bytwerk, *Julius Streicher* (New York, 1983); and D. M. Kelley, *22 Cells in Nuremberg* (New York, 1947), pp. 141–51, for a psychiatrist's opinion ('a true paranoid reaction').

23. IWM, FO 645, Box 162, testimony of Julius Streicher taken at Nuremberg, 8 September 1945, p. 15; A. Neave, *Nuremberg: A Personal Record of The Trial of the Major Nazi War Criminals in 1945–6* (London, 1978), p. 96; PRO, LCO 2/2982, memorandum for the IMT General Secretary from Major Neave, 24 October 1945, p. 8, and accompanying list of lawyers; Kelley, *22 Cells in Nuremberg*, p. 150.

24. IWM, FO 645, Box 162, testimony of Julius Streicher taken at Nuremberg, 17 October 1945, p. 8.

25. ibid., p. 19.

26. IWM, FO 645, Box 154, Streicher personality file, letter from Pokrovsky to Shawcross, 16 November 1945.

27. IWM, FO 645, Box 159, testimony of Otto Ohlendorf taken at Nuremberg, 24 October 1945, pp. 15–16.

28. IWM, FO 645, Box 162, testimony of Dieter Wisliceny taken at Nuremberg, 15 November 1945 (p.m.), pp. 7–9; von Lang, *Das Eichmann-Protokoll*, pp. 87–8. The story was repeated in the affidavit submitted to the tribunal signed by Wisliceny. See NA II, RG 238, Jackson papers, Box 16, affidavit of Dieter Wisliceny, 24 November 1945. The wording is not identical. In the affidavit Wisliceny made his description of the meeting with Eichmann briefer, while adding a clear statement about the jurisdictional competence of the different elements of the Himmler apparatus to assist the prosecution.

29. von Lang, *Das Eichmann-Protokoll*, pp. 69, 86. Eichmann repeated in his dictated 'memoirs' written in his time in Latin America in the 1950s, when he had no particular reason to misrepresent the date, that extermination began in the late summer of 1941.

30. IWM, FO 645, Box 162, testimony of Dieter Wisliceny taken at Nuremberg, 15 November 1945, p. 7.

31. IWM, FO 645, Box 156, testimony of Wilhelm Frick taken at Nuremberg, 9 October 1945, p. 10. The figure of nine million was clearly a misinterpret-

ation of the figure supplied by the World Jewish Congress for an estimate of the total European Jewish population. See G. Reitlinger, *The Final Solution: The Attempt to Exterminate the Jews of Europe 1939–1945* (London, 1953), p. 489. The figure of 'nine million' has been calculated more precisely since, at 8,861,800 Jews in Europe in 1939, but this degree of statistical accuracy is not possible given the difficulty of dealing with a variety of forms of census classification and inadequate census-taking. See the discussion in S. A. Diamond, 'Had the Holocaust Not Happened, How Many Jews Would be Alive Today? A Survey of Jewish Demography, 1890–2000', *Journal of Holocaust Education*, 6 (1997), pp. 35–7. The figures of those who were killed or died varies widely. Most estimates exceed five million and are consistent with Wisliceny's global figures (Jews transported plus Jews killed by security forces and the army in the east). See Y. Bauer, *A History of the Holocaust* (New York, 1982), p. 355, who estimates Jewish losses at 5,820,900.

32. IWM, FO 645, Box 159, testimony of Otto Ohlendorf taken at Nuremberg, 26 November 1945, p. 28.

33. NA II, RG 238, Jackson papers, Box 16, affidavit of Dieter Wisliceny, 24 November 1945, p. 6. These figures and subsequent figures come from two Wisliceny interrogations, on 15 November (a.m.) and 17 November 1945 (IWM, FO 645, Box 162).

34. IWM, FO 645, Box 162, testimony of Dieter Wisliceny taken at Nuremberg, 15 November 1945 (p.m.), p. 1.

35. IWM, FO 645, Box 162, testimony of Dieter Wisliceny taken at Nuremberg, 17 November 1945, p. 10.

36. M. Broszat (ed.), *Kommandant in Auschwitz. Autobiographische Aufzeichnungen von Rudolf Höss* (Stuttgart, 1961), pp. 7, 145. See also Gaskin, *Eyewitnesses at Nuremberg*, p. 56, testimony of Whitney Harris.

37. IWM, FO 645, Box 157, testimony of Rudolf Hoess taken at Nuremberg, 4 April 1946, pp. 11–12.

38. D. Dwork and R. Jan van Pelt, *Auschwitz: 1270 to the Present* (New York, 1996), pp. 277–83; E. Kogon, H. Langbein and A. Rückerl (eds.), *Nazi Mass Murder: A Documentary History of the Use of Poison Gas* (New Haven, 1993), pp. 145–6.

39. PRO, LCO 2/2980, report from Costello, Moscow embassy, 4 May 1945, 'German Extermination Camps'. On the Allies' knowledge of Auschwitz and its function see Breitman, *Official Secrets*, pp. 138–50; M. Gilbert, *Auschwitz and the Allies* (London, 1981), pp. 231ff.

40. NA II, RG 238, Jackson papers, Box 16, affidavit of Franz Blaha, 9 January 1946, p. 5. The story told by Franz (Frantisek) Blaha changed in some details between his liberation in May 1945 and his later testimony on

issues such as the use of poison gas at Dachau. See Kogon, Langbein and Rückerl, *Nazi Mass Murder*, pp. 203–4.

41. IWM, FO 645, Box 157, testimony of Rudolf Hoess taken at Nuremberg, 5 April 1946, p. 11.

42. G. M. Gilbert, *Nuremberg Diary* (London, 1948), p. 155.

43. Broszat, *Kommandant in Auschwitz*, p. 146.

44. Gilbert, *Nuremberg Diary*, pp. 160–61.

45. NA II, RG 238, Jackson papers, Box 3, letter from Ley for Dr Flicker [Pflücker is meant], 24 October 1945, p. 5.

46. Gilbert, *Nuremberg Diary*, p. 156.

47. PRO, WO 311/5, letter from Judge Advocate-General Western Command Branch to Military Department, Judge Advocate-General's Office, 1 May 1945, p. 1.

48. PRO, WO 309/1423, HQ BAOR to Judge Advocate-General's Office, 4 January 1946, enclosing interrogation reports from No. 1 Sub-Centre CSDIC, 10 December 1945. The conversation was recorded on 3 November 1945. The report was prefaced with a handwritten request that the source of the information should under no circumstances be revealed.

'I hope they hang *all*': Final Retribution

1. IWM, FO 645, Box 162, testimony of Fritz Wiedemann taken at Nuremberg, 18 October 1945, pp. 22–3.

2. IWM, FO 645, Box 155, testimony of Hjalmar Schacht taken at Nuremberg, 19 October 1945.

3. IWM, FO 645, Box 156, Office of US Chief of Counsel, Interrogation Division summary, 'Interrogation of Hans Frank', 14 November 1945; testimony of Hans Frank taken at Nuremberg, 7 September 1945, p. 23, for the reference to Christianity. See also Andrus, *The Infamous of Nuremberg*, p. 110, who recalled Father Sixtus O'Connor, the Catholic chaplain, saying to him: 'Frank has been saved. He has come back to the faith.'

4. IWM, FO 645, Box 156, testimony of Hermann Goering taken at Nuremberg, 19 October 1945, p. 3.

5. PRO, FO 1049/286, Advanced HQ (Berlin), Control Commission for Germany to BWCE, 6 December 1945; telegram to Control Commission, Berlin, 6 December 1945. It was suggested that lesser war criminals could be handed over to relatives or to the police for burial, but neither category of prisoner was to be released for anatomical examination.

6. PRO, FO 1049/286, Control Commission to BWCE, Nuremberg, 10 December 1945.

7. PRO, FO 1049/286, Deputy Military Governor, British Zone, to British Legal Division, 11 December 1945.

8. PRO, FO 945/346, General Robertson (Control Commission, Berlin) to Arthur Street (Foreign Office), 25 March 1946; Patrick Dean to R. Beaumont (Foreign Office), 3 April 1946, pp. 1–2; Street to Robertson, 30 April 1946. On the final fate of the bodies see H. J. Neumann, *Arthur Seyss-Inquart* (Vienna, 1970), p. 382. Neumann used the account reproduced in G. Steinbauer, *Ich war Verteidiger in Nürnberg* (Klagenfurt, 1950). No official record of the fate of corpses seems to have been kept, but the rumour has persisted that they were taken to Dachau to be burned in one of the ovens there. There would have been a grim symmetry in this final act of the drama, which may explain the survival of what is most likely myth.

9. NA II, RG 238, Jackson papers, Box 6, letter from Ernest Schoenfeld to Jackson, 1 December 1945.

10. NA II, RG 238, Jackson papers, Box 3, letter from H. G.-Z. to Jackson, 1 November 1945.

11. Cited in LHA, Hechler 1, p. 29. On Goering's suicide see B. E. Swearingen, *The Mystery of Hermann Goering's Suicide* (2nd edn., London, 1990), especially pp. 210–11.

12. PRO, LCO 2/2980, 'Memorandum of Proposals for the Prosecution and Punishment of Certain War Criminals and other Offenders', US War Department, 30 April 1945, pp. 11–12.

13. PRO, FO 1032/1860, 'Moral Rehabilitation of the German People', note by the Secretariat, Control Commission for Germany (British Element), 24 February 1946, p. 6; 'The Problem of Germany', memorandum from Research Division, Control Commission for Germany, to Secretariat, Advanced HQ (Berlin), 2 March 1946, p. 1.

14. IWM, FO 645, Box 162, testimony of Fritz Wiedemann taken at Nuremberg, 18 October 1945, pp 22–3.

15. PRO, FO 1049/286, Foreign Office minute by William Strang, 6 December 1945.

16. NA II, RG 238, Jackson papers, Box 3, Luise Jodl to Jackson, 19 August 1945.

Part II Interrogations: the Transcripts

Perspectives on the Fuehrer

1. IWM, Speer Collection, Box S 366, FIAT Evaluation Report 241, First Preliminary Report on Hjalmar Schacht, 31 July 1945, p. 4.

2. IWM, Speer Collection, Box S 369, FIAT Report 19, Parts I, II, and III, 20 August, 7 September and 1 October 1945.

3. This idea Hitler is thought to have borrowed from Karl Lueger, Mayor of Vienna when Hitler was an impressionable adolescent in the city before the First World War. See B. Hamann, *Hitler's Vienna: A Dictator's Apprenticeship* (Oxford, 1999), p. 300.

4. J. von Ribbentrop, *The Ribbentrop Memoirs*, introduced by A. Bullock (London, 1954), p. 175: 'I last spoke to Hitler one week before his death, and he said then that the Luftwaffe problem was the real military cause of the defeat.'

5. Paul Ludwig Troost, the Munich architect chosen to remodel the Reich Chancellery. See A. Speer, *Inside the Third Reich* (London, 1970), pp. 28, 39–41.

6. Fritz Todt (1891–1942), leader of the Organization Todt set up in 1933 to oversee major state construction projects, including the Autobahnen and the West Wall fortifications. Todt was appointed Minister of Armaments in 1940 and died in a plane crash on 8 February 1942.

7. Marshal Pietro Badoglio (1871–1956) was appointed chief of the Supreme General Staff in Mussolini's Italy in 1925. He resigned in 1940 following the Italian invasion of Greece, and helped to oust Mussolini in 1943. He became head of the government until June 1944.

8. Herbert Backe (1896–1947), State Secretary in the Agriculture Ministry from 1933 to 1944, when he became Minister until the end of the war. He committed suicide at Nuremberg on 6 April 1947.

9. Karl-Otto Saur, a former time-and-motion expert with the Krupp firm, became Technical Director of the Ministry of Armaments and Munitions under Albert Speer in 1942. After the war he became an important source of technical information on all aspects of the German industrial war effort. See, for example, Saur's analysis of the German 'armaments miracle' (*Wunder der Rüstung*) in IWM, Speer Collection, Box S 362, FD 3049/49, folder 4, report by Karl-Otto Saur, 'Gewaltaktionen 1940–1943', 23 November 1945, written in prison at Nuremberg.

10. Xaver Dorsch was a department head in the Speer Armaments Ministry, who undertook in 1944 to fulfil Hitler's demand for a gigantic programme

of underground construction to save German industry from bombing. He intrigued against Speer during 1944 and became a key figure in SS efforts to take control of the arms economy in the last months of war. See A. Speer, *The Slave State: Heinrich Himmler's Masterplan for SS Supremacy* (London, 1981), pp. 226–7, 230–32.

11. Special academies for training the future National Socialist elite. Four *Ordensburgen* were established, at Crossinsee, Marienburg, Sonthofen and Vogelsang. They were under the control of Robert Ley.

12. Walther Hewel (1900–1945), who participated as a young boy in the Hitler *Putsch* of 1923, became a member of Ribbentrop's private office in 1936, and in 1938 liaison officer between the Foreign Ministry and Hitler. He remained with Hitler in the bunker in 1945, and committed suicide on 2 May.

13. The Second Four Year Plan, announced at the Party Rally in September 1936, and formally established on 18 October with Hermann Goering as Plenipotentiary for the Four Year Plan. See D. Petzina, *Autarkiepolitik im Dritten Reich* (Stuttgart, 1968); R. J. Overy, 'The Four Year Plan', *German Business History Yearbook* (Frankfurt/Main, 2000), pp. 87–103.

14. Eva Braun (1912–1945), Hitler's mistress since 1933 and wife for one day after a marriage ceremony in the bunker on 29 April 1945. The following day she committed suicide by swallowing cyanide.

15. President Roosevelt died on 12 April 1945. See R. Reuth, *Goebbels* (London, 1993), pp. 353–6, on efforts to use the news to buoy up the home front.

16. Gottfried Semper was a nineteenth-century Austrian architect much admired by Hitler, creator of the Burgtheater on the Ringstrasse in Vienna. The Danish architect Theophil Hansen, who designed the Austrian Parliament building, was also revered by Hitler when he began to take an active interest in architecture. See Hamann, *Hitler's Vienna*, pp. 69–70.

17. Only a few such conferences survived in the record. See F. Gilbert (ed.), *Hitler Directs His War: The Secret Records of His Daily Military Conferences* (New York, 1950). The records were discovered at Berchtesgaden. Most had been burned by the SS, but a number of charred records survived. The stenographic reporting of these conferences in fact began in 1942, well before the date suggested by Speer, though the motive for doing so was the same – to have a clear record of the proceedings leading to the issue of operational orders.

18. Colonel-General Werner Freiherr von Fritsch (1880–1939) was commander-in-chief of the German army from 1935 to 1938, when he was the victim of a false accusation of homosexuality which forced his retirement. He died in the Polish campaign on 22 September 1939, when he deliberately exposed himself to fire.

19. Major-General Walter Warlimont (1895–1976) was deputy for operations under Jodl at Supreme Headquarters; General August Winter succeeded Warlimont as deputy for operations on 8 November 1944; General Walter Buhle (not Buhler) was Chief of the Army Staff attached to the OKW under Keitel as part of the reorganization of the army when Hitler assumed the role of commander-in-chief in December 1941; Major-General Walter Scherff was historian appointed to Supreme Headquarters.

20. Colonel-General Kurt Zeitzler (1895–1963) was chief-of-staff of the German army from September 1942 to July 1944, when he was finally replaced after regular disagreements with Hitler. His successor was Colonel-General Heinz Guderian (1888–1954), who had distinguished himself as a Panzer leader in the early campaigns of the war.

21. Field Marshal Erwin Rommel (1891–1944), a famous tank commander in the invasion of France, was appointed to command the Afrika Korps to assist the Italians in their war with the British Commonwealth in North Africa. He later led the defence of France against the D-Day landings, but killed himself following the attempt on Hitler's life in July 1944. Field Marshal Walter Model (1891–1945) succeeded Rommel and von Kluge in France in command of German armies. He failed to stem the tide and German forces were driven back into the Reich. On 21 April 1945 he shot himself. Field Marshal Ferdinand Schoerner (1892–1973) was a tough field commander and a favourite of Hitler. He led the defence of the Berlin area in 1945 and was later imprisoned by the Soviet authorities on war crimes charges. Field Marshal Albert Kesselring (1885–1960) was fortunate not to be in the dock at Nuremberg. He led an air fleet in the Battle of Britain, but later became Supreme Commander of German forces in Italy, where he authorized tough measures against partisans. He was sentenced to death for his part in anti-partisan measures in May 1947, but the sentence was commuted to life imprisonment. He was released in 1952. Neither Hans Hube nor Eduard Dietl was a field marshal; both were colonel-generals. Hube defended Sicily against the Allied invasion in 1943; Dietl was commander-in-chief of the XXth Mountain Army, active in Scandinavia, and was killed in an air crash in June 1944.

22. On the problems facing German forces in the Normandy invasion, see F. Ruge, *Rommel und die Invasion: Erinnerungen von Friedrich Ruge* (Stuttgart, 1959); on the deception plan see the recently published book by R. Hesketh, *Fortitude: The D-Day Deception Campaign*, introduced by N. West (London, 1999).

23. This was not strictly true. Hitler was often in Berlin, and chose to remain among the bombed ruins in the final weeks of the war.

24. The Waffen SS, or 'armed SS', was established in October/November 1939 as the military wing of the SS. By the end of the war 800,000 had served

in the many SS divisions. The SS units came under the control of the army field commanders, and did not have a distinct command structure, despite the post-war efforts by army spokesmen to argue that the SS and the regular army were separate institutions.

25. The Volkssturm was a popular militia set up in September 1944 in Germany to assist in the final stages of the defence of the Reich. Men of all ages not fighting at the front could be liable for service, but the units remained poorly armed and militarily ineffective.

26. The efforts to oust Speer from his post are explored in his *The Slave State*, pp. 51–9.

27. Speer is referring to Hitler, Churchill, Roosevelt and Stalin.

28. Heinrich Hoffmann (1885–1957) was Hitler's official photographer. Hitler met Eva Braun as a young assistant in Hoffmann's shop. He was tried before a German court in 1947 and sentenced to ten years.

29. Hermann Esser (1900–1981), co-founder of the German Workers' Party, predecessor of the NSDAP, was a notable anti-semite and sensation-seeker. He held a number of minor posts, including Vice-President of the Reichstag and Secretary of State for Tourism. He was not a major war criminal, but was tried and sentenced to five years by a German court in 1949.

30. Geli Raubal (1908–31) was Hitler's niece, daughter of his half-sister Angela. Geli almost certainly became Hitler's lover, but in September 1931 she killed herself after quarrelling violently with him. See the account in I. Kershaw, *Hitler, 1889–1936: Hubris* (London, 1998), pp. 351–5.

31. Leni Riefenstahl (1902–) was one of the few female film directors to succeed in 1930s Germany. She was commissioned by Hitler to film one of the Party rallies, and produced two films of the 1936 Berlin Olympics. Though a romantic link with Hitler was often rumoured, their relationship remained one of mutual admiration.

32. Baldur von Schirach (1907–74) was appointed leader of the Hitler Youth in 1931. In July 1941 he was demoted to become Gauleiter ('regional leader') of Vienna, where he presided over the transfer of Vienna's remaining Jewish population to the East.

33. Dietrich Eckart (1868–1923) was a well-known nationalist poet who joined the infant National Socialist Party and became an important influence on Hitler's early years as a politician. Eckart raised money to found the Party newspaper, *Völkischer Beobachter*, which he jointly edited for two years before his death.

34. Marshal Ion Antonescu (1886–1946) was appointed Prime Minister of Romania in September 1940, and became a virtual dictator until his arrest in August 1944 when Romania signed an armistice with the USSR. He was executed as a collaborator in 1946.

35. Adolf Wagner (1890–1944), Gauleiter of Upper Bavaria and an 'old fighter' of the Party.

36. See note 5 above.

37. Winifred Wagner (1891–1980), the English-born wife of Siegfried Wagner, the composer's son. She met Hitler in 1923 in Munich, and thereafter Hitler became a regular visitor at the Wagners' home, Haus Wahnfried.

38. Richard Wagner (1813–83) was one of the formative influences on the young Hitler. In Vienna before the First World War Hitler was a regular visitor to the Opera House to hear everything he could of Wagner's work. Wagner's widow, Cosima (1837–1930), still presided at Haus Wahnfried when Hitler became a visitor in the 1920s.

39. The Bayreuth Festival of Wagner's music was held annually in the Bavarian city where Wagner lived from 1876. Hitler made the festival into an annual pilgrimage for the National Socialist elite, and the festival continued through the war until 1944.

40. Hitler's half-sister Angela (not Angelika) (1883–1949) was the daughter of Hitler's father and his second wife, Franziska. She married Leo Raubal with whom she had one child, also called Angela (Geli), before his death in 1910.

41. Linz, the Austrian city near Hitler's birthplace, where he spent some of his childhood, was chosen by Hitler to become one of the major cities of the Third Reich. Here a vast new industrial complex was constructed, and plans laid for a national museum of art. On Hitler's architectural fantasies see J. Thies, 'Hitler's European Building Programme', *Journal of Contemporary History*, 13 (1978).

42. Josef Thorak and Arno Breker were two of Hitler's favourite sculptors. Both men produced the monumental torsos and nudes which became hallmarks of the 'Aryan' sculpture of the Third Reich.

43. Field Marshal August von Mackensen (1848–1945) was a flamboyant commander from the First World War who became the elder statesman of the German army after Hindenburg's death and was an admirer of the Hitler regime. It is more likely that Lammers is referring here to General Field Marshal Eberhard von Mackensen, who fought on the eastern and Italian fronts.

44. See note 20.

45. General Field Marshal Ewald von Kleist (1881–1954) served as a tank commander in the invasion of France in 1940, led the 1st Panzer Army in the Barbarossa campaign against the Soviet Union in 1941, and was the commander chosen by Hitler in the summer of 1942 to try to capture the Caucasian oilfields. Von Kleist was handed over to the Soviet authorities in 1948 and died six years later in a camp near Moscow.

46. General Field Marshal Wilhelm Ritter von Leeb (1876–1956) commanded an Army Group in the invasion of France, and was the commander of Army Group North in the invasion of the Soviet Union a year later. After arguing with Hitler about a defensive withdrawal around Leningrad, von Leeb was retired early in 1942, not without a handsome golden handshake.

47. General of Police Kurt Daluege (1897–1946) was an early member of the National Socialist Party and SA leader before transferring to the SS in 1928. He became head of the Ordnungspolizei ('order police') in 1936 and worked closely with Heydrich and the apparatus of the RSHA. He was appointed Deputy Protector of Bohemia in 1942. He was fortunate to avoid classification as a major war criminal. He was tried and hanged by the Czech authorities on 24 October 1946, a few days after the major war criminals.

48. General Field Marshal Walther von Reichenau (1884–1942) became one of Hitler's favourite military commanders. An enthusiast for the war effort, he commanded the 6th Army in Poland and France and during the Soviet campaign in 1941. He was promoted to commander of Army Group South in December 1941, but died of a heart attack in January 1942.

49. Reinhard Heydrich (1904–42) became a member of the SS in 1932 and rose quickly to become a leading figure in the reorganized police system in 1936. He was put in charge of the Security Police (*Sicherheitspolizei*) and of the Party's own intelligence agency, the SD. In 1939 he became head of the RSHA, and in 1941 was chosen to organize the genocide of the Jews. He was also appointed Deputy Protector of Bohemia in September 1941. He was assassinated by the Czech resistance in May 1942.

50. General Field Marshal Gerd von Rundstedt (1875–1953) was commander-in-chief of German armies in the invasion of France and commander of Army Group South for the Soviet invasion. After he was retired by Hitler in December 1941 he was appointed commander-in-chief of German armies in the west, a post that he held almost continuously to the end of the war.

51. Viktor Lutze (1890–1943) was an old fighter of the movement from the early 1920s, who became chief-of-staff of the SA following the murder of Ernst Roehm on 30 June 1934. He was killed in a partisan ambush in the occupied USSR in May 1943.

52. Josef 'Sepp' Dietrich (1892–1966) was a tough 'old fighter' from the 1920s who came to head Hitler's personal security in 1928. He had a successful career in the SS before becoming a leading general in the newly-formed Waffen SS in October 1939. He commanded an SS tank corps in France and the Soviet Union, and in December 1944 Hitler put him in command of the 6th Panzer Army for the Ardennes offensive. Dietrich was imprisoned by the Americans and interrogated at Nuremberg. In 1946 he was tried by a military court and condemned to twenty-five years' imprisonment, but was released after ten. He was then sentenced by a West German court to nineteen months for his part in the Roehm purge.

53. Colonel General Franz Halder (1884–1972) was a career soldier appointed as army chief-of-staff in August 1938. Though he distrusted Hitler's strategy and disliked interference in army affairs, Halder served his commander well in the first two years of war. He was finally dismissed in September 1942 following arguments with Hitler over the operations approaching Stalingrad. He was arrested following the July plot in 1944 and ended the war in a camp. He was an important source of technical military information for the Americans, and avoided criminal proceedings.

54. Colonel-General Hans Jeschonnek (1899–1943) was chief-of-staff of the German air force from 1939 to his suicide in August 1943 following the Soviet breakthrough after the Battle of Kursk and the Anglo-American destruction of Hamburg at the end of July 1943.

55. See note 21 above.

56. This is an error for Vice-Admiral Gunther Guse, chief of the naval staff from 1935 to 1938.

57. Flensburg was the north German city where Grand Admiral Doenitz (1891–1981) set up the successor government following Hitler's suicide in April 1945. General Jodl was one of those who moved to Flensburg and continued in office after the end of the war until the British closed the enclave down and arrested its leaders in the last week of May.

58. The attacks by RAF Bomber Command and the US Eighth Air Force over the period 25 July to 3 August 1943 created the worst destruction of life and urban area of any of the attacks hitherto. Total casualties were variously estimated at between 30,000 and 50,000. The Hamburg authorities and the Statistisches Reichsamt spent two years working out precise figures, and in March 1945 published a figure of 41,450 dead for the period from 25 July to 3 August. See O. Groehler, *Bombenkrieg gegen Deutschland* (Berlin, 1990), pp. 118–19.

'The world's worst criminal': Goering in the Third Reich

1. NA II, RG 238, Jackson papers, Box 1, letter from Carl Fritzsche, HQ, USFET, to Jackson, 14 August 1945, enclosing letter from Curt Reiss to Robert Murphy, dated 3 August 1945.

2. PRO, WO 208/4463, BWCE Special Report No. 10, 'Hermann Goering', 1 June 1934, p. 1.

3. PRO, LCO 2/2980, minutes of third meeting of BWCE, 5 June 1945, pp. 1, 4; minutes of meeting of BWCE, 15 June 1945, p. 2.

4 R. J. Overy, *Goering: 'the Iron Man'* (London, 1984), p. 235.

5. Alfred Rosenberg (1893–1946) was appointed head of the Einsatzstab Reichsleiter Rosenberg at the beginning of the war. The principal task of the new staff was to confiscate for Germany thousands of works of art of all kinds in the occupied areas.

6. From the summer of 1939 Hitler began to assemble a collection of paintings and sculpture, under the direction of Hans Posse, to be housed in magnificent art museums in Linz. The collection drew heavily on art confiscated from Jewish owners. See L. Nicholas, *The Rape of Europa: The Fate of Europe's Treasures in the Third Reich and the Second World War* (London, 1994), pp. 41–4.

7. Dr Kajetan Muehlmann, a Goering confidant, and State Secretary for the Arts in the Austrian government following the Anschluss. He was caught at the end of the war and held in custody for a number of years while experts pieced together the story of what was looted and by whom. See Nicholas, *The Rape of Europa*, pp. 422–3.

8. The hilltop abbey in central Italy which became the focal point of a fierce battle between German and Allied forces in the early months of 1944. The art stored at Monte Cassino was brought from Naples to make it safe from the bombing and shelling; 187 crates were sent north to the abbey, and then moved again as the German army retreated.

9. The so-called Salo Republic. Following the Italian surrender to the Allies in September 1943 a new regime was established in the German-occupied north known as the Italian Social Republic, led by Mussolini, who had been daringly rescued from captivity by German special forces.

10. This was a gift from the Italian government for Goering's birthday. Much of Goering's art was acquired in this way as businessmen, politicians and town councils sought to curry favour with the regime's leaders.

11. A reference to the crisis in the last days of the war when Goering, who had fled south to Bavaria, believed that Hitler was no longer capable of governing and that he should assume the leadership of the crumbling Reich. Hitler immediately ordered his arrest. See Bundesarchiv-Militärarchiv, Freiburg, RL1/5, telegram from Goering to Hitler (n.d.); telegram from Hitler to Goering, 23 April 1945.

12. The Allies spent a good deal of time working out exactly how wealthy Goering was. See PRO, WO 208/3785, MI6 personality file on Hermann Goering, card 1: 'is immensely rich. Owns: a game preserve in the "Hinteren Koenigsgebiet", valuable library and art collection, has 250 servants, a seaplane base, and vast estates.'

13. The hydrogenation plants for the manufacture of synthetic oil from coal. These were set up by the Four Year Plan organization from 1937 onwards in

collaboration with the German chemical giant IG Farbenindustrie. Investment was supplied partly by the state, partly by private industry.

14. German aircraft production was controlled from the Reich Air Ministry under the direction of the state secretary, Field Marshal Erhard Milch (1892–1972). In March 1944 a special 'Fighter Staff' was established in Speer's Armaments Ministry to oversee the production of fighter aircraft.

15. Flak is short for *Fliegerabwehrkanonen* ('anti-aircraft artillery').

16. On the decision to place armaments production underground, see R. J. Overy, 'World War II: the Bombing of Germany', in A. Stephens (ed.), *The War in the Air 1914–1994* (Canberra, 1994), pp. 128–9. Some 48.1 million square feet of underground floorspace was allocated for aircraft production, but by the end of the war only 8.4 million had been completed. See PRO, AIR/3873, British Bombing Survey Unit, 'German Experience in the Underground Transfer of War Industries', p. 12.

17. Karl-Otto Saur, Technical Director in the Armaments Ministry, was appointed head of the 'Fighter Staff' at Hitler's insistence. See A. Speer, *Inside the Third Reich* (London, 1970), pp. 332–3.

18. The Messerschmitt Me-262 jet fighter/fighter bomber, which was developed from 1938 onwards, but was only delivered for testing in April 1944 and flew its first combat sortie on 25 July 1944.

19. The Heinkel He-177 four-engined heavy bomber. First developed from a specification in 1937 for a German heavy bomber, the aircraft was plagued with technical difficulties, not least the insistence of the Air Ministry that it should have the four engines in two coupled pairs to allow the aircraft to dive-bomb. At Hitler's instigation the configuration was altered to four separate engines, and the new model saw service in small numbers in 1943 and 1944, but was never produced in the quantities necessary to mount a serious long-range bombing campaign. Over the war period 1,146 He-177s were produced; 573 were built in 1944 against a planned output of 1,651. Figures from BA-MA, RL3/167, Flugzeug-Programm, Plan 222, 1 September 1942; W. Baumbach, *Broken Swastika* (London, 1960), pp. 212–13.

20. Operational strength of the German single-engined fighter force and night-fighter force in December 1944 was considerably less than Goering remembered. The total strength was 3,516 aircraft (2,260 single-engined fighters, 1,256 night fighters), but the available serviceable aircraft totalled only 2,434 (1,521 and 913 respectively). In March 1944 the figure was much lower – a total strength of 2,251, with 1,519 available for operations. See C. Webster and N. Frankland, *The Strategic Air Offensive against Germany* (4 vols., London, 1961), pp. 501–2.

21. The precise figure for aircraft produced in 1944 is still open to dispute. The official figure of 36,103 from the post-war Bombing Survey reports

differs from the official German figure of 39,807. Almost 9,000 aircraft were destroyed in transit or at the factory airfields in 1944, so that the number actually accepted and flown by the German air force was close to the 30,000 suggested by Goering. Of the 39,000 produced, just over 30,000 were fighter aircraft.

22. In the winter of 1943–4 the so-called 'Baby Blitz' was directed at London. 'Operation Steinbock', as it was code-named, was undertaken by the IXth Fliegerkorps under Major-General Dietrich Peltz.

23. The Dornier Do-335 incorporated a radically new engine configuration, with engines and airscrews at either end of the fuselage. Developed in 1942 in response to a German Air Ministry requirement for an unarmed high-speed bomber, production versions were only available in the early months of 1945, too late to see operational experience.

24. The Jägerstab, or 'Fighter Staff', was activated on 1 March 1944 (see note 14 above).

25. Field Marshal Wolfram Freiherr von Richthofen, cousin of the famous 'Red Baron' of the First World War, became one of the most successful air commanders of the war. He commanded the airlift for the relief of Stalingrad in the winter of 1942/3, and was in command of Air Fleet 2 in Italy in 1943. He died on 12 July 1945.

26. Field Marshal Albert Kesselring was appointed Supreme Commander of German forces in Italy in December 1941, a post that he held until March 1945, when he became responsible for the defence of western Germany. Originally taken into the German air force from an army career, he was an operational air commander for only two years of war, from 1939 to 1941.

27. General Adolf Galland (1911–1996) served with the Kondor Legion in Spain, commanded the fighter force for the Battle of Britain, and became General of Fighters in 1944.

28. Major-General Dietrich Peltz was appointed *Angriffsführer England* ('attack leader, England') in March 1943, responsible for organizing special air units for retaliatory bomb attacks on England to try to persuade the RAF to abandon bombing. The campaign was hampered by a lack of aircraft and strong British defences, and little was achieved.

29. Arthur Seyss-Inquart (1892–1946) was a leader of the Austrian National Socialists, who briefly became Austrian Chancellor in March 1938 before Austria was incorporated into the Greater German Reich. He then became Reich Governor of Vienna, and provisional head of the provincial government. The region was renamed Ostmark, and following a law of 14 April 1939 Austria was fully integrated into the administrative structure of the Reich.

30. Kurt Schuschnigg (1897–1977) was Austrian Chancellor from 1934 to March 1938. A member of the Christian Social Party, Schuschnigg imposed

an authoritarian and corporatist system on Austria. After the Anschluss he was imprisoned in a camp until 1945. He eventually moved to the United States, where he adopted American citizenship and became a university professor.

31. The Saar Plebiscite was held in 1935 to determine the future of the German province which had been internationalized and placed under French control under the terms of the Treaty of Versailles. Supervised by a League of Nations force of British, Dutch, Swedish and Italian troops, the population voted by a proportion of 9:1 in favour of reuniting with Germany.

32. The Burgenland was a narrow strip of territory on the border between Austria and Hungary. Styria was the south-eastern province of Austria, bordering both Hungary and Yugoslavia.

33. Wilhelm Keppler (1882–1960) was one of the National Socialist Party's economic experts. He was made a special commissioner for economic affairs in 1933, and later became an official of Goering's Four Year Plan organization in charge of industrial fats and oils. He played some part in preparing the ground for the Anschluss, and was made a Reich Commissioner in the new province. He was tried at Nuremberg in the 'Ministries' trial in 1947 and sentenced to ten years in prison.

34. In 1918 the Austrian Germans, faced with the territorial fragmentation of the former Habsburg Empire in which they had been a privileged people, tried to establish a German–Austrian state without the approval of the victorious powers. Union was forbidden under the terms of the Treaty of Versailles.

Waging War

1. IWM, FO 645, Box 162, testimony of Fritz Wiedemann taken at Nuremberg, 9 October 1945, p. 23. A second version of the story appears in the testimony for 10 November 1945, p. 4. Wiedemann remembered Hitler saying on the same occasion that 'every generation has to go once to a war and now we have to make these things in the east with men who are now thirty-five years and the war in the west we shall make with the younger generation'.

2. IWM, FO 645, Box 162, testimony of Fritz Wiedemann taken at Nuremberg, 10 November 1945, p. 5.

3. ibid.

4. IWM, FO 645, Box 156, testimony of Hermann Goering taken at Nuremberg, 24 September 1945, p. 5.

5. See G. Gorodetsky, *The Grand Delusion: Stalin and the German Invasion of Russia* (London, 1999), especially Chs. 2–4.

6. IWM, Speer Collection, Box S 369, FIAT Report 19, Part II, examination

of Albert Speer, 'Nazi Foreign Policy and Military Leadership', 7 September 1945, p. 11.

7. IWM, FO 645, Box 152, personal file, Wilhelm Keitel, interrogation extract, 8 October 1945, p. 3. On the 'criminal orders' see G. Ueberschär and W. Wette (eds.), '*Unternehmen Barbarossa': Der deutsche Überfall auf die Sowjetunion 1941. Berichte, Analysen, Dokumente* (Paderborn, 1984), pp. 305–7, 313–14. Orders in May, June, August and September permitted the armed forces and security services to murder Communist officials, military commissars, Jews in the service of the Soviet state and all those engaged in partisan activities.

8. IWM, FO 645, Box 152, personal file, Wilhelm Keitel, interrogation analysis, 10 October 1945.

9. Sumner Welles, American Under-Secretary of State, visited Europe in March 1940 on a fact-finding tour for Roosevelt to see what prospects there were for a European settlement. Welles thought Ribbentrop 'very stupid'. See S. E. Hilton, 'The Welles Mission to Europe, February–March 1940: Illusion or Realism?', *Journal of American History*, 81 (1971), pp. 93–120.

10. Count Friedrich Werner von der Schulenburg (1875–1944) was German ambassador in Moscow from October 1934 to June 1941. He was a strong opponent of the German–Soviet war. He was chosen as Foreign Minister by the military conspirators for their proposed new government after the assassination of Hitler. The attempt, on 20 July 1944, failed and Schulenberg died in prison in November 1944.

11. On 27 June 1940 the Soviet Union sent Red Army units into the Romanian province of Bessarabia in order to secure a better strategic position on the Black Sea. See Gorodetsky, *Grand Delusion*, pp. 29–34.

12. The area of northern Bukovina was also annexed from Romania, to secure better Soviet railway communications across the central approaches to the Ukraine.

13. In July 1940 bombers of the German air force were stationed in Romania. In October a German military mission arrived, to be followed by German economic officials of the Four Year Plan, who tied Romanian industry closely to the war economic needs of the Reich.

14. Sir John Simon, the British Foreign Secretary, visited Berlin on 25/26 March 1935.

15. ADAP, Ser D, vol xv, doc 572, and 577. Ribbentrop was not entirely mistaken. He interviewed Leland Morris, the American chargé d'affaires, between 2:18 and 2:21 on 11 December 1941, reading out what amounted to a declaration of war, though it was couched in terms to suggest that the United States had deliberately put themselves in a state of war with Germany by persistent violations of neutrality, and that Germany was now regularizing what had hitherto existed only *de facto*.

16. Hitler spoke in the Reichstag on the afternoon of 11 December 1941, four days after the Japanese attack. During the speech he read out the declaration of war on the United States which Ribbentrop had earlier handed to the American chargé d'affaires.

17. There have been persistent rumours that the purges of the Red Army leadership in June 1937 were inspired by misleading information planted by German agents in Czechoslovakia and fed through to Moscow. The evidence is inconclusive. See C. Andrew and O. Gordievsky, *KGB: The Inside Story* (London, 1990), p. 106; A. C. Brown and C. B. Macdonald, *The Communist International and the Coming of World War II* (New York, 1981), pp. 437–9.

18. This view has been suggested in some of the recent Russian historiography of the purges, but the evidence is not yet substantial.

19. Anton Mussert (1894–1946) was the leader of the Dutch National Socialist Party. He collaborated with the German occupiers during the war and was arrested and hanged by the Dutch authorities in May 1946.

20. Oswald Mosley (1896–1980) was the leader of the British Union of Fascists, founded in 1935. A former Labour Party minister, he abandoned conventional politics during the slump of 1929–32 and tried to copy the rhetoric and symbols of the European fascist movements, with very limited success. During the war he was interned.

21. Leon Degrelle was the leader of the Belgian Rexist movement, founded in 1930. A firm disciple of Hitler, Degrelle went off with other Belgian volunteers to fight on the Eastern Front. He escaped at the end of the war to Argentina, then Spain. He was condemned to death *in absentia* by a Belgian court in 1946.

22. The Rhineland had been demilitarized under the terms of the Versailles Treaty. On 7 March 1936 German forces crossed the Rhine bridges to reoccupy the region, uncertain of whether French and British forces would be mobilized to evict them.

23. Emil Hacha (1872–1945) was President of Czechoslovakia from November 1938 until the German occupation in March 1939. On 15 March 1939 he was summoned to see Hitler, where after hours of bullying and threats to destroy Prague from the air he consented to invite the German army in to maintain 'order' in his country. He was made nominal head of the new Protectorate of Bohemia and Moravia, a position he remained in until 1945. He died in a Czech prison in June 1945.

24. Prince-Regent Paul (1893–1976) took over the throne of Yugoslavia following the assassination of his cousin King Alexander in 1934 until the child king, Peter, was old enough to succeed. Paul visited Berlin in June 1939, drawing Yugoslavia closer to the Axis powers. He was overthrown by army conspirators in March 1941, provoking a German invasion a few weeks later.

25. Ribbentrop made a two-day state visit to Paris on 6/7 December 1938, where a German–French Declaration was signed committing the two states to the peaceful settlement of disputes between them. Ribbentrop betrayed such an exaggerated vanity during the visit that the German ambassador to Paris thought him 'simply mad'. See M. Bloch, *Ribbentrop* (London, 1992), pp. 210–11.

26. Danzig, a former Prussian city, was declared a Free City under the League of Nations in 1919. The object was to provide the new state of Poland, carved out of former Polish territories in the German, Russian and Habsburg empires, with access to the Baltic. A 'corridor' of territory running through Prussia to the sea was also assigned to Poland. The formal demands made by Germany to Poland in 1939 were to renegotiate the future of Danzig and to allow Germany extra-territorial rights to a road and rail link across the corridor.

27. Bernardo Attolico (1880–1942) was Italian ambassador in Berlin from 1935 to 1940. He had the difficult task of telling Hitler on 25 August that Italy would not honour its pledges under the Pact of Steel, signed in May of that year, to fight at Germany's side if she were at war with Britain and France. The news, according to one witness, left Hitler 'completely bowled over'. See G. Engel, *Heeresadjutant bei Hitler 1938–1943: Aufzeichnungen des Majors Engel* (Stuttgart, 1974), p. 59.

28. An Anglo-Polish alliance was only formally signed on 25 August 1939. The guarantee to Poland was a verbal undertaking given by Chamberlain in March 1939.

29. On 6 October Hitler spoke in the Reichstag offering Britain and France the prospect of peace if he was allowed a free hand in eastern Europe. Speer's view that Churchill's presence in the British Cabinet may have prompted the offer is unlikely. Hitler had assumed for some time that Britain and France would declare war – if at all – to save face, but that they were not serious about a military conflict.

30. A reference to the visit of General Edmund Ironside to Warsaw in mid-July 1939. Far from being unfavourable, Ironside sent a telegram to London in which he insisted that 'the Poles are strong enough to resist'. See R. McLeod (ed.), *The Ironside Diaries, 1937–1940* (London, 1962), pp. 81–2.

31. The production programmes of the Four Year Plan, launched in 1936, took several years to plan and prepare fully. By 1939 many materials essential for the German war effort (synthetic oil, synthetic rubber, etc.) would not be available in the desired quantities until 1942–3.

32. The Ardennes offensive was a major spoiling attack launched by Hitler in December 1944 against American armies holding the Ardennes sector, in the hope of splitting American and British forces and driving towards Antwerp. Despite initial German successes in poor winter weather, the Allied line

re-formed, and with massive air support the German thrust was defeated in January 1945.

33. Field Marshal Werner von Blomberg (1878–1946) was chosen as Minister of Defence in Hitler's first Cabinet in 1933. He held the post, renamed Minister of War, in 1935, until February 1938, when he was forced to resign after marrying a woman whose indiscreet past was known to the Gestapo. He died in prison at Nuremberg in March 1946.

34. General Friedrich Hossbach (1894–1980) was Hitler's military adjutant from 1934 to 1938, and later served on the Eastern Front in command of the 4th Army; he was succeeded by General Rudolf Schmundt (1896–1944), whose notes on Hitler's military conferences were used as evidence at Nuremberg. Schmundt died of wounds sustained in the attempt on Hitler's life in July 1944.

35. The Maginot Line was a long series of static defences built by the French government between 1929 and 1939 along the border with Germany and Italy. The line was weakest opposite the Ardennes forest, and could not be built at all in the low-lying plain bordering Belgium.

36. The failure to prevent the British evacuation of troops from Dunkirk has been attributed to many things – Hitler's unwillingness to defeat Britain decisively, the mistaken claim by Goering that his air force could finish off the British on its own, the fear that French resistance would stiffen further south if too many divisions were diverted to deal with British forces: and so on. The natural defences available did make it difficult for German armour to advance swiftly.

37. The Labour Party politician Sir Stafford Cripps was sent as ambassador to Moscow in June 1940.

38. On 31 July 1940 Hitler hosted a meeting of the commanders-in-chief of the armed forces to discuss future strategy. During this meeting he announced that plans were to be prepared for a massive assault on the Soviet Union ('to smash the state heavily in one blow'). On German plans see J. Förster, 'Hitler Turns East – German War Policy in 1940 and 1941', in B. Wegner (ed.), *From Peace to War: Germany, Soviet Russia and the World, 1939–1941* (Oxford, 1997), pp. 117–24.

39. On 14 September 1940 Hitler postponed invasion to 27 September or 8 October. On 17 September he decided once again to postpone the operation, and on 12 October German forces were asked to keep up the pretence of a threat while preparing for a possible landing in the spring or early summer of 1941.

40. The raid into the Atlantic by the battleship *Bismarck* took place between 20 May and 27 May 1941, when the ship was sunk following an attack by British aircraft and surface vessels.

41. Keitel was mistaken in this view, though the German attack on London has often been seen as a revenge attack for the British bombing of Berlin in late August. German bombers had actually been attacking British urban targets since June 1940. See R. J. Overy, *The Battle* (London, 2000), pp. 67–72.

42. In particular wolfram, or tungsten, an important mineral in alloy steels for weapons.

43. This is most likely a mis-transcription for Rear-Admiral Otto Groos.

44. Plans to attack the Soviet Union predated the November visit by more than three months, but the discussions with Molotov, designed in German eyes as an opportunity to turn the Soviet Union eastwards towards the British Empire in India, showed Hitler that Soviet interests were in European security and the expansion of Soviet influence in the Black Sea region. See G. Gorodetsky, *Grand Delusion*, pp. 67–86, for the best discussion of the political crisis following the Molotov visit.

45. The German invasion of Yugoslavia, following the overthrow of Prince-Regent Paul in March 1941 and the installation of an anti-German regime, began on 6 April 1941 and was completed with the Yugoslav surrender on 17 April. Hungarian and Italian forces joined in the invasion, and Yugoslavia was broken up and partitioned between the three invading states and Bulgaria and Albania.

46. As German forces approached the outskirts of Moscow, the Red Army launched a counter-offensive on 5 December 1941 which pushed the German front back during three months of bitter fighting in sub-zero temperatures. See K. Reinhardt, *Moscow – the Turning Point: The Failure of Hitler's Strategy in the Winter of 1941–1942* (Oxford, 1992).

47. The Ploesti oilfields in Romania supplied Germany with a high proportion of its natural oil. They were attacked repeatedly by Allied bombers. The first attack, by American aircraft, came on 11 June 1942, with negligible results. The next attack, on 1 August 1943 by American B-24 Liberator bombers, caused severe damage; output was only restored after eight months, when bombing attacks were renewed. See R. C. Cooke and R. C. Nesbit, *Target: Hitler's Oil. Allied Attacks on German Oil Supplies 1939–1945* (London, 1985), pp. 82–96.

48. Field Marshal Gerd von Rundstedt was German Commander-in-Chief West when Allied forces invaded Normandy on 6 June. The German response to the invasion was hampered by the decision to divide armoured forces between Rommel, who was defending the French coastline, and von Rundstedt, who wanted to build a strong strategic reserve further inland to hurl into the battle at the decisive point.

49. Field Marshal Hugo Sperrle (1885–1953) commanded the German

Kondor Legion in the Spanish Civil War, and an air fleet in the Battle of Britain. He remained in command of German air forces in the west, but the poor performance of the air force during the invasion of France led to his dismissal in August 1944. He was interrogated at Nuremberg on the German bombing of civilians during the Blitz against London and other British cities.

50. When Keitel was interrogated the German commanders still had no idea that they had been duped by the Allied deception plan. Using German double agents a false Allied order of battle was fed through to German intelligence, suggesting that a whole army group (First US Army Group, or FUSAG) was stationed in south-east England waiting to attack north-eastern France.

51. Gestapo agents had discovered before the invasion that the BBC was to broadcast a coded message in two parts to warn the French resistance of imminent invasion. The lines of a poem by Paul Verlaine would be read out on the first or fifteenth day of the month in which invasion would happen, and additional lines broadcast just forty-eight hours prior to the actual invasion. The broadcast was intercepted by a German radio operator, and the message passed on to von Rundstedt's headquarters in Paris. The information was rejected on the grounds that no state would announce its intention to invade over the radio, and complete surprise was achieved by Allied forces on the morning of 6 June. See D. Kahn, *Hitler's Spies: German Military Intelligence in World War II* (London, 1978), pp. 505–11.

52. The attack on the synthetic oil (hydrogenation plants) began on 12 May 1944 and continued for much of that year, reducing the German output of aviation fuel by 95 per cent.

53. The Ludendorff Bridge across the Rhine at Remagen was scheduled for destruction as Allied forces approached. On 7 March the charges set failed to destroy the bridge and an American platoon crossed and held it under heavy German fire. The German officers deemed responsible for the failure were executed. The bridge was destroyed by German aircraft, but not before the American army was across in strength. By that time engineers had constructed a further sixty-two bridges across the river.

54. German armoured forces were commanded by SS General Sepp Dietrich and General Hasso Freiherr von Manteuffel (1897–1978).

Genocide

1. IWM, FO 645, Box 157, testimony of Rudolf Hoess taken at Nuremberg, 2 April 1945, p. 24.

2. IWM, FO 645, Box 156, testimony of Wilhelm Frick taken at Nuremberg, 9 October 1945, pp. 10–11. The figure of 9 million was in fact the total Jewish

population of Europe according to statistics supplied to the prosecution by the World Jewish Congress.

3. IWM, FO 645, Box 158, testimony of Werner Kirchert taken at Nuremberg, 6 November 1945, pp. 1–3.

4. On Polish documentation see E. Kogon, H. Langbein and A. Rückerl (eds.), *Nazi Mass Murder: A Documentary History of the Use of Poison Gas* (New Haven, Conn., 1993), pp. 144–5.

5. H. G. Adler, H. Langbein and E. Lingens-Reiner (eds.), *Auschwitz: Zeugnisse und Berichte* (Cologne, 1979), p. 312.

6. On Soviet occupation of Maidanek see J. Bridgman, *The End of the Holocaust: The Liberation of the Camps* (London, 1990), p. 19.

7. Dr Vojtěch Tuka was Prime Minister of Slovakia from October 1939 to September 1944; Šaňo Mach was appointed Minister of the Interior in 1940 and worked closely with Wisliceny.

8. Cardinal Secretary of State Maglione was a persistent critic of the German treatment of Catholic communities both inside and outside Germany.

9. Monseigneur Jozef Tiso (1887–1947), a Catholic priest, was appointed Prime Minister of Slovakia in October 1938, following the reorganization of the Czech state after the Munich Conference. In October 1939 he became President of the new state of Slovakia. He was later tried and executed by the new Czechoslovak regime in 1947.

10. Theodor Dannecker was a senior SS officer from the RSHA responsible for Jewish policy in France and, in 1943, Bulgaria. He negotiated the deal to transport Jews from the areas occupied by Bulgaria after Yugoslav and Greek defeat in 1941. Official Bulgarian statistics give a figure of 11,343 Jews deported from Macedonia and Thrace. See N. Rich, *Hitler's War Aims: The Establishment of the New Order* (2 vols., London, 1974), II, p. 262.

11. These were members of a special commando unit of the SS organized by Eichmann in March 1944 to deal with the Jews of Hungary. See H. Safrian, *Die Eichmann-Männer* (Vienna, 1993), p. 291.

12. The decision to end the extermination was finally taken at some point in September/October 1944. Extermination centres at Belzec, Chelmo, Sobibor and Treblinka had been closed down in 1943 and their facilities destroyed. The destruction of the Auschwitz crematoria was ordered by Himmler on 26 November 1944.

13. Kurt Becher (not Becker) was the SS officer responsible for the transport of Jews from Hungary. Israel Kasztner was a Hungarian Zionist and founder of the Hungarian Aid and Rescue Committee. He was at the centre of the negotiations with RSHA officials in Hungary in 1944 to pay $2 million to prevent any further deportations of Hungarian Jews to Auschwitz. This arrangement could not be met, but instead Himmler was offered 10,000 trucks

and other commodities as ransom for the remaining Hungarian Jews. This arrangement, too, came to nothing. The gas chambers were closed down in Auschwitz in October 1944, but the decision taken by Himmler was related to wider political issues than the negotiations with Kasztner. See Y. Bauer, *Jews for Sale? Nazi–Jewish Negotiations, 1933–1945* (New Haven, Conn., 1994), pp. 145–7, 162–4.

14. Theresienstadt was a concentration camp for Jews set up in Bohemia, north of Prague, where elderly Jews, Jewish war veterans and other special categories were sent. Eventually the camp became a staging-post for transport to Auschwitz. In 1945 fewer than 10,000 Jews remained there. Thousands perished in the camp from disease and food shortages, in addition to the thousands who were shipped east.

15. The disparity between Wisliceny's figure and the pre-war Jewish population of Poland is striking. The estimates put the 1939 population at approximately 3.3 million (the last Polish census was in 1931), but this does not account for emigration in the 1930s or for the numbers who came under Soviet rule in September 1939, which was imposed on areas of dense Jewish population. Jews were included among those deported from Soviet Poland in 1940–41, and significant numbers must be assumed to have fled eastwards in 1941 when the Germans advanced. Some Jews were killed by Poles after the Soviet authorities left. Wisliceny's figure must include Jews who were actually Soviet citizens in 1941 in Belorussia and Ukraine but were caught by the German security forces and local militias as they retreated. A final figure on the deaths of Polish and Soviet Jews is beyond accurate statistical recovery.

16. One estimate suggests that approximately 690,000 Belorussian Jews escaped or were deported eastwards, of whom an unknown proportion would have survived the attentions of the Soviet and German camp systems and murder squads. See G. Reitlinger, *The Final Solution: The Attempt to Exterminate the Jews of Europe, 1939–1945* (London, 1953), p. 498.

17. The Jewish population of Bohemia and Moravia was approximately 90,000, and the same number in Slovakia. The transport of 200,000 must include all those who were sent to Theresienstadt from elsewhere in Europe and then sent on from there to Auschwitz.

18. The Trianon Treaty was signed by the Allies and Hungary on 4 June 1920 at the Trianon palace at Versailles. Hungary lost about half her territory and two-thirds of her (mainly non-Magyar) population.

19. There were two Vienna Awards, both brokered by the German government. The first, in November 1938, granted Hungary most of the former Hungarian province of Ruthenia, ruled since 1920 by Czechoslovakia; the second, in August 1940, forced Romania to cede a large part of the former Hungarian area of Transylvania back to Hungary.

20. 'Nacht und Nebel' (Night and Fog) was the name given to a decree issued by Hitler on 7 December 1941 to deal with European resistance to German occupation. The security services were given the powers to make people 'disappear' without trial, sometimes to camps, sometimes for execution. See M. Moll, 'Führer-Erlasse', 1939–1945 (Stuttgart, 1997), p. 213, document 125: 'Verfolgung von Straftaten gegen das Reich oder die Besetzungsmacht in den besetzten Gebieten'.

21. Otto Pohl (1892–1951) was head of the SS Economic and Administrative Central Office (*Wirtschafts- und Verwaltungshauptamt*), responsible for the economic activities of the camp system, including the exploitation of labour and the expropriation of Jewish valuables and belongings during the genocide. He was hanged in 1951.

22. This was the figure that Hoess insisted on throughout his interrogations. The Soviet authorities later stated that 4 million had been exterminated there, but the more recent estimates suggest the figure may have been only 1.1 to 1.5 million. This disparity is difficult to explain. It may be that Eichmann knew of the numbers dispatched to the Polish camps, but not their exact destination, but this seems unlikely. The other camps, Belzec, Chelmo, Sobibor and Treblinka, accounted for an estimated 1.65 million Jews. A smaller camp in Belorussia, Maly Trostenets, may have accounted for a further 250,000. The total estimate for all the camps comes to approximately 3 million, which may be the source of Hoess's figure. This still leaves a further 2 million to reach the figure of 5 million claimed by Eichmann. More than 1 million were murdered on the Eastern Front in 1941–2, but these were not included in Eichmann's figure. This suggests that the number of deaths at Auschwitz and other camps must have been higher, which seems unlikely, or that estimates of the numbers killed outside the camp system have been far too low.

23. The first extermination rooms were set up in converted farm houses. The remaining crematoria were built during 1942.

24. Sachsenhausen concentration camp, located north of Berlin, was set up in 1936 to hold political prisoners and so-called 'asocials' (habitual criminals, homosexuals, vagrants, sex offenders, etc.).

25. More usually *Kapos*, supervisory personnel chosen from among the prisoners. They were allowed to live longer than the rest of the prisoners, secured better rations, and were, according to numerous testimonies, no less vicious and unscrupulous than the German guards.

26. The number of children who perished in the genocide has been estimated at 1.5 million. For a full account of their fate see D. Dwork, *Children with a Star: Jewish Youth in Nazi Europe* (New Haven, Conn., 1991).

The Hess Case

1. PRO, PREM 3 219/7, 'My Impressions of "X" [Hess]' by Major Sheppard, 21 May 1941, pp. 1–2.

2. PRO, PREM 3 219/7, Sir John Simon to the Foreign Office (forwarded to Churchill on 11 June 1941), 'Rudolf Hess – Preliminary Report', 10 June 1941, pp. 1–6.

3. IWM, Speer Collection, Box S 369, FIAT Report 19, Part I, examination of Albert Speer, 'Politicians and Politics in Nazi Germany', 20 August 1945, pp. 6–7.

4. ibid., p. 7.

5. IWM, FO 645, Box 151, memorandum from the committee of experts to the General Secretary, IMT, Brigadier-General William Mitchell, 20 November, 1945, p. 1. The memory loss was attributed to 'a tendency to exploit it to protect himself against examination'.

6. During the *Putsch* on 9 November 1923 in Munich, it was Hess's task to arrest the Bavarian ministers while Hitler started the 'national revolution'. This Hess did, holding them in the house of a pro-Nazi publisher. When the *Putsch* collapsed he took two of the ministers in a car to hide them in the mountains. He gave up the kidnapping, fled to Austria and returned in 1924 to face eighteen months in prison, of which he served six.

7. Willi Messerschmitt (1898–1978) was the designer of the main fighter aircraft of the German air force, the Me-109 and Me-110. Hess regularly piloted an Me-110 from the Messerschmitt factory and airfield at Augsburg. On this occasion Hess had persuaded the designer to modify an Me-110 on the pretext that he wanted to fly to Stavanger in Norway. Messerschmitt was fortunate to escape without serious penalty, since he was already at odds with the German Air Ministry. According to his own account, Goering came to Munich the following day and ordered Messerschmitt to meet him there. After an angry exchange, Goering told him that he 'should have noticed that the man was crazy'. Messerschmitt replied, 'How on earth am I supposed to know that a lunatic can have such a high position in the Third Reich?' See A. van Ishoven, *Messerschmitt* (London, 1975), p. 146.

8. A reference to the visit of the Soviet team of medical experts, who examined Hess on 15 November 1945.

The von Papen Case: Resistance and Compliance

1. IWM, FO 645, Box 160, testimony of Franz von Papen taken at Nuremberg, 12 October 1945, p. 1.
2. Heinrich Brüning (1885–1970) was German Chancellor from March 1930 until May 1932. In 1934 he emigrated to the United States, where he became a Harvard professor. He returned briefly to Germany in 1951 to teach at Cologne, but went back to America three years later.
3. PRO, FO 317/46777, minute by G. Harrison (Foreign Office), 'Capture of von Papen', 11 April 1945; interrogation of von Papen, 16 April 1945; SHAEF Special Interrogation Unit, 'Conversation with von Papen', 30 April 1945.
4. IWM, FO 645, Box 160, testimony of Franz von Papen taken at Nuremberg, 19 September 1945, p. 3.
5. Foreign and Commonwealth Office, *Nazi Gold: The London Conference* (London, 1998), pp. 580–83. Neither the Turkish authorities nor von Papen knew of the precise origin of the gold. A total of 249 gold bars were transferred to the Central Bank of the Turkish Republic in 1943.
6. On 2 December 1932 von Papen was forced to tender his resignation as Chancellor after his efforts to suspend the Constitution and rule by decree were frustrated by von Schleicher's opposition. Instead von Schleicher, Papen's Defence Minister, was appointed Chancellor in his place.
7. Von Papen was Minister President of Prussia, and Goering was made the Prussian Interior Minister. The conservative leadership assumed that Prussia would still play a disproportionate role in national politics, as it had done since 1871. It carried much less weight than expected.
8. The new Cabinet was dominated by conservative appointments: Schwerin von Krosigk as Finance Minister, von Neurath as Foreign Minister, Alfred Hugenberg, leader of the German National People's Party (DNVP), as Minister of Economics and Agriculture.
9. Field Marshal Werner von Blomberg (1878–1946) was German delegate at the Disarmament Conference in Geneva in January 1933. He was summoned back to Berlin and appointed Defence Minister in place of von Schleicher on 30 January 1933, two hours before the Hitler Cabinet was sworn in.
10. Captain Ernst Roehm (1887–1934) was leader of the SA from 1930. A tough, violent former soldier he turned the storm troopers into a 400,000-strong political army. He was made Minister without Portfolio in the Hitler Cabinet in December 1933, but on 30 June 1934 he and his immediate associates were murdered by SS assassins during the 'Night of the Long Knives' for an alleged conspiracy against Hitler.
11. Otto Meissner (1880–1953) was chief-of-staff to the President both

before and after 1933. He was one of the conservative officials around von Hindenburg who urged the risk of naming Hitler as Chancellor. Von Papen became a key player in the last days of January, when he indicated his preference for a Hitler-led Cabinet, in which he would play a dominant role. The best guide to the intricacies of the negotiations is H. A. Turner's *Hitler's Thirty Days to Power: January 1933* (London, 1996).

12. There is a confusion in the interrogator's mind here between the Emergency Powers granted in the wake of the Reichstag fire on 28 February 1933 and the Enabling Law of 23 March 1933 which gave the Cabinet the power to make laws without reference to Parliament. July 1934 saw the aftermath of the Roehm purge, which may explain the confusion of date.

13. The total death toll will never be known with certainty, but current figures suggest around 35,000 to 40,000 deaths. Some 350,000 were rendered homeless. Details in O. Groehler, *Bombenkrieg gegen Deutschland* (Berlin, 1990), pp. 411–12.

14. The 'Nuremberg Laws' were drawn up to define the status of Jews and to limit Jewish–German intermarriage. They were announced at a special session of the German parliament at the Party Rally in September 1935. The Law for the Protection of German Blood of 15 September 1935 banned marriage between Jews and Germans, and outlawed sexual relations outside marriage. The Reich Citizenship Law passed the same day confined German citizenship to those of 'German or kindred blood'.

15. This is a reference to von Papen's role as ambassador to Austria prior to the Anschluss.

16. Von Papen was ambassador to Turkey from April 1939.

17. This is an odd slip. Von Papen is perhaps thinking of the First World War, when German forces did fight against the Italians from 1915. He saw campaign service only briefly during the war, as a German staff officer with Turkish forces in Palestine in 1918.

18. A German–Vatican agreement was reached on 20 July 1933, thanks in part to von Papen's own efforts. The Concordat allowed the Catholic Church to continue to operate free of state interference.

19. On 17 June 1934 at the University of Marburg von Papen made a speech critical of the Nazi revolution, calling for the restoration of traditional moral values in politics. He survived the 'Night of the Long Knives' two weeks later, but his speech-writer did not.

20. Wilhelm von Ketteler, von Papen's personal assistant during his period as ambassador in Austria, disappeared on 13 March 1938, the day after the Anschluss, almost certainly murdered by the Gestapo. His mutilated corpse was fished out of the Danube a month later. See Franz von Papen, *Memoirs* (London, 1952), pp. 433–7.

21. Admiral Miklós Horthy was regent of Hungary from 1918 to 1944. He was held as a war criminal at 'Ashcan', and it was his treatment there that occasioned the poor relations between von Papen and Colonel Andrus. See F. von Papen, *Memoirs* (London, 1952), pp. 541–3.

Albert Speer: True Confessions?

1. PRO, WO 208/3152, MI14 report 'A General Survey of German Military War Production based on the Interrogations of Speer', 25–28 June 1945, p. 1.
2. G. Sereny, *Albert Speer: His Battle with Truth* (London, 1995). Less charitable to Speer, see the response to Sereny's book by D. van der Vat, *The Good Nazi: The Life and Lies of Albert Speer* (London, 1997).
3. IWM, FO 645, Box 161, testimony of Albert Speer taken at Nuremberg, 10 October 1945, p. 16.
4. Speer was poorly informed about economic policy. The Economics Ministry and Finance Ministry collaborated at the beginning of the war to raise taxes and to cut consumption by removing around 30 billion marks of purchasing power in the first year of war. The effect was to reduce per capita consumption very sharply in 1939–41, by a higher proportion than in Britain. Much surviving consumer production was in fact destined for the armed forces rather than the civilian market, but was classified as 'consumer goods output' for statistical simplicity. See R. J. Overy, *War and Economy in the Third Reich* (Oxford, 1994), pp. 26–8. By 1941 an average of 40–50 per cent of non-food consumer industries (textiles, leather, paper, etc.) went to the military.
5. German female labour had expanded considerably during the 1930s in response to the demands of rearmament and the reduction in the male agricultural workforce. Over 14 million German women worked in 1939, or 37 per cent of the workforce, a higher proportion than in Britain and the United States at any stage of the war. In addition there was a marked redistribution within the female workforce away from consumer goods to heavy industry and armaments. See E. Hancock, 'Employment in Wartime: the Experience of German Women during the Second World War', *War and Society*, 12 (1994) pp. 43–60, and Overy, *War and Economy in the Third Reich*, pp. 302–10.
6. Colonel General Georg Thomas was chief of the War Economy and Armaments Office at OKW; Friedrich Landfried was State Secretary in the Economics Ministry following the reorganization of the ministry in early 1938 and its integration with the Four Year Plan.
7. Paul Körner was State Secretary in the Prussian State Ministry under

Goering, and his deputy for the Four Year Plan. Körner co-ordinated the Plan and chaired the regular meetings of its officials between 1937 and 1942.

8. Rolf Wagenführ was an economist and statistician attached to the Reich Statistical Office. He became the chief source for the Allies of statistical data on the German war economy. He did not supply national income statistics. These were compiled for the American economic intelligence team by two German economists, Professor Karl Hettlage and Dr Ruth Grünig. On Wagenführ see IWM, FD 3057/49, FIAT Report 1312, 'Economic History of the Second World War' by Dr Rolf Wagenführ. On national income statistics see IWM, FD 3058/49, Wagemann Institute, National Income Estimates, 5 July 1945.

9. 'Indirect armaments' represented non-weapons military equipment, transport and communications, machinery for war industries and war-related construction. Much of the building programme and the supply of tools was completed by 1942, releasing more iron and steel for the building of finished weapons. The real achievement of the Speer Ministry was to use iron and steel with greater efficiency. In 1941, 100,000 tons of steel allocated to armaments produced only 10,000 tons of finished weapons; in 1944 the figure was 40,000 tons.

10. These 'new recruits' were forced foreign workers and prisoners-of-war who were placed under skilled German supervisory personnel. By 1944 some armaments factories employed up to 80 per cent foreign labour.

11. The BMW (Bayerische Motorenwerke) company converted to special machine tools and automated production of aero-engines in 1943, halving the man-hours per engine from 2,500 in 1941 to 1,250 in 1944. See IWM, FD 4969/45, BMW 'Ablauf der Lieferungen seit Kriegsbeginn' (n.d.), p. 25.

12. William Werner was director of the Auto-Union car company. Born in 1883 in New York of German parents, he worked in the American car industry before coming to Germany. In February 1941 he was appointed by the Air Ministry to investigate conditions in aero-engine production at BMW. He was then made head of the aero-engine section of a new Industrial Council set up in May 1941 to introduce rationalization of factory practices more extensively into aircraft production. See L. Budrass, *Flugzeugindustrie und Luftrüstung in Deutschland 1918–1945* (Düsseldorf, 1998), pp. 710–12.

13. The history of the Flugmotorenwerke Ostmark indicated how difficult it was to achieve effective collaboration between different elements of the war economic apparatus. Arguments between Speer and the Air Ministry over the supply of building materials and responsibility for construction led to endless delays when the factory was being built in 1941. The first engines were delivered not in 1944, but in 1943. The plant was then bombed and forced to disperse. See IWM, Speer Collection, FD 778/46, meetings of the Beirat (advisory council) of the Flugmotorenwerke Ostmark, 1941 to 1944.

14. Carl Krauch was a technical director of the IG Farben chemicals company. He became a section head in the Four Year Plan, responsible for synthetic production of oil and rubber, and the explosives programme.

15. The hydrogenation plants produced synthetic oil from lignite or 'brown coal'. The projected capture of the Soviet oilfields in the Caucasus would have made reliance on coal superfluous. Speer's assertion that no detailed analyses of the Soviet economic resources was carried out, and no economic experts attached to staffs in the east, is simply wrong.

16. Albert Vögler was director of the Vereinigte Stahlwerke (United Steel); Carl Krauch was a director of IG Farben; Hermann Röchling was a steel industrialist from the Saarland and an enthusiastic National Socialist.

17. The plans to attack the Soviet economy in the Urals area were far more extensive than Speer realized. Hitler's war directive for Barbarossa called for bomb attacks on the Soviet arms industry once the period of fast-moving mobile warfare had come to an end. In 1942 and 1943 the German air force developed a number of plans to attack economic targets, but each time lacked the resources or adequate long-range aircraft to do so.

18. The attacks on Britain were not mounted against civilian morale, but against economic and military targets, which were to be destroyed systematically once the RAF had been defeated over southern Britain. The failure to invade Britain in the autumn of 1940 led to a sustained bombing campaign conducted against major ports, industrial centres, and London, as an economic and administrative target. Demoralization was certainly an aim, but the Blitz was not intended to be a simple terror campaign for its own sake, even if its deadly consequences made it seem so.

19. Hungary supplied Germany with small amounts of natural oil right up to the end of the war. Upper Silesia produced coal, and iron and steel.

20. Karl-Otto Saur, Technical Director of Speer's Armaments Ministry.

21. Dr Robert Frank gave Speer his first architectural commission in 1933, and remained a close friend thereafter, safeguarding Speer's family at the end of the war.

22. A record of the conferences can be found in IWM, Speer Collection, Box S 363, Saur documents, 'Liste von Rüstungs-Besprechungen bei Adolf Hitler'. They show that Speer still regularly attended during 1944.

23. The Main Committees were set up by Speer shortly after becoming Armaments Minister in February 1942. Each one was responsible for overseeing the production of one major weapon category (e.g. submarines), and each was staffed largely by industrialists and technical experts.

24. The Arado Ar-234 was developed as a single-seater, four-engined reconnaissance and bomber aircraft, using four BMW 003A-1 jet engines. It was produced in very small quantities. A number flew reconnaissance sorties

over Britain and Italy, and a handful undertook bombing attacks on Allied positions during the Ardennes offensive of December 1944.

25. Franz Hofer was Gauleiter of South Tyrol.

26. Walther Rohland was a steel industrialist working for the Speer Ministry. In 1945 he was head of a special commission to keep Ruhr industry going.

27. Friedrich Florian, Gauleiter of Düsseldorf. For details of the argument see A. Speer, *Inside the Third Reich* (London, 1970), pp. 447–8.

28. A reference to the 'London Cage' where German scientists and officials were held and interrogated.

29. Franklin D'Olier, President of the Prudential Insurance Company, was appointed Chairman of the United States Strategic Bombing Survey in 1944. He did not visit Speer before the end of the war, but during the interlude of the Doenitz government at Flensburg.

30. Major-General Frederick L. Anderson was Deputy for Operations, United States Strategic and Tactical Air Forces Command. He was one of the main proponents of the Bombing Survey when it was established in 1944 and was involved in interrogating Speer in May 1945.

31. In August 1944 there were 7.65 million foreign workers in Germany, of whom 2.7 million worked in agriculture, and 0.43 million in mining; 1.94 million worked in the metal and chemical industries, together with 0.34 million prisoners-of-war. See U. Herbert, *Hitler's Foreign Workers: Enforced Foreign Labour in Germany under the Third Reich* (Cambridge, 1997), pp. 297–8.

32. This remark was disingenuous. The Speer Ministry set up the system of specialist committees that was responsible for ensuring that supplies of labour and raw materials reached the factories, and was also responsible for planning the projected flow of resources and monitoring their distribution and use.

Robert Ley: Profile of a Suicide

1. PRO, WO 208/4427, 7th Army Interrogation Center, Robert Ley personality file, report on Dr Ley, 29 May 1945, p. 1.

2. NA II, RG 238, Jackson papers, Box 3, note by Robert Ley (n.d.).

3. PRO, WO 208/4427, 7th Army Interrogation Center, report on Dr Ley, 29 May 1945, pp. 1–2.

4. IWM, FO 645, Box 155, 'Private Life of Ley. Brüninghoff, Notes through Interrogation Division', October 1945, pp. 2–8.

5. The Labour Front (Deutsche Arbeitsfront) was founded on 6 May 1933 following the compulsory disbanding of the trade unions. The Strength

through Joy movement (*Kraft durch Freude*) was established within the Labour Front on 27 November 1933.

6. Inga Ley shot herself on 29 December 1942 after a heavy drinking bout. According to Brüninghoff she had become depressed following complications in childbirth which left her drug-dependent.

7. The last presidential election was held on 10 April 1932, when von Hindenburg received 53 per cent of the votes cast. When he died in August 1934, Hitler fused the office of President and Chancellor into the single post of Fuehrer. A plebiscite to approve the change drew more than 90 per cent in favour.

8. The Enabling Law was passed by a two-thirds majority of the Reichstag on 23 March 1933, giving the Hitler Cabinet wide powers to rule by decree.

9. This was hardly the case. In the absence of any other labour organizations, and with the compulsory collection of dues, the voluntary aspect of membership was no more than nominal.

10. The Political Leaders (*Politische Leiter*) were the organizational and agitational leaders of the Party, under the general direction of Ley himself as head of Political Organization.

11. The Reichsbanner and Rotfront were the paramilitary wings of the two left-wing parties during the Weimar Republic.

12. Ley is here confusing the SA (Sturmabteilungen) and the SS (Schutzstaffel). The first was founded in late 1921 to protect Nazi Party meetings. The SS was set up as a separate elite paramilitary organization in 1929, responsible for safeguarding the person of Hitler himself.

13. Henry Morgenthau, Roosevelt's Secretary of the Treasury, whose views on the agrarianization of Germany were widely publicized.

14. Ilya Ehrenberg, the Soviet poet and writer, was a leading propagandist who helped to inspire the 'summer of hate' against the German invader in 1942.

Obeying Orders: Complicity and Denial

1. IWM, FO 645, Box 160, testimony of Joachim von Ribbentrop taken at Nuremberg, 10 September 1945, pp. 49–50, 51.

2. On these issues in general, see two collections of recent essays: K. H. Pohl (ed.), *Wehrmacht und Vernichtungspolitik. Militär im national-sozialistischen System* (Göttingen, 1999); H. Heer, K. Naumann (eds.), *War of Extermination: The German Military in World War II, 1941–1945.* (Oxford, 2000). The records of war crimes on the Western and Italian Fronts are available in the Public Record Office in the Foreign Office and War Office files.

3. Before 1939, seven main concentration camps were built. During the war a further sixteen camps were added, inside and outside Germany. Each camp spawned a network of sub-camps, usually for work purposes. There were 662 of these smaller camps by January 1945. See W. Sofsky, *The Order of Terror: The Concentration Camp* (London, 1997) for the best recent account of the camp system.

4. The Sachsenhausen camp was at Oranienburg, near Berlin. Dachau was in Bavaria, outside Munich. There was no major camp in Saxony. Frick may have been thinking of Sachsenburg in Thuringia. The nearest camps to the Saxon border were Flossenbürg in Bavaria and Theresienstadt across the frontier in Bohemia.

5. Operation Torch, the landings of American and British Commonwealth troops in Algeria and Morocco on 8 November 1942, shortly before the Red Army launched its devastating counter-attack against Axis forces on the approaches to Stalingrad.

6. Ribbentrop failed to recall that the so-called 'England-Committee' in the German Foreign Office advocated a short, sharp terror-bombing campaign against London in the autumn of 1940 to try to force Britain to sue for peace. See K. Maier, 'Die Luftschlacht um England', in K. Maier *et al.*, *Das Deutsche Reich und der Zweite Weltkrieg: Band II* (Stuttgart, 1979), p. 392.

7. Pierre Laval (1883–1945) became Prime Minister of France in April 1942 under Marshal Pétain. He worked sympathetically for the German cause and became a wanted man when his government collapsed in the summer of 1944. He was eventually arrested by the American army in Austria in July 1945, tried in Paris, and executed on 15 October 1945.

8. A reference to the Einsatzstab Reichsleiter Rosenberg, responsible for plundering European artistic and archaeological treasures for display in German museums.

9. The village of Lidice in Czechoslovakia was destroyed and all its male inhabitants murdered in retaliation for the attempted assassination of Himmler's deputy, Reinhard Heydrich, by Czech resistance on 29 May 1942. Heydrich died of his wounds a few days later. On 10 June the village, near Prague, was chosen as an example to the Czechs: 172 men were shot, the women were sent to camps or murdered and the children to camps or foster homes.

10. Under the terms of the Treaty of Versailles, signed outside Paris on 28 June 1919, Germany was compelled to accept the loss of a 'corridor' of territory through eastern Prussia to Poland. In addition, Upper Silesia was put under Allied control in order to determine by plebiscite which areas should be granted to Poland. The vote was held in March 1921 and as a consequence around half of the area returned to German rule, while the richer, industrialized region, came under Polish control.

11. The areas of Romania taken over by the Soviet Union in June 1940 following strong diplomatic pressure on Bucharest.

12. A reference to the appointment of Sir Stafford Cripps as British ambassador in Moscow in June 1940.

13. The order was distributed to units in early June 1941 by OKW.

14. The first of the so-called 'criminal orders' sent out from OKW on 13 May 1941, 'Decree concerning the implementation of Wartime Military Jurisdiction in the area of Operation Barbarossa'. Reproduced in T. Schulte, *The German Army and Nazi Policies in Occupied Russia* (Oxford, 1989), pp. 321–3.

15. The order signed by Keitel at OKW permitting German forces to execute 50–100 Soviet citizens for every German soldier killed by partisans. Human life, Keitel wrote, was cheap in the Soviet Union and terrorist tactics called for punishments of 'unusual severity'. See J. Förster, 'The Relation between Barbarossa as an Ideological War of Extermination and the Final Solution', in D. Cesarani (ed.), *The Final Solution: Origins and Implementation* (London, 1994), pp. 94–5.

16. This was not the case. The army rear areas (or *Korücks*) were controlled by military personnel. The areas far removed from the fighting – the Baltic states, Belorussia and the Ukraine – were given civilian authorities in 1941, but as German armies retreated the military-controlled rear areas trespassed on the regions of civilian administration.

Germany's Future

1. IWM, Speer Collection, Box S 366, FD 3055/49, FIAT Evaluation Report 241, 31 July 1945, 'First Preliminary Report on Hjalmar Schacht', p. 15.

2. ibid., p. 17.

3. ibid., p. 20.

4. PRO, WO 208/3791, Censorship Civil Communications, 30 October 1947, letter from J.J. to A.K., sent 25 October 1947, pp. 1–2.

5. PRO, FO 1032/1860, Control Commission for Germany (British Element), 'Moral Rehabilitation of the German People', note by Major-General P. M. Balfour, 24 February 1946, p. 7.

6. PRO, FO 1032/1860, Control Commission for Germany, R.D.R. Division to Secretariat, British Advanced HQ, 'The Problem of Germany – February 1946', p. 2.

7. PRO, FO 1032/1860, 'Moral Rehabilitation of the German People' (see note 5 above), p. 7.

8. This was the figure announced by Hitler in the Reichstag in 1939. The

actual amount was much lower. The Reich Finance Ministry budget statistics give a total of 48.8 milliards [= billion] for the budget years 1933/4 to 1938/9. See BAK, R2/21776–81, Reichsfinanzministerium, 'Entwicklung der Ausgaben in den Rechnungsjahren 1934–1939', 17 July 1939. The Reich Statistical Office produced a rather different figure after the war. In a report drawn up in 1947 it was calculated that between 1933 and August 1939 a total of 86.3 billion marks was made available for the government from savings, taxes and loans, and that of this total military expenditure in all its forms amounted to 57.8 billion, or 67 per cent, while much of the rest was spent on prestige projects such as motorways. See BAB, R3102/3602, 'Die gesteuerte Wehrwirtschaft 1933–1939' by A. Jessen, 25 February 1947, pp. 131–5. This figure includes 2 billion spent on the Reich Labour Service, which is not conventionally regarded as a form of military spending, though it did involve quasi-military training.

9. The line of fixed fortifications built along the German–French border in 1938 and 1939.

10. The Organisation Todt was set up in 1933 under the engineer Fritz Todt to undertake state construction projects, including the new system of motorways (Autobahnen) begun in 1934, and the West Wall fortifications. The Labour Service, which already existed before Hitler came to power, consisted of volunteer groups of young men to work on road repair and agricultural projects. In 1935 it was made compulsory for all men between the ages of eighteen and twenty-five. Labour Service was usually performed for a year before military service.

11. The process of standardization of non-military products began in 1938 as part of a programme to save resources for the war effort. The schedules of what could, and could not, be produced were remarkably detailed.

12. Estimates were made at the end of the war of the total quantity of rubble in the major cities. Some thirty-nine cities had in excess of 1 million cubic metres of rubble, but Berlin had an estimated 55 million and Hamburg 35 million cubic metres. See J. Diefendorf, *In the Wake of War: The Reconstruction of German Cities after World War II* (New York, 1993), pp. 14–15.

13. 'Mobilization' seems to be a mistranslation. Ley clearly means the improved mobility of the village with the addition of tractors and trucks. The 'people's tractor' was designed to be built in tens of thousands in large, purpose-built, mass-production plants.

14. The DAF was responsible for improving the productive performance of labour by introducing effective time-and-motion studies and a rational demarcation of jobs on the factory floor.

15. 'Labor initiative' refers to the scheme for workers to suggest improvements in work processes. Successful suggestions could earn bonuses or promotion.

16. After the war around 13 million Germans from eastern Europe entered the western zones of Germany as refugees, including the German populations of East Prussia and Silesia, which were incorporated into the modern state of Poland under agreements reached between the Allies at the Yalta and Potsdam Conferences in 1945.

17. Schacht's estimate was spot on. The total Reich debt on 8 May 1945 stood at 451.7 billion marks, including 388 billion of Reich loans, clearing debts to other states, etc. On currency in circulation he was remarkably well-informed. The total notes in circulation on 30 April 1945 amounted to 70.3 billion marks (8.7 billion in June 1939). See W. Boelcke, *Die Kosten von Hitlers Krieg* (Paderborn, 1985), pp. 102, 107.

Bibliography and Sources

Archive Sources

Public Record Office, Kew, London

Cabinet papers (classes CAB 128, 129, 130)
Foreign Office files (classes FO 371, 945, 1019, 1030, 1031, 1032, 1049, 1060)
Lord Chancellor's Office (class LCO 2)
Prime Minister's papers (classes PREM 3/219, 4/100, 8)
Treasury Solicitor files (class TS 26)
War Office files (classes WO 32, 205, 208, 219, 235, 309, 311)

Imperial War Museum, London

British Intelligence Objectives Sub-Committee papers
Cabinet Office, EDS papers
Combined Intelligence Objectives Sub-Committee papers
Foreign Office, International Military Tribunal files (class FO 645)
Krupp Collection (formerly housed at the Foreign and Commonwealth Office Library; originals now transferred to the Krupp archive in Essen)
Speer Collection, interrogation reports, Boxes S 362–9
Speer Collection, private firm's papers

Liddell Hart Archive, King's College, London

Hechler Collection

National Archives and Records Service II, College Park, Maryland

Record Group RG 107, classified correspondence of Assistant Secretary of War, John McCloy, Boxes 1–3; Secret correspondence, Secretary of War, H. L. Stimson, 1940–1945, Boxes 5, 15
Record Group RG 238, Judge Advocate-General's papers
  US Counsel for the Prosecution of Axis Criminality, Jackson Main Files
Record Group RG 332, United States Strategic Bombing Survey interrogations
Record Group RG 338, European Theater of Operations, US Army, 21st Army Group Interrogation Center

Published Sources

Adler, H. G., Langbein, H., and Lingens-Reiner, E. (eds.), *Auschwitz: Zeugnisse und Berichte* (Cologne, 1979)
Akten zur deutschen auswärtigen Politik 1918–1945, Serie C, D
Andrus, B., *The Infamous of Nuremberg* (London, 1969)
Annan, N., *Changing Enemies: The Defeat and Regeneration of Germany* (London, 1995)
Biddle, F., *In Brief Authority* (New York, 1962)
Broszat, M. (ed.), *Kommandant in Auschwitz. Autobiographische Aufzeichnungen von Rudolf Höss* (Stuttgart, 1961)
Campbell, T. M., and Herring, G. C. (eds.), *The Diaries of Edward R. Stettinius, Jr., 1943–1946* (New York, 1975)
Churchill, W. S., *The Second World War* (6 vols., London, 1948–54)
Clay, General L., *Decision in Germany* (New York, 1950)
Cooper, R. W., *The Nuremberg Trial* (London, 1947)
Dönitz, Admiral K., *Mein wechselvolles Leben* (Göttingen, 1975)
Foreign Relations of the United States (Washington, DC, annually)
Fritzsche, H., *The Sword in the Scales* (as told to Hildegaard Springer) (London, 1953)
Galbraith, J. K., *A Life in Our Times: Memoirs* (London, 1981)
Gaskin, H. (ed.), *Eyewitnesses at Nuremberg* (London, 1990)
Genoud, F. (ed.), *The Testament of Adolf Hitler: The Hitler–Bormann Documents* (London, 1961)
Gilbert, G. M., *Nuremberg Diary* (London, 1948)

Görlitz, W. (ed.), *Generalfeldmarschall Keitel: Verbrecher oder Offizier? Erinnerungen, Briefe, Dokumente des Chefs OKW* (Göttingen, 1961)

Hitler, A., *Hitler's Secret Book*, ed. L. Lochner (London, 1961)

——*Mein Kampf*, ed. D. C. Watt (London, 1969)

International Military Tribunal, *Nazi Conspiracy and Aggression* (11 vols., Washington, 1946–8)

——*The Trial of the Major War Criminals before the International Military Tribunal* (42 vols., Nuremberg, 1947)

Jackson, R. H., *International Conference on Military Trials* (Washington, DC, 1947)

——*The Nürnberg Case* (London, 1947)

Kelley, D. M., *22 Cells in Nuremberg: A Psychiatrist Examines the Nazi Criminals* (New York, 1947)

Kempner, R. M. W., *Ankläger einer Epoche: Lebenserrinerungen* (Frankfurt/Main, 1983)

Klimov, G., *The Terror Machine* (London, 1953)

Kogon, E., Langbein, H., and Rückerl, A. (eds.), *Nazi Mass Murder: A Documentary History of the Use of Poison Gas* (New Haven, Conn., 1993)

Lang, J. von (ed.), *Das Eichmann-Protokoll: Tonbandaufzeichnungen der israelischen Verhöre* (Berlin, 1982)

Marrus, M., *The Nuremberg War Crimes Trial 1945–1946: A Documentary History* (New York, 1997)

Meyer, G. (ed.), *Wehrmachtsverbrechen. Dokumente aus sowjetischen Archiven* (Cologne, 1997)

Muggeridge, M. (ed.), *Ciano's Diary 1939–1943* (London, 1947)

Neave, A., *Nuremberg: A Personal Record of the Trial of the Major Nazi War Criminals in 1945–6* (London, 1978)

Papen, F. von, *Memoirs* (London, 1952)

Processa Graziani: L'autodifesa dell' ex Maresciallo nel resoconto stenografico (Rome, 1948)

Raeder, Admiral E., *Mein Leben* (2 vols., Tübingen, 1957)

Redlich, S. (ed.), *War, Holocaust and Stalinism: A Documented History of the Jewish Anti-Fascist Committee in the USSR* (Luxemburg, 1995)

Ribbentrop, J. von, *The Ribbentrop Memoirs*, introduced by A. Bullock (London, 1954)

Schacht, H. H. G., *76 Jahre meines Lebens* (Bad Wörishofen, 1953)

Smith, B., *The American Road to Nuremberg: The Documentary Record 1944–1945* (Stanford, Calif., 1982)

Smith, H. A., 'The Great Experiment at Nuremberg', *Listener*, 34 (13 December 1945)

Speer, A., *Inside the Third Reich* (London, 1970)

——*Spandau: The Secret Diaries* (London, 1976)

——*The Slave State: Heinrich Himmler's Masterplan for SS Supremacy* (London, 1981)

Stave, B. M., Palmer, M., with Frank, L., *Witnesses to Nuremberg: An Oral History of American Participants at the War Crimes Trials* (New York, 1998)

Stern, J., *The Hidden Damage* (London, 1990)

Sudoplatov, P., *Special Tasks: The Memoirs of an Unwanted Witness – A Soviet Spymaster* (London, 1994)

Taylor, T., *Final Report to the Secretary of the Army on the Nuremberg War Crimes Trials under Control Council Law No. 10* (Washington, DC, 15 August 1949)

'Terminal': Record of the Proceedings of the Berlin Conference 17th July to 1st August, 1945 (HMSO, 1945)

West, R., *A Train of Powder* (London, 1955)

Williams, F., *A Prime Minister Remembers: The War and Post-war Memoirs of the Rt. Hon. Earl Attlee* (London, 1961)

Wilmot, C., 'Nuremberg: the Setting for the Trial', *Listener*, 34 (15 November, 1945)

Secondary Sources

Alford, K. D., *The Spoils of World War II: The American Military's Role in Stealing Europe's Treasures* (New York, 1994)

Andrew, C., and Gordievsky, O., *KGB: The Inside Story* (London, 1990)

Arendt, H., *Eichmann in Jerusalem: A Report on the Banality of Evil* (London, 1963)

Bankier, D. (ed.), *Probing the Depths of Nazi Anti-Semitism: German Society and the Persecution of the Jews 1933–1941* (Oxford, 2000)

Barkow, B., *Alfred Wiener and the Making of the Holocaust Library* (London, 1999)

Bauer, Y., *A History of the Holocaust* (New York, 1982)

——*Jews for Sale? Nazi-Jewish Negotiations, 1933–1945* (New Haven, Conn., 1994)

Baumbach, W., *Broken Swastika* (London, 1960)

Baumgartner-Tramer, F., 'Democracy and Character', *British Journal of Psychology*, 38 (1947)

Bezymenski, L., *The Death of Adolf Hitler: Unknown Documents from the Soviet Archives* (London, 1968)

Birn, R., 'Wehrmacht und Wehrmachtangehörigen in den deutschen Nachkriegsprozessen' in Müller, R.-D., and Volkmann, H.-E. (eds.), *Die Wehrmacht. Mythos und Realität* (Munich, 1999)

Black, P. R., *Ernst Kaltenbrunner: Ideological Soldier of the Third Reich* (Princeton, NJ, 1984)

Bloch, M., *Ribbentrop* (London, 1992)

Boelcke, W., *Die Kosten von Hitlers Krieg* (Paderborn, 1985)

Breitman, R., *Official Secrets: What the Nazis planned and what the British and Americans Knew* (London, 1998)

Bridgman, J., *The End of the Holocaust: The Liberation of the Camps* (London, 1990)

Browder, G., *Hitler's Enforcers* (New York, 1996)

Brown, A. C., and Macdonald, C. B., *The Communist International and the Coming of World War II* (New York, 1981)

Browning, C., *Ordinary Men: Reserve Police Battalion 101 and the Final Solution* (New York, 1992)

——*The Path to Genocide: Essays on Launching the Final Solution* (Cambridge, 1992)

Budrass, L., *Flugzeugindustrie und Luftrüstung in Deutschland 1918–1945* (Düsseldorf, 1998)

Burleigh, M., *Ethics and Extermination: Reflections on Nazi Genocide* (Cambridge, 1997)

——*The Third Reich: A New History* (London, 2000)

Burleigh, M., and Wippermann, W., *The Racial State: Germany 1933–1945* (Cambridge, 1991)

Burrin, P., *Hitler and the Jews* (London, 1989)

Bytwerk, R. L., *Julius Streicher* (New York, 1983)

Cesarani, D. (ed.), *The Final Solution: Origins and Implementation* (London, 1994)

Cohen, A., Cochavi, Y., and Gelber, Y. (eds.), *The Shoah and the War* (New York, 1992)

Conot, R. E., *Justice at Nuremberg* (London, 1983)

Cooke, R. C., and Nesbit, R. C., *Target: Hitler's Oil. Allied Attacks on German Oil Supplies 1939–1945* (London, 1985)

Davidson, E., *The Trial of the Germans: An Account of the Twenty-two Defendants before the International Military Tribunal at Nuremberg* (London, 1966)

Dennett, R., and Johnson, J. E. (eds.), *Negotiations with the Russians* (Boston, 1951)

Diamond, S. A., 'Had the Holocaust Not Happened, How Many Jews Would Be Alive Today? A Survey of Jewish Demography, 1890–2000', *Journal of Holocaust Education*, 6 (1997)

Diefendorf, J. M., *In the Wake of War: The Reconstruction of German Cities after World War II* (New York, 1993)

Diefendorf, J. M., Frohn, A., and Rupieper, H.-J. (eds.), *American Policy and the Reconstruction of West Germany, 1945–1955* (Cambridge, 1993)

Dwork, D., *Children with a Star: Jewish Youth in Nazi Europe* (New Haven, Conn., 1991)

Dwork, D., and van Pelt, R. Jan, *Auschwitz: 1270 to the Present* (New York, 1996)

Ellwood, D. W., *Italy, 1943–1945* (Leicester, 1985)

Engel, G., *Heeresadjutant bei Hitler 1938–1943: Aufzeichnungen des Majors Engel* (Stuttgart, 1974)

Feig, K. G., *Hitler's Death Camps: The Sanity of Madness* (New York, 1981)

Fest, J., *Speer: eine Biographie* (Berlin, 1999)

Fleming, G., *Hitler and the Final Solution* (London, 1985)

Foreign and Commonwealth Office, *Nazi Gold: The London Conference* (London, 1998)

Gaiba, F., *The Origins of Simultaneous Interpretation: The Nuremberg Trial* (Ottawa, 1998)

Gilbert, F. (ed.), *Hitler Directs His War: The Secret Records of His Daily Military Conferences* (New York, 1950)

Gilbert, M., *Auschwitz and the Allies* (London, 1981)

Ginsburgs, G., and Kudriavtsev, V. N. (eds.), *The Nuremberg Trial and International Law* (London, 1990)

Gitelman, Z., 'Politics and the Historiography of the Holocaust in the Soviet Union', in Z. Gitelman (ed.), *Bitter Legacy: Confronting the Holocaust in the USSR* (Bloomington, Indiana, 1997)

Goldhagen, D. J., *Hitler's Willing Executioners: Ordinary Germans and the Holocaust* (Boston, 1996)

Gorodetsky, G., *Grand Delusion: Stalin and the German Invasion of Russia* (London, 1999)

Grindrod, M., *The Rebuilding of Italy: Politics and Economics 1945–1955* (London, 1955)

Groehler, O., *Bombenkrieg gegen Deutschland* (Berlin, 1990)

Hamann, B., *Hitler's Vienna: A Dictator's Apprenticeship* (Oxford, 1999)

Hancock, E., 'Employment in Wartime: The Experience of German Women during the Second World War', *War and Society*, 12 (1994).

Harris, J., and Trow, M. J., *Hess: the British Conspiracy* (London, 1999)

Heer, H., and Naumann, K. (eds.), *War of Extermination. The German Military in World War II, 1941–1945* (Oxford, 2000)

Heinemann, J. L., *Hitler's First Foreign Minister: Constantin von Neurath, Diplomat and Statesman* (Berkeley, Calif., 1979)

Herbert, U., *Hitler's Foreign Workers: Enforced Foreign Labour in Germany under the Third Reich* (Cambridge, 1997)

Hesketh, R., *Fortitude: The D-Day Deception Campaign* (London, 1999)

Heydecker, J., and Leeb, J., *Der Nürnberger Prozess* (Cologne, 1979)

Hilberg, R., *The Destruction of the European Jews* (Chicago, 1967)

——*Perpetrators, Victims, Bystanders: The Jewish Catastrophe 1933–1945* (London, 1993)

Hilton, S. E., 'The Welles Mission to Europe, February–March 1940: Illusion or Realism?', *Journal of American History*, 81 (1971)

Hyde, H. Montgomery, *Norman Birkett: The Life of Lord Birkett of Ulverston* (London, 1964)

Irving, D., *Hess: The Missing Years 1941–1945* (London, 1987)

Ishoven, A. van, *Messerschmitt* (London, 1975)

Kahn, D., *Hitler's Spies: German Military Intelligence in World War II* (London, 1978)

Kenny, J. P., *Moral Aspects of Nuremberg* (Thomistic Studies No. 2, Dominican House of Studies, Washington, DC, 1949)

Kershaw, I., *The 'Hitler Myth': Image and Reality in the Third Reich* (Oxford, 1987)

——*Hitler* (London, 1991)

——*Hitler: 1889–1936, Hubris* (London, 1998)

——*Hitler: 1936–1945, Nemesis* (London, 2000)

Knight, F., 'The Sickness of Liberal Society', *Ethics*, 56 (1945)

Kochavi, A., 'Britain and the War Criminals Question at the Conclusion of the Second World War: the Military Dimension', *Journal of Holocaust Education*, 2 (1993)

——*Prelude to Nuremberg: Allied War Crimes Policy and the Quest for Punishment* (Chapel Hill, NC, 1998)

Lang, J. von, *The Secretary: Martin Bormann. The Man who Manipulated Hitler* (Athens, Ohio, 1979)

Levin, N., *The Jews in the Soviet Union since 1917* (2 vols., London, 1990)

Liddell Hart, B., *The Other Side of the Hill* (London, 1948)

Lifton, R. J., *The Nazi Doctors* (London, 1986)

Lipstadt, D., *Denying the Holocaust: The Growing Assault on Truth and Memory* (London, 1993)

Maier, K., 'Die Luftschlacht um England', in K. Maier *et al.*, *Das Deutsche Reich und der Zweite Weltkrieg: Band II* (Stuttgart, 1979)

Manchester, W., *The Arms of Krupp* (London, 1968)

Martens, S., *Hermann Göring: 'Erster Paladin des Führers' und 'Zweiter Mann im Reich'* (Paderborn, 1985)

Maser, W., *Nürnberg, Tribunal der Sieger* (Düsseldorf, 1977)

McIsaac, D., *Strategic Bombing in World War II* (vol. 1, New York, 1976)

McKale, D. M., *Hitler: The Survival Myth* (New York, 1981)

Mcleod, B. (ed.), *The Ironside Diaries, 1937-1940* (London, 1962)

Messerschmidt, M., 'Forward Defense: the "Memorandum of the Generals" for the Nuremberg Court', in Heer, H., and Naumann, K. (eds.), *War of Extermination: The German Military in World War II* (Oxford, 2000)

Morgenthau, H., 'The Ethics of Politics and the Ethics of Evil', *Ethics*, 56 (1945)

Müller, R.-D., and Volkmann, H.-E. (eds.), *Die Wehrmacht. Mythos und Realität* (Munich, 1999)

Naimark, N. M., *The Russians in Germany: A History of the Soviet Zone of Occupation, 1945-1949* (Cambridge, Mass., 1995)

Neliba, G., *Wilhelm Frick: Der Legalist des Unrechtsstaates: Eine politische Biographie* (Paderborn, 1992)

Neumann, H. J., *Arthur Seyss-Inquart* (Vienna, 1970)

Nicholas, L., *The Rape of Europa: The Fate of Europe's Treasures in the Third Reich and the Second World War* (London, 1994)

Overy, R. J., *Goering: 'the Iron Man'* (London, 1984).

——*War and Economy in the Third Reich* (Oxford, 1994)

——*Russia's War* (London, 1998)

——'World War II: the Bombing of Germany', in A. Stephens (ed.), *The War in the Air 1914–1994* (Canberra, 1994)

——'The Four Year Plan', *German Business History Yearbook* (Frankfurt/Main, 2000)

Padfield, P., *Himmler: Reichsführer SS* (London, 1990)

——*Hess: Flight for the Führer* (London, 1991)

Pawelczynska, A., *Values and Violence in Auschwitz*, trans. C. S. Leach (Berkeley, Calif., 1973)

Petropolous, J., *The Faustian Bargain: The Art World in Nazi Germany* (London, 2000)

Petrova, A., and Watson, P., *The Death of Hitler: the Final Words from Russia's Secret Archives* (London, 1995)

Petzina, D., *Autarkiepolitik im Dritten Reich* (Stuttgart, 1968)

Pohl, K.-H. (ed.), *Wehrmacht und Vernichtungspolitik. Militär im national-sozialistischen System* (Göttingen, 1999)

Reinhardt, K., *Moscow – the Turning Point: The Failure of Hitler's Strategy in the Winter of 1941–1942* (Oxford, 1992)

Reitlinger, G., *The Final Solution: The Attempt to Exterminate the Jews of Europe, 1939–1945* (London, 1953)

Reuth, R., *Goebbels* (London, 1993)

Rich, N., *Hitler's War Aims: The Establishment of the New Order*, 2 vols. (London, 1974)

Rosenbaum, R., *Explaining Hitler: The Search for the Origins of his Evil* (London, 1998)

Ruge, F., *Rommel und die Invasion: Erinnerungen von Friedrich Ruge* (Stuttgart, 1959)

Russell of Liverpool, Lord, *The Trial of Adolf Eichmann* (London, 1962)

Scheurig, B., *Alfred Jodl: Gehorsam und Verhängnis. Biographie* (Berlin, 1991)

Schleunes, K. A., 'An "International Solution" to the Jewish Problem, 1939', *Journal of Holocaust Education*, 2 (1993)

Schmidt, M., *Albert Speer: the End of a Myth* (New York, 1982)

Schmidt, R. F., *Rudolf Hess. 'Botengang eines Toren'? Der Flug nach Grossbritannien vom 10 Mai 1941* (Düsseldorf, 1997)

Schulte, T., *The German Army and Nazi Policies in Occupied Russia* (Oxford, 1989)

Seidl, A., *Der Fall Rudolf Hess 1941–1987* (Munich, 1988)

Sereny, G., *Into That Darkness: From Mercy Killing to Mass Murder* (London, 1974)

——*Albert Speer: His Battle with Truth* (London, 1995)

Simpson, A. P., *Hjalmar Schacht in Perspective* (The Hague, 1969)

Smelser, R., *Robert Ley: Hitler's Labor Front Leader* (Oxford, 1988)

Smith, B. F., *Reaching Judgement at Nuremberg* (London, 1977)

Sofsky, W., *The Order of Terror: The Concentration Camp* (London, 1997)

Solomon, P. H., *Soviet Criminal Justice under Stalin* (Cambridge, 1996)

Swearingen, B. E., *The Mystery of Hermann Goering's Suicide* (2nd edn., London, 1990)

Taylor, T., *The Anatomy of the Nuremberg Trials* (London, 1993)

Thies, J., 'Hitler's European Building Programme', *Journal of Contemporary History*, 13 (1978)

Thomas, H., *Doppelgängers: The Truth about the Bodies in the Berlin Bunker* (London, 1995)

Thompson, H. K., and Stutz, H. (eds.), *Doenitz and Nuremberg: A Reappraisal* (New York, 1976)

Trevor-Roper, H., *The Last Days of Hitler* (7th edn., London, 1995)

Turner, H. A., *Hitler's Thirty Days to Power: January 1933* (London, 1996)

Turner, I. D. (ed.), *Reconstruction in Post-War Germany* (Oxford, 1989)

Tusa, A. and J., *The Nuremberg Trial* (London, 1983)

Ueberschär, G., and Wette, W. (eds.), '*Unternehmen Barbarossa': Der deutsche Überfall auf die Sowjetunion 1941. Berichte, Analysen, Dokumente* (Paderborn, 1984)

Vaksberg, A., *The Prosecutor and the Prey: Vyshinsky and the 1930s Show Trials* (London, 1990)

——*Stalin Against the Jews* (New York, 1994)

van der Vat, D., *The Good Nazi: The Life and Times of Albert Speer* (London, 1997)

Webster, N., and Frankland, C., *The Strategic Air Offensive against Germany*, 4 vols. (London, 1961)

Wegner, B. (ed.), *From Peace to War: Germany, Soviet Russia and the World, 1939–1941* (Oxford, 1997)

Wieviorka, A. (ed.), *Les procès de Nuremberg et de Tokyo* (Paris, 1996)

Wilmowsky, T. von, *Warum wurde Krupp verurteilt? Legende und Justizirrtum* (Stuttgart, 1950)

Woetzel, R. K., *The Nuremberg Trials in International Law* (2nd edn., New York, 1962)

Woodward, L., *British Foreign Policy in the Second World War* (vol. 5, London, 1976)

Wright, J., and Stafford, P., 'Hitler, Britain and the Hossbach Memorandum', *Militärgeschichtliche Mitteilungen*, 42 (1987)

Zayas, A. M. de, *The Wehrmacht War Crimes Bureau, 1939–1945* (Lincoln, Nebr., 1989)

Transcript Sources

Document 1

IWM, Speer Collection, Box S 369, FIAT Report 19, Part III, exploitation of Albert Speer, 'Adolf Hitler', 19 October 1945

Document 2

PRO, FO 1031/102, Dr Karl Brandt, 'Women around Hitler', (n.d.), sent to Major E. Tilley, 6 February 1946

Document 3

IWM, FO 645, Box 159, paper prepared by Dr Hans Lammers, 'State Bonuses', 24 October 1945

Document 4

NA II, RG 332, United States Strategic Bombing Survey, Interview No. 62, Colonel General Alfred Jodl, 29 June 1945 (distributed 7 July 1945)

Document 5

IWM, FO 645, Box 156, testimony of Hermann Goering taken at Nuremberg, 8 October 1945

Document 6

NA II, RG 332, United States Strategic Bombing Survey, Interview No. 56, Hermann Goering, 29 June 1945 (distributed 6 July 1945)

Document 7

IWM, FO 645, Box 156, testimony of Hermann Goering taken at Nuremberg, 3 October 1945

Document 7b

IWM, FO 645, Box 156, testimony of Albert Goering taken at Nuremberg, 25 September 1945

Document 8

NA II, RG 238, Jackson papers, Box 4, memorandum for Jackson, 'Political Interrogation of von Ribbentrop' (n.d., but June 1945).

Document 9

IWM, Speer Collection, Box S 369, FIAT Report 19, Part II, examination of Albert Speer, 'Nazi Foreign Policy and Military Leadership', 7 September 1945

Document 10

NA II, RG 332, United States Strategic Bombing Survey, Interview No. 55, Field Marshal Wilhelm Keitel, 27 June 1945 (distributed 5 July 1945)

Document 11

IWM, FO 645, Box 162, testimony of Dieter Wisliceny taken at Nuremberg, 15 November 1945

Document 12

IWM, FO Box 645, Box 162, testimony of Dieter Wisliceny taken at Nuremberg, 17 November 1945 and 23 November 1945

Document 13

PRO, WO 309/1423, HQ BAOR to Judge Advocate General's Office, 4 January 1946 enclosing interrogation reports from No. 1 Sub-Centre CSDIC, 10 December 1945

Document 14

NA II, RG 238, Jackson papers, Box 16, affidavit of Franz Blaha taken at Nuremberg, 9 January 1946

Document 15

IWM, FO 645, Box 157, testimony of Rudolf Hoess taken at Nuremberg, 2 April 1946

Document 16

IWM, FO 645, Box 157, testimony of Otto Moll and Rudolf Hoess taken at Nuremberg, 16 April 1946

Document 17

IWM, FO 645, Box 157, testimony of Rudolf Hess taken at Nuremberg, 9 October 1945

Document 18

IWM, FO 645, Box 157, testimony of Rudolf Hess, Ingeborg Sperr and Hildegarde Fath taken at Nuremberg, 16 November 1945

Document 19

NA II, RG 238, Jackson papers, Box 2, 'Additional psychiatric comment on the Rudolph Hess case', report of the expert committee, (n.d., but December 1945?)

Document 20

IWM, FO 645, Box 160, testimony of Franz von Papen taken at Nuremberg, 3 September 1945

Document 21

IWM, FO 645, Box 160, testimony of Franz von Papen taken at Nuremberg, 12 October 1945

Document 22

IWM, Speer Collection, Box S 369, SHAEF G2 Office, interrogation of Albert Speer, 5th Session, 30 May 1945 (taken at SHAEF HQ in Paris)

Document 23

IWM, Speer Collection, Box S 369, SHAEF G2 Office, interrogation of Albert Speer, 7th Session, 1 June 1945, section 2

Document 24

IWM, Speer Collection, Box S 368, FD 3063/49, FIAT report 254–82, Stahl–Speer, 10 November 1945

Document 25

IWM, FO 645, Box 161, testimony of Albert Speer taken at Nuremberg, 2 November 1945

Document 26

IWM, FO 645, Box 161, testimony of Albert Speer taken by the Soviet delegation at Nuremberg, 14 November 1945

Document 27

NA II, RG 238, Jackson papers, Box 3, testament of Robert Ley (n.d., but August 1945).

Document 28

NA II, RG 238, Jackson papers, Box 3, translation of 'Ein Zwiegespräch' ['A Dialogue'] by Robert Ley, 14 August 1945

Document 29

NA II, RG 238, Jackson papers, Box 3, translation of a letter from Robert Ley to Dr Pflücker, 24 October 1945

Document 30

IWM, FO 645, Box 156, testimony of Wilhelm Frick taken at Nuremberg, 25 September 1945

Document 31

IWM, FO 645, Box 160, testimony of Joachim von Ribbentrop taken at Nuremberg, 10 September, 5 October and 7 October 1945

Document 32

IWM, FO 645, Box 156, testimony of General Heinz Guderian taken at Nuremberg, 5 November 1945

Document 33

PRO, WO 208/3154, SHAEF interrogation report, Dr Robert Ley 'Ideas on the Reconstruction of Housing in Germany', 7 July 1945

Document 34

IWM, Speer Collection, Box S 369, FIAT Interrogation Report, 'Second Preliminary Report on Dr Hjalmar Schacht', 7 September 1945

Index